LETTERS,
FICTIONS,
LIVES

LETTERS, FICTIONS, LIVES

Henry James
and
William Dean Howells

MICHAEL ANESKO

New York   Oxford • Oxford University Press   1997

Oxford University Press

Oxford   New York
Athens   Auckland   Bangkok   Bogota   Bombay   Buenos Aires
Calcutta   Cape Town   Dar es Salaam   Delhi   Florence   Hong Kong
Istanbul   Karachi   Kuala Lumpur   Madras   Madrid   Melbourne
Mexico City   Nairobi   Paris   Singapore   Taipei   Tokyo   Toronto   Warsaw

and associated companies in
Berlin   Ibadan

Copyright © 1997 by Oxford University Press, Inc.

Published by Oxford University Press, Inc.,
198 Madison Avenue, New York, New York 10016

Oxford is a registered trademark of Oxford University Press

Library of Congress Cataloging-in-Publication Data

James, Henry, 1843–1916.
[Correspondence. Selections]
Letters, fictions, lives : Henry James and William Dean Howells /
[edited by] Michael Anesko.
p.   cm.
Includes index.
ISBN 0-19-506119-5 (cloth)
1. James Henry, 1843–1916—Correspondence.   2. Authors,
American—19th century—Correspondence.   3. Authors, American—20th
century—Correspondence.   4. Howells, William Dean, 1837–1920—
Correspondence.   5. Novelists, American—19th century—
Correspondence.   6. Novelists, American—20th century—Correspondence.
7. Critics—United States—Correspondence.   8. Fiction—Authorship.
I. Howells, William Dean, 1837–1920.
II. Anesko, Michael.   III. Title.
PS2123.A435   1997
813'.4—dc21
[B]   97-11832

1 3 5 7 9 8 6 4 2

Printed in the United States of America
on acid-free paper

This book commemorates

the unabbreviated friendship of

S. and S.

Prologue

Chronologically at least, Howells had the last word, but time has favored James. At the hour of his death in 1920, Howells characteristically was at work, preparing a piece for *Harper's Monthly* ("The American James") in which he intended to commemorate their early friendship in Cambridge, their rambles at Fresh Pond, their beginning dialogue about "methods of fiction . . . the art we both adored." Howells honestly admitted that in those days he was much James's "junior" in such matters, a stance from which few critics have chosen to depart. As early as 1919 one comparative summary of their work curtly suggested that Howells "nowhere has the distinction of Henry James; and it may be doubted whether much of his fiction will long survive the test of changing interests and tastes."[1] The present volume of documents and commentary makes no particular claim to reverse this long-accepted priority, though it does seek to reveal new aspects of a vitally important literary friendship. Those aspects suggest that the personal and professional relationship between James and Howells was considerably more complex than is commonly believed. Epigrams have had a tendency to displace evidence, a point best illustrated by George Moore's famous quip that "Henry James went to France and read Tourgueneff," while "Howells stayed at home and read Henry James."[2] With very few exceptions, most critics have accepted Moore's logic of implied influence, assuming that a cosmopolitan James learned much more about the art of fiction from his European contemporaries than he ever could have gleaned from sources closer to home. In recent years sufficient allowance has been made for Hawthorne, but the full reach of James's American appropriations has not yet been measured. His was, after all, an admittedly grasping imagination.

If James went to France and read Turgenev, he also read William Dean Howells and remained unusually attentive to the complicated evolution of that writer's literary career. Neither James nor Howells came quickly to the writing of fiction, a fact that the modern reader (perhaps even desperately aware of their combined productivity) might easily overlook. Before that long, groaning shelf of novels was ever begun, both men served extended literary apprenticeships as travel writers and reviewers for the still relatively new American magazines of the post–Civil War era. Indeed, from 1865 to 1881 Howells's fortunes were directly linked to the *Atlantic Monthly,* the editorial ranks of which served as rungs on his literary ladder (and from which he frequently extended a helping hand to James). With varying degrees of interest, curiosity, and envy, each followed the other's tentative advances toward independent authorial professionalism.

In her still useful study of James's early career, Cornelia Pulsifer Kelley anticipated that "a task awaiting the future historian of American literature [would be] to determine not only Howells's early influence upon James but James's influence upon Howells."[3] This volume attempts to perform that task by reconstructing and evaluating documentary and textual evidence of their literary cross-fertilization. In different ways both Howells and James yearned for a realm of imaginative freedom, that "country of the blue" so tenderly evoked by James in the pages of "The Next Time." As their ongoing correspondence will show, neither man could find security in the competitive literary marketplace they jointly inhabited. Plagued by a restlessness that was more bourgeois than bohemian, Howells and James could only wander—and they could write. They did much of both, even to the extent of trespass. This book maps the paths of their transgressions, their achievements, and their careers.

To observe Henry James's sesquicentennial in 1993, hundreds of the writer's devotees from around the world converged on New York's Washington Square for a remarkable five-day series of lectures, symposia, dramatic readings, and other celebratory acts. From start to finish, those in attendance voiced their frustration over the limited range of James's letters currently available to scholars; in fact, the need for a complete edition of the Master's correspondence became virtually the sole topic on which critics of divergent theoretical persuasions could agree. This volume alone cannot satisfy their reiterated demand, but it may help to establish a new standard of scholarship for the presentation of James's epistolary texts, documents that have not always received the careful editorial attention they deserve.[4]

Of the 151 letters included in this volume—representing most of the extant correspondence between the two men—only half (76) have been printed elsewhere. The items previously unpublished are all James's (75). To a reader unfamiliar with James's peculiar habits, the fact that only 32 letters from Howells appear might be misleading. This lopsided tally does not relegate him to an inferior status among James's many correspondents. In fact, the reverse is true; scant as the number may seem, James preserved more letters from Howells than from anyone else outside his immediate family. As Leon Edel has shown, the Master's fireplace was his favored repository for correspondence; typically, he destroyed letters as soon as he answered them. On at least two occasions, with the ruthless deliberation of Savonarola, he made bonfires of others' postal vanities.[5]

Howells, fortunately, was less incendiary. When (after much debate) James's heirs finally gave permission for Percy Lubbock to assemble the first edition of the writer's correspondence—*The Letters of Henry James,* in two volumes (1920)—Howells eagerly pledged his support. "I have kept everything," he assured the family; "there must be some thousands of pages." In a postscript he added, "I am glad the letters will be allowed to tell the Life of H. J." Nothing else, he urged, "would have been fit."[6] Although Howells probably overestimated his true holdings, he had indeed preserved a run of James's letters that was almost unique in depth, longevity, and literary significance.[7]

Letters: from time to time, both men complained of their necessity. "God knows they *are* impossible," James lamented, "the great fatal, incurable, unpumpable leak of one's poor sinking bark." Still, he kept afloat, buoyed up by an epistolary energy that can only seem astonishing to our telephonic (and cybernetic) age. In spite of James's disclaimer that "letters, in the writing life, are the last things that get themselves written," scholars estimate that the Master composed more than twelve thousand of them; and his portion to Howells rank among the best. Even the occasional notes, dashed off at hurried moments, flicker with wit and style—which explains why they were lovingly preserved.

The full record of their relationship, however, cannot be traced exclusively in private correspondence. In reviewing each other's work, James and Howells were, in effect, writing public letters that even the prevailing habit of magazine anonymity could not entirely conceal. When read in sequence, their letters and published commentary provide a more complete record of critical response and reciprocity. The selection included in this volume represents each writer's most significant criticism of the other. To publish these documents together is not merely a matter of convenience: this new collection provides a valuable tool for historically informed comprehension and appreciation of both men's work.[8]

Notes

1. Walter C. Bronson, *A Short History of American Literature*, rev. ed. (Boston: D. C. Heath, 1919), 307.

2. George Moore, *Confessions of a Young Man* (1889; rpt. Montreal: McGill–Queens University Press, 1972), 152.

3. Cornelia Pulsifer Kelley, *The Early Development of Henry James* (1935; rev. ed. Urbana: University of Illinois Press, 1965), 75.

4. The accuracy of the most comprehensive edition now available, the four-volume *Henry James Letters*, edited by Leon Edel, has been questioned since the first installment appeared more than twenty years ago. In a summary view of the project, Philip Horne has concluded that Edel's work "is essential but inadequate. It is in his far-reaching unreliability that Professor Edel makes a comprehensive scholarly edition, daunting project as it is, an urgent necessity—despite the bulk of his four fat volumes. With a writer of the stature of Henry James his failings are a distressing anomaly, an error in need of correction" (*Cambridge Quarterly* 15 [1986]: 141). Also pertinent to the material published here is Christoph K. Lohmann and George Arms's "Commentary" (*Nineteenth-Century Fiction* 31 [1976–77]: 244–47); their critique of Edel's editorial procedure is based specifically on his published texts of letters addressed to Howells.

It should be noted that Howells's sesquicentennial celebration in 1987 also drew a crowd to Cambridge, Massachusetts: a gathering less numerous than James's, but still sufficiently eager to hear John Updike assess the Dean's career as an "anti-novelist." Ironically, Howells may be less popular, but his correspondence has been better served.

In contrast to the fallible (and much criticized) Harvard edition of James's letters, the six-volume *Selected Letters* (edited by George Arms et al.) has offered scholars little ground for complaint.

5. Altogether, I have located 182 items in public repositories: 138 from HJ to WDH, and 44 in exchange. Of the 12 WDH letters not published here, all but 2 can be found in Indiana University's six-volume *Selected Letters*. The 19 HJ letters omitted are mostly minor notes, such as invitations, travel directions, and the like.

6. WDH to Alice H. G. and Margaret Mary James, 26 Feb. 1917 (James Papers, Harvard).

7. On 4 October 1903 WDH told his sister Aurelia that for the purpose of planning his autobiography he had been "sorting, and filing or destroying thousands of old letters." "I am rich in autographs beyond the dreams of avarice," he proudly confessed, "and the letters are all interesting" (*SL* 5: 66). While it is unlikely that he would have discarded any of HJ's correspondence at this time, the possibility cannot entirely be ruled out.

8. For all of the reviews and essays, I have based this text upon their original serial publication. Until recently, the most complete source for WDH's commentary on HJ has been Albert Mordell, ed., *The Discovery of a Genius: William Dean Howells and Henry James* (New York: Twayne, 1961), which unfortunately reprints misattributed items and incomplete (unannotated) texts. Indiana University Press has issued three volumes of WDH's *Selected Literary Criticism*, ed. Ulrich Halfmann, Donald Pizer, and Ronald Gottesman (Bloomington, 1993), which include most of the Dean's widely dispersed critical observations about James. Likewise, most of HJ's commentary on WDH has been collected in the invaluable Library of America edition of his *Literary Criticism: Essays on Literature, American Writers, English Writers*, ed. Leon Edel (New York, 1984).

Acknowledgments

Publishing the material in this volume would not have been possible without the generous cooperation of the late Alexander R. James and William White Howells, to whom a new generation of readers and scholars surely will be grateful. At an early stage of my research, Warner Berthoff, David Nordloh, and Philip Horne read through transcriptions and annotations of the letters; their probing questions and seasoned editorial advice were invaluable. With Professor Nordloh's kind permission, I also had access to the voluminous files of the Howells Edition Center at Indiana University, where I compared my typescripts with a corresponding set compiled by a team of dedicated editors during their meticulous preparation of the six-volume *Selected Letters of William Dean Howells*. Their work established a model of scrupulously authoritative scholarship that I have attempted to emulate. If errors or embarrassments remain, they are mine alone.

In the time needed to complete this book, my debts to librarians and archivists have multiplied almost beyond measure. The Houghton Library at Harvard University has become a familiar and comfortable place to work, owing largely to the supportive enthusiasm of Richard Wendorf, Dennis Marnon, and Roger Stoddard and the prompt courtesies of the reading room staff, especially Susan Halpert, Denison Beach, Jennie Rathbun, Emily Walhout, Judith Wilson, and Melanie Wisner. Receiving the library's Houghton Mifflin Fellowship in Publishing History enabled me to check my work against the manuscripts one last time, and to supplement my research in the archives of Houghton Mifflin Company and its historical predecessors.

Thanks are also due to the American Council of Learned Societies, the Charles Warren Center for Studies in American History (Harvard), and the Institute for the Arts and Humanistic Studies (Pennsylvania State University), whose patronage gave me the freedom to complete my research and writing. The support of the Warren Center's former director, Bernard Bailyn, has meant more to me than any pecuniary award; his example as a scholar, teacher, and colleague remains an inspiration. I am grateful to Lawrence Buell, Andrew Delbanco, Susan Hunt, James Rambeau, Robert Secor, James L. W. West III, and

Christopher Wilson for believing in this project. A grant from the Hyder Rollins Fund, administered by Harvard's Department of English and American Literature and Language, helped subsidize the photographic embellishments to this volume.

The Houghton Library, the Brotherton Library (University of Leeds), and the Rutherford B. Hayes Presidential Center (Fremont, Ohio) have granted permission for documents in their collections to appear here.

My understanding of the complex relationship between Henry James and William Dean Howells has been enriched by the stimulus of eager students at Harvard and Penn State. Their continued questions give one hope.

Contents

Abbreviations

Throughout this volume, the following abbreviations are used in the notes and editorial apparatus. Complete bibliographical information for other published sources appears whenever such material is first cited.

AJ   Alice James
ALS   Autograph letter, signed
ANS   Autograph note, signed
CN   *The Complete Notebooks of Henry James*, ed. Leon Edel and Lyall H. Powers (New York: Oxford University Press, 1987)
CT   *The Complete Tales of Henry James*, 12 vols., ed. Leon Edel (Philadelphia: Lippincott, 1961–64)
CWJ   *The Correspondence of William James*, ed. Ignas K. Skrupskelis and Elizabeth M. Berkeley, 3 vols. (Charlottesville: University of Virginia Press, 1992–)
DAJ   *The Diary of Alice James*, ed. Leon Edel (1964; rpt. New York: Penguin Books, 1982)
HJ   Henry James
HJL   *Henry James Letters*, ed. Leon Edel, 4 vols. (Cambridge, Mass.: Belknap Press of Harvard University Press, 1974–84).
HJ Sr.   Henry James Senior
LHJ   *The Letters of Henry James*, ed. Percy Lubbock, 2 vols. (New York: Charles Scribner's Sons, 1920).
LiL   *Life in Letters of William Dean Howells*, ed. Mildred Howells, 2 vols. (Garden City, N.Y.: Doubleday, Doran, 1928).
Mrs. HJ Sr.   Mrs. Henry James Senior
SL   *Selected Letters of William Dean Howells*, ed. George Arms et al., 6 vols. (Boston: Twayne, 1979–83).
THJ   *The Tales of Henry James*, ed. Maqbool Aziz, 3 vols. (New York: Oxford University Press, 1973–).
TLS   Typescript letter, signed
WDH   William Dean Howells
WJ   William James

A Note on Editorial Procedure

The letters in this volume are printed in clear text in a form that best approximates the finished state of each manuscript. The accompanying textual apparatus records significant alterations made during the process of composition and emendations introduced by me.* Only when authorial inadvertence has jeopardized the clear sense of a letter have I intervened; consequently, eccentricities of spelling, punctuation, and the inconsistent use of emphasis have largely been retained (e.g., is n't). Obvious typographical errors introduced by Howells or by James's various stenographers have been silently emended. Except for those few documents estranged from the primary Harvard archive, each transcription has been checked against the manuscript three times; in the other cases, I have based the edited text upon photocopies of the originals.

The heading introducing each letter identifies the author and addressee, a full date when known (or a reasonable conjecture, based upon internal evidence), the place of composition, and the physical status and location of the manuscript. Since no printed text can reproduce the full range of authorial idiosyncrasies (such as James's habit of running his closing lines up the margins of his writing paper), I have adopted a few stylistic conventions to achieve an attractive presentation of the documents. Regardless of their placement in the originals, inside addresses appear on one or more lines directly below the editorial heading. Unless canceled by the author, printed letterhead that indicates the location of composition appears in small capitals. No effort has been made to distinguish the printed datelines of office stationery from holograph insertions. Italics and full capitals are used only when the author has underscored some portion of his manuscript for emphasis. An indented paragraph opens the body of each letter, even though both men occasionally began to write on the

---

*An encyclopedic textual record—which is beyond the scope of this volume—has been deposited with the Houghton Library at Harvard. For WDH's letters to HJ, the compilers of his *Selected Letters* have already provided one.

same line as their salutation. Likewise, all complimentary closings and signatures have been standardized irrespective of their widely varying locations in the originals. Indentations (and the long dashes sometimes employed to indicate new paragraphs) also have been made uniform. Underlined words—and, where significant, portions of words—have been set in italics.

LETTERS,
FICTIONS,
LIVES

part one

Arrivals and Departures

Biographical Overview

For much of their adult lives, Howells and James had to suffer the conjunction that made them into a collective noun: the grammar of literary history can be peculiar. While destiny brought the two men together, the formative circumstances of their early lives probably could not have been more dissimilar. William Dean Howells grew up in a series of frontier towns and villages, where he seldom had the benefit of formal education; he found a schoolroom wherever his improvident father occasionally set up shop to publish newspapers. The Jameses could afford to be more glamorously itinerant, since the family patriarch derived an annual income of ten thousand dollars from inherited property and investments. Whatever their later affinities, no one would ever suspect that Henry James could have written *My Year in a Log Cabin*. A familiar string of paired opposites describes these authors well: East/West, urban/rural, cosmopolitan/provincial, patrician/democratic. A reader of their correspondence will often feel the tensions suggested by such juxtapositions.

Beneath these obvious differences, though, less tangible correspondences exist. Paternal idealisms, inspired by the reformed Christian doctrines of Emmanuel Swedenborg, flickered brightly in both families. The spirit of utopian socialism suffuses almost all of Henry James Sr.'s published work (the true destiny of man, he fervently believed, could only be realized through society, not selfish individualism). Similarly, for a brief period in the early 1850s (commemorated by his son in *New Leaf Mills*), William Cooper Howells actually attempted to organize an Owenite community near Xenia, Ohio. Eureka Mills was no more successful than any of Henry James Sr.'s notoriously obscure books, but only through such "failure" could their sons come to appreciate the American meaning of "success."

What we are most likely to appreciate in these early letters James and Howells tend to deprecate: shoptalk. Their correspondence is full of it—and for good reason. Throughout this period (1867–80), Howells writes not merely as James's friend but also as influential literary editor of the *Atlantic Monthly*, in which capacity he eagerly seeks quality submissions (from a reliable source). Having been brought to Boston in 1866 as James T. Fields's assistant, Howells succeeds his illustrious predecessor in 1871, thereby rising to perhaps the most powerful and authoritative position in American letters. By devoting more of his time to travel writing and book reviewing, this author of conventionally romantic lyric poems has also come to recognize both the literary importance and professional value of a new kind of prose. He works to create a different style—more objective and clear, realistic, attuned to the immediacies of American life—and extends his range to experiment with new genres: short story, novel, and play.

By comparison, James's vocational path is deliberately less straightforward. Whereas Howells (with a growing family) seeks job security and the usual comforts of middle-class status, James prefers the distinction of remaining detached from particular places and institutions. Howells frequently uses company stationery; James's pen never touches it. The bachelor's letters chart his varied migrations—Cambridge, New York, Paris, London, Florence, Rome—even as they confirm his singular engagement to Art.

Where best to practice the art of fiction becomes a running theme here, one that reaches its inevitably divergent conclusion when Howells reviews his friend's critical biography of *Hawthorne*. (To refer to the author of *The Scarlet Letter* as "provincial"—and not once but a dozen times—was more than even a transplanted New Englander could bear.) Indeed, their differences illuminate not merely the *where* of novel writing but the *how*. Questions of plotting and problems of characterization occupy them almost as much as publishing calendars and editorial deadlines. Professional obligations require Howells and James to write letters *to* each other, but over time they seem increasingly to write novels *for* each other. Critically analyzing that pattern of discourse is the purpose of this introduction; the ensuing letters and documents help reveal it.

Parallel Chronology

This running table (carried forward in the second and third overview sections) briefly lists the major events in the lives of Howells and James, together with their most important publications. More complete bibliographical information (including serial publications) can be obtained from *A Bibliography of William Dean Howells*, compiled by William M. Gibson and George Arms (New York: New York Public Library, 1948); and *A Bibliography of Henry James*, third edition, compiled by Leon Edel and Dan H. Laurence and revised with the assistance of James Rambeau (Oxford: Clarendon Press, 1982).

	HOWELLS	JAMES	
1837	Born at Martin's Ferry, Ohio, March 1.		
1840–51	Father publishes newspapers in various smaller towns in Ohio; his Free Soil convictions are	Born in house adjacent to Washington Square, New York City, April 15.	1843

	HOWELLS	JAMES	
	seldom popular. WDH begins to set type at age nine.		
		During earliest childhood, family resides first in Windsor, England (where father suffers nervous collapse and Swedenborgian conversion), and later in Paris.	1843–45
		Family returns to New York; settles in Albany, city where paternal grandfather amassed fortune that enabled descendants to avoid careers in business or trade.	1845–47
1852	Family settles in Jefferson, where William Cooper Howells edits the Ashtabula *Sentinel*, giving voice to his abolitionist views.	Family moves to large house on Fourteenth Street in Manhattan. Household entertains such distinguished visitors as Bryant, Alcott, Emerson, and Thackeray.	1847–55
1853–57	Period of intense self-education. Learns Spanish, French, Latin, and German. Begins career in journalism, contributing to the *Sentinel, Ohio State Journal,* and other local papers.	Discouraged by utilitarian nature of American education, father takes family to Europe, where children study in various progressive academies and often with tutors and governesses.	1855–58
1858	City editor and columnist of the *Ohio State Journal* in Columbus.	Economic troubles bring family back to America. Jameses take up residence at Newport, Rhode Island. Friendship with Thomas Sergeant Perry.	1858–59
1859	*Poems of Two Friends*, with John James Piatt. Meets Elinor Mead, of Brattleboro, Vermont, who is visiting her cousin, Rutherford B. Hayes, in Columbus.	Another season in Geneva; abortive experiment taking mathematics classes at pre-engineering school.	1859–60
1860	James R. Lowell accepts WDH's poems for the *Atlantic*. WDH writes campaign biography of Lincoln. Makes first literary	Family returns to Newport. With WJ, schooled in art by William Morris Hunt. Befriends John La Farge.	1860–62

	HOWELLS	JAMES	
	pilgrimage to New England. Meets Lowell, Holmes, Hawthorne, Emerson, Thoreau, and (in New York City) Whitman. Visits Mead family in Vermont; becomes engaged to Elinor.		
1861	Appointed U.S. consul at Venice; sails for Italy in November. Lives in Venice for duration of Civil War and studies Italian art, language, and literature.		
1862	Marries Elinor Mead in Paris (December 24).		
1863	Articles on Venice begin to appear in *Boston Daily Advertiser*. Winifred Howells born (December 17).	Enters Harvard Law School; withdraws before end of first year to pursue literary career. Younger brothers enlist in Union Army.	1863
		Father brings rest of family to Boston. In February, *Continental Monthly* publishes first tale (unsigned), "A Tragedy of Error." Begins noticing books for the *North American Review*, edited by Cambridge neighbor Charles Eliot Norton.	1864
1865	Returns to United States and begins writing career in New York City. Joins staff of E. L. Godkin's new journal the *Nation*.	*Atlantic Monthly* publishes first signed tale, "The Story of a Year." Begins fifteen-year career reviewing books for the *Nation*.	1865
1866	Assistant editor of the *Atlantic*. Moves to Sacramento Street, Cambridge; meets HJ. *Venetian Life*.	Family moves to 20 Quincy Street, Cambridge. Becomes friends with WDH, who eagerly recruits work for the *Atlantic*.	1866

	HOWELLS	JAMES	
1867	*Italian Journeys.*		
1868	John Mead Howells born (August 14).		
		Sails to Europe for first independent grand tour: England, France, Switzerland, Italy. Through Charles Eliot Norton, meets many prominent British writers and intellectuals.	1869
1870	Lectures on modern Italian literature at Harvard.	Returns to Cambridge in May. Continues magazine work.	1870
1871	Succeeds James T. Fields as editor of the *Atlantic*. Attempts to expand range of magazine's literary contributors and social interests. *Suburban Sketches.*	Serializes first novel, *Watch and Ward*, in the *Atlantic*.	1871
1872	*Their Wedding Journey.* Builds new house at 37 Concord Avenue, Cambridge. Mildred Howells born (September 26).	Accompanies sister Alice and Aunt Catharine Walsh on tour of England and the Continent. Remains abroad to see if he can support himself by writing. Cultivates friendships among expatriate communities in Paris, Florence, and Rome.	1872–74
1873	*A Chance Acquaintance. Poems.*		
1875	*A Foregone Conclusion.*	Returns home with manuscript of *Roderick Hudson*, soon accepted by WDH for the *Atlantic*. Spends winter in New York assessing professional opportunities. Publishes first collections of tales (*A Passionate Pilgrim*) and travel pieces (*Transatlantic Sketches*).	1875
1876	Serializes "Private Theatricals" in the *Atlantic* (published in book form as *Mrs. Farrell*, 1921).	Engaged by New York *Tribune* as Paris correspondent. Becomes acquainted with remarkable	1876

	HOWELLS	JAMES	
	Writes campaign biography of Hayes. After disputed election, Hayes becomes nineteenth president.	circle of literary figures: Turgenev, Flaubert, Zola, Daudet, the Goncourts, Maupassant. When editor asks for more gossip and less critical observation, HJ resigns and moves to London.	
1877	Following the holiday success of *The Parlor Car* (published in time for Christmas 1876), WDH continues long career as writer of domestic farces and comedies with *Out of the Question* and *A Counterfeit Presentment*.	*The American*.	1877
		Brings out first book with Macmillan in England, *French Poets and Novelists*. The *Cornhill* publishes "Daisy Miller" to international acclaim. Tale is quickly pirated in America; nevertheless, authorized Harper pamphlet edition sells twenty thousand copies. *The Europeans*.	1878
1879	*The Lady of the Aroostook*.	Immersion in London society. *Confidence. Hawthorne*.	1879
1880	*The Undiscovered Country*.	Springtime in Florence, working on manuscript of *The Portrait of a Lady. Washington Square*.	1880

A Season in
Cambridge

Their earliest letters are probably unrecoverable, and so, too, were their memories of first meeting one another. Neither James nor Howells could speak with much precision about the beginnings of their friendship, but from what we do know, one conclusion seems inescapable: the personal and the professional were intermingled from the start. "We seem to have been presently always together," Howells recalled, "and always talking of methods of fiction, whether we walked the streets by day or night, or we sat together reading our stuff to each other."* What stayed in James's mind, significantly, was the "beautiful thrill" of editorial acceptance. "You showed me the way and opened me the door," he graciously acknowledged to Howells. "You published me at once—and paid me, above all, with a dazzling promptitude; magnificently, I felt, and so that nothing since has ever quite come up to it." James dated these memories to the summer of 1866 and credited Howells with "a frankness and sweetness of hospitality," the stout encouragement of vocational self-confidence, "that was really the making of me."

On two other autobiographical occasions late in life, James returned to this same moment in his career to renew his commemorative appreciation of Howells, "my super-excellent friend and confrère."[1] In 1866, however, Howells was still just a new name on the masthead of the *Atlantic*, to whom James addressed ("as I seem to remember, at his positive invitation") the most "presuming" of his fictional bids, a longish story called "Poor Richard." In retrospect, James could hardly distinguish between the joy of dedicating himself to the task of composition and the "ecstasy" of receiving Howells's "glittering" acceptance. The two aspects of authorship—private consecration to the muse and public recognition of achievement—melded in a "great comprehensive *fusion*," as James put it, "a perfect muddle of pleasure."[2]

---

*To avoid redundancy and clutter, quotations from documents printed in this volume will not be cited.

The pleasure of one's memories frequently increases in proportion to their being muddled; not surprisingly, James was much inclined to look back at his feeble fictional beginnings through a veil of nostalgia. Howells remembered that "Poor Richard" was submitted to him not by James but rather by James T. Fields, the magazine's editor and publisher. "Would you take it?" asked Fields. "Yes," Howells answered, "and all the stories you can get from the writer." Significantly, Howells's version of this event implies a degree of editorial reluctance (on Fields's part) rather than invitation, the need to get a second opinion before giving James his second chance to publish in the *Atlantic*. In a later essay, James, too, came round to this inevitable truth, owning that "from the first I found 'writing for the magazines' an art still more difficult than delightful." What baffled Fields, apparently, was how a writer still so young ("an author with his mother's milk scarce yet dry on his lips") could be so fixedly pessimistic: "Poor Richard," like so many other James titles, does not end happily, which could only register as an "apparent perversity" to the elder editorial imagination.[3] From a distance of fifty years, James could now see that throughout his friend's term as assistant editor, Howells must have intervened again and again—and usually to good effect.

In January 1867, for example, having known James for at most two or three months, Howells nevertheless recommended that the *Atlantic* take another of the early tales ("My Friend Bingham") even before "Poor Richard" was scheduled to appear. "I find it entirely acceptable," Howells emphasized (the adverb here affirming the tale's romantic ending), and he urged prompt publication. "If you haven't made up the March number entirely yet," he pressed Fields, "wouldn't it be well to get this story into it?"[4] The senior editor heeded this friendly advice, and "My Friend Bingham" ran in the March 1867 issue of the magazine. James's inference about Howells's repeated intervention was surely correct.[5]

While James's later autobiographical pieces cast a pall of bemused benignity over his youthful American years, his contemporaneous letters convey a more profound sense of alienation and vocational struggle. Howells was willing to attribute a veritable kindness to the streets and houses of Cambridge, Massachusetts, whence he had come, in the spring of 1866, to assume the assistant editorship of the *Atlantic Monthly*. James's response to the town was hardly one of comfort, perhaps because he was neither a newcomer nor gainfully employed. James abortively attended Harvard Law School in 1862–63, but then returned to his father's notoriously peripatetic household, which wandered for the next few years between Newport and Boston. In the fall of 1866, the elder James removed his family to the eastern fringe of Harvard Yard, where it remained until the end of his life. "We have taken a house here . . . in Quincy St," James told his boyhood friend Thomas Sergeant Perry, "and like it very well—better than town." Still, Cambridge was not Seville and Massachusetts was not Grenada (Perry was enjoying the Grand Tour): "you will see that I date from Cambridge," James warned, "and that you have not even now escaped from its bondage."[6]

A new acquaintance who may have helped reconcile James to *his* bondage was the assistant editor of the *Atlantic*. "Talking of talks," Howells noted, "young Henry James and I had a famous one last evening, two or three hours long, in which we settled the true principles of literary art. He is a very earnest fellow, and I think extremely gifted—gifted enough to do better than any one has yet done toward making us a real American novel."[7] Howells's faith may not have been misplaced, but neither was it automatically reciprocated. James's first recorded impression of Howells, in a letter to his sister, sounds somewhat more provisional. Urging Alice to read "a thing called *Lago Maggiore*" in the latest *Atlantic* (February 1867), James remarked that it was written "by a Mr. Howells who lives here, and is a very nice gentleman. If you haven't read it, do so; for it is very good."[8] Whereas Howells sounds openly enthusiastic, James's tone seems triflingly dry; he might have recommended Howells's essay, but he also misremembered its title ("Forza Maggiore"). To the author himself James was audibly more amiable (compare letter #1), and his published review of *Italian Journeys* is decidedly friendly. The writer of that volume (and the previously published *Venetian Life*) was not merely a "very nice gentleman," as James said privately, but a genuine "observer" whose work belonged "to literature and to the centre and core of it,—the region where men think and feel, and one may almost say breathe, in good prose, and where the classics stand on guard." One gathers that James, too, was keeping watch.

And so, of course, were others, especially the New England worthies who had offered Howells a provisional place among the literary elect. "You have enough in you to do honor to our literature," Lowell affirmed, at the same time that he admonished Howells to keep on "cultivating" himself.[9] Howells obediently kept up with current books and foreign languages, attended meetings of the Dante Society at Longfellow's, and at first declined a professorship (at Union College) but then agreed—at Lowell's and President Eliot's request—to deliver a series of lectures at Harvard on modern Italian literature. "That boy will know how to write if he goes on," Lowell bubbled over to Fields, "and then we old fellows will have to look about us."[10] Such patronage carried its price, however; naturally, Howells was flattered by the welcome that the Brahmins afforded him, but he was stung, too, by the condescension that frequently shadowed their scrupulous gentility.[11]

Whether such friction ever threatened his new friendship with James is difficult to say, but an impression of a kind of asymmetrical affection does emerge from the relatively sparse documentary record that survives. Animated conversations with James about art and literature crowd Howells's memories of these years; but in 1867 James could remark that nothing would be so useful to him "as the thought of having companions and a laborer with whom [he might] exchange feelings and ideas." Apparently, Howells could not fully compensate for the absence, as James put it, "of any really satisfactory society" in Cambridge. Approaching his mid-twenties, James felt too old to fraternize with the undergraduates; but the college tutors and faculty he found too preoccupied and, as he bluntly reported, "Longfellow, Lowell, Norton and co. [were] (in spite of great amiability), not at all to [his] taste." Howells, meanwhile, savored such Cantabrigian amiability almost daily, and he seems to have relished precisely what James failed to discover: "the wear and tear of living and talking and observing" by which "works of art shape themselves into completeness."[12]

Even without these benefits of society, James's art continued to flourish, in Howells's opinion, and the assistant editor broadcast his compliments to many correspondents. Despite his confidence that James had "every element of success in fiction," Howells prophetically recognized that his friend would first have to "create his audience"—a shrewd perception that would almost become a lifelong curse.[13] Feeling the pulse of the public was indeed one of the most valuable services Howells could render to James, although the latter's fierce ambition sometimes overpowered his gratitude. "When you've a fame as great as Hawthorne's," Howells once chided him, "you won't forget who was the first, warmest and truest of your admirers, will you?"

Until James published his first book of short stories in 1875, Howells confined his admiration to private letters. But in the years preceding the appearance of *A Passionate Pilgrim and Other Tales*, his endorsements grew stronger and stronger. "Harry James has just been here," Howells reported to Norton on 15 November 1868, "and left the manuscript of a story which he read me a week ago—the best thing, as I always say, that he has done yet." Within a year he could boast to Fields that "Gabrielle de Bergerac," which had just appeared in the *Atlantic*, marked "a great gain upon all that he's done before, in the popular estimation."[14] After James left Cambridge for his first solo European tour (1869–70), Howells continued to solicit work from him, although the literary fruits of foreign sojourn were delayed by James's deliberation (and occasional ill health). When those fruits at last were borne, however, in the shape of "Travelling Companions" (1870) and "A Passionate Pilgrim" (1871), Howells promptly gathered them up for the *Atlantic*.

Howells could now accommodate James in the magazine without deferring to anyone, for the new publisher had promised him the *Atlantic* editorship when Fields retired in 1871. Howells's literary ascent was as swift as it was remarkable, especially for a man from Ohio who had never finished grammar school. In 1860, when Howells first arrived in Boston to meet James Russell Lowell and the other New England literati, Oliver Wendell Holmes had quipped, somewhat derisively, "Well, James, this is something like the apostolic succession; this is the laying on of hands."[15] In little more than a decade, this subtle sarcasm would become a social fact, although Howells would never feel completely secure in his new elevation—nor would literary Boston let him. "People are so snobbish here!" Elinor complained after hosting a reception for Howells's fellow westerner Bret Harte, at which she tried to achieve "more variety than there is generally in Cambridge parties."[16] James clearly felt that he was doing Mrs. Howells a favor by attending, especially since he had reluctantly declined a competing invitation from his Florentine friend Lizzie Boott. "An opportunity to meet these marvellous creatures is, I suppose, not lightly to be thrown aside," he apologetically noted. "On the other hand I shall pine for the marvellous creatures assembled in your *atelier* and *salon*. But sich is life!"[17] For all of Howells's efforts to ingratiate himself with his Cambridge neighbors, and his earnest belief that the town was "full of appreciation and liberality," the Jameses and many others viewed his literary rise (à la *Silas Lapham*) with a mixture of envy and contempt.

While James was in Europe, he eagerly anticipated Howells's letters and copies of the *Atlantic* containing the new sketches his friend was writing. From Genoa, for example, he told his brother William that reading "A Pedestrian Tour" was an unmitigated pleasure. "I have enjoyed all [Howells's] things more even since being abroad than at home," he continued. "They are really American."[18] Perhaps for that very reason James was inclined to criticize them more severely after he himself returned to Cambridge. A portion of a later letter to Charles Eliot Norton is justifiably famous:

> Howells edits, and observes and produces—the latter in his own particular line with more and more perfection. His recent sketches in the *Atlantic*, collected into a volume, belong, I think, by the wondrous cunning of their manner, to very good literature. He seems to have resolved himself, however, into one who can write solely of what his fleshly eyes have seen; and for this reason I wish he were "located" where they would rest upon richer and fairer things than this immediate landscape. Looking about for myself, I conclude that the face of nature and civilization in this our country is to a certain point a very sufficient literary field. But it will yield its secrets only to a really *grasping* imagination. This I think Howells lacks. (Of course *I* don't!) To write well and worthily of American things one needs even more than elsewhere to be a *master*.[19]

Significantly, James's shrewd analysis merely amplifies a comment Howells already had made about his own work. In his letter to James of 2 January 1870, Howells admitted that his recent sketches were "rather small business"; but, having fallen naturally into doing them, he persuaded himself ("too fondly, perhaps") that they were "a new kind of study of our life, and I have an impression that they're to lead me to some higher sort of performance."[20] For Norton's ear, James deftly converts Howells's modesty into a reproach, a strategy he quite consistently adopted when comparing others' ambitions to his own. Still, James could play off Howells's title by calling his own second book *Transatlantic Sketches* (1875), just as he would appropriate the comic scene of a snowstorm in May that opens *Suburban Sketches* in the first chapter of *The Europeans* (1878). Grasping imagination, indeed!

The higher sort of performance to which *Suburban Sketches* would lead was authored by James as well as Howells, for both writers profited from the book's experimental realism, a closeness of observation that was nevertheless mitigated by a kind of idealized detachment. In such fictional chapters as "A Romance of Real Life" and "Scene," Howells deliberately manipulates his narrative point of view to vivify the consequences of romantic misperception. In his next book, *Their Wedding Journey* (1871), Howells adopts the same technique but more fully exploits its narrative potential by centering his attention on two of his most useful characters, Basil and Isabel March, playing one off against the other (and both, in turn, against the author, who maintains a kind of third-party presence). James was quick to realize that, drawn out over many pages, such an arrangement threatened to become tedious. But his aesthetic criticisms, however valid, were also informed by social factors. Renewed evidence of Howells's advancing career, especially his assumption of the *Atlantic* editorship, prompted James to anticipate an inevitable complacency in his literary work. James again confided his suspicions to Norton:

> Howells is now monarch absolute of the *Atlantic*, to the increase of his profit and comfort. His talent grows constantly in fineness, but hardly, I think, in range of application. I remember your saying some time ago that in a couple of years when he had read Sainte-Beuve etc. he would come to his best. But the trouble is he never will read Sainte-Beuve, nor care to. He has little intellectual curiosity; so here he stands with his admirable organ of style, like a poor man holding a diamond and wondering how he can use it. It's rather sad, I think, to see Americans of the younger sort so unconscious and unambitious of the commission to do the best.[21]

Within a year James would publish similar charges, directing them, however, not at Howells but at Nathaniel Hawthorne. The posthumous publication of Hawthorne's journals deepened James's sense of his genius, at the same time that they singularly diminished his sense of the writer's "general intellectual power." Judging them "with any real critical rigor," James insisted, the notebooks betrayed Hawthorne "as superficial, uninformed, incurious, inappreciative."[22] Even years of sustained European residence could not disturb the terrible simplicity of Hawthorne's imagination, the perpetual blandness of which simultaneously pleased and appalled his reviewer. James's aggressive attitude toward Hawthorne has often taken readers by surprise; but even more surprising, perhaps, is the parallel between his reproach of a venerable classic and his comments about a more vulnerable colleague. Citing the complex James/Hawthorne relation to exemplify theories of literary influence has become almost conventional among modern critics, few of whom notice that James's anxieties were hardly confined to his forebears.[23] Indeed, the American past, as James viewed it, presented him with almost nothing to be anxious about; small wonder, then, that he should pit himself against contemporary rivals, the most significant of whom was Howells.

"Let us make the most of Mr. Howells," urged Lowell when he reviewed *Suburban Sketches;* in these early years, Henry James consistently preferred to make the least, even though he shared Lowell's appreciation of the "singular delicacy" of Howells's genius and the "fastidious purity of his style."[24] Again using terms that he would later make notorious in *Hawthorne*, James whispered to Grace Norton that the "charming style and refined intentions" of *Their Wedding Journey* were "poorly and meagerly served by our American atmosphere." Howells definitely had a writer's gift ("a little divine spark of fancy that never quite goes out"), but it was ultimately betrayed by the poverty of American materials. "Through thick and thin I continue to enjoy him," James humorously added, "or rather thro' thinner and thinner."[25]

When James composed his infamous catalogue of the items of high civilization missing from the texture of American life, it may well be that he had Howells's work rather than Hawthorne's in mind, for in *Their Wedding Journey* Howells anticipates James's long string of negatives ("no Epsom nor Ascot!").

Somewhat less specific but every bit as satiric is Howells's depiction of the shallow basis for class distinction in the United States. On the riverboat from Manhattan to Albany, Howells (as narrator) observes two leisured families, both obviously on their way to Saratoga. One group is headed by a man of "sudden gains," a thriving man of business, the other by a "smoother rich man of inherited wealth," and the juxtaposition of the two American types leads the narrator to make this comparison:

> There was something pleasanter in the face of the hereditary aristocrat, but not so strong nor, altogether, so admirable; particularly if you reflected that he really represented nothing in the world, no great culture, no political influence, no civic aspiration, not even a pecuniary force, nothing but a social set, an alien club-life, a tradition of dining.

With a clever Hawthornian twist, Howells concludes that the "very highest pleasure that such an American's money can purchase is exile, and to this rich man doubtless Europe is a twice-told tale."[26] No wonder a would-be cosmopolitan like James was put on the defensive. In this particular passage, Howells had almost allegorized the presumptive distinction between his own social/literary situation and the more comfortably elite standing of an "aristocrat" like James, only to watch the distinction collapse. James's response was somewhat precocious but inevitable. Citing *Their Wedding Journey* as proof positive, James announced that Howells had "passed into the stage which . . . is the eventual fate of all secondary and tertiary talents—worked off his slender Primitive, found a place and an income, and now is destined to fade slowly and softly away in self-repetition and reconcilement to the commonplace."[27] And this from a man whose greatest work to date was *Watch and Ward!*

Indeed, if Howells had not found a place and an income on the staff of the *Atlantic*, James's first serial novel might never have been published (possibly to no one's great regret—not even the author's, since James later repudiated it). Expressions of gratitude, however, were unbecoming to an aggressively aspiring literary professional, and James seldom let one slip. Maintaining a strategic demeanor of entitlement was the young writer's most consistent approach to the marketplace, and his attitude, however risky, usually paid off. At a crucial moment in negotiating terms for *Watch and Ward*, James even had the cheek to assure James T. Fields that "the story is one of the greatest works of 'this or any age.'"[28] Fortunately, Howells was there to mediate such flourishes in the event that his friend's irony misfired. Not everyone at the *Atlantic* was so charitable.[29] If Howells could presume upon the terms of his employment to secure publication, James could presume upon the terms of his acquaintance.

This fundamental difference helps explain the pattern of asymmetrical affection that becomes legible in the surviving documents from these early years. Most literary historians have assumed that in order to advance his own career, James deliberately concealed his true feelings about Howells's work. Such critics usually base their conclusions on the censorious letters written to others (like the Nortons), which the absence of encouraging letters to Howells cannot answer. Although it has become rather fashionable to interpret others' silences for them, in James's case such procedures are probably unnecessary. Reticence is a vice of which James has seldom been accused; and the argumentative dialogue that soon begins between the two writers—once they commit themselves to the novel as a preferred form—suggests that neither was afraid of the other's criticism. On the contrary, Howells and James may well have figured as optimal implied readers for each other. Their published texts (both fiction and criticism) often seem to take up where their private letters leave off, and, as one critic has noticed, "astringent innuendo sometimes emerges from their well-bred phrases."[30]

Many of those phrases reflect particular concern about the sufficiency of the United States as a field for narrative art. After renewed residence in Europe, James's breezy confidence in American possibilities gave way to profound skepticism. To document this, one need only compare his early letters to Thomas Sergeant Perry ("We are Americans born. . . . I look upon it as a great blessing; and I think that to be an American is an excellent preparation for culture") with the complaints of the struggling expatriate artist Theobald in "The Madonna of the Future," who exclaims, "We are the disinherited of Art. We are condemned to be superficial! We are excluded from the magic circle. The soil of American perception is a poor little barren, artificial deposit."[31] The auditor of this confession, another American whose name is given only as H——, rejects Theobald's desperate assertions by challenging him, in patriotic fashion, to get to work. "Nothing is so idle as to talk about our want of a nutritive soil, or opportunity, of inspiration, and all the rest of it," he responds. "The worthy part is to do something fine! There's no law in our glorious Constitution against that. Invent, create, achieve!" (*THJ* 2: 205). After many years of contemplation, however, Theobald still confronts a blank canvas in his Florentine studio, while his intended model, the once seraphic Serafina, has visibly aged and swollen to the pasta-fed proportions of a Mamma Leone. When H—— confronts Theobald with these unfortunate realities, the artist (rather like Hawthorne's Owen Warland in "The Artist of the Beautiful") cannot withstand the shock of disillusion, falls ill, and dies.

Theobald's abortive career is really an exhausted protest against market forces, which are vulgarly embodied in the story by another "artist" whose apparently limitless supply of animal figurines caters to a limitlessly prurient demand. Describing his inventory of ersatz terra-cotta cats and monkeys (cast in various poses of "sentimental conjunction"), he boasts to H——, "You will do me the honour to admit that I have handled my subjects with delicacy. Eh, it was needed, signore! I have been free, but not licentious. Just a hint, you know!" (*THJ* 2: 227). Shrewd businessman that he is, this nameless sculptor knows a potential customer when he sees one. Indeed, James's canniest move here is to suggest the real complicity between the narrator's aesthetic smugness and the Italian's cynical complacency. Both men advocate a debased kind of realism: the narrator simply deals in facts, with what his fleshly eyes can see, while the "artist" proudly shapes his figures from life, with what his eyes have seen of the flesh. "Contemplation," for him, is routine: the monkeys frolic in a private menagerie; for the cats, he just looks out of his shop's back window. His satire is quite deliberate: "Cats and monkeys,—monkeys and cats,—all human life is there!" "Truly," he says, "I don't know whether the cats and monkeys imitate us, or whether it's we who imitate them" (*THJ* 2: 226–27).

Ironically, the narrator resolves this paradox by literally behaving like one of the sculptor's "expressive little brutes," for he has already dealt Theobald a fatal blow by brutally exposing his cherished illusions to the withering truth of Serafina's slatternly transfiguration (*THJ* 2: 227). "My poor friend," he says mockingly, "you've *dawdled!* She's an old, old woman—for a Madonna!" (*THJ* 2: 221). Retrospectively acknowledging his tactless accusation, H—— nevertheless disguises his literalism as "a piece of *brusquerie*" (*THJ* 2: 221), shifting to a foreign idiom to camouflage this aggressively American trait. Significantly, the sculptor also utters his first words in the tale in "that fantastic French in which Italians so freely indulge" (*THJ* 2: 224). In spite of external differences, the two men speak the same language; their common tongue is vulgar. Throughout the tale, the narrator views Serafina in animal rather than ideal terms; to him she is provocatively fleshly and coarse. After Theobald has introduced him to his intended model, H—— cannot help asking himself, "What was the relation of this singular couple?" (*THJ* 2: 219), precisely the leading question that the sculptor's lewd figurines are intended to provoke. As the narrator struggles inconclusively to find an answer, his innocent surmises yield to morally ambiguous hypotheses. When he later discovers Serafina in the company of the swarthy artist, H—— irresistibly lets his imagination run to pornographic extremes. Entering her apartment unannounced, the American witnesses the couple sharing a late-night supper, which confirms his suspicions of intimacy. The American's gaze is specifically attracted to the would-be Madonna: "With one hand she held in her lap a plate of smoking maccaroni; with the other she had lifted high in air one of the pendulous filaments of this succulent compound, and was in the act of slipping it gently down her throat" (*THJ* 2: 223). Presumably, his conclusion about their relation is less savory than the fettucini.

As editor of the *Atlantic*, Howells gladly published "The Madonna of the Future," but he found the "cats and monkeys philosophy" rather hard to swallow, especially since James ended the story by repeating the sculptor's sour exclamation that his animal subjects represent the totality of human life. If, as Kenneth Lynn has suggested, James deliberately modeled his narrator after Howells, perhaps the editor had good reason to complain.[32] Indeed, if Lynn is right, the implications of the story are even more profound than he suggests, for he specifically disavows the most important link between H—— and the sleazy purveyor of cats and monkeys. What connects these two characters is not merely lack of imagination and exaggerated respect for productivity but rather a more insidious commitment to the market as a final arbiter of artistic value. Just before he meets the sculptor for a second time to hear his cynical reprise, the narrator himself repeats a phrase Theobald first utters about Michelangelo: "He did his best at a venture." In this iteration, "venture" modulates to convey economic (rather than heroic) significance, and the painter's tribute becomes instead a kind of mocking epitaph, further reinforced by Serafina's announcement that she has just emptied her pockets "for a nine days' mass for his soul" (*THJ*

2: 231). The story's despairing tone derives less from its "cats and monkeys philosophy" than from its stubborn insistence upon exchange value in the assessment of Theobald's ill-fated career.

To his credit, the narrator resists one final exchange by refusing to gratify public curiosity about Theobald's (nonexistent) Madonna. At the painter's funeral, H——— is greeted by Mrs. Coventry, high priestess of an aesthetic salon, who had previously discouraged the narrator from taking Theobald's talent seriously. Having botched a commission from her twenty years earlier, Theobald becomes an easy target for her prophetic slander. "There are people who doubt whether there is any picture to be seen," she confides to the narrator, but if the long-awaited Madonna does exist, Mrs. Coventry fancies that one would find it "very like the picture in that tale of Balzac's,—a mere mass of incoherent scratches and daubs, a jumble of dead paint!" (*THJ* 2: 215). Not surprisingly, Theobald berates Mrs. Coventry as a philistine; to her, connoisseurship is simply a matter of possession rather than appreciation. As private patron and public consumer, she personifies two formidable aspects of the market, and to repudiate her is, presumably, to defy capitalism's encroaching claims upon artistic genius. Yet the narrator can repudiate Mrs. Coventry only on her own terms by asserting an exclusive claim to Theobald's legacy. When she inquires whether he has seen the Madonna, the narrator affirms, "I've seen her . . . she's mine,—by bequest. But I shall never show her to you." And he justifies this restrictive attitude by rudely, albeit correctly, exclaiming, "My dear Mrs. Coventry, you'd not understand her!" (*THJ* 2: 231).

For readers of Howells and James, this particular exchange assumes unusual importance because either one, or both, or neither of them may have written it. This authorial ambiguity greatly complicates the conventional wisdom about the publication history of this tale, which (replicating the story's interior logic) pits a bravely cosmopolitan author against his prudish editor.[33] After four months of renewed contact with European soil, James sent his story to the *Atlantic* in the summer of 1872. Always pressed for space, Howells found the manuscript too long to print in a single number, and he insisted that cuts be made once it was set in type. In unexpurgated form the tale charmed the entire James family, though its length afforded them two evenings' entertainment in Quincy Street. "Willy pronounced it very *distingué*, Mother charming, Alice exquisite." But Henry James Sr., who reported their reactions, also told of reservations, and his letter to James Jr. is worth quoting at length:

> Mr. Howells couldn't agree to give 25 pages of one number of the magazine to it, that was positive. And then besides he had a decided shrinking from one episode— that in which Theobald tells of his love for, and his visit from the Titian-ic beauty, and his subsequent disgust of his worthlessness—as being risky for the magazine; and then moreover he objected to the interview at the end between the writer and the old English neighbor [Mrs. Coventry], as rubbing into the reader what was sufficiently evident without it. On both the first and second points, we all thought that while Howells *in general* is too timid, there was good ground for his timidity in the present case. Both Mother & Alice shrank from both the episodes as not helping the understanding of the story along, and as being scary in themselves.

Willy thought the second quite unnecessary & superfluous, and thought the first if it had not been so much detailed but had been condensed into half a column, would perhaps do. But I thought they were both utterly uncalled for by the actual necessities of the tale, while they would both alike confer upon it a disagreeable musky odour strikingly at war with its unworldly beauty. I went to Howells accordingly this morning & told him that if he would consent to publish the whole tale in one piece, I would take upon me the responsibility of striking out the two episodes. He agreed, and he has made the connection of the parts perfect, so that no one would even dream of anything stricken out. . . . I ought to say also that Howells admires the story very much, thinks it very beautiful, and only objects to these episodes as being too much fashioned upon French literature. He thought also that the first one was very well done except for the details.[34]

Presumably, the narrator's final rebuke of Mrs. Coventry was much more explicit than the serial version implies, aggressively "rubbing into the reader" James's disdain for an audience both philistine and female. As the text stands, however, Mrs. Coventry merely affects a certain indifference to her interlocutor's "reprehensible rudeness"; the narrator terminates their brief conversation by turning away from her and saying, by way of excuse, that he is "sad and vexed and bitter" (*THJ* 2: 231). As emended, then, the story shields Mrs. Coventry from complicity in Theobald's demise, a privilege that Howells may have insisted upon out of deference to the *Atlantic*'s largely feminine audience. As published, the tale may silence the narrator's vexation and bitterness, but (twice) it voices the Italian sculptor's cynical measure of shallow public taste. His ejaculations do not convey full narrative authority, but they do smudge the exaggerated fastidiousness of Mrs. Coventry and, indeed, of the narrator himself. At least for a week after Theobald's death, H—— is troubled by "a fantastic, impertinent murmur, 'Cats and monkeys, monkeys and cats; all human life is there!' " (*THJ* 2: 232).

Howells, too, was troubled by this line (singling it out for adverse criticism both in a letter to James and in his 1875 review of *A Passionate Pilgrim and Other Tales*), but he let it stand. As we have seen, Howells was not alone in suggesting revisions to "The Madonna of the Future," even though James tended to place responsibility for expurgation with his editor. "With such a standard of propriety it makes it a bad look out ahead for imaginative writing," James told his father. "For what class of minds is it," he wondered, "that such very timorous scruples are thought necessary?" (To which one would have to answer: a class that included the entire James family, for censorious reactions extended to every one of them; the women, in particular, found parts of the work "scary.") The whole affair was sobering but also enlightening to James. He had to admit that "Howells has a better notion of the allowances of the common public than I have," and he was grateful that the editor performed the revision personally, "for of course he will have done it neatly."[35] In fact, James must have been more than usually satisfied, for when he republished "The Madonna of the Future" two years later, he did not restore any of the deleted passages, even though these had been reserved for him by Howells and returned to Quincy Street.

Even without them, the tale remains a fantasy of impertinence (to paraphrase its closing line), deflating both a sentimentalized means of production and a vulgarized marketplace of consumption. Romantic genius and enlightened patronage are equally illusory. Theobald's canvas may be a "mere dead blank," but as such it serves simultaneously as a foil to and mirror of the narrator's implicitly depraved curiosity (*THJ* 2: 228). H—— is not surprised by his discovery in "the little room it seemed such cruel irony to call a studio" (Mrs. Coventry's skepticism has proven powerfully contagious), but neither is he prepared for Theobald's final words of forgiveness: " 'You were right,' he said with a pitiful smile, 'I'm a dawdler! I'm a failure! I shall do nothing more in this world. You opened my eyes, and, though the truth is bitter, I bear you no grudge. Amen!' " (*THJ* 2: 229, 228). The narrator's reaction, telling enough, is to insist that Theobald immediately accompany him to dinner, as if the painter's words were a prayer of thanksgiving. Amen! Consumption, literally, is the only available mechanism for alleviating the narrator's profound discomfort when he is confronted with Theobald's revelation of his mortal wound. Of course, the invitation is declined. Theobald succumbs to brain fever and the Madonna's future is indefinitely postponed.

More incisively than some of his other early stories, "The Madonna of the Future" describes what James elsewhere refers to as the "complex fate" of being an American, especially an American artist, eager to distinguish himself and his culture yet temperamentally disassociated from the United States and liable to indulge a "superstitious valuation of Europe."[36] The reciprocal tendency, which James seemed to fear less and Howells more, was superstitiously to devalue America. Many readers have indulged James by uncritically appropriating his own definitions; it has been relatively simple, then, to contrast James's complex fate with Howells's presumably more simple one. Indeed, James himself specifically invited this distinction and encouraged his contemporaries to patronize Howells's confidence in America's sufficiency as a narrative field. Howells's fate, however, was in some ways even more complex than James's insofar as he had to come to terms not only with Europe but also (and perhaps more formidably) with Boston.

Complex Fates

As Lewis P. Simpson and others have suggested, Howells's elected affinity for New England culture was always being undermined (perhaps subconsciously) by a nagging sense of its illiberal social origins. To accept the social contingencies of that culture meant, for Howells, to betray the more egalitarian ethos of his boyhood on the Ohio frontier and the idealized concept of literary vocation that he had formed there.[1] Whatever the psychic cost, however, Howells willingly made the sacrifice in order to secure his hard-won literary status. He readily adopted the prejudices of his neighbors, as *Suburban Sketches* makes evident; when the Irish began to move into Sacramento Street, it was time for the Howellses to move out. In "A Pedestrian Tour" (1869) the author, self-consciously Yankee, pretends to mock

> the spiritual desolation occasioned by the settlement of an Irish family in one of our suburban neighborhoods. The householders view with fear and jealousy the erection of any dwelling of less than a stated cost, as portending a possible advent of Irish; and when the calamitous race actually appears, a mortal pang strikes to the bottom of every pocket. Values tremble throughout that neighborhood, to which the new-comers communicate a species of moral dry-rot.

To fellow readers of the *Atlantic*, this was supposed to be an inside joke, but there was little humor in Howells's revelation to Norton that "Sacramento street has lately become much less desirable than it was: Irish have moved in, and I think it would be the part of prudence to sell the house if I could find a good purchaser. I'm afraid it will depreciate on my hands."[2]

The Quincy Street neighbors of another Irish family—the Jameses—probably had less to worry about when those newcomers arrived in 1866. For one thing, they came from Newport, not from Dublin; and no whiff of Roman Catholicism came with them, only a rather diffuse aroma of Swedenborgianism. With its prodigious gifts of mind and money, the James family found a ready place in Cambridge. Indeed, among the younger Jameses the community's social blandness often provoked a yearning for exile rather than the desire for acceptance that Howells more poignantly felt. If it is true (as William James once observed) that the James family virtually constituted a sovereign nation in itself, then it must also be confessed that the family was highly jealous of its borders. James's mother made the point in 1873, when Henry was traveling in Europe, by detailing to him the family's social itinerary:

> We are to entertain to-morrow at dinner, the Aldriches! & the Howells! Don't you wish you were here? I would ask Sargy [Perry], but he says that Aldrich always reminded him of a rotten apple. The association at the dinner table would not be agreeable.[3]

How volubly those exclamation points speak! And yet, at the appointed hour their implicit condescension may have been inaudible to Howells, who reported to James that he and his wife had a "merry time" with his parents. The incongruity is significant, not because it justifies an indictment of hypocrisy against the Jameses but rather because it vivifies the real social contradictions of Howells's literary situation. As editor of the *Atlantic* his cultural power was indisputable, but as a man of letters transplanted from the frontier, his cultural legitimacy was peculiarly vulnerable—and he knew it.

Just two weeks before the engagement in Quincy Street, Howells had written home to Ohio about the progress of his first real novel, *A Chance Acquaintance*, which had started its run in the magazine. "People speak to me of it more than of Their Wedding Journey," he noted:

> I am glad I have done it for one reason if for no other: it sets me forever outside of the rank of mere *culturists*, followers of an elegant literature, and proves that I have sympathy with the true spirit of Democracy. Sometimes I've doubted whether I had, but when I came to look the matter over in writing this story, I doubted no longer.[4]

Presumably in this story Howells repudiates "the rank of mere culturists" through the character of Miles Arbuton, a fastidious Bostonian whose discriminating conscience prevents him from "encouraging people whom he might have to drop for reasons of society."[5] Chance nevertheless challenges his habitual reserve by acquainting him with Kitty Ellison, a charming young woman from Eriecreek, New York, where something close to "perfect democracy" governs both social and political relations. Together with her native self-reliance, frontier conditions encourage in Kitty the "unsnubbed fearlessness of a heart which did not suspect a sense of social difference in others, or imagine itself misprized for anything but a fault" (*ACQ* 37). Romantically combining these two opposing types (and mapping their repercussions), Howells again develops his plot around holiday travel (as in *Their Wedding Journey*), but this novel marks a significant advance over its modest predecessor, as James was quick to recognize.

The surviving letters from 1873 convey the first relatively full exchange of their views on narrative art, which heretofore had been displaced between the covers of their respective books. In *Watch and Ward*, for example, James's heroine recommends a current novel to the rather supercilious minister, Hubert Lawrence, who has been flirting with her. The hero of the "silly" book she proffers, also a minister, falls in love with "a fair Papist." Converting her to the true faith is not easy, but finally succeeding he "baptizes her with his own hands one week, and marries her the next." Lawrence scoffs at the improbable plot. "Heaven preserve us!" he exclaims, "what a hotch-potch!"

> "Is that what they are doing nowadays? I very seldom read a novel, but when I glance into one, I 'm sure to find some such stuff as that! Nothing irritates me so as the flatness of people's imagination. Common life—I don't say it 's a vision of bliss, but it 's better than that!"

Substituting himself for the misguided novelist, the minister proposes an alternative design. " 'Why did n't he marry her first and convert her afterwards?' " he asks. " 'Is n't a clergyman after all, before all, a man? I mean to write a novel about a priest who falls in love with a pretty Mahometan and swears by Allah to win her.' "[6] Howells attempts in his own work to redeem Lawrence's aesthetic priorities from the jaded manner of their none too serious advocate. More than once in *Their Wedding Journey* Howells himself steps forward to confess a predilection for the stuff of ordinary lives. After placing the Marches aboard a railroad car whose other everyday occupants sympathetically absorb their attention, the author addresses the reader in the first person:

> As in literature the true artist will shun the use even of real events if they are of an improbable character, so the sincere observer of man will not desire to look upon his heroic or occasional phases, but will seek him in his habitual moods of vacancy and tiresomeness. To me, at any rate, he is at such times very precious; and I never perceive him to be so much a man and a brother as when I feel the pressure of his vast, natural, unaffected dulness. Then I am able to enter confidently into his life and inhabit there, to think his shallow thoughts, to be moved by his dumb, stupid desires, to be dimly illumined by his stinted inspirations, to share his foolish prejudices, to practise his obtuse selfishness.[7]

How carefully Howells read (and revised) the foregoing passage from *Watch and Ward* is also suggested by the donnée of *A Foregone Conclusion*, already begun while *A Chance Acquaintance* was running in the magazine. "The hero is a Venetian priest," he bubbled over to James, "in love with an American girl. There's richness!" Undissuaded by his friend's cosmopolitan irony, Howells deliberately converted James's facetious improbabilities into creditable fictions. Their critical dialogue now began in earnest.

More than one critic has remarked that Howells might have had James in mind when he delineated the overly refined figure of Miles Arbuton;[8] but the biographical parallels between that fictional character and his author's friendly competitor are probably less important than the suggestive impact *A Chance Acquaintance* had upon James's subsequent work. James vigorously responded more than once to this story as it ran serially in the *Atlantic,* and though not all of his reactions (including, perhaps, his most generous) have survived, their recurrence testifies to pregnant interest. Most significantly perhaps, Howells's independently minded heroine arrested James's imagination and provoked envious praise. Recognizing Kitty Ellison as a distinctively American type, James prophesied that Howells could take out "an unassailable patent" on the American girl. She was a property subject to infringement, however, and in the coming years no one would encroach upon her more forcefully than James himself, whose various appropriations took the form of Daisy Miller, Isabel Archer, and numerous other spirited young women.

James's reaction to Howells's next book did not come piecemeal through letters but rather in the unusual form of twin (unsigned) reviews. In both of these James did not restrict his attention to *A Foregone Conclusion;* rather, he took up Howells's latest novel as the cumulative product of the author's imaginative development: reaching back, as it did, to the Italy of *Venetian Life* and reproducing, in even more vivid form, the type of puckish heroine "patented" in *A Chance Acquaintance.* Significantly, to James the new volume marked a clear advance over its other fictional predecessors; for the first time Howells had shown that he could "embrace a dramatic situation with . . . true imaginative force." Indeed, this published view is consonant with his earlier private reservation about *A Chance Acquaintance,* in which (as James alleged) Howells had slighted the dramatic possibilities inherent in his juxtaposition of opposing character types. Kitty was truly rounded, remarkably complete, but James found Arbuton "a shade too scurvy," his particular moral shabbiness incongruent with his patrician social antecedents. (In the novel's denouement, Arbuton "cuts" Kitty—in spite of his professed affection for her—when he finds himself in the company of two more fashionable Boston women; consequently, their engagement is irreparably severed.) As a result of this imbalance, James admonished, "you rather resent [Kitty's] drama—her own part in it being so very perfectly analysed—having a hero who was coming to *that!* I was hoping," James prophetically added, "that it was she who was to affront him." As James would soon demonstrate, the captivating idea of "a certain young woman affronting her destiny" started him off on *The Portrait of a Lady.* [9]

Throughout his life, James could never resist the impulse to rewrite novels written by others, a habit that cost him more than one friendship (most famously with H. G. Wells).[10] The same imperious urge surfaces in these early letters to Howells, usually cloaked with apologies ("I didn't mean to dig so deep," etc.); but unlike some of James's later correspondents, Howells accepted criticism genially and constructively. Though some scholars have simply viewed James's epistolary aggressions as evidence of a superior disregard for Howells, these critical gestures offer perhaps the truest measure of artistic friendship, for they presume an inherent elasticity of temper and eagerly seek to elicit a spirited response. Simultaneously, they signal a genuine engagement and a provocative challenge, both at considerable remove from the rather smug condescension of James's earlier remarks to the Nortons and other long-term residents of literary Cambridge. If Howells had remained a "tertiary talent," as James incorrectly anticipated only a few years before, these letters would never have been written.

The best evidence to support this claim comes not from James's correspondence but from his fiction. Quickened appreciation for the specifically national quality of a Howells heroine ("the delicate, nervous, emancipated young woman begotten of our institutions and our climate, and equipped with a lovely face

and an irritable moral consciousness") probably did as much for James, imaginatively, as the memory of his cousin Minny Temple, whose untimely death (in
1870) unleashed a flood of fictional possibilities. The peculiar intensity of this
necrophilic family romance has often been cited as an inspiration for *The Portrait of a Lady*, whose admirable heroine indeed shares many qualities with those
James attributed to Minny Temple.[11] Kitty Ellison, however, not only resembles
Isabel Archer but quite literally anticipates her story. At the decisive midpoint
of *A Chance Acquaintance*, Kitty takes stock of her relationship with Arbuton, a
process that Howells conveys through interior monologue. "It had begun like a
romance," she muses; "she had pleased her fancy, if not her heart, with the
poetry of it; but at last she felt exiled and strange in his presence." To be sure,
the transcription of Kitty's consciousness does not effloresce into chapter 42 of
The Portrait, but it does prefigure that momentous scene in certain ways. "She
had no right to a different result," Howells continues,

> even through any deep feeling in the matter; but while she owned, with her half-
> sad, half-comical consciousness, that she had been tacitly claiming and expecting
> too much, she softly pitied herself, with a kind of impersonal compassion, as if it
> were some other girl whose pretty dream had been broken. Its ruin involved the
> loss of another ideal; for she was aware that there had been gradually rising in her
> mind an image of Boston, different alike from the holy place of her childhood, the
> sacred city of the antislavery heroes and martyrs, and from the jesting, easy, sympa-
> thetic Boston of Mr. and Mrs. March. The new Boston with which Mr. Arbuton
> inspired her was a Boston of mysterious prejudices and lofty reservations; a Boston
> of high and difficult tastes, that found its social ideal in the Old World, and that
> shrank from contact with the reality of this; a Boston as alien as Europe to her
> simple experiences, and that seemed to be proud only of the things that were
> unlike other American things; a Boston that would rather perish by fire and sword
> than be suspected of vulgarity; a critical, fastidious, and reluctant Boston, dissatis-
> fied with the rest of the hemisphere, and gelidly self-satisfied in so far as it was not
> in the least the Boston of her fond preconceptions.

As we know, James would bravely extend such self-examination to fill an entire
chapter. Howells stops short of this—the record of Kitty's thoughts make only
for a long pause in an ongoing dialogue—but his comparatively abbreviated use
of the technique is justified by the nature of the relationship itself. As the book's
title indicates, hers is a chance acquaintance. Unlike Isabel, Kitty is not trapped
in a suffocating marriage; indeed, she prophetically imagines what might happen
if she were:

> "Sometimes, Fanny," she said, now, after a long pause, speaking in behalf of that
> other girl she had been thinking of, "it seems to me as if Mr. Arbuton were all
> gloves and slim umbrella,—the mere husk of well-dressed culture and good man-
> ners. His looks *do* promise everything; but O dear me! I should be sorry for any
> one that was in love with him. Just imagine some girl meeting with such a man,
> and taking a fancy to him! I suppose she never would quite believe but that he
> must somehow be what she first thought him, and she would go down to her grave
> believing that she had failed to understand him. What a curious story it would
> make!" (ACQ 91–92)

When she is challenged by her aunt to write such a story, Kitty disqualifies herself on the grounds that it would be too unpleasant and difficult. "The only way you could show his character," Kitty asserts, "would be to have her do and say hateful things to him, when she couldn't help it, and then repent of it, while he was impassively perfect through everything" (*ACQ* 92). James, of course, would find another way that, ironically, was already mapped out by Howells: consistently internalizing the "hateful" action through the heroine's prolonged meditation, indulging the instinct for melodrama while avoiding its conventional form.

The architectonic refinement of *The Portrait of a Lady* was humbly preceded by another novel that also benefited from the example of Howells: *Washington Square* (1880). Indeed, James's epistolary responses to *A Chance Acquaintance* outline an identifiable précis of this story, which also involves the mismatch of character types, a broken engagement, and, especially, the inviting challenge of a morally recreant suitor (Morris Townsend). If James did feel personally impugned by Howells's character of Arbuton, in *Washington Square* he deliberately placed a similarly "scurvy" character at considerable remove from the assured status of the cosmopolitan gentry. As his name implies, Townsend lives on the ruffled fringe of society, sustained by sentimentally vulnerable women who sponsor his romantic exploits. Townsend's career has indeed been transatlantic, but conceit and misplaced social ambition have taken him further than anything else. These same motives lead him to Washington Square, where he deceptively courts a plain and unassuming heiress, Catherine Sloper. As the young woman's father dryly observes, Townsend's tenor voice is "very taking—very taking."[12] The adjective threatens to become transitive at any moment.

Curiously enough, James also suggests that the mercenary Townsend is a kind of realist manqué, a pedestrian observer of pedestrian things. His first solitary encounter with Catherine reads more like an interview than a romantic tryst. "Tell me about yourself," he asks journalistically; "give me a little sketch." When their talk indifferently turns to literature, Townsend affirms that books are "tiresome things; only, as he said, you had to read a good many before you found it out. He had been to places that people had written books about, and they were not a bit like the descriptions. To see for yourself—that was the great thing; he always tried to see for himself" (*WS* 32–33). To convey this rather threadbare realist credo, James shifts from direct to indirect discourse, a strategy that deliberately undermines Townsend's representational legitimacy. Furtively displacing Townsend's cleverness through the objectified third-person, this narrative mode compromises his authenticity.

As Dr. Sloper quickly senses, Townsend has grasping instincts, but not a truly grasping imagination: he is more than content (as James once said of Howells) to deal with what his fleshly eyes can see. Materially, at least, they take in a great deal. To interpret the novel by paraphrasing from James's letters is not to say that *Washington Square* is a retributive roman à clef. Townsend is not an allegorical Howells, even though (by the end of the book) he somewhat uncomfortably begins to resemble him. A little too plump and much too socially familiar, Townsend embodies a patrician culture's worst fears of predatory democracy.

As we have seen, Howells became the target of similar anxieties, especially after he came to assume a position of real cultural power as the editor of the *Atlantic Monthly*. Private correspondence among Howells's contemporary Bostonians registers the same peculiar combination of resentment and fear that Townsend inspires in Dr. Sloper. These feelings became especially audible once the ambitious young man from Ohio began to extend the frontier of the magazine's cultural geography beyond New England. James, of course, already had sneered at Howells's editorial ambition and modest literary accomplishments; undeniable evidence of his growing popularity in the 1870s provoked others to respond in kind. Even though they genially entertained Howells at their dinner tables, literary Cantabrigians nevertheless entertained lingering doubts about his cultural credentials. As Charles Eliot Norton reported to Lowell in 1874, "Howells came in to dine . . . plump and with ease shining out of his eyes. He has passed his poetic stage, and bids fair to be a popular American author. As for art in American letters,—recent numbers of the 'Atlantic Monthly' forbid one to think of it."[13]

The suspicious condescension James (and many others) first felt toward Howells resurfaces in Dr. Sloper's attitude toward Townsend. To the skeptical physician, Townsend is squandering his bachelor artfulness on a "subject" disproportionately meager. Much like James's version of America in *Hawthorne*, written shortly prior to *Washington Square*, Catherine Sloper can only be defined in negative terms. Though she is not ugly (the narrator informs us), neither is she attractive; while she is not clever, neither is she abnormally deficient; if there is nothing to be proud of in the poor girl, neither is there anything to be ashamed of. Catalogued in a manner almost worthy of Tocqueville, James's sketch of Catherine is composed of erasures rather than definitive strokes. From her father's cynically cosmopolitan point of view, only the prospect of a fabulous inheritance could possibly attract a suitor's attentions. Catherine's fortune is handsome, whereas she is plain. A commonplace child, she epitomizes the democratic average, which helps to explain (even if it cannot fully justify) the doctor's—and James's—cruelly ironic treatment of her.

Throughout the novel, James's narrative vocabulary again modulates between aesthetic and economic emphases. Appreciation develops as a major theme of the book—an issue vivified by the failure of both Dr. Sloper and Townsend to comprehend Catherine's human worth in anything but material terms. As a woman, Catherine is (almost) trapped by the false romanticism of the marriage market; but the men uniformly are trapped by the distorting realism of the capitalist market, where all values reductively become tokens for exchange. Even though James does permit his heroine to grow in moral stature by the end of the novel, he stubbornly refuses to indulge her mediocrity. Catherine Sloper is the madonna without a future. On the novel's last page, she takes up her needlework "for life, as it were" (WS 189).

If *Washington Square* looks back to *A Chance Acquaintance*, James's novel also takes an important cue from *A Foregone Conclusion*. By displacing the imagination for melodrama into a character (Mrs. Penniman) who presumes to know far more than she really does, James playfully aggravates and satirizes the banality of the kind of plot his novel willfully aborts. James's published remarks about Florida Vervain's mother (in *A Foregone Conclusion*) can easily be transposed to describe the function of the histrionic *ficelle* in *Washington Square*. With her "lively hospitality to the things that don't happen, and her serene unconsciousness of the things that do," Mrs. Vervain impressed upon James "the way human levity hovers about the edge of all painful occurrences. Her scatter-brained geniality deepens the picture of her daughter's brooding preoccupations, and there is much sustained humor in making her know so much less of the story in which she plays a part than we do." Oblivious to her own self-indulgence, which frequently verges on cruelty, Aunt Penniman in *Washington Square* is both more and less knowledgeable than her pitiable niece. She thinks herself a woman of the world, but (unlike Catherine) she cannot imagine any other world than the gas-lit stage of star-crossed love.

Lavinia Penniman's treacherous fidelity to Townsend enforces a greater loneliness on Catherine, who nevertheless declines, after much inner torment, to accommodate the willfulness of others. Appropriately, Dr. Sloper's last words in the novel express his surprise at her hard-won resolution, when she stubbornly refuses to submit to his authority. Even his announced intention of compromising the terms of her inheritance cannot swerve her. "Upon my word," he exclaims, "I had no idea how obstinate you are!" That Catherine herself knows this to be true gives her (and the reader) "a certain joy" (*WS* 176). Like so many other James novels, *Washington Square* finds its pleasures in frustration.

Having turned Townsend away for the last time, Catherine sits alone in her parlor and resumes her distaff artistry, quietly applying the needle to the "morsel of fancy-work" that becomes her celibate alternative to social intercourse (*WS* 189). In spite of obvious restrictions, Catherine achieves palpable dignity through renunciation, maintaining a sad but necessary independence. Her isolated status at the novel's end closely resembles that of many other Jamesian protagonists—artist-figures in particular—whose visionary integrity can only be purchased at the expense of public recognition. James had not yet resigned himself to such a fate; but in writing *Washington Square* the author had come to a pivotal moment in his career. Like his heroine, James was contending with problems of (literary) inheritance and influence; the novel's rather confused texture innocently reflects this, as James experiments with and variously indulges one narrative mode after another: the realism of Balzac, the irony of Austen, the psychological moralism of Hawthorne.[14]

Above all, however, *Washington Square* adopts Howells's shrewd technique of "making small things do great service," as James put it in his first review of *A Foregone Conclusion*. The "monotonous" surface of American life required a serious literary artist to discover salient values "where a less devoted glance would see little more than an arid blank." So long as she remains an emblem of vacuity to the other characters, Catherine Sloper provokes a strikingly similar dilemma of perception. While it is easy to confuse the author's narrative voice with Dr. Sloper's caustically ironic attitude (indeed, the novel at first seems to invite such confusion), Catherine finally emerges as an authentic heroine through a marked shift in James's stylistic allegiance. Only by displacing or silencing the intrusively

conventional mannerisms of others (the ironic interjections and cynical confidences of Sloper or the melodramatic outbursts of Mrs. Penniman) can one hope
to hear and appreciate the more restrained voice preferred by Catherine. As
James writes, "Poor Catherine's dignity was not aggressive; it never sat in state;
but if you pushed far enough you could find it" (WS 176). Her value, at once
human and aesthetic, consists in remaining inconspicuous.

The Larger
Success

While *A Chance Acquaintance* was running through the *Atlantic*, James remarked to his sister that he was relishing every installment. "But what a pity," he added, "that with such pretty art, [Howells] can't embrace a larger piece of the world."[1] By now James's complaint was a familiar one. *Suburban Sketches, Their Wedding Journey, A Chance Acquaintance*: all had suffered from the same want of largeness and scope. An impoverished cultural landscape—which had been, as James viewed it, the debilitating curse of Hawthorne—continued to plague the American artist. And yet Howells had managed to publish three sizable books in as many years, and a fourth was on the way.[2] (At this rate he was outproducing, if not outperforming, Hawthorne himself.) For all his copious magazine scribbling, James had not yet brought out a single volume, although his editor had generously encouraged him to gather some short stories together and promised to intercede with a publisher on behalf of the venture. The elder Henry James also volunteered to perform a similar office for his son. While he appreciated the sincerity of their offers, the ambitious younger James preferred to wait. He wanted, in particular, to grapple with the marketplace firsthand, to dispense with (even friendly) intermediaries, and to start himself, as he put it, "on a remunerative and perfectly practical literary basis."[3] James wanted to profit by the example of Howells's early career as editor and author, at the same time that he intended to escape what he viewed as the inherent limitations of his friend's literary situation.

Because Howells had wedded his fortunes to one periodical, bartering a certain kind of freedom for the security of assured publication and a weekly paycheck, his work could hardly be expected to transcend the restrictive limits of the *Atlantic*'s largely feminine readership. No truly ambitious writer, James felt, could survive the contradiction between the free exercise of creative imagination and the rigorous enforcement of squeamish editorial scruples, which he memorably described as myopic demands for the representation of "virtuous and aspiring characters," a so-called "happy ending," and the "distribution at the last of prizes, pensions, wives, babies, millions, appended paragraphs, and cheerful remarks."[4] During the first dozen years of his own career, James wrote scores of blistering reviews, the nominal subjects of which frequently served only as a pretext for him to deride the imbecility of the novel's usual audience and the conventional expectations it presupposed. Historically, novel reading by women often had been deplored as a threat to feminine virtue; but in his early reviews James completely reversed the logic of this argument, according to Anne T. Margolis, "insinuating that it was literature which needed protection from women readers and not vice versa."[5]

Much derided (by James and many others since) for actively embracing genteel editorial standards, Howells conveniently lent himself to easy but superficial comparison. His actual relationship to the reading public, and its impact on his own conception of professional authorship, was much more complex (and far less passive) than is commonly understood.[6] As Richard Brodhead has recently observed, "To edit the *Atlantic* is not, for Howells, to buy into a secondary form of literary life. To manage this institution is to occupy what he knows as literature's central place of power: it is to realize himself *in* the literary in the most compelling way he is able to imagine it."[7] While James's career has seemed distinctively modern to later critics (especially Lionel Trilling) because of his apparently radical disjunction or alienation from any given institutional setting, Howells has almost always been approached through the commercial matrix of his publishing affiliations; and hostility toward that presumably genteel environment has tinged most assessments of his work with a combination of resentment and despair.[8] The recoverable sequence of the Howells–James correspondence should force us to recognize that James's displacement from sites of cultural power was more illusory than real, a self-preserving construction largely of his own making. Exerting different kinds of pressure, the literary marketplace deeply implicated both men in a complex—and sometimes overlapping—series of social and aesthetic negotiations.

James was more interested in testing (and stretching) the limits of the market rather than defining them. As early as 1872 he turned aside some advice offered both by Howells and his brother William about the "over-refinement" of his magazine style. Admitting that they were right to discourage him, James nevertheless preferred not to compromise:

> Beyond a certain point this would not be desirable . . . for me at least, who must give up the ambition of ever being a free-going & light-paced enough writer to please the multitude. The multitude, I am more & more convinced, has absolutely no taste—none at least that a thinking man is bound to defer to. To write for the few who have is doubtless to lose money—but I am not afraid of starving.[9]

The minor scuffle with the *Atlantic* about possibly salacious passages in "The Madonna of the Future" (1873) reminded James that insufficient refinement could also be a problem. On that account he sent another sexually suggestive tale, "Madame de Mauves," to New York's *Galaxy* later in the same year.[10]

The necessity—and the freedom—to place material elsewhere were stimuli Howells seldom felt in his career, perhaps to his detriment. Some biographical critics have alleged that because of his considerable daily workload as an editor,

Howells sacrificed the opportunity to learn and develop the art of fiction more completely. According to George N. Bennett, the serious question of whether Howells's editorial responsibilities might prevent him from realizing his "full potentialities as an author seems not to have occurred to him with any real force."[11] While such assertions are questionable (Howells did, after all, resign from the *Atlantic* in 1881, confessing that he was "fearfully tired of editorial work, and impatient . . . to devote [him]self to authorship"),[12] another, more subtle implication of running the magazine may have been that under its aegis Howells was denied the help of serious criticism from other writers who were dependent upon his goodwill. The example of James both supports and refutes this proposition. At first he directs his pointed analysis of Howells's intellectual limitations to others; once established as a novelist in his own right, however, he challenges his editor directly—and bluntly—about matters of form, character, and technique. In more psychological terms, the social visibility attached to editing the *Atlantic* actually may have heightened Howells's cultural insecurities, as the infamous debacle at the Whittier Birthday Dinner illustrates.[13] The benefits of Howells's affiliation with the *Atlantic* are at once obvious and ambiguous.

As James began to devote himself more exclusively to the writing of fiction, he quickly recognized that one periodical (even the most prestigious) could not hope to keep pace with his production. Just as important, he came to see that active competition for his work would measurably enhance both his economic and artistic leverage. James readily adapted to the logic of the marketplace, as his preliminary thoughts about serializing his first full-length novel make clear. With an invitation from the editor of *Scribner's Magazine* in hand, James nevertheless felt that, in deference to years of consistent support and encouragement, he should give Howells the right of first refusal of the story. "I am pretty sure the *Atlantic* would like equally well with *Scribner* to have my story," James confided to his parents, which "I should prefer to appearing there. It must depend on the money question, however, entirely and whichever will pay best shall have the story, and if the *Atlantic* will pay as much as the other, I ought, properly, to take up with *it*."[14] Howells agreeably matched the competition's offer (twelve hundred dollars for twelve installments), thereby securing the rights to *Roderick Hudson*.

Deliberate apprenticeship, continued residence abroad, and perhaps the grudgingly formidable example of Howells's fertile "native-grown" imagination all predisposed James to tackle a large, "international" subject for his first full-length novel. Though flagrantly derivative and leaning heavily on Hawthorne's *Marble Faun* (1860), with its quartet of characters transplanted to the American art colony in Rome, James's book also takes certain cues from *A Foregone Conclusion*, especially as it repudiates or frustrates romantic notions of genius. Howells's novel locates this principle in the European figure of Don Ippolito, a Venetian priest, whose faith comes to grief in his yearning for America and his unreciprocated desire for Florida Vervain, the exuberant young heroine who so impressed James. *Roderick Hudson*, on the other hand, bestows the ambiguous distinction of genius upon its title character, an aspiring sculptor from singularly uninspiring Northampton, Massachusetts. Both egoists are shadowed by more cerebral types, observer figures who compete with and finally displace the nominal protagonists. In the nervously autobiographical Ferris (who serves as American consul to Venice during the Civil War), Howells captures the essence of residual Puritanism, incapable of reconciling self-conscious social virtue with largely unconscious sexual desire. James's Rowland Mallett suffers from a very similar internal disjunction that renders him at once prurient and fastidious.

Roderick Hudson directly followed Howells's novel as the leading serialized fiction in the *Atlantic,* and in more ways than one it picks up where *A Foregone Conclusion* leaves off. Whereas Howells begins his story in Venice only to return, in the closing chapter, to America, James reverses the migration by beginning in New England and quickly transporting his cast of characters to Italy. By bringing Ferris and Florida Vervain back to the United States, Howells also makes it possible for them to discover their love for one another and to marry. In both his notices, James objected to the tidiness of this conclusion, which he would have preferred to keep open-ended, trustfully surrendering "Florida Vervain's subsequent fortunes to the imagination of the reader." Without the benefit of knowing James's opinion, Howells privately agreed with it, for he told Charles Eliot Norton that he wanted the tale to end with Florida's rejection of the misguided priest. "If I had been perfectly my own master—it's a little droll, but true, that even in such a matter one isn't—the story would have ended with Don Ippolito's rejection. But I suppose that it is well to work for others in some measure," Howells continued, "and I feel pretty sure that I deepened the shadows by going on, and achieved a completer verity, also." Kenneth Lynn interprets this remark to mean that the owners of the *Atlantic,* wary of disappointing subscribers, obliged the author to tack on a happy ending to his story. But this is only one of several possibilities; the same pressure could have come from Howells's wife or others who occasionally reviewed and criticized his work in manuscript. More straightforwardly, his phrasing could also imply that he had willingly internalized, and wanted to respect, the narrative expectations he associated with the common reader.[15]

Any number of critics have eagerly contrasted Howells's readerly indulgence with James's writerly condescension, much to the former's disadvantage; but the full range of available evidence does not consistently uphold this attractively simple distinction. In his later editorial contributions to *Harper's,* of course, Howells's antagonism toward conventional romanticism and sentimentality became almost notorious. But it is worth remembering that neither does his early fiction always seek to appease the common appetite for a narrative resolution rung in to the sound of church bells. Kitty Ellison abruptly ends her brief engagement in *A Chance Acquaintance*; more than Don Ippolito's death sours the future happiness of Florida Vervain and Henry Ferris in *A Foregone Conclusion*; and in Howells's next novel, *Private Theatricals* (serialized in 1875–76), the heroine's overwrought flirtations exhaust even her most ardent admirers. Though she is cast as Juliet in the book's final scene, her story conspicuously ends without an available Romeo. Suspecting that the bulk of his readers were women, Howells nevertheless decided to make this novel, as he told James T. Fields, "more of an experiment upon my public than I've ventured before," perhaps to see how far his audience would indulge the "little freedoms" of a deliberately self-aggrandizing female protagonist.[16]

Howells's experiment did not please everyone—least of all the author himself—and he chose not to reprint the serial in volume form despite lucrative offers from his publisher.[17] Even as it ran through the magazine, however, *Private Theatricals* did excite much comment. "Brilliant" was the word James kept hearing; and such reports made him eager to review the book. That occasion would also serve to return a favor, for Howells had recently lavished much praise on James's first collection of fiction, *A Passionate Pilgrim and Other Tales* (1875). When the decision not to publish *Private Theatricals* left James without a book to review, he paid Howells an even higher compliment by refashioning his story in *The Europeans* (1878). Though James considered Howells's suppression of the novel a great mistake (news of a pirated German translation made its way even to the purlieus of Kensington), the forfeit left him free to poach. Perhaps to disguise his indebtedness, as well as to multiply his opportunities for satire, James located his quaint novella in the 1830s (so as to "play havoc," as he told his editor, with "a mouldering & ascetic old Puritan family"), but significant parallels between the two books abound.

After he had finished reading *A Chance Acquaintance*, James told Howells that his characters were better than the scenery, which they heroically struggle to find picturesque. "Vivid figures will always kill the finest background in the world," he advised; in *The Europeans* James applies that principle with deliberate vengeance, using sharp-tongued cosmopolitan characters to expose the social vacuity of provincial New England. Such a strategy had also been part of Howells's "experiment" in *Private Theatricals*, which exploits the contemporary vogue for local color by subverting the usually rather pious sympathies of that mode. (Howells arguably took an even greater risk by making the narrative voice directly accountable for such comic heresies.) At the beginning of his novel, Howells describes the Yankee farmers of West Pekin in terms of humorous desolation. "If they have no thoughts," he observes, "they have not the irrelevance and superfluity of words."

> They are a signally silent race. I have seen two of them, old neighbors, meet after an absence, and when they had hornily rattled their callous palms together, stand staring at each other, their dry, serrated lips falling apart, their jaws mutely working up and down, their pale-blue eyes vacantly winking, and their weather-beaten faces as wholly discharged of expression as the gable ends of two barns confronting each other from opposite sides of the road. . . .[18]

With strokes like this, Howells's realism, previously a matter of delicacy, could become almost grotesque: a cross between Edgar Allan Poe and Sarah Orne Jewett. Keeping his focus more on the country gentry, James permits his Europeanized protagonist to offer this assessment of New England character:

> "No, they are not gay," Felix admitted. "They are sober; they are even severe. They are of a pensive cast; they take things hard. I think there is something the matter with them; they have some melancholy memory or some depressing expectation. It 's not the epicurean temperament. My uncle, Mr. Wentworth, is a tremendously

high-toned old fellow; he looks as if he were undergoing martyrdom, not by fire, but by freezing."[19]

Looking out of her hotel window, which cheerfully overlooks a cemetery in downtown Boston, Felix's sister, Eugenia, glances at the most typical element in the New England landscape ("a tall wooden church-spire, painted white"); it strikes her as "the ugliest thing she had ever seen" (*TE* 876). A curtain of heavy white snow (falling on the twelfth of May!) cannot shroud its grim presence. In both novels local color becomes a brittle annoyance.

Not even the flaming romance of multiple marriages can take the chill out of James's narrative, which ends for the Baroness Eugenia in self-imposed exile. Her primly fastidious (would-be) lover, Robert Acton, catches Eugenia fibbing, and instead marries "a particularly nice young girl" (*TE* 1038). There is safety, at least, in anonymity. Like Belle Farrell before her, Eugenia finds her coquettish temperament incompatible with provincial culture. Mrs. Farrell returns to Boston to launch an acting career; Eugenia merely continues hers by returning to Germany, where a morganatic marriage has condemned her to play a rather sterile role. Still, disappointed by the narrow scope of a man like Acton, she concludes that "Europe seems to me much larger than America" (*TE* 1038). As Robert Emmet Long has suggested, viewed chronologically, *Private Theatricals* and *The Europeans* "form an interesting transition—from regional realism to an international satire of manners."[20]

As is the case with Zenobia in Hawthorne's *Blithedale Romance*, a deceptively Arcadian setting only exaggerates Belle Farrell's histrionic excesses. But the novel's flippant contrasts between urban sophistication and rural simplicity, which are intended to be comic, frequently have the opposite effect; as in Hawthorne's romance, a fundamental dislocation of the culture's social and sexual energies betrays itself through nervous laughter. The middle-class wives who spend the summer at Woodward Farm gladly become "widows" five days out of seven; and the husbands who arrive on weekends seem only to look forward to the Monday morning train that will carry them back to Boston. Howells notes:

> It may not have been so dull a life for the ladies as men would flatter themselves; they all seemed to like it and not a woman among them was eager to get back to her own house and its cares. Perhaps the remembrance of these cares was the secret of her present content; perhaps women, when remanded to a comparatively natural state, are more easily satisfied than men. (*MF* 11)

Though probably intended as a consolation, this conjecture also invites the reader to question what is "natural" about such bifurcated lives. In her defiance of conventional domesticity, the one real widow in this novel, Mrs. Farrell, poses a similar question, which Howells finally seems determined to suppress. At first she inspires animated defenses from her male companions. "[Y]ou want to hem her in," one of them charges his mother, "with the same dread and misapprehension that imprison her life in your brutal Boston. She longs for a breath of free mountain air, and you stifle her with your dense social atmosphere" (*MF* 37). Eventually, however, the maternal skeptic (Mrs. Gilbert) assumes the role of the implied reader. Even though Mrs. Farrell's other suitor lamentably describes marriage as an institution that "narrows the destiny of half the world," America, at least, would seem to be better off for the restriction (*MF* 73). The dutiful matriarch symbolizes the country itself. "When I order a great ideal picture of America from you," Mrs. Gilbert teases a farm girl who (vainly) aspires to a career in art, "you shall paint me your mother's portrait. Only in these days they'll say it isn't in the least like America. No matter: it's like what she has been and hasn't forgotten how to be again" (*MF* 109). Having unleashed an unruly heroine, Howells conservatively transforms the novel into a vehicle of feminine containment. Which is just what many of his readers—especially women—seemed to want: "Your Mrs. Farrell is terrific," Fanny Kemble (an actress herself) told the author, "—do for pity's sake give her the Small Pox—she deserves it" (*LiL* 1: 205). By sending Mrs. Farrell back to Boston, Howells may have exceeded that request.

James, too, occasionally responded to queries from readers. To one of his transatlantic correspondents he apologized for the frenzied nuptials that take place in the final paragraph of *The Europeans*. "The offhand marrying in the end was *commandé*—likewise the length of the tale. I *do* incline to melancholy endings," he added, "but it had been a part of the bargain with Howells that *this* termination should be cheerful and that there should be distinct matrimony."[21] That happy bargain had been struck, at least in part, because of Howells's disappointment with the ending of *The American*, which frustrates Christopher Newman's desire to marry a beautiful French noblewoman, Claire de Cintré. The exchange between editor and author on this point was particularly significant to Howells, an inference that seems plausible even though his letters to James from this period apparently do not survive.[22] From the amplitude of James's defensive responses (which do), the signs and effects of creative misreading emerge. While James obviously fretted over the increasingly narrow cultural patriotism that his editor seemed to favor—a subject soon renewed (and intensified) by the Hawthorne biography in 1879—we should also recognize that these letters measurably deepened Howells's understanding of human tragedy and the forms in which fiction might express it. Explicating his own novel, James located the real interest of *The American* in "its exemplification of one of those insuperable difficulties which present themselves in people's lives & from which the only issue is by forfeiture—by losing something." He told Howells, "We are each the product of circumstances [and] there are tall stone walls which fatally divide us." To a man then finding favor by writing slight parlor comedies like *A Counterfeit Presentment*, such a pessimistic philosophy must have seemed alien indeed.[23] But if James could not always serve as a model, his artistic preference for dealing with "the tragedies in life" was nevertheless an important counterweight for Howells. Precisely because most of his editorial reactions to *The American* are lost, we should listen more attentively for delayed responses that become audible in his fiction.

Even without his letters to James, some firsthand evidence of Howells's enthusiasm for the novel does exist. Beginning with the very first installment, *The American* pleased him through its vivid portrayal—and qualified sanction—of the national character. What more could an editor want during the country's centennial year? "I am glad you like *The American*," Howells affirmed to John Hay. "The fact that Harry James could write likingly of such a fellow-countryman as Newman is the most hopeful thing in his literary history, since *Gabrielle de Bergerac*."[24] When he reviewed A *Passionate Pilgrim and Other Tales* the year before, Howells had remarked upon the consistency of that volume—unusual for a collection of short stories—which was largely achieved through James's deployment of a comparative point of view. "The American who has known Europe much can never again see his country with the single eye of his old ante-European days," Howells autobiographically noted. "For good or for evil," he added (paraphrasing Hawthorne), "the light of the Old World is always on her face; and his fellow-countrymen have their shadows cast by it."[25]

For both personal and professional reasons, Howells openly worried about his friend's expatriation; and he was hardly alone in fearing that James might lose the ability—even the desire—to deal directly with American subjects. Among the few reservations Howells publicly expressed about A *Passionate Pilgrim* was the author's apparent predilection for addressing himself "less to men and women in their mere humanity, than to a certain kind of cultivated people, who, well as they are in some ways, and indispensable as their appreciation is, are often a little narrow in their sympathies and poverty-stricken in the simple emotions; who are so, or try to be so, which is quite as bad, or worse." As we have seen, Howells himself was hardly devoid of prejudice; but his sensitivity to the finer shades of social discrimination, made even more acute by his move to Boston, equipped him to register even the feeblest pulse of blue blood. Better, perhaps, than James, he understood the risks of purchasing originality at the expense of readership. In its claims for representativeness, then, *The American* appealed to Howells's profoundly democratic sympathies.

The novel richly preserves James's immediate impressions of Paris, where he worked as resident correspondent for the New York *Tribune* (1875–76) and scribbled away at short stories and reviews for American magazines. Introduced to the cosmopolitan enclave of French realists, of whom the Russian Turgenev was also a member, James enjoyed teasing Howells with gossip about their naughty work-in-progress, but (even admitting a greater aesthetic latitude) James also carefully distanced himself from "their wares." Whatever immoralities are implied by *The American*, their origins are distinctly un-American. "Cheated" out of marriage to a French noblewoman, the New World hero (Christopher Newman) nevertheless lets "the insolent foreigner go," as James said, "out of his good nature." Even without a conventionally happy ending, James intended to flatter the cultural nationalism of *Atlantic* readers. When Newman's western vernacular got out of hand (William James warned his brother that certain infelicitous phrases attributed to the hero would "make the reader's flesh creep"), the author gave Howells carte blanche to tidy things up and expressed his gratitude for such editorial intervention. The novel works hard to redeem Newman of his innocent vulgarity and unvarnished materialism. Unburdened by the past, his character remains elastic and amenable to change; the arrogant Bellegardes, on the other hand, are blighted by the "history" in which they claim to take such pride. As James told another disappointed reader (Howells was not alone), "It

seemed to me that in putting it into Newman's power to forgive & contemptu-
ously 'let off' the haughty Bellegardes, I was doing quite the most dramatic &
inspiring thing."[26]

In retrospect, Howells probably agreed, for in his next novel, *The Lady of the
Aroostook* (1879), he takes up a similar theme and fashions a rather humorous
response to James's more pessimistic assertions. This neglected novel (which, for
years after its publication, was one of the author's most popular) recapitulates—
and radically clarifies—many of the important problems of narrative art that
Howells and James struggled with through the 1870s: how best to represent the
American woman, dramatize the contrast between national cultures, and advance the development of credible psychological realism. Conceived by Howells
just at the time that "Daisy Miller" made her audacious appearance, Lydia Blood
(the "lady" of Howells's title) could well be Miss Miller's cousin. Another remarkably self-reliant American heroine, she embarks for Europe (unchaperoned)
on board a ship whose other passengers all wear trousers.[27]

As in James's more famous "study" of the American girl, questions of social
(and sexual) decorum preoccupy the other characters. Lydia's voyaging acquaintance with Harvard-educated Mr. Staniford is less a matter of chance than of
fate, but the connection between this book and *A Chance Acquaintance* is otherwise linear. In *The Lady of the Aroostook*, however, republican romance triumphs
democratically over Bostonian reserve; the considerable social barriers that divide Staniford and "Lurella" (as he condescendingly refers to her) are not—
contra *The American*—insuperable. When James expatiated to Howells about
the impossibility of marrying his ill-starred lovers, he significantly raised the
question of where such a couple might live. Fatally pampered by Paris, Claire de
Cintré "couldn't have lived in New York," James emphasized; and "Newman,
after his marriage (or rather *she*, after it) couldn't have dwelt in France. There
would have been nothing left," he depressingly suggested, "but a farm out West."
Should it come as any surprise, then, that after their marriage Lydia and Staniford strike out for a ranch in California?

The joke was not lost on Thomas Wentworth Higginson, who noted that
while James busied himself with "international episodes" (the title of his fictional follow up to "Daisy Miller"), Howells's real subjects were "inter-oceanic
episodes." Higginson was not deceived by the outward similarities in the work
of these two writers (for example, the frequent shift in setting, from America to
Europe), nor did he give the usual aesthetic priority to James's transatlantic
material. "The truth is," he lamented, "that Mr. James's cosmopolitanism is, after
all, limited: to be really cosmopolitan, a man must be at home even in his own
country." And here Howells had a definite advantage. To "trace American 'society' in its formative process, you must go to Howells," Higginson insisted; "he
alone shows you the essential forces in action." Even in *The Lady of the Aroostook*, which carries its story to Europe, Howells develops his most important
social contrasts through a "dialogue between the Atlantic and Pacific slopes,"
between the (overly) cultivated East and the (refreshingly) uncultivated West.[28]

James's delight in this book was not confined to his letters. While he glow-
ingly reported that *The Lady of the Aroostook* was "the most brilliant thing"

Howells had yet written, James would also reflect some of that brilliance in *The Portrait of a Lady*, which he had already begun in 1879 and was very anxious to complete. If the characters of Howells's novel share many attributes with those of "Daisy Miller," they also anticipate, to a remarkable degree, the more significant figures of *The Portrait*. Something of a professional dilettante, like James's Osmond, Staniford also manifests the romantic curiosity of Ralph Touchett. He confesses a tremendous eagerness "to know what a girl of [Lydia Blood's] traditions thinks about the world when she first sees it. Her mind," as he says to his companion, Dunham, "must be in most respects an unbroken wilderness."[29] Like the author of *The Portrait*, he is captivated by the prospect of a young woman affronting her destiny and can only wonder (as James asked in his preface), "What will she *do?*" When Staniford formulates an answer to that question, he freely exploits the vogue of "Daisy Miller" and provides an uncanny précis of Isabel Archer's future career. "If she were literary," he quips,

> she would be like those vulgar little persons of genius in the magazine stories. She would have read all sorts of impossible things up in her village. She would have been discovered by some aesthetic summer boarder, who had happened to identify her with the gifted Daisy Dawn, and she would be going out on the aesthetic's money for the further expansion of her spirit in Europe. Somebody would be obliged to fall in love with her, and she would sacrifice her career for a man who was her inferior, as we should be subtly given to understand at the close. (*LA* 91)

By reversing Staniford's first premise and freely indulging Isabel's preferences for romantic (but ethically serious) literature, James incorporates and redeems this projected parody of his work-in-progress.

For any reader familiar with James's more celebrated novel, *The Lady of the Aroostook* will probably seem like déjà vu all over again, which should only underscore the importance of Howells's chronological priority. Details of characterization and snatches of discourse confirm a friendly intertextual dialogue in process. While the correspondence of Lydia's aunt (Mrs. Erwin) is "exasperatingly vacuous and diffuse," the telegrams of Isabel's relative (Mrs. Touchett) are tersely ambiguous—and similarly inscrutable. But one thing is clear: both women mean business. "Under these conditions [Mrs. Erwin's script is excitedly illegible] it was no light labor to get at her meaning," Howells writes, "but the sum of her letter [initiating the action in the first chapter] was that she wished Lydia to come out to her at once" (*LA* 34). James employs a similar epistolary device in the opening scene of *The Portrait* to announce Isabel's embarkation at the behest of Mrs. Touchett, but here the information is conveyed in clipped, confusing phrases: "Changed hotel, very bad, impudent clerk, address here. Taken sister's girl, died last year, go to Europe, two sisters, quite independent." To which Ralph Touchett says to Lord Warburton, "Over that my father and I have scarcely stopped puzzling; it seems to admit of so many interpretations." To old Mr. Touchett, however, at least one inference is inescapable: the hotel clerk has certainly taken "a dressing" from his indomitable wife.[30]

In both novels humor assuages a latent anxiety about the transposition of gender roles. Far from being passive or merely reactive, the protagonists (and even lesser female characters such as Henrietta Stackpole) tend to subordinate their male companions into conventionally feminine attitudes. It is hardly accidental that Isabel's moment of self-recognition comes after she glimpses her husband, seated, in the presence of another woman. What James dramatizes Howells confides more directly to the reader: "From time to time a man must show his hand, but save for one supreme exigency a woman need never show hers." Such power may indeed be circumscribed by cultural definitions of virtue, but within that limited sphere a woman's prerogatives strike the author as enviable: unlike men, women "need not account for what they do not do" (*LA* 53). By dramatizing the inner life of such characters, making heroic the otherwise passive operations of consciousness, Howells and James enhanced the illusion of psychological realism at the same time that they tried to vindicate a particular mode of literary production as a distinctively masculine pursuit.[31]

In one of the book's most famous conversations, Isabel and Madame Merle exchange opinions about the nature of reality and the posture of the self in a world of material appurtenances. "What do you call one's self?" Madame Merle interposes. "Where does it begin? where does it end? It overflows into everything that belongs to us—and then it flows back again. . . . I have a great respect for *things!*" Disagreeing, of course, Isabel urges, "I don't know whether I succeed in expressing myself, but I know that nothing else expresses me. Nothing that belongs to me is any measure of me; on the contrary, it's a limit, a barrier, and a perfectly arbitrary one" (*PL* 397–98). Howells's characters, on the other hand, are more content to live with their hypocrisies; but they also ask questions. "Do you ever find yourself struggling very hard to be what you think people think you are?" Staniford asks his companion.

> "Oh, yes," replied Lydia. "But I thought no one else did."
> "Everybody does the thing that we think no one else does," said Staniford, sententiously.
> "I don't know whether I quite like it," said Lydia. "It seems like hypocrisy. It used to worry me. Sometimes I wondered if I had any real self. I seemed to be just what people made me, and a different person to each." (*LA* 125–26)

Sometime later, Staniford advises Lydia that when she arrives in Italy she will finally have to recognize her latently aristocratic bearing. "You will go about in a dream of some self of yours that was native there in other days," he gaily prophesies: "you will recognize sisters and cousins in the patrician ladies when you see their portraits in the palaces where you used to live in such state" (*LA* 161). Already envisioned as the portrait of a lady, Lydia Blood inevitably provokes Staniford to ask himself a very Jamesian question: "What would she do with these ideals of hers in that depraved Old World,—so long past trouble for its sins as to have got a sort of sweetness and innocence in them,—where her facts would be utterly irreconcilable with her ideals, and equally incomprehensible?" (*LA* 216).

In the turbulent wake of "Daisy Miller," which, as Howells told Lowell, sharply divided the reading public into opposing factions, the author was eager to extend the debate about cultural nationalism in order to give James a better hearing. "His art is an honor to us," Howells believed, "and his patriotism—which has been duly questioned—is of the wholesome kind that doesn't blink our little foibles."[32] With the appearance of *Hawthorne* just months away, Howells's concern could not have been better timed. Nor could his confidence survive intact after he was obliged to review the biography, especially commissioned for Macmillan's "English Men of Letters" series. Despite a willingness to indulge James's cosmopolitan temper (and to allow for his contractual obligation to write for a British audience), Howells perfectly understood how offensive *Hawthorne* would prove to many American readers: "we wait," he grimly noted, "with the patience and security of a spectator at an *auto da fé*, to see." Most of the book's other reviewers were only too glad to apply the torch (Thomas Sergeant Perry was a lone—and predictable—exception), though James quickly attributed their flag-waving criticism to "vanity, vulgarity & ignorance. I thought they would protest a good deal at my calling New England life unfurnished," he told another friend, "but I didn't expect they would lose their heads and their manners at such a rate. We are surely the most-thin-skinned idiots in the world, & I blush for my compatriots."[33]

Although the *Atlantic*, too, was offended by the tone of *Hawthorne* and took the author to task for overstating the terms of American provinciality, classifying Howells with the other thin-skinned idiots was a mistake James did not make. His epistolary remonstrance to Howells, in some respects pointedly aggressive, should not blind us to his real expressions of gratitude. What James may not have fully appreciated, however, was the ironic position in which his book left Howells, who (as the voice of the *Atlantic*) felt obliged to defend American (and specifically New England) values. Behind the mask of fictional narrative, Howells had more than once suggested that what passed for culture in Boston left something to be desired. When *A Chance Acquaintance* first appeared, James's mother reported that the family's neighbors were up in arms about "the Boston man," Miles Arbuton, "which it is said must have been conceived in pique. Howells disclaims having intended him as a typical Bostonian, but I must say it looks very like it."[34] After Mark Twain's humbling debacle at the Whittier Birthday Dinner (1877), Howells needed no reminder of the Trojan forms that cultural punishment could take in the Athens of America. As Alfred Kazin once said, Howells learned his sense of social fact "the hard way," as only a provincial could, which gave him honest credentials to lay the groundwork for a literature attuned to the realities of class distinction in America.[35] If Howells felt the sting of James's condescending attitude, he nevertheless had to admire the courage of a writer willing to defy complacent expectations and to question cultural platitudes.

The occasion of *Hawthorne* also presented both writers with renewed occasion for significant misreading. Emphasizing Hawthorne's frequently declared preference for the romance (as opposed to the novel), Howells took exception to James's theoretical premise that history and art were covalent, that a "complex social machinery" was necessary "to set a writer in motion." In response to the long list of things that James claimed were missing from the texture of American life—castles, courts, and abbeys—Howells simply pointed out that no one "would have known less what to do with that dreary and worn-out paraphernalia than Hawthorne," and he refused to admit that their absence could be detrimental to American fiction. In this Howells was actually reiterating a word of advice already received, for together with his praise for *The Lady of the Aroostook,* James had urged the author to do that book one better, to "attack the great field of American life on as many sides as you can." "Plunge into it," he insisted, "don't be afraid, & you will do even better things than this." If the theory propelling the Hawthorne biography were true, however, one might well ask into what, exactly, could Howells plunge? If American society were truly as vacant as James seemed to suggest, what would a writer discover on "the great field of American life"? (Precious little, he would have had to admit, if he were thinking of *Washington Square.* Writing the book, he told Howells, made him "feel acutely the want of the 'paraphernalia.' ") James, of course, was simultaneously defending his own novelistic preferences and his willing surrender to the cosmopolitan appeal of London. "The die is cast & the deed is done," he flatly wrote of his confirmed expatriation—to which he added, ambiguously, "The harm, I mean, is done." To many of James's fiercest critics, however, the harm was just beginning; defending James's patriotism became one of Howells's chief preoccupations for the next forty years. For much of that time, he fought a losing battle.[36]

Coincidentally, perhaps, Howells's imaginative inclinations already anticipated James's advice. When James praised *The Lady of the Aroostook* in terms of measured fulfillment ("I don't see how your manner can go farther"), he also expressed the hope that the author would do "something a little larger." Howells, too, was beginning to chafe at his admittedly self-imposed limitations: the restricted range and number of his characters; his reliance on steamship and railroad timetables to establish narrative action. Spending stretches of two summers among the Shakers in central Massachusetts inspired Howells (in 1877) to begin a novel about the question of spiritualism entitled *The Undiscovered Country.* The author himself recognized this book as a significant departure from his previous work in terms of both subject and narrative complexity. In contrast to his earlier courtship novels, *The Undiscovered Country* does not schematically align character with social condition; rather, it mediates that relation through more richly detailed evocation of discrete symbolic environments: the shabby boardinghouse where Dr. Boynton and his daughter Egeria first "perform"; the grim country tavern where they are waylaid; the disturbingly unnatural Shaker village in which they find sanctuary. To be sure, Howells's artistic control over these materials is inconsistent. James was among the first to consider this novel "more ambitious but less charming" than others by the author;[37] but whatever James's doubts about *The Undiscovered Country,* its subject had "the merit of being real, actual & American," a representativeness that an author in exile considered of utmost importance. Shifting to the imperative, he issued Howells a worthy command. "Continue to Americanize & to *realize:* that is your mission;—& if you stick to it you will become the Zola of the U.S.A."

In writing *The Undiscovered Country*, Howells could hardly lay claim to that particular laurel, which he may not have coveted anyway. But whatever its faults (and James was quick to detail them), the book did reveal an unsuspected dimension of Howells's literary imagination. "As a mere story it is very slight," Charles Eliot Norton likewise discerned, "but in the delineation of character he has before done nothing so good as Dr. Boynton. It is a genuinely imaginative creation, and shows a range of thought, and a power of speculation hardly indicated by his previous work."[38] To James's annoyance, Howells surrendered the more serious implications of his theme by refusing to exploit fully the spiritualistic idiosyncrasies he had so fortuitously chosen to depict. The novel's realism was both too literal and too self-conscious, as a footnote in the text rather baldly reveals.[39] At the same time, Howells could not rid himself of certain idealizing tendencies (ending the book with "suburban matrimony," for example), which now struck James as tediously repetitive. The "ventilation" James looked for in Howells's work was still short-winded.

Together with his rather shrill criticism of American culture in *Hawthorne*, these variously disparaging comments to Howells suggest the urgency of James's need to legitimate his status as an American writer who found himself chronically in absentia. Admitting that in *The Undiscovered Country* Howells had hit upon "something really new and unworked," James nevertheless added that "an intense aversion to spiritualistic material" would never lead him to attempt a similar donnée. First hearing of Howells's next project, *Dr. Breen's Practice*, James could "applaud" the subject, but not "envy" it; he could even presuppose the plot (incorrectly). With *The Bostonians* (a book much concerned with spiritualism, a "lady-doctor," and the status of women generally) just a few years ahead of him, James's deprecating remarks about these subjects cannot conceal a fundamental indebtedness. The tenacity of James's epistolary erasures seems only to make his novel's pentimento more obvious. The step from the Boyntons' run-down boarding house to Miss Birdseye's is very short indeed.[40]

One particularly significant consequence of James's expatriation was the necessary enlargement of the market for his literary work. Even when he had confined his publications to America, the pages of the *Atlantic* (and the incomparable friendliness of its editor) could not retain his absolute loyalty. Now that London was his adopted home, approaching British magazines and publishers was inevitable; and after the unanticipated success of "Daisy Miller," such approaches were generously welcomed. The *Cornhill* agreed to publish some of James's work simultaneously with its appearance in *Harper's*, immediately doubling the author's profits; and *Macmillan's* soon offered to do the same. Although the *Atlantic* took pride in making exclusive arrangements for its serials (a tradition Howells vigorously respected),[41] James mounted a persistent campaign to liberalize the magazine's policy. As early as 1877 Frederic Macmillan had made overtures to publish James in tandem with the *Atlantic*, but the author realized that this was premature. He valued the offer, however, "as a sign of extension," knowing it would "serve for the next time."[42] James was soon making direct appeals to his American editor, implying that he could work this new familiarity with British publishers to their mutual advantage. "Why don't you take measures to issue your own things here as well as at home?" he asked. Never one to ignore professional opportunities, Howells responded eagerly to James's reports of British enthusiasm for *A Chance Acquaintance* and *Private Theatricals* (which had been pirated in German translation) and sent a synopsis of *The Undiscovered Country* across the ocean, hoping that James could persuade a London periodical to take it. Negotiations with Leslie Stephen, Thackeray's successor at the *Cornhill*, did not immediately bear fruit—for Howells, that is. Since his editor now seemed willing to entertain the idea of simultaneous publication, James quickly proposed this for his own work-in-progress, *The Portrait of a Lady*, assuring Howells, "I can always be your novelist if I can publish here also." Cognizant of its implications for giving definite shape—and weight—to his career, James was especially eager to afford his longest story to date the widest possible audience. "I must try and seek a larger success than I have yet obtained," he bluntly told his editor, "in doing something on a larger scale than I have yet done. I am greatly in need of it—of the larger success."

Although some of Howells's books had previously appeared in England (*Venetian Life*, in fact, came out first in London), his transatlantic success was still quite modest. Very few Englishmen (perhaps a few more Englishwomen) subscribed to the *Atlantic*; and since no British publishers had an independent relationship with Howells, they had little incentive to market his titles aggressively. Only small numbers of sheets were imported from America for binding and distribution. After 1882, however, when David Douglas of Edinburgh began to issue Howells's books in a popularly priced format, the author's reputation spread quite rapidly. Within just a few years, his fame equaled (and his sales considerably exceeded) James's. Even the culturally conservative *Westminster Review* took note, observing that "Mr. Howells has had as friendly a reception from the British public within the past two or three years as he could well wish; the attractions of Mr. Douglas's pocket edition combining with those of the novelist's style, humour, and piquant narrative to lead even temperate novel-readers into prolonged dissipation."[43]

Such manifestations of success were nowhere in evidence just four years earlier, when Alexandra Sutherland Orr published a remarkably discerning essay on Howells in the *Contemporary Review* (which James promptly posted to his friend in America). Significantly distinguishing him and James as the foremost American novelists of the day, Orr also had to admit that while James was already familiar to many English readers, Howells was virtually unknown. Her piece was much more than a friendly advertisement, however. Among her other salient insights, she shrewdly sensed that it was "in their treatment of the female sex" that the two writers gave "emphasis to each other" and revealed their interdependence. She also recognized an important priority in Howells's work and stressed one aspect of it in particular that James had deliberately—and persistently—underestimated: the implicit, though artfully understated, recognition by Howells of the "complex fate" of being an American. The phrase famously belongs to James; but, as Orr suggestively demonstrates, Howells intuitively understood the range of its cultural implications.[44] Her argument is worth quoting at length because it applies equally to the fiction of both writers. "Mr. Howells' women," she observed,

> have often another and a peculiar interest in our eyes—the interest of their broken relation to the Old World. The consequences of the rupture are not always understood, yet in whatever degree they assert themselves they give to the individual life the pathos of a lost inheritance. An existence cut off from its historic past is impoverished by the fact, whether consciously or not; and the rebound of the higher American nature when brought into contact with the records of this past, sufficiently proves how real, if unconscious, has been the need of it. This need is most active in the young, to whom the actual is always the unreal, and the craving of the imagination part of the material desire of life. It may show itself in the mere consequences of aesthetic starvation, as in the contracted nature of Lydia Blood; or as an actual want, as in Florida Vervain's pathetic groping for some social tradition applicable to the minor moralities of her European life; or as a want not only felt but understood, as in Kitty Ellison's rapid appropriation of all romantic material to her imaginative use. And the indications thus supplied by Mr. Howells' heroines are confirmed by those of Mr. James.[45]

Even though Howells eventually would cede the "international theme" to James and come to identify it as the expatriate's distinctive province ("It is preeminently and indefeasibly your ground," he argued in 1886; "you made it, as if it were a bit of the Back Bay"), his magnanimity has not always been properly appreciated.

Howells's attitude, however, was not always so generous. In response to James's prickly defense of his anglophilic *Hawthorne*, Howells nervously retaliated with *A Fearful Responsibility* (1881), an overwrought novella in which every motive is confused save one: the book clearly betrays a distrust of Europe generally and a disdain for Great Britain in particular. "What a great thing it is *not* to be an Englishman!" Howells exclaimed after finishing the story. "It's a sort of patent of nobility."[46] In his story Howells casts vitriolic aspersions at a supercilious English painter (Mr. Rose-Black) who, with Venice supplying a romantic backdrop, chases an attractive young American woman (Lily Mayhew), thus aggravating her nominal guardians, Professor and Mrs. Owen Elmore, recently arrived from a college town in upstate New York. Perhaps too much addicted to academic posturing (his wife calls his ideas "perverted"), Elmore freely indulges his patriotism at the expense of Rose-Black. "I have been wondering," the professor muses, "if, in his phenomenal way, he is not a final expression of the national genius,—the stupid contempt for the rights of others; the tacit denial of the rights of any people who are at English mercy; the assumption that the courtesies and decencies of life are for use exclusively towards Englishmen." If Howells had kept his anglophobia within quotation marks, he might have succeeded in perpetrating this rather crude satire. But he appended to Elmore's remarks an authorial aside that was even more stinging, which cost him the goodwill of at least one English reader. "This was in that embittered old wartime," Howells adds (referring to the anguished 1860s, when British neutrality greatly encouraged the Confederacy):

we have since learned how forbearing and generous and amiable Englishmen are; how they never take advantage of any one they believe stronger than themselves, or fail in consideration for those they imagine their superiors; how you have but to show yourself successful in order to win their respect, and even affection.[47]

When Orr came across this passage in the copy of *A Fearful Responsibility* Howells had sent her, she promptly notified the author that their amiable correspondence, just then beginning to flourish, could not possibly continue.[48]

Significantly, Howells had begun this story immediately after resigning his editorial post at the *Atlantic*. "I am glad you like A Fearf. Resp.," he wrote his sister. "You are right: it was the first fruits of my emancipation."[49] The writer's choice of words here resonates simultaneously at many levels. "Emancipation" neatly evokes the Civil War era in which the story is set, at the same time that Howells's personal appropriation of it would seem to equate his editorship with a form of capitalist slavery from which he has at long last been liberated. In a more indirect way, Howells may also have been revealing a latent desire to emancipate himself from James's influence and to distinguish his own diligent labors on native ground from James's easier success in literary London. At a time when his authorial ambitions were cresting, encouraging him at last to break free of magazine work, Howells's failure to gain a foothold in England by "simultaning" either *The Undiscovered Country* or *Dr. Breen's Practice* must have hurt his professional pride, especially after he heard James boast of the "absurd facility" with which success abroad could be won. Indeed, Howells's reluctance to concede defeat in this matter might even suggest a hint of suspected betrayal; for months James persisted in assuming that the *Cornhill* planned to serialize one of Howells's titles well after those negotiations had collapsed. Partly by urging Howells on Leslie Stephen, James had eked from the *Atlantic* the concession of "simultaning" *The Portrait of a Lady*, an unusual arrangement that probably cost the American editor dearly in his (already) strained relations with the magazine's tightfisted owners. But the reciprocity Howells anticipated from England did not materialize. Of course, James was not directly responsible for this outcome, but he was necessarily implicated in Howells's disappointment: Stephen's primary excuse for deferring acceptance of *Dr. Breen's Practice* was the fact that, contrary to expectation, *Washington Square* ballooned to six installments instead of the three James had promised, thereby diminishing the magazine's flexibility and, in effect, edging Howells out.[50]

To discover, in this competitive environment, that the author of *A Fearful Responsibility* should attempt to rewrite *Washington Square* may not come as much of a surprise. Unlike James's Dr. Sloper, whose conscious jealousy is frankly financial, Elmore feels compelled jealously to safeguard the morals (not the money) of the young woman under his charge. While James orchestrates his drama according to a strict geometry of relation (Sloper, Catherine, Townsend, and Mrs. Penniman occupy the four fixed corners of *Washington Square*), Howells's more confused plot betrays a sprawling absence of control. Elmore thinks he knows who the enemy is, although his nativist suspicions eventually target a string of variously threatening European suitors: Captain Ehrhardt, the dashing

Austrian soldier whom Lily innocently encourages; Rose-Black, the obnoxious dilettante from the supercivilized depths of Mayfair; and Herbert Andersen, a harmless Dane, who (like all the rest) utterly falls for the American beauty. Because Elmore cannot discover a single focus for his anxieties, the symptoms of a kind of eroticized paranoia become manifest. The intimidating masculine assertiveness he simultaneously fears and envies may well be a projection of his own repressed desire. Like a malignant tumor, his increasingly morbid sense of responsibility grows out of all proportion to the real ethical content of his relatively benign situation. (Captain Ehrhardt's intentions seem, in the end, to be honorable; and poor Mr. Andersen even has a mother in tow to guarantee his blonde-and-blue-eyed respectability.) Whereas James, decidedly celibate, could experiment with the pre-Freudian implications of Dr. Sloper's selfish family romance, Howells could not yet take up directly the theme of father–daughter conflict and marital disappointment: his own anxieties, at least, were all too real. As she advanced through adolescence, Howells's oldest child, Winifred, collapsed into chronic physical and mental illness; she suffered her first breakdown (at the age of sixteen) just as her father was struggling to complete *A Fearful Responsibility*. Outwardly the story conforms to the stylized narrative of American girlhood that Howells and James had already made so familiar; inwardly, however, its psychology is disturbingly autobiographical.[51]

Ripe with confusion, this novella (typically ignored or dismissed by critics) deserves a certain kind of scrutiny precisely because it fails to overmaster its contemporaneous rival. Like James's story, Howells's is set in a past not yet displaced from memory, a time removed just far enough from the present to allow for certain authorial indulgences. Elmore and his wife depart war-torn America for Europe because his frail health disqualifies him for military service under Lincoln, but feelings of guilt shadow his conscience (and Howells's narrative) from start to finish. Using a rather self-conscious mode of address, Howells tells the reader that Elmore "submitted to expatriation as he best could; and in Italy he fought for our cause against the English, whom he found everywhere all but in arms against us" (*AFR* 5). In its nominal subject and subliminal motive, *A Fearful Responsibility* is a tale of displaced aggression, which helps to explain both its occasional strengths and peculiar lapses as a work of art.

Expatriation transforms Elmore into a kind of deracinated Sloper. Ostensibly at work on a history of Venice (also one of Howells's pet projects), Elmore's professional commitment to research softens with the enforced leisure of foreign residence; but his inquiring mind—like the doctor's, always craving for verification—redirects itself away from the past and into the lives of others. More so than James's steely physician (whose surgical mind—and sarcastic tongue—cuts sharply), Elmore willingly indulges the more poetic possibilities of what the author refers to as his "novel responsibility." Sloper, too, we should recall, possesses a certain narrative curiosity: amused by Catherine's romantic resolution to see Townsend (in spite of her father's sternly negative injunction), the doctor declares, "By Jove . . . I believe she will stick—I believe she will stick!" This "idea of Catherine 'sticking' appeared to have a comical side," James adds, "and to offer a prospect of entertainment. He determined, as he said to himself, to see it out" (*WS* 99). Less cynically, no doubt, Howells's professor still cannot repress "a degree of sympathy with [Captain Ehrhardt,] the bold young fellow who had overstepped the conventional proprieties in the ardor of a romantic impulse, and he could see how this very boldness, while it had a terror, would have a charm for the girl. There was no necessity," Howells stipulates, "except for the purpose of holding Mrs. Elmore in check, to look at it in an ugly light" (*AFR* 51).

Both stories, then, explore the limits (and the cost) of expository determinism, imposed by characters who read—almost live—for the plot with a sort of misogynist vengeance; and each rejects the false authority of its self-inscribed narrator. Dr. Sloper takes his convictions, unrepentantly, to the grave. Almost as grimly, Elmore simply returns to America, but he remains plagued by doubts about his negative interference in Lily's affairs. The American girl, frustrated in European romance, eventually resettles in Omaha, taking up a clergyman, as it were, for life. (Following the pattern set by James's heroine, she first must reject an old flame who—much like the middle-aged Townsend, veiled in luxurious whiskers—is no longer straight and slim.) Ironically, Howells's struggle to redeem the final sterility of *Washington Square* cannot fully succeed because he does not allow Lily Mayhew to assert herself through even passive resistance to Elmore's paranoid design. Her resignation cannot achieve the same measure of quiet dignity as Catherine Sloper's because the author gives priority instead to the male protagonist's psychic torment. After Lily leaves for the West, Elmore irresistibly takes up his own morsel of fancy work, his fantastic mental embroidery of her posited relations with the Austrian suitor he insistently turned away: "what he so passionately and sorrowfully longed for accomplished itself continually in his dreams," Howells writes, "but only in his dreams" (*AFR* 163).

Notes

A Season in Cambridge

1. HJ, "Mr. and Mrs. James T. Fields" [1915], in *Literary Criticism*, 2 vols., ed. Leon Edel (New York: Library of America, 1984), 1: 168.

2. *Notes of a Son and Brother* [1914] in HJ, *Autobiography*, ed. F. W. Dupee (New York: Criterion Books, 1956), 494.

3. HJ, "Mr. and Mrs. James T. Fields," 170. James might have spurred his memory by exhuming one of the earliest letters Howells addressed to him, which solicited contributions for the magazine. "What we want," Howells wrote (quoting Fields), "is short, *cheerful* stories."

4. WDH to James T. Fields, 4 January 1867, *SL* 1: 273.

5. Only once did WDH lose an argument with Fields about James's work; and the story in dispute ("A Light Man") was soon printed elsewhere. See WDH, "Recollections of an *Atlantic* Editorship," *Atlantic* 100 (November 1907): 599; and letter #2, in which he regrets not having the story for the magazine.

6. HJ to Thomas Sergeant Perry, 1 December 1866, *HJL* 1: 67.

7. WDH to Edmund C. Stedman, 5 December 1866, *SL* 1: 271.

8. HJ to AJ, 3 February [1867], *HJL* 1: 69.

9. James Russell Lowell to WDH, 28 July 1864, *Letters of James Russell Lowell*, 2 vols., ed. Charles Eliot Norton (New York: Harper & Brothers, 1894), 1: 338.

10. James Russell Lowell to James T. Fields, 20 December 1868, *Letters of James Russell Lowell*, 2: 13.

11. For extended analyses of WDH's uneasy relation to the Brahmin establishment, see Kenneth S. Lynn, *William Dean Howells: An American Life* (New York: Harcourt Brace Jovanovich, 1971), 91–97, 194–96; and Lewis P. Simpson, "The Treason of William Dean Howells," in his *Man of Letters in New England and the South: Essays on the History of the Literary Vocation in America* (Baton Rouge: Louisiana State University Press, 1973), 85–128.

12. HJ to Thomas Sergeant Perry, 20 September and 15 August 1867, *HJL* 1: 77, 72, 77.

13. WDH to Charles Eliot Norton, 10 August 1867, *SL* 1: 283.

14. WDH to Charles Eliot Norton, 12 and 15 November 1868, *LiL* 1: 137; WDH to James T. Fields, 24 August 1869, *SL* 1: 335.

15. WDH, *Literary Friends and Acquaintance: A Personal Retrospect of American Author-ship* (1901; rpt. Bloomington: Indiana University Press, 1968), 36.

16. Elinor Mead Howells to Aurelia and Victoria Howells, [17 March 1871], *If Not Literature: Letters of Elinor Mead Howells*, ed. Ginette de B. Merrill and George Arms (Columbus: Ohio State University Press, 1988), 138.

17. HJ to Elizabeth Boott, [24 February 1871], *HJL* 1: 255. Edel incorrectly dates this letter April 1871.

18. HJ to WJ, 13 February [1870], *CWJ* 1: 146. See also HJ to AJ, 10 March [1869]; HJ to WJ, 26 April [1869]; HJ to WJ, 30 October [1869]; HJ to AJ, 7 November [1869]; *HJL* 1: 97, 113, 159, 171.

19. HJ to Charles Eliot Norton, 16 January 1871, *HJL* 1: 252.

20. Throughout *Suburban Sketches*, as one critic has noticed, "we sense that [How-ells's] enthusiasm for small everyday things could not altogether offset a feeling of regret that there were no more exciting things to write about." See Olov W. Fryckstedt, *In Quest of America: A Study of Howells's Early Development as a Novelist* (Cambridge, Mass.: Harvard University Press, 1958), 100.

21. HJ to Charles Eliot Norton, 9 August 1871, *HJL* 1: 262.

22. HJ, review of *Passages from the French and Italian Note-Books of Nathaniel Haw-thorne* (1872), in *Literary Criticism* 1: 307–8. While Hawthorne could almost be forgiven these lapses (a result of his stubborn antebellum provincialism), a later writer such as Howells apparently had no excuse, in James's view.

23. Even Alfred Habegger, who has vigorously contextualized James and Howells in relation to popular women's fiction of the nineteenth century, slights their debts to one another and prefers to see both in conflict with the gendered traditions of the domestic novel. See *Gender, Fantasy, and Realism in American Literature* (New York: Columbia University Press, 1982) and, even more pointedly, *Henry James and the "Woman Business"* (New York: Cambridge University Press, 1989).

24. James Russell Lowell, review of *Suburban Sketches*, *North American Review* 112 (1871): 237, 236.

25. HJ to Grace Norton, 27 November 1871, *HJL* 1: 264.

26. WDH, *Their Wedding Journey* (1871; rpt. Bloomington: Indiana University Press, 1968), 43. The corresponding passage from *Hawthorne* (1879) is too famous to quote at length; see *Literary Criticism* 1: 351–52.

27. HJ to Grace Norton, 27 November [1871], *HJL* 1: 264.

28. HJ to James T. Fields, 15 November [1870], *HJL* 1: 249.

29. A curiously apologetic letter from HJ Sr. to James T. Fields hints at the real possibility that James Jr. had his enemies in the *Atlantic's* precincts. The father's charac-teristically intemperate prose offers a glimpse behind the facade of gentility scrupulously maintained by most nineteenth-century publishers. The target of his invective was proba-bly Thomas Wentworth Higginson or, more remotely, Oliver Wendell Holmes. "I had no sooner left your sanctum yesterday," the elder James wrote,

than I was afflicted to remember how I had profaned it by my unmeasured talk about poor H. Please forget it utterly. I don't know how it is with better men, but the parental sentiment is so fiendish a thing with me, that if any one attempt to slay my young, especially in a clandestine way, or out of a pious regard (e.g.) to the welfare of the souls comprehender in the diocese of the Atlantic Monthly, I can't help devoting him bag and baggage with all my vows to the infernal gods. I am not aware of my animus until I catch—as yesterday—a courteous ear; then the unholy fire flames forth at such a rate as to leave me no doubt or reflection where it was originally lighted. Please pray for your sinful & suffering but cordial friend, Henry James.

HJ Sr. to James T. Fields, 2 May 1868 (Houghton Mifflin Archive, Harvard).

30. Patricia Kane, "Mutual Perspective: James and Howells as Critics of Each Other's Fiction," *Minnesota Review* 7 (1967): 331.

31. HJ to Thomas Sergeant Perry, 20 September [1867], *HJL* 1: 77; HJ, "The Madonna of the Future," in *THJ* 2: 205. Hereafter cited parenthetically.

32. Kenneth S. Lynn, *William Dean Howells*, 214.

33. See, for example, Oscar Cargill, "Henry James's 'Moral Policeman': William Dean Howells," *American Literature* 29 (January 1958): 371–98.

34. HJ Sr. to HJ, 14 January [1873] (James Papers, Harvard). Aziz includes this text in his introduction (*THJ* 2: xxxviii–ix) but misprints some key passages.

35. HJ to HJ Sr., 1 February [1873], *HJL* 1: 333, 334.

36. HJ to Charles Eliot Norton, 4 February 1872, *HJL* 1: 274.

Complex Fates

1. As Simpson explains, "Howells' sense of his betrayal is subtle; but it appears, when we examine his feelings for his vocation in some detail, that it centered in his relation to New England" (*The Man of Letters in New England and the South*, 86–87).

2. "A Pedestrian Tour" first appeared in an issue of the *Atlantic* (24 [November 1869]: 591–603); this text is from *Suburban Sketches* (1870; rpt., new and enlarged ed. Boston: James R. Osgood & Co., 1875) 70–71. WDH to Charles Eliot Norton, 7 November 1869, *SL* 1: 345. Just a few months earlier (in a letter to James) Howells boasted of the absence of "intellectual vulgarity" in Cambridge, delighting in the town's superabundance of "appreciation and liberality"; without a hint of ironic self-reflection, he then moved on to disparage the sorry traces of the Celtic invasion.

3. Mrs. HJ Sr. to HJ, 27 April [1873] (James Papers, Harvard).

4. WDH to William C. Howells, 20 April 1873, *SL* 2: 24.

5. WDH, *A Chance Acquaintance* (1873; rpt. Bloomington: Indiana University Press, 1971), 11; hereafter cited parenthetically as *ACQ*.

6. HJ, *Watch and Ward* (1871), in *Novels, 1871–1880*, ed. William T. Stafford (New York: Library of America, 1983), 104–5. Although as a serial this novel ran in tandem with *Their Wedding Journey*, James delivered the manuscript of *Watch and Ward* to the *Atlantic* just as Howells was beginning to write his travel novel.

7. In a previous chapter of the book, after recording snatches of overheard dialogue in the style of a printed play, Howells parenthetically exclaims, "Ah! poor Real Life, which I love, can I make others share the delight I find in thy foolish and insipid face?" (*Their Wedding Journey*, 55, 42).

8. Olov Fryckstedt, for example, was the first to observe that Arbuton's negative reactions to the scenery of the Saint Lawrence Valley closely echo the opinions James had voiced in two travel articles ("Quebec" and "Niagara") published in the *Nation* in 1871. Whereas James and Arbuton find the landscape devoid of meaningful literary or historical associations, Howells's heroine promptly recalls Longfellow's historical epic *Evangeline* (*In Quest of America*, 139). Lynn follows the same line of argument in his biography of Howells (*William Dean Howells*, 215–16).

9. The phrase comes from HJ's 1908 preface to the novel, written for the New York Edition (*Literary Criticism* 2: 1076).

10. See *Henry James and H. G. Wells: A Record of Their Friendship, Their Debate on the Art of Fiction, and Their Quarrel,* ed. Leon Edel and Gordon N. Ray (London: Rupert Hart-Davis, 1958).

11. See HJ to Mrs. HJ Sr., 26 March 1870; HJ to WJ, 29 March 1870; and HJ to Grace Norton, 1 April 1870; all in *HJL* 1: 218–32.

12. HJ, *Washington Square,* in *Novels, 1881–1886,* ed. William T. Stafford (New York: Library of America, 1985), 41; hereafter cited parenthetically as WS.

13. Charles Eliot Norton to James Russell Lowell, 6 February 1874, *The Letters of Charles Eliot Norton,* 2 vols., ed. Sara Norton and M. A. DeWolfe Howe (Boston: Houghton Mifflin, 1913), 2: 33.

14. Millicent Bell persuasively develops this point in "Style as Subject: *Washington Square,*" *Sewanee Review* 83 (1975): 19–38; see also her later revision of this essay in *Meaning in Henry James* (Cambridge, Mass.: Harvard University Press, 1991), 65–79.

The Larger Success

1. HJ to AJ, 25 April [1873], *HJL* 1: 373.

2. Between the lines of James's twice-told praise for *A Foregone Conclusion,* one can also detect "a hint of envy," according to Cornelia P. Kelley, "for James realized that Howells with three novels to his credit had, though he had started later, 'arrived' before him, and he approached his own fiction writing with a new determination which was not, however, to bear fruit for some time" (*The Early Development of Henry James,* 204–5).

3. HJ to HJ Sr., 22 December [1873], *HJL* 1: 422. In the same missive HJ wrote, "Alice's letter contained an adjuration to me, from Howells, to print a volume of short stories. Good advice, doubtless, but I must wait, to apply it, till I get home, when I shall attempt also to put forth a volume of articles and letters about Europe."

4. HJ, "The Art of Fiction" [1884], in *Literary Criticism* 1: 48.

5. Anne T. Margolis, *Henry James and the Problem of Audience: An International Act* (Ann Arbor, Mich.: UMI Research Press, 1985), 8.

6. According to Laurel T. Goldman, much of the twentieth-century criticism that "finally destroyed Howells' reputation was based on a prejudice which misrepresented the American reading public and Howells' relationship with it." That prejudice not only pilloried Howells as a willing prisoner of feminine taste but also, with unembarrassed misogyny, defined such taste as intrinsically incompatible with high formal and aesthetic standards. A survey of actual responses to Howells's fiction, preserved in the voluminous archive of letters addressed to him, revealed that he "was read by more types than young girls and their mothers." See "A Different View of the Iron Madonna: William Dean Howells and His Magazine Readers," *New England Quarterly* 50 (1977): 564, 576.

7. Richard H. Brodhead, *The School of Hawthorne* (New York: Oxford University Press, 1986), 86; for further comparison with James, see pp. 108–10.

8. Trilling's essay on Howells, which repeats and confirms James's early derogations, has surely been the most influential. In the confident first-person plural, Trilling writes, "almost in the degree that we admire James and defend his artistic practice, we are committed to resist Howells." See "William Dean Howells and the Roots of Modern Taste," in *The Opposing Self* (1955; rpt. New York: Harcourt Brace Jovanovich, 1978), 67–91; quotation, 76. That Howells himself was James's first admirer and defender goes unremarked.

9. HJ to WJ, 22 September [1872], *CWJ* 1: 170.

10. Admitting that the editor's hands were already full with other of his manuscripts, HJ told his father that Howells "would not publish the *Galaxy* story on account of the subject, I'm afraid. (It's needless to say that *I* think the subject all right—in fact very fine!)" See HJ to HJ Sr., 26 October [1873], *HJL* 1: 406.

11. George N. Bennett, *William Dean Howells: The Development of a Novelist* (Norman: University of Oklahoma Press, 1959), 87.

12. WDH to William C. Howells, 13 February 1881, *SL* 2: 275.

13. Suggestive accounts of this event can be found in Lynn, *William Dean Howells*, 168–78, and Henry Nash Smith, *Mark Twain: The Development of a Writer* (Cambridge, Mass.: Harvard University Press, 1962), 92–112. See also *Mark Twain–Howells Letters*, 2 vols., ed. Henry Nash Smith and William H. Gibson (Cambridge, Mass.: Belknap Press of Harvard University Press, 1960), 1: 210–15.

14. HJ to his parents, 3 April [1874], *HJL* 1: 435.

15. WDH to Charles Eliot Norton, 12 December 1874, quoted in *SL* 2: 78n2; see Lynn, *William Dean Howells*, 231. Norton himself may have influenced Howells, for earlier in the same year he had complained to Lowell about the story's projected outline. "I hope it is pretty & good," he wrote, "but Howells lacks the sort of imagination to fuse such incongruous elements in his melting-pot." Charles Eliot Norton to James Russell Lowell, 23 February 1874 (Lowell Papers, Harvard).

16. WDH to James T. Fields, 22 November 1875, and WDH to Charles Dudley Warner, 5 January 1876, *SL* 2: 110, 117.

17. James R. Osgood knew that maintaining an appearance of incessant productivity by keeping an author's name before the public was a key element to literary success. While Howells deliberately withheld *Private Theatricals*, James succumbed to similar entreaties from his publisher and agreed to issue *Watch and Ward* (first serialized in 1871) because it seemed "a good way of turning an honest penny." With his list of book-length fictions steadily growing, and a definite (albeit limited) audience established, James realized (with Osgood's help) that his "early things will be sure to be rummaged out; and as they are there it is best to take hold of them myself and put them in order" (HJ to HJ Sr., 19 April [1878], *HJL* 2: 167). Ironically, his newfound marketplace wisdom did not prevent the piracy of "Daisy Miller" just three months after James wrote this letter.

18. WDH, *Mrs. Farrell* (New York: Harper & Brothers, 1921), 3; hereafter cited parenthetically as *MF*. In response to this opening scene, Charles Dudley Warner exclaimed to the author, "You've hit the hill farmer between wind and water. I know him. If he ever reads your description, which is not likely, he will murder you. Of course you never expect to go into the country again after this. Nor into any summer boarding house. How dare you make it so true?" (*SL* 2: 110n2).

19. HJ, *The Europeans*, in *Novels, 1871–1880*, 902–3; hereafter cited parenthetically as *TE*.

20. Robert Emmet Long, *The Great Succession: Henry James and the Legacy of Hawthorne* (Pittsburgh, Pa.: University of Pittsburgh Press, 1979), 58. The same author extends this comparison in *Henry James: The Early Novels* (Boston: Twayne, 1983), 69.

21. HJ to Elizabeth Boott, 30 October [1878], *HJL* 2: 189.

22. Though frustrating, the loss (or destruction) of these letters should not be construed as a sign of their irrelevance to James; none written to him by his brother William survives from this period either. That correlation might even suggest that a trove of particularly important documents awaits discovery.

23. Hearing a rumor that WDH was being considered by President Rutherford B. Hayes for the ambassadorship to Switzerland, HJ wrote approvingly to Thomas Sergeant Perry on 18 April 1877, "It is interesting to hear that Howells may come to Berne; and

between ourselves I am glad in so far as it may interrupt his 'comedies.' I thought the last ["Out of the Question"] (in spite of pretty touches) a feeble piece of work for a man of his years—and sex!" (*HJL* 2: 108).

24. WDH to John Hay, 22 February 1877, *SL* 2: 158.

25. In 1879 WDH wrote to James Russell Lowell about Americans' painfully acute self-consciousness: "I have come to understand fully what Hawthorne meant when he said to me that he would like to see some part of America on which the shadow of Europe had not fallen" (*SL* 2: 231). In *Literary Friends and Acquaintance* Howells recounted more fully the conversation he had in 1860 with the shy genius from Concord, who was very "curious about the West, which he seemed to fancy much more purely American" than his native New England. Hawthorne "said he would like to see some part of the country on which the shadow, or, if I must be precise, the damned shadow, of Europe had not fallen" (49).

26. HJ to Elizabeth Boott, 26 May [1877] (James Papers, Harvard). Perhaps more significantly, many reviewers of *The American* also complained about the denouement. Lowell offered HJ a word of consolation, saying that he liked best "precisely what [others] found fault with, I mean the conclusion. It seemed to me in keeping with your hero's character as I understood it and therefore done with deliberation. Wasn't I right?" James Russell Lowell to HJ, 9 September 1878, *New Letters of James Russell Lowell*, ed. M. A. DeWolfe Howe (New York: Harper & Brothers, 1932), 236.

27. Among other similarities between Howells's novel and "Daisy Miller," Annette Kar clearly establishes parallels between the characters and the values they represent: Lydia and Daisy (social innocence), Staniford and Winterbourne (social arrogance), Hicks and Giovanelli (social disreputability). See "Archetypes of American Innocence: Lydia Blood and Daisy Miller," *American Quarterly* 5 (1953): 31–38.

28. Thomas Wentworth Higginson, *Short Studies of American Authors* (Boston: Lee & Shepard, 1880), 35–36, 57, 36–37. The chapters of this short but highly suggestive book first appeared in 1879 in the Boston weekly *The Literary World*. Many of Higginson's remarks have become staples of modern criticism. See, for example, John W. Crowley, "An Interoceanic Episode: *The Lady of the Aroostook*," *American Literature* 49 (May 1977): 180–91.

29. WDH, *The Lady of the Aroostook* (Boston: Houghton, Osgood, 1879) 82–83; hereafter cited parenthetically as *LA*.

30. HJ, *The Portrait of a Lady*, in *Novels, 1881–1886*, 201; hereafter cited parenthetically as *PL*.

31. A number of recent works have persuasively established the connection between gender anxiety and the priorities of realism. See, for example, Eric Cheyfitz, "A *Hazard of New Fortunes*: The Romance of Self-Realization," in *American Realism: New Essays*, ed. Eric J. Sundquist (Baltimore, Md.: Johns Hopkins University Press, 1982), 42–65; Daniel Borus, *Writing Realism: Howells, James, and Norris in the Mass Market* (Chapel Hill: University of North Carolina Press, 1989), esp. 65–99; and Michael Davitt Bell, *The Problem of American Realism: Studies in the Cultural History of a Literary Idea* (Chicago: University of Chicago Press, 1993), 17–38.

32. WDH to James Russell Lowell, 22 June 1879, *SL* 2: 231. According to one view, WDH defended "Daisy Miller" because he realized that the public could easily confuse Winterbourne's sentiments—detached, cynical, censorious—for those of James. See David D. Hirsch, "William Dean Howells and Daisy Miller," *English Language Notes* 1 (December 1963): 123–28.

33. HJ to Elizabeth Boott, 22 February [1880] (James Papers, Harvard). Perry, whose partisanship went back to their shared Newport boyhood, said of James, "We find in this

book a certain period of New England life judged in no unfriendly spirit by a man who looks upon it with as much impartiality as he would, for instance, look upon any period of French history. . . . His irony, so far as it appears at all, is of the gentlest kind." Perry's notice appeared in the *International Review* 8 (April 1880): 447–50; quotation, 448.

34. Mrs. HJ Sr. to HJ, 25 May [1873] (James Papers, Harvard).

35. Here is Kazin on the novel of manners: "This sense of the social texture, when it identifies *with* the dominant class yet holds out the suggestion that literary intelligence can help with the human values, when it enjoys the existing arrangements of society more than it disapproves of its cruelties—this is what makes the novel of manners possible at all in our society." "Howells the Bostonian," *Clio* 3 (1974): 225.

36. As Richard Foley has written, "Howells spared no effort to create critical interest in James, to stimulate the public to read him, and to cajole and shame Americans into paying the homage due an author whom he considered the greatest American artist in fiction of his day." See his *Criticism in American Periodicals of the Works of Henry James from 1866 to 1916* (Washington, D.C.: Catholic University of America Press, 1944), 163.

37. HJ to Thomas Sergeant Perry, 26 July [1880], in Virginia Harlow, *Thomas Sergeant Perry: A Biography* (Durham, N.C.: Duke University Press, 1950), 308.

38. Charles Eliot Norton to James Russell Lowell, 27 June 1880, *Letters of Charles Eliot Norton* 2: 110.

39. Still worried, perhaps, that the characters of *Private Theatricals* may have libeled identifiable people, Howells included an explicit disclaimer in *The Undiscovered Country*: "In placing some passages of his story among the Shakers of an easily recognizable locality, the author has avoided the study of personal traits, and he wishes explicitly to state that his Shakers are imaginary in everything but their truth, charity, and purity of life, and that scarcely less lovable quaintness to which no realism could do perfect justice." WDH, *The Undiscovered Country* (Boston: Houghton, Mifflin, 1880), 161n1.

40. While a number of recent critics have rediscovered Howells's novel as an important link between Hawthorne's *Blithedale Romance* and James's *Bostonians* (see Long, *The Great Succession*, and Brodhead, *The School of Hawthorne*), at least one has also noted that in manuscript Howells's hero (Ford) was first called Gifford, the same name that James had used for his skeptical antagonist in "Professor Fargo," a short story about mesmerism first serialized in the *Galaxy* (1874). Far from being strictly linear, the descent of this theme from Hawthorne suggests a more complicated pattern of appropriation and revision in which neither Howells nor James can be viewed as a passive conduit. See Kermit Vanderbilt, *The Achievement of William Dean Howells* (Princeton, N.J.: Princeton University Press, 1968), 47n32.

41. In 1875, for example, WDH declined Julian Hawthorne's series of historical sketches, *Saxon Studies*, which was also appearing in the *Contemporary Review* (London). "I am not in a position to take Hawthorne's serial," he told Osgood, "even if I cared to publish a story coming out simultaneously elsewhere." *Appleton's Journal* of New York was less discriminating, for it printed one of Hawthorne's installments in October of that year. WDH to James R. Osgood, 27 January 1875 (Howells Papers, Harvard).

42. HJ to AJ, 29 December [1877], *HJL* 2: 148.

43. "Mr. Howells' Novels," *Westminster Review* n.s. 66 (October 1884): 348. Scott Bennett reports that by 1885 Douglas had printed 131,000 copies of fourteen Howells titles. By that date James's combined sales in Great Britain totaled no more than 33,000 copies. See "David Douglas and the British Publication of W. D. Howells' Works," *Studies in Bibliography* 25 (1972): 121; and Leon Edel and Dan H. Laurence, with James Rambeau, *A Bibliography of Henry James*, 3d rev. ed. (New York: Oxford University Press, 1982).

44. James coined the phrase in a letter (4 Feb. 1872) to Charles Eliot Norton expressing his desire to go abroad and join the Nortons in Europe:

> I confess that my best company now-a-days is that of various vague moonshiny
> dreams of getting to your side of the world with what speed I may.—I carry the
> desire . . . to a morbid pitch, and I exaggerate the merits of Europe. It's the same
> world there after all and Italy isn't the absolute any more than Massachusetts. It's
> a complex fate, being an American, and one of the responsibilities it entails is
> fighting against a superstitious valuation of Europe. (*HJL* 1: 273–74)

45. A[lexandra (Leighton) Sutherland] Orr, "International Novelists and Mr. Howells," *Contemporary Review* 37 (1880): 745.

46. WDH to Thomas Wentworth Higginson, 14 August 1881, *SL* 2: 292.

47. WDH, A *Fearful Responsibility and Other Stories* (Boston: James R. Osgood & Co.,
1881), 100; hereafter cited parenthetically as *AFR*.

48. "There is something . . . in the book which embarrasses me gravely," she wrote,
"both with reference to itself and to any other you may be kind enough to intend to
send me, and that is, the contempt for my countrypeople which you express . . . no
longer dramatically or humorously, but seriously, and in your own name." Alexandra
Leighton Sutherland Orr to WDH, 18 October [1881] (Howells Papers, Harvard).

49. WDH to Anne H. Fréchette, 14 August 1881, *SL* 2: 293.

50. On 14 April 1880 Stephen apologized to Howells for their misunderstanding by
tipping his editorial hand: "Meanwhile I may as well tell you that Henry James has
exceeded the length of his story originally proposed. He will begin in June & last through
six numbers ie. till *November*" (Howells Papers, Harvard).

51. John W. Crowley provides the best account of Winifred's sadly mysterious condition in "Winifred Howells and the Economy of Pain," *Old Northwest* 10 (Spring 1984):
41–75.

Letters and Documents

I.

JAMES TO HOWELLS, 10 May 1867, Cambridge

ALS Houghton
bMS Am 1784 (253) 1

Cambridge—May 10th

Dear Howells—

Thanks again for your papers.[1]—They are utterly charming, & a 100 times the most graceful, witty and poetical things yet written in this land. I especially liked the chapter on Ferrara.—*Que n'y suis-je-pas!*[2] But they are all delightful and I await the rest. Your manner seems to me quite your own & yet it reminds one vaguely of all kinds of pleasant & poignant associations. Thou hast the gift—"go always!" I like the real levity of your lightness & the real feeling of your soberness; and I admire the delicacy of your touch always & everywhere.

—The worst of it is that it is almost *too* sympathetic. You intimate, you suggest so many of the refinements of the reality, that the reader's soul is racked by this superfluous enjoyment. But as I say, I think I can stand another batch.

—Yours always
H. J. jr

Henry James, *review of* Italian Journeys, North American Review 106 (*January 1868*): 336–39.

Under favor of his work on "Venetian Life,"[1] Mr. Howells took his place as one of the most charming of American writers and most satisfactory of American

1. Portions of WDH's *Italian Journeys* (1867) that had recently appeared in the *Nation* and the *Atlantic Monthly*.
2. If only I were there!
1. WDH's first important book, published in London and New York (1866).

William Dean Howells, editor of the *Atlantic Monthly* (1875). By permission of the Houghton Library, Harvard University.

Henry James in the 1890s. By permission of the Houghton Library, Harvard University.

travellers. He is assuredly not one of those who journey from Dan to Beersheba only to cry out that all is barren. Thanks to the keenness of his observation and the vivacity of his sympathies, he treads afresh the most frequently trodden routes, without on the one hand growing cynical over his little or his great disappointments, or taking refuge on the other in the well-known alternative of the Baron Munchausen.[2] Mr. Howells has an eye for the small things of nature, of art, and of human life, which enables him to extract sweetness and profit from adventures the most prosaic, and which prove him a very worthy successor of the author of the "Sentimental Journey."[3]

Mr. Howells is in fact a sentimental traveller. He takes things as he finds them and as history has made them; he presses them into the service of no theory, nor scourges them into the following of his prejudices; he takes them as a man of the world, who is not a little a moralist,—a gentle moralist, a good deal a humorist, and most of all a poet; and he leaves them,—he leaves them as the man of real literary power and the delicate artist alone know how to leave them, with new memories mingling, for our common delight, with the old memories that are the accumulation of ages, and with a fresh touch of color modestly gleaming amid the masses of local and historical coloring. It is for this solid literary merit that Mr. Howells's writing is valuable,—and the more valuable that it is so rarely found in books of travel in our own tongue. Nothing is more slipshod and slovenly than the style in which publications of this kind are habitually composed. Letters and diaries are simply strung into succession and transferred to print. If the writer is a clever person, an observer, an explorer, an intelligent devotee of the picturesque, his work will doubtless furnish a considerable amount of entertaining reading; but there will yet be something essentially common in its character. The book will be diffuse, overgrown, shapeless; it will not belong to literature. This charm of style Mr. Howells's two books on Italy possess in perfection; they belong to literature and to the centre and core of it,—the region where men think and feel, and one may almost say breathe, in good prose, and where the classics stand on guard. Mr. Howells is not an economist, a statistician, an historian, or a propagandist in any interest; he is simply an observer, responsible only to a kindly heart, a lively fancy, and a healthy conscience. It may therefore indeed be admitted that there was a smaller chance than in the opposite case of his book being ill written. He might notice what he pleased and mention what he pleased, and do it in just the manner that pleased him. He was under no necessity of sacrificing his style to facts; he might under strong provocation—provocation of which the sympathetic reader will feel the force—sacrifice facts to his style. But this privilege, of course, enforces a corresponding obligation, such as a man of so acute literary conscience as our

2. Rudolph Erich Raspe (1737–94), *Baron Munchausen's Narrative of His Marvellous Travels and Campaigns in Russia* (1785), a record of grossly exaggerated stories attributed to Baron Münchhausen (1720–97), a German mercenary in the Russian army.

3. Laurence Sterne (1713–68), whose *A Sentimental Journey Through France and Italy* appeared in the year of his death.

author would be the first to admit and to discharge. He must have felt the importance of making his book, by so much as it was not to be a work of strict information, a work of generous and unalloyed entertainment.

These "Italian Journeys" are a record of some dozen excursions made to various parts of the peninsula during a long residence in Venice. They take the reader over roads much travelled, and conduct him to shrines worn by the feet— to say nothing of the knees—of thousands of pilgrims, no small number of whom, in these latter days, have imparted their impressions to the world. But it is plain that the world is no more weary of reading about Italy than it is of visiting it; and that so long as that deeply interesting country continues to stand in its actual relation, aesthetically and intellectually, to the rest of civilization, the topic will not grow threadbare. There befell a happy moment in history when Italy got the start of the rest of Christendom; and the ground gained, during that splendid advance, the other nations have never been able to recover. We go to Italy to gaze upon certain of the highest achievements of human power,—achievements, moreover, which, from their visible and tangible nature, are particularly well adapted to represent to the imagination the *maximum* of man's creative force. So wide is the interval between the great Italian monuments of art and the works of the colder genius of the neighboring nations, that we find ourselves willing to look upon the former as the ideal and the perfection of human effort, and to invest the country of their birth with a sort of half-sacred character. This is, indeed, but half the story. Through the more recent past of Italy there gleams the stupendous image of a remoter past; behind the splendid efflorescence of the Renaissance we detect the fulness of a prime which, for human effort and human will, is to the great aesthetic explosion of the sixteenth century very much what the latter is to the present time. And then, beside the glories of Italy, we think of her sufferings; and, beside the masterworks of art, we think of the favors of Nature; and, along with these profane matters, we think of the Church,—until, betwixt admiration and longing and pity and reverence, it is little wonder that we are charmed and touched beyond healing.

In the simplest manner possible, and without declamation or rhetoric or affectation of any kind, but with an exquisite alternation of natural pathos and humor, Mr. Howells reflects this constant mute eloquence of Italian life. As to what estimate he finally formed of the Italian character he has left us uncertain; but one feels that he deals gently and tenderly with the foibles and vices of the land, for the sake of its rich and inexhaustible beauty, and of the pleasure which he absorbs with every breath. It is doubtless unfortunate for the Italians, and unfavorable to an exact appreciation of their intrinsic merits, that you cannot think of them or write of them in the same judicial manner as you do of other people,—as from equal to equal,—but that the imagination insists upon having a voice in the matter, and making you generous rather than just. Mr. Howells has perhaps not wholly resisted this temptation; and his tendency, like that of most sensitive spirits brought to know Italy, is to feel—even when he does not express it—that much is to be forgiven the people, because they are *so* picturesque. Mr. Howells is by no means indifferent, however, to the human element in all that he sees. Many of the best passages in his book, and the most delicate touches, bear upon the common roadside figures which he met, and upon the manners and morals of the populace. He observes on their behalf a vast number of small things; and he ignores, for their sake, a large number of great ones. He is not fond of generalizing, nor of offering views and opinions. A certain poetical inconclusiveness pervades his book. He relates what he saw with his own eyes, and what he thereupon felt and fancied; and his work has thus a thoroughly personal flavor. It is, in fact, a series of small personal adventures,—adventures so slight and rapid that nothing comes of them but the impression of the moment, and, as a final result, the pleasant chapter which records them. These chapters, of course, differ in interest and merit, according to their subject, but the charm of manner is never absent; and it is strongest when the author surrenders himself most completely to his faculty for composition, and works his matter over into the perfection of form, as in the episode entitled "Forza Maggiore," a real masterpiece of light writing. Things slight and simple and impermanent all put on a hasty comeliness at the approach of his pen.

Mr. Howells is, in short, a descriptive writer in a sense and with a perfection that, in our view, can be claimed for no American writer except Hawthorne. Hawthorne, indeed, was perfection, but he was only half descriptive. He kept an eye on an unseen world, and his points of contact with this actual sphere were few and slight. One feels through all his descriptions,—we speak especially of his book on England,—that he was not a man of the world,—of this world which we after all love so much better than any other. But Hawthorne cannot be disposed of in a paragraph, and we confine ourselves to our own author. Mr. Howells is the master of certain refinements of style, of certain exquisite intentions (intentions in which humor generally plays a large part), such as are but little practised in these days of crude and precipitate writing. At the close of a very forcible and living description of certain insufferable French *commis-voyageurs*[4] on the steamer from Genoa to Naples, "They wore their hats at dinner," writes Mr. Howells; "but always went away, after soup, deadly pale." It would be difficult to give in three lines a better picture of unconscious vulgarity than is furnished by this conjunction of abject frailties with impertinent assumptions.

And so at Capri, "after we had inspected the ruins of the emperor's villa, a clownish imbecile of a woman, *professing to be the wife of the peasant who had made the excavations,* came forth out of a cleft in the rock and received tribute of us; why, I do not know." The sketch is as complete as it is rapid, and a hoary world of extortion and of stupefied sufferance is unveiled with a single gesture. In all things Mr. Howells's touch is light, but none the less sure for its lightness. It is the touch of a writer who is a master in his own line, and we have not so many writers and masters that we can afford not to recognize real excellence. It is our own loss when we look vacantly at those things which make life pleasant. Mr. Howells has the qualities which make literature a delightful element in

4. Traveling businessmen.

life,—taste and culture and imagination, and the incapacity to be common. We cannot but feel that one for whom literature has done so much is destined to repay his benefactor with interest.

2.

HOWELLS TO JAMES, 26 June, 18 and 24   ALS Houghton
July 1869, Cambridge   bMS Am 1094 (229)

Cambridge,
June 26, 1869.

My dear James:

I had it in my heart to answer you as soon as I'd read your letter;[1] but I hadn't it in my power; and so your missive has lain upon my table to reproach me, and I've endured torments from it. You see that although you had used me very ill in not writing me sooner, my resentment was all melted away by the air of homesickness in your letter, and for a day I really flattered myself that there was some reason why you should be so fond of me. But that is past now, and the Light Man himself could not address you more coldly than this husband and father.[2] I don't know but I've got a touch of that diarist's style; I confess the idea of him fascinated me. He's one of your best worst ones; and I'm sorry we hadn't him for the Atlantic; though it is good policy for you to send something to the Galaxy now and then. I'll enclose some scraps of print, by which you'll see that Gabriele de Bergerac[3] is thought well of by those whose good opinion ought not to be of any consequence, but is. It really promises to make a greater impression than anything else you've done in the Atlantic.

I suppose I was right to carry your letter to your brother, and that he was wrong to show it at once to the rest of your family. Wherever the error is, it is now too late to repair it. Here we enjoyed it all; and Mrs. Howells hunted up the April Atlantic and read Door Step Acquaintance over again.[4] Just at present, however, we are thinking of things that make even my literature seem unimportant. Mrs. Howells's father[5] has lain very sick for the last three weeks, and it is very uncertain yet whether he will recover. From day to day he was not expected to live; she has been with him for nearly two weeks, at Brattleboro',

1. Not extant.

2. HJ, "A Light Man," *Galaxy* (July 1869); the story, told in diary form, of an ambitious but superficial young man, Maximus Austin, who seeks to inherit a fortune first designated for his close friend, Theodore Lisle.

3. HJ, "Gabrielle de Bergerac," *Atlantic* (July–September 1869).

4. WDH, "Door Step Acquaintance," *Atlantic* (April 1869). Other influential literary figures—including James Russell Lowell (1819–91) and the publisher Melancthon M. Hurd (1828–1912)—echoed HJ's apparently encouraging judgment of the piece, which eventually resulted in *Suburban Sketches* (New York: Hurd & Houghton, 1871).

5. Larkin Goldsmith Mead Sr. (1795–1869), a lawyer and prominent citizen of Brattleboro, Vermont; father of Elinor Gertrude Mead (1837–1910), who married WDH in Paris in 1862.

whence she now writes me that there is a little change in him for the better. Add to these anxieties the horrible tumult of this Jubilee business,[6] and the largely increased editorial business, and you have some thing like an excuse for my not answering you at once. I will enclose what I've written about the Jubilee, which will tell a long story in itself, and help to say also what I've been doing.— The summer has passed very quietly in Cambridge, and as like twenty other summers as possible. Thanks to a slow, but uninterrupted spring, and a good deal of wet weather since the foliage started, we are a thought leafier than usual; and you may guess how pleasant it is in that little grove over the way from us, and in fact in every part of the common-place old town—which like some plain girls has a charm quite independent of beauty. Even in Cambridge, I enter quite into the spirit of your home sickness, and feel the fascination which you miss. The town has very few positive advantages; but it is a prodigious satisfaction to "feel that meeting any" acquaintance upon the street, you are well-nigh sure of meeting some person who is not common or mean in his mind, but is full of appreciation and liberality. This appears to me the character of the whole population. I should think there was less intellectual vulgarity here—the worst sort, by the way—than any where else in the world. And yet it's a hard place to live in, expensive, inconvenient, and at times quite desolate. My own stay here seems often drawing to a close for these reasons, and yet I should be exceedingly unhappy anywhere else, I'm afraid. At any rate, I don't think we shall remain much longer in this neighborhood.[7] All Ireland seems to be poured out upon it, and there is such a clamor of Irish children about us all day, that I suspect my "exquisite English," as I've seen it called in the newspapers, will yet be written with a brogue.—

July 18.—You see I am not a ready writer—of letters at least. Till now, I've not seen the hour when I could sit down with a clean conscience to finish this—or if it at any time my conscience was clean my head was empty. Since I began to write—three weeks ago—Mr. Mead has died, and I have been to Brattleboro' to see laid in the ground all that was left of the kind, cheerful, simple old man. He was one who felt so friendly toward the whole world that he imagined it a good one, and led the very happiest life here. He was—

> —"So full of summer warmth, so glad,
> So healthy, sound, and clear and whole,
> His memory scarce can make me sad."[8]

But after all it has been a depressing experience, and my wife has felt it deeply. We have now Mrs. Mead[9] with us, and are trying what we can to keep up the

6. The World's Peace Jubilee, celebrated in Boston in June 1869, was the subject of WDH's "Jubilee Days," *Atlantic* (August 1869).

7. The Howells family, then residing in Sacramento Street, moved in 1873 to a house that WDH had built at 37 Concord Avenue.

8. Alfred, Lord Tennyson (1809–92), "The Miller's Daughter," ll. 14–16.

9. Mary Jane Noyes Mead (1806–76), widow of Larkin Mead Sr. and sister of John Humphrey Noyes (1811–86), founder of the utopian Oneida community.

illusion of mere absence to her.—For a man who never intended to recognize death as among the possibilities, except in an abstract and general sort of way, I have within a year, seen enough of it to convince me of an error in my theory of life.[10] It can never again seem the alien far-off thing it once did; and yet acquaintance with it, has robbed it of something of its terrors. Shall I say it has been at once realized and unsubstantialized? I had always thought to find death in the dead; but they are "but as pictures"; I feel the operation of a principle which seemed improbable, formerly but I am not frightened at its effect as I had always thought to be. I don't mean, of course, that I don't fear to die—God knows I do—but in other times, the mere imagination of death was enough to fill me with unspeakable anguish.—I had hardly got back from my father-in-law's funeral, when our baby's nurse was called away to her little son, in Charlestown, who after a day's sickness died. Mrs. Howells was still at Brattleboro', and you may guess my troubles in taking care of our boy[11] in the nurse's absence. It was sad enough, but even more absurd than sad;—a bachelor and childless man can never understand it all. I walked the floor nearly the whole night, in flowing robes of white, and threshed my brains to contrive diversions for the little ruffian whom nothing could persuade to drop asleep; and next day, to please the poor soul who had lost the whole world she lived for, in her son, I went to see him. It was a wonderful contrast to the scene, I had just witnessed at Brattleboro', where ages of Puritanism had strengthened and restrained the mourners from every display of their grief. The little one lay there on a kind of couch, with candles and vases of flowers about him—an awful, beautiful vision, hallowing and honoring the shabby room, as the most triumphal aspect of life could not have done, and presently the mother cast herself upon him, and bewailed him with a wild heart-rending poetry of anguish. I could not bear it; I broke down, and cried as heartily as she did.—Well, you've had enough of all this, which has lately occupied me to the exclusion of nearly every thing else; and which I hope you'll forgive my writing about; it had to be this or nothing.

I saw your family shortly before they left for Pomfret, and I've since had a little note from your father saying that they were well and most contented with their place. I miss them a good deal—not because I saw them very often, but because it was a pleasure to be able to see them when time favored.—Nearly every one is out of town, in Europe, or in the country,—Lowell alone of the "few immortal names," is left. He called at my house, yesterday, and I walked down town with him the windy, sunny forenoon—down Oxford street; and I wish I could picture you here the beauty of those willows, which line the deserted railway track, as the breeze took them and tossed up the white of their

---

10. The preceding summer, WDH's mother had fallen seriously ill, but he willingly believed the reassuring messages he first received from his family about her condition. When word finally came that she was failing, WDH, conscience-stricken, left immediately for Ohio, only to arrive at his mother's bedside three hours after she had died.

11. John Mead Howells (1868–1959), only son of WDH.

leaves. What a lovely bit of wildness it is, along there!—though there's pro-
vokingly little of it, and it's as hollow and false as a stage-scene,—absolutely
nothing but a few willows, with a growth of lady's-slipper hiding empty tomato
cans and other rubbish about their roots.[12]—I'm not sure that the August Atlantic will reach you, and so I shall tear out the installment of Gabrielle and Jubilee
Days and send them in this letter. Your story is universally praised, and is ac-
counted the best thing you've done. There seems at last to be a general waking-
up to your merits; but when you've a fame as great as Hawthorne's, you wont
forget who was the first, warmest and truest of your admirers, will you?—I'm
writing now and have nearly finished something I call a "Pedestrian Tour," and
which is nothing but an impudent attempt to interest people in a stroll I take
from Sacramento street up through the Brickyards and the Irish village of Dublin near by, and so down through North Avenue. If the public will stand this, I
shall consider my fortune made; and shall go on to write out a paper on "Pleasure Excursions" to different places in and near Boston.[13] The Nation hasn't
pronounced yet upon Jubilee Days—should it be adverse perhaps I sha'n't feel
encouraged to go on. Horrible, is n't it, to have only one critic for 40,000,000
of people?—I don't know whether you'll have heard of the honor conferred on
me by the new President of Harvard;[14] but at any rate I'll do myself the pleasure
to tell you of it. He's asked me to deliver one set of lectures in a course to post-
graduates; and accordingly I'm to lecture along with Lowell, Child and Whitney.
Ci pensi![15] Of course I take modern Italian literature, not knowing anything
else, and feeling secure in the general ignorance concerning that.—Now for an
honor the new President of the United States[16] did Winny[17] at the Jubilee. He
kissed her!—She was very anxious to see him, for reasons of her own, and I led
her near the sofa, where he sat, and told her to ask a certain friendly-looking
old gentleman who sat near Grant to show her the President. He did more: he
led her up to Grant, "And the Presentdent," says Winny, "he took me in his
arms, and said I was a nice little girl, and kissed me; and then the Presentdent's
son kissed me, and laughed at me; and so I ran away." She was very proud for a
day or two, and proposed to "save" the cheek Grant kissed as long as she lived;
but really only kept it sacred for a half-day.—She sends her best love to you,

12. These impressions figure in "A Pedestrian Tour," *Atlantic* (November 1869), another serial
installment of *Suburban Sketches*.
13. WDH, "A Day's Pleasure," *Atlantic* (July–September 1870), also included in *Suburban
Sketches*.
14. Charles W. Eliot (1834–1926), named president of Harvard in 1869, invited WDH, James
Russell Lowell, Professor William D. Whitney of Yale, and others to deliver a series of talks on
modern literature. WDH gave his first lecture on "New Italian Literature" on 16 May 1870; accepting reappointment the following year, he took "Modern Italian Poetry and Comedy" for his
subject.
15. Think of it!
16. Ulysses S. Grant (1822–85), elected eighteenth president of the United States in 1868.
17. Winifred Howells (1863–89), elder daughter of WDH.

and the enclosed tin-type, which she had taken on the Jubilee grounds about an hour after being kissed. It's uncommonly precious, on that account.—The boy is not able to express the friendship he feels for you, but I make bold to send his regards. He grows strong and troublesome, which is all we could wish, I suppose.

July 24. Waiting the receipt of your address from your father, I add a few more lines to this letter, which seems not to grow better with age.—We have lately amused ourselves with the simple joys of a trip down the harbor to Nantasket beach, where we had adventures dear to timid souls—such as getting softly aground in the mud off the pier. The trip was voted a great success, and we mean to take many another like it. Yesterday I got a very tame horse and drove my womenkind over to Lexington—a lovely road, full of that safe wildness which pleases me. In Lexington we added a final charm to the excursion by enquiring the price of board at the hotel, and making ourselves believe for a moment, that we'd go out and spend some weeks there. It was with a kind of dismay that I learnt the pleasure was quite within my means.—You'll have heard from other sources, no doubt, before this letter reaches you, that your brother Wilkie and Arthur Sedgwick[18] have rowed in open boats from Boston to Mt Desert.—I've read the last proof of your Gabrielle, and it's really magnificent—as Mrs. Howells, a very difficult critic, declares. Aren't you going to send us anything about your travels? Do.

Well, good-bye. Write, if youve the heart after reading this—Europe has no such gift as a letter from you to bestow. Mrs. Howells sends her regards, and I am

Ever yours
W. D. Howells.

P. S. Give my best love to the Nortons[19] when you see them. I suppose I must send you this stupidissima letter. And I'm alarmed to find that I've lost the scraps about your story that I intended to send—except one that I enclose.

Give our best love to the Nortons. Mislike me not for my letter, but believe me ever affectionately yours

W. D. H.

I mail an August by this post.

18. Garth Wilkinson James (1845–83), HJ's brother, and Arthur George Sedgwick (1844–1915), a Cambridge friend of HJ and a regular contributor to the *Nation* at this time.

19. Charles Eliot Norton (1827–1908), coeditor with Lowell of the *North American Review*, and his family were then touring in Italy.

3.

HOWELLS TO JAMES, 2 January and 6   ALS Houghton
March 1870, Cambridge   bMS Am 1094 (230)

Cambridge
January 2, 1870

My dear James:

I may as well *start* a letter to you, and trust fortune for the opportunity of finishing it. I'm not only very busy, but my wrist has somehow got out of order, so that it's a pain for me to write. The doctor encourages me to think that it's lead-poisoning from the pipe that goes from the pump to the well in our kitchen, but this flattering belief I can't indulge. However, it's certainly stiff writing—the wrist is—and it takes the opportunity of resting to ache a great deal. So you see I have some reason for neglecting you. I wanted to write the moment I got your last letter,[1] for I felt that that was the only way to get another just like it; but I couldn't. All I could do was to ask your news from time to time of your family, and I hope they've mentioned my infirmity to you. I'm not to blame if they haven't, for according to my wont, I've complained about it to everybody. And aproposito of your family, I saw them last night when I went to fetch Mary Mead,[2] who had been dining with them. I don't know whether your sister[3] is really so much better than she used to be, but she looks so, and I've found a very great resemblance to you in her—a fact you've both reason to be proud of. Your father was well, and your mother, as you'll doubtless know from them long before this reaches you. I don't go to any other house, except Lowell's, with so much content; though I miss you, my dear fellow, horribly. There's a slouch hat of yours (that you used sometimes to wear when you came to our house in bad weather) that I see now and then on the hall table, and that suggests you in such a way as to give me an intolerable longing for you. I suppose that if the truth were known, I like you enormously; and of course I'm flattered when you pretend to care for me. So please be thanked for asking us to remain in Cambridge, on your account. I really think we shouldn't want to go away if we could, though in looking about for another house, we talk Boston a great deal.—In this sentimental strain I interrupted myself to go down to the post-office, where I got an Italian fotograf Mr. Norton had sent me—a charming picture of an ox-cart loaded with oak boughs and two peasants atop. I had a letter from Miss Grace[4] day before yesterday.—Where you are now, or whether you will see the Nortons or not before you get this, I haven't the smallest

1. Not extant.

2. Mary Noyes Mead (1844–1910), WDH's sister-in-law.

3. Alice James (1848–92), only daughter of Henry James Sr. (1811–82) and Mary Walsh James (1810–82), suffered from neurasthenia most of her life.

4. Grace Norton (1834–1926), Charles Eliot Norton's sister, a devoted friend and lifelong correspondent of HJ.

notion. I think I could write a little more comfortably if I knew in what land this missive would hit you. Would it might be at Sorrento. To have it read on the terraces overlooking the gulf would almost give me a sniff of the orange-trees, and a glimpse of Capri. Do look up my Antonino Occhio d'Argento, if you would have a good boatman and a thorough rascal while you're at Sorrento. And kiss the pretty muletress that beats your donkey up to the palace of Timberio (as they call Tiberius) at Capri, and dances the Tarantella for you at the inn there.[5] But that it was a sin not proper for a married man, and that my wife and sister-in-law were by, myself had kissed the maid (if I may call her so). I write this to give you an idea of what a mocking and profligate character I am at heart; but really the girl was pretty, and I'm sorry I can't remember her name. On the whole I think Capri the quaintest experience of Italian travel. Pompeii being the strangest. As to the latter place, I let you and the Norton's go there of my free-will, but for other people I envy 'em enough to kill 'em.—I suppose it's in pity of me who think longingly of the places you look on (with bored thoughts sometimes) that we're having such an Italian winter in Cambridge. It's now the 2d of January; a mild October rain is falling, and we've had only one fall of snow and scarce any cold weather. The frost's all out of the ground as in late April. It's really extraordinary, and fills one with old-wife dreads of sickness which must follow such uncommon clemency of the heavens. You imagine of course the gayety of Sacramento street under this sopper of a rain.

Now, you think I've been keeping you from literature long enough. Well, there isn't so much to tell about literature as one at your distance would believe. A new magazine has been started, under the editorship of the Rev. E. E. Hale,[6] by Hurd and Houghton, called Old and New, which has not been enviably good. But it has a chance to grow much better, which isn't the case with the A. M.[7] unless you will write for it. And by the way, why don't you? As the matter goes you're in great danger of having your private letters stolen and published. "What we want," says Mr. Fields,[8] with perfect truth, "is short, *cheerful* stories." And our experience of you is quite in that way of fiction. In all seriousness (as people say who think they've been ironical or playful), I wish you could send us something. Any sketch of what you see or do, would be welcome—I'd almost print an art criticism for you.—Our latest literary event is Lowell's new poem The Cathedral,[9] which I like better than anything I've read for a very long time. I wonder if you get the Atlantic, and if you've seen the poem yet? I doubt if you'd like it as much as I do—your father doesn't. The little paper which your father

5. An episode related by WDH in the tenth chapter ("Capri and Capriotes") of *Italian Journeys*.

6. Edward Everett Hale (1822–1909), a Unitarian clergyman and great-nephew of Nathan Hale, also wrote short stories (most famously "The Man Without a Country" [1863]) and essays on religious and historical subjects.

7. *Atlantic Monthly*.

8. James T. Fields (1817–81), renowned Boston publisher and editor of the *Atlantic*, appointed WDH as his assistant in 1866.

9. Published in the *Atlantic* 25 (January 1870): 1–15.

gave us for January on Woman[10] has been much liked, and I'm instigating him to write more for the magazine.—The N. A. Review is to be cut down to two hundred pages hereafter. Every Saturday is published with very handsome illustrations, now. Generally the literary world is dull, and is I suspect awaiting the appearance of my volume of Atlantic sketches which is to be published in the spring.[11] I sent you one of these sketches (Pedestrian Tour) before it appeared in the November number. Since, I have done By Horse-Car to Boston; and I have in type A Romance of Real Life which records a droll and curious experience of mine. In some ways these things seem rather small business to me; but I fell naturally into doing them; I persuaded myself (too fondly, perhaps) that they're a new kind of study of our life, and I have an impression that they're to lead me to some higher sort of performance. They're not easy to do, but cost me a great deal of work. They seem to be pretty well liked, and I'm told are looked for by readers.—So sweet is it to talk of oneself!—I could go on in this strain for hours and hours.

March 6.

You see how long it takes me to finish a letter. I hope you don't despise me more than half as much as I loathe myself; but I should be glad if you felt something more than the pity I have for your poor unworthy friend. I'm celebrating the presence of your mother in our house by resuming this letter to you. She has come to call, with a perseverance worthy of a better cause, through all the mud and melting snow that shut out Sacramento street from the rest of the world, and she tells me of your being again in England, and of your great homesickness for Italy. Well, I partly understand that; but I think Italy has gone harder with you than she did with me. I find that I'm even ceasing be jealous of other people for loving her, and boasting of her favors. It was n't perhaps a true passion I had for her after all.

A great many things have happened since I began to write this letter. I've been sick a bed for the first time in ten years,—not seriously sick, but very tediously and painfully; and our little boy was dangerously attacked with bronchitis. But all's well now, and these woes are part of the whole incredible past. They originally interrupted my letter to you, however.—Several nights I couldn't sleep, and read till morning. Without this tremendous occasion, I suppose I never should have looked into Erckmann-Chatrian's books;[12] but John Fiske[13]

---

10. Henry James Sr., "The Woman Thou Gavest Me," *Atlantic* (January 1870): 66–72. The elder James's later contributions on the subject of women included: "Is Marriage Holy?" (March 1870): 360–68; and "The Logic of Marriage and Murder" (June 1870): 744–49.

11. *Suburban Sketches* was published 19 December 1870, although 1871 is listed on the title page as the year of publication.

12. Emile Erckmann (1822–99) and Alexandre Chatrian (1826–90) jointly authored a popular series of historical novels; *L'Ami Fritz* (1864) was not part of the series but met with equal success.

13. John Fiske (1842–1901), WDH's Cambridge neighbor, philosopher and historian at Harvard, soon became a leading American advocate of the new evolutionary theories of Charles Darwin and Herbert Spencer.

happened to bring me some of them, and I read them with such rapture, that I
fire away about them to everybody that lets me talk to him. I think they're
amazingly good, and I marvel at the partnership that produced them. I think I
never read a more *pleasing* book than *L'Ami Fritz*—unless it's Björnson's Fisher-
maiden,[14] though that's lovely in such a very different way. What a wonderful
atmosphere of springtime in *L'Ami F.*! The impulse to go and find a cherry-tree
in blossom, and to make love to some blonde person was hardly to be resisted
even by an enthusiast lying on his back in bed with an abcess on his bowels. As
for Björnson, his little romances so enchanted me that I must needs write about
them, and if you've so much patience, you can read my mind in the April
Atlantic.—The Romance of Real Life has made all the impression it merited;
but I could not help being amused with one adverse criticism in view of the fact
that the whole thing was a record of actual experience. The critic praised the
style, but said very justly "Mr. Howells has no invention."—Now you are settled,
not to say soaking up that water-cure, why couldn't you do something for us in
the way of stories, or anything else you've a mind to write? Mr. Fields spoke of
the matter only the other day, and I promised to stir you up. So please consider
yourself appealed to in the most moving terms by an editor in great suffering.

Mrs. Howells lends me her powerful hand in finishing this letter, for my own
hand is still somewhat lame. I do not know that I have so much gossip to tell
you about Cambridge as you get from your own family. In fact the winter has
been very quiet as far as my own family is concerned. We have seen scarcely
anybody but the doctor, who came twice a day for a month—and though we
like him very well as a man we dont consider that in seeing him so often we
have exactly been in society. After living within a gunshot of Mr. John Fiske for
several years I am beginning to get somewhat acquainted with him, and take as
kindly to him as anyone can I suppose who has no idea what positive philosophy
is. He has almost a fashion of coming to see us lately, and I find him a very
simple-hearted fellow. We have also given each other dinners, and I suppose
that in case of a wedding or a funeral we might depend upon each other for the
common civilities of life—though this is venturing to say a good deal for Cambridge you will no doubt consider. When we went to the Fiske's we expected to
meet Mr. Dennett,[15] but he failed to appear, and I have seen him only once
since he came to live amongst us, and that was when I called upon him, immediately after his arrival. He sustains his character of recluse with great rigor, and
indeed has lately lost a sister. Mr. Gurney,[16] however, told me the other day that
he came often to dine with him. He still writes for the Nation, and it would be
a great loss to everybody if he ceased to do so. I am really sorry not to be able

14. Björnstjerne Björnson (1832–1910), author of *The Fisher-Maiden* (1868), had his book reviewed by WDH, together with *Arne* (1858) and *A Happy Boy* (1860), in the *Atlantic* (April 1870).
15. John R. Dennett (1837–74), chief literary critic of the *Nation*, was noted for his severity.
16. Ephraim Whitman Gurney (1829–86), assistant professor of philosophy at Harvard, replaced
Charles Eliot Norton as coeditor of the *North American Review* in 1868.

to make his acquaintance. Our great excitement at present is Fechter[17]—and I am wholly his—as far as Hamlet goes. I have not seen him in any other character. I wonder if you have seen him in Europe and how you like him. To my thinking he is almost a perfect actor—almost as good as Joe Jefferson[18] with his realistic and untheatrical ways. I was not only interested in his Hamlet, but thrilled and transported by it. I have never seen Booth[19] yet, whose friends of course rage against Fechter.

I believe there is little or nothing to tell you about literature. I think we grow more poverty-stricken in that direction every day. Editorially I have a pretty good survey of the whole field, and the prospect is a discouraging one. The signs of growth are very small and feeble, while there are some striking instances of dwindling. There is no sort of freshness in the things that are sent us at least. One of the new Spring books is a collection of Mr. Bret. Harte's stories from the Overland,[20] which are very good indeed so far as they go—but he has eked out the book with some old and inferior writings of his. Miss Phelps[21] has produced a novel, Hedged In, that is written in her most gasping shuddering style, and discomforts me exceedingly, though I dare say Miss Phelps likes it, and it is pretty sure to sell twenty thousand. Mrs. Prescott Spofford[22] is exclusively engaged on Frank Leslie,[23] and all the magazines and newspapers continue to grind out the usual amount of fiction and poetry. The latest of the Magazines, Old and New, is a sort of diluted Putnam,[24] if you can imagine it, and one must be a very good Unitarian or a very bad critic to like it. I see this letter is getting to be fearfully cynical, and I seek in vain for a cheerful topic with which to close it up. I will substitute something that is to us, at least, very exciting. I told you in the January number of this letter that we were looking about for a new house. I have now to tell you that we are still looking without an immediate prospect of finding any. For a while our dream was to live near Porter's Station so that we might get easily to and from Boston by the steamcars, but now we rave of a house near the Square so that we may enjoy Cambridge society, Mrs. Howells having got very much better and having some faint

---

17. Charles A. Fechter (1824–79), the popular English actor, was then touring the United States.

18. Joseph Jefferson (1829–1905), an American actor, best remembered for his role in Dion Boucicault's *Rip Van Winkle* (1865).

19. Edwin Booth (1833–93), the celebrated American Shakespearean actor.

20. *The Luck of Roaring Camp and Other Sketches* (1870). Bret Harte (1836–1902), editor of San Francisco's *Overland Monthly* (1868–70), became an overnight sensation with the title story. The next year James T. Fields offered Harte the unprecedented sum of ten thousand dollars for the use of ten short stories in the *Atlantic*.

21. Elizabeth Stuart Phelps (1844–1911) authored many popular novels; her most famous work, *The Gates Ajar*, appeared in 1868.

22. Harriet Prescott Spofford (1835–1921), another popular fiction writer.

23. *Frank Leslie's Illustrated Newspaper* (1855–1922), founded by Frank Leslie (1821–80), the publisher.

24. *Putnam's Monthly Magazine*, published by G. P. Putnam & Sons.

aspirations in that direction. Our project is to have Mrs Mead and Mary[25] come and live with us, and we shall take a larger house than we otherwise should. We have even thought of building—but not in our lucid intervals, and taking into consideration our peculiarities it would not be at all amazing if the whole thing were abandoned. At any rate you need not expect to find us living in a North Avenue palace when you come back. But come back nevertheless. I miss you more and more, and now, when the weather begins to open and the streets all about to reek with the thaw I have a wild longing to take a walk with you, as I used to do in other days.

Mrs. Howells relinquishes the pen that I may assure in my own feeble hand how delighted I am that you're to return next fall. Let me beseech you to use me better than I deserve, and to write very soon. I am joined by my whole family in love to you, and I am

affectionately yours
W. D. Howells.

Winny sends a kiss. "But tell him I think I wont marry him. He'll be an old man by the time I'm grown up."

This is a great lot of stuff hardly better than nothing.

4.

HOWELLS TO JAMES, 1 September 1872, Boston   ALS Houghton
bMS Am 1094 (232)

OFFICE OF "THE ATLANTIC MONTHLY,"
NO. 124, TREMONT STREET, BOSTON,
September 1, 1872.

My dear James:

If I attempted a letter of the generous length of yours,[1] I should feel bound to give it up at the start, but if you'll let me begin with four modest pages, I think you may hear from me soon, at any rate.

—The days go by here very much as usual, and with that strong family like-ness to each other which would enable one to recognize a Cambridge day any-where; but their going has at least brought the long terrible summer to an end, and that's some merit. Mrs. Howells and Winny have been home some weeks from Princeton, where they spent two perfectly satisfactory months,[2] and now we're all together again, and expect to be five instead of four before the end of

25. Elinor's mother and sister, Mary Noyes Mead.
1. Not extant.
2. WDH's family was summering at Princeton, Massachusetts, a small agricultural village north-west of Worcester.

September.[3] In the meantime, we take a very great interest in the new house which this daring family has begun to build. The lot is part of Mr. Parsons's[4] garden, on Concord Avenue, and not far from the Observatory grounds. The cellar is dug, and the lumber is partly on the ground, and every day Winny and Bua[5] and I visit the place, they to play on the sand and boards, and I to watch the cellar wall abuilding, and admire at myself for giving employment to four men, two boys and two horses. The money's all somehow to come out of me, but as yet, the future house and the opportunity of letting the poor earn their bread, seem to be freely bestowed upon me by some good power outside of me. My satisfaction is marred by nothing but occasional thoughts of my story,[6] which I brought to a close in July with such triumphal feelings that I would not have exchanged my prospect of immortality through it for the fame of Shakespeare. Now I regard it with cold abhorrence, and work it over, shuddering. This too must pass away: anyhow I begin printing in January, and I dare say I shall be ready to agree, and more, with anybody who praises it. Your own story—Guest's Confession—opens in the October number, and closes in November. I think I shall put the Florentine story into January.[7] G.'s C. reads excellently, I assure you, and I'm certain will make favor for you. On some accounts I'm sorry you couldn't have brought out a volume this fall; it would have served to assemble the liking and reputation you've won. I think yet you might make a successful book of the romantic tales.—I have seen something more than usual of Perry, lately; and I'm working hard to get him the sub-editorship of the N. A. Review.[8] It depends upon the problematical chief, for the publishers are quite willing. I think it a pity Perry should go to N. Y., and be Dennettized.[9] One Dennett's enough—and to spare. The Nation has regularly brought me your letters,[10] and I've liked them, as I like everything of yours. If you asked me, I should say you tended a little too much to the metaphysical expression of travel, as opposed to the graphic; but this tendency is what I heard Lowell praise when I objected to it before.—At present they have no chief on the N. A. R. The October number was left *planted*, by both the late editors,[11] and I'm putting it together from such

3. WDH's daughter Mildred (1872–1966) was born on 26 September.

4. Theophilus Parsons (1797–1882), Dane Professor of Law at Harvard (1848–69), sold WDH a building lot at 37 Concord Avenue.

5. Affectionate nickname for John Mead Howells.

6. *A Chance Acquaintance* ran in the *Atlantic* from January to June 1873.

7. HJ's story "The Madonna of the Future" did not appear in the *Atlantic* until March 1873.

8. Thomas Sergeant Perry (1845–1928), a close friend of both HJ and WDH, became affiliated with the *North American Review* through WDH's intervention with James R. Osgood & Company, the publisher. Perry brought out the magazine from January 1873 through January 1874, when Henry Adams (1838–1918) returned from Europe and resumed his editorship, a post he held from 1870 to 1876.

9. John R. Dennett was then chief literary critic for the *Nation*.

10. At irregular intervals, from July through November 1872, the *Nation* ran HJ's six-part series of travel sketches entitled "A European Summer."

11. James Russell Lowell and Henry Adams.

material as I can get, and proof-reading it. My friend Boyesen has been here all summer, but has now gone back to Urbana. I'm to print a Norwegian story for him next year.[12] What do you intend to do for literature in '73?—a year destined to be famous.—I send love from my wife with my own to your whole party, and I hope you'll write as promptly as I have written. I see your people rather often, now; but I have long seasons of non-intercourse with mankind when I feel too inert to transact the social pleasures, though I've always the grace to be ashamed of myself.

Yours evermore,
W. D. H.

P. S. Of course, it's all right about Miss Blagden's poem.[13] It was good enough to print; but my chief pleasure in printing it would have been the thought that it gratified the Bootts.[14] To whom, by the way, please remember me cordially, in any communication you have with them.—The weather is so fresh that I've a fire in my stove this morning; and if you were here, we might take the longest and briskest walk of the year without discomfort.—Alas! how the years go by, and how little they leave behind. When I think of the walks we have taken, we seem less substantial in the past than the shadows of the clouds that drifted over the same autumnal paths. Sometimes the whole intolerable mystery of the thing comes over me suffocatingly—and I don't feel as if a first-class notice in The Nation were worth striving for. But this of course is disease. I hope you are happy, and that you are putting by for the public a store of the honey you find on those Swiss mountain sides. But I don't envy you those acclivities, but O my lagoons of Venice, and the seaweedy smell of the shallows!—these I do begrudge. Ricorditi di me [15]—when you lie there in your boat, and at least say, Poor Howells, he liked Venice, though perhaps he didn't understand her.

---

12. Hjalmar Hjorth Boyesen (1848–95) emigrated from Norway in 1869 and became a professor of German at Urbana College, a Swedenborgian school, in Ohio. His novella "Gunnar" appeared in the *Atlantic* (July–December 1873).

13. Isabella Blagden (1816–73), an Englishwoman long resident in Florence, wrote poems and novels; she was an intimate of the Brownings' literary circle and a neighbor of Francis and Elizabeth Boott.

14. Francis Boott (1813–1904), an American expatriate composer, and his daughter Elizabeth (1846–88) resided in Florence. HJ, too, was a close friend of the family; his observation of them informs the treatment of Gilbert Osmond and his daughter Pansy in *The Portrait of a Lady* (1881).

15. Remember me.

5.

HOWELLS TO JAMES, 28 October 1872, Boston   ALS Houghton
bMS Am 1094 (233)

. . . "THE ATLANTIC MONTHLY," . . .

BOSTON,

Oct. 28, 1872.

My dear James:

I asked them to send you the check some time ago, so that by now I hope
you have it. The story I'm going to print in February.[1] Your "Guest's Confession"
has on the whole been received with more favor than anything else you've
printed in the Atlantic; and though I don't give up my early favorites, I see
many reasons why G's. C. should be generally liked. Mrs. Howells, who is not a
"genial critic"—of her husband's writings, at any rate—praises it very highly;
says your people both speak and act from motives of their own; and the different
scenes are intense, and the whole plot new and good. Whereupon I enviously
point out that somehow the end does not come with a click, and that there's a
certain obscurity in Mrs. Beck's fate, so that your brother and I disputed as to
whom she marries.[2] I think you don't make your young man generous enough
to merit that good girl. Nevertheless I admire the story greatly.—The first chapter of my own story[3] is in proof, and it seems not altogether loathsome. Perry,
who is of a cool temperament, and of a vast experience in novel-reading, has
been so good as to read the whole thing in MS., and has had the face to pretend
that he likes it.—By the way, that excellent young man is to have charge of the
N. A. Review for the present, at any rate, my machinations having succeeded.
He has taken rooms in Boston, and has set to work. I think it's just the work
for him.—I dare say your family have written you of our happiness, at the prospect of which I hinted. We have a little daughter, now a month old, whom we
call Mildred. She bids fair to be the prettiest of the children, and for the time
being is all that ought to be expected of a young lady of her age. My wife is
very well, indeed, and we are so blest that some sort of retribution must be in
store for us.—Cambridge goes forward at the accustomed pace, with some slight
symptoms of a social awakening. I was at a small affair at the Ashburner's,[4] the
other night, and met the habitual friends. Sedgwick is back again, and is to
resume his work on the Atlantic, and is otherwise going to take out letters-of-

---

1. "The Madonna of the Future," *Atlantic* (March 1873).

2. In HJ's story both duplicitous John Guest and wealthy Mr. Crawford court Mrs. Clara Beck,
Laura Guest's companion. In the final scene, the narrator observes Mrs. Beck adding a lump of sugar
to Crawford's tea—a symbol of her favor? "His eye met mine," the narrator concludes, "and I fancied
he looked sheepish." See *THJ* 2:201.

3. *A Chance Acquaintance*.

4. Anne (1807–94) and Grace (1814–93) Ashburner were the English maiden aunts of Susan
(Sedgwick) Norton, the wife of Charles Eliot Norton. They had come to America to care for Susan
after the death of her parents.

marque for a privateering cruise on the high seas of political literature.[5]—Prof. Child[6] is "comfortably sick" with a low fever which threatens to keep him indoors for a couple of months.—I've just come in from a long walk up North Avenue, in which I missed you abominably. It's been a very cool, sunny, sparkling day, and the clear evening seemed to demand you by a strength of association that shewed me how long you and I had been friends. We have known each other for about six years, and in the meantime I am thirty five years old. In the spring my new pantaloons measured 32 inches in the waist; those that just came home measure 34. So we go. A man booked for obesity must not sentimentalize about a long standing friendship. Otherwise I should rejoice in ours. But I should like to hear from you. We all send love.

Yours ever
W. D. Howells.

6.

HOWELLS TO JAMES, 10 March 1873, Cambridge

ALS Houghton
bMS Am 1094 (234)

Cambridge,
March 10, 1873.

My dear James:

I hope you'll be properly affected by the size of this sheet: it's extent is an emblem of my friendship for you, for I'm reducing the size of my notepaper generally.

First let me thank you with all my heart for your criticism on my story—rather, on my heroine. It came too late for the magazine; but I have been able to check the young person a little before handing her down to the latest posterity in book form.[1] Her pertness was but another proof of the contrariness of her sex: I meant her to be everything that was lovely, and went on protesting that she was so, but she preferred being saucy to the young man, especially in that second number. Afterwards I think she is at least all I profess for her. I like her because she seems to me a character; the man, I own is a simulacrum. Well or ill advisedly I conceived the notion of confronting two extreme American types: the conventional and the unconventional. These always disgust each other, but I amused myself with the notion of their falling in love, which would not be impossible, if they were both young and good looking. Now conventionality is,

5. Arthur G. Sedgwick began his "Politics" department for the *Atlantic* in January 1872.

6. Francis James Child (1825–96), professor of English at Harvard, a Cambridge neighbor of WDH affectionately remembered in *Literary Friends and Acquaintance* (1900).

1. HJ's letter criticizing the serial version of *A Chance Acquaintance* is not extant, although his letter of 22 June 1873 contains incidental remarks about the story. WDH's revisions of the serial, conveniently tallied in the Indiana University Press edition of the novel ("Emendations," 175–84), reveal the extent to which he heeded HJ's advice to "check" Kitty Ellison.

in our condition of things, in itself a caricature; I did my best for the young man, but his nature was against him, and he is the stick you see. Of course the girl must be attracted by what is elegant and fine in him, and provoked to any sort of reprisal by his necessary cool assumption of superiority. She cannot very well help "sassing" him, though she feels that this puts her at a disadvantage, and makes her seem the aggressor. I have tried to let this explain itself to the reader as much as I can; but it is a kind of thing that scarcely admits of dramatic demonstration, and I feel that the whole thing is weighed down with comment. However, I've learnt a great deal in writing the story, and if it does not destroy my public, I shall be weaponed better than ever for the field of romance. And I am already thirty pages advanced on a new story,[2] in which, blessed be heaven, there is no problem but the sweet old one of how they shall get married. In this case I'm sorry to say they don't solve it, for the hero is a Venetian priest in love with an American girl. There's richness! And now peace to me and my work. I've been burning to tell you how much I like your "Madonna,"[3] and to report the undissenting voice of acclaim with which it has been hailed. Ever so many people have spoken of it, the Delphic Dennett[4] alone remaining mum. Truly it has been a success, and justly, for it is a bravely solid and excellent piece of work. All like the well-managed pathos of it, the dissertations on pictures, the tragic, most poetical central fact, and I hope that many feel with me its unity and completeness. Every figure in it is a real character, and has some business there. The sole blemish on it to my mind is the insistance on the cats and monkeys philosophy.[5] I don't think you ought to have let that *artista* appear a second time, and, I confess, to have the cs and ms for a refrain at the close, marred the fine harmony of what went before, till I managed to forget them. I have your Roman romance,[6] and I shall print it very soon. I like it, but I shall tell you more about it when I get it in print. I'm glad that we're to hear from you every month, and I rejoice that you think of doing a serial for next year. Whether you'll find Venice a good working climate, I'm not sure. I'd rather do my loafing there. But it's delicious in early summer, and with sea-baths, I don't see why you shouldn't get on.—All the family at Casa Howells are well; but they have had their colds and other woes this winter. My wife in particular has been very delicate, though with a little promise of spring she's at least gaining

2. *A Foregone Conclusion*, published in 1874.

3. "The Madonna of the Future," *Atlantic* (March 1873).

4. John R. Dennett, literary critic of the *Nation*.

5. In HJ's story the pathetic romantic idealism of the American expatriate painter Theobald is tellingly contrasted with the sordid productivity of an Italian sculptor who markets animal figurines in suggestive human poses. Addressing the narrator, the sculptor asks, "What do you say to my types, signore? The idea is bold; does it strike you as happy? Cats and monkeys,—monkeys and cats,—all human life is there! Human life, of course, I mean, viewed with the eye of the satirist!" (THJ 2:226). After Theobald's death—and the revelation that his long-awaited portrait of the Madonna remains a blank, cracked canvas—the narrator again recalls the sculptor's cynical observation, which concludes the story. WDH repeated this mild censure of the story in his 1875 *Atlantic* review of HJ's *A Passionate Pilgrim and Other Tales*, reprinted in this book.

6. "The Last of the Valerii," *Atlantic* (January 1874).

courage if not health again. She agrees with you about Kitty's pertness, and is otherwise my terriblest critic, as always. The children are all that a fond papa could desire. The two oldest you know, but little maid Mildred is the jolliest and prettiest of all. She is really a little beauty, and as amiable as the day is long.—The house gets on as well as could be expected in a winter which has forbidden plastering. It's all finished outside, and we're to be in it—if we put our faith in carpenters—by the first of June.—You divine truly that I have seen no one this winter. The other night I went to one of the Rev. Peabody receptions, and to-morrow we're invited to the Golden Wedding of Dr. and Mrs. Palfrey.[7] About once in three weeks Mr. Longfellow[8] has regularly taken pity on me, and had me to dinner. This is the whole story. I don't know whether anything's been going on or not, but I love all my fellow men here as heartily as if I had met the whole human family once a week. I thank you for not telling me too much about Rome. Such things are hard to bear. I hate the American in Europe,— because I am not he. At times the longing is almost intolerable with me, and if I could see any way of keeping the bird in the hand while I clutched at those in the bush, I should go. I have a scheme for work some day in Italy which I hope to carry out.[9] It would take me there just about the time the children should be studying French and music, and keep me there five years. M'aspetti! Intanto Le reverisco![10] Mrs Howells and the children join me in love.

Yours ever
W. D. Howells.

P. S. I'm glad Osgood is to get out a volume for you.[11]

Imagine getting up this morning and finding a heavy snow storm in full blast. It was almost heart-breaking. We've now had three months of snow, and sleighing.

---

7. Andrew P. Peabody (1811–93) and John Gorham Palfrey (1796–1881) were both Unitarian ministers; Peabody edited the *North American Review* from 1852 to 1861.

8. Henry Wadsworth Longfellow (1807–82), revered poet and Professor of Modern Languages and Belles Lettres at Harvard.

9. WDH had planned to write a history of Venice, a project he worked on intermittently for many years but never finished.

10. Wait for me! Meanwhile I send you my regards!

11. HJ's first collection of stories, *A Passionate Pilgrim*, and a travel volume, *Transatlantic Sketches*, were published by James R. Osgood & Company in 1875. At this time Osgood was continuing the business of Ticknor & Fields, the Boston publishing firm that rose to prominence in the antebellum period. In 1878 he went into partnership with Henry Oscar Houghton (1823–95) to form Houghton, Osgood & Company. When that partnership was dissolved in 1880, Osgood again went into business on his own, reforming James R. Osgood & Company. That firm filed for bankruptcy in 1885, at which point Osgood became affiliated with Harper & Brothers of New York. Because Osgood was such an influential publishing figure for both HJ and WDH, the chronology of his affiliations acquires some importance. See Carl Weber, *The Rise and Fall of James Ripley Osgood* (Waterville, Me.: Colby College Press, 1959); and Ellen Ballou, *The Building of the House: Houghton Mifflin's Formative Years* (Boston: Houghton Mifflin, 1970).

7.

HOWELLS TO JAMES, 12 May 1873, Boston

ALS Houghton
bMS Am 1094 (235)

. . . THE ATLANTIC MONTHLY, . . .

BOSTON,

May 12, 1873.

My dear James:

"A Roman Holiday" (which I have butchered your Carnival to make) is cast for the July number,[1] and it was put in type for June, but it came out eleven pages instead of five or six. I can only keep my word to you to print a contribution every month if you keep within bounds. I want to have your name appear regularly, but it is a brute matter of space, and not an affair of the heart, with the printers, though I would willingly give you half the magazine. I like the A R. H. very much indeed, and the Roman Rides are still better—more in the vein, and richer-toned. That is delicious, about that infernal scoundrel's experience as héros de roman![2] If the black drop of envy could kill, he lives no longer. But alas! it is not Rome alone that works such wonders; youth helps, which is going; money which I never had, nor social courage. It is a plebeian as well as a senile spite that I vent.—Your paper was good all through, and this I said to myself before your letter came to confirm me in my liking by its generous praises of my story.[3] It will go into the August Atlantic.—I'm glad you like that IV part, and I needn't be ashamed to own that I thought it well managed.—If you have been vexed by Dennett's curt and most unfair treatment of your Gautier,[4] let me tell you that it has united all other voices in your favor and honor. It has been universally liked by everybody here.

1. "A Roman Holiday," *Atlantic* (July 1873); presumably HJ's original title for the article was "A Roman Carnival." When he prepared his text for book publication, HJ did not restore any passages that WDH may have cut; in fact, a few more minor deletions were made before the piece appeared in *Transatlantic Sketches* (1875).

2. In "Roman Rides" (*Atlantic* [August 1873]) HJ invents a dilettantish companion who remarks that a day spent riding in the campagna makes him feel as if he were "reading an odd chapter in the history of a person very much more of a *héros de roman* than myself" (191).

3. HJ's letter praising the serial version of *A Chance Acquaintance* is not extant; see letter #8, however, for his further comments about WDH's novel.

4. John R. Dennett of the *Nation* had scoffed at HJ's sympathetic treatment of Théophile Gautier (1811–72) in an essay HJ had published in the *North American Review* (April 1873). According to Dennett,

> Mr. James's criticism of Gautier is very kind. "If there are sermons in stones," he remarks, "there are profitable reflections to be made even on Théophile Gautier; notably this one— that a man's supreme use in this world is to master his intellectual instrument and play it in perfection." Persons in imperfect sympathy with the general view here implied will feel like suggesting that the supreme use of some men in this world, considering what a world it is, is to throw away their intellectual instrument and never play anything on it. But Mr. James's essay makes it plainer than would be supposed by most who have listened to British–American sermons over Gautier's remains, that Gautier was hardly one of these players after all, though certainly no fit company for St. Cecilia. A wonderful world we shall have, though,

Events are much rarer than great genius in Cambridge, as you know. However, we have the divine Keeler[5] back again, and that is something. He comes back from the arbitration of the Alabama claims with a formulated philosophy of Epicurean type, and is really delightful joking. Aldrich,[6] Perry, Fiske and rest are very well; I will pass round your messages. Fiske will probably go abroad in August. Mrs. Edwards, one of his sectaries, gives him $1000 towards his expenses.[7] Isn't that handsome? I hope Perry will be able to keep the North American; they have at least made no other arrangement about it.—We dined with the Aldriches at your father's, the other day, and had a merry time.—There has been a slight rash of dinners and parties in Cambridge, this spring, but the eruption has yielded to treatment, and all is now quiet again. We look soon to have the Nortons back. I rowed on Fresh Pond with Keeler, last week, and to-day, I rode round it with my wife. It's very well, let me tell you, though it's not Roman. The landscape was in the tender beauty of its most virginal green; the low western sun struck across the grass orchards (where scarcely a stubborn bough has budded yet,) and it was fairly *ridente*[8]—but with tears somewhere, too. O it breaks my heart to have the spring again—what a rapture, what a pang it is!—The Howellses are well, and united in their love to you.—The new house, which is pretty enough, is hurrying forward.—I have written nearly a hundred and fifty pages of my new story,[9] and am getting the people together. It goes just now no smoother than true love's course, but I hope and strive.—Don't make your sketches more than 30 pages of your Ms., if you can help.

Yours ever
W. D. Howells.

---

when "art for art's sake" is the rule that guides our pickers and stealers and our young addle-pates.

See [John R. Dennett], "The North American Review for April," *Nation* 16 (24 April 1873): 289.

Before receiving this letter from WDH, HJ questioned his brother about the authorship of the *Nation* notice: "The general style of the article didn't read like Dennett, though the phrases about my thing were obscure enough for him. Whoever he is, he is very silly." See HJ to WJ, 19 May [1873], *CWJ* 1: 204.

5. Ralph Keeler (1840–73), a journalist, had been in Geneva covering the proceedings of the international Tribunal of Arbitration, charged with settling the claims of restitution for damages suffered by the United States because of Great Britain's support of the Confederacy during the Civil War. The CSS *Alabama,* built to Southern specifications at the Laird Shipyards in Liverpool, had been notoriously effective in harassing the Northern merchant marine, destroying sixty-nine vessels between 1862 and 1864.

6. Thomas Bailey Aldrich (1836–1907), Boston novelist and minor poet, succeeded WDH as editor of the *Atlantic* (1881–90).

7. Mrs. M. A. Edwards's patronage of John Fiske is documented in John Spencer Clarke, *The Life and Letters of John Fiske,* 2 vols. (Boston: Houghton Mifflin, 1917), 1: 406–7; see also Milton Berman *John Fiske: The Evolution of a Popularizer* (Cambridge, Mass.: Harvard University Press, 1961), 133.

8. Laughing.

9. *A Foregone Conclusion.*

Thank you again with all my heart for what you say of my story. You see with kind eyes; but I really hoped that I had put something to be seen. That chapter cost me infinite pains.

8.

JAMES TO HOWELLS, 22 June 1873, Berne   ALS Houghton
bMS Am 1784 (253) 2

Berne, Switz. June 22$^{\underline{d}}$

My veritably dear Howells—

Your letter of May 12$^{\underline{th}}$ came to me a week ago (after a journey to Florence & back) & gave me exquisite pleasure. I found it in the Montreux post office & wandered further till I found the edge of an open vineyard by the lake & there I sat down with my legs hanging over the azure flood & broke the seal. Thank you for everything: for liking my writing and for being glad I like yours. Your letter made me homesick & when you told of the orchards by Fresh Pond I hung my head for melancholy. What is the meaning of this destiny of desolate exile—this dreary necessity of having month after month to do without our friends for the sake of this arrogant old Europe which so little befriends us? This is a hot Sunday afternoon: from my window I look out across the rushing Aar at some beautiful undivided meadows backed by black pine woods & blue mountains: but I would rather be taking up my hat & stick & going to invite myself to tea with you. I left Italy a couple of weeks since, & since then have been taking gloomy views of things. I feel as if I had left my "genius" behind in Rome. But I suppose I am well away from Rome just now; the Roman (& even the Florentine) lotus had become, with the warm weather, an indigestible diet. I heard from my mother a day or two since that your Book is having a sale—bless it![1] I haven't yet seen the last part & should like to get the volume as a whole. Would it trouble you to have it sent by post to *Brown, Shipley & Co London?*— Your fifth Part I extremely relished; it was admirably touched. I wished the talk in which the offer was made had been given (instead of the mere resumé) but I suppose you had good & sufficient reasons for doing as you did. But your work is a Success & Kitty a creation. I have envied you greatly, as I read, the delight of feeling her grow so real and complete, so true & charming. I think, in bringing her through with such unerring felicity, your imagination has *fait ses preuves.*[2] —I wish I could talk over her successor with you, sitting on the pine-needles by Fresh Pond. This is odiously impossible: but at least let me hear what you can, as the thing goes on. I suppose it's to begin with January.—Are you in

1. *A Chance Acquaintance*; HJ's mother noted that three thousand copies had already been sold. "There is a good deal of criticism of the Boston man [Miles Arbuton]," she added, "which it is said must have been conceived in pique. Howells disclaims having intended him as a typical Bostonian, but I must say it looks very like it." Mrs. HJ Sr. to HJ, 25 May [1873] (James Papers, Harvard).

2. Made its mark.

the new house yet? Let me know how it's arranged—that is where your library & the *dining room* are, that I may sometimes drop in in a vision. I've just seen Aldrich's *Marjory Daw* in the *Revue*,[3] looking as natural as if begotten in the Gallic brain. It's a pretty compliment to have translated it & well-deserved. Perhaps they'll try you next.[4]—I can fancy that Keeler should be more divine than ever. I suppose the recent letter in the *Nation* about Sir A. Cockburn was his.[5] It was very well said & he has learned to write at least like a mortal. I should like to tell you a vast deal about myself, & I believe you would like to hear it. But as far as *vastness* goes I should have to invent it & it's too hot for such work. I send you another (& for the present last) travelling-piece—about Perugia &c.[6] It goes with this, in another cover: a safe journey to it. I hope you may squeeze it in this year. It numbers (in pages) more than your desire; but I think it is within bounds as you will see there is an elision of several.—I have done in all these months since I've been abroad much less writing than I hoped. Rome, for direct working, was not good—too many distractions & a languefying atmosphere. But for "impressions" it was priceless, & I've got a lot duskily garnered away somewhere under my waning (that's an *n*, not a *v*) *chevelure*[7] which some day may make some figure. I shall make the coming year more productive or retire from business altogether. Believe in me yet awhile longer & I shall reward your faith by dribblings somewhat less meagre.—I'm very glad to hear of Fiske's coming out & of his friend's generosity. His long labors richly deserve it.[8]—I say nothing about the Fire.[9] I can't trouble you with vain ejaculations & inquiries which my letters from home will probably already have answered. At this rate, apparently, the Lord loveth Boston immeasurably. But what a grim old Jehovah it is!—Are you to be in Cambridge for the Summer? May it be happy & kindly for your wife & children, wherever spent. Commend me tenderly to your wife, & recall me to the expanding memories of Winny & Booa. My blessing, dear Howells, on all your affections, labors & desires. Write a word when you can (B. & S. London) & believe me always

faithfully yours,
H. James jr

3. The *Revue des Deux Mondes* published a translation of Thomas Bailey Aldrich's short story in 1873.

4. The *Revue* would soon begin to publish translations of HJ's stories, the first of which, "Le Dernier des Valerius" ("The Last of the Valerii"), appeared on 15 November 1875.

5. Sir Alexander Cockburn (1802–80), Lord Chief Justice of England, arbitrated the *Alabama* claims. The letter ("Sir A. Cockburn's Embarrassments," *Nation* 16 [22 May 1873]: 353–54) is signed "K."

6. "A Chain of Italian Cities," *Atlantic* (February 1874).

7. Head of hair.

8. With the financial assistance of Mrs. M. A. Edwards (see letter #7, note 7), John Fiske was preparing to embark for Europe.

9. On the night of 9 November 1872, fire had destroyed the commercial center of Boston. HJ's belated acknowledgment of the catastrophe may have been sparked by reading WDH's account, "Among the Ruins," in the January 1873 issue of the *Atlantic*.

9.

HOWELLS TO JAMES, 26 August 1873, Boston   ALS Houghton
bMS Am 1094 (236)

. . . "THE ATLANTIC MONTHLY," . . .

BOSTON,

Aug. 26, 1873.

My dear James:

I have just finished your Chain of Cities, which with the Villeggiatura, I shall publish before the year's out.[1] The last is much the best, for the Chain is a little too much drawn out in the direction of things that cannot be felt by the many readers who have never seen them; it's meagre, too, whereas the Villeggiatura is richly full, and has certain luxuries of sentiment that gave me a poignant pleasure. They are both good enough; but I wish you would write for the Atlantic as unlaboriously as you seem to write your Nation letters, putting all the minor observation and comment that you can into them.—Your brother[2] tells me that you are not so well as you have been, which I'm truly sorry to hear, but I hope it's merely *cose passagiere.*[3] Here, we are in very reasonable repair, but for a sprinkling of whooping-cough among the children. We are in our new house, with which we are vastly content. We have done some aesthetic wall-papering, thanks to Wm. Morris whose wall papers are so much better than his poems;[4] and my library is all in chestnut, with a three-story mantle-piece, after Eastlake[5]—set with tiles, and standing very solidly on a tiled hearth, while overhead is a frescoed ceiling. I try not to be proud.—Directly after I got your last letter I sent you my book,[6] which I hope you received. You would be amused at the letters I get—some forty, now—from people unknown to me—begging for a sequel. The trouble is that they are of such various minds as to what the end ought to be. Miss Lane writes us from Quebec that half a dozen gentleman have called, to see the rooms in which Kitty lived.[7] This, I take it, is being a novelist in dead earnest, and I am pushing forward my Venetian priest's story all I can; but I shall hardly begin printing it before next summer.[8] In the meantime Osgood is going to bring out a volume of poetry for me in October.[9]—I have

---

1. "A Chain of Italian Cities," *Atlantic* (February 1874). The "Villeggiatura" to which WDH refers was an article on "Roman Neighborhoods" published in the *Atlantic* (December 1873).

2. William James (1842–1910), HJ's elder brother.

3. A passing thing.

4. William Morris (1834–96), English poet, utopian socialist, and founder of the Arts and Crafts movement in interior design.

5. Sir Charles Eastlake (1793–1865), probably the most ornate designer of the Victorian age.

6. *A Chance Acquaintance.*

7. Miss Lane kept a boardinghouse at 44½ Anne Street in Quebec; WDH's father stayed there when he became American consul in 1874.

8. *A Foregone Conclusion.*

9. *Poems* (Boston: James R. Osgood & Co., 1873), favorably reviewed by HJ in the *Independent* 26 (8 January 1874): 9.

seldom known Cambridge so empty as this summer—possibly because I've been in it all the time. Just now when the crickets are prophesying autumn with heart-breaking solemnity, I'm getting ready to go west for three weeks, with Winny.—Next year we are to have new type for the magazine, and it is otherwise to be brightened up. What is to be done with the North American—whether it is to be left with Perry, or to be given to Norton or Adams—isn't decided. I believe they're all three willing to take it. Of Perry one has only very brief glimpses at rare intervals; he spends all his time at Miss Cabot's[10] country retreat.

Mrs. Howells and all the children join me in love to you.—I wish this were not such a stupid letter.

Affectionately yours,
W. D. Howells.

10.

JAMES TO HOWELLS, 9 September 1873, Homburg   ALS Houghton
bMS Am 1784 (253) 3

Homburg. Sept. 9th
5 Kisseleff-Strasse.

Dear Howells—

I have been meaning for many days to write & tell you that your book[1] came safely & very speedily to hand; but have put it off for reasons doubtless not good enough to bear telling. The work is at any rate by this time the better digested. I had great pleasure in reading it over, & I have great pleasure now in recurring to it. It gains largely on being read all at once and certain places which at first I thought amenable to restriction (or rather certain features—as zum beispiel[2] a want of interfusion between the "scenery" element in the book & the dramatic) cease, quite, to seem so in the volume. But your people are better than their background; you have done your best for the latter but your story is intrinsically more interesting. This of course, however. Vivid figures will always kill the finest background in the world.—Kitty is certainly extremely happy—more so even than I feel perfectly easy in telling you; for she belongs to that class of eminent felicities which an artist doesn't indefinitely repeat. Don't be disappointed, then, if people don't like her later-born sisters just as relishingly. If they do, however, you will have taken out an unassailable patent as story-teller & shown—what is the great thing—that you conceive the particular as part of the general. The successful thing in Kitty is her *completeness*: she is singularly palpable and rounded and you couldn't, to this end, have imagined anything better than the

10. Thomas Sergeant Perry married Lilla Cabot (1848–1933), an author and painter, in April 1874.
    1. *A Chance Acquaintance*.
    2. For example.

particular antecedents you have given her. So! in the House of Fable she stands firm on her little pedestal. I congratulate you!—Arbuton I think, now that I know the end, decidedly a shade too scurvy. The charm of Kitty, as one thinks of her, is that she suggests a type—a blessed one, and the interest of the tale as one gets into it is the foreshadowing of a conflict between her type and another. But at the last, the man's peculiar shabbiness undermines this interest by making you think that she had simply happened to get hold of a particularly mean individual—one, indeed, that she wouldn't have even temporarily felt any serious emotion about.[3] I know that a great part of the idea of the story is that she shall be impressed by his unessential qualities; but as it stands, you rather resent her drama—her own part in it being so very perfectly analysed—having a hero who was coming to *that!* I was hoping that it was she who was to affront him. She does, indeed, by her shabby clothes; but this is an accident; that she should have done something, I mean, which even had she been dressed to perfection, would have left him puzzled, at loss, feeling that she wasn't for him. This wouldn't, indeed, have, necessarily implied his being snubbed, but was that inherent in your plan? Your drama, as you saw it, I suppose was the irreconcilability of the two results of such opposed antecedents & not a verdict on one or the other.—But you'll be amused at my "something", and ask me to draw it up for you. Heaven deliver me! Your own at least is very neatly executed.—But I didn't mean to dig so deep. How are the Venetian Priest and his fair one coming on? I suppose they're to begin in January & that you're giving them touch upon touch & line upon line.[4] I wish you quiet days and propitious moods. The wish for the former sounds sarcastic: for I suppose Cambridge is still Cambridge, in your new house as well as your old. That your new roof covers you is almost all I've heard about you in a long time. The Arctic explorations of my own family have made their letters rare and slow to arrive.[5]

I wrote you from Berne, in June & you got the letter, because you sent me the book: but don't let that be the only answer. I sent you also a paper ("A Chain of Cities") which I trust you received & can sooner or later use.[6] I've not had a very productive summer—directly at least; but indirectly, yes; as I came here unwell & shall be leaving permanently better as I trust, & apt for turning productive, evermore. There isn't much to say about my summer. It has been ten quiet weeks of Germany. ——

3. Compare WDH's remarks about HJ's "Guest's Confession" in letter #5.

4. WDH serialized *A Foregone Conclusion* in the *Atlantic* from July to December 1874.

5. In the summer of 1873, Alice James, together with various New York cousins and her venerable Aunt Katherine Walsh, toured Quebec, the lower St. Lawrence valley, and the maritime provinces of Canada, where they were joined by her parents. During her stay in Quebec, Alice James resided at "the Misses Lane's boarding house, wh. has lately been made famous by Mr. Howells story . . . [and] slept in the room in which 'Kitty' is supposed to have dwelt, & wh. looks into the Ursuline convent." See AJ to Annie Ashburner, 26 September 1873, in *The Death and Letters of Alice James: Selected Correspondence Edited, with a Biographical Essay*, ed. Ruth Bernard Yeazell (Berkeley: University of California Press, 1981), 55–56.

6. "A Chain of Italian Cities" first appeared in the *Atlantic* (February 1874).

Even while I wrote, half an hour ago, came your letter of Aug. 26. Your 40 letters about your story make me blush over all the foregoing stuff. But with them & Miss Lane's reports, you needn't heed late-coming praise or blame. I'm sorry your Venetian priest is still so far off.—So my Chain of Cities did arrive. I'm sorry it seems "meagre"—an idea that makes me weep salt tears. This, how-ever, I fondly hope, was less owing to my own poverty than to a constant fear to amplify and make it too long.—I'm very glad to get news of you, but your letter was cruelly brief. But I suppose such things must be with editors and householders. I'm glad your house is so good, and should like vastly this horrible afternoon (a foretaste of November) to spend an hour before that wonderful fire-place. Farewell. I shall send you more things in these coming months, and I shall heed your advice about unlaboriousness. I know I'm too ponderous. But the art of making *substance* light is hard. Love to your wife & kids.

Yours always
H. James jr.

P. S. I start again very soon for Italy: but oh, blasé human soul! with hardly more palpitation than if I were going to take the horse-car at the corner!

11.

JAMES TO HOWELLS, 18 October 1873, Florence   ALS Harvard
                                                          bMS Am 1784 (253) 4

Florence Oct. 18th

Dear Howells—

I send you another bundle of hieroglyphics (apart from this, in a second cover) with hopes that matters are not immutably disposed against its coming to the front early rather than late.[1] If it suits you to have me figure in your january number, if my two last sketches are printed & my story is too long for the purpose—*if* all this is blessed fact—here's your chance. Siena, you'll see is my theme & I have tried to remain brief. My only fear is you'll find me too brief. Bald, however, I have tried not to be, nor yet too artfully curled and anointed. In short, consider me discreetly light and agreeably grave and print me when you can!

—I am distinctly in Italy again, as you see, & am spending three or four weeks in Florence previous to settling in Rome for the winter. If I could have my wish I think I should remain quietly by the Arno & write enchanting stories; but my brother is at present crossing the ocean to join me (as of course you know) and Rome is his goal.[2] I had last winter there a bad time for work; but I

1. "Siena," *Atlantic* (June 1874). The other contributions were "Roman Neighborhoods" (December 1873), "A Chain of Italian Cities" (February 1874), and "The Last of the Valerii" (January 1874).
2. WJ arrived in Florence in late October.

must, can & shall do better now.—I wrote you some five weeks ago from Homburg, just at the moment your last letter reached me. Mine I suppose you duly received.—I know nothing about you now save that you are watching the autumn days drop like bright-colored leaves. My memory is full of uneffaced Cambridge Octobers, & every now and then I drop a tear on them & I seem to hear a little leafy rustle deep down in my spiritual parts and to see a dim haze before my eyes. Here yet, it is frank summer, but I don't complain, for I don't like cold weather any better as I grow older. If I only overtake the warmth yet in Rome I shall have had almost ten months of it at a stretch. Envy me, ma non troppo;[3] for there are uncountable drearinesses in exile. In some future remission of it I'll tell you them.

—What are you to be doing this winter, before that picturesque fire-place? Is your novel[4] coming on in a manner to make life tolerable? And your wife, without the consolations of authorship, does she find the days pass lightly? Of course they do when they march with the patter of one's children's feet. What I meant was,—is she well & a happy housewife? My love & compliments. Whom shall you see this winter whom you've not seen before?—When you wrote you were going to Ohio; was it done & done prosperously?[5] Ohio! I make this vague purposeless exclamation, simply as a Florentine.—I hope you will extend some social charity to my people this winter, who, with my brother W$^{\underline{m}}$ now also absent, will be very lonely.—Do you often see the Nortons—& what of Charles? I hope this winter to find Lowell in Rome. Oh for a man to talk a bit with!— Farewell. With every good wish & tender invocation upon your wife your children & your genius—

Yours

H. J. jr

12.

HOWELLS TO JAMES, 5 December 1873, Boston · · · · · · · · · · ALS Houghton
bMS Am 1094 (237)

. . . THE ATLANTIC MONTHLY, . . .

BOSTON,

Dec. 5, 1873.

My dear James:

Today, I met your mother on the Corso, in the vicinity of the Mercato Tom-Brewero, and she gave me your news, as you Italians say.[1] Part of these was that you had been writing a notice of my poetry for the North American, but that

---

3. But not too much.
4. *A Foregone Conclusion.*
5. With his daughter Winifred, WDH had visited Columbus, Ohio, in September 1873.
1. Mildred Howells notes that "the Mercato Tom-Brewero" was WDH's Italianate designation of the local shop where most of literary Cambridge bought their groceries. See *LiL* 1: 179–80.

you had been anticipated by another "party"—and the review was at home, in MS. and I might read it there before it was sent off to seek its fortune.[2] This I did with great consolation and thankfulness, for the leaf that has been commonly bestowed upon my poetical works by the critics of this continent has not been the laurel leaf—rather rue, or cypress. You have indeed treated my poor little book with a gracious kindness which I shall not forget; and I hope it isn't immodest to add with the first real discernment that has been shown by its critics. Thanks; and whilst I am in the way of it let me thank you also for what you say in your last letter both in praise and in blame of A Ch. Acq. Your strictures are fairly made, and I know that I ran along the edge of a knife-blade to reach that dénouement. Sometimes it seems to me all clumsily wrong; and I have the motive as clearly before me, as I had at first, and feel that nothing could drive me from that conclusion. But much is to be said against it, and you have said it very justly. As to the new story,[3] it draws near the end, with I hope, a gathering intensity. I long to get it all once fairly on paper, so that I can view it as a whole, and begin to clean it up a bit. The effects are still so much in the rough, so much at loose ends, that I have a certain *brivido*[4] in touching it, and I should like to jump the rest down at once. I have to work at it so interruptedly, too, that the pleasure of working at it is greatly marred.—Excuse, as Artemus Ward says, the apparent egotism.[5]—I have your Last of the Valerii in the January no., and I like it very much. It did not strike me so favorably in MS. as it does in print; but now I think it excellent. By the way, I hope you wont send any of your stories to Scribner's. We have of course no claim upon you, but we have hitherto been able to print all the stories you have sent, and so it shall be hereafter. Scribner is trying to lure away all our contributors, with the syren song of Doctor Holland, and my professional pride is touched.[6] Your Chain of

2. A brief notice of WDH's *Poems* (1873) appeared in the January 1874 *North American Review*. The *Independent* (8 January 1874) published HJ's longer appreciation, which included the following summation:

> Mr. Howells's verse is a tissue of light reflections from an experience closely interfused with native impulse. Discriminating readers, we think, will enjoy tracing out these reflections and lingering over them. They speak of the author's early youth having been passed in undisturbed intimacy with a peculiarly characteristic phase of American scenery; and then of this youthful quietude having expanded into the experience, full of mingled relief and regret, of an intensely European way of life. Ohio and Italy commingle their suggestions in Mr. Howells's pages in a harmony altogether original.

3. *A Foregone Conclusion*.
4. Shudder.
5. Artemus Ward, the stage name of Charles Farrar Browne (1834–67), was a popular humorist and author.
6. WDH anticipated HJ's desire to find a wider market for his literary wares but was not altogether successful in restraining the competition. Dr. Josiah Holland (1819–81), founder and editor of *Scribner's*, was a popular lecturer and author of sentimental novels. He is best remembered as WDH's most vigorous adversary in the "realism war" and, together with his wife, Elizabeth Luna Chapin (1823–96), as one of Emily Dickinson's closest friends and correspondents. See Edwin H. Cady, *The Road to Realism: The Early Years 1837–1885 of William Dean Howells* (Syracuse, N.Y.: Syracuse University Press, 1956), 122–25, 169–70.

Cities goes into the February, and your Siena, which is charming, into the March no.[7]—And what do you think of our dear old Atlantic's being sold! But it changes nothing but the publisher's imprint; even the editor remains the same. Aldrich and I had a Black Thursday when we heard our periodicals were in a state of barter, and scarcely knew whether we were to be sold with them or not. But we were both made over. I am sorry to part with Osgood, who was a good master; but Hurd and Houghton promise me fair, and you know they were my first publishers.[8] The printing will hereafter be done at the Riverside Press; and if you were again in Cambridge, I hope we should have many a stretch across the flats together.[9] In one's own company it is not a merry walk, especially in winter. But I console myself with thinking that it is business and not pleasure, anyway.—The social season in Cambridge opens with some sprightliness. I was at your brother Wilkie's Infare,[10] which was full of enjoyment for me, and apparently for everybody else. I seem to be dining out a good deal, too; even to-night I am going to Col. Dodge's[11] on Quincy street. Dinner at 7—what do you think of that for our simple Cambridge?—I haven't fairly got used yet to the Nortons' being at home, and I haven't seen Charles more than twice. He is better in health, but he comes home with a dreadfully high standard for us all. We may attain it as blessed spirits a thousand years hence.[12]—The fall-and-winter Englishman is beginning to appear. I have met him twice—at your house and at the Gurney's: a very peaceful Briton, indeed, and disposed to inform himself.[13] To this end he has bought my "works", as I'm given to know. There is also a Russian amongst us, studying bugs with Agassiz—one Baron Osten-something, whom I want to be calling Gregory Ivanovich, out of Turgénieff.[14]—Our babes

7. "Siena" did not appear until June.

8. To raise desperately needed capital, James R. Osgood sold *Every Saturday* (edited by Thomas Bailey Aldrich) and the *Atlantic* to Hurd & Houghton for twenty thousand dollars.

9. Henry O. Houghton's Riverside Press occupied a large site in a low-lying area of Cambridgeport. The editorial offices of the *Atlantic* were moved here from Boston after the sale of the magazine.

10. On 12 November Garth Wilkinson James ("Wilkie") married Caroline Eames Cary in Milwaukee; they came to Cambridge directly after their wedding. To celebrate both their nuptials and their arrival, Mrs. Henry James Sr. hosted a large party at 20 Quincy Street on the evening of 20 November. In spite of the festivities, neither parent much cared for their new daughter-in-law: as HJ Sr. bluntly remarked, "I can't for the life of me imagine why Wilky fell in love with her." See HJ Sr. to WJ & HJ, 21 November 1873, quoted in Jane Maher, *Biography of Broken Fortunes: Wilkie and Bob, Brothers of William, Henry, and Alice James* (Hamden, Conn.: Archon Books, 1986), 125.

11. Theodore A. Dodge (1842–95), brevetted colonel in the Union Army, wrote several books on the Civil War.

12. Charles Eliot Norton's biographer agreed with this estimate, referring to his subject as an "apostle of culture in a democracy." See Kermit Vanderbilt, *Charles Eliot Norton: Apostle of Culture in a Democracy* (Cambridge, Mass.: Belknap Press of Harvard University Press, 1959).

13. George Charles Brodrick (1831–1903), an English barrister who turned to journalism, was visiting the United States as correspondent for the London *Times*.

14. Carl Robert Romanovich von der Osten-Sacken (1828–1906) was doing research under the supervision of Louis Agassiz (1807–73), the famous Harvard biologist. He had recently served as a member of the Russian Legation to the United States (1856–62) and as Russian consul general in New York (1862–71). The reference to Turgenev is whimsical.

are all well, and Mrs. Howells sends you her warmest regards.—My sister Annie, whom perhaps you remember is spending the winter in Boston as a correspondent for some western papers.[15]—No more at present.

Affectionately yours
W. D. Howells.

Love to your brother.

13.

JAMES TO HOWELLS, 9 January 1874, Florence   ALS Houghton
                                                             bMS Am 1784 (253) 5

Florence Jan 9th 74.

Dear Howells—

Your good letter of a month ago reached me some ten days since, just as I was leaving Rome, & I have just been reading it over, under these less balmy skies. My brother had a mild stroke of malaria, in consequence of which the doctor ordered him away, under penalty of being probably worse; so he retreated upon Florence as the next best thing, & I have followed him to keep him company. From the Cambridge point of view I suppose Florence ought to be a very tolerable *pis aller*,[1] even from Rome: but I confess to utter corruption from that terrible Roman charm, Florence seems to me a vulgar little village and life not worth the living away from the Corso and the Pincio. With time however I don't despair of settling down, doggedly, to my hard fate. Meanwhile, to beguile the heavy hours, I turn to conversation with you. Many thanks for your letter, which was most agreeable. The news of the sale of the *Atlantic* set me wondering about you & I needed your own word for it that you are contented to soothe my startled sympathies. All prosperity to the new dispensation and fame and fortune to both of us. I'm sorry you have to go and watch your flock across the sands of Dee, as it were, but I suppose there is a daily excitement in it.[2] I have just received the new Atlantic, which makes a very handsome appearance. I don't like the new type as well as the old, which was remarkably pretty; but the cover and the paper make one feel as if one were ministering to the highest culture of the Age. Give Aldrich my compliments on his novel, which opens out most agreeably.[3] There is something in all the regular New England scenes

15. With WDH's help, Anne T. Howells (1844–1938) had begun sending regular columns to various Ohio newspapers and a New York magazine, *Hearth and Home*, as Boston correspondent.

1. Last resort.

2. HJ's image for WDH's daily journey through the flats of Cambridge to his new editorial office at the Riverside Press. In Charles Kingsley's "The Sands of Dee" (1849), a maiden sent to call the cattle home is swept from a treacherous sandbar by the rising tide (*Poems* [London: Macmillan, 1907], 246).

3. Thomas Bailey Aldrich's *Prudence Palfrey* was serialized in the *Atlantic* (January–June 1874).

and subjects, in fiction, which strikes in a chill upon my soul; but with A., I imagine, we shall get a great deal of prettiness. But for heaven's sake, do hurry up with your Venetian priest; he can't help, at the worst, being prettier than Parson Wibird.[4]

Thank you for speaking well of my own tale;[5] it reads agreeably enough, though I suppose that to many readers, it will seem rather idle. Let me explain without further delay the nature of the package which will go with this, in another cover. It is the 1st half of a tale in two parts, for use at your convenience.[6] I have been reading it to my brother who pronounces it "quite brilliant." I was on the point of sending it to Scribner, but your words in deprecation of this course have made me face about. I am much obliged for the esteem implied in them; but it remains true, in a general way, that I can't really get on without extracting tribute from that source.[7] It's a mere *money* question. The *Atlantic* can't publish as many stories for me as I ought & expect to be writing. At home, it could, for then I needed scantier revenues. But now, with all the francs it takes to live in these lovely climes, I need more strings to my bow and more irons always on the fire. But I heartily promise you that the *Atlantic* shall have the best things I do; & it is because this *Eugene Pickering* (being perhaps unusually happy in subject) is probably better than its next follower will be, that I now make it over to you. The second half will follow by the next mail: heaven's blessings attend it.———

I should like to gossip to you about Rome, which in this last month I have been spending there, laid hold of me again with a really cruel fascination. But talking is vain, for the thing can't be described; it must be *felt*, as a daily, daily blessing. I believe that if I could live there for two or three years I should finally, by my doings—my thinkings & feelings & scribblings—quadruple the circulation of the *Atlantic*. Don't you want to pension me, for the purpose?— But you remember it all, more or less, of course. Nay, I thought I did, even from last spring: but it all came rushing back, in a wondrous wave, and melted me into daily stupefaction. It's either very good for one, or very bad: I don't know which. My sternly scientific brother thinks the latter; & there is indeed much in that view. Thank your stars at all events, that you are not living in a place whereof the delight demoralizes; and when you are buffeting the breezes in that Campagna which leads to Riverside, reflect with complacency that you are not a cringing parasite of the Beautiful. Florence, after Rome, seems tame and flat and infernally cold. It's cruel after basking for a month on the Pincio to wake up in the region of chapped lips and chillblains. But happily, even the Floren-

4. WDH's A *Foregone Conclusion* did not begin serialization until July 1874. Parson Wibird Hawkins is a retiring minister in Aldrich's novel.

5. "The Last of the Valerii."

6. "Eugene Pickering," *Atlantic* (October–November 1874).

7. HJ's story "Adina" would appear in *Scribner's Monthly* from May to June 1874. *Scribner's* published four other HJ stories and the novel *Confidence* before Josiah G. Holland's death and the magazine's merger into the *Century* in 1881.

tine winter is short and before long I hope to be sniffing the vernal breath of the Tuscan poderes.[8]

—I'm very sorry the N.A.R. couldn't give a corner to my notice of your poems. It was written quite from my tenderer part, & I think would have found assenting readers. But I trust it may still find them somewhere.[9]

—I think I have no news for you. In Rome I saw few people, & here I bid fair to see no one. No one, that is, save Lowell, who is lingering here on his way to Rome & with whom I lately passed an evening. He was very jolly, tho' homesick, & taking Europe with the sobriety of maturity. He says he positively can't work here—& like Bryant and May's matches won't go off unless struck on his own box.[10] He goes home in July, & if that will start him up, let him hurry.—I'm not surprised at your finding Charles Norton an impracticable comrade. He seemed to me to be ripening for home discomfort, when I last saw him. But I suppose you are tired of the theme. Whom *do* you see, then?—You'll see me, I apprehend, before very long: that is I hope to manage to stay abroad another six months & to turn up in Cambridge toward the close of next summer. I don't know that I shall undertake the winter in Cambridge; but I shall spend the autumn there. We shall have plenty to talk about—the more that in that case, I shall remain in Italy till almost the last.—Farewell! My affectionate regards to your wife & blessings on all your house. Yours, dear H.,

always,

H. James jr.

14.

JAMES TO HOWELLS, 10 March 1874, Florence   ALS Houghton
                                                              bMS Am 1784 (253) 6

Florence March 10$\underline{^{th}}$

Dear Howells—

This is grim business, and yet I must be brief. Your dear friend Dr. Holland has just proposed to me to write a novel for *Scribner,* beginning in November next. To write a novel I incline & have been long inclining: but I feel as if there were a definite understanding between us that if I do so, the *Atlantic* should have the offer of it. I have therefore sent through my father a refusal to Dr. H., to be retained or forwarded according to your response. Will the *Atlantic* have my novel, when written? Dr. H's offer is a comfortable one—the novel accepted at rate (that is if terms agree,) and to begin, as I say, in November & last till the November following. He asks me to name terms, and I should name

    8. Farms, countryside.

    9. HJ's review appeared in the *Independent* (8 January 1874).

    10. Since 1855 the British firm of Bryant & May held sole rights for the manufacture of safety matches in the United Kingdom. See Patrick Beaver, *The Match Makers* (London: H. Melland, 1985), 28–29.

$1200. If the Atlantic desires a story for the year and will give as much I of course embrace in preference the Atlantic. Sentimentally I should prefer the A.; but as things stand with me, I have no right to let it be anything but a pure money question. Will you, when you have weighed the matter, send me a line through my father or better, perhaps, communicate with him *viva voce?*—This is not a love-letter & I won't gossip. I expect to be in Europe &, I hope, in Italy, till midsummer. I sent you lately, at three or four weeks' interval, the two parts of a tale.[1] You have them, I hope? Farewell, with all tender wishes to your person & household.

> Yours ever,
> H. James jr

15.

JAMES TO HOWELLS, 3 May 1874, Florence

ALS Houghton
bMS Am 1784 (253) 7

Florence, Piazza Sta. Maria Novella
May 3$\underline{d}$.

Dear Howells—

I rec'd some days ago from my father the little note you had sent him,[1] signifying your acceptance of my story for next year's *Atlantic*, & have had it at heart ever since to drop you a line in consequence.—I'm extremely glad that my thing is destined to see the light in the Atlantic rather than in t'other place & am very well satisfied with the terms. My story[2] is to be on a theme I have had in my head a long time & once attempted to write something about. The theme is interesting, & if I do as I intend & hope, I think the tale must please. It shall, at any rate have all my pains. The opening chapters take place in America & the people are of our glorious race; but they are soon transplanted to Rome, where things are to go on famously. Ecco.[3] Particulars, including name, (which however I incline to have simply that of the hero), on a future occasion. Suffice it that I promise you some tall writing. My only fear is that it may turn out taller than broad. That is, I thank you especially for the clause in the contract as to the numbers being less than twelve. As I desire above all things to write close, & avoid padding and prolixity, it may be that I shall have told my tale by the 8$\underline{th}$ or 9$\underline{th}$ number. But there is time enough to take its measure scientifically. I don't see how, in parts of the length of Aldrich's *Prudence Palfrey* (my protagonist is *not* named Publicius Parsons,)[4] it can help stretching out a

---

1. "Eugene Pickering."
1. Not extant.
2. *Roderick Hudson* first appeared in the *Atlantic* (January–December 1875).
3. There you are.
4. HJ's alliterative irony is aimed at Aldrich's title character and his fictional minister, Parson Wibird.

good piece.—Of Aldrich's tale, I'm sorry to say I've lost the thread, through missing a number of the magazine, & shall have, like Dennett, to wait till it's finished.—Why do you continue to treat me as if I didn't care to hear from you? I have a vague sense of unnumbered notes, despatched to you as an editor, but in which your human side was sufficiently recognized to have won from you some faint response. If you knew how dismally and solitudinously I sit here just now before my window, ignorant of a friendly voice, & waiting for the rain-swept piazza to look at last as if it would allow me to go forth to my lonely pranzo[5] at a mercenary trattoria[6]—you would repent of your coldness. I suppose I ought to write you a letter flamboyant with local color; but the local color just now, as I say, is the blackest shade of the pluvious, & my soul reflects its hue. My brother will have talked to you about Florence and about me, sufficiently too, I suppose, for the present.[7] Florence has become by this time to me an old story—though like all real masterpieces one reads & re-reads it with pleasure. I am here now but for a few weeks longer, & then I shall leave Italy—for many a year, I imagine. With ineffable regret for many reasons; contentedly enough for others. But we shall have a chance before long to talk of all this. I return home at the end of the summer (& hope to bring my tale with me substantially completed).[8] To many of the things of home I shall return with pleasure—especially to the less isolated, more freely working– & talking–life.—Don't wait for this, however, to let me hear from you; but write me meanwhile, if it's only to tell me you're glad I'm coming. I have had no personal news of you in an age, but I trust you are nestling in prosperity. It's a hundred years since I heard of your wife's health: but I trust it is good, even at the advanced age which this makes her. What are you doing, planning, hoping? I suppose your Venetian tale[9] is almost off your hands—I long to have it on mine. (I'm delighted by the way to hear you like "Eugene Pickering:" *do*, oh do, if possible put him through in a single number.) Lowell has just passed through on his way to Paris. I got great pleasure from his poem,[10] which he read me in bits. I'm impatient to see it all together. Farewell, dear Howells; the rivulets on the piazza run thin, & I must trudge across & quaff the straw-covered fiaschetto:[11] I shall do it, be sure, to your health, your gentilissima sposa's[12] & your childrens'.

Yours always
H. J. jr

5. Dinner.
6. Restaurant.
7. WJ had returned to Cambridge at the end of March 1874.
8. In his 1907 preface to the New York Edition of the novel, HJ recalled that *Roderick Hudson* "was earnestly pursued during a summer partly spent in the Black Forest and (as I had returned to America early in September) during three months passed near Boston" (*Literary Criticism* 2: 1041).
9. A *Foregone Conclusion*.
10. Lowell's elegy "Agassiz" appeared in the *Atlantic* (May 1874).
11. Flask of wine.
12. Gracious wife's.

Henry James, *review of* A Foregone Conclusion, Nation 20 (*7 January 1875*): *12–13*.

Mr. Howells in his new novel returns to his first love, and treats once more of Venice and Venetian figures. His constancy has not betrayed him, for 'A Foregone Conclusion' is already rapidly making its way. A novelist is always safer for laying his scene in his own country, and the best that can be said of his errors of tone and proportion, when he deals with foreign manners, is that the home reader is rarely wise enough to measure them. But in Venice Mr. Howells is almost at home, and if his book contains any false touches, we, for our part, have not had the skill to discover them. His Venetian hero is not only a very vivid human being, but a distinct Italian, with his subtle race-qualities artfully interwoven with his personal ones. We confess, however, that in spite of this evidence of the author's ability to depict a consistent and natural member of the Latin family, we should have grudged him a heroine of foreign blood. Not the least charm of the charming heroines he has already offered us has been their delicately native quality. They have been American women in the scientific sense of the term, and the author, intensely American in the character of his talent, is probably never so spontaneous, so much himself, as when he represents the delicate, nervous, emancipated young woman begotten of our institutions and our climate, and equipped with a lovely face and an irritable moral consciousness. Mr. Howells's tales have appeared in the pages of the *Atlantic Monthly,* and the young ladies who figure in them are the actual young ladies who attentively peruse that magazine. We are thankful accordingly, in 'A Foregone Conclusion,' for a heroine named after one of the States of the Union, and characterized by what we may call a national aroma. The relation of a heroine to a hero can only be, of course, to be adored by him; but the specific interest of the circumstance in this case resides in the fact that the hero is a priest, and that one has a natural curiosity to know how an American girl of the typical free-stepping, clear-speaking cast receives a declaration from a sallow Italian ecclesiastic. It is characteristic of Mr. Howells's manner as a story-teller, of his preference of fine shades to heavy masses, of his dislike to *les grands moyens,*[1] that Florida Vervain's attitude is one of benignant, almost caressing, pity. The author's choice here seems to us very happy; any other tone on the young girl's part would have been relatively a trifle vulgar. Absolute scorn would have made poor Don Ippolito's tragedy too brutally tragical, and an answering passion, even with all imaginable obstructions, would have had a quality less poignant than his sense that in her very kindness the woman he loves is most inaccessible. Don Ippolito dies of a broken heart, and Florida Vervain prospers extremely—even to the point of marrying, at Providence, R. I., an American gentleman whom, in spite of his having in his favor that he does not stand in a disagreeably false position, the reader is likely to care less for than for the shabby Venetian ecclesiastic.

---

1. Take things to extremes; i.e., resort to melodrama.

This story is admirably told, and leads one to expect very considerable things from Mr. Howells as a novelist. He has given himself a narrow stage, or rather a scanty *dramatis personæ* (for he has all glowing Venice for a back scene), and he has attempted to depict but a single situation. But between his four persons the drama is complete and the interest acute. It is all a most remarkable piece of elaboration. Mr. Howells had already shown that he lacked nothing that art can give in the way of finish and ingenuity of manner; but he has now proved that he can embrace a dramatic situation with the true imaginative force—give us not only its mechanical structure, but its atmosphere, its meaning, its poetry. The climax of Don Ippolito's history in the present volume is related with masterly force and warmth, and the whole portrait betrays a singular genius for detail. It is made up of a series of extremely minute points, which melt into each other like scattered water-drops. Their unity is in their subdued poetic suggestiveness, their being the work of a writer whose observation always projects some vague tremulous shadow into the realm of fancy. The image of Don Ippolito, if we are not mistaken, will stand in a niche of its own in the gallery of portraits of humble souls. The best figure the author had drawn hitherto was that charmingly positive young lady, Miss Kitty Ellison, in 'A Chance Acquaintance'; but he has given it a very harmonious companion in the Florida Vervain of the present tale. Miss Vervain is positive also, and in the manner of her positiveness she is a singularly original invention. She is more fantastic than her predecessor, but she is hardly less lifelike, and she is a remarkably picturesque study of a complex nature. Her image is poetical, which is a considerable compliment, as things are managed now in fiction (where the only escape from bread-and-butter and commonplace is into golden hair and promiscuous felony). In the finest scene in the book, when Florida has learned to what extent Don Ippolito has staked his happiness upon his impossible passion, she, in a truly superb movement of pity, seizes his head in her hands and kisses it. Given the persons and the circumstances, this seems to us an extremely fine imaginative stroke, for it helps not only to complete one's idea of the young girl, but the fact of the deed being possible and natural throws a vivid side-light on the helpless, childish, touching personality of the priest. We believe, however, that it has had the good fortune to create something like a scandal. There are really some readers who are in urgent need of a tonic regimen! If Mr. Howells continues to strike notes of this degree of resonance, he will presently find himself a very eminent story-teller; and meanwhile he may find an agreeable stimulus in the thought that he has provoked a discussion.

A matter which it is doubtless very possible to discuss, but in which we ourselves should be on the protesting side, is the felicity of the episodes related in the last twenty pages of the tale. After the hero's death the action is transplanted to America, and the conclusion takes place in the shadow of the Fifth Avenue Hotel. We have found these pages out of tune with their predecessors, and we suspect that this will be the verdict of readers with the finer ear. The philosophy of such matters is very ethereal, and one can hardly do more than take one's stand on the "I do not like you, Doctor Fell" principle.[2] One labors under the disadvantage, too, that the author's defence will be much more categorical than the reader's complaint, and that the complaint itself lays one open to the charge of siding against one's own flesh and blood. We should risk it, then, and almost be willing, for the sake of keeping a singularly perfect composition intact, to pass for a disloyal citizen. And then the author can point triumphantly to 'A Chance Acquaintance' as proof that a very American tale may be also a very charming one. Of this there is no doubt; but everything is relative, and the great point is, as the French say, not to *mêler les genres*.[3] We renounce the argument, but in reading over 'A Foregone Conclusion' we shall close the work when the hero dies—when old Veneranda comes to the door and shakes her hands in Ferris's face and smites him, as it were, with the announcement. The author, however, is thoroughly consistent, for in stamping his tale at the last with the American local seal he is simply expressing his own literary temperament. We have always thought Mr. Howells's, in spite of his Italian affiliations, a most characteristically American talent; or rather not in spite of them, but in a manner on account of them, for he takes Italy as no Italian surely ever took it—as your enterprising Yankee alone is at pains to take it. American literature is immature, but it has, in prose and verse alike, a savor of its own, and we have often thought that this might be a theme for various interesting reflections. If we undertook to make a few, we should find Mr. Howells a capital text. He reminds us how much our native-grown imaginative effort is a matter of details, of fine shades, of pale colors, a making of small things do great service. Civilization with us is monotonous, and in the way of contrasts, of salient points, of chiaroscuro, we have to take what we can get. We have to look for these things in fields where a less devoted glance would see little more than an arid blank, and, at the last, we manage to find them. All this refines and sharpens our perceptions, makes us in a literary way, on our own scale, very delicate, and stimulates greatly our sense of proportion and form. Mr. Lowell and Mr. Longfellow among the poets, and Mr. Howells, Bret Harte, and Mr. Aldrich among the story-tellers (the latter writer, indeed, in verse as well as in prose), have all preeminently the instinct of style and shape. It is true, in general, that the conditions here indicated give American writing a limited authority, but they often give it a great charm—how great a charm, may be measured in the volume before us. 'A Foregone Conclusion' puts us for the moment, at least, in

---

2. Thomas Brown (1663–1704) had been threatened with expulsion from Christ Church College, Oxford, by the dean, Dr. John Fell, who promised to forgive him if he could deliver an impromptu translation from the Latin of Martial's thirty-second epigram, which Brown rendered as follows:

> I do not love thee, Dr. Fell:
> The reason why I cannot tell;
> But this I know, and know full well:
> I do not love thee, Dr. Fell.

3. Mix two different literary genres.

good humor with the American manner. At a time when the English novel has come in general to mean a ponderous, shapeless, diffuse piece of machinery, "padded" to within an inch of its life, without style, without taste, without a touch of the divine spark, and effective, when it is effective, only by a sort of brutal dead-weight, there may be pride as well as pleasure in reading this admirably-balanced and polished composition, with its distinct literary flavor, its grace and its humor, its delicate art and its perfume of poetry, its extreme elaboration, and yet its studied compactness. And if Mr. Howells adheres in the future to his own standard, we shall have pleasure as well as pride.

Henry James, *review of* A Foregone Conclusion, North American Review *120 (January 1875): 207–14.*

Those who, a couple of years ago, read "A Chance Acquaintance" will find much interest in learning how the author has justified the liberal fame awarded that performance. Having tried other literary forms with remarkable success, Mr. Howells finally proved himself an accomplished story-teller, and the critic lurking in even the kindliest reader will be glad to ascertain whether this consummation was due chiefly to chance or to skill. "A Chance Acquaintance" was indeed not only a very charming book, but a peculiarly happy hit; the fancy of people at large was vastly tickled by the situation it depicted; the hero and heroine were speedily promoted to the distinction of types, and you became likely to overhear discussions as to the probability of their main adventures wherever men and women were socially assembled. Kitty Ellison and her weak-kneed lover, we find, are still objects of current allusion, and it would be premature, even if it were possible, wholly to supersede them; but even if Mr. Howells was not again to hit just that nail, he was welcome to drive in another beside it and to supply the happy creations we have mentioned with successors who should divide our admiration. We had little doubt ourselves that he would on this occasion reach whatever mark he had aimed at; for, with all respect to the good fortune of his former novel, it seemed to us very maliciously contrived to play its part. It would have been a question in our minds, indeed, whether it was not even too delicate a piece of work for general circulation,—whether it had not too literary a quality to please that great majority of people who prefer to swallow their literature without tasting. But the best things in this line hit the happy medium, and it seems to have turned out, experimentally, that Mr. Howells managed at once to give his book a loose enough texture to let the more simply-judging kind fancy they were looking at a vivid fragment of social history itself, and yet to infuse it with a lurking artfulness which should endear it to the initiated. It rarely happens that what is called a popular success is achieved by such delicate means; with so little forcing of the tone or mounting of the high horse. People at large do not flock every day to look at a sober cabinet-picture. Mr. Howells continues to practise the cabinet-picture manner, though in his present work he has introduced certain broader touches. He has returned to the ground of his first literary achievements, and introduced us again to that charming half-merry, half-melancholy Venice which most Americans know better through his pages than through any others. He did this, in a measure, we think, at his risk; partly because there was a chance of disturbing an impression which, in so far as he was the author of it, had had time to grow very tranquil and mellow; and partly because there has come to be a not unfounded mistrust of the Italian element in light literature. Italy has been made to supply so much of the easy picturesqueness, the crude local color of poetry and the drama, that a use of this expedient is vaguely regarded as a sort of unlawful short-cut to success,—one of those coarsely mechanical moves at chess which, if you will, are strictly within the rules of the game, but which offer an antagonist strong provocation to fold up the board. Italians have been, from Mrs. Radcliffe down, among the stock-properties of romance;[1] their associations are melodramatic, their very names are supposed to go a great way toward getting you into a credulous humor, and they are treated, as we may say, as bits of coloring-matter, which if placed in solution in the clear water of uninspired prose are warranted to suffuse it instantaneously with the most delectable hues. The growing refinement of the romancer's art has led this to be considered a rather gross device, calculated only to delude the simplest imaginations, and we may say that the presumption is now directly against an Italian in a novel, until he has pulled off his slouched hat and mantle and shown us features and limbs that an Anglo-Saxon would acknowledge. Mr. Howells's temerity has gone so far as to offer us a priest of the suspected race,—a priest with a dead-pale complexion, a blue chin, a dreamy eye, and a name in *elli*.[2] The burden of proof is upon him that we shall believe in him, but he casts it off triumphantly at an early stage of the narrative, and we confess that our faith in Don Ippolito becomes at last really poignant and importunate.

"A Venetian priest in love with an American girl,—there's richness, as Mr. Squeers said!"—such was the formula by which we were first gossipingly made acquainted with the subject of "A Foregone Conclusion."[3] An amiable American widow, travelling in Italy with her daughter, lingers on in Venice into the deeper picturesqueness of the early summer. With that intellectual thriftiness that characterizes many of her class (though indeed in Mrs. Vervain it is perhaps only a graceful anomaly the more), she desires to provide the young girl with instruction in Italian, and requests the consul of her native land (characteristically again) to point her out a teacher. The consul finds himself interested in a young ecclesiastic, with an odd mechanical turn, who has come to bespeak the consular patronage for some fanciful device in gunnery, and whose only wealth is a little store of English, or rather Irish, phrases, imparted by a fellow-priest from Dublin. Having been obliged to give the poor fellow the cold shoulder as an inventor, he is prompt in offering him a friendly hand as an Italian master,

1. Ann Radcliffe (1764–1823), leading exponent of the Gothic novel, set her most famous stories in Italy, including *A Sicilian Romance* (1790), *The Mysteries of Udolpho* (1794), and *The Italian* (1797).

2. That is, a familiar Italian surname.

3. Compare letter #6, WDH to HJ, 10 March 1873.

and Don Ippolito is introduced to Miss Vervain. Miss Vervain is charming, and the young priest discovers it to his cost. He falls in love with her, offers himself, is greeted with the inevitable horror provoked by such a proposition from such a source, feels the deep displeasure he must have caused, but finds he is only the more in love, resists, protests, rebels, takes it all terribly hard, becomes intolerably miserable, and falls fatally ill, while the young girl and her mother hurry away from Venice. Such is a rapid outline of Mr. Howells's story, which, it will be seen, is simple in the extreme,—is an air played on a single string, but an air exquisitely modulated. Though the author has not broken ground widely, he has sunk his shaft deep. The little drama goes on altogether between four persons,— chiefly, indeed, between two,—but on its limited scale it is singularly complete, and the interest gains sensibly from compression. Mr. Howells's touch is almost that of a miniature-painter; every stroke in "A Foregone Conclusion" plays its definite part, though sometimes the eye needs to linger a moment to perceive it. It is not often that a young lady in a novel is the resultant of so many fine intentions as the figure of Florida Vervain. The interest of the matter depends greatly, of course, on the quality of the two persons thus dramatically confronted, and here the author has shown a deep imaginative force. Florida Vervain and her lover form, as a couple, a more effective combination even than Kitty Ellison and Mr. Arbuton; for Florida, in a wholly different line, is as good—or all but as good—as the sweetheart of that sadly incapable suitor; and Don Ippolito is not only a finer fellow than the gentleman from Boston, but he is more acutely felt, we think, and better understood on the author's part. Don Ippolito is a real creation,—a most vivid, complete, and appealing one; of how many touches and retouches, how many caressing, enhancing strokes he is made up, each reader must observe for himself. He is in every situation a distinct personal image, and we never lose the sense of the author's seeing him in his habit as he lived,—"moving up and down the room with his sliding step, like some tall, gaunt, unhappy girl,"—and verging upon that quasi-hallucination with regard to him which is the law of the really creative fancy. His childish mildness, his courtesy, his innocence, which provokes a smile, but never a laugh, his meagre experience, his general helplessness, are rendered with an unerring hand: there is no crookedness in the drawing, from beginning to end. We have wondered, for ourselves, whether we should not have been content to fancy him a better Catholic and more intellectually at rest in his priestly office,—so that his passion for the strange and lovely girl who is so suddenly thrust before him should, by itself, be left to account for his terrible trouble; but it is evident, on the other hand, that his confiding her his doubts and his inward rebellion forms the common ground on which they come closely together, and the picture of his state of mind has too much truthful color not to justify itself. He is a representation of extreme moral simplicity, and his figure might have been simpler if he had been a consenting priest, rather than a protesting one. But, though he might have been in a way more picturesque, he would not have been more interesting; and the charm of the portrait is in its suffering us to feel with him, and its offering nothing that we find mentally disagreeable,—as we should have found the suggestion of prayers stupidly mumbled and of the *odeur de sacristie*.[4] The key to Don Ippolito's mental strainings and yearnings is in his fancy for mechanics, which is a singularly happy stroke in the picture. It indicates the intolerable *discomfort* of his position, as distinguished from the deeper unrest of passionate scepticism, and by giving a sort of homely practical basis to his possible emancipation, makes him relapse into bondage only more tragical. It is a hard case, and Mr. Howells has written nothing better—nothing which more distinctly marks his faculty as a story-teller—than the pages in which he traces it to its climax. The poor caged youth, straining to the end of his chain, pacing round his narrow circle, gazing at the unattainable outer world, bruising himself in the effort to reach it and falling back to hide himself and die unpitied,—is a figure which haunts the imagination and claims a permanent place in one's melancholy memories.

The character of Florida Vervain contributes greatly to the dusky, angular relief of Don Ippolito. This young lady is a singularly original conception, and we remember no heroine in fiction in whom it is proposed to interest us on just such terms. "Her husband laughed," we are told at the close of the book, "to find her protecting and serving [her children] with the same tigerish tenderness, the same haughty humility, as that with which she used to care for poor Mrs. Vervain; and he perceived that this was merely the direction away from herself of that intense arrogance of nature which, but for her power and need of loving, would have made her intolerable. What she chiefly exacted from them, in return for her fierce devotedness, was the truth in everything; she was content they should be rather less fond of her than of their father, whom, indeed, they found much more amusing." A heroine who ripens into this sort of wife and mother is rather an exception among the tender sisterhood. Mr. Howells has attempted to enlist our imagination on behalf of a young girl who is positively unsympathetic, and who has an appearance of chilling rigidity and even of almost sinister reserve. He has brilliantly succeeded, and his heroine just escapes being disagreeable, to be fascinating. She is a poet's invention, and yet she is extremely real,—as real, in her way, as that Kitty Ellison whom she so little resembles. In these two figures Mr. Howells has bravely notched the opposite ends of his measure, and there is pleasure in reflecting on the succession of charming girls arrayed, potentially, along the intermediate line. He has outlined his field; we hope he will fill it up. His women are always most sensibly women; their motions, their accents, their ideas, savor essentially of the sex; he is one of the few writers who hold a key to feminine logic and detect a method in feminine madness. It deepens, of course, immeasurably, the tragedy of Don Ippolito's sentimental folly, that Florida Vervain should be the high-and-mighty young lady she is, and gives an additional edge to the peculiar cruelty of his situation,—the fact that, being what he is, he is of necessity, as a lover, repulsive. But Florida is a complex personage, and the tale depends in a measure in her having been able to listen

---

4. Aroma of the sacristy.

to him in a pitying, maternal fashion, out of the abundance of her characteristic strength. There is no doubt that, from the moment she learns he has dreamed she might love him, he becomes hopelessly disagreeable to her; but the author has ventured on delicate ground in attempting to measure the degree in which passionate pity might qualify her repulsion. It is ground which, to our sense, he treads very firmly; but the episode of Miss Vervain's seizing the young priest's head and caressing it will probably provoke as much discussion as to its verisimilitude as young Arbuton's famous repudiation of the object of his refined affections. For our part, we think Miss Vervain's embrace was more natural than otherwise—for Miss Vervain; and, natural or not, it is admirably poetic. The poetry of the tale is limited to the priest and his pupil. Mrs. Vervain is a humorous creation, and in intention a very happy one. The kindly, garrulous, military widow, with her lively hospitality to the things that don't happen, and her serene unconsciousness of the things that do, is a sort of image of the way human levity hovers about the edge of all painful occurrences. Her scatter-brained geniality deepens the picture of her daughter's brooding preoccupations, and there is much sustained humor in making her know so much less of the story in which she plays a part than we do. Her loquacity, however, at times, strikes us as of a trifle too shrill a pitch, and her manner may be charged with lacking the repose, if not of the Veres of Vere, at least of the Veres of Providence. But there is a really ludicrous image suggested by the juxtaposition of her near-sightedness and her cheerful ignorance of Don Ippolito's situation, in which, at the same time, she takes so friendly an interest. She *overlooks* the tragedy going on under her nose, just as she overlooks the footstool on which she stumbles when she comes into a room. This touch proves that with a genuine artist, like Mr. Howells, there is an unfailing cohesion of all ingredients. Ferris, the consul, whose ultimately successful passion for Miss Vervain balances the sad heart-history of the priest, will probably find—has, we believe, already found—less favor than his companions, and will be reputed to have come too easily by his good fortune. He is an attempt at a portrait of a rough, frank, and rather sardonic humorist, touched with the *sans gêne*[5] of the artist and even of the Bohemian. He is meant to be a good fellow in intention and a likable one in person; but we think the author has rather over-emphasized his irony and his acerbity. He holds his own firmly enough, however, as a make-weight in the action, and it is not till Don Ippolito passes out of the tale and the scale descends with a jerk into his quarter that most readers—feminine readers at least—shake their heads unmistakably. Mr. Howells's conclusion—his last twenty pages—will, we imagine, make him a good many dissenters,—among those, at least, whose enjoyment has been an enjoyment of his art. The story passes into another tone, and the new tone seems to *jurer*,[6] as the French say, with the old. It passes out of Venice and the exquisite Venetian suggestiveness, over to Providence, to New York, to the Fifth Avenue Hotel, and the Academy of Design. We ourselves regret the transition,

5. Unconventionality.
6. Clash.

though the motive of our regrets is difficult to define. It is a transition from the ideal to the real, to the vulgar, from soft to hard, from charming color to something which is not color. Providence and the Fifth Avenue Hotel certainly have their rights; but we doubt whether their rights, in an essentially romantic theme, reside in a commixture with the suggestions offered us in such a picture as this:—

> "The portal was a tall arch of Venetian Gothic, tipped with a carven flame; steps of white Istrian stone descended to the level of the lowest ebb, irregularly embossed with barnacles and dabbling long fringes of soft green sea-mosses in the rising and falling tide. Swarms of water-bugs and beetles played over the edges of the steps, and crabs scuttled sidewise into deeper water at the approach of a gondola. A length of stone-capped brick wall, to which patches of stucco still clung stretched from the gate on either hand, under cover of an ivy that flung its mesh of shining green from within, where there lurked a lovely garden, stately, spacious for Venice, and full of a delicious half-sad surprise for whoso opened upon it. In the midst it had a broken fountain, with a marble naiad standing on a shell, and looking saucier than the sculptor meant, from having lost the point of her nose; nymphs and fauns and shepherds and shepherdesses, her kinsfolk, coquetted in and out among the greenery in flirtation not to be embarrassed by the fracture of an arm or the casting of a leg or so; one lady had no head, but she was the boldest of all. In this garden there were some mulberry and pomegranate trees, several of which hung about the fountain with seats in their shade, and, for the rest, there seemed to be mostly roses and oleanders, with other shrubs of the kind that made the greatest show of blossom and cost the least for tendance."

It was in this garden that Don Ippolito told his love. We are aware that to consider Providence and New York not worthy to be mentioned in the same breath with it is a strictly conservative view of the case, and the author of "Their Wedding Journey" and "A Chance Acquaintance" has already proved himself, where American local color is concerned, a thoroughgoing radical. We may ground our objection to the dubious element, in this instance, on saying that the story is Don Ippolito's, and that in virtue of that fact it should not have floated beyond the horizon of the lagoons. It is the poor priest's property, as it were; we grudge even the reversion of it to Mr. Ferris. We confess even to a regret at seeing it survive Don Ippolito at all, and should have advocated a trustful surrender of Florida Vervain's subsequent fortunes to the imagination of the reader. But we have no desire to expatiate restrictively on a work in which, at the worst, the imagination finds such abundant pasture. "A Foregone Conclusion" will take its place as a singularly perfect production. That the author was an artist his other books had proved, but his art ripens and sweetens in the sun of success. His manner has now refined itself till it gives one a sense of pure *quality* which it really taxes the ingenuity to express. There is not a word in the present volume as to which he has not known consummately well what he was about; there is an exquisite intellectual comfort in feeling one's self in such hands. Mr. Howells has ranked himself with the few writers on whom one counts with luxurious certainty, and this little masterpiece confirms our security.

16.

JAMES TO HOWELLS, 13 January 1875, New York   ALS Houghton
                                                           bMS Am 1784 (253) 8

111 east 25$\underline{^{th}}$ st.
Jan. 13$\underline{^{th}}$

Dear Howells—

I have just received your telegram[1] about the proof,[2] which went this a.m. I was in the country when they came, & they had been lying two days on my table, but I despatched them as soon as possible on my return. Don't lose courage about sending me more; I have made probably my only absence for the winter. I hope this has not seriously bothered you.—I found also your letter[3] which gave me all the pleasure I had given you. My notices of the F. C.[4] were written most pleasurably to myself.—

I am glad you are dining out & liking Boston. I'm afraid the tender grace of a day that is dead will not revisit *this* stagnant heart. But I come back to N. Y. (from near Philadelphia, to be sure,) with a real relish. I feel vastly at home here & really like it. Pourvu que ça dure![5] I have been staying at Mrs. Owen Wister's & having Fanny Kemble read Calderon for me in tête à tête of a morning.[6] How is that for high? She had on a cap & spectacles, but her voice is divine. I see a little of Sedgwick[7] & dine with him at theatrical chop-houses. Naughty Bohemian! Would that I were either! Farewell.

—I seem to have books enough on my hands for the Nation just now, but if you would like a notice of Emerson's *Parnassus*, I might try it.[8] In a week or two begins the annual exhibit of watercolors at the Academy. Would you like a

1. Not extant.

2. HJ was proofreading sheets for the serialization of *Roderick Hudson* in the *Atlantic* (January–December 1875).

3. Not extant.

4. *A Foregone Conclusion*; for HJ's notices, see two preceding selections.

5. Provided it lasts!

6. Frances Anne (Fanny) Kemble (1809–93) was a celebrated actress and author. Her daughter, Sarah Butler Wister (1835–1908), was the mother of the American novelist Owen Wister (1860–1938), best remembered for *The Virginian* (1902). The work Mrs. Kemble privately read for HJ was by the Spanish dramatist Pedro Calderón de la Barca (1600–1681).

7. Arthur G. Sedgwick.

8. WDH did publish a review of *Parnassus* ("Recent Literature," *Atlantic*, 35 [April 1875]: 495–96), but there is no evidence to suggest that HJ wrote it. Neither is it likely that WDH himself would have been quite so critical of Ralph Waldo Emerson (1803–82), the celebrated Transcendentalist poet and essayist. *Parnassus* consisted of a collection of Emerson's favorite poems and lines of verse by other hands, things he had copied down for future reference and therefore presumably of more general interest. But, the *Atlantic* reviewer warned, "we fear that any one who set out to discover Mr. Emerson's judgment of poetry by this book would have to be satisfied with a very general induction" (496).

couple of pages on it, if I can supply them?[9]—It may interest you to know that the N. has dropped noticing the magazines, a competent hand not appearing.[10] I have looked up Lathrop, but hardly seen him & I'm afraid he finds his experiment here not a bed of roses.[11] With love a casa[12]—

Yours
H. J. jr.

William Dean Howells, review of A Passionate Pilgrim and Other Tales, Atlantic Monthly 35 *(April 1875): 490–95.*

Mr. Henry James, Jr., has so long been a writer of magazine stories, that most readers will realize with surprise the fact that he now presents them for the first time in book form. He has already made his public. Since his earliest appearance in The Atlantic people have strongly liked and disliked his writing; but those who know his stories, whether they like them or not, have constantly increased in number, and it has therefore been a winning game with him. He has not had to struggle with indifference, that subtlest enemy of literary reputations. The strongly characteristic qualities of his work, and its instantly recognizable traits, made it at once a question for every one whether it was an offense or a pleasure. To ourselves it has been a very great pleasure, the highest pleasure that a new, decided, and earnest talent can give; and we have no complaint against this collection of stories graver than that it does not offer the author's whole range. We have read them all again and again, and they remain to us a marvel of delightful workmanship. In richness of expression and splendor of literary performance, we may compare him with the greatest, and find none greater than he; as a piece of mere diction, for example, The Romance of Certain Old Clothes in this volume is unsurpassed. No writer has a style more distinctly his own than Mr. James, and few have the abundance and felicity of his vocabulary; the precision with which he fits the word to the thought is exquisite; his phrase is generous and ample. Something of an old-time stateliness distinguishes his style, and in a certain weight of manner he is like the writers of an age when literature was a far politer thing than it is now. In a reverent ideal of work, too, he is to be rated with the first. His aim is high; he respects his material; he is full of his

9. HJ's notice, "On Some Pictures Lately Exhibited," appeared in the *Galaxy* (20 [July 1875]: 89–97).

10. The *Nation's* literary columnist, John R. Dennett, had recently died.

11. George Parsons Lathrop (1851–98) had studied law at Columbia but was trying to make a living as a freelance writer. WDH would soon hire him as an associate editor of the *Atlantic*. Son-in-law of Nathaniel Hawthorne (1804–64), he wrote a book entitled A *Study of Hawthorne* (1876) that served as the starting point for HJ's critical biography *Hawthorne*, which was published in 1879. HJ may also be insinuating a sly remark about Lathrop's incipient marital difficulties; he and Rose Hawthorne eventually separated in 1881.

12. To your house.

theme; the latter-day sins of flippancy, slovenliness, and insincerity are immeasurably far from him.

In the present volume we have one class of his romances or novelettes: those in which American character is modified or interpreted by the conditions of European life, and the contact with European personages. Not all the stories of this sort that Mr. James has written are included in this book, and one of the stories admitted—The Romance of Certain Old Clothes—belongs rather to another group, to the more strictly romantic tales, of which the author has printed several in these pages; the scene is in America, and in this also it differs from its present neighbors. There is otherwise uncommon unity in the volume, though it has at first glance that desultory air which no collection of short stories can escape. The same purpose of contrast and suggestion runs through A Passionate Pilgrim, Eugene Pickering, The Madonna of the Future, and Madame de Mauves, and they have all the same point of view. The American who has known Europe much can never again see his country with the single eye of his old ante-European days. For good or for evil, the light of the Old World is always on her face; and his fellow-countrymen have their shadows cast by it. This is inevitable; there may be an advantage in it, but if there is none, it is still inevitable. It may make a man think better or worse of America; it may be refinement or it may be anxiety; there may be no compensation in it for the loss of that tranquil indifference to Europe which untraveled Americans feel, or it may be the very mood in which an American may best understand his fellow-Americans. More and more, in any case, it pervades our literature, and it seems to us the mood in which Mr. James's work, more than that of any other American, is done. His attitude is not that of a mere admirer of Europe and contemner of America—our best suffers no disparagement in his stories; you perceive simply that he is most contented when he is able to confront his people with situations impossible here, and you fancy in him a mistrust of such mechanism as the cis-Atlantic world can offer the romancer.

However this may be, his book is well worth the carefullest study any of our critics can give it. The tales are all freshly and vigorously conceived, and each is very striking in a very different way, while undoubtedly A Passionate Pilgrim is the best of all. In this Mr. James has seized upon what seems a very common motive, in a hero with a claim to an English estate, but the character of the hero idealizes the situation: the sordid illusion of the ordinary American heir to English property becomes in him a poetic passion, and we are made to feel an instant tenderness for the gentle visionary who fancies himself to have been misborn in our hurried, eager world, but who owes to his American birth the very rapture he feels in gray England. The character is painted with the finest sense of its charm and its deficiency, and the story that grows out of it is very touching. Our readers will remember how, in the company of the supposed narrator, Clement Searle goes down from London to the lovely old country-place to which he has relinquished all notion of pretending, but which he fondly longs to see; and they will never have forgotten the tragedy of his reception and expulsion by his English cousin. The proprietary Searle stands for that intense

English sense of property which the mere dream of the American has unpardonably outraged, and which in his case wreaks itself in an atrocious piece of savagery. He is imagined with an extraordinary sort of vividness which leaves the redness of his complexion like a stain on the memory; and yet we believe we realize better the dullish kindness, the timid sweetness of the not-at-once handsome sister who falls in love with the poor American cousin. The atmosphere of the story, which is at first that of a novel, changes to the finer air of romance during the scenes at Lockley Park, and you gladly accede to all the romantic conditions, for the sake of otherwise unattainable effects. It is good and true that Searle should not be shocked out of his unrequited affection for England by his cousin's brutality, but should die at Oxford, as he does, in ardent loyalty to his ideal; and it is one of the fortunate inspirations of the tale to confront him there with that decayed and reprobate Englishman in whom abides a longing for the New World as hopeless and unfounded as his own passion for the Old. The character of Miss Searle is drawn with peculiar sweetness and firmness; there is a strange charm in the generous devotion masked by her trepidations and proprieties, and the desired poignant touch is given when at the end she comes only in time to stand by Searle's death-bed. Throughout the story there are great breadths of deliciously sympathetic description. At Oxford the author lights his page with all the rich and mellow picturesqueness of the ancient university town, but we do not know that he is happier there than in his sketches of Lockley Park and Hampton Court, or his study of the old London inn. Everywhere he conveys to you the rapture of his own seeing; one reads such a passage as this with the keen transport that the author felt in looking on the scene itself:—

"The little village of Hampton Court stands clustered about the broad entrance of Bushey Park. After we had dined we lounged along into the hazy vista of the great avenue of horse-chestnuts. There is a rare emotion, familiar to every intelligent traveler, in which the mind, with a great, passionate throb, achieves a magical synthesis of its impressions. You feel England; you feel Italy. The reflection for the moment has an extraordinary poignancy. I had known it from time to time in Italy, and had opened my soul to it as to the spirit of the Lord. Since my arrival in England I had been waiting for it to come. A bottle of excellent Burgundy at dinner had perhaps unlocked to it the gates of sense; it came now with a conquering tread. Just the scene around me was the England of my visions. Over against us, amid the deep-hued bloom of its ordered gardens, the dark red palace, with its formal copings and its vacant windows, seemed to tell of a proud and splendid past; the little village nestling between park and palace, around a patch of turfy common, with its tavern of gentility, its ivy-towered church, its parsonage, retained to my modernized fancy the lurking semblance of a feudal hamlet. It was in this dark, composite light that I had read all English prose; it was this mild, moist air that had blown from the verses of English poets; beneath these broad acres of rain-deepened greenness a thousand honored dead lay buried."

A strain of humor which so pleasantly characterizes the descriptions of the

London inn, tinges more sarcastically the admirable portrait of the shabby Rawson at Oxford, and also colors this likeness of a tramp—a fellow-man who has not had his picture better done:—

"As we sat, there came trudging along the road an individual whom from afar I recognized as a member of the genus 'tramp.' I had read of the British tramp, but I had never yet encountered him, and I brought my historic consciousness to bear upon the present specimen. As he approached us he slackened pace and finally halted, touching his cap. He was a man of middle age, clad in a greasy bonnet, with greasy earlocks depending from its sides. Round his neck was a grimy red scarf, tucked into his waistcoat; his coat and trousers had a remote affinity with those of a reduced hostler. In one hand he had a stick; on his arm he bore a tattered basket, with a handful of withered green stuff in the bottom. His face was pale, haggard, and degraded beyond description,—a singular mixture of brutality and finesse. He had a history. From what height had he fallen, from what depth had he risen? Never was a form of rascally beggarhood more complete. There was a merciless fixedness of outline about him, which filled me with a kind of awe. I felt as if I were in the presence of a personage—an artist in vagrancy.

" 'For God's sake, gentlemen,' he said, in that raucous tone of weather-beaten poverty suggestive of chronic sore-throat exacerbated by perpetual gin,—'for God's sake, gentlemen, have pity on a poor fern-collector!'—turning up his stale dandelions. 'Food hasn't passed my lips, gentlemen, in the last three days.'

"We gaped responsive, in the precious pity of guileless Yankeeism. 'I wonder,' thought I, 'if half a crown would be enough?' And our fasting botanist went limping away through the park with a mystery of satirical gratitude superadded to his general mystery."

Mr. James does not often suffer his sense of the ludicrous to relax the sometimes over-serious industry of his analyses, and when he has once done so, he seems to repent it. Yet we are sure that the poetic value of A Passionate Pilgrim is enhanced by the unwonted interfusion of humor, albeit the humor is apt to be a little too scornful. The tale is in high degree imaginative, and its fascination grows upon you in the reading and the retrospect, exquisitely contenting you with it as a new, fine, and beautiful invention.

In imaginative strength it surpasses the other principal story of the book. In Madame de Mauves the spring of the whole action is the idea of an American girl who will have none but a French nobleman for her husband. It is not a vulgar adoration of rank in her, but a young girl's belief that ancient lineage, circumstances of the highest civilization, and opportunities of the greatest refinement, must result in the noblest type of character. Grant the premises, and the effect of her emergence into the cruel daylight of facts is unquestionably tremendous: M. le Baron de Mauves is frankly unfaithful to his American wife, and, finding her too dismal in her despair, advises her to take a lover. A difficulty with so French a situation is that only a French writer can carry due conviction of it to the reader. M. de Mauves, indeed, justifies himself to the reader's sense of likelihood with great consistency, and he is an extremely suggestive conjecture. Of course, he utterly misconceives his wife's character and that of all her race, and perceives little and understands nothing not of his own tradition:—

"They talked for a while about various things, and M. de Mauves gave a humorous account of his visit to America. His tone was not soothing to Longmore's excited sensibilities. He seemed to consider the country a gigantic joke, and his urbanity only went so far as to admit that it was not a bad one. Longmore was not, by habit, an aggressive apologist for our institutions; but the baron's narrative confirmed his worst impressions of French superficiality. He had understood nothing, he had felt nothing, he had learned nothing; and our hero, glancing askance at his aristocratic profile, declared that if the chief merit of a long pedigree was to leave one so vaingloriously stupid, he thanked his stars that the Longmores had emerged from obscurity in the present century, in the person of an enterprising lumber merchant. M. de Mauves dwelt of course on that prime oddity of ours, the liberty allowed to young girls; and related the history of his researches into the 'opportunities' it presented to French noblemen,—researches in which, during a fortnight's stay, he seemed to have spent many agreeable hours. 'I am bound to admit,' he said, 'that in every case I was disarmed by the extreme candor of the young lady, and that they took care of themselves to better purpose than I have seen some mammas in France take care of them.' Longmore greeted this handsome concession with the grimmest of smiles, and damned his impertinent patronage."

This is all very good character, and here is something from the baron that is delicious:—

"I remember that, not long after our marriage, Madame de Mauves undertook to read me one day a certain Wordsworth,—a poet highly esteemed, it appears, *chez vous*. It seemed to me that she took me by the nape of the neck and forced my head for half an hour over a basin of *soupe aux choux*, and that one ought to ventilate the drawing-room before any one called."

The baron's sister, in her candid promotion of an intrigue between Madame de Mauves and Longmore, we cannot quite account for even by the fact that she hated them both. But Madame de Mauves is the strength of the story, and if Mr. James has not always painted the kind of women that women like to meet in fiction, he has richly atoned in her lovely nature for all default. She is the finally successful expression of an ideal of woman which has always been a homage, perhaps not to all kinds of women, but certainly to the sex. We are thinking of the heroine of Poor Richard, of Miss Guest in Guest's Confession, of Gabrielle de Bergerac in the story of that name, and other gravely sweet girls of this author's imagining. Madame de Mauves is of the same race, and she is the finest,—as truly American as she is womanly; and in a peculiar fragrance of character, in her purity, her courage, her inflexible high-mindedness, wholly of our civilization and almost of our climate, so different are her virtues from the virtues of the women of any other nation.

The Madonna of the Future is almost as perfect a piece of work, in its way, as A Passionate Pilgrim. It is a more romantic conception than Madame de Mauves, and yet more real. Like A Passionate Pilgrim, it distinguishes itself among Mr. James's stories as something that not only arrests the curiosity, stirs the fancy, and interests the artistic sense, but deeply touches the heart. It is more than usually relieved, too, by the author's humorous recognition of the pathetic absurdity of poor Theobald, and there is something unusually good in the patience with which the handsome, common-minded Italian woman of his twenty years' adoration is set before us. Our pity that his life should have slipped away from him in devout study of this vulgar beauty, and that she should grow old and he should die before he has made a line to celebrate her perfection or seize his ideal, is vastly heightened by the author's rigid justice to her; she is not caricatured by a light or a shadow, and her dim sense of Theobald's goodness and purity is even flattered into prominence. In all essentials one has from this story the solid satisfaction given by work in which the conception is fine, and the expression nowhere falls below it—if we except one point that seems to us rather essential, in a thing so carefully tempered and closely wrought. The reiteration of the Italian figure-maker's philosophy, "Cats and monkeys, monkeys and cats; all human life is there," is apparently of but wandering purport, and to end the pensive strain of the romance with it is to strike a jarring note that leaves the reader's mind out of tune. Sometimes even the ladies and gentlemen of Mr. James's stories are allowed a certain excess or violence in which the end to be achieved is not distinctly discernible, or the effect so reluctantly responds to the intention as to leave merely the sense of the excess.

Eugene Pickering is, like Madame de Mauves, one of those realistic subjects which we find less real than the author's romantic inspirations. There is no fault with the treatment; that is thoroughly admirable, full of spirit, wit, and strength; but there is a fancifulness in the outlines of Pickering's history and the fact of his strange betrothal which seems to belong to an old-fashioned stage-play method of fiction rather than to such a modern affair as that between the unsophisticated American and Madame Blumenthal; it did not need that machinery to produce this effect, thanks to common conditions of ours that often enough keep young men as guileless as Pickering, and as fit for sacrifice at such shrines as hers. However, something must always be granted to the story-teller by way of premises; if we exacted from Mr. James only that lie should make his premises fascinating, we should have nothing to ask here. His start, in fact, is always superb; he possesses himself of your interest at once, and he never relinquishes it till the end; though there he may sometimes leave your curiosity not quite satisfied on points such as a story-teller assumes to make clear. What, for example, were exactly the tortuous workings of Madame Blumenthal's mind in her self-contradictory behavior towards Pickering? These things must be at least unmistakably suggested.

Since Hawthorne's Donatello,[1] any attempt to touch what seems to be the remaining paganism in Italian character must accuse itself a little, but The Last of the Valerii is a study of this sort that need really have nothing on its con-

---

1. In *The Marble Faun* (1860) Hawthorne makes pointed comparisons between the innocently animated character of Donatello and the Marble Faun of Praxiteles.

science. It is an eminently poetic conceit, though it appeals to a lighter sort of emotions than any other story in Mr. James's book; it is an airy fabric woven from those bewitching glimpses of the impossible which life in Italy affords, and which those who have enjoyed them are perfectly right to overvalue. It has just the right tint of ideal trouble in it which no living writer could have imparted more skillfully than it is here done. If the story is of slighter material than the others, the subtlety of its texture gives it a surpassing charm and makes it worthy to be named along with the only other purely romantic tale in the book.

To our thinking, Mr. James has been conspicuously fortunate in placing his Romance of Certain Old Clothes in that eighteenth-century New England when the country, still colonial, was no longer rigidly puritanic, and when a love of splendor and accumulating wealth had created social conditions very different from those conventionally attributed to New England. It is among such bravely dressing provincials as Copley used to paint, and as dwelt in fine town mansions in Boston, or the handsome country-places which still remember their faded grandeur along Brattle Street in Cambridge, that Mr. James finds the circumstance and material of his personages; and we greatly enjoy the novelty of this conception of what not only might, but must have existed hereabouts in times which we are too prone to fancy all close-cropped and sad-colored. The tale is written with heat, and rapidly advances from point to point, with a constantly mounting interest. The sisterly rivalry is shown with due boldness, but without excess, and the character of Viola is sketched with a vigor that conveys a full sense of her selfish, luxurious beauty. The scene between her and Perdita when the engagement of the latter is betrayed, the scene in which she unrolls the stuff of the wedding-dress and confronts herself in the glass with it falling from her shoulder, and that in which she hastily tries the garment on after her sister's marriage, are pictures as full of character as they are of color. The most is made of Perdita where she lies dying, and bids her husband keep her fine clothes for her little girl; it is very affecting indeed, and all the more so for the explicit human-nature of the dying wife's foreboding. In the whole course of the story nothing is urged, nothing is dwelt upon; and all our story-tellers, including Mr. James himself, could profitably take a lesson from it in this respect. At other times he has a tendency to expatiate upon his characters too much, and not to trust his reader's perception enough. For the sake of a more dramatic presentation of his persons, he has told most of the stories in this book as things falling within the notice of the assumed narrator; an excellent device; though it would be better if the assumed narrator were able to keep himself from seeming to patronize the simpler-hearted heroes, and from openly rising above them in a worldly way.

But this is a very little matter, and none of our discontents with Mr. James bear any comparison to the pleasure we have had in here renewing our acquaintance with stories as distinctly characteristic as anything in literature. It is indeed a marvelous first book in which the author can invite his critic to the same sort of reflection that criticism bestows upon the claims of the great reputations; but one cannot dismiss this volume with less and not slight it. Like it or not, you must own that here is something positive, original, individual, the result of long and studious effort in a well-considered line, and mounting in its own way to great achievement. We have a reproachful sense of leaving the immense suggestiveness of the book scarcely touched, and we must ask the reader to supply our default from the stories themselves. He may be assured that nothing more novel in our literature has yet fallen in his way; and we are certain that he will not close the book without a lively sense of its force. We can promise him, also, his own perplexities about it, among which may be a whimsical doubt whether Mr. James has not too habitually addressed himself less to men and women in their mere humanity, than to a certain kind of cultivated people, who, well as they are in some ways, and indispensable as their appreciation is, are often a little narrow in their sympathies and poverty-stricken in the simple emotions; who are so, or try to be so, which is quite as bad, or worse.

17.

JAMES TO HOWELLS, 19 or 26 March 1875, New York   ALS Hayes

III east 25th st.
Friday evening.

Dear Howells—

I read this morning your notice of A P. P.[1] &—well, I survive to tell the tale! If kindness could kill I should be safely out of the way of ever challenging your ingenuity again. Never was friendship so ingenious—never was ingenuity of so ample a flow! I am so new to criticism (as a subject,) that this rare sensation has suggested many thoughts, & I discern a virtue even in being overpraised. I lift up my hanging head little by little & try to earn the laurel for the future, even if it be so much too umbrageous now. Meanwhile I thank you most heartily. May your fancy never slumber when you again read anything of mine!

I hope to be in Cambridge for two or three days about April 10th, if by that time there is any symptom whatever of sprouting grass or swelling buds. We will take a walk together & you will help my town-wearied eyes to discover them. I will bring with me the "balance" as they say here, of my novel[2] or at least the greater part of it. I hear rumors that you are coming this way (i.e. to New Jersey:) I hope it won't be at just that time. Of course you won't be here, with whatever brevity, without looking me up. The wheel of life revolves, here, but it doesn't turn up any great prizes. I lead a very quiet life & dwell rather in memories & hopes than in present emotions. With love to your house,

Yours ever—more than ever—
H. James jr.

1. A *Passionate Pilgrim*; for WDH's notice, see previous selection.
2. *Roderick Hudson*.

18.

JAMES TO HOWELLS, 3 February 1876, Paris   ALS Houghton
                                                       bMS Am 1784 (253) 9

Paris, Rue de Luxembourg, 29.
Feb. 3$^{\underline{d}}$

Dear Howells—

Ambiguous tho' it sounds, I was sorry to get your letter of the 16$^{\underline{th}}$ ult.[1] Shortly after coming to Paris, finding it a matter of prime necessity to get a novel on the stocks immediately, I wrote to F. P. Church,[2] offering him one for the *Galaxy*, to begin in March, & I was just sending off my first instalment of MS.[3] when your letter arrived. (The thing has been delayed to April.) It did not even occur to me to write to you about it, as I took for granted that the *Atlantic* could begin nothing till June or *July*, & it was the money question solely that had to determine me. If I had received your letter some weeks before I think my extreme preference to have the thing appear in the *Atlantic* might have induced me to wait till the time you mention. But even of this I am not sure, as by beginning in April my story, making nine long numbers, may terminate & appear in a volume by next Xmas. This, with the prompter monthly income (I have demanded $150 a number,) is a momentous consideration. The story is "The American"—the one I spoke to you about (but which, by the way, runs a little differently from your memory of it.) It was the only subject mature enough in my mind to use immediately. It has in fact perhaps been used somewhat prematurely; & I hope you find enough faults in it to console you for not having it in the *Atlantic*. There are two things to add. One is that the insufferable *nonchalance*, neglect & ill-manners of the Churches have left me very much in the dark as to whether my conditions are acceptable to them: & I have written to them that if they are not satisfied they are immediately to forward my parcel to you. The other is that I would, at any rate, rather give a novel to the *Atlantic* next year, (beginning, that is, in January) than this. So far as one party can make a bargain, I hereby covenant to do so. I expect to have the last half of the summer & the autumn to work on such a tale; for I shall have obviously to settle down and produce my yearly romance. I am sorry, on many accounts that the thing for the present stands as it does, but I couldn't wait. I hope you will find something that will serve your turn.

—Why didn't you tell me the name of the author of the very charming notice of *R. H.* in the last *Atlantic*, which I saw today at Galignani's? I don't recognise you, & I don't suspect Mrs. Wister. Was it Lathrop?[4] If so please assure

1. Not extant.
2. Francis Pharcellus Church (1839–1906), at this time coeditor with his brother, William Conant Church (1836–1917), of the *Galaxy* magazine (1866–78).
3. *The American*.
4. George Parsons Lathrop did write the review of *Roderick Hudson* for the *Atlantic* (37 [February 1876]: 237–38).

him of my gratitude. I am doing as I would be done by & not reading your story in pieces. Will you mail me the volume when it appears? I should like to notice it.[5]

—Yes, I see a good deal of Tourguéneff & am excellent friends with him. He has been very kind to me & has inspired me with an extreme regard. He is everything that one could desire—robust, sympathetic, modest, simple, profound, intelligent, naïf—in fine angelic. He has also made me acquainted with G. Flaubert, to whom I have likewise taken a great fancy, & at whose house I have seen the little *coterie* of the young realists in fiction.[6] They are all charming talkers—though as editor of the austere *Atlantic* it would startle you to hear some of their projected subjects. The other day Edmond de Goncourt (the best of them) said he had been lately working very well on his novel—he had got upon an episode that greatly interested him, and into which he was going very far. *Flaubert:* "What is it?" *E. de G.* "A whore-house *de province.*"[7]

I oughtn't to give you any news—you yourself were so brief. Indeed I have no news to give: I lead a quiet life, & find Paris more like Cambridge than you probably enviously suppose. I like it—(Paris)—much, & find it an excellent place to work.—I am glad my *Tribune* letters amuse you.—They are most impudently light-weighted, but that was part of the bargain.[8] I find as I grow older, that the only serious work I can do is in story-spinning.—Farewell. With a friendly memory of your wife & children

Yours very truly
H. James jr.

5. WDH's serial *Private Theatricals* ran in the *Atlantic* from November 1875 through May 1876, but was not published in volume form—as *Mrs. Farrell*—until 1921. WDH had been threatened with a possible lawsuit because of his unflattering description of a New England country retreat, and he chose to drop the book publication.

6. During his year in Paris (1875–76), HJ became acquainted with many of the notable European writers of his time, including the expatriate Ivan Turgenev (1818–83), Gustave Flaubert (1821–80), and his coterie of disciples, including Edmond de Goncourt (1822–96) and Emile Zola (1840–1902). Celebrated for their extraordinary realism, the novels of Goncourt and his brother Jules (1830–70) were frequently viewed as human documents based on dossiers they assembled about persons and events. For HJ's record of his time in Paris, see *CN*, 215–17.

7. Goncourt's novel was *La Fille Elisa* (1877), which HJ reviewed (unfavorably) for the *Nation*. See *Literary Criticism* 2: 403–4.

8. During his year in Paris, HJ was a correspondent for the New York *Tribune*, his only regular stint as a journalist. When his articles proved to be too literary, insufficiently "newsy" (as his publisher put it), HJ gave up the job. The episode became the basis for HJ's story "The Next Time" (1895). See HJ, *Parisian Sketches: Letters to the New York Tribune, 1875–1876*, ed. Leon Edel and Ilse Dusoir Lind (New York: New York University Press, 1957), ix–xxxvii, 209–27; see also *CN*, 109–10, 123–25.

19.

JAMES TO HOWELLS, 4 April 1876, Paris   ALS Houghton
                                                    bMS Am 1784 (253) 10

                                                    29 Rue de Luxembourg
                                                    April 4$\underline{\text{th}}$

Dear Howells—

I am very glad now that you have got hold of my story,[1] & I wish you all
prosperity & satisfaction with it. I am very well pleased that you should have
made your proposal to Church—whose own conduct, however, remains to me a
mystery. *Enfin,*[2] all's well that ends well. I hope you will think my story does,
since the beginning pleases you. I have been suspending work upon it while its
fate was in the balance, but I shall now send you another instalment in a very
few days & the following ones as regularly & speedily as possible.

What shall I tell you? My windows are open, the spring is becoming serious, & the soft hum of this good old Paris comes into my sunny rooms, whence,
thro' an open door, I see my porter, the virtuous Adrien, making up my bed in
an alcove of voluminous blue chintz. I like Paris, I like alcoves, I like even
porters—abhorred race as they generally are. In these simple likings my life flows
gently on. I see a good many people, but no one intimately. I saw Tourguéneff a
couple of days since, since receiving your letter, but had no chance to give him
your message, as 'twas in a crowd; but I shall do so. He is a most worthy man, &
purely a genius. I don't remember what I told you about the "realists" to make
you thank God you are not a Frenchman[3]—the only one I really know is Flaubert, to whom I have taken a great fancy. He is a very solid old fellow—quite a
man. But I like the man better than the artist. The other day came to see me
C. D. Warner,[4] from Munich—very amiable & diffusing into the Parisian air a
sensible savor of Hartford. We dined together, & I shall see him again. I have
heard several times from home that your story[5] is extremely *brilliant:* that is the
word that is always used. It is a very good one, methinks. Your list of your other
achievements & projects almost takes my breath away—comme vous y allez![6]
But I shall be in my single person a crowded audience to your comedy. Farewell.

1. *The American* ran serially in the *Atlantic* from June 1876 through May 1877.
2. In short.
3. See letter #18 for the source of WDH's shuddering patriotism.
4. Charles Dudley Warner (1829–1900), a prolific American editor and author, was a neighbor
of Mark Twain's at Hartford, Connecticut. WDH had given him HJ's address in Paris.
5. *Private Theatricals* (published in 1921 as Mrs. *Farrell*).
6. How you move on! In addition to *Private Theatricals*, WDH was finishing two plays, *The
Parlor Car* and *Out of the Question*, both serialized in the *Atlantic*. That spring WDH and Mark
Twain agreed to collaborate on an experiment in corporate authorship, in which a single plot would
be submitted to twelve different writers, each of whom would then write a story from it (*Mark
Twain–Howells Letters* 1: 129–31). WDH was also commissioned to write a campaign biography for
Rutherford B. Hayes, the Republican candidate who captured the presidency in the bitterly con-
tested election of 1876.

My love to your wife & children. Say a word of friendship for me to Lathrop & believe me

always yours
Henry James jr.

20.

JAMES TO HOWELLS, 28 May 1876, Paris   ALS Houghton
bMS Am 1784 (253) 11

29 Rue de Luxembourg.
May 28 th

Dear Howells—

I have just received (an hour ago) your letter of May 14 th.[1] I shall be very glad to do my best to divide my story so that it will make 12 nos., & I think I shall probably succeed.[2] Of course 26 pp. is an impossible instalment for the magazine. I had no idea the 2 d number would make so much; though I half expected your remonstrance. I shall endeavor to give you about 14 pp., & to keep doing it for 7 or 8 months more. I sent you the other day a 4 th Part, a portion of which, I suppose, you will allot to the 5 th.

My heart was touched by your regret that I hadn't given you "a great deal of my news"—though my reason suggested that I couldn't have given you what there was not to give. "La plus belle fille du monde ne peut donner que ce qu'elle a."[3] I turn out news in very small quantities—it is impossible to imagine an existence less pervaded with any sort of *chiaroscuro*. I am turning into an old, and very contented, Parisian: I feel as if I had struck roots into the Parisian soil, & were likely to let them grow tangled & tenacious there. It is a very comfortable & profitable place, on the whole—I mean, especially, on its general & cosmopolitan side. Of pure Parisianism I see absolutely nothing. The great merit of the place is that one can arrange one's life here exactly as one pleases—that there are facilities for every kind of habit & taste, & that everything is accepted & understood. Paris itself meanwhile is a sort of painted background which keeps shifting & changing, & which is always there, to be looked at when you please, & to be most easily & comfortably ignored when you don't. All this, if you were only here, you would feel much better than I can tell you—& you would write some happy piece of your prose about it which would make me feel it better, afresh. *Ergo*, come—when you can! I shall probably be here still. Of course every good thing is still better in spring, & in spite of much mean weather I have been liking Paris these last weeks more than ever. In fact I have accepted destiny here, under the vernal influence. If you sometimes read

1. Not extant.
2. HJ originally planned to serialize *The American* in nine installments.
3. The loveliest girl in the world can only give what she has.

my poor letters in the *Tribune,* you get a notion of some of the things I see & do. I suppose also you get some gossip about me from Quincy St. Besides this there is not a great deal to tell. I have seen a certain number of people all winter who have helped to pass the time, but I have formed but one or two relations of permanent value, & which I desire to perpetuate. I have seen almost nothing of the literary fraternity, & there are fifty reasons why I should not become intimate with them. I don't like their wares, & they don't like any others; & besides, they are not *accueillants.*[4] Tourguéneff is worth the whole heap of them, & yet he himself swallows them down in a manner that excites my extreme wonder. But he is the most loveable of men & takes all things easily. He is so pure & strong a genius that he doesn't need to be on the defensive as regards his opinions & enjoyments. The mistakes he may make don't hurt him. His modesty & naïveté are simply infantine. I gave him some time since the message you sent him, & he bade me to thank you very kindly & to say that he had the most agreeable memory of your two books. He has just gone to Russia to bury himself for two or three months on his estate, & try & finish a long novel he has for three or four years been working upon.[5] I hope to heaven he may. I suspect he works little here.

—I interrupted this a couple of hours since to go out & pay a visit to Gustave Flaubert, it being his time of receiving, & his last Sunday in Paris, & I owing him a farewell. *He* is a very fine old fellow, & the most interesting man & strongest artist of his circle. I had him for an hour alone & then came in his "following," talking much of Emile Zola's catastrophe—Zola having just had a serial novel for which he was being handsomely paid interrupted on account of protests from provincial subscribers against its indecency. The opinion apparently was that it was a bore, but that it could only do the book good on its appearance in a volume.[6] Among your tribulations as editor, I take it that this particular one at least is not in store for you.[7] On my way down from Flaubert's I met poor Zola climbing the staircase, looking very pale and sombre, & I saluted him with the flourish natural to a contributor who has just been invited to make his novel last longer yet.

—Warner[8] has come back to Paris, after an apparently rapturous fortnight in

4. Hospitable.

5. *Virgin Soil* (1877).

6. In June 1876 *Le Bien publique* suspended Zola's *L'Assommoir* not for reasons of morality but because of the novel's unflattering portrayal of the working class. A competitor, *La République des lettres,* published the remainder. The book soon became a bestseller and brought Zola both celebrity and fortune.

7. In 1869 WDH's decision to publish "The True Story of Lady Byron's Life" by Harriet Beecher Stowe (1811–96) cost the *Atlantic* fifteen thousand subscribers. Defending himself (and Stowe's article, which accused Byron of committing incest with his half-sister), WDH wrote to his father, "The world needed to know just how base, filthy and mean Byron was, in order that all glamour should be forever removed from his literature" (WDH to William Cooper Howells, 22 Sept. 1869, *SL* 1: 340).

8. Charles Dudley Warner.

London, & the other morning breakfasted with me—but I have not seen him since, & I imagine he has reverted to London. He is conspicuously amiable. I have seen no other Americans all winter—men at least. There are no men here to see but horribly effeminate & empty-pated little *crevés*.[9] But there are some very nice women.—I went yesterday to see a lady whom & whose *intérieur* it is a vast pity you shouldn't behold, for professional purposes: a certain Baroness Blaze de Bury—a (supposed) illegitimate daughter of Lord Brougham.[10] She lives in a queer old mouldy, musty rez de chaussée[11] in the depths of the Faubourg St. Germain, is the grossest & most audacious lion-huntress in all creation & has two most extraordinary little French, emancipated daughters. One of these, wearing a Spanish mantilla, & got up apparently to dance the cachacha, presently asked me what I thought of *incest* as a subject for a novel—adding that it had against it that it was getting, in families, so terribly common. *Basta!* But both figures and setting are a curious picture.—I rejoice in the dawning of your dramatic day, & wish I might be at the Première of your piece at Daly's.[12] I give it my tenderest good wishes—but I wish you had told me more about it, & about your comedy. Why (since the dramatic door stands so wide open to you,) do you print the latter before having it acted? This, from a Parisian point of view, seems quite monstrous.—Your inquiry "Why I don't go to Spain?" is sublime—is what Philip Van Artevelde says of the Lake of Como, "softly sublime, profusely fair!"[13] I shall spend my summer in the most tranquil & frugal hole I can unearth in France, & have no prospect of travelling for some time to come. The Waverley Oaks[14] seem strangely far away—yet I remember them well, & the day we went there. I am sorry I am not to see your novel sooner, but I applaud your energy in proposing to change it.[15] The printed thing always seems to me dead and done with. I suppose you will write something about Philadelphia[16]—I hope so, as otherwise I am afraid I shall know nothing about it. I

---

9. Shrimps, pygmies.

10. Henry Peter Brougham (1778–1868), Lord Chancellor of England (1830–34), was a noted Whig orator, legal reformer, and social eccentric; he lived in France for most of the last thirty years of his life. The Baroness Marie Blaze de Bury (née Pauline Rose Stewart) wrote novels and critical essays in English and French.

11. Ground-floor apartment.

12. WDH's first one-act play, "The Parlor Car," was written for Augustin Daly (1838–99), a prominent theatrical manager and entrepreneur, who later would also have dealings with HJ. Daly announced WDH's play for the 1876–77 season, but it was never produced. See *The Complete Plays of W. D. Howells*, ed. Walter J. Meserve (New York: New York University Press, 1960), 23–24.

13. From the "Lay of Elena" interlude to Sir Henry Taylor's *Philip van Artevelde* (1834). See *The Works of Sir Henry Taylor*, 5 vols. (London: Henry S. King & Co., 1877), 1: 187.

14. A wooded site at Belmont favored for picnics and country outings.

15. *Private Theatricals*; WDH abandoned his efforts to revise the serial for book publication (see letter #18, note 5).

16. HJ refers to the United States Centennial Exhibition, which opened at Philadelphia on 10 May 1876. WDH published "A Sennight of the Centennial" in the *Atlantic* (38 [July 1876]: 92–107).

salute your wife & children a thousand times & wish you an easy & happy summer & abundant inspiration.

Yours very faithfully
H James jr

21.

JAMES TO HOWELLS, 3 July 1876, Paris

ALS Houghton
bMS Am 1784 (253) 12

July 3$\underline{^d}$
Paris Rue de Luxembourg, 29.

Dear Howells—

Here—in another cover—is another batch of my story[1]—good luck to it! I have just been reading you in the last Atlantic, on the Centennial,[2] & loving you, as ever. There are a thousand charming touches in your piece, & you made me almost wonder whether I mightn't almost wish that I could visit Philadelphia *ces jours-ci.*[3] This was a triumph. I wrote you a long letter some weeks since, & I hope it will strike you as answerable. I suppose you are among your Shakers by this time, & with a fair amount of leisure.[4] Give me an hour of it. I leave Paris ten days hence for the country—I don't know where—whence I shall despatch you the rest of my MS. It is very well printed. (Will you excuse my sordidly alluding to money matters an instant—& remarking that I will take it kindly of you if you cause it to be noted that albeit my tale is published in 12 parts, I would prefer to have it paid for as at first intended in 9 instalments. I mention this as a precaution: it is probably the intention of the publishers.) Tell me what is thought of Bret Harte's novel[5]—I have it, but am keeping it to read under a French tree. Tell me also whether you would (having my novel) have too much of me in an *article* on Danl. Deronda—8 or 10 pages?[6] Will you let me hear of this by Sept 1st? (Address always 29 Rue de Luxembourg.) I should like to propose an article on George Sand,[7] but the disposition I once had to write it is

---

1. *The American.*

2. "A Sennight of the Centennial," *Atlantic* (July 1876).

3. One of these days.

4. WDH spent the summer at Shirley Village, Massachusetts, where he studied the social life of a Shaker community. These observations would inform his treatment of the Shakers in *The Undiscovered Country* (1880).

5. *Gabriel Conroy: A Novel* (1876).

6. WDH published HJ's critical exchange on George Eliot's novel, "Daniel Deronda: A Conversation," in the *Atlantic* (December 1876).

7. Masculine pseudonym of French novelist Aurore Dupin, Baronne Dudevant (1804–76). HJ had recently completed several notices of Sand's life and work: "Parisian Topics," New York *Tribune* (1 July 1876); "George Sand," New York *Tribune* (22 July 1876); and ["M. Taine's Letter on George Sand"], an unsigned note in the *Nation* (27 July 1876). A longer critical essay, "George Sand," would appear in the *Galaxy* (July 1877).

defunct. I suppose you are fictionizing—Dio vi benedicat.[8] I salute a 1000 times your wife & children & desire their health, & with all good wishes to yourself am

yours always
H. J. jr.

22.

JAMES TO HOWELLS, 24 October 1876, Paris

ALS Houghton
bMS Am 1784 (253) 13

29 Rue de Luxembourg.
Oct. 24th

Dear Howells—

Many thanks for your letter[1] & the promise of *Hayes*,[2] which I shall expect. Thanks also for your good opinion of the notice of *D. D.*,[3] which charmed & reassured me. I was rather afraid that you would think its form beneath the majesty of the theme. Many thanks, furthermore, for your continuing to like the *American*, of which I shall send you by the next mail another instalment. (I sent you one by the last, & I shall very soon send you the closing pages.) Your appeal on the subject of the *dénoûement* fairly set me trembling, & I have to take my courage in both hands to answer you. In a word Mme de C.[4] doesn't marry Newman, & I couldn't possibly, possibly, have made her do it. The whole pivot of the dénoûement was, in the conception of the tale, in his losing her; I am pretty sure this will make itself clear to you when you read the last quarter of the book. My subject was: an American letting the insolent foreigner go, out of his good nature, after the insolent foreigner had wronged him & *he* had held him in his power. To show the good nature I must show the wrong & the wrong of course is that the American is cheated out of Mme de Cintré. That he should only have been scared, & made to fear, for a while, he was going to lose her, would have been insufficient—non è vero?[5] The subject is sad certainly, but it all holds together. But in my next novel[6] I promise you there shall be much marrying. Apropos of this I have it on my conscience to mention that I am in correspondence with Scribner about a serial to begin in their magazine in June

8. God bless you.
1. Not extant.
2. WDH's campaign biography of his wife's cousin, Rutherford B. Hayes (1822–93), the Republican governor of Ohio who narrowly won the presidency in November. The *Sketch of the Life and Character of Rutherford B. Hayes* was published in Boston by Hurd & Houghton on 15 September 1876.
3. "Daniel Deronda: A Conversation," *Atlantic* (December 1876).
4. Claire de Cintré, the French heroine of *The American*.
5. Isn't that so?
6. *The Europeans* (1878).

next.[7] Nothing is yet settled, but I suppose something will be. The vision of a serial in Scribner does not, I may frankly say, aesthetically delight me; but it is the best thing I can do, so long as having a perpetual serial running has defined itself as a financial necessity for me. When my novels (if they ever do) bring me enough money to carry me over the intervals I shall be very glad to stick to the *Atlantic*. Or I would undertake to do this if I could simply have money down for my MS., leaving the Magazine to publish at its leisure. My novel is to be an *Americana*—the adventures in Europe of a female Newman, who of course equally triumphs over the insolent foreigner.[8]—Yes, I couldn't help translating those croquet-verses of Turgenieff,[9] tho' I don't share the Russian eagerness for war. T. himself is full of it, & I suspect it is coming. The air is full of it & all the world here expects it.—I think I shall thrive more effectually than here in London, to which city I propose before long to emigrate—if I don't go to Italy. But I shan't, at any rate, winter here. You manage to tell me very little about yourself. What are you writing?

Yours very truly, with love at your fireside,
H. James jr.

23.

JAMES TO HOWELLS, 18 December 1876, London   ALS Houghton
bMS Am 1784 (253) 14

3 Bolton St. Piccadilly W.
Dec. 18th.

Dear Howells.

Your letter of Nov. 10th[1] lies open before me, & as I glance over it I derive new satisfaction from your good opinion of my tale.[2] I send you herewith the 11th part, which I have been keeping to post in England, as I never feel that I can take precautions enough. It is shorter than most or than any: & the 12th, which will soon follow, will likewise be brief. I trust that, to the end, the thing will seem to you to carry itself properly. I rec'd. a few days since a letter from my brother Wm., in which he speaks of some phrases (on Newman's part) as

---

7. *Scribner's* was still eager to enlist HJ as a contributor, but nothing came of this plan.

8. HJ's preliminary sketch of *The Portrait of a Lady* (1881).

9. In the *Nation* (23 [5 October 1876]: 213) HJ had anonymously contributed a verse translation of a belligerent poem by Turgenev, in which the Russian writer pictures a complicitous Queen Victoria playing croquet with the bloody heads of Christians massacred by the Ottoman Turks in Bulgaria. In spite of reports of widespread violence—it was later estimated that twelve thousand Bulgarians died—the British government under Disraeli refused to intervene. In December 1876 reforms were pressed upon Turkey at an international conference in Constantinople, but the Ottoman rulers refused to accept them. The result was the Russo-Turkish War of 1877–78.

1. Not extant.

2. *The American*.

being so shocking as to make "the reader's flesh creep." Two or three that he quotes are indeed infelicitous, as I perceive as soon as my attention is called to them. He mentions having persuaded you to omit one or two of the same sort. I am very glad you have done so, & would give you *carte blanche*.[3] It is all along of my not seeing a proof—which is a great disadvantage. There are many things which, as they stand printed, I should have changed. *Ma che vuole?*[4] Here I have no one to try any thing on, or to ask how things sound. —

Àpropos of my Scribner project, let me say now that it is abandoned. They lately wrote me that my novel could begin not in June, but only in November, & then conditionally. So I have retreated. Once I wait so long as that, I prefer to wait for the *Atlantic*, & hereby bestow on you my next-generated romance. Only I should like you to let me know as far in advance as possible when you should be able to begin it.[5] —

You see I have changed my sky: as far as sky goes, for the worse. But as regards other things, I imagine, for the better. I like London, in so far as thro' the present fog-blanket I can puzzle it out, & I suspect that in the long run I shall prosper here. Just now it is rather lugubrious, as I know few people & the change from glittering, charming, civilized Paris is rude. But I shall scribble better here, which you will agree with me is every thing. I hope that *you* are scribbling well in spite of the political turmoil.[6] I am so much out of it here that I don't pretend to understand the rights and wrongs & don't risk an opinion. I can imagine that the suspense is very wearisome & depressing.—What are you doing? I am sorry you haven't sent me Hayes, any how. I heard from my mother that poor Lathrop's wife[7] has been very ill, & at Somerville. Pray give him my friendliest regards & assure him of my sympathy. I hope by this time she is

3. Because WJ's letter to HJ is not extant, it is impossible to know exactly which phrases he found objectionable or which WDH might have altered for use in the *Atlantic*. A later letter to HJ's mother suggests that Newman's crude manner of speaking—his decidedly Western idiom—was the source of irritation. "Tell [William] I thank him much for his strictures on some of Newman's speeches in *The American* of which I quite admit the justice. It is all along of my not seeing proof—I should have let none of those things pass. The story, as it stands, is full of things I should have altered; but I think none of them are so inalterable but that I shall be easily able in preparing the volume, to remove effectually, by a few verbal corrections, that Newmanesque taint on which William dwells" (*HJL* 2: 87).

4. What can I say?

5. HJ postponed his study of "an *Americana*—the adventures in Europe of a female Newman" (*The Portrait of a Lady*), and instead next wrote *The Europeans* for the *Atlantic* (July–October 1878).

6. In the disputed presidential election of 1876, the first since the Civil War in which the defeated Southern states cast ballots, conflicting electoral returns from a number of states left the outcome undecided. A congressional commission ultimately awarded all twenty disputed electoral votes to the Republican candidate, Rutherford B. Hayes, who edged out his Democratic opponent, Samuel J. Tilden (1814–86), by a single vote. WDH had written a campaign biography of Hayes; see letter #22, note 2.

7. Rose Hawthorne (1851–1926), daughter of Nathaniel Hawthorne, married George Parsons Lathrop in 1871.

restored to health & to her home. I trust your own fireside is tranquil & Mrs. Howells reasonably vigorous. Give my love to her & believe me

always faithfully yr's,
H. James jr.

24.

JAMES TO HOWELLS, 2 February 1877, London   ALS Houghton
                                                            bMS Am 1784 (253) 15

3 Bolton St Piccadilly W.
Feb. 2$^{\underline{d}}$

Dear Howells.—

I sent you a few lines three days since with my last bundle of copy; but now comes your letter of Jan. 20$^{\underline{th}}$[1] which prompts me to send a few more.——I quite understand that you should not be able to begin another serial by H.J.jr until after the lapse of a year at least. Your readers & your contributors would alike remonstrate. I shall be glad, however, if you could begin to print a *six-months' tale* sooner than a longer one, to do something of those dimensions. But I should not make use of the subject I had in mind when I last alluded to this matter—that is essentially not compressible into so small a compass. It is the portrait of the character & recital of the adventures of a woman—a great swell, psychologically; a *grande nature*—accompanied with many "developments."[2] I would rather wait and do it when I can have full elbow room. But I will excogi-tate something for the shorter story, & shall endeavor to make it something of an "objective," dramatic & picturesque sort.[3] Only let me know well in advance when you should commence publication. In January '78?—I agree with you in thinking that a year seems a long time for a novel to drag thro' a magazine—especially a short novel that only fills one volume when republished. But I think that the real trouble is not that any novel that the Atlantic would publish in a year is too long, but that it is chopped up in too fine pieces. Properly such a thing as the *American* should have been put thro' in 5 or 6 months, in numbers of 30 or 35 pages. To wait a month for a 20 minutes' nibble at it, would, it seems to me, if I were a reader, put me into a fatally bad humor with it. I have just been making this reflection apropos of your little "Comedy"—which is extremely pretty & entertaining.[4] But one wants to go through with it. Your young-lady talk is marvellous—it's as if the devil himself were sitting in your

1. Neither letter extant.
2. Another anticipation of *The Portrait of a Lady*.
3. This eventually became *The Europeans*, which was published in four installments.
4. WDH's play *Out of the Question* appeared in three installments of the *Atlantic* (February–April 1877).

inkstand. *He* only could have made you know that one girl would say that another's walking from the station was *ghastly!!*[5]

Yours ever
H. J. jr.

25.

JAMES TO HOWELLS, 30 March 1877, London

ALS Houghton
bMS Am 1784 (253) 16

3 Bolton St. W.
March 30th

Dear Howells—

I am supposed to be busily scribbling for lucre this morning; but I must write you three lines of acknowledgment of your welcome long letter.[1] It's most interesting portion was naturally your stricture on the close of my tale,[2] which I accept with saintly meekness. These are matters which one feels about as one may, or as one can. I quite understand that as an editor you should go in for "cheerful endings"; but I am sorry that as a private reader you are not struck with the inevitability of the *American* dénoûement. I fancied that most folks would feel that M$^{\underline{me}}$ de Cintré *couldn't*, when the pivot came, marry Mr. N.; and what the few persons who have spoken to me of the tale have expressed to me (e.g. Mrs. Kemble t'other day) was the fear that I should really put the marriage through. *Voyons;*[3] it would have been impossible: they would have been an impossible couple, with an impossible problem before them. For instance—to speak very materially—where could they have lived? It was all very well for Newman to talk of giving her the whole world to choose from: but Asia & Africa being counted out, what would Europe & America have offered? M$^{\underline{me}}$ de C. couldn't have lived in New York; depend upon it; & Newman, after his marriage (or rather *she*, after it) couldn't have dwelt in France. There would have been nothing left but a farm out West.[4] No, the interest of the subject was, for me, (without my being at all a pessimist) its exemplification of one of those insuperable difficulties which present themselves in people's lives & from which the only issue is by forfeiture—by losing something. It was cruelly hard for poor N. to lose, certainly: but *que diable allait-il faire dans cette galère?*[5] We

5. See *The Complete Plays of W. D. Howells*, 36.
1. Not extant.
2. WDH apparently objected to the unhappy close of *The American*, in which Christopher Newman fails to win the acceptance of Claire de Cintré.
3. Come now.
4. WDH may have taken this cue to arrive at his conclusion for *The Lady of the Aroostook* (1879), in which, after their marriage, Lydia Blood and James Staniford settle on a ranch in California.
5. What the devil was he supposed to do in this situation? The line from the second act of Molière's *Fourberies de Scapin* (1671) has been rendered idiomatically.

are each the product of circumstances & there are tall stone walls which fatally divide us. I have written my story from Newman's side of the wall, & I understand so well how Mme de Cintré couldn't really scramble over from *her* side! If I had represented her as doing so I should have made a prettier ending, certainly; but I should have felt as if I were throwing a rather vulgar sop to readers who don't really know the world & who don't measure the merit of a novel by its correspondence to the same. Such readers assuredly have a right to their entertainment, but I don't believe it is in me to give them, in a satisfactory way, what they require.—I don't think that "tragedies" have the presumption against them as much as you appear to; & I see no logical reason why they shouldn't be as *long* as comedies. In the drama they are usually allowed to be longer—non è vero?[6]

—But whether the *Atlantic* ought to print unlimited tragedy is another question—which you are doubtless quite right in regarding as you do. Of course you couldn't have, for the present, another evaporated marriage from me! I suspect it is the tragedies in life that arrest my attention more than the other things & say more to my imagination; but, on the other hand, if I fix my eyes on a sunspot I think I am able to see the prismatic colors in it. You shall have the brightest possible sun-spot for the 4–number tale of 1878.[7] It shall fairly put your readers eyes out. The idea of doing what you propose much pleases me; & I agree to squeeze my buxom muse, as you happily call her, into a 100 of your pages. I will lace her so tight that she shall have the neatest little figure in the world. It shall be a very joyous little romance. I am afraid I can't tell you at this moment what it will be; for my dusky fancy contains nothing joyous enough: but I will invoke the jocund muse & come up to time. I shall probably develop an idea that I have, about a genial, charming youth of a Bohemianish pattern, who comes back from foreign parts into the midst of a mouldering & ascetic old Puritan family of his kindred (scene, imaginary locality in New England 1830,) & by his gayety & sweet audacity smooths out their rugosities, heals their dyspepsia & dissipates their troubles. *All* the women fall in love with him (& he with them—his amatory powers are boundless;) but even for a happy ending he can't marry them all. But he marries the prettiest, & from a romantic quality of Xtian. charity, produces a picturesque imbroglio (for the sake of the picturesque I shall play havoc with the New England background of 1830!) under cover of which the other maidens pair off with the swains who have hitherto been starved out: after which the beneficent cousin departs for Bohemia (*with his bride, oh yes!*) in a vaporous rosy cloud, to scatter new benefactions over man-, & especially, woman-, kind! —(Pray don't mention this stuff to any one. It would be meant, roughly speaking, as a picture of the conversion of a dusky, dreary domestic circle to epicureanism. But I may be able to make nothing of it. The merit would be in the amount of *color* I should be able to infuse into it.) — But I shall give you it, or its equivalent, by Nov. next. It was quite by accident

6. Isn't that so?
7. *The Europeans.*

I didn't mention the name of your admiress. Nay there are two of them! The one I spoke of, I think, is Lady Clarke[8]—a handsome charming woman, of a certain age, the wife of a retired & invalid diplomatist who lives chiefly on her estate in Scotland. She "takes in" the *Atlantic* & seems to affect you much. The other is Mrs. Coltman, a modest, blushing & pleasing woman, who also has the *Atlantic*, & who can best be identified by saying that she is the sister of the widow of A. H. Clough,[9] the poet—Lowell's friend. She is to take me some day soon down to Eton & show me an inside-view of the school, where her rosy little British boys are. Both of these ladies descanted to me on the *Atlantic* & your productions & said nary a word to me of my own masterpieces: whereby I consider my present action magnanimous! Àpropos: the young girl in your comedy[10] is extremely charming; quite adorable, in fact; & extremely real. You make them wonderfully well.

—What more shall I say?—Yes, I find London much to my taste—entertaining, interesting, inspiring, even. But I am not, as you seem to imply, in the least in the thick of it. If I were to tell you whom I see, it would make a tolerably various list: but the people only pass before me panoramically, & I have no relations with them. I dined yesterday in comp'y. with Browning[11] at Smalley's[12]—where were also Huxley & his wife[13] & the editor & editress of the *Daily News*:[14] among the cleverest people I have met here. Smalley has a charming house & wife, & is a very creditable American representative; more so than the minister,[15] who, I am told, has never returned a dinner since he has been here. Browning is a great chatterer but no *Sordello* at all.—We are lost in admiration of Mr. Hayes; may his shadow never grow less! Blessings on your home.

Yours always truly
H. James jr.

8. Lady Clark (d. 1897), formerly Charlotte Coltman, daughter of the Honorable Sir T. J. Coltman, was married to Sir John Forbes Clark (1821–1910). HJ was a frequent guest at their country estate in Tillypronie, Scotland.

9. Arthur Hugh Clough (1819–61), whose "Amours de Voyage" was first published in the *Atlantic* (1858) by James Russell Lowell. His widow, Blanche Smith Clough, edited the *Prose Remains of Arthur Hugh Clough* (Macmillan, 1888), including a brief memoir and selections from his letters.

10. Leslie Bellingham, WDH's affectionate incarnation of American girlhood in *Out of the Question*.

11. Robert Browning (1812–89), English poet much admired by HJ, was the author of *Sordello* (1840), a narrative poem notorious at the time for its presumed obscurity.

12. George Washburn Smalley (1833–1916) was at this time London correspondent for the New York *Tribune*. He and his wife, Phoebe Garnaut Smalley, were close friends of HJ during their years in London.

13. Thomas Henry Huxley (1825–95), the English naturalist, and his wife, H. A. (Heathorn) Huxley.

14. Frank Harrison Hill (1830–1910) and his wife, Jane Dalzell Finlay Hill (d. 1904).

15. Edwards Pierrepont (1817–92) served as U.S. ambassador to Great Britain in 1876–77.

26.

JAMES TO HOWELLS, 6 May 1878, London

ALS Houghton
bMS Am 1784 (253) 127

3 Bolton St. May 6$\underline{^{th}}$

Dear Howells—

I post you to day the 3d Part of the "Europeans:" the *last* will presently follow. Good luck to them all!—

—I hope that this will not find you in a midMay like the one described at the beginning of my tale.[1] I wish I could give you—that is, that you could take with me—a week of this beautiful English spring—all sprinkled with young lambs & primroses. I have just been spending two or three days in the Isle of Wight in company with *six* Boston ladies, whom I conveyed *en masse* about the island.[2] It was very amusing—especially ordering tea & toast for them at the "Dolphin"—or I think it was the "Beagle." If I feared not to be personal I would "do" the episode for the *Atlantic*; or better still, furnish you with the facts, so that you might do it; for you would be the one for this.—Last night I was at a dinner party, where a clever & charming old lady, staying in the house, said to me—"Go & take that book on that table; it's so charming; you must read it." I go & take it up, & find A "Chance Acquaintance"; and then I sit down beside her & we sing its praises for ten grand minutes—which is a good while to devote to a subject in London. She wanted to know (believing it to be real) what the book was which Arbuton says "one of us might have written."[3] I doubt whether you will remember that touch, but Mrs. Duncan Stewart[4] appreciated it highly.—I heard from my brother W$\underline{^m}$ the other day that your play seemed very charming in representation, & I hope that you yourself felt the charm in the

---

1. *The Europeans* opens as a mid-May blizzard descends on Boston, an example of HJ's ironic infusion of local color.

2. In a letter of 1 May 1878 to WJ, HJ also mentioned this excursion. With London empty for Easter, HJ wrote, "I profited by the stillness to run down for a couple of days to the Isle of Wight and call upon our little friend Miss Peabody—a design I had entertained more or less ever since she came to England. I had proceeded on the hypothesis that she was in solitude and desolation; but I found her *très-entourée*, having with her four other American women beside her mother, who is much better" (CWJ 1: 300). Miss Peabody was probably Maria (or Mary) Peabody, an acquaintance of Alice James, and the daughter of Andrew Preston Peabody. See DAJ 110.

3. In chapter 8 of *A Chance Acquaintance* Miles Arbuton and Kitty Ellison converse about a book called '*Details*': "just the history," as Kitty says, "of a week in the life of some young people who happen together in an old New-England country-house; nothing extraordinary, little, every-day things told so exquisitely, and all fading naturally away without any particular result, only the full meaning of everything brought out." Arbuton, whose tastes are more urbane, offers this summary of the author: "He's a very ordinary sort of man,—not what one would exactly call a gentleman, you know, in his belongings,—and yet his books have nothing of the shop, nothing professionally literary, about them. It seems as if almost any of us might have written them." See *A Chance Acquaintance* (Indiana University Press edition), 98–99.

4. Mrs. Duncan Stewart (1797–1884), wife of a Liverpool merchant.

region of your purse-strings.[5] Are you on your way to Belmont—are you to arrive there this summer?[6] With many greetings to your wife—

ever faithfully yours
H. James jr.

27.

JAMES TO HOWELLS, May–June 1878 London   ALS Houghton
bMS Am 1784 (253) 17

11 KENSINGTON PARK GARDENS, W.
Saturday.

Dear Mr James,[1]

Will you be so very kind as to tell me, as I have no doubt you know, what is the title of that novel of Howells's which in the German translation is called "Ein Bühnenspiel ohne Coulissen"?[2] We know there is such a book because a friend of my sister's has reviewed it, and received Mr. Howells's acknowledgement of the fact.[3] But nobody seems to have seen the original; and our bookseller through whom I have tried to get it with other of Howells's works, tells me that his American agent cannot trace it by the German name. I think this is humbug; but there is no help for it. A mere post-card on the subject will make me,

Your's much obliged,
A. Orr.

I was very sorry to have our talk cut short the other Sunday, though I believe the interrupter was a good young fellow in the main, and I am not without

5. WJ's letter is not extant, but HJ's response reveals a more critical attitude toward WDH's theatrical enterprise (*A Counterfeit Presentment*). "I am very glad that Howells's play seemed so pretty, on the stage," HJ wrote. "Much of the dialogue, as it read, was certainly charming; but I should have been afraid of the slimness & un-scenic quality of the plot." HJ goes on to describe his own mastery of the French dramatists—Dumas, Augier, and Sardou—"whom it is greatly lacking to Howells—by the way—to have studied." See HJ to WJ, 1 May [1878], *CWJ* 1: 301.

6. Construction of Red Top, WDH's Belmont home, had begun in 1877. Designed by McKim, Mead, & Bigelow, Red Top reflected the combined tastes of WDH and his wife, even though the house remained the property of Charles Fairchild (1838–1910), a Boston financier, from whom they rented it.

1. This autograph letter, sent to HJ by Alexandra (Leighton) Sutherland Orr (1828–1903), was subsequently mailed to WDH, after HJ added his own postscript. Orr later published a flattering overview of WDH's work entitled "International Novelists and Mr. Howells" (*Contemporary Review* 37 [1880]: 741–65).

2. The unauthorized German translation (Berlin and Stuttgart, 1878) of WDH's *Private Theatricals*, the serialized novel he chose not to publish in volume form.

3. The reviewer, Heinrich Homberger (1838–90), had previously published an appreciative essay on "William Dean Howells" in *Deutsche Rundschau* (June 1877), which was brought to WDH's notice by Thomas Sergeant Perry. Homberger's review of *Private Theatricals* appeared in the Berlin weekly *Magazin für die Literatur des Auslandes* (12 October 1878).

interest in him. But if he had been another *you*, two *is* company, and three none.

[*The letter continues in HJ's hand.*]

Dear H.——

I enclose you the above, tender *p.s.* & all, to show you how wrong you are not to republish "*P. T.*" & what a clamor there is for it in Kensingtonian circles. The letter is from Mrs. Sutherland Orr, a remarkably charming & intelligent woman, sister of Sir Frederick Leighton,[4] President of the R. Academy, & an *intimissima*[5] of Browning. I wrote you lately.

> Many greetings
> H. J. jr

Mrs. O. is *not* the same one I told you about in my last at the dinner party.[6]

28.

JAMES TO HOWELLS, 29 December 1878, Ferrybridge   ALS Houghton
bMS Am 1784 (253) 23

FRYSTON HALL,
FERRYBRIDGE.
Dec. 29$\frac{\text{th}}{}$

Dear Howells—

I am so very glad you liked my tale[1] & forwarded my note to H., O & Co.,[2] from whom I rec'd. a prompt response. Although the tale has no plot, it has, as one may say, a scheme, & I think will be readable enough. You tickle me where I itch when you call me an "artist"; for I confess that if I didn't think I had it in me to be one I shouldn't care to try and make anything of this more or less miserable spectacle of life.—These are graceless allusions, however, for this convivial season; the more especially as I am spending it in considerable revelry. I am passing Xmas week amid the Yorkshire snows, being now at my 2$\frac{\text{d}}{}$ country-house,[3] with thoughts of going on to a third. It is a pleasantish life for a few days, seasoned with an element that we Yankees & storytellers are bound to find

4. Frederick, Lord Leighton (1830–96), British painter and sculptor, president of the Royal Academy of Arts.
5. Confidante.
6. See letter #26.
1. "The Pension Beaurepas," *Atlantic* (April 1879).
2. Houghton, Osgood & Company, the Boston publishers of the *Atlantic*. In all likelihood, HJ had requested payment for the story upon receipt of the manuscript instead of waiting for its publication.
3. Fryston Hall was the Yorkshire country house of Richard Monckton Milnes, Lord Houghton (1809–85), famous for his generosity to geniuses in distress. HJ had come there from Thornes House, where he was the guest of Charles George Milnes Gaskell (1842–1919).

"picturesque", & exhibiting the English character & manners quite at their best. On the whole, however, I enjoy the houses themselves perhaps even more than the people—enjoy their delightful libraries, & those various treasures & comforts accumulated by well-living generations which had discovered "culture" even before it was discovered in Boston. It is 7 p.m.; I am sitting by my bedroom fire in an ancient panelled chamber, waiting till I hear the dinner dressing-bell. There it comes & I must close. I sent Mrs. Howells a *Cornhill* the other day, & will immediately after I return to town send her the sequel.[4] I hope you have had a gentle Xmas & your share, morally & metaphysically too, of plum-pudding. My blessing on your New Year.

Ever faithfully yours
H. James jr

29.

JAMES TO HOWELLS, 7 April 1879, London   ALS Houghton
                                                  bMS Am 1784 (253) 18

April 7$\underline{th}$
3, BOLTON STREET,
PICCADILLY. W.

Dear Howells—

The amazingly poor little notice of your novel in the last (at least my last) *Nation*,[1] makes me feel that I must no longer delay to send you three words of greeting & tell you with what high relish & extreme appreciation I have read it. (I wish you had sent it to me: you ought to have done so, considering all the things I have sent you. I have had to go and buy it—for eight terrible shillings. If you could only appreciate *that* compliment! But do send it, as it is; I want a copy to lend.) It is the most brilliant thing you have done, & I don't see how your own manner can go farther. I sometimes wish in this manner for something a little larger—for a little more *ventilation*, as it were; but in this case the merit & the charm quite run away with the defect, & I have no desire but to praise, compliment & congratulate you! All the last part in especial is richly

---

4. These issues (December 1878–January 1879) contained the two installments of "An International Episode."

1. The *Nation* objected to WDH's choice of a commonplace subject in *The Lady of the Aroostook*. "Like Mr. James," George E. Woodberry noted, "Mr. Howells is a realist—he copies life; and realism in literature, although not so plainly a disappointment as in art, is quite as unsatisfactory." According to this view, the idealizing tendency of imagination was regrettably absent from WDH's novel: "What is valuable in literature is not the miniature of life, but the illumination of life by the imagination; not common things set in the light of common day, but the revelation of what is hidden in common things by the light that never was on sea or land." See the *Nation* 28 (20 March 1879): 205.

successful—& the very ultimate portion triumphant. Bravo & go on—you have only to do so. You are sure of your manner now; you have brought it to a capital point & you have only to apply it. But apply it largely & freely—attack the great field of American life on as many sides as you can. Plunge into it, don't be afraid, & you will do even better things than this.—Over here, I am greatly struck with the extreme *freshness* of your book; (don't take the term amiss)—I mean that newness & directness of personal impression, of feeling as to what you write about, which is the most precious thing in literature—& which is in such vivid contrast with the staleness of tone & flatness of note of most of the writing here. But in America, I must add,—*je ne vois que vous!*[2] I see with great pleasure that your book is largely successful.[3]—I have no great news. I have just got my "Pension Beaurepas," & am wincing over some of the misprints—especially the missing of my cherished little opposition between Beaurepas & Bonrepos.[4] But che vuole,[5] you'll say, with my hand?—The English spring is coming in after a winter of all the devils, & life assumes a sufficiently tolerable aspect. London continues to possess & please me; I have passed a bargain with it forever. The die is cast & the deed is done. The harm, I mean, is done. You can live elsewhere *before* you have ever lived here—but not after. Not that it is any great "harm" to live in this multitudinous world-centre. ——— You will see, I hope unresentfully, that I am to begin before long (in August) a short novel in *Scribner.*[6] They wrote me a couple of months ago a sudden & advantageous proposal, with which I closed. It's to be but a small affair—like the *Europeans.* I had however a notion of offering it to you before assenting to Holland, but as this would have cost a month's uncertainty I decided I couldn't afford it. You must ask me for something. I am expanding considerably (in a literary sense) over here. Farewell, dear Howells. With every blessing—

Yours ever
H. James.

I must squeeze in many salutations to Mrs. Howells & the little—or the big—H.'s.[7]

2. I see only you!

3. Publisher's records indicate that by April 1879 five printings of the novel were needed to meet the demand. Within the first year of publication, 9,427 copies were sold. See Houghton, Osgood Copyright Accounts Ledger: 1876–1881, p. 147 (Houghton Mifflin Archive, Harvard).

4. "The Pension Beaurepas," *Atlantic* (April 1879). In the serialized version of the story, the chief competitor of Mme Beaurepas is named Mme "Bonrep*as*," occluding HJ's intended witticism. When HJ revised this tale for publication in 1880, he changed the name altogether to "Chamousset." For this and other textual variants, see *THJ* 3: 482–508. For his copy text the editor of this volume claims to follow the *Atlantic* version, but he silently alters the spelling of "Bonrepas" to conform to HJ's original intention: "Bonrepos."

5. What would you have?

6. *Confidence* was serialized in *Scribner's Monthly* (August 1879–January 1880) but published as a volume by Houghton, Osgood in 1880.

7. HJ's postscript is written up the narrow left margin of his first sheet of notepaper.

30.

JAMES TO HOWELLS, 17 June 1879, London   ALS Houghton
bMS Am 1784 (253) 20

June 17th.
3, BOLTON STREET,
PICCADILLY. W.

Dear Howells.

Many thanks for the flattering note of the fair Washingtonian.[1] These responsive throbs & thrills are very gratifying—as you of course have known for a long time.

I had been meaning to write a word of answer to your letter of the other day,[2] which was extremely pleasant, in all ways.—I am delighted to hear of the flourishing condition of my fame in the U. S. & feel as if it were a gt. shame that I shouldn't be there to reap a little the harvest of my glory. My fame indeed seems to do very well everywhere—the proportions it has acquired here are a constant surprise to me; it is only my fortune that leaves to be desired.—I hope very much to send you sometime in the autumn a *short* story[3] (size of the *Pension B;*). I don't see my way just now to promising anything larger, & for such a purpose I have a very good subject—a real subject—not a mere pretext like the P.B.—*en tête.*[4] I am pledged to write a long novel as soon as possible, & am obliged to delay it only because I can't literally afford it. Working slowly & painfully as I do I need for such a purpose a longish stretch of time during which I am free to do nothing else, & such liberal periods don't present themselves— I have always to keep the pot-a-boiling. The aforesaid fame, expanding through two hemispheres, is represented by a pecuniary equivalent almost grotesquely small. Your account of the vogue of *D. M.* & the *I. E.*,[5] for instance, embittered my spirit when I reflected that it had awakened no echo (to speak of) in my pocket. I have made 200 $ by the whole American career of D. M. & nothing at all by the Episode (beyond what was paid—a very moderate sum—for the use of it in Harper's Magazine). The truth is I am a very bad bargainer & I was born to be victimized by the pitiless race of publishers.[6] Excuse this sordid plaint; &

1. Possibly Clara Stone Hay (1849–1914), a fellow Ohioan and the wife of John Hay (1838–1905), diplomat, poet, and man of letters.

2. Not extant.

3. HJ never wrote this story; he turned instead to *The Portrait of a Lady.*

4. In mind.

5. "Daisy Miller" and "An International Episode," both published by Harper & Brothers in inexpensive paper wrappers, achieved wide circulation. "Daisy Miller," first serialized in the *Cornhill* (June–July 1878), was also pirated by two American periodicals: *Littell's Living Age* (6 and 27 July 1878) and the *Home Journal* (31 July, 7 and 14 August 1878).

6. HJ's confession does not wholly square with the version of events he presented to his mother. On the heels of the unprecedented success of "Daisy Miller," HJ deliberately wrote "An International

don't indeed take it too hard, for after all I shall have made this year much more than I have ever made before, & shall little by little do better still.—Don't regret having declined the *Episode:* I never offered it to you. You mistake in thinking it to be the same as a certain novel about a Europeanizing heroine touching which I wrote you. That is quite another affair & is a very long story. It is the same as the novel I just now spoke of which I am waiting to write, & which, begun some time, since has remained an aching fragment.[7]—Why don't you take measures to issue your own things here as well as at home? It would be, I shld. think, well worth your while. The other day at a brilliant dinner party a lady sitting next me began eagerly—"You who are an American, *do* you know anything about Mr. Howells?—You know him personally? Oh, tell me *everything* about him. His books have enchanted me! &c". I painted you in the tenderest tints, & I imagine there are many—or would be, if you would give them a chance—who would have the same bright yearning as my neighbor, who was not young or pretty, but who was a clever old woman of the world. What has struck me here, is the almost absurd facility of success. Here are 15 years that I have been addressing the American public, & at the end of a few months I appear to have gone as far with this one as I ever got at home.—I am very happy to hear of your teeming projects for work—the blessing of nature & the smile of circumstance rest upon them all.[8] I remember very well your children's "deserted city," with its bushy vistas & grassy cross-roads. I used very often to play there—alone! Won't you dine with me on the 20th, to meet Turgenieff? I wish you might, indeed. He is in England for a few days, & I have asked John Fiske to meet him, who will tell you of him. A happy summer & a bushel of compliments to your house.

Ever yours
H. James jr

Episode" as a counterpart to it and quickly sold it to the *Cornhill* and *Harper's* for simultaneous publication in December 1878. Between both sources HJ received £95 ($460)—"more money," he told his mother, "than I have ever got for so little labor." The Harpers purchased all rights to "An International Episode" for $200, but decided to market the story directly as an addition to their inexpensive "Half-Hour Series," in which "Daisy Miller" had appeared. See HJ to Mrs. HJ Sr., 29 September 1878 (James Papers, Harvard).

7. *The Portrait of a Lady.*

8. In addition to finishing his serialization of *The Undiscovered Country*, which ran in the *Atlantic* (January–July 1880), WDH began work on several other projects at this time. *A Woman's Reason* was already started but continued to give him trouble and was eventually shelved until 1882; in July 1879 he reported that "A Fearful Responsibility" was under way; by 4 January 1880 parts of *Dr. Breen's Practice* were drafted.

31.

JAMES TO HOWELLS, 14 or 15 July 1879, London   ALS Houghton
                                                    bMS Am 1784 (253) 24

REFORM CLUB,
PALL MALL. S. W.

My dear Howells.—

Your letter of June 29ᵗʰ,[1] asking me for a novel for next year came to me three days since, & I have been thinking over your proposal. I am under certain pledges to the *Cornhill* & *Macmillan*; but having sifted them out & boiled them down, I have come to the conclusion that I may properly undertake to furnish you a glowing romance[2] about the time you propose. That is if my conditions suit you. These bear on two or three points. For instance I have a desire that the next *long* story I write be *really* a long one—i.e. as long as the *American* at least—though very preferably told in a smaller number of longer instalments. As you speak of having 4 novels in one year I am afraid that this *won't* suit you. I think that what I should like would be 6 or 7 numbers of 25 pages apiece. I should also like to begin about the middle of the year—June or July—hardly before, & not later.

—I shall also feel inspired, probably, to ask more for my tale than I have done for any of its predecessors. If I publish in *Macmillan* or the *Cornhill* I can double my profits by appearing also in *Harper*, & I shall have, to a certain extent, to remember this in arranging to appear in one periodical exclusively.[3] But I shall not, in this respect, be at all unreasonable. You had better let me know how these things suit you before you announce me: especially the matter of length. I don't feel as if it would be worth my while to pledge myself so long in advance to furnish a *short* novel—a thing like the *Europeans* or like *Confidence*, now appearing in *Scribner*. I must try & seek a larger success than I have yet obtained in doing something on a larger scale than I have yet done. I am greatly in need of it—of the larger success.

Yours ever
H. James jr

1. Not extant.
2. *The Portrait of a Lady.*
3. HJ had recently discovered the pecuniary advantage of simultaneous publication in English and American magazines. "The Diary of a Man of Fifty" had just appeared in both *Harper's Monthly* and *Macmillan's Magazine* (July 1879); *Washington Square* would soon follow in *Harper's Monthly* and the *Cornhill* (July–November 1880).

32.

JAMES TO HOWELLS, 22 July 1879, London   ALS Houghton
                                                          bMS Am 1784 (253) 21

July 22$\underline{d}$

REFORM CLUB,
PALL MALL. S. W.

Dear Howells—

Immediately after receiving yesterday your letter of July 9$\underline{th}$[1] I went to see both Leslie Stephen & Fredk. Macmillan.[2] The latter told me that their magazine had just made arrangements for fiction in the autumn (a novel of Mrs. Oliphant[3] &c,) & that he didn't see his way, though he should like to, to taking your novel. But to Leslie Stephen I blew upon the trumpet of your fame such a long & mellow blast that I left him with a lively desire to have your work for the *Cornhill* & an intention to write you straightaway. I told him your plot, & he is well aware of your merits. There is no intrinsic obstacle—the only difficulty will hinge upon the time of beginning. But he will write you about this, & I greatly hope the thing will be arranged.[4] I am extremely glad you have desired to present yourself here—it is high time & it is well worth your while. I wish good luck to the negotiations; Stephen, on his side, will not, I think, be difficult.—Your *donnée* strikes me as very promising, though I confess I can't disembarrass myself of an intense aversion to spiritualistic material, which has always seemed to me terribly sordid & dreary. But your subject has the merit of being real, actual & American, & this is a great quality. Continue to Americanize & to *realize:* that is your mission;—& if you stick to it you will become the Zola of the U.S.A.—which I consider a great function.—I wrote you but a few days since about your proposal for my novel, & am glad you hold to it. I suppose I shall hear from you in answer to my letter. I am afraid you are all roasting alive, while we are living under a cold water-spout.

Yours ever
H. James jr

1. Not extant.
2. Leslie Stephen (1832–1904) was editor of the *Cornhill*; Frederick Macmillan (1851–1936) was the heir apparent in the Macmillan family's publishing empire.
3. Margaret Wilson Oliphant (1828–97), English novelist and historical writer. Her lengthy novel *He That Will Not When He May* required thirteen installments in *Macmillan's Magazine* (November 1879–November 1880).
4. From HJ's description of the subject, it seems that WDH first wanted to arrange simultaneous publication for *The Undiscovered Country*, the first installment of which began in the January 1880 issue of the *Atlantic*. A series of letters from Leslie Stephen to WDH show that the American's hopes for British serialization of this and other works were repeatedly frustrated by conflicting publication schedules. Both *Dr. Breen's Practice* and *A Modern Instance* were later discussed as possibilities, but neither could be delivered at times that would suit Stephen's needs. See Leslie Stephen to WDH, 10 December 1879, 14 April 1880, 29 November 1880, and 4 January 1881 (Howells Papers,

33.

JAMES TO HOWELLS, 19 August 1879, London   ALS Houghton
bMS Am 1784 (253) 22

My address is always here.
3, BOLTON STREET,
PICCADILLY. W.
Aug. 19$\underline{th}$

My dear Howells—

Without waiting for your answer to my letter of some time since (I forget exactly when,) I think it better to write to you again. Shortly after I wrote before, the Macmillans came down upon me with the assurance that they hold me definitely pledged to furnish them a serial for next year. They are perfectly willing to *simultane*, & if you can be brought to do so, the thing can easily be settled. Your note to me about "simultaning" your own next novel has led me to believe that you might be so brought. (You will let me hear by the way, I hope, what has come of my visit to Leslie Stephen—he himself has left town.) With my chance here & my chance at home, it is very difficult for me not to wish to bring out in both places at once, & escape the bad economy of lavishing a valuable fiction upon a single public. If objection to simultaneous publication is a matter of dignity with the *Atlantic*, there is no reason why it should be more difficult than Blackwood, Fraser, the *Cornhill* & Macmillan.[1] I hope it won't, as this will, in this case & all others to come, greatly simplify the producing-question with me—I can always be your novelist if I can publish here also. Try & think I am worth it—worth having on those terms. If you will see it so, I engage to produce the most immortal & fortune-making (all round) works. Will you kindly let me know about this as soon as possible.—I am spending this cold, wet, dismal summer, as you see, in this big, empty wilderness of paving-stones. It's horribly un-rural & little natural, but I go abroad (to Paris) for the autumn, on Sept. 1$\underline{st}$. I have lately seen several times our friend Clemens,[2] on his way back to Hartford. He seemed to me a most excellent pleasant fellow—& what they call here very "quaint." Quaint he is! & his two ladies[3] charming.

Yours ever faithfully—
H. James jr

Harvard); and WDH to Lawrence Barrett, 11 April 1880, in *Staging Howells: Plays and Correspondence with Lawrence Barrett*, ed. George Arms et al. (Albuquerque: University of New Mexico Press, 1994), 129–30.

1. The leading British literary monthlies.
2. Samuel Langhorne Clemens ("Mark Twain") (1835–1910) had been traveling with his family in Europe since April 1878.
3. Probably Clemens's daughters, Susy (1872–96) and Clara (1874–1964).

34.

JAMES TO HOWELLS, 23 August 1879, London   ALS Houghton
                                                            bMS Am 1784 (253) 19

April 23$\frac{d}{}$[1]

REFORM CLUB,
PALL MALL. S. W.

Dear Howells,—

If I had only kept over my letter of three or four days since, 24 hours, I should have written it, to better purpose, with yours of the 8$\underline{th}$[2] before me. I learn by this, to my satisfaction, that you are willing, with regard to my projected serial, to entertain the idea of simultaneity, & I hasten to be explicit, as you say, in respect to my terms in this case. Considering that the instalments are to be long ones, & the thing is to appear nearly a year hence, by which time I hope to have achieved a surcease of reputation, I don't see how I can ask less than $250 a number—the same price that was paid for the *Europeans*, & that Scribner pays me for the *Confidence*, which is in short instalments. I hope this will suit Osgood,[3] & that you will find yourselves able to consent to the simultaneity of appearance with Macmillan of which I treated in my letter of three days ago. I dwelt so on this in that letter, that it doesn't seem to me worthwhile to say at present anything about terms for exclusive publication, as in case the simultaneous business doesn't suit you I fear I should have to postpone writing a novel for the *Atlantic* alone. But I trust it will suit. I don't pretend to fix the *number* of instalments, more than to say, *probably* not less than six, & more than eight. Also it *may* be that I shall have to ask you to begin in *June*: but this I shall know later. I don't know that there is anything else to settle or to touch upon. I think I told you that my title would (probably) be "The Portrait of a Lady." But on this meanwhile please observe complete silence. And do let me hear from you at your 1$\underline{st}$ commodity.

—I am so very glad that Leslie Stephen wrote to you immediately & I hope your matter may be settled.[4] I should have liked to see the "wonderful ladies" at your hotel: but verily there are such everywhere![5]

Yours
H. J. jr

1. HJ's dating of this letter is clearly erroneous.

2. Not extant.

3. In 1878 James Ripley Osgood had merged his publishing firm with Henry O. Houghton's to become Houghton, Osgood & Company, thereby restoring Osgood's connection to the *Atlantic*.

4. Because of outstanding commitments, the *Cornhill* could not begin *The Undiscovered Country* in January 1880, and WDH dropped the question of simultaneous publication for that novel. See letter #32, note 4.

5. As was customary, WDH and his family spent a week at the seashore in early August 1879.

35.

JAMES TO HOWELLS, 31 October 1879, Paris

ALS Houghton
bMS Am 1784 (253) 126

Paris. 42 Rue Cambon.
Oct. 31st.

My dear Howells—

I have no less than *three* notes from you[1] to thank you for, the last of which appeared (excuse my inadvertance, which, in a serial writer addressing an editor, is natural; I mean *arrived*) a few days since, accompanied by a graceful missive from your wife, for which I beg you to express to her my gratitude, & by a little picture of your house, which is evidently a very fascinating structure.[2] The point to be settled between us was whether my next year's novel[3] should begin in *July*. It appears now, after much delay, that *Macmillan* would greatly prefer *August*. There are various good reasons for this, & I have assented to it. I hope you will be able to do the same, & that it won't incommode you. *August* then let it be—my 1st instalment will appear in Macmillan for *August, 1880,* & you will proceed accordingly. As usual, I haven't much news for you, as I don't, as you know, fabricate the article in large quantities. A man in my situation can only entertain his friends by getting married or by dying, & I fear the one event is as distant as I hope the other to be. Tell Mrs. Howells I am much flattered by her strictures on my photo., as what conviction can be more delightful than that a charming woman has examined one's image with care? As for my *eyes*, in the said photog., it may be that you—or rather your wife,—can't see into them; but for all that, meanwhile, they are looking straight at *her*. I had flattered myself that the face had the happy expression consequent upon such an occupation.

—I am spending the autumn in this place, which on the whole, familiarity never makes stale, & am not without a hope of spending three or four weeks in Italy before I return to England. Much as I have learned to appreciate the latter country as a residence I freely confess that I shall enjoy it the more, when I return, for having been for some time absent from it. At the same time, absence from London makes me feel how fond I am of it. It operates in the same way with regard to my native land, which I hope to behold again some ten months hence. If no unexpected obstacles present themselves I shall go home for a long visit, about that period; & then I shall climb your graceful slope, & if Mrs. Howells will allow me, sit in her loggia.—I wrote you some time since (before the matter of my long novel was settled,) that I should send you a short tale (25 pages) this autumn. I have not on account of the other project abandoned this one, & shall probably send you the story in question (a good one) within two

1. None extant.
2. WDH and his family had moved into Red Top, at Belmont, in 1878.
3. *The Portrait of a Lady.*

or three weeks.[4] I hope the fact of my appearing later on a larger scale will not render it superfluous. Farewell, my old one, as they say here. Carry yourself well, as they also say; &, as they further express it, salute your wife & children a 1000 times for me. I hope you are working, & doing everything else, happily.

"All to you"
H. James jr

I am glad to see you Tauchnitized[5]—your last book forms one of the ornaments of *the Boulevarde*.

36.

JAMES TO HOWELLS, 3 January 1880, London   ALS Houghton
bMS Am 1784 (253) 25

Jan. 3$\underline{d}$ 1880.
3, BOLTON STREET,
PICCADILLY. W.

My dear Howells.

I have just received your note of the 21$\underline{st}$,[1] enclosing the report of the Holmes breakfast.[2] This must have been a wonderful affair & I should have greatly liked to be in the thick of it. But since then you have had affairs more wonderful still. Three days ago, in a country-house in Yorkshire,[3] I beheld in a Leeds paper the telegram announcing the destruction by fire of poor H. & O's premises.[4] I have learned no further details, & am quite in the dark as to the consequences of the thing upon their business. May they be as light as possible. I am afraid Osgood will begin to believe in his evil star. But what I chiefly wish to express (for there are natural limits to one's sympathy with one's publishers,) is the hope that *you* are not injured or compromised by it, & that the *Atlantic* is not shaken. Are your books or plates burned up? For mine it doesn't matter—

4. Probably "A Bundle of Letters," which first appeared in the *Parisian* (18 December 1879), an English-language weekly published in Paris. The story was quickly pirated in America by Loring of Boston and George Munro in the Seaside Library. See *A Bibliography of Henry James*, 47–49.

5. Samuel L. Clemens had brought WDH to the attention of Christian Bernhard Tauchnitz (1816–95), a continental publisher of books for English-speaking tourists abroad. After negotiating the matter with WDH, Tauchnitz brought out *A Foregone Conclusion* and *The Lady of the Aroostook*. Since 1878 he had also published HJ's work. Even in the absence of international copyright, Tauchnitz paid his authors modest sums for the right to reprint their material.

1. Not extant.

2. WDH had organized a testimonial breakfast for Oliver Wendell Holmes (1809–94), the self-proclaimed Autocrat of the Breakfast Table, on 3 December 1879. See John T. Morse Jr., *Life and Letters of Oliver Wendell Holmes*, 2 vols. (Boston: Houghton, Mifflin, 1896), 2: 43–44.

3. HJ had spent New Year's at Thornes House in Wakefield as the guest of Charles Milnes Gaskell.

4. On the night of 28 December 1879, fire destroyed the Boston offices of Houghton, Osgood & Company. The company's inventory at the Riverside Press was not affected.

they sell so little. I hope, however, to hear that the plates (including those of a book they are now printing for me—*Confidence*—) were not in Boston but at the Riverside, which would seem their natural place. At the best, though, it must have knocked you all about a good deal; & for whatever in commodity you may have suffered, you have my lively sympathy. Do write me a line when you can, projecting a ray of lurid light upon the causes & consequences of the event. I suppose the firm will pick itself up, & build again. — As a compensatory topic, I have been reading your "Undiscovered Country,"[5] & discovering in it all sorts of excellent points. You have got hold of something really new & unworked, & you work it in this first number with admirable effect. I view with a certain slight alarm the 2 young men friends who chaff each other (as they have become rather familiar figures in your graceful page;)[6] but doubtless I am on a false scent, & the reluctant Egeria, is in any case a most interesting invention— a real *trouvaille*.[7] I blush to record that my short story has perforce stretched itself into a long one—three nos.—& I have (virtually) sold it to the persuasive *Scribner*, who however will probably not publish it for a year.[8] I tried to squeeze it down for you, but it was no use. It seemed to me absurd to offer you anything in more than one instalment—when I am to give you so many instalments later in the year.[9] The fotog. is like you, but not brilliantly so; though it testifies to your blooming youth. Such as it is, however, I thank you for it; & shall show it to the British matron, but not give it to her. In France I tried to be agreeable to the local ladies by having you (in Tauchnitz) charmingly bound & presenting you to them—a good turn that you rendered me. But you will be both amazed & amused to learn that in wishing to do the same to a young girl, (a charming French one,) I was sternly checked. The "F. G." & the "L. of the A."[10] were declared unadapted to the perusal of this class—one as representing a priest in love, & the other a young girl alone for weeks with a lot of men. Write me what you can about the fire, & receive the wishes of the season for Mrs. H. & all the house—

Ever

H. *James jr*

5. Serialized in the *Atlantic* (January–July 1880).

6. In *The Undiscovered Country* this conflict surfaces between the poor journalist Ford and his friend Phillips, a genial (and wealthy) collector and man-about-town. Rivalries based on class and vocation also figure in *A Foregone Conclusion* (Henry Ferris, the painter/consul in Venice, and Don Ippolito, a hapless priest); *Private Theatricals*, published in 1921 as *Mrs. Farrell* (William Gilbert, an aggressive New York lawyer, and Wayne Easton, a reticent man of leisure); and *The Lady of the Aroostook* (Charles Dunham, an unpretentious bourgoise, and James Staniford, a Boston aesthete).

7. Discovery or find.

8. HJ eventually sold *Washington Square* to the *Cornhill* and *Harper's Monthly*, where it appeared in six installments.

9. *The Portrait of a Lady*.

10. *A Foregone Conclusion* and *The Lady of the Aroostook*.

William Dean Howells, review of Hawthorne, Atlantic Monthly 45 *(February 1880): 282–85.*

Mr. James's book on Hawthorne, in Morley's English Men of Letters series,[1] merits far closer examination and carefuller notice than we can give it here, alike for the interest of its subject, the peculiarity of its point of view, and the charm and distinction of its literature. An American author writing of an American author for an English public incurs risks with his fellow-countrymen which Mr. James must have faced, and is much more likely to possess the foreigner whom he addresses with a clear idea of our conditions than to please the civilization whose portrait is taken. Forty-six, fifty, sixty-four, are not dates so remote, nor are Salem and Concord societies so extinct, that the people of those periods and places can be safely described as provincial, not once, but a dozen times; and we foresee, without any very powerful prophetic lens, that Mr. James will be in some quarters promptly attainted of high treason. For ourselves, we will be content with saying that the provinciality strikes us as somewhat over-insisted upon, and that, speaking from the point of not being at all provincial ourselves, we think the epithet is sometimes mistaken. If it is not provincial for an Englishman to be English or a Frenchman French, then it is not so for an American to be American; and if Hawthorne was "exquisitely provincial," one had better take one's chance of universality with him than with almost any Londoner or Parisian of his time. Provinciality, we understand it, is a thing of the mind or the soul; but if it is a thing of the experiences, then that is another matter, and there is no quarrel. Hawthorne undoubtedly saw less of the world in New England than one sees in Europe, but he was no cockney, as Europeans are apt to be.

At the same time we must not be thought to deny the value and delightfulness of those chapters on Salem and Brook Farm[2] and Concord. They are not very close in description, and the places seem deliciously divined rather than studied. But where they are used unjustly, there will doubtless be abundant defense; and if Salem or Brook Farm be mute, the welkin will probably respond to the cries of certain critics who lie in wait to make life sorrowful to any one dealing lightly with the memory of Thoreau or the presence of the poet Channing. What will happen to a writer who says of the former that he was "worse than provincial, he was parochial," and of the latter that he resembled the former in "having produced literary compositions more esteemed by the few than by the many," we wait with the patience and security of a spectator at an *auto da fé,* to see. But even an unimbattled outsider may suggest that the essential

1. John Morley (1838–1923), stateman, essayist, and biographer, served as general editor of Macmillan's popular "English Men of Letters" series.
2. The Brook Farm Institute of Agriculture and Education (1841–47) was a utopian experiment in communal living in which many New England literary intellectuals took an interest. Some, including Hawthorne and William Henry Channing (1810–84), took up residence there for a time, while others, including Ralph Waldo Emerson (1803–82), Henry David Thoreau (1817–62), and Margaret Fuller (1810–50) were occasional visitors.

large-mindedness of Concord, as expressed in literature, is not sufficiently recognized, although it is thoroughly felt. The treatment of the culture foible and of the colorless æsthetic joys, the attribution of "a great deal of Concord five and thirty years ago" to the remark of a visitor of Hawthorne that Margaret Fuller "had risen perceptibly into a higher state of being since their last meeting," are exquisite,—too exquisite, we fear, for the sense of most Englishmen, and not too fine only for the rarefied local consciousness which they may sting. Emerson is indeed devoutly and amply honored, and there is something particularly sweet and tender in the characterization of such surviving Brook Farmers as the author remembers to have met; but even in speaking of Emerson, Mr. James has the real misfortune to call his grand poem for the dedication of the monument to Concord Fight a "little hymn."[3] It is little as Milton's sonnet on Shakespeare is little.

We think, too, that in his conscience against brag and *chauvinism* Mr. James puts too slight a value upon some of Hawthorne's work. It is not enough to say of a book so wholly unexampled and unrivaled as The Scarlet Letter that it was "the finest piece of imaginative writing put forth in" America; as if it had its parallel in any literature. When he comes to speak of the romances in detail, he repairs this defect of estimation in some degree; but here again his strictures seem somewhat mistaken. No one better than Mr. James knows the radical difference between a romance and a novel, but he speaks now of Hawthorne's novels, and now of his romances, throughout, as if the terms were convertible; whereas the romance and the novel are as distinct as the poem and the novel. Mr. James excepts to the people in The Scarlet Letter, because they are rather types than persons, rather conditions of the mind than characters; as if it were not almost precisely the business of the romance to deal with types and mental conditions. Hawthorne's fictions being always and essentially, in conception and performance, romances, and not novels, something of all Mr. James's special criticism is invalidated by the confusion which, for some reason not made clear, he permits himself. Nevertheless, his analysis of the several books and of the shorter tales is most interesting; and though we should ourselves place The Blithedale Romance before The House of the Seven Gables, and should rank it much higher than Mr. James seems to do, we find ourselves consenting oftener than dissenting as we read his judgments. An admirably clear and just piece of criticism, we think, is that in which he pronounces upon the slighter and cheaper *motif* of Septimius Felton. But here there are not grounds for final sentence; it is possible, if that book had received the author's last touches, it might have been, after all, a playful and gentle piece of irony rather than a tragedy.

3. Emerson's "Concord Hymn: Sung at the Completion of the Battle Monument, April 19, 1836," the last stanza of which is best remembered:

> By the rude bridge that arched the flood,
> Their flag to April's breeze unfurled,
> Here once the embattled farmers stood,
> And fired the shot heard round the world.

What gives us entire satisfaction, however, is Mr. James's characterization, or illustration, of Hawthorne's own nature. He finds him an innocent, affectionate heart, extremely domestic, a life of definite, high purposes singularly unbaffled, and an "unperplexed intellect." The black problem of evil, with which his Puritan ancestors wrestled concretely, in groans and despair, and which darkens with its portentous shadow nearly everything that Hawthorne wrote, has become his literary material; or, in Mr. James's finer and more luminous phrase, he "transmutes this heavy moral burden into the very substance of the imagination." This strikes us as beautifully reasonable and true, and we will not cloud it with comment of ours. But satisfactorily as Mr. James declares Hawthorne's personality in large, we do not find him sufficient as to minor details and facts. His defect, or his error, appears oftenest in his discussion of the note-books, where he makes plain to himself the simple, domestic, democratic qualities in Hawthorne, and yet maintains that he sets down slight and little aspects of nature because his world is small and vacant. Hawthorne noted these because he loved them, and as a great painter, however full and vast his world is, continues to jot down whatever strikes him as picturesque and characteristic. The disposition to allege this inadequate reason comes partly from that confusion of the novelist's and the romancer's work of which we have spoken, and partly from a theory, boldly propounded, that it needs a long history and "a complex social machinery to set a writer in motion." Hawthorne himself shared, or seemed to share, this illusion, and wrote The Marble Faun, so inferior, with its foreign scene, to the New England romances, to prove the absurdity of it. As a romancer, the twelve years of boyhood which he spent in the wild solitudes of Maine were probably of greater advantage to him than if they had been passed at Eton and Oxford. At least, until some other civilization has produced a romantic genius at all comparable to his, we must believe this. After leaving out all those novelistic "properties," as sovereigns, courts, aristocracy, gentry, castles, cottages, cathedrals, abbeys, universities, museums, political class, Epsoms, and Ascots, by the absence of which Mr. James suggests our poverty to the English conception, we have the whole of human life remaining, and a social structure presenting the only fresh and novel opportunities left to fiction, opportunities manifold and inexhaustible. No man would have known less what to do with that dreary and worn-out paraphernalia than Hawthorne.

We can only speak of the excellent comment upon Hawthorne's Old Home, and the skillful and manly way in which Mr. James treats of that delicate subject to his English audience. Skillful and manly the whole book is,—a miracle of tact and of self-respect, which the author need not fear to trust to the best of either of his publics. There is nothing to regret in the attitude of the book; and its literature is always a high pleasure, scarcely marred by some evidences of hurry, and such *writerish* passages as that in which *sin* is spoken of as "this baleful substantive with its attendant adjective."

It is a delightful and excellent essay, refined and delicate in perception, generous in feeling, and a worthy study of the unique romancer whom its closing words present with justice so subtle and expression so rich:—

"He was a beautiful, natural, original genius, and his life had been singularly exempt from worldly preoccupations and vulgar efforts. It had been as pure, as simple, as unsophisticated, as his work. He had lived primarily in his domestic affections, which were of the tenderest kind; and then—without eagerness, without pretension, but with a great deal of quiet devotion—in his charming art. His work will remain; it is too original and exquisite to pass away; among the men of imagination he will always have his niche. No one has had just that vision of life, and no one has had a literary form that more successfully expressed his vision. He was not a moralist, and he was not simply a poet. The moralists are weightier, denser, richer, in a sense; the poets are more purely inconclusive and irresponsible. He combined in a singular degree the spontaneity of the imagination with a haunting care for moral problems. Man's conscience was his theme, but he saw it in the light of a creative fancy which added, out of its own substance, an interest, and, I may almost say, an importance."

37.

JAMES TO HOWELLS, 31 January 1880, London   ALS Houghton
bMS Am 1784 (253) 26

Jan. 31st
3, BOLTON STREET,
PICCADILLY. W.

My dear Howells—

Your letter of Jan. 19th,[1] & its inclosure (your review of my *Hawthorne*) came to me last night, & I must thank you without delay for each of them.

I am very happy to hear the effects of the fire[2] were so minimized by the moment at which it took place; & evidently, both in your letter & in your article, you had been writing in a smokeless air. Your review of my book is very handsome & friendly & commands my liveliest gratitude. Of course your graceful strictures seem to yourself more valid than they do to me. The little book was a tolerably deliberate & meditated performance, & I should be prepared to do battle for most of the convictions expressed. It is quite true I use the word provincial too many times—I hated myself for't, even while I did it (just as I overdo the epithet "dusky".) But I don't at all agree with you in thinking that "if it is not provincial for an Englishman to be English, a Frenchman French &c, so it is not provincial for an American to be American." So it is not provincial for a Russian, an Australian, a Portuguese, a Dane, a Laplander, to savour of their respective countries: that would be where this argument would land you. I think it is extremely provincial for a Russian to be very Russian, a Portuguese very Portuguese &c; for the simple reason that certain national types are essentially & intrinsically provincial. I sympathize even less with your protest against the idea that it takes an old civilization to set a novelist in motion—a proposi-

1. Not extant.
2. See letter #36, note 4.

tion that seems to me so true as to be a truism. It is on manners, customs, usages, habits, forms, upon all these things matured & established, that a novelist lives—they are the very stuff his work is made of; & in saying that in the absence of those "dreary & worn-out paraphernalia" which I enumerate as being wanting in American society,[3] "we have simply the whole of human life left," you beg (to my sense) the question. I should say we had just so much less of it as these same "paraphernalia" represent, & I think they represent an enormous quantity of it. I shall feel refuted only when we have produced (setting the present high company—yourself & me—for obvious reasons, apart) a gentleman who strikes me as a novelist—as belonging to the family of Balzac & Thackeray.[4] Of course, in the absence of this godsend, it is but a harmless amusement that we should reason about it, & maintain that if right were right he should already be here. I will freely admit that such a genius will get on *only* by agreeing with your view of the case—to do something great he must feel as you feel about it. But then I doubt whether such a genius—a man of the faculty of Balzac & Thackeray—*could* agree with you! When he does I will lie flat on my stomach & do him homage—in the very centre of the contributors' club,[5] or on the threshold of the Magazine, or in any public place you may appoint!—But I didn't mean to wrangle with you—I meant only to thank you & to express my sense of how happily you turn those things.

—I am greatly amused at your picture of the contributing blood-hounds whom you are holding in check. I wish, immensely, that you would let them fly at me—though there is no reason, certainly, that the decent public should be bespattered, periodically, with my gore.—However my tender (or rather my very tough) flesh is prescient already of the Higginsonian fangs.[6] Happy man, to be

3. The offending passage reads:
The negative side of the spectacle on which Hawthorne looked out, in his contemplative saunterings and reveries, might, indeed, with a little ingenuity, be made almost ludicrous; one might enumerate the items of high civilization, as it exists in other countries, which are absent from the texture of American life, until it should become a wonder to know what was left. No State, in the European sense of the word, and indeed barely a specific national name. No sovereign, no court, no personal loyalty, no aristocracy, no church, no clergy, no army, no diplomatic service, no country gentlemen, no palaces, no castles, nor manors, nor old country-houses, nor parsonages, nor thatched cottages nor ivied ruins; no cathedrals, nor abbeys, nor little Norman churches; no great Universities nor public schools—no Oxford, nor Eton, nor Harrow; no literature, no novels, no museums, no pictures, no political society, no sporting class—no Epsom nor Ascot! (*Literary Criticism* 1: 351–52)
4. Honoré de Balzac (1799–1850), French novelist greatly admired by HJ, and William Makepeace Thackeray (1811–63), Victorian novelist and satirist.
5. A column in the *Atlantic* containing brief reviews, commentary, and personal notes by and about regular contributors to the magazine. WDH originated the feature in 1877.
6. HJ's *Hawthorne* provoked lively responses in the American press; many reviewers, like WDH, were annoyed by the patronizing attitude HJ seemed to show toward Hawthorne, an attitude they equated with an anti-American, or excessively Anglophilic, demeanor. One of HJ's sterner critics, Thomas Wentworth Higginson (1823–1911), may have been suppressed by WDH, but it is likely that a hostile review in *Scribner's Monthly* (19 [April 1880]: 943–44), is from his pen. From the first page, the review complains, "[I]t is apparent . . . that Mr. James lacks the underlying characteristic

going, like that, to see your plays acted.[7] It is a sensation I am dying, (though as yet not trying,) to cultivate. What a tremendous quantity of work you must get through in these years! I am impatient for the next *Atlantic*.[8] What is your *Cornhill* novel about?[9] I am to precede it with a poorish story in three numbers—a tale purely American, the writing of which made me feel acutely the want of the "paraphernalia."[10] I *must* add, however, (to return for a moment to this) that I applaud & esteem you highly for not feeling it; i.e. the want. You are entirely right—magnificently & heroically right—to do so, & on the day you make your readers—I mean the readers who know & appreciate the paraphernalia—do the same, you will be the American Balzac. That's a great mission—go in for it! Wherever you go, receive, & distribute among your wife & children, the blessing of

yours ever—
H. James jr

38.

JAMES TO HOWELLS, 18 April 1880, Florence   ALS Houghton
bMS Am 1784 (253) 27

Florence, April 18$\underline{\text{th}}$

Carino Amico[1]—

The most caressing epithets of a caressing language are not out of place in regard to the particular motive of my writing to you. My imagination seeks eagerly for anything that will ease me off a little & rob my letter of its sting. This sting resides, brutally speaking, in my earnest wish that you may find it not fatally inconvenient to begin my promised serial[2] in *October* instead of *August!* A postponement of two whole months!—the thing will probably have to you an impudent sound. But I throw myself on your mercy & urge upon your attention that the story shall be a 100 per cent better by each day that you have to

---

which a good biographer must have, namely, sympathy. Mr. James shows no sympathy whatever with the United States, New England or Hawthorne. It is not now his fault; it has become his misfortune" (943). In an essay first published in November 1879, Higginson had remarked upon HJ's "indifference to careful local coloring," especially when the scene was laid in the United States. "When he draws Americans in Europe," Higginson charged, "he is at home; when he brings Europeans across the Atlantic, he never seems quite sure of his ground, except in Newport, which is in some respects the least American spot on this continent." See his *Short Studies of American Authors*, 56.

7. WDH's *Yorick's Love*, staged by Lawrence Barrett (1838–91), opened in Boston on 20 January after initial performances in Philadelphia.

8. WDH's *Undiscovered Country* was appearing serially.

9. HJ had thought that the *Cornill* was to publish *The Undiscovered Country*; see letter #32, note 4.

10. The *Cornhill* published *Washington Square* in six installments (June–November 1880).

1. Dear Friend.

2. *The Portrait of a Lady.*

wait. My motives for this petition are twofold. In the first place I withdrew a month ago from London & its uproar, its distractions & interruptions, in order to concentrate myself upon my work. But if London is uproarious, Italy is insidious, perfidious, fertile in pretexts for one's haunting its lovely sights & scenes rather than one's writing-table; so that, in respect to my novel, it has been a month lost rather than gained. In the second place I think I wrote you before that I lately finished a serial tale for the *Cornhill*.[3] This has proved by the editor's measurement longer than by my own, so that instead of running through 4 numbers, it will extend to *six*. As it begins in *June* this will make it terminate in *November*; & it will be agreeable to *Macmillan* that the novel for them & you, shall not begin till the thing in the *Cornhill* is virtually leaving the scene. Behold, dear Howells, my reasons; I trust they will seem to you worthy of a compatriot & a Christian, & that the delay won't cause you any material discomfort. It will leave me a chance to get forward a good deal further than I should otherwise do, before beginning to publish. I shall assume that I have touched you by this appeal, & shall proceed in consequence; but a line in answer (to 3 Bolton St. Piccadilly,) will nevertheless be very welcome.

—Come back to Italy as soon as you can: but don't come with a masterpiece suspended in the air by the tenderest portions of its texture; or else forbid yourself the pleasure of paying your proper respects to this land of loveliness.—I have just come back from a ten days' run to Rome & Naples, & shall be in this place for the longer or shorter time that I remain absent from England. Florence is delightful, as usual, but I am lacerated with the effort of tearing myself away from Rome, where I feared I shouldn't do much work, but which is, to Florence, as sunlight unto moonlight.—I hope that, putting aside the untoward incident embodied in this letter, everything is well with you. I read your current novel[4] with pleasure, but I don't think the subject fruitful, & I suspect that much of the public will agree with me. I make bold to say this because, as the thing will be finished by this time, it won't matter that my rude words discourage you. Also, I am in a fine position to talk about the public's agreeing with me!—But if you do, sometimes, I don't care about the others! Greet me your wife & children, & believe me

your devotissimo—
H. James jr

3. *Washington Square.*
4. *The Undiscovered Country.*

39.

ALS Houghton
                                                                bMS Am 1784 (253) 28

3, BOLTON STREET,
PICCADILLY. W.
June 6<u>th</u>

Dear Howells.

   You received my request like an angel, & I am duly grateful. You shall have
the opening sheets of the story, printed, in abundantly good time for your own
use. The instalments may prove rather shorter than I proposed, owing to the
apparently limited capacity of Macmillan; but they will be quite as long, probably as you care to have them. I returned from Italy about a fortnight since, & a
few days ago sent you the *Contemporary*, as I promised, with Mrs. Sutherland
Orr's article on your books.[1] You will probably have seen it, but I wished to keep
my promise. The article will have helped to make you more known here; it
seems very kindly in tone & more discriminating than I usually find such things.
The writer is a pleasant, clever, accomplished woman, in bad health, with no
eyesight, & of rather a philosophic turn. Her paper is a good forerunner to your
tale in the *Cornhill*.[2] (I sent you by the way the opening of my own short story
in that periodical.)[3] I hear you are having a furious inception, as the papers say,
of summer; but I trust it will burn itself out. I envy you your visit to Washington[4] & should be glad to hear of your adventures. I am expecting my brother
here next week;[5] I hope he may lately have seen you.—Love to your house (I
don't mean Houghton & Mifflin!)[6]

                                                                Faithfully yours
                                                                H. James jr

   1. A[lexandra (Leighton) Sutherland] Orr, "International Novelists and Mr. Howells," *Contemporary Review* 37 (1880): 741–65. Speaking of Howells and James, Orr wrote:
   [T]hey are probably the first American novelists who have regarded their countrymen from
   the distance which allows of their being critically drawn. We all know and appreciate this
   perspective in Mr. James's work; the English public has yet to know and appreciate it in that
   of Mr. Howells; and it is the more striking in his case that he is in all respects the more
   American of the two. He is, in fact, the strongest exponent of that union of national feeling
   and extra-national judgment which constitutes the representative quality of their genius.
   (742)
   2. HJ was still unaware that WDH's plans for simultaneous publication of his work had fallen
through.
   3. The first *Cornhill* installment of *Washington Square* appeared in June 1880.
   4. WDH and his family had been guests at the White House. President Rutherford B. Hayes
was Elinor Mead Howells's cousin.
   5. William James arrived in London in early June and stayed with HJ for a month before going
to the continent for a summer holiday.
   6. The partnership of Houghton, Osgood & Company was dissolved in May 1880. Houghton,
Mifflin & Company retained the *Atlantic* and all the prior firm's copyright contracts; James R. Osgood & Company (1880–85) became an independent enterprise and mounted an aggressive campaign to acquire new titles from established *Atlantic* writers, including WDH and HJ.

40.

JAMES TO HOWELLS, 20 July 1880, London

ALS Houghton
bMS Am 1784 (253) 29

3, BOLTON STREET,
PICCADILLY. W.
July 20$^{\underline{th}}$

Dear Howells.

I send you to day 48 printed pages of my novel[1]—which should have gone to you five days since, but that just as I received the sheets from the printer I was taken with a sharp attack of illness which kept me in bed for three days, unable to use a pen. This is the first moment I have got my wits about me again. (I had a terrible siege of neuralgic pain in my head, to which, I am sorry to say, I am wofully liable.)

What you have herewith are the sheets of Macmillan containing the 1st part (number) of the story & the greater portion of the second number. You shall have in two or three days the rest of the second & the whole of the third. After that the sequel will flow freely. You will see that the 1st part is *very* long (26¼ pages of *Macmillan*) (which will make, I shld. say, just about the same of the *Atlantic.*) The following numbers will, as a general thing, probably be shorter by two or three pages. I wrote you that *October* was the month fixed for beginning here; but I am afraid I did not make as clear to you as I ought (as I was indeed myself rather inattentive to the fact at the time) that for the *Atlantic* this must mean the NOVEMBER number. It is only by your publishing a fortnight after Macmillan, rather than a fortnight before, that I can secure the English copyright: an indispensable boon. This is what Harper is doing with my little *Washington Square*, which beginning in the *Cornhill* in *June*, began in Harper in July. Don't worry about the *P. of a L.* being stolen in the few days interval of time that may elapse between the October *Macmillan* arriving in New York, & the *Atlantic* coming out: for Houghton & Mifflin will please immediately have the thing copyrighted for me, & each number of Macmillan will contain (as the current *Cornhills* do) a footnote duly setting forth that I have taken out the American copyright & will have my pound of flesh from whomsoever infringes it. In *November* then I look for you to begin. I feel as if I had done nothing but delay & disappoint you with regard to this production; but you see what it is to have given me a boundless faith in your *bonté.*[2] Prove it once more.

I am much obliged to you for the pretty volume of the *Undiscovered*, which I immediately read with greater comfort & consequence than in the magazine.[3] My first impression of it remains, however (& you have probably found it the general impression)—that it is the least *entertaining* of your books. The subject

1. During the serial run of *The Portrait of a Lady*, HJ sent WDH page proofs, printed by Macmillan, with his corrections.
2. Kindness.
3. Houghton, Mifflin & Company published *The Undiscovered Country* in June 1880.

is interesting & the character of Boynton very finely conceived; but the spirit-ism, which at the beginning one looks to see more illustrated, vanishes from the scene, & the Shakerism which comes in, seems arbitrary & unaccounted for. You strike me, once you have brought in Shakerism, as not having made quite enough of it—not made it grotesque, or pictorial, or whatever-it-may-be, enough; as having described it too un-ironically & as if you were a Shaker yourself. (Perhaps you are—unbeknown to your correspondents & contribu-tors!!—& that this is the secret of the book!) Furthermore, I think Egeria is the least individual & personal of your heroines; and I resent her suburban matri-mony with Mr. Ford (whom I don't care for, either,) at the end. On the other hand the subject is a larger & heavier one than you have yet tried, & you have carried it off with great ease & the flexibility which shows how well you have learned your art. Excuse this diatribe, which is really cool as accompanying an appeal, on my own part, to your consideration. I have as usual no personal news. The only important things that can happen to me are to die and to marry, and as yet I do neither. I shall in any case do the former first; then, in the next world, I shall marry Helen of Troy. My brother has been spending a month with me & has left for Switzerland. I shall be writing you again in a few days.

Yours ever faithfully
H. *James jr*

41.

JAMES TO HOWELLS, 18 August 1880, London

ALS Houghton
bMS Am 1784 (253) 30

REFORM CLUB,
PALL MALL. S. W.
Aug. 18th

Dear Howells—

I am afraid I have caused you a good deal of disappointment, but I hope, & believe, you will find that it rests on no very serious basis. On the receipt, this morning, of your note of the 5th, I immediately went & asked the Macmillans whether it would be possible to telegraph you, as you desired, that you were free to begin my novel[1] in *October*. The result of my conversation was I sent you half an hour afterwards the telegram that Houghton & Mifflin will by this time have received.[2] The Macmillans could only reiterate to me that by priority of publication in the U. S., I lose my right to take out the English copyright & this we both agreed it would be a grievous pity I should do. In other words I should suffer a serious damage here & get no corresponding gain at home, where

---

1. *The Portrait of a Lady.*
2. Neither WDH's note nor HJ's telegram is extant.

my copyright if taken out beforehand is not invalidated by the English priority of publication, & holds good even if my novel should be begun in Dec. or January. You will of course answer that my "gain" will be in accommodating myself to the conditions that you prefer & in particular to the understanding that I first had with you. As to this understanding, I admit that I was culpably unbusiness-like. I had not informed myself until I wrote you about the matter a month ago, that it was necessary *your* date shld. be November. When I was reminded of this by Fredk. Macmillan it came to me wholly as an after-thought—but at the same time as one to which you would not object. I was extremely sorry I had not made a point of it before, but I consoled myself with thinking that any objections you would make to it, you would have felt before equally. These objections do not seem to me grave as compared with the disad-vantage it would be to me that you should publish in America first. The newspa-pers may speak of my story, but as they can't steal it, I should think their speak-ing of it will only advertise it. This, I admit, however, is a view I cannot impose on Houghton & Mifflin—who are open to take the ground that I have misled them, & that it is not worth their while to publish the novel on these condi-tions. If they make up their mind to this they will of course [*one-half sheet of the letter is missing at this point*] to recognise the fact that I had not made the thing plain at first. But I shall proceed on the favourable hypothesis, & go on sending you copy (I expect to send you another packet in a few days) as if you accepted the November condition. I earnestly hope the inconvenience of your doing this will not be appreciable. I add nothing more, as I wish to [*remainder of letter is missing*].

42.

JAMES TO HOWELLS, 11 September 1880, Dover   ALS Houghton
                                                          bMS Am 1784 (253) 31

Dover, Sept. 11<u>th</u>

Dear Howells.

   I send you herewith another piece of my novel[1]—having been—as regards essentials—partially reassured by your telegram of some days ago.[2] That is, I am now at rest as regards H., M & Co.[3] keeping the story (which I confess I was not before;) but until I hear from you—I suppose you will have written,—I shall not be at rest as to their estimation of the damage my inadvertence will have caused them. I cannot, honestly, however, think it will be great. *Macmillan* is deeply ignored in the U.S.A., & its arrival there will precede the *Atlantic* by a barely appreciable time. But basta!—I have just (i.e. an hour ago,) heard from

---

1. *The Portrait of a Lady.*
2. Not extant.
3. Houghton, Mifflin & Company, new publishers of the *Atlantic*.

Grace Norton, & she speaks of your having been at Ashfield with your "delightful daughter," & of "your never having been more charming."[4] All this makes me regret I was not also there, instead of at dull Dover, where the only entertainment is to see the seasick passengers arrive from France. G.N. also speaks of your writing a story about a "lady-doctor"! I applaud you that subject— it is rich in actuality—though I cannot, I think, on the whole, say I envy you it. Of course the hero is a patient whom she attends?[5] I hear the *Undiscovered Country* is, against your forecast, a great success;[6] on which I much congratulate you. Your popularity at least I envy.—You will see that the instalments of my novel are at least as long as I first proposed. It will take *12* numbers.[7]

In haste, yours ever—
H. James jr

43.

JAMES TO HOWELLS, 20 September 1880, London

ALS Houghton
bMS Am 1784 (253) 32

Sept. 20th
REFORM CLUB,
PALL MALL. S. W.

Dear Howells.

I have delayed answering your card of Sept. 1st,[1] because I was in the country when it reached me[2] & I wished to think over, in the light of London, your proposal in reference to "crowding" the tale. I do not believe, when you appreciate the length of the individual instalments, that you will desire to do so, & I trust you won't think me unaccommodating if I say that now that it is settled that you publish on the month following *Macmillan* I would much rather the whole thing, & its component parts, should march in that order to the end. It is better & safer for me, & I cannot think that you will suffer from relinquishing the idea. My separate instalments will be not of minimum, but of maximum, length, & contain in all probability as much of the tale as you will *ever* desire

4. WDH and his daughter Winifred had visited the Nortons at their summer place at Ashfield, Massachusetts. None of Grace Norton's letters to HJ survives.

5. HJ's surmise about the plot of *Dr. Breen's Practice* (1881) was incorrect. The "hero" is another physician to whose experience Grace Breen defers, but whose proposal of marriage she rejects. She marries instead Mr. Libby, a cultivated young industrialist.

6. As of October 1880 Houghton, Mifflin reported sales of 8,226 copies (Copyright Accounts Ledger: 1876–81, p. 146 [Houghton Mifflin Archive, Harvard]).

7. Ultimately, *The Portrait of a Lady* ran to fourteen installments.

1. Not extant.

2. HJ passed the previous weeks first at Kenilworth, with his friend Mrs. Carter, then with Sir James John Trevor Lawrence (1831–1913), a Tory M.P. from Surrey, before moving on to the channel town of Dover.

to present to your readers at once. As you speak of your wishing to "crowd" 5 numbers as only a remote contingency I hope this frowning reply will not appreciably disappoint you. I thank you for your advice not to think further of our misunderstanding, & shall succeed in obeying it.—I wrote you about a week ago from the sea-side, & sent you a couple of bundles of copy which I trust will soon be reaching you.—I am sorry—very sorry—that you were obliged to decline the invitation for the presidential journey[3]—as the loss strikes me as being inflicted on light literature as well as on yourself. But the decision proves your riches— your resources. Apropos of riches, what a fortune you must be making! I congratulate you heartily on the circulation of the U. C.[4]—which I liked better than you appear to suppose.—I suppose you are basking in a golden haze & that in these September days Belmont justifies its name. If you see my brother, soon, he will give you news of me.[5]

Yours very truly—
H. James jr

44.

JAMES TO HOWELLS, 11 November 1880, London

ALS Houghton
bMS Am 1784 (253) 33

Nov. 11th
REFORM CLUB,
PALL MALL. S. W.

Dear Howells

I send you by this post the 5th (March) instalment of my fiction.[1] It is something shorter (a page or two) than its predecessors, & will make about 24 of your pages.—I have hardly time to do more than despatch it, with many compliments.

I hope it will find you in health & heart & looking a New England winter calmly in the face. The face of the winter here is invisible—veiled in muggy rains & glutinous fogs! I hope to escape for a part of it to some continental sunshine.[2]—I see by the way that the *Atlantic* prospectus announces my tale to terminate *early* in 1881. This, I suppose, is a piece of publishers' rose-colour, for I thought I had been explicit as to its longitude—12 months: a majestic length.—If you are ever moved to make me a present, send me once in a while some good American book: for instance, at Xmas, Aldrich's *Stillwater Tragedy*

---

3. President Rutherford B. Hayes had invited WDH to accompany a group of almost twenty men and women on a two-month tour of the West (including seven hundred miles by stagecoach).

4. *The Undiscovered Country.*

5. WJ had recently returned to Cambridge from Europe.

1. *The Portrait of a Lady.*

2. HJ left for Italy in February 1881, where he finished writing *The Portrait.*

(your pretty article about which[3]—*tissu d' air!*[4]—I read in the last magazine.) Or even, if you think well of it the *Grandissimes*,[5] which I see described as a lovely thing. Don't send the G.'s unless *you* esteem it—I prefer the Tragedy. Bien des choses chez vouz![6]

Ever yours
H. James jr

45.

JAMES TO HOWELLS, 5 December 1880, London   ALS Houghton
                                                    bMS Am 1784 (253) 34

Dec. 5th.
3, BOLTON STREET,
PICCADILLY. W.

Dear Howells.

I didn't mean to put the screw on you to the extent of *two* volumes of native fiction, & am much obliged to you for your generosity.[1] I shall not attempt to read the books just now, but keep them for the larger leisure of a journey abroad, later in the winter. Dizzy's "Endymion",[2] which is the actuality of the hour here, has almost fatally disgusted me with the literary form to which it pretends to belong. Can the novel be a thing of virtue, when such a contemptibly bad novel as that is capable of being written—& read? Perhaps, however, Aldrich & the Grandissimo will reconcile me to this branch of art. I asked you about the latter because I had observed one or two notices of him which seemed to indicate (in

---

3. In the November 1880 *Atlantic*, WDH reviewed Thomas Bailey Aldrich's novel *The Stillwater Tragedy* (1880) in the context of a general appraisal of "Mr. Aldrich's Fiction." In spite of Aldrich's choice of subject—a strike in a New England manufacturing town and its violent social consequences—WDH noted that "Mr. Aldrich seems to have a preference for looking at life through literature, and for giving not so much the likeness of what he might see if he rejected this medium as the likeness of something that has pleased him in books. He cannot deny himself the suggestion of traits endeared by literary association, as he cannot deny himself the pleasure of making witty and humorous remarks upon his action and people. This is English usage, sanctioned by all the great novelists, and yet we cannot help thinking it a vice." See "Mr. Aldrich's Fiction," *Atlantic* 46 (November 1880): 45.

4. In the most delicate style.

5. WDH never reviewed *The Grandissimes: A Story of Creole Life* (1880) by George Washington Cable (1844–1925), but he told the author it was a "noble and beautiful book." See WDH to Cable, 2 October 1881, *LiL* 1: 302; see also Kjell Ekström, "The Cable–Howells Correspondence," *Studia Neophilogica* 22 (1950): 53–54.

6. Best regards to your house!

1. WDH sent HJ both volumes mentioned in the preceding letter: Thomas Bailey Aldrich's *Stillwater Tragedy* (1880) and George Washington Cable's *Grandissimes* (1880).

2. The latest novel by Benjamin Disraeli (1804–81), British statesman and author.

superlative terms) that the G.A.N.[3] had at last arrived; but from the moment that public opinion had not forced him on your own perusal, I was willing to give the G.A.N. another chance.—Your strictures on my own story seem to me well-founded (don't say that I don't take criticism like an angel.) The girl is over-analysed, & her journalistic friend *seems* (whether she is or not) over drawn.[4] But in defense of the former fault I will say that I intended to make a young woman about whom there should be a great deal to tell & as to whom such telling should be interesting; & also that I think she is analysed once for all in the early part of the book & doesn't turn herself inside out quite so much afterwards. (So at least it seems to me—perhaps you will not agree with me). Miss Stackpole is not I think really exaggerated—but 99 readers out of a 100 will think her so: which amounts to the same thing. She is the result of an impression made upon me by a variety of encounters & acquaintances made during the last few years; an impression which I had often said to myself could not be exaggerated. But one must have received the impression, & the home-staying American doubtless does not do so as strongly as the expatriated; it is over here that it offers itself in its utmost relief.—That you think well of Lord W.[5] makes me regret more than I already do that he is after all but a secondary figure. I have made rather too much of his radicalism in the beginning—there is no particular use for it later.—I must have been strangely vague as to *all* the conditions of my story when I first corresponded with you about it, & I am glad to have wrung from you the confession that you expected it to be in six numbers, for this will teach me to be more explicit in future.[6] I certainly supposed I had been so in this case—the great feature of my projected tale being that it was to be long—longer than its predecessors. Six months, for a regular novel, is a very small allowance—I mean for dealing with a long period of time & introducing a number of figures. You make your own stories fit into it, but it is only by contracting the duration of the action to a few weeks. Has not this been the case in all of them? Write one that covers a longer stretch of months or years, and I think you will see that it will immediately take more of the magazine. I believed that in this case you positively desired something voluminous & I believed equally that I had announced my voluminosity well in advance. I am afraid that it will be a characteristic of my future productions (in, I hope, a

3. The Great American Novel, first heralded by John W. De Forest (1826–1906) in an article of that title, published in the *Nation* 6 (9 January 1868): 27–29.

4. Isabel Archer, the heroine of *The Portrait of a Lady,* and her newspaper correspondent friend, Henrietta Stackpole, a study in comic excess.

5. Lord Warburton, rejected English suitor of Isabel Archer.

6. HJ's letter of 14 or 15 July (#31) did not specify exactly the number of installments he would need for *The Portrait,* but he did suggest that the story would be on a larger scale than his previous work. WDH had been looking for a six-month commitment from HJ; HJ wrote to Frederick Macmillan, 22 July [1879]: "I am to furnish Howells a story for the last half of 1880. . . ." See *The Correspondence of Henry James and the House of Macmillan, 1877–1914,* ed. Rayburn S. Moore (London: Macmillan, 1993), 38.

reasonable measure;) but I will be careful to put the points on my i's.—I complain of you that you will never write to me save of the weather—as if you had just been introduced to me at an evening party! That is very well: especially as you describe it beautifully—but I would rather you told me what you are doing, writing, enjoying, suffering, hearing, seeing. About all these things you are very mysterious. Your description of the impudent Cambridge winter, however, is vivid—with the earth like a stone & the sky like a feather. Here the earth is like a Persian rug—a hearth-rug, well besprinkled with soot.—I hear every now and then that you are soon coming abroad; but I sincerely hope you won't have the perversity to take just the time when I am coming home, as I hope (this time seriously,) to do next year. Your wife, I am sure, would not do this. Tell her I believe it, & remain

faithfully yours
H. James jr

I think you may be sure Mrs. Orr got your book: but I will make a point of *ascertaining.* [7]

---

7. In recognition of her favorable assessment of his work, WDH probably sent Alexandra Leighton Orr a copy of *The Undiscovered Country* (see letter #27, note 1; and letter #39, note 1).

part two

Fearful
Responsibilities

Biographical
Overview

After years of cumulative experiment, both writers are poised to achieve their first major novelistic triumphs. A *Modern Instance* and *The Portrait of a Lady* firmly establish Howells and James as American exemplars of the realist school of fiction, a link irrevocably confirmed by the former's essay on "Henry James, Jr." in the *Century* (November 1882).

After the deaths of both his parents that same year, James commits himself to permanent life abroad. ("I have made my choice," he had already affirmed in his notebook, "and God knows that I have now no time to waste. My choice is the old world—my choice, my need, my life" [CN 214]). In 1884 Alice James joins her brother in England, where she will live as an invalid for the rest of her life. *The Bostonians* confirms James's predilection for exile, but *The Princess Casamassima* suggests that London life can also be alienating. The failure of both books prompts James to reassess his commitment to the novel as a preferred genre. He begins a new career. Abandoning his quarters in Piccadilly, he signs a twenty-one-year lease on a more spacious flat in fashionable Kensington (34 De Vere Gardens West), from which he launches an ill-starred campaign for success on the London stage. After years of deferred hope, he is greeted by jeers at the premiere of *Guy Domville* in January 1895 and flees from the theater. To complete his escape, he reconsecrates himself to the art of fiction. "It is now indeed that I may do the work of my life," he confides to his journal. "And I will" (CN 109).

Fortunately, Howells is there to assist him, especially with strategies on how best to market his work. In this Howells has become expert (through necessity as well as by instinct), as he has moved from magazine to magazine and publisher to publisher. After Howells leaves the *Atlantic*, first James R. Osgood and then the Harper brothers "monopolize" the writer, paying him a generous annual salary in exchange for the first option to publish his work (stipulating that he produce at least one full-length novel a year). Never one to shrink from work, Howells routinely satisfies the terms of his contract. He is punctual and prolific. The shelf of books grows longer year by year.

Much like the good fortune of Silas Lapham, however, Howells's security proves rather deceptive. A looming sense of despair shadows the writer, even as he enjoys the hard-won fruits of literary fame. In a public sphere besmirched by labor violence, the unrestrained forces of industrial capitalism seem to be corrupting the social basis of democracy in America. More privately but no less poignantly, illness and psychological trauma beset his family, prompting a harrowing (and expensive) quest for diagnoses, treatments, and cures—none of which, in the end, proves effective. Two days after her father's fifty-second birthday, his elder daughter, Winifred, dies.

In the closing chapters of *A Hazard of New Fortunes*, a policeman's bullet pierces the heart of Conrad Dryfoos as he tries to shelter the maimed (but still defiant) radical Lindau from an assault by strikebreakers. The death of his only son almost breaks the stony heart of old man Dryfoos, who has always sneered at Conrad's liberal Christian sympathies; but the novel stubbornly refuses to affirm the prospect of inevitable moral transformation. Indeterminacy supplants the older verities. Similarly bereft, Howells can no longer take refuge in the certainty of progress or a conveniently providential view of American history. When the United States declares war on Spain in 1898, the patriot/politicians spew the rhetoric of freedom, but Howells suspects that their language only cloaks a dangerous lust for imperial conquest. The newspapers universally proclaim the war a Manichaean struggle between muscular democracy and decrepit monarchy, between the New World and the Old; Howells privately laments that so much blood is shed in a battle over coaling stations. Less cynically perhaps, his fictions of the nineties give voice to a jumble of confused emotions: inward grief and guilt (*The Quality of Mercy, The Shadow of a Dream*), outward disaffection with the country's social aims (*A Traveller from Altruria*), and the unrequitable nostalgia of advancing middle age (*The Landlord at Lion's Head*).

As their lives are marked by death and their careers by disappointment, both Howells and James find the consolations of friendship more precious.

Parallel Chronology

	HOWELLS	JAMES	
1881	Resigns editorship of the *Atlantic*. Suffers breakdown while finishing *A Modern Instance*. *A Fearful Responsibility, and Other Stories. Doctor Breen's Practice*.	Returns to United States (October), where he is encouraged by the "reasonable show of fame" his literary achievements have won. *The Portrait of a Lady*.	1881
1882	Trip to Europe with family: growing concern about Winifred's health. Declines professorship at Johns Hopkins.	Death of both parents: Mary Robertson James in January; Henry James Sr. in December. After mother's funeral, HJ	1882

	HOWELLS	JAMES	
	A Modern Instance. Essay on James in the *Century* provokes international controversy about literary realism and modern letters.	spends summer and autumn in the French provinces, gathering material for new series of travel sketches.	
1883	Returns to Boston. *A Woman's Reason.*	Called home by father's illness (December 1882), HJ named his executor. Against William James's objections, HJ revokes father's will to ensure that all children receive equitable share of inheritance. HJ surrenders his portion to Alice.	1883
1884	Buys house in Back Bay, Boston.	*Portraits of Places. A Little Tour in France. Tales of Three Cities.* "The Art of Fiction."	1884
1885	Collapse of James R. Osgood & Company; WDH signs lucrative long-term contract with Harper & Brothers. *The Rise of Silas Lapham. Tuscan Cities.*	Because of Osgood's failure, lengthy serialization of *The Bostonians* earns HJ nothing.	1885
1886	Begins "Editor's Study" in *Harper's Monthly. Indian Summer.* Declines Smith professorship at Harvard (held earlier by Longfellow and Lowell). Haymarket riot in Chicago.	*The Bostonians. The Princess Casamassima.* Alice James takes up residence in London.	1886
1887	Letter to New York *Tribune* (November 6) requesting clemency for men jailed after bombing of Haymarket Square. *The Minister's Charge.*	Spends winter in Italy, especially Florence and Venice.	1887
1888	Moves family to New York City. *April Hopes.*	*The Reverberator. Partial Portraits. The Aspern Papers.*	1888
1889	Winifred dies (March 3). *Annie Kilburn.*	*A London Life.*	1889

	HOWELLS	JAMES	
1890	Moves to Boston for the year. *A Hazard of New Fortunes. The Shadow of a Dream. A Boy's Town.*	*The Tragic Muse.* The *Atlantic* rejects "The Pupil" (later serialized in England by *Longman's*). HJ abandons novel writing in abortive experiment as playwright (1890–95); engages Wolcott Balestier as theatrical agent.	1890
1891	Returns to New York. *Winifred Howells* (privately published memorial volume). *Criticism and Fiction. An Imperative Duty.*	Dramatic version of *The American* a modest success; other plays circulated but not produced. Death of Balestier.	1891
1892	Lets Harper contract expire. Coedits *Cosmopolitan*, December 1891–June 1892. Attempts to transform magazine into a center of literary radicalism but runs afoul of millionaire-owner's wishes. *The Quality of Mercy.*	*The Lesson of the Master.* Death of Alice James (March 6).	1892
1893	*The World of Chance. The Coast of Bohemia. My Year in a Log Cabin.*	*The Real Thing and Other Tales. The Private Life. Essays in London and Elsewhere.*	1893
1894	Trip to France to visit son in Paris; afternoon in Whistler's garden. Father dies. *A Traveller from Altruria.*	*The Wheel of Time. Theatricals: Two Comedies. Theatricals: Second Series.*	1894
1895	*My Literary Passions. Stops of Various Quills.* Begins regular contributions to *Harper's Weekly.*	HJ hooted off stage at premiere of *Guy Domville* (January 5). *Terminations.*	1895
1896	*The Day of Their Wedding. A Parting and a Meeting. Impressions and Experiences.*	*Embarrassments.*	1896
1897	*The Landlord at Lion's Head. An Open-Eyed Conspiracy.* Journeys to Carlsbad, Germany; sees HJ in London on return.	*The Spoils of Poynton. What Maisie Knew.* Signs twenty-one-year lease for Lamb House in Rye, Sussex. Engages stenographer for dictation.	1897

	HOWELLS	JAMES	
1898	*The Story of a Play.* Continues "American Letter" in *Literature* (May 1898–November 1899).	*In the Cage. The Two Magics* (includes "The Turn of the Screw"). Begins "American Letter" in *Literature* (March–July). Engages James B. Pinker as literary agent.	1898

"Those Badly Assorted
Siamese Twins"

In his holiday letter of 1880 James complained about the paucity of personal news and professional gossip that Howells had been providing. James would hardly have suspected that his friend's reticence concealed a growing discontent with his comfortably prosperous literary situation; but by the end of that year, Howells had resolved to sever the primary bond that tied him to Boston. Resigning from the *Atlantic* granted Howells greater freedom; in these altered circumstances, the novelist recognized a profound need to break new ground. In some of his other letters dating from this time he spoke almost resentfully of the "international" subject that, by now, he seemed condemned to repeat. Praising another novel for its vivid depiction of New York (not, incidentally, *Washington Square*), Howells envied the author for having that field to himself. "No one can say that you are working up the tracts of those badly assorted Siamese twins, J. and H., who happened to treat inter-continental passion (or bi-continental passion) before you." [1] In writing *A Modern Instance,* Howells was attempting to defeat what had already become a customary classification and distance himself from a comparison in which he would always suffer. As *The Portrait of a Lady* sailed majestically through number after number of the magazine, Howells surely recognized that James was laying more exclusive claim to the trans-Atlantic novel of manners—if not, indeed, exhausting the genre.

Like James, Howells was eager to tackle something on a larger scale, but he was still somewhat unsure of his ability to manage the Great American Novel (a subject that the two writers gingerly tossed back and forth). Trying to justify his extended analysis of Isabel Archer (Howells had alleged this nondramatic exposition took up too much space), James asserted that his conception of the story could not be contained within the small compass that his editor typically had favored. Confronted by the massive reality of the Victorian triple-decker, which was still the standard format for distributing fiction in England (via the circulating libraries), James knew he could not compete successfully with other writers by presenting abbreviated works like *The Europeans* or *Confidence.* [2] To have only six installments for the periodical run of a book was insufficient. "You make your own stories fit into it," he told Howells, "but it is only by contracting the duration of the action to a few weeks. Has not this been the case in all of them? Write one that covers a longer stretch of months or years, and I think you will see that it will immediately take more of the magazine." Timely advice, considering that *A Modern Instance* was on the boards and would stretch to eleven numbers in the *Century*, the longest work Howells had yet written.

As he worked on this novel through 1881, Howells gladly posted his progress quantitatively: six hundred pages by August, nine hundred in September, more than fourteen hundred by early November—just to the point where Bartley Hubbard deserts his family (Marcia Gaylord and the couple's newborn child) and lights out for the territories. Here Howells famously broke down physically and imaginatively. Bedridden for over two months, he despaired of finishing the book. "I have made a long story of A Modern Instance," the author confessed to John Hay, "and I am just now slowly and painfully reaching the end. Since my sickness, I work with difficulty, and the result I fancy lacks texture."[3] As Howells suspected, the novel rather limps to its conclusion, largely by suppressing Hubbard's character and substituting the anguished affections of Ben Halleck (who for years has been in love with Marcia but has been paralyzed by a divided conscience) and the pious moralities of Eustace Atherton, a respectable Boston lawyer who chastises the invalid Halleck for compromising his sense of duty. The frequent complaint relating to the novel's irresolution did not bother James, who quipped that *A Modern Instance* was "the Yankee *Romola*." At last Howells seemed to be living and working up to his potential. By sundering his ties to the *Atlantic*, he had won the freedom, as James put it, to "enlarge a little his studies and his field,"[4] a benefit immediately realized in this impressive chronicle of American social disorder and ethical uncertainty.

The notoriety of its subject matter quickly brought *A Modern Instance* to the attention of columnists and reviewers, who greeted the book with both praise and alarm. Even though Howells appears to retreat behind the conventional pieties of Atherton, thereby buttressing the conservative view that a casually civil basis for the marriage contract represented a threat to civilization, a few discerning readers, such as Horace E. Scudder of the *Atlantic*, understood that "to regard *A Modern Instance* as a tract against the divorce laws" would be "unjust": the book was, rather, "a demonstration of a state of society of which the divorce laws are the index." A greater number of reviews alleged that Howells had dishonored the novelist's art by dealing with the sordid problems of commonplace people. As London's *Academy* aphorized, "A depressing, dreary book, with all its ability and good intentions."[5]

Not coincidentally, a number of literary paragraphers had used similar words to describe *The Portrait of a Lady*,[6] which now seemed to anticipate Howells's novel. Both titles were accepted (rather grudgingly) as representative examples of a new school of fiction, typically modern, self-consciously American, and regrettably unconventional. For readers accustomed to brisk sensation, this newer mode of storytelling was too slow, too cerebral, too much wanting in intensity. *A Modern Instance* "had great dramatic capabilities," one notice lamented: "that Mr. Howells has not availed himself of them is due in great measure to the same defects which mar *The Portrait of a Lady*—to too much attention to details, too much commonplace, too much analysis."[7] With Howells no longer at the helm, the *Atlantic* also began to consider the writers in tandem, posing rhetorical questions to its readers: "Is it a fanciful likeness which we detect between The Portrait of a Lady and Dr. Breen's Practice?"[8] Even if the answer were a rhetorical "yes," the inevitability of comparison was itself more immediately significant. The authors' mutual friends tended to minimize the importance of such judgments, even to disbelieve them. (As John Hay said—perhaps a little disingenuously—to Howells, "You have chosen fields so different that there is hardly any rivalry.")[9] But despite their mutually deliberate recent efforts at differentiating themselves, to many readers James and Howells still resembled a pair of literary Siamese twins. And they were joined even more inexorably after the appearance of a laudatory article about "Henry James, Jr." in the November 1882 issue of the *Century*, for the essay (replete with a full-page lithograph of James's profile) carried the byline of W. D. Howells.

Notes accompanying the letters accurately trace the uproar occasioned by this perceptive overview of James's career, which also advanced Howells's judgments about the current status of the novel. In the hands of a new generation of writers (among whom James was preeminent), the art of fiction, Howells alleged, had become "a finer art" because its ablest practitioners studied human nature "in its wonted aspects" and disdained the intrusive narrative mannerisms that had been freely indulged by the early Victorians. Howells's comparisons were hardly invidious (as James immediately recognized), but they were remarkably inflammable, especially in Britain, and a journalistic firestorm quickly ensued. Though Howells obviously took much abuse for his remarks, many critics gleefully turned their sights on James, since he was already a familiar (though hardly popular) commodity in London. The offense committed by Howells was political, not merely aesthetic, according to the *Quarterly Review*, which extended its rather satirical indictment to include James. "Whatever may be the differences of opinion as to the value of the new 'school,' " the *Review* charged,

> it must be acknowledged on all sides that a novelist enjoys an immense advantage in being a contributor to an illustrated magazine, which is ready not only to publish his works, but to issue elaborate articles on their merits—accompanied, as we have said, by that most affecting of souvenirs, a "portrait of the author," duly softened and idealized. The art of puffery gets "finer" every day, whatever we may think about the art of novel-writing.[10]

With genuine surprise and regret, Howells came to see the perverse effect brought on by his ample praise. Partly because his own work was just then being published in Great Britain, Howells probably benefited from the ongoing controversy (as did the *Century*, whose editor was predictably elated).[11] James's situation was considerably more vulnerable and his hold on an audience less secure; while he tried to dismiss the ruckus as nothing more than "idiotic commotion," its lingering implications continued to depress him.[12] Others shared his concern. Henry Adams, for example, exchanged the following confidence with John Hay: "I admit also to a shudder at the ghastly fate of Harry James and

Howells. The mutual admiration business is not booming just now. Between ourselves, there is in it always an air of fatuous self-satisfaction fatal to the most grovelling genius."[13] Adams may have overstated the case, which was neither wholly fatuous nor fatal, but he perceptively appreciated the latent risks of Howells's continued proprietorship of James's reputation.

By 1886, when both *The Bostonians* and *The Princess Casamassima* failed to regain the independent momentum James had worked so hard to establish, he belatedly recognized the need to disentangle himself from Howells. James's penetrating essay "William Dean Howells," which appeared in *Harper's Weekly* in June of that year, betrays a profound compulsion to maneuver around and to deny reciprocity with its subject (a stance for which the author immediately confided his apologies). Without denying the salience of James's particular judgments, most of which have indeed become standard (particularly with respect to the "innocence" of Howells's novels, which, James alleged, collectively revealed "so small a perception of evil"), we should recognize that his remarks have almost always been cited out of context, and that the distancing severity of some of them can be attributed (at least in part) to a nagging sense of his own professional insecurity. "I had a horror of appearing too mutual & reciprocal," he forthrightly told Howells, and "cultivated (in your own interest) a coldness which I didn't feel." It would be easy—but inaccurate—to interpret this statement as just another example of James's polite disingenuousness. Rather, the evidence confirming a genuinely apologetic attitude becomes more cogent when we consider that James's most telling criticisms of Howells were, in fact, almost plagiaristically derivative.

Three years before James published his essay, an imposing article on the subject of "American Literature in England" appeared in *Blackwood's*. Contributed (anonymously) by Margaret Oliphant, this piece was intended to be a review essay of Howells's collected works, then newly published by David Douglas. After the appearance of the soon-to-become notorious *Century* article, however, Oliphant felt obliged to recast her subject in more derisively comparative terms. Responding to Howells's infamous judgments about his Victorian predecessors, she quickly dispatched the American upstart with aggressive understatement. "When a writer of fiction commits himself so terribly as to allege that the art of which he is a professor is finer than the art of Thackeray, the punishment which he prepares for himself is so prodigious that it becomes ridiculous," she wrote. "But no one we believe will be cruel enough to make the suggested comparison, and measure Mr Howells against Thackeray. He is so far safe in the inferiority of his stature." Freed from the obligation of that comparison, however, she immediately proceeded to measure Howells against one of his own contemporaries, Henry James, and to vindicate James in the process.

With surprising specificity, Oliphant's biting remarks anticipate James's more generous summations about Howells's democratic temperament and the self-consciously "American" quality of his work. But the particularity of James's indebtedness can best be discerned in her comments about *A Modern Instance* and the alleged vulgarity of that novel's conception of evil. Whereas James cheerfully accepted Howells's representativeness and admitted that "what is most remarkable, or most, at least, the peculiar sign, in his effort as a novelist [was] his unerring sentiment of the American character," Oliphant preferred a more invidious approach to reach the same conclusion. "He is a better type of the American novelist than Mr James," she sharply asserted, "by right of being less accomplished, and moving within a more contracted circle of observation." (Or, as James would have it, "People are always wanting a writer of Mr. Howells's temperament to see certain things that he doesn't.") "An artist," Oliphant continued,

> when he possesses the conditions of greatness—a writer, when he has in any degree that indescribable addition to all gifts which we call genius—is thereby disqualified from being a type of any class or country. He becomes himself a recognisable power, but he is not a specimen any longer. Mr Howells, however, is not too great to be a specimen. For all we know he is the very best example of the American novelist *pur sang* that we are likely to attain to.

To buttress this point of view, Oliphant analyzes Howells's major fictions at considerable length, frequently comparing them (more or less intelligently) with James's. Some of her most arresting comments are reserved for Bartley Hubbard. "He is a sort of vulgar Tito," she pregnantly begins (to Howells himself James had described A *Modern Instance* as "the Yankee *Romola*"),

> without any of the tragic elements involved in George Eliot's great and terrible conception,—dropping from dishonesty to dishonesty, from indulgence to indulgence, with no more heroic result than that of getting fat and slightly dissipated, and losing character. . . . His other sins do not strike us as very heavy. He drinks a great deal of beer . . . and this is, no doubt, a mistake. But he has his trials.

By which she means being married to Marcia Gaylord. Again anticipating James, Oliphant exhibits small patience for Howells's women, whom she finds devoid of Jamesian "curiosity and interest," frustratingly impervious even to the finer influences of Europe.[14]

James himself always pretended to be impervious or indifferent to popular "criticism" (as he ironically called it), but in the turbid wake of Howells's *Century* essay, the journals and newspapers firmly arrested his attention. Almost helplessly, his letters become analytical bibliographies, compilations of opinions he professed to ignore but eagerly kept pace with. In the spring of 1883 he told Howells that articles about the two of them were running "thick as blackberries" (and most were just as thorny); every day the two Americans were being "immolated on the altar of Thackeray & Dickens." Partly to pluck his own brand from the burning, James contributed his essay on Howells to *Harper's Weekly*, borrowing from (and, typically, improving upon) earlier commentary. Influentially, Lionel Trilling accorded James's essay particularly privileged status for defining the ground of modern indifference to Howells, but he himself was indifferent to the fact that others had given James a running start. Understandably, the tartness of James's observations has contributed to his preeminence (his style, as usual, makes quotation irresistible); but even his essay's most frequently cited passage betrays considerable obligation to the viewpoint Oliphant first expressed:

> If American life is on the whole, as I make no doubt whatever, more innocent than that of any other country, nowhere is the fact more patent than in Mr. Howells's novels, which exhibit so constant a study of the actual and so small a perception of evil. His women, in particular, are of the best—except, indeed, in the sense of being the best to live with. Purity of life, fineness of conscience, benevolence of motive, decency of speech, good-nature, kindness, charity, tolerance (though, indeed, there is little but each other's manners for the people to tolerate), govern all the scene; the only immoralities are aberrations of thought, like that of Silas Lapham, or excesses of beer, like that of Bartley Hubbard.

If, as Oliphant said, Bartley had his trials, so too did Henry James—particularly after Howells had sung his praises (to the detriment of Henry Esmond and Little Nell). James's answering refrain was bound to be less than harmonious, especially in view of the discordant critical environment from which it emerged.

That James never chose to reprint "William Dean Howells" even though he had an immediate opportunity (Macmillan published *Partial Portraits*, a collection of his most recent criticism, just two years later, in 1888) considerably amplifies his private disavowal. Apologizing for the "rather dry tone" of his essay, James presumed upon the geniality of Howells's good nature, knowing that his friend would "read between the lines" and draw appropriately sympathetic inferences. Through the ongoing dialogue of their novels, both James and Howells invited their readers to do the same, for their critical cross-examinations continued to spill over into the pages of their fiction, often with humorous effect.

Howells had brought his family to Europe in 1882, where he planned to finish his next novel, *A Woman's Reason*, as well as to complete a touring itinerary that would enable him to write another book of travel, *Tuscan Cities*. The death of James's father, meanwhile, forced his son to return to America for a year, reversing the usual geography of the novelists' transatlantic correspondence. Strangely occupying the other's accustomed territory did neither writer much good, and each struggled to overcome an aggravating sense of imaginative dispossession. Elinor Mead Howells wrote back to the States that her husband considered "his new story a sort of failure," and the author himself admitted to Mark Twain that *A Woman's Reason* bore "the fatal marks of haste and distraction."[15] Likewise, a certain desperation creeps into the notebook entries James made after leaving his familiar London perch; these private jottings fervently express more hope than conviction that his next novel, *The Bostonians*, would "show that I *can* write an American story" (CN 19).[16]

By focusing on the confused situation of women in American life, both these novels attempt to dramatize newly problematic social conditions. Some critics have remarked that as a result of its depiction of Helen Harkness's precarious economic circumstances, *A Woman's Reason* foreshadows Howells's growing awareness of social inequality in the United States and his willingness to seek remedies for it through his fiction. By contrast, *The Bostonians* despairs of a middling sameness in America that threatens to reduce all cultural discourse to the level of advertisement; equality becomes a token of flatness rather than an abused social ideal. Another way of accounting for such differences is to see that *A Woman's Reason* fundamentally reverses the donnée of *A Portrait of a Lady* to tell the story of a young woman who is stripped of (rather than blessed with) an inheritance. In both instances the Jamesian question ("What will she do?") motivates the plot, but while *The Portrait* becomes a study of romantic (and economic) excess, Howells's novel (or, rather, the better part of it) willingly portrays the kind of social dinginess from which James instinctively retreated.

While Howells was living abroad, the Jamesian international novel became a kind of foil for his own work-in-progress. Simply by losing her privileged economic status in New England society, Helen Harkness finds herself expatriated. The narrative summarizes her reflections after she takes a room in a boarding house: "Here in the heart of Boston, she was as remote from the Boston she had always known as if it were a thousand miles away; from herself of the time when she lived in that far-off Boston she seemed divided by centuries."[17] However, in contrast to Isabel Archer's tormented rambles through the blood-stained streets of Rome, the humble byways of the South End and Cambridgeport cannot sustain much melodramatic brooding; in the New World history is more of a nuisance, like dust from the horsecars. A similarly ironic reversal affects the romantic choices of the novels' respective heroines. Isabel Archer famously spurns her steadfast American lover, Caspar Goodwood, in James's final pages; by contrast, the English nobleman Lord Rainford must suffer Helen Harkness's rejection—but not before he has a chance to deliver an arresting judgment about his recent American acquaintances. When Helen teases him about his inability to understand her country (she quotes from *Martin Chuzzlewit*, perhaps to answer the outcry over Howells's reputed disparagement of Dickens), Lord Rainford alleges that for him to criticize the United States would be ungracious, if not superfluous, since Americans were so good at it themselves. "They talk about London," he sharply observes,

> and about Paris, and about Rome; there seems to be quite a passion for Italy; but they don't seem interested in their own country. I can't make it out. It isn't as if they were cosmopolitan; that isn't quite the impression, though—excuse my saying so—they try to give it. They always seem to have been reading the *Fortnightly* and the *Saturday Review*, and the *Spectator*, and the *Revue des Deux Mondes*, and the last French and English books. It's very odd! Upon my word, at one dinner the Americans got to talking to one another about some question of local finance in pounds, shillings, and pence. I don't understand it. (*AWR* 142–43)

A Woman's Reason brims with ironic touches of this kind, in passages which could almost masquerade as affectionately satiric paraphrases of James's letters.

James, too, proved adept at insinuating Howells into the fictional world of *The Bostonians*. Indeed, Verena Tarrant's climactic performance at the Music Hall and her projected future as a crowd-pleasing orator on behalf of women's rights depend entirely upon the successful delivery of a lecture called "A Woman's Reason" ("her most promising effort," in Olive Chancellor's view).[18] Basil Ransom, on the other hand, is "simply sickened" by Verena's impending triumph, for he already senses that, with such twaddle, "she would become 'widely popular,'" an unacceptable fate (for women, at least) in his chauvinist scale of values. Ransom determines to circumvent this outcome by any means, and Verena unwittingly shapes his intentions by joking that "she didn't see how he could stop her unless he kidnapped her" (*TB* 1164). James's nominal hero literally ransoms her career, as he impels her to desert not only Olive Chancellor but also the assembled multitude that eagerly awaits Verena's much-heralded performance.

The language of piracy furnishes a kind of subtext for *The Bostonians*, starting with Ransom's name and ending with his forcible appropriation of Verena; and well it might, since in developing his story James himself had borrowed freely from Howells's *Undiscovered Country* and, to a lesser extent, *Dr. Breen's Practice*. About both those novels James had confessed certain misgivings, as we have seen. Yet in setting out to prove that he could write a truly American tale, the anxious expatriate inevitably had to confront—and subtly challenge—the literary precedent that Howells (and Hawthorne before him) had established. Spiritualism and "lady-doctors" had seemed to James unpromising subjects—at least until he, too, had occasion to make use of them.

While a number of recent critics have rediscovered *The Undiscovered Country* as a pivotal link in the literary genealogy of *The Bostonians*, in their haste to work back to Hawthorne's *Blithedale Romance* as a common inspiration, most commentators have underestimated the amplitude of Howells's broader influence. Less obvious, in some ways, but no less important is the connection between James's book and the journalistic world of *A Modern Instance*; for in both novels the disruptive agency of publicity, namely, its catalytic tendency to convert private emotion into public spectacle, commands greater scrutiny than the comparatively topical interest of mesmerism or women's rights. James himself confessed as much in his notebook, when he remarked that in the American tale he projected there had ("indispensably") to be "a type of newspaper man—the man whose ideal is the energetic reporter" (*CN* 19). Typically, it was Howells who made Matthias Pardon and Selah Tarrant indispensable to *The Bostonians*, for in fleshing out Bartley Hubbard, he was one of our first novelists to discern the peculiar social significance of the modern newspaper and to gauge its effects on American manners.

Because James and Howells shared each other's company during the months in which the author was shepherding *A Modern Instance* through the press, almost no epistolary exchanges about the novel survive. In a diary entry for 18 August 1882, Howells noted that he and his friend had walked home together through the streets of London, James "talking to me most of the way about A Mod. Instance, wh. he is reading,"[19] but the absence of more specific detail renders it impossible to infer James's reactions. More telling, perhaps, is an editorial from the New York *Tribune* (probably written by their mutual friend John Hay) which James sent on to Howells the following spring. In the midst of the international uproar over Howells's *Century* article, the *Tribune* attempted to offer a more balanced assessment of the undeniably hostile shift in public opinion that had taken place regarding America's two leading novelists. Foreign residence had always left James vulnerable to attack (as his study of Hawthorne amply demonstrated), but the pronounced antagonism toward Howells was something wholly unanticipated, and it could not be explained entirely as a reaction against his support of Jamesian realism and narrative objectivity. The hidden animus, the *Tribune* suspected, was Howells's insight into the debased character of Hubbard, the newspaperman who shamelessly sacrifices conscience for the sake of sensational copy. Small wonder that a hundred petty journalists mercilessly spilled printer's ink to defame the novelist. As the *Tribune* observed with obvious relish, "He has gone to the bottom of their vulgar little souls and turned them inside out."[20]

Three weeks after clipping this editorial for his friend, James sent his publisher a detailed scenario of *The Bostonians* and elaborated (in his private journal) upon a similar intention for his novel. "I should like to *bafouer* the vulgarity and hideousness of this," he noted, "the impudent invasion of privacy—the extinction of all conception of privacy, etc." (*CN* 19). When James began to compose his story, however, he realized that newspapermen (such as Bartley Hubbard and Matthias Pardon) were not singularly culpable for these depressing developments: they had willing accomplices among a demoralized citizenry. Through the character of Verena's father, Selah Tarrant, James discovered an even more ample vehicle for ridiculing the state of the nation, for Tarrant extinguishes privacy by capitalizing upon it, wringing surplus value out of domestic sensibility. Cloaking himself in the mantle of benevolent reform, so characteristic of latter-day transcendentalism, Tarrant affects moral loftiness while keeping his gaze on the main chance. As James cleverly says, "he never saw so much as when he had his eyes fixed on the cornice" (*TB* 896).

In some of his later novels (notably *A Hazard of New Fortunes* and *The Quality of Mercy*) Howells, too, would analyze the parasitic relation between newsmen and their subjects, but *The Bostonians* achieves peculiar vividness because James suggestively eroticizes the world of publicity. Recognizing the power of print to blur any distinction between the private self and its public representations, James satirically unmasks Tarrant's irrepressible desire to distend and expose himself to the world. After describing Tarrant's incessant perambulations, his haunting of horsecars and railway stations, the novelist remarks that "the places that knew him best were the offices of the newspapers and the vestibules of the hotels—the big marble-paved chambers of informal reunion which offer to the streets, through high glass plates, the sight of the American citizen suspended by his heels." Tarrant, though, is no Hurstwood; his circuit affords a few proto-Dreiserian glimpses of "shaggy-backed men in strange hats" writing letters in hotel lobbies, but his real destination is the citadel of journalism, a mission which, as James describes it, becomes pornographically comic:

> The *penetralia* of the daily press were, however, still more fascinating, and the fact that they were less accessible, that here he found barriers in his path, only added to the zest of forcing an entrance. He abounded in pretexts; he even sometimes brought contributions; he was persistent and penetrating, he was known as the irrepressible Tarrant. He hung about, sat too long, took up the time of busy people, edged into the printing-rooms when he had been eliminated from the office, talked with the compositors till they set up his remarks by mistake, and to the newsboy when the compositors had turned their backs. He was always trying to find out

what was "going in"; he would have liked to go in himself, bodily, and failing in this, he hoped to get advertisements inserted gratis. (*TB* 897)

Correspondingly, the unflappable columnist Matthias Pardon, whose indelicacy has become synonymous with his vocation, shares this charged fantasy of boundless reproduction, of fluid dispersal through the medium of print. If *The Bostonians* succeeds at all, it does so on the strength of its perversities, its deliberately lurid touches of local color. Burdened by centuries of accumulated repressiveness, James's New Englanders helplessly betray their largely misdirected sexual energies, the various manifestations of which afford an embarrassment of satiric riches. As a prospective husband for Verena (indeed, of all her suitors he is the elder Tarrant's favorite), Pardon harbors no proprietary jealousy; his "passion," James remarks, includes "a remarkable disposition to share the object of his affection with the American people" (*TB* 917).

Not surprisingly, in matters of sexuality the Jamesian muse could dally where a more angelic Howells feared to tread. Selah Tarrant's naked yearning for physical insertion and promiscuous circulation only reminds us that Bartley Hubbard's cravings tend to be oral rather than libidinal. Early in *A Modern Instance,* Marcia Gaylord falls to her knees and fervently presses her lips to a doorknob that the young man has just touched with his hand (a scene also witnessed, reproachfully, by her aging father). While jealousy and passion inflame much of this novel, they also exhaust themselves in it about halfway through; the denouement twitches with more decorous ambiguity. A century of criticism has never tired of repeating Howells's own admission that there could be no "palpitating divans" in his fiction, especially since the magazines in which he serialized his work understandably sought to respect their family readership by maintaining genteel standards of propriety. If his own conscience ever strayed, he noted with some relief, the mindful presence of his wife and children would correct him and keep his fictional representations of sex within bounds.[21] Almost as if to remind him of the claims his family made for a stable income and upwardly mobile respectability, Howells created domestic counterparts in his fiction—for example, the autobiographical couple of Basil and Isabel March—to whom he returned in book after book and through whom he dramatized the familiar bourgeois dialectic of masculine impulse and feminine decorum, physical appetite and conscientious restraint.

James, on the other hand, had an almost morbid awareness—as a confirmed bachelor—of the limits that conventional marriage could impose on the creative imagination. ("The only important things that can happen to me," he once quipped to Howells, "are to die and to marry, and as yet I do neither. I shall in any case do the former first.") If, by eloping with Ransom, Verena is destined to be silenced and sacrificed in *The Bostonians,* there are many corresponding male victims in James's stories: Mark Ambient, for example, in "The Author of 'Beltraffio'" (1884); or Henry St. George in "The Lesson of the Master" (1888), who compromises his artistry (and himself) in the marketplace in order to satisfy the social imperatives of "placing one's children and dressing one's wife."[22]

When Howells and his family returned to Europe in 1882, both those middle-class objectives were much on his mind, as a flurry of surviving notes from James attests. Indeed, the cosmopolitan bachelor of Bolton Street proved an invaluable repository of information about French tutors and fashionable shops, and he clearly took a kind of proprietary pleasure in showing Howells the ropes of London. To Grace Norton, however, James confided a rather different view of the situation. "Howells is here," he reported back to Cambridge, "& I have inducted him & his impedimenta (terrible ones *I* should find some of them!) into lodgings in South Kensington & where he expects to spend some weeks, I believe, finishing a novel. His industry is wonderful, & I am told the *Modern Instance* which I have not yet read, has all the elements of a great success."[23] That Howells could produce anything under these conditions of travel was astonishing, if not altogether enviable, to James, who grudgingly understood that the author's "impedimenta" might well present claims more pressing than those of a work-in-progress. In fact, as James may have anticipated, the manuscript in question that Howells was struggling to complete (*A Woman's Reason*) remained unfinished, put off by the author until his family took up a quieter autumn residence in Switzerland. With all its obvious flaws (especially the implausibly contrived, romantic plot), *A Woman's Reason* could easily have been penned by James's ironically styled "Master," a writer both made and unmade by a feminine reading audience and the "mercenary muse" whom he has "led to the altar of literature"—and lucre.[24]

Privately James could joke about Howells's familial obligations and count his blessings for having none of them; but a number of critics (going back even to Henry Adams) have complained about the pallor of female characters like Isabel Archer and attributed their unreality to the novelist's failure to marry.[25] James may never have really known a woman, but he did know the French novel—not bad, perhaps, as surrogates go. Leaving Paris for London in December 1876, James had few regrets about putting some distance between himself and the circle of French realists with whom he had come to associate—and, up to a point, admire. Their self-proclaimed zeal for observation often led them to look for subject matter in very queer corners, which sometimes gave James pause; his affinity for their professionalism, on the other hand, never wavered, as a formidable series of discerning reviews and essays about them attests. James's abiding respect for technical proficiency and formal experiment permitted him to recommend certain writers and approve of certain works that made many other Anglo-American readers (including Howells) shudder.[26]

The Art of
Fiction

A signal instance of James's more tolerant cosmopolitanism can be found in his 1880 review of *Nana,* a book that gave him almost scandalous occasion for probing "the deep mystery of . . . French taste." The same predilection for "uncleanness" that could push Zola's novel into thirty-nine editions within six months of its publication James found surprisingly dull. But if the Frenchman was almost tediously indecent, which James freely admitted, he was also methodical, authorial qualities that made the great naturalist doubly exceptional in the English-speaking world. "A novelist with a system, a passionate conviction, a great plan—incontestable attributes of M. Zola—is not now to be easily found in England or the United States," James regretted, "where the storyteller's art is almost exclusively feminine, is mainly in the hands of timid (even when very accomplished) women, whose acquaintance with life is severely restricted, and who are not conspicuous for general views." At precisely this point Howells and James would seem irrevocably to part company. Whereas James repeatedly deplored the wholesale evasion of adult sexuality in the English novel and the marketplace imperative to write for an audience composed almost exclusively of "young unmarried ladies," Howells apparently took satisfaction in the fact that in "our civilization" (as he put it) the novel "always addresses a mixed company" and therefore must be respectful of innocent decency. "In what fatal hour," Howells queried ironically in the "Editor's Study" (the monthly literary column that he wrote for *Harper's Magazine* from 1886 to 1892), "did the Young Girl arise and seal the lips of Fiction, with a touch of her finger, to some of the most vital interests of life?" Absolving the Young Girl of responsibility, Howells blandly asserts that writers who complain of her limiting influence have misplaced their frustration, for, simply put, the "manners of the novel have been improving with those of its readers." By definition, for Howells, the serious novelist assumes an obligation for the moral stewardship of society; if a writer proposes "to deal with certain phases of life," his audience has the right to expect "a sort of scientific decorum."[1]

James, of course, dissented from this view and openly chided his friend for

insisting "more upon the restrictions & limitations, the *a priori* formulas & interdictions, of our common art, than upon that priceless freedom which is to me
the thing that makes it worth practising." Reminding Howells (in January 1888)
that "a grain of example is worth a ton of precept," James found more diplomatic
phrasing for an opinion that he had voiced to Robert Louis Stevenson three
months before. "I wish [Howells] would 'quit' [the "Editor's Study"]," James then
bluntly urged, "and content himself with writing the novel as he thinks it should
be and not talking about it: he does the one so much better than the other."[2]
For James, this complaint had become habitual. The stubborn provincialism of
many of Howells's "monthly polemics" (anticipated, perhaps, by his 1880 review
of *Hawthorne*) diminished their potential value at the same time that they frustrated James's desire for the development of Anglo-American literary fraternity.
"I am surprised sometimes, at the things you notice & seem to care about,"
James confessed to Howells. "One should move in a diviner air."[3]

Whereas James could aver in 1883 that Alphonse Daudet's *Numa Roumestan*
was a masterpiece, Howells strenuously objected to what he called the book's
"bad French morality." "Think of a mother," he exclaimed to John Hay, "who in
order to reconcile her daughter to her husband's falsehood, cold-bloodedly tells
her, with the father's consent, that her idolized father had also been false. It's
atrocious."[4] Howells probably communicated a similar opinion to James (in a
letter no longer extant); no wonder that, writing from France a year later, James
would describe Howells's "simplicity of mind" ("in artistic and literary questions") as simply "inexpressible." It should be remembered, however, that James
also considered his Parisian associates, including Daudet, "strangely corrupt and
prodigiously ignorant," exquisitely provincial (for all their worldliness) in matters of taste.[5]

Implicitly positioning himself between these two extremes, James deliberately
mediated the contested space remaining, territory in which his own form of
realism could artfully take refuge in the suggestive depths of English euphemism.
Two tales that James wrote later in the decade, "The Liar" and "A London Life,"
derive significantly from Daudet's licentious donnée. But of the latter story James
wrote in his journal, "to make something of it I must modify it essentially—as I
can't, and besides, don't particularly want to, depict in an American magazine,
a woman carrying on adulteries under her daughter's eyes." Sounding more like
Howells, perhaps, than the author of *Numa*, James added, "That case, I imagine,
is in America so rare as to be almost abnormal."[6]

With its express concern for the typical and socially representative, James's
private judgment could easily be mistaken for one of Howells's more notorious
public pronouncements in the "Editor's Study." To compare the Anglo-
American and French treatment of sensuality in fiction, Howells penned an
imaginary dialogue between a resentful author like James (envious of Gallic li-
cense) and an amiable critic like himself (more content with the respectable
status quo). "See how free those French fellows are!" the writer rebelliously
laments. "Shall we always be shut up to our tradition of decency?" "Do you
think," his more circumspect friend inquires, "it's much worse than being shut
up to their tradition of indecency?"

Then the novelist began to reflect, and he remembered how sick the invariable motive of the French novel made him. He perceived finally that, convention for convention, ours was not only more tolerable, but on the whole was truer to life, not only to its complexion, but also to its texture. No one will pretend that there is not vicious love beneath the surface of our society; if he did, the fetid explosions of the divorce trials would refute him; but if he pretended that it was in any just sense characteristic of our society, he could be still more easily refuted.[7]

In all likelihood Howells's audience would have seen through this mask of anonymity, since James frequently had defended the continental novel—indeed, the art of fiction generally in a well-known essay of that name—by appealing to an ideal of artistic freedom that detached the author from any obligation morally to instruct or elevate his readers. At least part of Howells's strategy, then, was to temper the cosmopolitan emphasis of James's position and thus to reassure the American magazine readership that expatriation had not alienated James from middle-class values.

In the pages of the "Editor's Study" it was not especially difficult for Howells to retain the advantage in this somewhat one-sided conversation. In the more indulgent world of his fiction, however, Howells could let James appear to have the upper hand. In the middle of *Indian Summer,* for example, one of Howells's genial sojourners in Europe suggests that, as a cast of characters, the colony of Americans in Florence comprises "a very interesting group—almost dramatic." Colville, the protagonist, quickly extends the literary analogy to fiction. "Oh, call us a passage from a modern novel," he teases, "if you're in the romantic mood. One of Mr. James's." "Don't you think we ought to be rather more of the great world for that?" his interlocutress replies. "I hardly feel up to Mr. James. I should have said Howells. Only nothing happens in that case!"[8] Not surprisingly, many readers have been content to read this passage as a rather bald confession on Howells's part, an admission of inferior status. But the real humor of the exchange depends upon what follows in the conversation. "If it's only Howells," Colville deprecates, "there's no reason why I shouldn't go with Miss Graham to show her the view of Florence from the cypress grove up yonder." The range of implicit allusion here is as amusing as it is wide. Since it's only Howells, there can be no danger for Imogene Graham (unlike Daisy Miller) in accepting an unchaperoned escort. Since it's only Howells, innocent American freedom successfully transports itself from the verandahs of Prairie des Vaches, Indiana, to the villas of Tuscany. Since it's only Howells, the view from "up yonder" will not ominously signify latent evil, as it does in *The Portrait of a Lady,* in which (with brooding portentousness) James describes Osmond's cypress-shrouded house, perched high above the red-tiled rooftops of Florence and the ocher-stained water of the Arno. Beyond these differing connotations of perspective, even more telling is the simple directness of Howells's style, which (again in contrast to James's) is briskly conversational, replete with contractions and colloquialisms. As John Updike has noted, the title itself (evoking a season—and a vernacular nomenclature—peculiar to America) posits a claim against the novel's outwardly Jamesian, trans-Atlantic territory.[9]

With its central figure a middle-aged man coming to terms with the emptiness of his life, *Indian Summer* usually figures in comparative criticism as a rather lame anticipation of one of James's late masterworks, *The Ambassadors* (1903).[10] Since James admittedly based the character of Lambert Strether on Howells himself, such comparison is admittedly tempting, but it is not altogether fair or historically justified. In fact, fully to appreciate *Indian Summer* we have to reverse the conventional logic and thus see Howells (as Updike recommends) subjecting James's earlier work to ironical cross-examination. The challenge comes promptly in chapter 3, when Colville and the expatriate Unitarian minister Mr. Waters trade friendly remarks about their Florentine compatriots. "I'm bound to say," Waters begins,

> "that I don't find our countrymen so aggressive, so loud as our international novelists would make out. I haven't met any of their peculiar heroines as yet, sir."
> Colville could not help laughing. "I wish *I* had. But perhaps they avoid people of our years and discretion, or else take such a filial attitude toward us that we can't recognize them."
> "Perhaps, perhaps," cried the old gentleman, with cheerful assent.
> "I was talking with one of our German friends here just now, and he complained that the American girls—especially the rich ones—seem very calculating and worldly and conventional. I told him I didn't know how to account for that. I tried to give him some notion of the ennobling influences of society in Newport, as I've had glimpses of it." (*IS* 617)

Howells's sarcasm would seem to take aim at (if not actually to deflate) the kind of romantic heroine James had celebrated in *The Portrait of a Lady*, a woman uncorrupted by the luxury of wealth. (James's imagination, we should recall, reverently traced the moral genealogy of Isabel Archer back to the unconventional spontaneity of his Newport cousin Minny Temple.) In *Indian Summer*, Howells seeks to answer or rehabilitate Isabel's tragedy of renunciation by exposing a similar heroine's self-sacrifice as a deluded but correctable form of self-indulgence. Captivated by the image of Colville's martyred youth (at forty-one, he has never married since his first love spurned him seventeen years before), Imogene Graham yearns to "help him complete the destiny, grand and beautiful as it would have been, which another had arrested" (*IS* 767). Sounding very much like Isabel, she must defend her improbable lover against a battery of skeptical realists. "I should despise him if he were merely a society man," she splutters to one antagonist. "I have seen enough of them. I think it's better to be intellectual and good" (*IS* 764). These elements of benign parody make *Indian Summer* one of Howells's most charming books; even James looked forward to its appearance when he heard from T. S. Perry that the novel would be set in Europe.[11]

Whatever his early enthusiasm, James's final response to *Indian Summer* was rather cool, perhaps because of its modestly self-reflexive satire. Howells's perpetual comedy, voiced mostly through the amiable figure of Colville, struck James as too forcibly contrived. The novel's protagonist, he alleged, was "so irrepressibly and happily facetious as to make one wonder whether the author is not prompting him a little, and whether he could be quite so amusing without help from outside." Given his situation, though, Colville needs all the help he can get, as the contest for his affection between Evalina Bowen and Imogene Graham becomes increasingly shrill. What James would strenuously internalize in the character of Strether—the elegiac conflict between lost youth and prosaic middle age—Howells effectively displaces through the paired female company his hero keeps. Like Owen Elmore before her, Mrs. Bowen, Colville's widowed contemporary, has accepted the fearful responsibility of social stewardship for a young American girl whose romantic impulses make her elder's role familiarly unenviable. With Colville as their common object of desire, the once cordial relation between the two women sours into a crossfire of possessive resentment and sexual jealousy. Viewed from the distaff side, then, *Indian Summer* curiously prefigures *The Awkward Age, not The Ambassadors.*[12]

Embracing the myth of domestic virtue was almost inevitable for Howells (as it was for Mark Twain and many other writers, male and female, of the Gilded Age), but his surrender was not altogether complete, as any reader of *A Modern Instance* or *Indian Summer* will quickly sense. Informed psychological criticism has come to see *A Modern Instance* as a barely concealed revolt against a whole cluster of cultural norms, perhaps even as a retributive examination of the psychic costs that a patriarchal society can inflict upon men in their presumably natural roles as husbands, fathers, and economic providers.[13] Because of its outwardly comic tenor, *Indian Summer* is somewhat more deceptive; but as Oscar Firkins has suggested, through their "morbid entanglement [Mrs. Bowen and Imogene] develop capacities for suffering and even for wrath and cruelty which seem alien alike to the book's temper and their own."[14] Wrath and cruelty are not, however, alien to the book's chosen setting: a ravaged country that embodies "the lesson of noble endurance," an Italy that has only become "more and more civilized" under a tyranny of restraint. As Reverend Waters remarks, "[I]n simply outgrowing the different sorts of despotism that had fastened upon them, till their broken bonds fell away without positive effort on their part, [the Italians] showed a greater sublimity than if they had violently conquered their freedom" (IS 652). What might be called Pyhrric surrender (to the forces of time and history) is indeed the novel's most significant theme.

Not coincidentally, the author transposes the personal and the political as he assesses the implications of Mrs. Bowen's standing *in loco parentis* to her younger rival. "There is no reason why one woman should establish another woman over her," Howells writes, "but nearly all women do it in one sort or another, from love of a voluntary submission, or from a fear of their own ignorance, if they are younger and more inexperienced than their lieges." The author, however, cannot resist adding a sly codicil: "Neither the one passion nor the other seems to reduce them to a like passivity as regards their husbands" (IS 679–80). For Imogene, however, libidinal willfulness takes precedence over dutiful subordination: "I wish to *defy* the world," she openly exclaims to Colville, ridiculing his—and Mrs. Bowen's—concern for respectable appearances (IS 783). The tangible sign of her defiance is a stolen kiss, which paralyzes Colville's sanative judgment. "When he thought of perhaps refusing her caresses, he imagined the shock it would give her, and the look of grief and mystification that would come into her eyes, and he found himself incapable of that cruel rectitude." Unlike Isabel Archer, whose "cruel rectitude" (one might say) transports her away from Goodwood's last embrace, Colville cannot bring himself "to fly from Florence and shun [Imogene] altogether" (*IS* 784). Colville would rather submit than renounce; but, then, he reads Heine and not Goethe.[15]

In marked contrast to the chill Puritanism of James's *Portrait*, a warm haze of Catholic indulgence pervades *Indian Summer*. Even Reverend Waters, echoing the book's central motif, confesses that, were he to live his life over again, he would trade in his Unitarian collar for the more comfortable vestments of Anglicanism. In contrast to some of Howells's other books (such as *The Rise of Silas Lapham*), where the issue of self-sacrifice is pitched in more drastic terms, *Indian Summer* approaches this subject in a more relaxed fashion. While James typically employs the international novel to sharpen cultural contrasts, Howells uses it here to soften moral inflexibility. Colville's self-reproaches are as charmingly ineffective as they are provincially inevitable: he almost takes pleasure in imagining himself a "newly invented kind of scoundrel" for encouraging Imogene's advances. As the novel coyly puts it, he vibrates "between an instinctive conviction of monstrous wickedness and a logical and well-reasoned perception that he had all the facts and materials for a perfectly good conscience" (*IS* 784). Small wonder that William James, ever the lover of paradox, found *Indian Summer* an exquisite delight. As he confessed to the author, "How you tread the narrow line of nature's truth so infallibly is more than I can understand."[16]

William was not the only member of the James clan who viewed Howells's recent work with appreciative wonder. After the public disparagement he suffered on account of *The Bostonians* (which, critics alleged, obviously defamed certain respectable citizens of that fair city),[17] brother Henry read *The Rise of Silas Lapham* with something approaching awe. Every literate person in London ("including myself") admired "the truth and power" of the novel, James told Grace Norton. "But what hideousness of life!" he immediately continued. "They don't revile Howells when he does America, and such an America as that, and why do they revile me? The 'Bostonians' is sugar-cake, compared with it."[18] However, the tinge of astonished resentment evident here did not prevent James from complimenting Howells through the agency of their common publisher, whom he implored to tell the author that *Silas Lapham* was "tremendously good—life & reality caught in the very fact."[19]

Had his own recent work been treated more favorably in the United States, James might not have remarked upon Howells's apparent immunity from public censure. But the expatriate novelist anxiously sensed that the modest tide of popular favor he briefly enjoyed (first marked in 1879 by the auspicious piracy of "Daisy Miller") was now beginning to ebb. The transatlantic success of *The Portrait of a Lady* seemed to solidify James's sense of authorial command ("I, too, am 'someone' here," he proudly wrote back to England from the nation's capital in 1882; it is worth remembering that he was not utterly deaf even to the more vulgar appeals of celebrity),[20] but when his next two serials (*The Bostonians* and *The Princess Casamassima* [1885–86]) failed to generate "an audible echo or reverberation of any kind," an ominous foreboding overtook him. "If I had not my bread and butter to earn," he confided to Howells, "I should lay down my pen tomorrow—hard as it is, at my age, to confess one's self a rather offensive fiasco."

Other circumstances exacerbated the author's growing pessimism, most notably the business failure (in 1885) of James Ripley Osgood, the affable New Englander who had been publishing James and Howells since the early years of the decade. While Howells managed to survive Osgood's collapse without pecuniary harm, James never received the substantial sum of four thousand dollars owed him upon completion of the serial run of *The Bostonians*. Almost overnight his most lucrative contract to date became a worthless scrap of paper, and he had to scramble unaccustomedly to find a decent home for his newly orphaned novel. This turning point in their professional lives warrants scrutiny given that the consequences for James and Howells were so markedly different. While James, remote from the scene, suffered acutely from his ignorance about Osgood's affairs, Howells was in a position to profit from what we would now call insider information. Forewarned of the publisher's impending catastrophe, Howells had already begun independent negotiations with the New York firm of Harper & Brothers, with whom he eventually concluded an extremely lucrative contract.[21] Sitting in comparative darkness, James lacked this competitive advantage, though he was eager to glean whatever information he could. "Do let me know," James quickly wrote to their mutual friend Edmund Gosse, "if you hear anything of interest from W. D. H. about his connection with the Osgood infamy."[22]

James also pressed his brother William to make similar inquiries. Even before receiving this request from London, William instinctively took the initiative the day he received word of Osgood's insolvency. Writing to Howells, he correctly surmised that "Harry will no doubt be rather impatient to learn whether he is likely to lose much by Osgood's failure." "If you know in your own case," he asked Howells, "how matters are to stand, can't you tip him a line of information? Or can you tell me how to find out?" A week later William repeated this request with an aggravated tone of desperation. "I suppose you know how Osgood's affairs are going," he again suggested to Howells. "I know absolutely nothing, nor of the thing to be done under such circumstances. Do you suppose it would lessen Harry's risks in any way if I were to put his interests into a lawyer's hands to look after?"[23] Finding Howells's response to William unsatisfactory, James appealed directly to his confrere and expressed "a friendly hope" that Osgood's bankruptcy "has not fallen heavily upon *you*." "I am sorry to say," he confessed, "that my own connection with the defunct has not been one on which I could congratulate myself," and then proceeded to append the "sordid details" of his loss. A rather touching example of Jamesian indirection, this letter was nevertheless a serious plea for help.

No evidence survives to suggest that Howells responded directly to James's missive. Interpreting his curious silence is not simple, especially in the light (or, perhaps more suggestively, the shadow) of *Silas Lapham*, the financial plot of which pivots on an uncannily analogous withholding of evidence, and which Howells had finished writing only two months before. At that very same moment, in fact, he had just concluded his first tentative negotiations with the Harpers, finding the prospects "extremely gratifying."[24] The temptation to conceal certain facts, to take advantage of privileged information, is precisely what Silas Lapham must confront and, ultimately, resist. When William James had urged Howells to "tip [Henry] a line," he unwittingly hit upon the device that Howells had used to salvage the stature of his novel's protagonist, whose "rise" is predicated upon his recognition that a higher moral law should supersede the statutory capitalist principle of *caveat emptor,* which otherwise would prevent the collapse of his business empire. In his time of crisis Lapham refuses to defraud an investor who is eager to sink a fortune in his namesake mineral paint, an enterprise that has become ruinously vulnerable to outside competition. "All I had to do was to keep quiet about that other company," Lapham admits to his conscientious wife.

> But I had to tell him how I stood. I had to tell him about it, and what I wanted to do. He began to back water in a minute, and the next morning I saw that it was up with him. He's gone back to New York. I've lost my last chance. Now all I've got to do is to save the pieces.[25]

Given the rapacious tendencies of nineteenth-century economic life, Lapham's tidy self-sacrifice has seemed to many critics rather improbable.[26] Indeed, what Howells could accomplish in fiction he may not have been able to replicate in life, when the pressure of Osgood's collapse put him to an uncomfortably similar test. Rather like Lapham, Howells at first refused to believe that his publisher's troubles would prove insurmountable; after all, the "puissant Osgood" (as Howells had described him) had survived many tough scrapes before. Perhaps for that reason he did not respond to his absent friend's early alarm. To William James, at least, Howells conveyed an optimistic view of the situation, for on the ninth of June the novelist's brother sent congratulatory intimations to London. "I'm very glad you're not to lose by Osgood," he reported promisingly to Henry; "Howells was here a few days since—called him a perfectly *honest* man, so far as he knew."[27]

Osgood may have been honest, but he was no longer credit-worthy. By early June Howells already knew that Benjamin Ticknor, Osgood's former associate, was organizing a new company and wanted very much to keep both American writers on his list by offering to pay "any royalties or other indebtedness that are now in arrears."[28] Howells quickly maneuvered to secure his own interests, and Ticknor agreed to continue the $150 weekly salary the author had been receiving from Osgood through March of the following year and immediately to make up all his back pay (over $1,700). In exchange Howells granted Ticknor the right to publish *Silas Lapham* as a volume and to keep the other titles on Osgood's list (*Indian Summer, A Woman's Reason, A Modern Instance, Dr. Breen's Practice, A Fearful Responsibility,* and various small books of travel and dramatic farces).[29] Somewhat ironically, the obvious popularity of *Silas Lapham* (which was still appearing serially in the *Century*) gave Howells particular leverage, for it was in anticipation of publishing the author's future work that Ticknor agreed to such generous terms. When, two months later, Howells concluded a separate arrangement with the Harpers, Ticknor understandably was aggrieved; if this author pretended to believe in Reverend Sewell's theory of the economy of pain, his publisher was getting more than his share.[30]

To measure the true extent of Howells's knowledge (or the manipulative uses to which it may have been put) is, of course, difficult; and it would be a mistake to assert that he deliberately sought to profit at James's expense. But it is hard to deny that, within a few short months, Howells gained precisely what James irrevocably lost: the security of a long-term commitment (and guaranteed income) from a reputable publisher. As the novelist who would go on to write *The World of Chance* (1893), a lachrymose story about the vicissitudes of publishing, Howells was getting a pretty good view of such caprice at first hand. His recent experience, however, might also have revealed a sense of his own complicity in the outcomes that the marketplace dictated. Benjamin Ticknor may well have had other reasons for canceling James's contract for *The Bostonians*, but, considering the shaky finances of his struggling new company, the expensive campaign to keep Howells surely would have figured into his thinking. Though Ticknor was reluctant to lose either writer from his list, even a quick glance at the firm's publishing records would have reminded him that Howells was the safer bet: his books outsold James's by at least three to one.[31] Howells aggressively (and successfully) worked every advantage with Ticknor, renegotiating his already favorable contracts and securing his seventy-five-hundred-dollar salary—only to give all his future books to the rival Harpers; James's sole bid to get better terms for *The Bostonians* miserably backfired. Capped by the prosperous career of *Silas Lapham*, Howells's income in 1885 rose to new heights; James, however, could say only one thing: "This year has been disastrous."[32]

Such stark differences can belie latent similarities, for Howells, too, had his share of setbacks that year—especially after his daughter Winifred's health broke down that autumn, on the eve of her social debut in Boston. Looking back on this period of his life, at any rate, Howells told an interviewer that just when his affairs were flush and "prospering, his work marching as well as heart could wish, suddenly, and without apparent cause, the status seemed wholly wrong." In his own words, "The bottom dropped out."[33] Understandably, critics and biographers have had some difficulty ascertaining the precise meaning of this confession, which seems to carry with it dark hints of a Swedenborgian "vastation" or more secular nervous breakdown.[34] Almost nothing in Howells's correspondence from this time warrants such a conclusion, however; his letters brim with the customary literary chatter, outline plans for the usual meandering summer vacation (the Berkshires, the Maine coast, the White Mountains), actually speak favorably about the family's general health and well-being. (Winny's relapse did not occur until October.) But if they are obsessed with good humor, these letters are also obsessed with money; indirectly, at least, they lend credence to Lewis Simpson's assertion that "in the very midst of success and power" Howells was overcome by "a suspicion—irrational but compelling"—that "he had betrayed the ideal of literary life in America."[35]

To a considerable extent, that ideal depended upon the artist's jealous preservation of his freedom, which the depressing hegemony of bourgeois culture historically had threatened. For James the best solution was simply to live abroad, although he could never fully escape the marketplace imperatives to secure a public and sell his work. Howells, on the other hand, wanted to make use of the very aspects of American life that James found so repugnant—the pedestrian life of the new urban middle class, of which his family was very much a part— and therefore had a trickier compromise to work out (the reality of which he was only too well aware). At the same time that evidence of the culture's widening inequality began seriously to irritate his social conscience, the private demands of family life seemingly required him to endure a life of persistent contradiction. "Ah! The expenses!" he exclaimed only half-facetiously to one correspondent on a spring day in 1885. "I am on fire, and I *must boil*. . . . I must give my daughter her chance in this despicable world,—where I'm so much better for having had none; I must get my boy through school and into college,—where I'm so much wiser for not having been!"[36] Even as he grew increasingly critical of the plutocratic concentration of wealth made possible by the noncompetitive tendencies of industrial capitalism, Howells recognized (and could not resist) the pecuniary advantage of "monopolizing" himself as a cultural commodity.[37]

"Nobody knew the business of authorship better than Howells," Edwin Cady confidently affirmed. "[C]ertainly like no one before, and possibly like no one after," he discovered "how to make writing pay steadily, fully, even handsomely without selling out either his artistic or civic conscience."[38] The facts of the novelist's success are probably indisputable, but Cady's rather homiletic conclusion is not. No one doubted it more than Howells himself. Almost from the moment that he signed his lucrative long-term contract with the Harpers, an inward sense that he had made a kind of Faustian bargain overtook him. "I am a coward," he said in an unusually revealing moment, "and all kinds of a tacit liar—not because I don't love the truth, heaven knows, but because I'm afraid to tell it very often." Even if Howells meant these words in jest, the humor takes on a blackish tinge when we recognize that no one has ever given a better summary judgment of his whole career.[39]

In spite of Howells's nascent advocacy of literary realism, critics on both sides of the Atlantic had already discerned in his stories a "leaning to rose-colour." As the *Westminster Review* sharply noted in 1884, "after promising to give us sound realistic work, embodying both observation and meditation on life, he has descended to the function of producing lollipops."[40] While the treacly resolution of *A Woman's Reason* may have prompted this particular remark (James, too, we should recall, had warned against a tendency toward "factitious glosses"), many of the author's later books also disappoint the readerly expectations they simultaneously invite. With the possible exception of the Marches (whose irrepressible badinage effectually justifies their complacency), his characters seldom respond fully to the dramatic possibilities with which their lives are invested; their credibility diminishes almost in direct proportion to the realized pressure of social and economic circumstance that bears down upon them. The most critically aware figures become the most mired by inconsequence; the gestures that would make them truly memorable routinely evade or escape them. Ironically, the novels become politically inert at the same time that their documentary value becomes historically significant. The "truth" toward which they aspire (echoing Howells's phrase) takes the form of a tacit lie, a consoling half-truth, that his circumspect editors and audience presumably would find more acceptable. As Alfred Kazin has suggested, the most important thing about Howells's "sometimes enervating literary career is that one cannot imagine him writing without an audience, writing against the current, writing in advance of his time. He is the professional writer to perfection," utterly—almost too exquisitely—attuned to the demands of the marketplace.[41]

In this, perhaps, he was not alone. At least one observer in the 1880s recognized Howells and James (and, not incidentally, F. Marion Crawford) as "the most distinctly professional novelists in America," an epithet they earned by virtue of their incessant productivity. Horace E. Scudder went on to describe these writers (with a certain class-bound irony) as "knights of labor who never seem dissatisfied with their lot, never work less than twenty-four hours a day,— it is impossible that they can accomplish all they do in less time,—and never seem to be engaged on any strike or boycotting lark."[42] This tendency (or need) to define literary labor in opposition to manual work was something that both Howells and James struggled with most of their professional lives; but the particular historical circumstances of this crucial decade forced each to confront a central vocational paradox in separate ways. If, as literary historians have recently observed, the practice of realism also became a strategy for defining the social position of the writer, the divergent examples of James and Howells should remind us that such claims to cultural authority could manifest themselves in radically different forms.[43] While it seemed to many of their contemporaries that their careers thus far had run in tandem, by 1890 their work deliberately resisted obvious parallelism.

More profoundly than James, Howells understood and accepted literature as a social institution; consequently he was more willing to establish himself within a relatively public sphere of literary production and to abide by the normative values it promulgated. James's frustration with that sphere drove him, at least temporarily, to abandon the novel in favor of the drama (a form in which he mistakenly assumed that he could exercise more direct control over his material and his audience) and, ultimately, to consecrate himself to a more exclusively private conception of art. Even to speak of the public's "taste" became, for James, a hopeless contradiction: as he pointedly advised one friend, "look at Mr. Smith's bookstalls & you'll see." The novelist admitted,

> Certainly I must, as a peintre de moeurs & de caractère, be exasperating in my poor way, but it isn't—I think—in trying to give what the main public & *gros* reader want that I shall seek the right remedy. They "want" simply bottomless niaiserie. . . . Give them what one wants oneself—it's the only way: *follow* them & they lead one by a straight grand highway to abysses of vulgarity.

In his literary columns and private letters Howells, on the other hand, increasingly deprecated "what people call 'art.'" He preferred the natural to the mannered, even at the risk of skirting the abyss James so desperately feared. "I like nearness to life," he forthrightly declared, life "portrayed with conscience, with knowledge, both deep and quick, and with a most satisfying, self-respectful simplicity and clearness, which is the only 'art' worth having."[44]

Some time would pass, however, before these differences became especially noticeable in their work. In the meantime, their mutual commitment to the documentary project of realism led both James and Howells to take to the streets with notebook and pencil in hand. Freshness and vitality of direct observation were what James complimented in *The Minister's Charge* (Howells's next novel); perhaps it should come as no surprise that the creator of Millicent Henning (that robust, cocknified foil to the title figure of *The Princess Casamassima*) could almost imagine himself writing the part of Howells's street-smart 'Manda Grier. In the "Editor's Study," James's friend would reciprocate, recommending *The Princess Casamassima* as "the greatest novel of the year" published in English, a generous attempt to make up for the book's otherwise lukewarm reception. As William promptly reported to his brother, "Howells told me the other night that he had written a rousing eulogy of your *Princess* for the next Harper, and he had n't a fault to find with it"—praise that also might have been merited because the author seemed to be taking up a theme that Howells had recommended to him in 1882 ("to paint in some story the present phase of change in England"). A handful of other glowing tributes arrived from Lowell and George du Maurier, but public criticism of the novel (especially in England) tended to be scornful.[45]

The Minister's Charge provoked a similar response in America; indeed, becoming conspicuous targets for "printed animosity" inspired in both men a new level of frankness and sympathy in their correspondence, which increasingly sought to compensate for what James called "the stupidity of the age." Though he could hardly relish adverse criticism, Howells at least could take comfort in his salary from the Harpers. James, however, had greater cause for alarm, which he famously expressed in his 1888 New Year's letter to Howells; he now feared that *The Bostonians* and *The Princess Casamassima* had "reduced the desire, & the demand, for [his] productions to zero." To help remedy this, Howells consistently lauded James's latest fictions in his *Harper* column—and not just by repeating the usual twaddle of magazine puffery. He courageously affirmed: "It is in a way discreditable to our time that a writer of such quality should ever have grudging welcome; the fact impeaches not only our intelligence, but our sense of the artistic." Howells correctly prophesied that future readers would look back with astonishment at the disappointing facts of James's contemporaneous reception.

Howells could also admire *The Princess* for the way in which James had tried to resolve the same narrative dilemma posed by *The Minister's Charge:* how to represent and make credible the intelligent awareness of social disorder through a character deprived of educational advantage. Analyzing that problem would become the focus of James's explanatory preface to *The Princess Casamassima* in the New York Edition (1908), which ends up being much more than an apology for Hyacinth Robinson's unusual perspicacity; in addition, James offers here his most detailed elaboration of the structural significance of a novel's center of consciousness and the particular pleasure that results from "placing advantageously, placing right in the middle of the light, the most polished of possible mirrors of the subject."[46] In writing *The Minister's Charge*, Howells eventually discovered that the diminished intellectual luster of Lemuel Barker, his rusticated protagonist, could not adequately reflect the subject that had come to occupy him; he therefore displaced that subject—the problem of social "complicity"—into the consciousness (and verbal performance) of his American exemplar of Victorian doubt, the Reverend David Sewell, whose credentials afford him a climactic opportunity to deliver a sermon on that theme. Howells closes the novel with an indirect report of this oratorical triumph (which reverberates through the newspapers as far west as Chicago) and necessarily inculpates his audience in its most pressing implication. "If a community was corrupt, if an age was immoral," Howells solemnly intones, "it was not because of the vicious, but the virtuous who fancied themselves indifferent spectators."[47]

This explicitly political turn in Howells's thinking has often been credited to his reading of Tolstoy, but he could have been challenged just as forcefully by some of the more perceptive criticism his own work thus far had elicited. As one observer noted in 1883, while Howells was "heartily democratic in his theories, his tastes and sympathies nevertheless seem[ed] to lead dangerously toward aristocratic exclusiveness." (Too much, in other words, like James.) From this point forward, at any rate, Howells largely accepted the artistic agenda laid out for him here: to shift "from trifles to principles"; to break through "the external crust of character traits to the real springs of national character itself"; to "put his hand effectively upon our peculiar national problems." Pursuing an insight that modern historians have only recently begun to take seriously, this same critic recognized that Howells's work implicitly betrayed a much broader shift in social values, contingent upon a newly emergent hierarchy of professional status. "That floating stratum of culture which, in some of our older cities, is separating and refining itself from the industrous multitudes is refining away, with much that is indeed coarse-grained and uncultivated, nearly all that is intrinsically American in our life"—a remark that significantly anticipates both a major theme in almost all of Howells's later fiction (beginning with *The Rise of Silas Lapham*) and the thesis of Lawrence Levine's *Highbrow/Lowbrow*. [48]

We can sense Howells's ambivalent relation to his most critical insights about American culture through the way in which Lemuel Barker becomes cognizant of invidious distinction. After a series of misadventures (which briefly lands him in jail), Barker eventually takes a porter's job at a boarding house, the shabbiness of which escapes his notice. An ungraduated sense of urban luxury overwhelms Barker when he first arrives in Boston; but the discriminating attitude of Howells's narrative voice never fails to remind us of the kind of social knowledge the young man has yet to gain.

> At the hotel, Lemuel remained in much of his original belief in the fashion and social grandeur of the ladies who formed the majority of Mrs. Harmon's guests. Our womankind are prone to a sort of helpless intimacy with those who serve them; the ladies had an instinctive perception of Lemuel's trustiness, and readily gave him their confidence and much of their history. He came to know them without being at all able to classify them with reference to society at large, as of that large tribe among us who have revolted from domestic care, and have skillfully

unseated the black rider who remains mounted behind the husband of the average lady-boarder. (TMC 137–38)

The narrative reserves comparative judgment to itself—or, rather, invites the reader to share in this exercise of discriminating observation. From the confident tone of the passage, we can assume that the author, too, has an "instinctive perception" of his audience's "trustiness": they will accept the specific criterion for classification (the absence of a serviceable, and significantly anonymous, African-American) and recognize the economic distinction that Barker cannot measure. Howells's realism will not allow him to attribute such keen perception to his innocent protagonist, but neither does it necessarily enhance our sympathy for a doltish young man from the provinces. As with *Silas Lapham*, Howells encourages his audience to make reading an act of liberal condescension.

Contrary to his instinctive egalitarianism, Barker eventually learns "that there were sorts of honest work in the world which one must not do if he would keep his self-respect through the consideration of others." Although this degrading ideology of labor provokes in him "a turmoil of suspicions," he nevertheless internalizes it and begins to esteem "the boarders at the St. Albans in the degree that he thought them enlightened enough to contemn him for his station" (TMC 172–73). Howells intends his readers to feel the pathos of this ironic self-sacrifice and thereby to recognize their own complicity in its consequences; but the novel never effectively repudiates the implicit fatalism of its psychological representations. "Endowed as he is with some kind of genius," Barker is still "a kind of fool," John De Forest pregnantly told Howells. "He can't rise (except in mere fits of resultless longing) above his birth-line."[49] Compromised by its own ways of knowing, the novel resists the political implications it wants most to convey.

Try as he might, Barker will never be one of those people on whom nothing is lost; but neither is he (in contrast to James's Hyacinth Robinson) one of those people on whom nothing rubs off. Whatever its embarrassments, Barker is much more at home with his intrinsic vulgarity than James's sad little hero—who, though a bastard by birth, behaves (as Irving Howe once noted) as if he were immaculate in conception.[50] In spite of his initiation to culture in the Brahmin household of the Coreys (like Sewell, carried forward from *The Rise of Silas Lapham*), Barker never completely surrenders a kind of stubborn self-reliance which the legacy of accumulated leisured has dissipated among the comfortable Bostonians with whom he comes to live. As Bromfield Corey, the mild-mannered patriarch, says of him, "He's as true as a Tuscan peasant, as proud as an Indian, and as quick as a Yankee." Without a hint of irony, the old man delights in "seeing the great variety of human nature there is in every human being here. Our life," he happily declares, "isn't stratified; perhaps it never will be. At any rate, for the present, we're all in vertical sections" (TMC 261–62). In spite of this atmosphere of complacent pluralism, the Corey household cannot retain Barker for very long. A premature engagement restricts him to getting "work that should not take him too far away from the kind of people his betrothed was used to," a decision that invokes both "pity and respect" in Reverend Sewell, who is even somewhat relieved that "life had already taught this wisdom, this resignation," to the young man (*TMC* 300). Whether Howells, too, endorses this conservative subordination of personal ambition to social duty remains an open question (Sewell's judgment seems less reliable here than in *Silas Lapham*). In *The Princess Casamassima* James subordinates Hyacinth's "duty" (his anarchist pledge to commit murder) to private despair: the assassin's bullet pierces his own heart.

In different ways both Lemuel Barker and Hyacinth Robinson are artists manqué: the former a failed poet (who first comes to the city because of Sewell's misplaced adulation of his verse), the latter a would-be man of letters whose aesthetic instincts must largely be satisfied in binding the work of others. Coincidentally, perhaps, both young men experience a kind of aesthetic awakening in the libraries of their respective aristocratic patrons; but, as envisioned by James and Howells, the immediate reactions of their quickened sensibilities contrast significantly. For Robinson, the treasure-filled library at Medley—"row upon row of finely-lettered backs"—becomes a secular sanctuary from poverty and his tormented awareness of inequality. To be locked within its luxurious brown walls (and beneath its "dimly gilt" ceiling) constitutes "his vision of true happiness."[51] In Bromfield Corey's library (similarly decorated with "Italian saints and martyrs in their baroque or gothic frames of dim gold" and "low shelves with their ranks of luxurious bindings"), Barker's revelations do not inspire the same sense of isolated contentment. He wonders at first that neither of Corey's daughters can find the time to read to their father (the service for which he has been hired), "not knowing," as Howells writes, "the disability for mutual help that riches bring." It is not long, however, before Barker sees "that they could not have rendered nor their father have received from his family the duty which he was paid to do, as they must have done if they had been poorer" (*TMC* 258). For James the library serves as an ideal place of refuge; for Howells there is no escape from the cash nexus.

Complicity

In his published remarks about *The Princess Casamassima*, Howells took great pity on the "troubled soul" of the "little, morbid, manly" bookbinder, who finds himself drawn into an anarchist conspiracy. The critic's attitude was prophetic, for within six months he found himself urging clemency for a group of men who had been convicted for the anarchist bombing of Chicago's Haymarket Square in May 1886. Not even circumstantial evidence could link the accused prisoners to the scene of violence, but a frenzied public was eager for retribution and discounted their alibis. As Howells bitterly observed, the trial put the interests of the newspapers before those of justice. Seven men faced the death penalty; another was to serve fifteen years in the state penitentiary. When an appeal for a writ of error was set aside by the Illinois Supreme Court, Howells (notably alone among the nation's literary figures) petitioned the governor of Illinois to commute their sentences and wrote a public letter to the New York *Tribune* urging others to do the same. Even before his letter was printed, one of the condemned men had committed suicide; two were spared when Governor Richard J. Oglesby commuted their sentences to life imprisonment; the other four were hanged a week later.[1]

In the sorrowful wake of this event, Howells penned another letter (apparently never sent) which nevertheless testifies to a vital link between his literary and social priorities. What Howells demanded of the artist (truthful treatment of material) was precisely what he expected of a court of law or any other democratic institution (a proper regard for the evidence) in conducting its proceedings. Howells denigrated romance and sentimentality because their promiscuous indulgence by popular writers paralleled, in a literary sense, the violation of public trust that he had witnessed in the nation's economic and political life. The four men hanged in Chicago "would be alive today," Howells wrote, "if one thousandth part of the means employed to compass their death had been used by the people to inquire into the question of their guilt; for, under the forms of law, their trial has not been a trial by justice, but a trial by passion, by terror, by prejudice, by newspaper." The same agencies—passion and terror—that Howells decried in best-selling novels for seducing almost every intelligent reader to some degree he also held responsible for the gravest miscarriage of justice the nation had yet seen. On November 11, 1887, four men died, "in the prime of the first Republic the world has ever known, for their opinion's sake."[2]

When Howells said (in the same unposted letter) that he looked forward to a time when journalism might cease so that history could begin, he anticipated a judgment that James would render more comically in *The Reverberator* (1888). James's novelistic jeu d'esprit innocently turns away from matters of political injustice, but its satire (like Howells's pessimism) derives completely from contemporaneous events. Somewhat ironically, this story about unwanted publicity is the closest thing to a roman à clef that James ever wrote.[3] As professional men of letters, both Howells and James knew firsthand the potentially corrosive effects of a journalistic age; indeed, Bartley Hubbard and Matthias Pardon rank among its first inky apostles. Defending art from the invasion of the newspaper was no simple task, since the genteel monthly magazines from which both men derived so much of their income faced increasing competition from an ever-widening array of print media, and inexorably felt pressured to adopt the new devices that seemed to attract a wider readership. Not even the venerable *Atlantic* could hold out forever against accepting paid advertisements or employing illustrators, from abbreviating stories and serial installments or running chatty columns about its contributors' personal affairs. Irresistibly, these circumstances inspired both writers to chronicle the troubling (though frequently comic) incongruity between the ideal life of letters and the modern realities of the literary vocation. "The mere sight of my name in a newspaper," James wryly confessed upon completing *The Reverberator*, "still causes me torture & anguish. You may say that with that degree of sensibility one has no business to write—& indeed I often think I have none."[4]

"The Man of Letters as a Man of Business" was the oxymoronic title Howells chose for his most important essay on this subject; but by the time that piece first appeared in 1892, both writers already had explored this vocational contradiction in numerous works of fiction. In story after story, James took up multifarious aspects of this conflict between "art" and "the world"—which didn't prevent him also from devoting a sprawling novel, *The Tragic Muse* (1890), to the same donnée ("one of the half-dozen great primary motives," he later said, available to an artist).[5] In *The World of Chance* (1893) Howells, too, composed a novel around that conflict, though it was eminently foreshadowed by a much greater work, *A Hazard of New Fortunes* (1889–90). A presumption of incompatibility—or "binary opposition" as some theoreticians would say—hovers behind most of James's melodramatic parables about the social (mis)construction of art. Success is always failure in a world devoid of taste; following in the footsteps of the huge, flat-footed public can never lead to the gates of paradise (or "the country of the blue" invoked by the narrator at the conclusion of "The Next Time"). As soon as he finished *The Tragic Muse*, James proclaimed to his brother that he was utterly "divorced" from any concern for the novel's sale or popularity: "One must go one's own way & know what one's about & have a general plan & a private religion—in short have made up one's mind as to *ce qui en est* with a public the draggling after which simply leads one in the gutter. One has always a 'public' enough if one has an audible vibration—even if it shld. only come for one's self."[6] "The Lesson of the Master" (1888), "The Real Thing" (1892), "Greville Fane" (1892), "The Middle Years" (1893), "The Next Time" (1895): all of these tales forcibly echo this conclusion; each is a study in contrast and social antagonism.

For Howells, on the other hand, the fable of the artist usually becomes a more desperate study in social complicity. Because he was less inclined to privilege art above other values, Howells rarely grants his fictional writers, painters, and sculptors the kind of immunity that James frequently bestows. In Howells's world, the production (and, even more so, the passive appreciation) of art is always shadowed by some kind of social cost. For James art always seems to possess an absolute surplus value that can never really be calculated; for Howells art typically assumes an exchange value, even though the market seldom can find its true equivalent. Recognizing this nettlesome inequality often becomes a source of pain in Howells's work; in James's fiction the same disproportion contributes to more brilliant displays of irony and satire.

In a letter to James (10 October 1888) Howells famously recorded his growing disenchantment with the more smiling aspects of American life, remarking that unless it based itself "anew on a real equality," our predatory culture would never fulfill its democratic promise. For fifty years he had optimistically remained "content with 'civilization' and its ability to come out all right in the end," but now Howells grimly felt that it was "coming out all wrong." He blandly confessed, however, to the hypocritical indulgence of wearing a fur-lined overcoat and living in all the luxury his money could buy. Resorting to family autobiography was a path Howells could least resist when it came to writing fiction. In *A Hazard of New Fortunes* the conceited polymath Angus Beaton purchases a new fur-lined overcoat for himself rather than send his earnings home to the invalid father from whom he has borrowed money. Beaton's selfishness exemplifies only one dimension of the author's troubled conscience; indeed, a major strength of the novel is the confident freedom with which Howells distributes his imaginative energy among an unusually wide variety of characters. No one understood this virtue better than James, whose astonishingly perceptive epistolary response to the novel probably represents the highest commendation Howells ever received. Only James's "birthday" tribute to his friend can rival the appreciative wonder of this letter.

In a sort of preface to these gratifying remarks, James penned his first words of praise for the book in a dispatch to William. Finding *Hazard* "so prodigiously good & able, & so beyond what [Howells] at one time seemed in danger of reducing himself to," James announced that he intended to write the author "a gushing letter about it not a day later than tomorrow." True to his word, the next day James filled both sides of twenty-six sheets with his inimitable bounding scrawl—a letter remarkable not only for its length but also for the fidelity with which the novelist's critical script conforms to his private judgment. Naturally, to Howells his tone is somewhat more genial; but James does not gloss over his reservations or simply withhold them, Januslike, to gloat over them with other correspondents, as he once routinely had done. Instead, he can observe (ungrammatically) Howells's want of form ("there's a whole quarter of the heaven upon which, in the matter of composition, you seem to be consciously—*is* it consciously?—to have turned your back"), without dulling the edge of his remark to William that his friend had purchased his "abundance & facility . . . by throwing the whole question of form, style & composition over board into the deep sea—from which, on my side, I am perpetually trying to fish them up."[7]

It is worth remembering that James probably had not hooked them yet: whatever its other merits, neither economy of form nor concision of statement are obvious features of *The Tragic Muse* (although William did pay his brother a characteristically backhanded compliment by observing, "Your sentences are straighter and simpler than before, and your felicities of observation are on every page"—all 882 of them).[8] Howells, too, could joke about his friend's habitual expository excrescences, the witty parenthetical elaborations that give James's books from this period an almost suffocating richness of literary ornamentation (and truly Victorian heft). In their seemingly endless search for a place to live in New York, Basil and Isabel March are abashed by the material splendor of Mrs. Grosvenor Green's furnished flat, in which the "items of high civilization" are everywhere apparent:

> The front of the upright piano had what March called a short-skirted portière on it, and the top was covered with vases, with dragon candlesticks, and with Jap fans, which also expanded themselves bat-wise on the walls between the etchings and the water-colors. The floors were covered with filling, and then rugs, and then skins; the easy-chairs all had tidies, Armenian and Turkish and Persian; the lounges and sofas had embroidered cushions hidden under tidies. The radiator was concealed by a Jap screen, and over the top of this some Arab scarfs were flung. There was a superabundance of clocks. China pugs guarded the hearth; a brass sunflower smiled from the top of either andiron, and a brass peacock spread its tail before them inside a high filigree fender; on one side was a coal-hod in repoussé brass, and on the other a wrought-iron wood basket. Some red Japanese bird-kites were stuck about in the necks of spelter vases, a crimson Jap umbrella hung opened beneath the chandelier, and each globe had a shade of yellow silk.
>
> March, when he had recovered his self-command a little in the presence of the agglomeration, comforted himself by calling the bric-à-brac Jamescracks, as if this was their full name.[9]

The pun immediately strikes its target with the capital letter; but we can also read Howells's ridiculous catalogue, full of cumbersome aesthetic detail, as a belatedly sardonic reply to its negative counterpart in James's *Hawthorne*. Exaggeratedly cosmopolitan, Mrs. Grosvenor Green's America is anything but empty. Europeanized taste has denatured everything indigenous (as Hawthorne himself feared it would): a simple "wood" basket is dysfunctional wrought-iron; what should be a tin coalhod is instead repoussé brass. (And the mistress of it all, poor dear, is on her way back to Paris to renew her study of "art"!) As a finishing touch, Basil March, the author's occasional stand-in, cannot resist taking the apartment, in spite (or perhaps even because) of his wife's strenuous objections to its shameless excess.

All humor aside, *A Hazard of New Fortunes* and *The Tragic Muse* jointly recognize what Howells called "the very latest facts of society and art, and of that queer flirtation between them that can never be a marriage." The peculiar problem of vocation that the artist faces in a capitalist order lends poignance to the broader comedy of both novels, if indeed Howells's book can warrant that generic classification. Perhaps in response to the depressing reception accorded *The Bostonians* and *The Princess Casamassima*, after 1886 James largely abandoned his calculated experiment with naturalism—almost at the very moment that, with the Haymarket Affair an irresistible stimulus, Howells began to compile his most searching critical investigations of middle-class life. Thomas Hardy doubtless was too severe when, after reading *The Reverberator*, he noted that "James's subjects are those one could be interested in at moments when there is nothing larger to think of," but the comparative slightness of that novel (and even the ungainly *Tragic Muse*) did not go unremarked by others.[10]

Whatever comic assurance *Hazard* offers is nervous and fleeting. Perpetually assaulted by the realities of the modern city, the Marches cannot sustain their attitude of theatrical voyeurism in relation to it. "Their point of view," Howells writes,

> was singularly unchanged, and their impressions of New York remained the same that they had been fifteen years before: huge, noisy, ugly, kindly, it seemed to them now as it seemed then. The main difference was that they saw it more now as a life, and then they only regarded it a spectacle; and March could not release himself from a sense of complicity with it, no matter what whimsical, or alien, or critical attitude he took. A sense of the striving and the suffering deeply possessed him; and this grew the more intense as he gained some knowledge of the forces at work—forces of pity, of destruction, of perdition, of salvation. (*HNF* 305–6)

By now *complicity* has become a keyword (as Raymond Williams would say) in Howells's novelistic vocabulary, not merely sociological but theological in its overtones. Howells greatly enlarges the scope of his fiction by committing himself to search out the implications of this idea; but it can also incite him, as William James trenchantly observed, to fits of "queer spasmodic moralism."[11] Howells could avoid that problem in *A Hazard of New Fortunes* by distributing his critical views among a range of different characters who successfully exhibit the power of their author's capably dialogic imagination.[12] Indeed, the elder James exempted this novel from the qualification just cited. "The steady unflagging flow of it is something wonderful," he testified. "Ah! my dear Howells, it's worth something to be able to write such a book, and its so peculiarly *yours* too, flavored with your idiosyncrasy. (The book is so d———d humane!). . . . The year which shall have witnessed the apparition of your 'Hazard of New Fortunes,' of Harry's 'Tragic Muse,' and of *my* 'Psychology' will indeed be a memorable one in American Literature!!"[13]

In different ways, both of *Hazard*'s immediate predecessors, *April Hopes* (1888) and *Annie Kilburn* (1889), take their cue from *The Minister's Charge*, in which the concept of complicity first achieves thematic prominence. In *Annie*

Kilburn the writer's attempt to manifest immediate social relevance is possibly too obvious (as his first choice for a title, *The Upper and the Nether Millstones,* mordantly suggests). If Tolstoy was indeed a primary inspiration for the book (a number of critics detect a deliberate homology between *Anna Karenina* and the latter title), the brittle result tends to confirm James's charge that Howells could only make the great Russian into a bore.[14] The heroine's aggrieved sense of her own superfluousness is too forced to be truly convincing; her anxious scruples verge on self-pity, which occasionally provokes even the author to make light of her. Deliberately forgoing her comfortable life among the colony of (Jamesian) expatriates in Rome, she returns to America, as she says, to "try to do some good." Much to her surprise, however, from the moment she arrives in her native town of Hatboro', Massachusetts,

> the difficulty of being helpful to anything or any one increased upon her with every new fact that she had learned about it and the people in it. To her they seemed terribly self-sufficing. They seemed occupied and prosperous, from her front parlour window; she did not see anybody going by who appeared to be in need of her; and she shrank from a more thorough exploration of the place. She found she had fancied necessity coming to her and taking away her good works, as it were, in a basket. . . .[15]

Without knowing it, perhaps, Miss Kilburn is really a first cousin to James's more tortured Bostonian, Olive Chancellor, who has always wanted "to know intimately some *very* poor girl" (*TB* 832).

April Hopes is a much slyer novel, outwardly unconcerned with upper or nether millstones, except insofar as such a terrible apparatus may be set in motion by the "tortuous feminine mind" (as James immediately discerned). A very different reader, however, confidently could assume that the novel was intended to satirize the "useless, amiable and purposeless life certain wealthy Americans lead." Hamlin Garland's opinion may have been off base—as Howells himself said—but it was not altogether wrong.[16] As an acute register of social nuance and class-based perceptions of selfhood, *April Hopes* is unsurpassed in Howells's extensive canon. The novel opens amid the regalia of Harvard commencement week: lavish spreads under the embracing elms of the Yard; courtly displays of privilege and romance; the colorful festivities of Class Day. The nomenclature antedates the author's figurative use of it, but his characters don't need uppercase letters to appreciate this event's exclusionary social significance. "Well, it makes you feel that you *have* got a country, after all," the heroine's mother gratefully sighs. Mrs. Pasmer delivers this affirmation (we are told) as "a sort of apostrophe to her European self."[17] Her sense of security is put to the test, however, when she is obliged to gauge the uncertain social status of a handsome young graduate, Dan Mavering, who focuses his sights on her daughter. In the deceptively relaxed atmosphere of America, cosmopolitanism enforces severe habits of discrimination. Citizenship, in Mrs. Pasmer's country at least, is a privilege that not even a Harvard diploma automatically can guarantee.

In a clever set piece of Howellsian realism, the author suggestively evokes the incongruity between nature's benign leveling tendencies and society's unnatural stratifications. Collegiate tradition demands that an ordinary American elm display color out of season. The wreath of flowers that adorns the Class Day Tree is not just a pastoral indulgence, however, but rather the envied prize in a fiercely competitive scramble which belies the illusion of Arcadia in this grove of academe. Segregated in concentric circles about the tree, the various classes of undergraduates tensely await the signal; when the Marshal pitches his cap in the air, they all converge and clamber desperately to ascend the tree in pursuit of the fragile trophy. Whatever desultory reading these college men have done, they seem to know Spencer's *First Principles*. Those who are pulled down helplessly serve as the base for a swarming pyramid of kicking legs and snatching arms; inadvertently, the contest becomes a physical lesson in social Darwinism.

A warm June sun beats down on everyone, but the genteel artifice of Class Day transforms its rude energy into "painted light," just as carefully arranged tiers of spectators help to conceal the plebeian brick of the college buildings.

> The sun had not been oppressive at any time during the day, though the crowded buildings had been close and warm, and now it lay like a painted light on the grass and paths over which they passed to the entrance of the grounds around the Tree. Holden Chapel, which enclosed the space on the right as they went in, shed back the sun from its brick-red flank, rising unrelieved in its venerable ugliness by any touch of the festive preparations; but to their left and diagonally across from them high stagings supported tiers of seats along the equally unlovely red bulks of Hollis and of Harvard. These seats, and the windows in the stories above them, were densely packed with people, mostly young girls dressed in a thousand enchanting shades and colors, and bonneted and hatted to the last effect of fashion. They were like vast terraces of flowers to the swift glance, and here and there some brilliant parasol, spread to catch the sun on the higher ranks, was like a flaunting poppy, rising to the light and lolling out above the blooms of lower stature. But the parasols were few, for the two halls flung wide curtains of shade over the greater part of the spectators, and across to the foot of the chapel, while a piece of carpentry whose simplicity seems part of the Class Day tradition shut out the glare and the uninvited public, striving to penetrate the enclosure next the street. (AH 344–45)

When James returned to Cambridge almost twenty years later, he considered the Harvard campus too democratically permeable, still insufficiently guarded by gates or formidable enclosures. Howells, on the other hand, had already sensed their strategic superfluity; whenever necessary, the institution's personnel dependably could discourage most would-be invaders. When one member of the party recalls that on Class Day young women used to dance on the green, the passing of the custom is greeted with general relief. "I think it's just as well," one professor's wife tellingly remarks, "It was always a ridiculous affectation of simplicity." Similarly struck by the oddness of the idea, Dan murmurs to Alice Pasmer, "It must have been rather public." "It doesn't seem as if it could ever have been in character quite," the young woman responds (AH 336). She is wise beyond her twenty-one sheltered years.

The trials of keeping decorously "in character" occupy much of the rest of this novel, surely one of Howells's most derisive comedies. Its "happy" ending compares only with that of *The Bostonians* as a portent of discord. The romantic egotism of both young people threatens to wed them to moral absolutes rather than to each other. This is particularly true of Alice Pasmer, who is aptly described by a New York friend as "moybid." With her penchant for self-sacrifice, Alice easily imagines herself joining an Anglican sisterhood: as they did for so many other listless Americans of this period, the rituals (and sublimated sexuality) of Anglo-Catholicism exert a magnetic attraction for her.[18] "She isn't moybid in the usual sense of the woyd," Miss Anderson nasally remarks, "but she expects more of herself and of the woyld generally than anybody's going to get out of it" (*AH* 374–75). Her pronunciation may differ from the Master's, but the young woman from Brooklyn is only telling us what James had recently said in print, namely, that Howells's women in particular were of the best—"except, indeed, in the sense of being the best to live with." Inspired, perhaps, by James's cue, in *April Hopes* Howells makes that desperate virtue an almost comic necessity. Their respective infatuations deny his love-struck couple the insight into life's provisionality that the choric figure of Mrs. Brinkley offers. "We all have twenty different characters," she says at one point (sounding very much like *The Portrait*'s knowing Madame Merle), "more characters than gowns—and we put them on and take them off just as often for different occasions" (*AH* 592). If, as Howells later claimed, *April Hopes* was the first novel he completed "with the distinct consciousness that he was writing as a realist," he had good reason to thank James for helping him to that recognition.[19]

Just as the vagaries of New England's springtime weather undercut the title of *April Hopes* with incipient despair, the death of Winifred Howells (in March 1889) casts a pall over most of her father's work dating from these years. "When a man loses a loved child everything that is most tender in him must be infinitely lacerated," James wrote consolingly (and prophetically). The loss of his only son afflicts old Dryfoos at the end of *Hazard*; ghostly visitations from the repressed unconscious shatter any semblance of normalcy in *The Shadow of a Dream* (1890); in *The Quality of Mercy* (1892) the guilt-ridden protagonist is haunted by the memory of an elder daughter whose death and symptoms of acute anorexia nervosa bear an almost terrible resemblance to Winifred's. A decade after this book appeared, Grace Norton told James that a melancholy Howells recently had paid her a visit and confessed that he lived "under the dominion of 'fear.'" James confirmed this: "I've always known [that Howells had] a strange, sad kind of subterraneous crepuscular *alter ego*, a sort of 'down cellar' (where they keep the apples of discord) of gloom and apprehension." The marvel was how thoroughly his friend concealed it: "real as this condition in him is," James thought, "it is yet a thing disconnected, in a manner, from his *operative* self," which cheerfully went about the business of writing novels year in and year out. At the same time, James suspected that Howells's fiction secretly fed from this troubled source of psychic energy; the man's work valiantly tried to correct and compensate for his treacherous anxieties—a judgment not significantly improved upon by even the most informed psychoanalytic criticism of Howells's life and fiction.[20]

About such anguish Howells tended to be reticent; James, on the other hand, seemed to relish what he called the "imagination of disaster," his inclination to see life as "ferocious and sinister," permeated by a tragic sense of evil.[21] At least temporarily, though, Howells could share that point of view; nothing else explains the inception of *The Shadow of a Dream*, which occupies such an anomalous place in this author's rather sprightly canon. (Howells himself acknowledged the story's strangeness: he called it "a queer thing.")[22] When critics even bother to notice this work, they typically invoke it to qualify James's famous remark that Howells's perception of evil was minimal.[23] From an aesthetic standpoint, however, this eschatological approach to the *nouvelle* may be the least interesting way of interpreting it. More arresting, in some ways, is the story's experimental narrative technique, which employs a youthful (and rather censorious) Basil March as first-person narrator—an unusual deviation for Howells—and carefully circumscribes the rational boundaries of his omniscience. Structurally the work divides into three sections, each of which focuses on one of the characters implicated in the plot's triangular possibilities of wedded love and illicit passion. *The Shadow of a Dream*, then, can be said to reflect James's influence rather than to repudiate his judgment, for it immediately invites comparison with some of the shorter works (especially "A London Life" and "The Liar") that Howells had recently commended for their "clutch upon the unconscious motives which are scarcely more than impulses, instincts."

The lurid premise of "A London Life" (1888), for example, is the exposure of a young American woman to the presumed adultery (and possible divorce) of her sister and British brother-in-law, whose flagrant behavior torments her proper New England conscience. A penniless dependent in their household, Laura Wing nevertheless rebukes her sister, Selina, for violating the sacred trust of marriage and compromising her children's innocence. By restricting the point of view largely to the voice of wounded propriety, however, James frees the reader to question the validity of Laura's dutiful apprehensions, which assume an almost biblical majesty in their wrathful judgment. "You are all blind and senseless and heartless," she shouts at Selina's admittedly vulgar husband. "[G]lowing like a young prophetess [she exclaims,] 'There is a curse on you and there will be a judgment!' " (CT 7: 118). Are her fears justified or is she simply a provincial prude, feverishly making herself the victim of her culture's moralistic stereotypes? "Was she all wrong after all," she later wonders, "—was she cruel by being too rigid?" Should she instead

> propose to herself to "allow" more and more, and to allow ever, and to smooth things down by gentleness, by sympathy, by not looking at them too hard? It was not the first time the just measure of things seemed to slip from her hands as she became conscious of possible, or rather of very actual, differences of standard and usage. (165)

Basil March and his wife face a similar dilemma of "just measure" in *Shadow*, when they are condemned to interpret Douglas Faulkner's unspeakable dream of his wife's adultery and his best friend's betrayal. Reflecting on the terrible prospect that life might simply be a "series of stupid, blundering accidents," March solemnly meditates:

We who were nowhere when the foundations of the earth were laid, and knew not who had laid the measures of it, or stretched the line upon it, could only feel that our little corner of recognition afforded no perspective of the infinite plan; and we left those others to their place in it, not without commiseration, but certainly without trying to account for what had happened to them, or with any hope of ever offering a justification of it.[24]

While Laura Wing is tempted to play the role of an Old Testament Jehovah, March (borrowing his cadences from the Book of Job) significantly wants to renounce that responsibility.

As with so many of his other novels and tales, "A London Life" reflects James's melodramatic preference for teasing the reader with the revelation of extramarital secrets. Howells, always more circumspect, excels instead in the depiction of intramarital confidences. Appropriately enough, Selina and Lionel Berrington never once occupy the same room or carriage in James's tale. Basil and Isabel March are inseparable; even when they are not directly engaged in dialogue, their mental processes are telepathically synchronized. Without knowing it, old Mrs. Faulkner describes their marriage quite well when, paraphrasing Swedenborg, she affirms her belief that "one man and one woman shall live together to all eternity in a union that will make them one personality" (*SD* 90).

For the Marches that mystical prospect seems relatively benign, but for the others more sinister implications arise from the eruption of subconscious jealousy and the impotence of vicarious knowledge. Tormented by a vision of Hermia's infidelity, Faulkner at last succumbs to a psychosomatic paralysis of the heart as he sits in an "old neglected garden by the sea." In this Poelike setting, his final gesture, all the while glaring at the Reverend James Nevil (her supposed lover), is to push his wife away "with a look of fierce rejection" (*SD* 86, 42). These dramatic details remain wholly suggestive, however, for Dr. Wingate, Faulkner's medical confidante, refuses to divulge the painful narrative of his patient's recurrent nightmare until much later in the story. (Then it is revealed that the stricken man has repeatedly envisioned Hermia and Nevil exchanging vows in the same church where his own livid corpse awaits burial.) In the meantime, the other characters truly must contend with the shadow—or, rather, the shadows—of the dream that each separately constructs according to his (skeptical) or her (romantic) temperament. None, however, finally achieves complete expiation from imagined guilt. Nevil dies unable to profess the love he indeed feels for Hermia; she follows him to the grave within a year. As Basil March concludes, "we become so bewildered before the mere meaninglessness of events, at times, that it is a relief to believe in a cruel and unjust providence rather than in none at all" (*SD* 113). While Laura Wing can remove at last to the green shores of the Rappahanock (safer ground, morally, than the embankment of the Thames), the Marches must content themselves with the consolations of a rather withered puritanical philosophy. "I can conceive of no hate that could have framed a law so dreadful as the law of death," Howells wrote a month after Winny's death. "I must believe that Love did it."[25]

After that event, a bereaved father could not find the right words to thank

James for his letter of condolence, which Howells quoted with helpless pride to several other correspondents: "To be young & gentle & do no harm, & only to pay for it as if it were a crime." James's touching summary of Winifred's short life also serves uncannily as a prophecy of his own creative work. Betrayed innocence had always been one of the author's favorite themes, but in the nineties doomed and dying children populate James's fiction as never before. "The Pupil" (1891), *The Other House* (1896), *What Maisie Knew* (1897), *The Awkward Age* (1899), and most famously "The Turn of the Screw" (1898) all depict what James elsewhere referred to as "youth & high brightness so massacred in their flower."

The untimely passing of Wolcott Balestier provoked that particular remark, but a host of other sorrowful events contributed to James's elegiac mood in these years. His invalid sister, Alice, died of breast cancer in 1892; less than two years later two close literary friends were also gone: Constance Fenimore Woolson committed suicide in Venice, and tuberculosis claimed Robert Louis Stevenson on a far-off hilltop in Samoa. Closer to home, James had good reason to mourn not only his personal career ambitions but the fate of literature as well. The publishing world seemed increasingly inhospitable to his work. "Criticism" (James used quotes advisedly) was degenerating into the puerile exercise of publicity, a commodity that flowed through the periodical press "like a river that has burst its dikes."[26] After five sorry years his abortive experiment with the theater ended in public humiliation. Occasionally despondent and discouraged, James turned to Howells for support and advice, which the latter helpfully bestowed. Without flinching, Howells could honor his friend's literary superiority. The "aspiring eyes" of a new generation, he claimed, were fixed on James and no one else (not even on the Harpers' editorially anointed dean of American letters). Much has been written about Howells's generous encouragement of younger talent (Hamlin Garland, Stephen Crane, Henry Blake Fuller, Frank Norris, and many others); it has been easier to forget that without his help one rather mature writer might never have enjoyed his so-called major phase.[27] Through published comment and private exhortation, Howells diligently insisted upon James's preeminent craftsmanship and modernity, keeping outlets open to him that otherwise would have been closed.

Howells's detailed knowledge of the literary marketplace invariably found its way into his fiction, too. Never one to pass up opportunities, in businesslike fashion he transformed his sobering essay on "The Man of Letters as a Man of Business" into a parodic novel, *The World of Chance* (1893). Like *The Tragic Muse*, the book reveals that artistic success is always a socially contingent value. But in spite of its satiric content—which echoes some of James's more whimsical tales of the literary life ("Sir Domenick Ferrand" and "The Private Life" both appeared in 1892)—the novel mordantly despairs of reconciling private ambition and public good. Populated with literary aspirants and disappointed social reformers, *The World of Chance* superficially resembles *A Hazard of New Fortunes*, but it sourly suggests an even narrower prospect for human betterment (or vocational satisfaction). Neither the protagonist's romantic egotism nor the failed utopianism of the book's morbid socialists effectively challenges the inscrutable force exerted by the modern city. "Their common ignorance of what it was all for was like a bond," Howells writes (anticipating Dreiser), "and they clung involuntarily together in their unwieldy multitude because of the want of meaning, and prospered on, suffered on, through vast cyclones of excitement that whirled them round and round, and made a kind of pleasant-drunkenness in their brains, and consoled them for never resting and never arriving."[28]

The incessant flux of the novel partly reflects the author's own restlessness, which distinguished him (James said with mirthful accuracy) as "the most addressless man I know." Finding Boston and Cambridge insupportable after Winny's death, Howells at last decided to move his family to New York. With Holmesian wit he told his friends at the hub of the universe that, after departing Boston, his address would be simply the solar system.[29] For many years no fixed orbit could hold him; except for their stays in a summer house at Kittery Point (which the author purchased in 1902), the family lived a largely nomadic existence. Atypically, however, Howells's fluctuating professional affiliations kept pace with his domestic jostle. His highly visible status as the nation's leading man of letters brought him offers that reflect the era's rapidly changing marketplace for intellectual property, which was now greatly expanding because of technological developments and the passage of international copyright legislation. With his contract with the Harpers due to expire, Howells serialized *The Quality of Mercy* (1891–92) in S. S. McClure's newspaper syndicate, potentially reaching a mass urban audience that stretched from Boston to Chicago. McClure also proposed joint ownership of a new literary magazine, which Howells would also edit; this temptation he managed to refuse. Instead, the writer formed a dazzling misalliance with John Brisben Walker, mercurial publisher of the *Cosmopolitan Magazine*, which Howells edited jointly for a brief period (March–June 1892) and where he serialized his most outspoken socialist views in *A Traveller from Altruria*. Next in line was Edward Bok, enterprising editor of the *Ladies' Home Journal*, who secured *The Coast of Bohemia* and a sort of readerly autobiography, *My Literary Passions*. Not to be completely disowned of the figurehead they had done so much to create, the Harpers responded with attractive offers for another volume of autobiography (*Literary Friends and Acquaintance*), various novellas and longer fictions and, lastly, a new occasional literary department ("Life and Letters") in their weekly magazine.

The competitive advantages of freelancing did not accrue without attendant anxieties. Predictably receiving a fixed salary had always been the author's best hedge against the world of chance; indeed, such reasoning furnished his primary motive for accepting the associate editorship of Walker's magazine.[30] When that arrangement collapsed, Howells had to push his work (and himself) much more aggressively, a situation which made him yearn for the guilty comfort of being "monopolized." The scramble only reminded him of the perversities of the marketplace and sharpened his increasingly bitter awareness of the caprice of literary fame. As his Altrurian visitor to America would observe, "plutocratic prosperity, the selfish joy of having, at the necessary cost of those who cannot have, is blighted by the feeling of insecurity, which every man here has in his secret soul."[31] In February 1895 Mrs. Howells made a startling confession: "[E]very magazine, except Harper" had refused "a story or even a paper" from her husband, announcing that they were full for two years to come; "unless Harper orders one," she grimly anticipated, "we shall have to step down and out." (By way of consolation, she added, "Harry James—whose play has just been hissed in London—is in a worse case").[32] Elinor's gloom may have been premature, but her remarks suggest how misleading the more smiling aspects of Howells's success could be.

The turbulent waters off the coast of Bohemia became more navigable when the Harpers persuaded Howells to rejoin their payroll as an occasional correspondent for the *Weekly*. "It has been trying for me of late to place my work," he wrote his sister Aurelia in April 1895, "and though I shall now have to do more work, I shall be less anxious."[33] Ironically, the better part of Howells's problem resulted from what James aptly described as his astounding "activity & fecundity," the sheer volume of work he was capable of producing (and the limited space available to him in appropriate periodical outlets). The disappointing experiment with newspaper syndication had not greatly affected public demand for his fiction. Indeed, none of Howells's later titles would ever match the surprisingly large circulation—upwards of twenty thousand copies—enjoyed by *A Hazard of New Fortunes*. Moreover, in straying from his accustomed venues, Howells became increasingly self-conscious about fixing his prospective audience. Deprived of former confidence, he even made nervous queries: "We appeal to the intelligent American woman rather than to the intellectual type," the editor of the *Ladies' Home Journal* was obliged to explain.[34] Just to make sure of *his* appeal, perhaps, Howells supplied *The Coast of Bohemia* with both: a natively "intelligent" girl from the country and an "intellectual" urban aesthette. Rather neatly, when the artist-hero of that novel attempts a portrait of one, his brushwork unwittingly displays the attractive features of the other—a dubious writer's professional wish fulfillment of satisfactory representation.

Unquestionably, James's fiasco with the theater dwarfed his friend's occasional insecurity about venturing beyond his accustomed audience. "I have found the theatre always a snare," Howells admitted prophetically, "yet, how I should like to do a successful play!" Smitten with the same desire, James pressed on, producing script after script, but he failed repeatedly to find an actor-manager willing to take them on. Finally, George Alexander surrendered, agreed to produce *Guy Domville*, and the author's hapless fate was sealed. "Poor H.J. is having a play at last bro't out," William James told Howells on the eve of the first performance, "—or rather has had it bro't out at Alexander's theatre some 4 or 5 hours ago, if nothing at last befel to prevent. So he stands by now damned or saved—I hope on bended knee the latter."[35] Even his brother's prayerful attitude could not save James from that night's debacle, toward which he had edged with grim foreboding.

Almost as if he were participating vicariously, only months earlier Howells had finished *The Story of a Play*, which often reads like a paraphrase of James's comments about his recent theatrical experience. "Whether he liked it or not," Howells's protagonist reflects (with a pragmatism James never really achieved), he was part of the thing which in its entirety meant high-kicking and toe-practice, as well as the expression of the most mystical passions of the heart. There was an austerity in him which the fact offended, and he did what he could to appease this austerity by reflecting that it was the drama and never the theatre that he loved; but for the time this was useless. He saw that if he wrote dramas he could not hold aloof from the theatre, nor from actors and actresses—heavies and juveniles, and emotionals and soubrettes. He must know them, and more intimately; and at first he must be subject to them, however he mastered them at last; he must flatter their oddities and indulge their caprices.[36]

Somewhat less modestly, in his letters James had referred to the stage as "a kingdom to conquer—a kingdom forsooth of ignorant brutes of managers and dense *cabotins* of actors." Privately he wailed, "I *may* be meant for the Drama— God knows!—but I certainly wasn't meant for the Theatre."[37] Howells refuses to indulge his playwright in such melodramatic outbursts, though a few are given instead to Brice Maxwell's headstrong wife. Following a tack James himself had taken in *The Tragic Muse*, where the elusive character of Gabriel Nash hurls the most pointed barbs at contemporary philistinism, Howells equips the ancillary character with a biting tongue and then allows her husband's common sense to assuage her. Like James's earlier novel, *The Story of a Play* is largely a story of tolerable compromise. Having endured his own harrowing experience on stage, however, James (predictably) found the book disappointing. "The mutual indulgences of the whole thing," he commented, "fairly bathe the prospect in something like a suffusion of that 'romantic' to which the author's theory of the novel offers so little hospitality." Stricter realism could only be less happy.

James's infatuation with the theater was more distressing because it was far more insecure. Five years of effort went largely unrewarded, frustrating his golden dream of making "more money than literature has ever consented, or evidently *will* ever consent, to yield me." Hooted from the stage at the premiere of *Guy Domville*, James heroically summoned all his inner resources to regain his writerly equilibrium. Not incidentally, he also found solace in rereading Howells's "benignant" letters, which greatly "soothed & cheered & comforted" him. Even more stimulating was the prospect of seeing his old friend face to face, anticipations of which frequently become the focus of their later correspondence. With Howells threatening to pass through London like a whirlwind in 1897, James pleads, "won't you all . . . dine or lunch or, at the very least, tea with me?" However brief the communion, their meeting that autumn was remarkably auspicious, especially restorative of James's professional confidence. "I felt myself, somehow perishing in my pride or rotting ungathered, like an old maid against the wall & on her lonely bench," he confided to Howells. "Well, I'm *not* an old maid (for the blessed trade) quite yet. And you *were* Don Quixote!"

Arming James to joust with the Harpers was only one of many things the two men talked about as they walked through Kensington Gardens "in the soft lap, & under the motherly apron, of the dear old muffling fog" that late October morning. The visit lasted "only just six hours," as James told his sister-in-law, but it "came, in fact, at quite a psychological moment" and served him well "in an illuminating professional (i.e., commercial) way."[38] In such an exchange of confidences, it is likely that Howells also would have told James of his recent— and unsuccessful—effort to persuade Houghton, Mifflin of Boston to issue his books in a uniform collected edition, information that would serve James admirably years later when his own New York Edition faced a similarly uphill battle. How diligently James followed Howells's lead in professional matters can be measured in his repeated expressions of gratitude for its benefit. Howells even got misplaced credit for the Master's hiring an amanuensis and taking up the practice of dictation, which soon became his fixed routine.[39]

Notes

"Those Badly Assorted Siamese Twins"

1. WDH to William H. Bishop, 21 March 1880, SL 2: 246. WDH was expressing his pleasure in Bishop's novel *The House of a Merchant Prince*, which was serialized in the *Atlantic* (February–December 1882); an earlier book entitled *Detmold; A Romance* (1879) was defrauded of a decent sale, according to WDH, because it was unfavorably compared to "Daisy Miller" and *The Lady of the Aroostook*.

2. The latter title, published in 1879, would be almost completely insignificant if it were not a curious example of James's trying—and failing—to write a Howells novel, a romantic comedy based on sprightly dialogue. See Cornelia P. Kelley, *The Early Development of Henry James* (1935; rev. ed. Urbana: University of Illinois Press, 1965), 277.

3. WDH to John Hay, 2 April 1882, SL 3: 16.

4. HJ to Thomas Sergeant Perry, 16 February 1881, HJL 2: 341.

5. [Horace E. Scudder], review of *A Modern Instance*, *Atlantic* 50 (November 1882): 712; E. Purcell, review of *A Modern Instance*, *Academy* 22 (14 October 1882): 274. As Scudder recognized, the typical novel reader (the skimming turner of pages) would probably carry away the impression "that the author was unnecessarily at pains in portraying the features of people whom one does not care to number among his intimate associates" (710).

6. As the *Athenaeum* tersely put it, "It is impossible not to feel that Mr. James has at last contrived to write a dull book." Roger Gard reprints this and many other contemporary reviews in *Henry James: The Critical Heritage* (New York: Barnes & Noble, 1968), 93–125; quotation, 97.

7. Arthur Tilley, "The New School of Fiction," *National and English Review* 1 (April 1883): 267. Other notices observed, more specifically, that both stories explored the problematic psychology of modern marriage; one shrewdly suggested that Ralph Touchett's role as the invalid-observer in *The Portrait of a Lady* prefigured that of Ben Halleck in Howells's novel (*Athenaeum*, No. 2867 [7 October 1882]: 461).

8. [Horace E. Scudder], review of *The Portrait of a Lady* and *Dr. Breen's Practice*, *Atlantic* 49 (January 1882): 128.

9. John Hay to WDH, 31 December 1881, quoted in SL 3: 14n5. Two months later Constance Fenimore Woolson told HJ that she had "never been able to comprehend how anyone could possibly compare" him and WDH. "I like to think that you like Mr.

Howells," she added, "he has such a warm generous feeling for you" (*HJL* 3: 530). More caustically, Henry Adams offered a telling judgment on the two novelists' common weakness: credible characterization. "Howells cannot deal with gentlemen or ladies; he always slips up. James knows almost nothing of women but the mere outside; he never had a wife." Privately Thomas Sergeant Perry was of the same opinion: both Howells and James were deficient, he wrote, "in their sympathy with & knowledge of men. . . . But after all it is pardoned because women are the main novel readers, & unmarried girls who know men less than they know their own sex." See Henry Adams to John Hay, 24 September 1883, in *The Letters of Henry Adams*, 6 vols., ed. J. C. Levenson et al. (Cambridge, Mass.: Belknap Press of Harvard University Press, 1982–88), 2: 513; see also Thomas Sergeant Perry to Hercules Warren Fay, n.d., in Harlow, *Thomas Sergeant Perry*, 101.

10. [Louis John Jennings], "American Novels," *Quarterly Review* 155 (January 1883): 219.

11. Joseph A. Dowling has shown that Edwin Cady was mistaken when he asserted that the 1882 *Century* article ruined WDH's critical standing abroad. According to Dowling, "the evidence in the reviews indicates a steady increase in Howells' reputation through the 1880s with the high point being reached, probably, in 1885 with the publication of *The Rise of Silas Lapham*." See "W. D. Howells' Literary Reputation in England, 1882–1897," *Dalhousie Review* 45 (1965): 278. On 6 December 1882, Richard Watson Gilder reported to WDH, "We have all been rejoicing in the row which you have stirred up in London" (Howells Papers, Harvard).

12. HJ to George W. Smalley, 21 February [1883], *HJL* 2: 406. Many of HJ's other letters from this time reveal his need to distance himself from WDH's tribute.

13. Henry Adams to John Hay, 6 January 1884, in *The Letters of Henry Adams*, 2: 527.

14. [Margaret Oliphant], "American Literature in England," *Blackwood's* 133 (January 1883): 144, 145, 160, 153.

15. Elinor Mead Howells to Anne H. Fréchette, 17 February 1883, in *If Not Literature*, 253; WDH to Clemens, 10 February 1883, in *Mark Twain–Howells Letters* 1: 425.

16. The following letter from HJ to John Hay, written in the spring of 1882 (several months before WDH's departure), neatly captures and reflects the mutual problem of geography:

> As I write this I look out on Louisburg Square, where Howells has pitched his tent, & I reflect, with envy, that he has the advantage of not wanting to go abroad, finding his native land more than sufficient for literary purposes. He is right in being shy of the dismal fate of trying to live in two countries—in two worlds—at once. There is a woeful intellectual straddle in the attempt, & my poor legs ache with it.

HJ to John Hay, 5 April 1882, in *Henry James and John Hay: The Record of a Friendship*, ed. George Monteiro (Providence, R.I.: Brown University Press, 1965), 87.

17. WDH, *A Woman's Reason* (Boston: James R. Osgood & Co., 1883), 159; hereafter cited parenthetically as *AWR*.

18. HJ, *The Bostonians*, in *Novels, 1881–1886*, 1163; hereafter cited parenthetically as *TB*.

19. WDH, entry for 18 [August 1882], London Notebook (Howells Papers, Harvard).

20. "The Case of Mr. Howells," New York *Tribune*, 18 March 1883, 6:3; see also letter #59, note 12.

21. WDH to John Hay, 18 March 1882, *SL* 3: 12.

22. HJ, "The Lesson of the Master," CT 7: 239.

23. HJ to Grace Norton, 2 August [1882] (James Papers, Harvard). After spending time with the Howellses in Italy, Constance Fenimore Woolson also expressed marked reservations about Elinor's influence on her husband. "You once remarked to me," she wrote HJ on 7 May 1883,

> that Mrs. Hay occasionally expressed herself with a singular lack of cultivation. What, then, do you say of Mrs. Howells? (I have not known her until this past winter.) It seems to me that Mrs. Hay has at least a large, and even noble, nature; that she is above the petty things of life. Small feminine malice, and everlasting little jealousies. . . . For herself, [Mrs. Howells] is happy (or should be; though she never seems to be *very* happy about anything), because Mr. Howells is entirely devoted to her, markedly so; and he thinks everything she says, and does, most admirable.

HJ's response to these observations has not survived; he destroyed his letters to Woolson. See *HJL* 3: 551–52.

24. HJ, "The Lesson of the Master," CT 7: 262. Aptly enough, WDH may have turned HJ's veiled condescension to account when he published *A Little Swiss Sojourn* several years later. In his letter of 15 October 1882, HJ rhapsodized so excessively about the landscape around Montreux (vainly quoting—and misquoting—Ruskin and Arnold) that he felt obliged to apologize. "I don't mean to exult over you," HJ pleaded. In his sketch, WDH similarly describes the ambiance of Montreux and notes, in particular, the place's "extreme suitability to the purposes of the international novelist," pointedly adding that "a young man of cultivated sympaties and disdainful tastes could have a very pleasant time there." See *A Little Swiss Sojourn* (New York: Harper & Brothers, 1892), 103.

25. Indeed, somewhat fantastically, Alfred Habegger has claimed that almost all of James's heroines "have been lamed in secret by their author," who should therefore be held accountable for "a covert act of force directed against women." See *Henry James and the "Women Business,"* 26, 230.

26. For this reason modern taste has privileged HJ's literary criticism over that of all his contemporaries. See, for example, Robert P. Falk, "The Literary Criticism of the Genteel Decades: 1870–1900," in *The Development of American Literary Criticism*, ed. Floyd Stovall (Chapel Hill: University of North Carolina Press, 1955), 113–57.

The Art of Fiction

1. HJ, review of *Nana* by Emile Zola [1880], *Literary Criticism* 2: 865, 868; WDH, *Criticism and Fiction* (New York: Harper & Brothers, 1891), 149 154, 155.

2. HJ to Robert Louis Stevenson, 1 October 1887, *HJL* 3: 204. It should be remembered that Stevenson had taken *A Modern Instance* as a personal affront and quarreled bitterly with Howells about the issue of divorce. James's tone may partially reflect the hostility of his letter's recipient.

3. In August 1880 HJ had made a similar complaint to Thomas Sergeant Perry, whose favorable review of *Hawthorne* had provoked a remonstrance from Howells. "I am very sorry Howells turns the cold shoulder to your observations upon the flatness of our native literature," James wrote, "but am not surprised. The principles on which he edits the *Atlantic* indicate a low standard, certainly, & the vulgarity of that magazine often calls a patriotic blush to my cheek." See Harlow, *Thomas Sergeant Perry*, 308.

4. WDH to John Hay, 30 July 1883, *SL* 3: 74–75.

5. HJ to Grace Norton, 23 February 1884, *HJL* 2: 33.

6. HJ, entry for 20 June 1887, *CN* 37. HJ's essay "Alphonse Daudet" first appeared in the *Century* (26 [August 1883]: 498–509) and is reprinted in *Literary Criticism* 2: 223–49.

7. WDH, *Criticism and Fiction*, 150–51; the dialogue first appeared in *Harper's* (79 [June 1889]: 151–52).

8. WDH, *Indian Summer* [1886], in *Novels, 1875–1886*, 754; hereafter cited parenthetically as *IS*.

9. Quite persuasively, Updike suggests that "*Indian Summer* is the culmination of Howells's transatlantic, Jamesian mode. It holds, we might fancy, a touch of friendly challenge, of riposte to the narratives of Americans abroad that had brought Henry James his one strong dose of popular success." See "Rereading 'Indian Summer,'" *New York Review of Books* 37 (1 February 1990): 13.

10. According to Robert Emmet Long, "*Indian Summer* and *The Ambassadors* deal with the same equations-America vs. Europe; sobriety vs. youth and romance; Howells opts for sobriety and resignation (with a note of genial irony), but in James, these conflicts are strenuously challenging on either side, dramatic and sharply focussed. The difference is that James imagined these distinctions boldly, and searched their cultural implications—while Howells did not." See "'The Ambassadors' and the Genteel Tradition: James's Correction of Hawthorne and Howells," *New England Quarterly* 42 (1969): 48.

11. HJ to T. S. Perry, 6 March [1884], in Harlow, *Thomas Sergeant Perry*, 316. See also Barbara C. Ewell, "Parodic Echoes of *The Portrait of a Lady* in Howells's *Indian Summer*," *Tulane Studies in English* 22 (1977): 117–31.

12. More immediately, its influence can be felt in HJ's "Louisa Pallant" (1888) in which the title figure uses her daughter to shield herself from the male narrator, whose proposal of marriage she had refused many years earlier. Now widowed (like Mrs. Bowen), she wishes to conceal her feelings of love for him for fear that he would scorn her affection as false. To redeem his opinion of her, Louisa Pallant is willing to denounce her own daughter, in whom she now recognizes what were once her own most worldly ambitions. In his notebook jotting for this tale, HJ reminded himself, "They may all be Americans—in Europe: since Howells writes to me that I do the 'international' far better than anything else." HJ even contemplated setting the story in Florence, but then decided upon Hamburg (*CN* 34–35).

13. See John W. Crowley, *The Black Heart's Truth: The Early Career of W. D. Howells* (Chapel Hill: University of North Carolina Press, 1985), 110–49.

14. Oscar W. Firkins, *William Dean Howells: A Study* (Cambridge, Mass.: Harvard University Press, 1924), 124.

15. At an early point in the novel, Colville and Imogene banter about a story of Heine's (from *Florentine Nights* [1837]) in which a young man discovers his true love in the form of a fallen statue, lying amid the ruins of a neglected garden. WDH (and some of his readers) would also have remembered HJ's "Last of the Valerii," a much darker and melodramatic tale built around a similar motif, which he published in the *Atlantic* in 1874. Colville's quick remark that "morbid impulses are one of the luxuries of youth" may indirectly repudiate the sordid implications of HJ's story, in which the hero becomes psychosexually enslaved to a statue of Juno unearthed at his Roman villa (*IS* 660–62).

16. WJ to WDH, 21 July 1886, in *The Letters of William James*, ed. Henry James, 2 vols. (Boston: Atlantic Monthly Press, 1920), 1: 253.

17. "I wish people would buy my books more & ask for my signature less," James complained to one of Osgood's partners. "The rumpus about the *Bostonians* will, I trust,

help the former consummation. But the charges in regard to this serial's containing 'personalities' is idiotic & baseless: there is not the smallest, faintest portrait in the book." HJ to Benjamin Ticknor [1885] (Ticknor Papers, Library of Congress).

18. HJ to Grace Norton, 9 December [1885], *HJL* 3: 106. Significantly, he was not alone in this opinion. "How dare you speak out your beliefs as you do?" John W. De Forest wonderingly inquired of Howells. "You spare neither manhood nor womanhood, & especially not the latter, though it furnishes four fifths of *our* novel-reading public. It is a wonder that the females of America, at least the common born & bred of them, do not stone you in the streets." De Forest to WDH, 6 December 1886, quoted in *SL* 3: 170n2.

19. HJ to Mr. [Benjamin] Ticknor, 30 January [1885] (Berg Collection, New York Public Library).

20. HJ to Sir John Clark, 8 January [1882], *HJL* 2: 367.

21. Harper's was not ashamed of advertising its coup. As WDH wryly noted to Mark Twain, "You will have heard from the din of the newspapers that I have contracted to take all of Harper & Bro.'s money in return for certain literary services." For exclusive serial rights to WDH's future productions (one novel-length work a year), Harper's agreed to pay him an annual salary of ten thousand dollars, together with a 12.5 percent royalty on the sale of published volumes. For his new column (the "Editor's Study") in *Harper's Monthly*, he was to receive an additional three thousand dollars yearly. Any additional contributions to Harper publications would fetch advantageous prices: fifty dollars per thousand words in the *Monthly*, thirty dollars per thousand in the *Weekly*. WDH's Memorandum of Agreement with Harper's is dated 6 October 1885, Harper Contract Books 5: 280–84; see *The Archives of Harper and Brothers, 1817–1914* (Teaneck, N.J.: Chadwyck-Healey Microfilm Edition, 1982), reel 2. See also *Mark Twain–Howells Letters*, 2: 537; and Edwin H. Cady, *The Realist at War: The Mature Years 1885–1920 of William Dean Howells* (Syracuse, N.Y.: Syracuse University Press, 1958), 1–3.

22. HJ to Edmund Gosse, 27 May [1885], in *Selected Letters of Henry James to Edmund Gosse, 1882–1915*, ed. Rayburn S. Moore (Baton Rouge: Louisiana State University Press, 1988), 38.

23. WJ to WDH, 5 and 12 May [18]85 (Howells Papers, Harvard).

24. WDH to Joseph W. Harper Jr., 13 March 1885, *SL* 3: 119. In a postscript, he added an open-ended conditional clause ("Of course, if J. R. O. & Co. are only in a trance, poor fellows—") which, avoiding the subjunctive, does not seem contrary to fact.

25. WDH, *The Rise of Silas Lapham*, in *Novels, 1881–1886*, 1188.

26. S. Foster summarizes the issue well: "Although Howells is not directly didactic, by giving his novel a traditionally Christian framework—a pattern of sin, guilt, retribution, and regeneration—he compels us to recognize a moral relationship between cause and effect, and a difference between 'good' and 'bad' behaviour, even while he implies that these are relative distinctions." See "W. D. Howells: *The Rise of Silas Lapham* (1885)," in *The Monster in the Mirror: Studies in Nineteenth-Century Realism*, ed. D. A. Williams (Oxford: Oxford University Press for the University of Hull, 1978), 169–70.

27. WJ to HJ, 9 June [1885], *CWJ* 2: 20–21.

28. Benjamin H. Ticknor to WDH, 1 June 1885 (Howells Papers, Harvard).

29. Memorandum of Agreement between Ticknor & Co. & WDH, 20 July 1885 (Howells Papers, Harvard). For the first four novels listed, Howells had already received generous advances on future royalties; the rate of payment on all his other books was now to increase to an unusually advantageous 16⅔ percent.

30. "Parting company with you will be a great sorrow to me," Ticknor told WDH on 1 August 1885. "I want to postpone the evil day as long as possible & gather all the

crumbs that I may from your bounteous table in the meantime." A month later he voiced his disappointment more emphatically. It was only in the hope of getting WDH's future work, he now made clear, "that we waived the old contracts; of course you didn't promise anything but we wanted to have everything satisfactory to you & have put ourselves in your hands accordingly." Benjamin H. Ticknor to WDH, 10 September 1885 (Howells Papers, Harvard).

31. Admittedly, Osgood had not yet brought out a novel by HJ—only collections of stories, travel writing, and the (comic) dramatic version of *Daisy Miller*. Nevertheless, while demand for WDH's books usually pushed them into multiple editions, James's sales seldom exhausted even a modest first printing of fifteen hundred copies.

32. HJ to WJ, 21 August [1885], *CWJ* 2: 25. For details of HJ's failed negotiations with Ticknor, see Michael Anesko, *"Friction with the Market": Henry James and the Profession of Authorship* (New York: Oxford University Press, 1986), 101–7.

33. Quoted in Marrion Wilcox, "The Works of William Dean Howells," *Harper's Weekly* 40 (4 July 1896): 656.

34. Edwin H. Cady himself admits that the "psychic event which occurred to make all this true is essentially unknowable" (*The Road to Realism: The Early Years 1837–1885 of William Dean Howells* [Syracuse, N.Y.: Syracuse University Press, 1956], 245), but he inclines toward the Swedenborgian explanation. Kenneth Lynn, on the other hand, alleges that the author "could not rise to the challenge of his conscience" in working out the plot of *Silas Lapham* and therefore "collapsed, borne down by the questions and problems of American society that he might have dealt with, but had not" (*William Dean Howells*, 280).

35. Simpson, *The Man of Letters in New England and the South*, 86.

36. WDH to James Parton, 27 March 1885, *SL* 3: 119–20.

37. Osgood's bankruptcy immediately brought home the urgency of these contradictions, for a week after the publisher's collapse became public Howells arranged a meeting with Roswell Smith, owner of the *Century*, from whom he expected to receive "a conditional offer." In anticipation of their conversation, Howells jotted down several questions that vividly illustrate the contrary nature of his situation:

    I. Whether he is ready to monopolize me.
    II. Whether he could put all that I write in *The Century*.
    III. Could he leave me free in choice of subjects?
    IV. That I could not go on under O[sgood]'s contract except for the stories stipulated for.
    V. What percentage on books?
    VI. Go abroad and write a history, when sick of stories.

See "Questions noted down to put to Mr. Roswell Smith, in expectation of a conditional offer from him, Monday evening, May 11, [18]85" (Howells Papers, Harvard).

38. Cady, *The Realist at War*, 187. Recent assessments generally support this claim, though they are more divided about its implications. See James L. W. West III, *American Authors and the Literary Marketplace Since 1900* (Philadelphia: University of Pennsylvania Press, 1988), 118–19; see also Christopher P. Wilson, "Markets and Fictions: Howells' Infernal Juggle," *American Literary Realism* 20 (1988): 2–22.

39. WDH was noting the similarity between himself and Ezra Wendell, the antihero of *In War Time* by S. Weir Mitchell (WDH to Mitchell, 20 October 1885, *SL* 3: 132).

40. "Mr. Howells's Novels," *Westminster Review*, n.s. 66 (October 1884): 351. Less acerbically, a shrewd American critic made the same point, declaring that Howells was incapable of writing tragedy: "his novels have all the vivacity and lightness of diction

belonging to romantic comedy, and any termination other than a happy one ill accords with their movement when considered in reference to action." See G. H. Badger, "Howells as an Interpreter of American Life," *International Review* 14 (1883): 382.

41. Kazin, "Howells the Bostonian," 223.

42. Horace E. Scudder, "James, Crawford, and Howells," *Atlantic* 57 (June 1886): 850. From a slightly different angle, a waggish writer for *Life* could distort the economics of publishing to satirize both literary popularity and literary labor. A squib called "Some Figures" ran this way:

> It is said that T. B. Aldrich gets $1,200 for a poem. We are able to state with equal truth that Whittier is paid $14,000 for each of his poems, and Bret Harte not less than $17,500; that Mr. Howells receives $288,000 for a serial novel, while H. James, Jr., cannot command more than $192,000.25 for the same sort of work. E. P. Roe's price varies from half to three-quarters of a million. (*Life* 8 [22 July 1886]: 60)

43. See, for example, Amy Kaplan, *The Social Construction of American Realism* (Chicago: University of Chicago Press, 1988), 13; Daniel Borus, *Writing Realism*, 65–77; and Richard Brodhead, *Cultures of Letters: Scenes of Reading and Writing in Nineteenth-Century America* (Chicago: University of Chicago Press, 1993), 1–12.

44. HJ to Mrs. Hugh Bell, 7 February [1890] (James Papers, Texas); WDH to S. Weir Mitchell, 20 October 1885, *SL* 3: 132.

45. WJ to HJ, 10 March 1887, *CWJ* 2: 59. Lowell's appreciative response (dated 30 November 1886) can be found in *New Letters of James Russell Lowell*, 296–97; but du Maurier's, still unpublished, deserves quotation. Writing from Paris, he asserted:

> No English book I have read for years either by yourself or any one else has wrapped me up so completely, or held me so intent[ly]. It is a surprise for me that you should have this knowledge of the lower walks of London life—I had always associated you more with Casamassimas & Lady Auroras than with Millicents! And I feel that after the touching & delightful hero, Millicent is the best character in the book, where all are so good. In spite of her Cockney vulgarity on which you have insisted with the truest and rightest instinct, and of her infidelity (which is not confirmed) she is truly loveable, and her friendship for Hyacinth, with its admirable background of foggy streets & gaslighted shops has attracted & delighted me almost more than anything else. (George du Maurier to HJ, [1 November 1886], James Papers, Harvard)

46. HJ, Preface to *The Princess Casamassima*, in *Literary Criticism* 2: 1095.

47. WDH, *The Minister's Charge; or, The Apprenticeship of Lemuel Barker*, in *Novels, 1886–1888*, ed. Don L. Cook (New York: Library of America, 1978), 309; hereafter cited parenthetically as *TMC*.

48. G. H. Badger, "Howells as an Interpreter of American Life," 383, 386; Lawrence W. Levine, *Highbrow/Lowbrow: The Emergence of Cultural Hierarchy in American Life* (Cambridge, Mass.: Harvard University Press, 1988). Among other recent works that reflect this orientation, the most influential have been Alan Trachtenberg's *Incorporation of America* (New York: Hill & Wang, 1982) and Warren Susman's *Culture as History* (New York: Pantheon, 1984). The standard account of Tolstoy's influence on Howells is Bennett's *William Dean Howells: The Development of a Novelist*, 164–71, which has been qualified by Sarah B. Daugherty, "Howells, Tolstoy, and the Limits of Realism: The Case of *Annie Kilburn*," *American Literary Realism* 19 (Fall 1986): 21–41.

49. "He gets engaged," De Forest continued, "like a nigger whitewasher, without a

dollar in his pocket, to a girl as poor as himself & a hopeless invalid. He has no radical self-command & no effective forethought." De Forest to WDH, 6 December 1886, quoted in *SL* 3: 170–71n5.

50. Irving Howe, *Politics and the Novel* (New York: Horizon Press, 1957), 152.

51. HJ, *The Princess Casamassima*, in *Novels, 1886–1890*, ed. Daniel Mark Fogel (New York: Library of America, 1989), 259–60.

Complicity

1. WJ was among those who refused to sign a petition, even though it was circulated by his brother-in-law, William M. Salter, then head of the Society for Ethical Culture in Chicago. In WJ's view, the riot in Chicago had "nothing to do with knights of labor" but was instead "the work of pathological germans & poles" (WJ to HJ, 9 May [18]86, *CWJ* 2: 40). In 1893 Governor John P. Altgeld granted clemency to the surviving Haymarket prisoners.

2. WDH to the Editor of the New York *Tribune*, 12 November 1887, *SL* 3: 201–4; WDH's earlier letter appears on page 199 of the same edition. On the pernicious effects of sensational fiction, see *The Rise of Silas Lapham*, 1086; see also *Criticism and Fiction*, chapters 18–19.

3. An entry in HJ's notebook amply documents the parallels between the events of his novel and a scandal provoked in Venice by the publication of a gossipy letter written by a young American woman (*CN* 40–43).

4. HJ to Robert Underwood Johnson, 16 January 1888 (American Academy of Arts and Letters Archives, New York). Considering the storm of abuse he suffered for publishing his plea for clemency, WDH had every reason to savor James's novel. "What a squalid and vulgar oligarchy of half-bred scribblers we live under!" he complained to one sympathetic friend. "Somehow their power must be broken." See WDH to William M. Salter, 24 November 1887, in Howard A. Wilson, "William Dean Howells's Unpublished Letters About the Haymarket Affair," *Journal of the Illinois State Historical Society* 56 (1963): 15.

5. HJ, Preface to *The Tragic Muse* (1908), in *Literary Criticism* 2: 1,103.

6. HJ to WJ, 23 July 1890, *CWJ* 2: 145.

7. HJ to WJ, 16 May 1890, *CWJ* 2: 135–36. Characteristically, Percy Lubbock omitted this passage in the first published text of this letter (compare *LHJ* 1: 162).

8. WJ to HJ, 26 June 1890, *CWJ* 2: 143.

9. WDH, *A Hazard of New Fortunes* (1889; rpt. Bloomington: Indiana University Press, 1976), 49; hereafter cited parenthetically as *HNF*.

10. Thomas Hardy, journal entry for July 1888. A reviewer for the *Athenaeum* made a similar comment about *The Tragic Muse*: "The story, if we may say so, is for the most part negative—a history of occurrences that do not occur, unions that perpetually hang fire, passions that come to nothing, aspirations—political and intellectual—that have no fruition, with other episodes of a clever but barren quality." See *Henry James: The Critical Heritage*, 186, 195.

11. WJ to HJ, [June 1890], *CWJ* 2: 138. See also William McMurray, "The Concept of Complicity in Howells' Fiction," *New England Quarterly* 35 (1962): 489–95.

12. Curiously, HJ singled out old Dryfoos for special praise, the one character whom WDH felt compelled to demonize through authorial intervention. In a notable exception to the book's dramatic technique, the narrative voice (rather than one of the other characters) editorializes about the man's "moral decay," brought on by the corrupting power of capital (*HNF* 263–64).

13. WJ to WDH, 20 August 1890, *The Letters of William James* 1: 298–99.

14. As George Bennett rightly observes, the novel "gives the effect of being curiously remote from the issue of the conflict between capital and labor which it raises in discussion. Howells seems to offer an intelligently sympathetic expression of regret to a patient suffering from a disease whose pains he himself has never endured. His attitude is sincere, but it is intellectualized" (*William Dean Howells*, 177). See also HJ to WJ, 1 October 1887, CWJ 2: 75.

15. WDH, *Annie Kilburn*, in *Novels, 1886–1888*, 645, 672.

16. Garland's review of the novel is quoted in SL 3: 220–21n1, together with WDH's response.

17. WDH, *April Hopes*, in *Novels, 1886–1888*, 334; hereafter cited parenthetically as AH.

18. T. J. Jackson Lears analyzes this phenomenon in *No Place of Grace: Antimodernism and the Transformation of American Culture, 1880–1920* (New York: Pantheon, 1981), 184–215. Perhaps to the detriment of his general argument, Lears accepts the conventional view of WDH as the prissy and complacent representative of a feminized culture, and therefore finds him largely insensitive to the "weightlessness" of middle-class life. More careful attention to WDH's fiction should have suggested the opposite. Twenty years earlier Richard Foster anticipated Lears's thesis precisely by locating in Howells's work a profound recognition of "the severance of the commercially structured present from the ways of life of the traditional past" and, concomitantly, "the displacement of the intellectual as the traditional spokesman for intelligence and responsibility in the arena of public action." By manipulating the conventional forms of bourgeois life (dinners, teas, theaters, parlor cars, country hotels, and urban boarding houses), WDH was able, according to Foster, "to accumulate his larger panorama: a world of present cultural formlessness ironically juxtaposed with a background of felt organic traditions." See "The Contemporaneity of Howells," *New England Quarterly* 32 (1959): 59, 56.

19. Marrion Wilcox, "The Works of William Dean Howells," *Harper's Weekly* 40 (4 July 1896): 655. Paul John Eakin traces Alice Pasmer's lineage back to James's early review of *A Foregone Conclusion*, in which he first called attention to the "irritable moral consciousness" of WDH's heroines. See *The New England Girl: Cultural Ideals in Hawthorne, Stowe, Howells and James* (Athens: University of Georgia Press, 1976), 125.

20. HJ to Grace Norton, 13 December 1903, HJL 4: 300.

21. HJ to Arthur C. Benson, 29 June 1896, in *Letters to A. C. Benson and Auguste Monod*, ed. E. F. Benson (New York: Charles Scribner's Sons, 1930), 35.

22. WDH to William C. Howells, 24 November 1889, SL 3: 263.

23. See, for example, Andrew Delbanco, "Howells and the Suppression of Knowledge," *Southern Review*, n.s. 19 (1983): 765–84.

24. *The Shadow of a Dream* (1890; rpt. Bloomington: Indiana University Press, 1970), 59; hereafter cited parenthetically as SD.

25. WDH to Moncure D. Conway, 7 April 1889, SL 3: 250.

26. HJ, "The Science of Criticism" [1891], in *Literary Criticism* 1: 95.

27. At least that much can be said about one novel from this period, for without Howells's literal inspiration James would never have found the germ for *The Ambassadors*. The remark he made in Whistler's Paris garden to Jonathan Sturges—"Live all you can: it's a mistake not to"—found its way (through delayed report) into James's scribbler and immediately struck the Master as a ripe and promising subject. "It touches me," James noted, "I can see him—I can hear him." The vibration was audible in part because Howells had already confided an important impression of his brief visit to Paris (pitifully truncated in June 1894 by the sudden decline in health of his father back in Ohio, to

whom he immediately returned). "I fell in love with Paris on sight," Howells confessed. "For the first time I got the notion of something denser on the other side"—not easy for a patriotic man of fifty-seven to admit. To his son WDH struck a note more characteristic of Waymarsh than of Strether. "Perhaps it was as well I was called home," he wrote on 27 July 1894 (*LiL* 2: 52). "The poison of Europe was getting into my soul. You must look out for that. They live much more fully than we do. Life here is still for the future,—it is a land of Emersons—and I like a little present moment in mine. When I think of the Whistler garden!"

See HJ, notebook entry for 31 October 1895, CN 140–42; and also the twenty-thousand-word "Project of Novel" (CN 541–76) submitted to Harper & Brothers in 1900, which represents HJ's first elaboration of the book.

28. WDH, *The World of Chance* (New York: Harper & Brothers, 1893), 214.

29. WDH to Thomas Bailey Aldrich, 17 June 1891, *LiL* 2: 18.

30. See WDH to William Cooper Howells, 20 December 1891, *LiL* 2: 20. Walker had proposed an annual salary of fifteen thousand dollars—exceeding even the Harpers' fabled generosity. For other details of WDH's tenure with the magazine, see D. M. Rein, "Howells at *The Cosmopolitan*," *American Literature* 21 (March 1949): 49–55; and Cady, *The Realist at War*, 177–89.

31. WDH, "Letters of an Altrurian Traveller: A Bit of Altruria in New York" [1893], in *The Altrurian Romances* (Bloomington: Indiana University Press, 1968), 230.

32. Elinor M. Howells to Anne H. Fréchette, 16 February [1895], in *If Not Literature*, 275.

33. WDH to Aurelia H. Howells, 21 April 1895, *SL* 4: 103.

34. Edward W. Bok, *The Americanization of Edward Bok: An Autobiography* (New York: Charles Scribner's Sons, 1920), 374–75. WDH extricated himself from a proposal to write for *Munsey's Magazine*, another mass-circulation periodical, by telling its editor, "I have a serious doubt whether I could hit the preferences of your public, and I dread this unconscious straining out of my natural bent." WDH to Frank A. Munsey, 4 March 1894, *SL* 4: 62.

35. WJ to WDH, 5 January [18]95 (Howells Papers, Harvard).

36. WDH, *The Story of a Play* (New York: Harper & Brothers, 1898), 216–17.

37. HJ to Robert Louis Stevenson, 18 February 1891; and HJ to Elizabeth Lewis, [15? December 1894], *HJL* 3: 336, 496.

38. HJ to Alice H. G. James, 1 December 1897, *HJL* 4: 65.

39. As WDH told Mark Twain, "I was amused when I was in London last fall, to have James tell that he had taken to dictating all his fiction because he heard that I always dictated. He makes it go, but if there could be anything worse for me than a typewriter, it would be a human typewriter." See WDH to Clemens, 23 October 1898, in *Mark Twain–Howells Letters* 2: 681.

Letters and
Documents

46.

JAMES TO HOWELLS, 4 October 1881, London

ALS Houghton
bMS Am 1784 (253) 35

Oct. 4th

THE REFORM CLUB

Dear Howells.

I expect to see you so soon (I embark for Quebec—on the 20th) that I could at a pinch forbear to write to you. But I won't forego the pleasure of letting you know a little in advance, what satisfaction the history of your Doctress[1] gives me. I came back last night from a month in Scotland,[2] & found the October Atlantic on my table; whereupon, though weary with travel I waked early this morning on purpose to read your contribution in bed—in my little London-dusky back bedroom, where I can never read at such hours without a pair of candles. They burned low while I said to myself that barring perhaps the *Foregone Conclusion*, this is your best thing. It is full of vivacity, of reality, of the feeling of life & human nature, of happy touches of all sorts; & the way you have put yourself into the petticoats of your heroine has an almost uncanny ability. I must confess to you that she affects me painfully, & so do the manners & customs of her companions,[3]—but quite apart from this I have enjoyed

1. *Dr. Breen's Practice*, the heroine of which, Dr. Grace Breen, gives the book its title. The novel ran in the *Atlantic* (August–December 1881).

2. HJ had visited at Tillypronie with Sir John and Lady Clark, and then at Edinburgh, where he was the guest of Archibald Philip Primrose, fifth earl of Rosebery (1847–1929), later foreign secretary and prime minister.

3. HJ probably had in mind Mrs. Louise Maynard, a rather silly and self-indulgent invalid, whom Dr. Breen unsuccessfully attends.

the keenness & instinctive "naturalism" of the whole thing. I don't think you have done anything yet with so fine a point.

—I don't send you this as a bribe to be "attentive" to me after I arrive, but merely to express my satisfaction with you in instalments as I can't help reading you so—more shame to me!—I hope to be in Cambridge about Nov. 1st, & will lose no time in coming out to see you. You will find me fat & scant o'breath, & very middle-aged, but eminently amenable to kind treatment. One of the last impressions I shall carry from here is the remarkable interest & sympathy about poor Garfield's end.[4] It made me feel as if I were already in the U. S., & helps a little to bridge the dreadful sea. Don't be on the wharf but be at your door with Mrs. H. at the window.

> Yours ever
> H. James jr

47.

JAMES TO HOWELLS, 1 November 1881, Cambridge   ALS Houghton
bMS Am 1784 (253) 36

20 Quincy St. Nov. 1st

My dear Howells

Eccomi quà![1] I arrived here last night, after spending two days (& more) in the pathless wilds of Canada, subsequent to landing at Rimouski. I promptly opened your note,[2] & assure you that I shall be delighted to see you. To see you here—but even more to see you in your own house. Say I came & took a look at you on *Thursday* afternoon! If I don't hear from you that you are to be absent or engaged I will do so. It will remind me of old days. Intanto,[3] with general salutes,

> your devotissimo
> H. James jr

Tuesday p.m.

4. President James A. Garfield (1831–81) had been mortally wounded by a disappointed office seeker on 2 July, but he did not die until 19 September.
   1. Here I am!
   2. Not extant.
   3. In the meantime.

48.

JAMES TO HOWELLS, 6 December 1881, New York   ALS Houghton
bMS Am 1784 (253) 38

Tuesday.
115 EAST 25TH STREET

Dear Howells

I must not let another hour pass without wishing you joy of your I trust placid convalescence.[1] I came off hurriedly to this place (to attend the funeral of a near relative,)[2] on Thursday night last, & since then have been uninterruptedly given up to family duties & to the social ministrations of Godkin,[3] with whom I am staying. Even now I am writing with one eye on the clock, for an impending appointment. This therefore is not a letter; it is merely a scribbled stop-gap, to tell you that I shall very immediately write, that I envelop you with good wishes & that I am not the neglectful brute I seem. I earnestly hope that you are well out of the woods—& can see the sky & the horizon. You have had an odious moment, but I believe you now to be given over to the amiable languor of a repentant invalid. I won't speak of New York to-day, but I will to-morrow or next day. It is very diverting & tremendously metropolitan. Si diverti anche Lei![4] Congratulate your wife & children for me & believe me

ever your devotissimo
H James jr

Dec. 6*th*.

49.

JAMES TO HOWELLS, 3 January 1882, New York   ALS Houghton
bMS Am 1784 (253) 37

36 Irving Place[1]
Tuesday—

Dear Howells.

Who is it that writes as well as you—almost, & yet is not you? I have been reading the notice of T. P. in the Atlantic with unbounded and grateful

1. WDH had been bedridden since mid-November. His illness has usually been interpreted as a nervous breakdown, occasioned by the traumatic subject matter of *A Modern Instance* (see Cady, *The Road to Realism*, 208–10; and Lynn, *William Dean Howells*, 253–54), but other letters suggest that he suffered from a urinary-tract infection (see *SL* 2: 301–2).

2. Mary Helen James (1840–81), a cousin of HJ.

3. Edwin L. Godkin (1831–1902), founder and editor of the *Nation*.

4. May you also be enjoying yourself!

1. HJ returned to New York after spending Christmas in Cambridge; his friend Godkin had left town for the holidays, however, and he took lodgings in a hotel. See HJ to Whitelaw Reid, 26 December [1881], in *Parisian Sketches*, 223.

relish.[2] It would be fatuous for me to praise it, but let me at least beg you, whoever the author is, to tell him I thank him from my heart & consider him the most charming fellow in the world. Whoever he is, I say; & especially if he is Lathrop!

Yours ever truly

H James jr

P. S. I have had it at heart ever since I heard the fact, to drop you a hint of my pleasure in learning that you're lightened of your editorial burden.[3] Honestly, I feel a thrill of almost physical satisfaction in the thought of that genius of yours now having its ease & its leisure to go & do one good thing after another, through all the coming years. Heaven's blessing attend it!

50.

JAMES TO HOWELLS, 9 January 1882, Washington, D. C.   ALS Houghton
bMS Am 1784 (253) 39

(723 Fifteenth St.)
METROPOLITAN CLUB
WASHINGTON, D. C.
Jan. 9th 1882.

My dear Howells.

Only a word of greeting & to hope you continue to ameliorate. If you could breathe this bright & balmy air (which I confess appears to-day for the 1st time,) I think that your physics & your morals would equally revive. Perhaps however you have something like it; & in any case, I trust, your health is restored & your genius rekindled. I should be glad to think too that you are by this time domiciled in Boston—& no longer looking out on those deflowered gardens

2. Horace E. Scudder (1838–1902) wrote the penetrating review of *The Portrait of a Lady* and *Dr. Breen's Practice* that appeared in the *Atlantic* (49 [January 1882]: 126–30). In his remarks Scudder anticipated the emphasis on the novel's structure that HJ himself would make in his 1907 preface to the New York Edition. "The artist gives us this advantage," Scudder wrote,

that all the elaboration of his work looks distinctly to the perfection of the central figure. . . . By a fine concentration of attention upon the heroine, Mr. James impresses us with her importance, and the other characters, involved as they are with her life, fall back into sec-ondary positions. It is much to have seized and held firmly so elusive a conception, and our admiration is increased when reflection shows that, individual as Isabel is in the painting, one may fairly take her as representative of womanly life to-day. The fine purpose of her freedom, the resolution with which she seeks to be the maker of her destiny, the subtle weakness into which all this betrays her, the apparent helplessness of her ultimate position, and the conjectured escape only through patient forbearance,—what are all these, if not attributes of womanly life expended under current conditions? (127)

3. WDH had decided to resign the editorship of the *Atlantic* as of 1 March 1881.

which encircle that melancholy monument.[1] I spent, after leaving you, a few rather eventless days in New York, & two or three more of a perhaps richer complexion—enriched, at dinner, &c, by the presence of the Philadelphian fair—at Butler Place[2] with Mrs. Wister, who told me that she shed salt tears when she heard of your leaving the *Atlantic,* though she *does* think you are too hard on the upper classes, & too soft on the lower. What shall I tell you about Washington?—you know more about it, I think, than I. It is quite too awfully queer—& is what is called by the London vulgar rather rum-looking. But it seems to me to promise well for the genial psychologist—there are plenty of people to see, & every one is most good natured & conversible. I will let you know my further impressions at a later period. If you can scribble at all, do let me hear of it. Remember that it is never too late to mend, & recall me to your wife & children.

Ever yours
H James jr

51.

JAMES TO HOWELLS, 28 July 1882, London ALS Houghton
bMS Am 1784 (253) 40

3 Bolton St, Piccadilly W.
July 28$^{\underline{th}}$

Dear Howells.

Welcome to old England[1] & to such rest & refreshment as an I trust not too abominable voyage may have caused you to yearn for! I hope that neither Mrs. Howells nor any other of you is knocked up, & that if you are, the sight of these dusky shores will ease off the situation. Do let me know at your first convenient moment, after the perusal of this, when I may prepare to do the honours of the metropolis for you. I have taken for you a set of very good rooms at *No. 18 Pelham Crescent, South Kensington. S. W.* This is not the Bloomsbury Region, but I shrank from that—for reasons I will impart. I will also, in the freedom of conversation, tell you why I took these;—roughly speaking, it was because I *knew* them to be good, whereas I didn't know it of others. I engaged them only for a week, so that you can easily quit them if they don't suit or if they

---

1. To be closer to his doctor, WDH had been residing temporarily at a boardinghouse in Cambridge at 7 Garden Street, overlooking the Cambridge Common (where a granite-templed statue of Lincoln was recently erected to commemorate native sons killed in the Civil War).

2. The Germantown, Pennsylvania, home of Mrs. Sarah Butler Wister, the daughter of HJ's friend Fanny Kemble.

1. WDH and his family had sailed from Quebec on 22 July and arrived at Liverpool two days after HJ posted this welcome. The family came straight to London on 31 July and stayed until 18 September 1882.

are too dear. They are dearer than some & cheaper than others: *i.e.* 4 guineas ($21) a week for a drawing-room, dining room & three good bedrooms, in a quiet, salubrious, genteel, but unfashionable, situation. As soon as you telegraph me by what train you come, I will let your landlady know, order your dinner (or your lunch,) &c, & then come to Euston to meet you. There are two ways of coming from Liverpool: —to the Euston Station, or to St. Pancras. Take the former! You will without difficulty get a carriage to yourselves; a shilling to the Guard will make it *sure*. You are much expected here the fame of your advent preceding you, though the town unfortunately is rapidly emptying itself. I repeat my hope that you have suffered no sea-change, & await your news.

> Ever yours
> H James jr

52.

JAMES TO HOWELLS, 1 August 1882, London[1]   ANS Houghton
bMS Am 1784 (253) 41

W. D. Howells, Esq.
18 Pelham Crescent
South Kensington. S. W.

When you come to morrow, do bring with you, if not inconvenient, the sheets of the *Modern Instance*.[2]

> H. J. jr.

53.

JAMES TO HOWELLS, 12 August 1882, London   ALS Houghton
bMS Am 1784 (253) 47

3 Bolton St. W.

Dear Howells.

I was in hopes you would turn up yesterday afternoon, as you couldn't come the day before, that I might conduct you to the importunate Athenaeum; & I was on the point, an hour ago, of telegraphing you to come for the same purpose *to-day*, when I got a telegram from my brother Bob,[1] announcing his arrival in town some time to-day & probable re-departure, with my assistance, for York-

---

1. Postmark cancel.

2. WDH's novel *A Modern Instance* was running serially in the *Century* (December 1881–October 1882).

1. Robertson James (1846–1910), HJ's youngest brother.

shire: which, as I myself go into the country at 6 o'clock, would leave us little opportunity for our visit. I go down into Bucks. this evening & return either Monday morning or on Tuesday early—in time to meet you & Winnie, for Loseley,[2] at the WATERLOO *station for the 10.35 train to* GUILDFORD. Be there five or ten minutes before, & take your two *return*-tickets for the said Guildford. In the meantime, if the spirit moves you, don't wait for me to go with you to the Athenaeum, but enter it yourself & be at home—breakfast, lunch, dine, write letters, read books, use all the conveniences. Only give your name to the hall-porter, as you go in, once for all, that he may know who you are.—I forwarded you a letter this a.m. I hope you all flourish, & that Mrs. Howells enamours herself a little of the metropolis.

Yours ever
H James jr

Aug. 12th

54.

JAMES TO HOWELLS, 19 August 1882, London

ALS Houghton
bMS Am 1784 (253) 42

3 Bolton St. W.
Aug. 19th

Dear Howells.

I go out of town tonight, to stop till Monday a.m.—with regret at missing your visit yesterday—(Osgood[1] I saw this morning.) You had better call for me about 7. on Monday evening, & we will go & dine together at the Athenaeum—or rather at the United Service Club (opposite) where during the annual window-washing of the A., the members & guests are relegated.—Stay, I just remember that you dine with the Century on Monday—so that we must say *Tuesday*—when I hope you will be free, & when I shall *not* have to go (as on Monday p.m.) to visit four haggard spinsters (compatriots & cousins)[2] who have descended upon Bloomsbury & upon *me*.—The present, I delight to say, is my last visit to the Country, so that next week we must take some walk or excursion; & I shall also see your wife.—Your novel[3] is admirable to the end, (which

---

2. Loseley House, an imposing Tudor structure in Surrey (and an inspiration for Gardencourt in *The Portrait of a Lady*), was the country residence of Sir John Rose (1820–88). Like Gardencourt's owner, Daniel Touchett, Sir John Rose was an expatriate banker (originally from Canada) who had been settled in England for many years. His wife, Charlotte Temple Rose, was the sister of Robert Emmet Temple (1808–54), who had married HJ's aunt, Catharine Margaret James (1820–54).

1. James R. Osgood, the Boston publisher.
2. HJ's visitors remain unidentified.
3. *A Modern Instance*.

I haven't quite reached,) of an extraordinary reality. I will talk to you about it. It is the Yankee *Romola!*[4]

Yours ever
H James jr

I have confided myself to *Osgood!*[5]

55.

JAMES TO HOWELLS, 14 September 1882, Paris   ALS Houghton
bMS Am 1784 (253) 43

Sept. 14th
GRAND HOTEL
12, BOULEVARD DES CAPUCINES
PARIS

Dear Howells

I meant to drop you a line of farewell before leaving London, which I quitted on Tuesday afternoon; but constant & extreme occupation left me but little time—or rather none at all. Here is a word to supplement our very hasty parting on Sunday afternoon. Its purpose is to tell you not to leave me long without news, & above all to give me some *general* address, if you have one, where I may at any time communicate with you. I came on Tuesday p.m. to *Dover* & slept, & proceeded yesterday to Paris, over a glassy channel. I shall be here 3 or 4 days & then go down for a fortnight into Touraine; after which I shall again be here for October. Here is some information which may help you. If you come to the Lake of Geneva *via* Paris, you can (after sleeping as many or as few nights as you please in the latter place,) go on at 8.55 in the morning, of course, (by the line of Paris-Lyons,) to Dijon, which you reach at 2.24 in the afternoon. Rest there 24 hours & see a very picturesque old town, & the next day, at 2.40 in the afternoon, go on by Pontarlier to *Lausanne,* which you reach at 9.25 in the evening. You have thus two very easy days. At Lausanne you are an hour's boat-sail, or less by train, from Montreux, or whatever your station is. A very good place for information touristical is *Cook's* office, Ludgate Hill. I hope London is giving you more rest. Love to every one.

Ever yours
H. James jr

I met my brother[1] on Sunday, & he left also on Tuesday p.m. You had better address always 3 Bolton St. It will see but a short delay.

---

4. *Romola* (1863) was the sixth novel written by George Eliot (Mary Ann Evans) (1819–90).

5. To bolster his position as an independent publisher of current fiction, James R. Osgood negotiated long-term contracts with both WDH and HJ.

1. WJ, who was enroute to Venice.

London Yankees, 1882. Autographs of American authors and men of letters (including James and Howells) who attended a banquet hosted by the convivial publisher James R. Osgood. By permission of the Houghton Library, Harvard University.

56.

HOWELLS TO JAMES, 4 October 1882, Villeneuve   ALS Houghton
                                                               bMS Am 1094 (238)

Le Clos, près Villeneuve, Vaud.
October 4, 1882.

My dear James:

We have now been rained in here two weeks; but the damp air is so good, and the lake and mountains so amiable that we are hardly even impatient with our imprisonment. If you happen to know the region, you can place our pension very near the Hotel Byron, and realize us on the right in going toward Montreux. Le Clos was formerly the country place of the family of Mlle Colomb, who were substantial people of Vevey, of the Brahminical caste. The house is full of old books, and smells equally of them, and the three cats and big dog which M'lle keeps. She is intelligent, witty, and I think one of the very most sensible people I ever saw: she has sense enough to be a man. Her cousin, Mme. Grenier *(veuve)*[1] and Mme. Grenier's son and daughter are our fellow-boarders: the mother is one of those exquisite persons, who keep a pretty gentleness and a young habit of blushing, far into their gray hairs; the daughter is *jolie*[2] (she gurgles it far down in her throat) and the son goes a great deal to the chase, and speaks Italian with me. We all struggle with French, the children more or less hopefully; and though I say it, we are an interesting household. I consider myself, especially fictionable, and I am sorry you are not here to study me in the character of a thoroughly bourgeois American: a man who had once some poetical possibilities, but who finds himself more and more commonplace in surroundings that twenty years ago appealed not in vain to something fine in him. I daily put on more *sitzfleisch*,[3] and feel hopelessly middle-aged, when I meet the pretty girls walking up from Chillon to gather the crimson leaves of the Virginia creeper, which hangs its splendor from all the walls here. Somewhere, deep within my awkward bulk, I know that I am as young and stylish and slim as any of them, but I know also that I don't look it.—England seems an age away, and of all that happened during our seven weeks in London, I remember your kindness most distinctly. I think you did not realize how good you were to us; but we did. The day we left we had a note from your brother,[4] and I was very sorry we should not have seen him.—I am working hard at my story[5] here,

---

1. A widow.
2. Pretty.
3. Extra pounds resulting from a sedentary life.
4. William James.
5. A *Woman's Reason* (1883), first begun in 1878. Back in London, on 9 September WDH had written to Edmund Gosse (1849–1928) about the difficulty he was having with the novel:

> I have written but a hundred pages of it in six weeks, and I have had such a good time that I have been unable to do so much even as kill a consumptive girl, or make a lover homesick enough to start home from China and get wrecked on an atoll in the South Pacific: he is

which takes shape very slowly and reluctantly. I shall never again I hope, attempt to finish a thing so long thrown aside.

All the family join me in love to you.

Yours ever
W. D. Howells

57.

JAMES TO HOWELLS, 15 October 1882, Bordeaux

ALS Houghton
bMS Am 1784 (253) 44

Bordeaux, Oct. 15$\underline{^{th}}$

My dear Howells.

Il me tardait,[1] as they say here (& even in your *pays de Vaud*,[2] I suppose,) to know what had become of you. Your letter came to me at this place, two days ago, & my imagination draws a long breath at being able to give you a local habitation. From what you say it must be a very pleasant one, though I am afraid you are sadly under water. I know your region well, & have lived about all around you—notably at the Hotel Byron, & at Glion, above Montreux, which is lovely in summer, when the blue lake shines through the walnut-trees which cover the hill as you go up. I suppose you will have walked (unless your *sitzfleisch* fears the ascent) up to the church at Montreux, which looks so well on the hillside, & about which Ruskin has somewhere written a charming passage (in *Modern Painters*.)[3] I have roamed all over the hills above you, & scaled the

---

still shamelessly hanging around Hong-Kong, and I have thrown away no end of geography and geology on his atoll. As long as I dine out four times a week, he will not budge; and I am resolved to try what effect a Swiss pension will have on him. (*SL* 3: 30)

1. I have been longing.

2. Region around Vaud, Switzerland.

3. John Ruskin (1819–1900), influential moralist and art historian. In part V, chapter 20 ("The Mountain Glory") of *Modern Painters*, first published in 1860, Ruskin records this anecdote:

I cannot leave this part of my subject without recording a slight incident, which happened to myself, singularly illustrative of the religious character of the Alpine peasant when under favourable circumstances of teaching. I was coming down one evening from the Rochers de Naye, above Montreux, having been at work among the limestone rocks, where I could get no water, and both weary and thirsty. Coming to a spring at a turn of the path, conducted, as usual, by the herdsmen into a hollowed pine-trunk, I stooped to it, and drank deeply: as I raised my head, drawing breath heavily, some one behind me said, "Celui qui boira de cette eau-ci, aura encore soif." [Whosoever drinketh of this water shall thirst again.] I turned, not understanding for the moment what was meant; and saw one of the hill-peasants, probably returning to his châlet from the market-place at Vevay [*sic*] or Villeneuve. As I looked at him with an uncomprehending expression, he went on with the verse:—"Mais celui qui boira de l'eau que je lui donnerai, n'aura jamais soif." [But whosoever drinketh of the water that I shall give him shall never thirst (John 4:13–14).]

I doubt if this would have been thought of, or said, by even the most intelligent lowland peasant. The thought might have occurred to him, but the frankness of address, and expecta-

Dent de Jaman & the Rochers de Naye. (Vide M. Arnold's *Obermann* for "Jaman's lonely peak.")[4] I don't mean to exult over you, who, I gather, don't both mountaineer & pursue a serial; but simply to show you that I place you. I congratulate you on your interesting household, though I confess I find it hard to get up an interest in a Swiss—much more in a *Suissesse*. They had produced but one person of distinction, & poor William Tell has lately been found out to be a myth! Haven't your ladies a *commencement de goître?*[5] If they haven't, they ought to have, to give you the real local colour. They do however probably give you good coffee and luscious honey, which, when you eat it, gets into your hair & shoes! I should have liked to know the perils, penalties, & I trust pleasures, of the journey from London, & you must tell me them some day. It's well you didn't try to cross the Alps, as Noah's ark would appear to have been the only vehicle. I appreciate your moralizings about middle-age & one's inevitable *embourgeoisement*, for I was a hundred-&-fifty last week! I have never felt so little young as since I undertook this youthful errand (in which you were my sponsor) of doing the French picturesque for *Harper*. For that is what brings me to these latitudes. I have assented to a proposal from Laffan[6] to write not two or three articles—but enough to make a book, & after having pursued this elusive volume through Touraine, I am making desperate snatches at it in these southern cities.—I go tomorrow to Toulouse, Carcassone, Narbonne, &c. I don't feel very successful, & find less material than I expected. But I shall put it through, & return to Paris by the end of the month. Touraine is charming, but revolutions & Napoleons have abolished the antique, in general, in France, to a degree that surprises—& much discomposes—me. There is no more to my purpose at Bordeaux than there would be at Fitchburg, & I am not even consoled by good claret, as what I am given here is very much what you would get at F.—that is if you can get any there. Do let me hear about you as you go; write, above all, as soon as you reach Italy. I hope Mrs. Howells enjoys the repose of Leman's shores—rest both from America & from England. I hear from my brother,[7] at Venice, who expects you there, but speaks of rain. I adjure Winnie & Pilar,[8] both of whom, with their brother, I embrace, to go bravely at

---

tion of being at once understood without a word of preparative explanation, as if the language of the Bible were familiar in all men, mark, I think, the mountaineer.

See *The Works of Ruskin*, Library Edition, 39 vols. (New York: Longmans, Green, 1904), 6: 432–33.

4. HJ captures the mood of two poems by Matthew Arnold (1822–88), "Stanzas in Memory of the Author of 'Obermann' " (1852) and "Obermann Once More" (1868), but the phrase is not a literal quotation from either.

5. Incipient symptoms of goiter; viz., swelling of the thyroid.

6. William Mackay Laffan (1848–1909), recently appointed London agent for Harper & Brothers. On 7 September HJ had met Laffan at a dinner sponsored by James R. Osgood, which WDH also attended. HJ eventually placed the serial installments of *A Little Tour in France* (1884) with the *Atlantic* (July–November 1883; February, April–May 1884) rather than with *Harper's Monthly*.

7. WJ; in a letter of the same date back to him, HJ enclosed the preceding one from "Howells, just received, which will show you where he is. I don't know when he thinks of starting for Venice." See HJ to WJ, 15 October [1882], *CWJ* 1: 334.

8. Pilar (occasionally written as Pilla or Pillà) was Mildred Howells's nickname.

their French—it will give them a great sense of conversational power. Love to all.

> Ever yours
> H James jr

William Dean Howells, "Henry James, Jr.," Century Magazine 25 (November 1882): 25–29.

The events of Mr. James's life—as we agree to understand events—may be told in a very few words. His race is Irish on his father's side and Scotch on his mother's, to which mingled strains the generalizer may attribute, if he likes, that union of vivid expression and dispassionate analysis which has characterized his work from the first. There are none of those early struggles with poverty, which render the lives of so many distinguished Americans monotonous reading, to record in his case: the cabin hearth-fire did not light him to the youthful pursuit of literature; he had from the start all those advantages which, when they go too far, become limitations.

He was born in New York city in the year 1843, and his first lessons in life and letters were the best which the metropolis—so small in the perspective diminishing to that date—could afford. In his twelfth year his family went abroad, and after some stay in England made a long sojourn in France and Switzerland. They returned to America in 1860, placing themselves at Newport,[1] and for a year or two Mr. James was at the Harvard Law School, where, perhaps, he did not study a great deal of law. His father removed from Newport to Cambridge in 1866, and there Mr. James remained till he went abroad, three years later, for the residence in England and Italy which, with infrequent visits home, has continued ever since.

It was during these three years of his Cambridge life that I became acquainted with his work. He had already printed a tale—"The Story of a Year"—in the "Atlantic Monthly," when I was asked to be Mr. Fields's assistant in the management, and it was my fortune to read Mr. James's second contribution in manuscript. "Would you take it?" asked my chief. "Yes, and all the stories you can get from the writer." One is much securer of one's judgment at twenty-nine than, say, at forty-five; but if this was a mistake of mine I am not yet old enough to regret it. The story was called "Poor Richard," and it dealt with the conscience of a man very much in love with a woman who loved his rival. He told this rival a lie, which sent him away to his death on the field,—in that day nearly every fictitious personage had something to do with the war,—but Poor Richard's lie did not win him his love. It still seems to me that the situation was strongly and finely felt. One's pity went, as it should, with the liar; but the

---

1. The peregrinations of the James family were somewhat more complicated than WDH's statement suggests. The Jameses first took up residence at Newport in 1858, when financial panic brought them back to America. They crossed the ocean again in the autumn of the following year, and then returned to Rhode Island in 1860.

whole story had a pathos which lingers in my mind equally with a sense of the new literary qualities which gave me such delight in it. I admired, as we must in all that Mr. James has written, the finished workmanship in which there is no loss of vigor; the luminous and uncommon use of words, the originality of phrase, the whole clear and beautiful style, which I confess I weakly liked the better for the occasional gallicisms remaining from an inveterate habit of French. Those who know the writings of Mr. Henry James will recognize the inherited felicity of diction which is so striking in the writings of Mr. Henry James, Jr. The son's diction is not so racy as the father's; it lacks its daring, but it is as fortunate and graphic; and I cannot give it greater praise than this, though it has, when he will, a splendor and state which is wholly its own.

Mr. James is now so universally recognized that I shall seem to be making an unwarrantable claim when I express my belief that the popularity of his stories was once largely confined to Mr. Fields's assistant. They had characteristics which forbade any editor to refuse them; and there are no anecdotes of thrice-rejected manuscripts finally printed to tell of him; his work was at once success-ful with all the magazines. But with the readers of "The Atlantic," of "Harper's," of "Lippincott's," of "The Galaxy," of "The Century," it was another affair. The flavor was so strange, that, with rare exceptions, they had to "learn to like" it. Probably few writers have in the same degree compelled the liking of their read-ers. He was reluctantly accepted, partly through a mistake as to his attitude— through the confusion of his point of view with his private opinion—in the reader's mind. This confusion caused the tears of rage which bedewed our conti-nent in behalf of the "average American girl" supposed to be satirized in Daisy Miller, and prevented the perception of the fact that, so far as the average American girl was studied at all in Daisy Miller, her indestructible innocence, her invulnerable new-worldliness, had never been so delicately appreciated. It was so plain that Mr. James disliked her vulgar conditions, that the very people to whom he revealed her essential sweetness and light were furious that he should have seemed not to see what existed through him. In other words, they would have liked him better if he had been a worse artist—if he had been a little more confidential.

But that artistic impartiality which puzzled so many in the treatment of Daisy Miller is one of the qualities most valuable in the eyes of those who care how things are done, and I am not sure that it is not Mr. James's most characteristic quality. As "frost performs the effect of fire," this impartiality comes at last to the same result as sympathy. We may be quite sure that Mr. James does not like the peculiar phase of our civilization typified in Henrietta Stackpole; but he treats her with such exquisite justice that he lets *us* like her. It is an extreme case, but I confidently allege it in proof.

His impartiality is part of the reserve with which he works in most respects, and which at first glance makes us say that he is wanting in humor. But I feel pretty certain that Mr. James has not been able to disinherit himself to this degree. We Americans are terribly in earnest about making ourselves, individu-ally and collectively; but I fancy that our prevailing mood in the face of all problems is that of an abiding faith which can afford to be funny. He has himself indicated that we have, as a nation, as a people, our joke, and every one of us is in the joke more or less. We may, some of us, dislike it extremely, disapprove it wholly, and even abhor it, but we are in the joke all the same, and no one of us is safe from becoming the great American humorist at any given moment. The danger is not apparent in Mr. James's case, and I confess that I read him with a relief in the comparative immunity that he affords from the national facetiousness. Many of his people are humorously imagined, or rather humorously *seen*, like Daisy Miller's mother, but these do not give a dominant color; the business in hand is commonly serious, and the droll people are subordinated. They abound, nevertheless, and many of them are perfectly new finds, like Mr. Tristram in "The American," the bill-paying father in the "Pension Beaurepas," the anxiously Europeanizing mother in the same story, the amusing little Madame de Belgarde, Henrietta Stackpole, and even Newman himself. But though Mr. James portrays the humorous in character, he is decidedly not on humorous terms with his reader; he ignores rather than recognizes the fact that they are both in the joke.

If we take him at all we must take him on his own ground, for clearly he will not come to ours. We must make concessions to him, not in this respect only, but in several others, chief among which is the motive for reading fiction. By example, at least, he teaches that it is the pursuit and not the end which should give us pleasure; for he often prefers to leave us to our own conjectures in regard to the fate of the people in whom he has interested us. There is no question, of course, but he could tell the story of Isabel in "The Portrait of a Lady" to the end, yet he does not tell it. We must agree, then, to take what seems a fragment instead of a whole, and to find, when we can, a name for this new kind in fiction. Evidently it is the character, not the fate, of his people which occupies him; when he has fully developed their character he leaves them to what destiny the reader pleases.

The analytic tendency seems to have increased with him as his work has gone on. Some of the earlier tales were very dramatic: "A Passionate Pilgrim," which I should rank above all his other short stories, and for certain rich poetical qualities, above everything else that he has done, is eminently dramatic. But I do not find much that I should call dramatic in "The Portrait of a Lady," while I do find in it an amount of analysis which I should call superabundance if it were not all such good literature. The novelist's main business is to possess his reader with a due conception of his characters and the situations in which they find themselves. If he does more or less than this he equally fails. I have sometimes thought that Mr. James's danger was to do more, but when I have been ready to declare this excess an error of his method I have hesitated. Could anything be superfluous that had given me so much pleasure as I read? Certainly from only one point of view, and this a rather narrow, technical one. It seems to me that an enlightened criticism will recognize in Mr. James's fiction a metaphysical genius working to aesthetic results, and will not be disposed to deny it any method it chooses to employ. No other novelist, except George Eliot, has dealt so largely in analysis of motive, has so fully explained and commented upon the springs of action in the persons of the drama, both before and after the facts. These novelists are more alike than any others in their processes, but with George Eliot an ethical purpose is dominant, and with Mr. James an artistic purpose. I do not know just how it should be stated of two such noble and generous types of character as Dorothea and Isabel Archer, but I think that we sympathize with the former in grand aims that chiefly concern others, and with the latter in beautiful dreams that primarily concern herself. Both are unselfish and devoted women, sublimely true to a mistaken ideal in their marriages; but, though they come to this common martyrdom, the original difference in them remains. Isabel has her great weaknesses, as Dorothea had, but these seem to me, on the whole, the most nobly intentioned women in modern fiction; and I think Isabel is the more subtly divined of the two. If we speak of mere character- ization, we must not fail to acknowledge the perfection of Gilbert Osmond. It is a profound stroke to make him an American by birth. No European could realize so fully in his own life the ideal of a European *dilettante* in all the meaning of that cheapened word; as no European could so deeply and tenderly feel the sweetness and loveliness of the English past as the sick American, Searle, in "The Passionate Pilgrim."

What is called the international novel is popularly dated from the publication of "Daisy Miller," though "Roderick Hudson" and "The American" had gone before; but it really began in the beautiful story which I have just named. Mr. James, who invented this species in fiction, first contrasted in the "Passionate Pilgrim" the New World and Old World moods, ideals, and prejudices, and he did it there with a richness of poetic effect which he has since never equalled. I own that I regret the loss of the poetry, but you cannot ask a man to keep on being a poet for you; it's hardly for him to choose; yet I compare rather discon- tentedly in my own mind such impassioned creations as Searle and the painter in "The Madonna of the Future" with "Daisy Miller," of whose slight, thin per- sonality I also feel the indefinable charm, and of the tragedy of whose innocence I recognize the delicate pathos. Looking back, to those early stories, where Mr. James stood at the dividing ways of the novel and the romance, I am sometimes sorry that he declared even superficially for the former. His best efforts seem to me those of romance; his best types have an ideal development, like Isabel and Claire Belgarde and Bessy Alden and poor Daisy and even Newman. But, doubt- less, he has chosen wisely; perhaps the romance is an outworn form, and would not lend itself to the reproduction of even the ideality of modern life. I myself waver somewhat in my preference—if it is a preference—when I think of such people as Lord Warburton and the Touchetts, whom I take to be all decidedly of this world. The first of these especially interested me as a probable type of the English nobleman, who amiably accepts the existing situation with all its possibilities of political and social change, and insists not at all upon the surviv- ing feudalities, but means to be a manly and simple gentleman in any event. An American is not able to pronounce as to the verity of the type; I only know that it seems probable and that it is charming. It makes one wish that it were in Mr. James's way to paint in some story the present phase of change in En- gland. A titled personage is still mainly an inconceivable being to us; he is like a goblin or a fairy in a storybook. How does he comport himself in the face of all the changes and modifications that have taken place and that still impend? We can hardly imagine a lord taking his nobility seriously; it is some hint of the conditional frame of Lord Warburton's mind that makes him imaginable and delightful to us.

It is not my purpose here to review any of Mr. James's books; I like better to speak of his people than of the conduct of his novels, and I wish to recognize the fineness with which he has touched-in the pretty primness of Osmond's daughter and the mild devotedness of Mr. Rosier. A masterly hand is as often manifest in the treatment of such subordinate figures as in that of the principal persons, and Mr. James does them unerringly. This is felt in the more important character of Valentin Belgarde, a fascinating character in spite of its defects,— perhaps on account of them—and a sort of French Lord Warburton, but wittier, and not so good. "These are my ideas," says his sister-in-law, at the end of a number of inanities. "Ah, you call them ideas!" he returns, which is delicious and makes you love him. He, too, has his moments of misgiving, apparently in regard to his nobility, and his acceptance of Newman on the basis of something like "manhood suffrage" is very charming. It is of course difficult for a remote plebeian to verify the pictures of legitimist society in "The American," but there is the probable suggestion in them of conditions and principles, and want of principles, of which we get glimpses in our travels abroad; at any rate, they reveal another and not impossible world, and it is fine to have Newman discover that the opinions and criticisms of our world are so absolutely valueless in that sphere that his knowledge of the infamous crime of the mother and brother of his betrothed will have no effect whatever upon them in their own circle if he explodes it there. This seems like aristocracy indeed! and one admires, almost respects, its survival in our day. But I always regretted that Newman's discovery seemed the precursor of his magnanimous resolution not to avenge himself; it weakened the effect of this, with which it had really nothing to do. Upon the whole, however, Newman is an adequate and satisfying representative of Americanism, with his generous matrimonial ambition, his vast good-nature, and his thorough good sense and right feeling. We must be very hard to please if we are not pleased with him. He is not the "cultivated American" who redeems us from time to time in the eyes of Europe; but he is unquestionably more national, and it is observable that his unaffected fellow-countrymen and women fare very well at Mr. James's hands always; it is the Europeanizing sort like the critical little Bostonian in the "Bundle of Letters," the ladies shocked at Daisy Miller, the mother in the "Pension Beaurepas" who goes about trying to be of the "native" world everywhere, Madame Merle and Gilbert Osmond, Miss Light and her mother, who have reason to complain, if any one has. Doubtless Mr. James does not mean to satirize such Americans, but it is interesting to note how they strike such a keen observer. We are certainly not allowed to like them, and the other sort find somehow a place in our affections along with his good Europeans. It is a little odd, by the way, that in all the printed talk about Mr. James—and there has been no end of it—his power of engaging your preference for certain of his people has been so little commented on. Perhaps it is because he makes no obvious appeal for them; but one likes such men as Lord Warburton, Newman,

Valentin, the artistic brother in "The Europeans," and Ralph Touchett, and such women as Isabel, Claire Belgarde, Mrs. Tristram, and certain others, with a thoroughness that is one of the best testimonies to their vitality. This comes about through their own qualities, and is not affected by insinuation or by downright *petting*, such as we find in Dickens nearly always and in Thackeray too often.

The art of fiction has, in fact, become a finer art in our day than it was with Dickens and Thackeray. We could not suffer the confidential attitude of the latter now, nor the mannerism of the former, any more than we could endure the prolixity of Richardson or the coarseness of Fielding. These great men are of the past—they and their methods and interests; even Trollope and Reade are not of the present. The new school derives from Hawthorne and George Eliot rather than any others; but it studies human nature much more in its wonted aspects, and finds its ethical and dramatic examples in the operation of lighter but not really less vital motives. The moving accident is certainly not its trade; and it prefers to avoid all manner of dire catastrophes. It is largely influenced by French fiction in form; but it is the realism of Daudet rather than the realism of Zola that prevails with it, and it has a soul of its own which is above the business of recording the rather brutish pursuit of a woman by a man, which seems to be the chief end of the French novelist. This school, which is so largely of the future as well as the present, finds its chief exemplar in Mr. James; it is he who is shaping and directing American fiction, at least. It is the ambition of the younger contributors to write like him; he has his following more distinctly recognizable than that of any other English-writing novelist. Whether he will so far control this following as to decide the nature of the novel with us remains to be seen. Will the reader be content to accept a novel which is an analytic study rather than a story, which is apt to leave him arbiter of the destiny of the author's creations? Will he find his account in the unflagging interest of their development? Mr. James's growing popularity seems to suggest that this may be the case; but the work of Mr. James's imitators will have much to do with the final result.

In the meantime it is not surprising that he has his imitators. Whatever exceptions we take to his methods or his results, we cannot deny him a very great literary genius. To me there is a perpetual delight in his way of saying things, and I cannot wonder that younger men try to catch the trick of it. The disappointing thing for them is that it is not a trick, but an inherent virtue. His style is, upon the whole, better than that of any other novelist I know; it is always easy, without being trivial, and it is often stately, without being stiff; it gives a charm to everything he writes; and he has written so much and in such various directions, that we should be judging him very incompletely if we considered him only as a novelist. His book of European sketches must rank him with the most enlightened and agreeable travelers; and it might be fitly supplemented from his uncollected papers with a volume of American sketches.[2] In

---

2. *Transatlantic Sketches* (Boston: James R. Osgood and Co., 1875). HJ incorporated four American travel pieces in *Portraits of Places* (London: Macmillan, 1883).

his essays on modern French writers he indicates his critical range and grasp;[3] but he scarcely does more, as his criticisms in "The Atlantic" and "The Nation" and elsewhere could abundantly testify.

There are indeed those who insist that criticism is his true vocation, and are impatient of his devotion to fiction; but I suspect that these admirers are mistaken. A novelist he is not, after the old fashion, or after any fashion but his own; yet since he has finally made his public in his own way of storytelling—or call it character-painting if you prefer,—it must be conceded that he has chosen best for himself and his readers in choosing the form of fiction for what he has to say. It is, after all, what a writer has to say rather than what he has to tell that we care for nowadays. In one manner or other the stories were all told long ago; and now we want merely to know what the novelist thinks about persons and situations. Mr. James gratifies this philosophic desire. If he sometimes forbears to tell us what he thinks of the last state of his people, it is perhaps because that does not interest him, and a large-minded criticism might well insist that it was childish to demand that it must interest him.

I am not sure that my criticism is sufficiently large-minded for this. I own that I like a finished story; but then also I like those which Mr. James seems not to finish. This is probably the position of most of his readers, who cannot very logically account for either preference. We can only make sure that we have here an annalist, or analyst, as we choose, who fascinates us from his first page to his last, whose narrative or whose comment may enter into any minuteness of detail without fatiguing us, and can only truly grieve us when it ceases.

58.

JAMES TO HOWELLS, 27 November 1882, London

ALS Houghton
bMS Am 1784 (253) 49

3 Bolton St. Piccadilly W.
Nov. 27th

My dear Howells.

It is not a "literary form" but a perfect verity that your letter[1] this a.m. found me on the point of writing to you. Were you dissolved in Alpine torrents or frozen in Alpine snows—had you grown stiff over your current serial,[2] or had you stealthily returned to a Boston suburb? These wonderments had passed through my mind, & I am delighted to have them answered. More seriously, I figured you fled to Italia nostra[3]—I don't know however but that I envy you that pleasure the more as still impending. Of course you have been under the

---

3. *French Poets and Novelists* (London: Macmillan, 1878).

1. Not extant.

2. *A Woman's Reason* did not begin its run in the *Century* until the next year (February–October 1883).

3. Our own Italy.

spout of heaven, as we all have been, but I am afraid it has been held more directly over your little corner of creation than over some others. May a sunny Italian winter make up for it.—I trust at least that the wetness of the world has only watered your ink—i.e. made it flow as freely as was necessary. Do you go to Italy with your novel finished? I wish you that joy. I hope the brevity of your mention of your wife's illness[4] is the measure of its duration & gravity. May she be speedily as well as she likes! Please to give her my kind remembrances.—I came back from Paris (where after coming up from my six weeks in the provinces I had been since Nov. 1$\underline{st}$) just a week ago—so that I missed the little breeze produced, as I am told, by the *November* Century.[5] I see in the last *Academy* that you have never seen the magazine—of which I should long since have sent you a copy did I not suppose that the publishers had the civility to do so.[6] I send you one to-day, that is as soon as I can procure it (having given all my own away)—with the hideous misprints in my *Venice* corrected.[7] You are accused of having sacrificed—in your patriotic passion for the works of H.J.jr—*Vanity Fair* & *Henry Esmond*[8] to *Daisy Miller* and *Poor Richard!* The indictment is rubbish—all your text says is that the "confidential" manner of Thackeray would not be tolerable to-day in a younger school, which should attempt to reproduce it. Such at least is all I see in it & all you ever meant to put. When I say "you are accused" all I mean to allude to is a nasty little paragraph in the *World*

4. Elinor Howells had suffered an attack of erysipelas.

5. WDH's *Century* article on HJ (see above) provoked an outpouring of retributive journalism—especially in England—because of the negative comparisons WDH made to the work of Thackeray and Charles Dickens (1812–70).

6. HJ was confused about his source but right about his information. The *Athenaeum* ran the following item in its columns of "Literary Gossip":

> Mr. W. D. Howells, who is writing his new novel in a retired place in Switzerland has known nothing of the animated discussion which his remarks in the November number of the *Century Magazine* have called forth from the English press. He writes to a friend who has called his attention to the subject that he has not even seen the magazine itself, and cannot recollect what he said about Dickens and Thackeray. But he is sure that he has been misprinted or misunderstood if he seems to be disrespectful to those great writers. "I always thought myself," he says, "quite unapproached in my appreciation of the great qualities of Dickens and Thackeray, and I can hardly believe that I have 'arraigned' them. I suspect that no Englishman can rate them higher than I do." The eminent novelist goes on to say that he only waits to see the *Century Magazine* and "what my offence in it against the great shades amounts to," to write further on the subject; and he is now determined, on the earliest opportunity, to carry out a design which has long been in his thoughts, namely, "to say my say about the art of Dickens and Thackeray in full." Next to a new novel from the pen of Mr. Howells, no contribution of his to literature would be more welcome than such a study.

(no. 2874 [25 November 1882]: 700)

The "friend" to whom WDH wrote, and who made sure this item got published, was Edmund Gosse, who was trying to help both HJ and WDH weather the storm of journalistic abuse that came in the wake of WDH's *Century* article. See WDH to Edmund Gosse, 16 November 1882, in *Transatlantic Dialogue: Selected American Correspondence of Edmund Gosse*, ed. Paul F. Mattheisen and Michael Millgate (Austin: University of Texas Press, 1965), 104–5.

7. HJ's article "Venice" also appeared in the November 1882 number of the *Century*.

8. Two of Thackeray's novels.

which accuses Warner[9] you & me of being linked in the most drivelling mutual admiration, & which accuses me individually of a "tepid, invertebrate, captain's-biscuit" style![10] Of the articles in the S. R. & P. M. I have seen only the former.[11] Warner's article on England exposes him, I think; it seems to me crude, boyish & not well written—especially for an editor of Men of Letters. But don't

9. Charles Dudley Warner, editor of Houghton, Mifflin's "American Men of Letters" series, had also contributed an article to the November *Century* on "England." His piece begins with a quotation from Benjamin Franklin, describing the country as a "petty island which, compared to America is but a stepping-stone in a brook, scarce enough of it above water to keep one's shoes dry" (134). The aggressive attitude of Warner's article is also apparent in his final reflections on literature:

> We used to be irritated at what we called the snobbishness of English critics of a certain school; we are so no longer, for we see that its criticism is only the result of ignorance,—simply of inability to understand. . . . I only refer to it to say that we should not be too hard on the "Saturday Review" critic when he is complaining of the American dialect in the English that Mr. Howells writes. How can the Englishman be expected to come into sympathy with the fiction that has New England for its subject,—from Hawthorne's down to that of our present novelists,—when he is ignorant of the whole background on which it is cast; when all the social conditions are an enigma to him; when, if he has, historically, some conception of Puritan society, he cannot have a glimmer of comprehension of the subtle modifications and changes it has undergone in a century? (141)

10. On 8 November 1882 the London *World* noted that the latest issue of the *Century* contains contributions from each member of that intellectual trinity, which it is the proper thing for all would-be "cultured" Americans to bow down and worship, and which constitutes in itself a fully-qualified Mutual Admiration Society. Mr. Henry James jun. writes of "Venice" in his usual tepid, invertebrate, captain's-biscuit style; and Mr. W. D. Howells writes of "Henry James Jr.," and places him at the head of the "new school" of fiction, which is, it seems, a very fine thing. Poor old Dickens and Thackeray are kicked out of court. . . . Let us burn our *éditions de luxe*, and fill our shelves with dime copies of *Daisy Miller* or *Their Wedding Journey*. (15:1)

11. A brief essay on "The Modern Novel" in the *Saturday Review* (54 [11 November 1882]: 633–34) takes issue with WDH's presumed claims for the superiority of contemporary fiction. Remarking on the multiple offenses of the November *Century*, the reviewer observes that "Mr. Howells writes an essay on Mr. James, and to the praise he gives to the manner of that delicate and graceful writer we can freely say 'ditto.' But he has also much to say about the modern school of fiction, which he considers, as is not indeed surprising, immeasurably superior to its predecessors." WDH's "moderation" in pressing this claim is even "more surprising, because in the same number of the same magazine a Mr. Warner, presumably also an American, snaps his fingers at England and all her works past, present, and to come" (633). In a review of *A Modern Instance*, the *Pall Mall Gazette* (14 November 1882) dryly observed:

> In the current number of a leading American periodical the author of "A Modern Instance" thus delivers himself upon the novelist's art:—"It is, after all, what a writer has to say, rather than what he has to tell, that we care for nowadays. In one manner or other the stories were all told long ago; and now we want merely to hear what the novelist thinks about persons and situations." No proposition so eminently disputable was ever perhaps so confidently laid down; but Mr. Howells has in one sense earned the right to take this tone. He practices what he preaches, if ever man did. He has a good deal "to say" in "A Modern Instance," and excellently well in many respects does he say it; but he has certainly very little "to tell."

Speaking more generally (and, by implication, including James), the reviewer suggests that the modern American school of novelists are in error in supposing, as they evidently do suppose, that it is solely to their analytic power that the great masters of moral analysis—that Balzac, that Thackeray, that Hawthorne owe their immortality. It is by the imaginative use of this power that they have won their crowns. (4, 5)

let the other matter bother you; it is infinitesimally small & the affair of ¾'s of a minute. I don't know whether your Scotch publisher[12] sends you (as he ought, if you wish them—I never do) notices of your M. I.,[13] but there is no doubt that you are rapidly coming very distinctly before the British public. You have only to go on.—I saw a good deal of John Hay, & C. King[14] in Paris, & got on beautifully with them both. Hay is an excellent fellow, & King is a charmer. He charms all the bricàbrac out of the shops. I made a goodly tour in France, to do it in *Harper*, & was informed on my return to Paris that Harper didn't want it! Laffan, who put me up to it, is much abashed. Write me as soon as you rest, somewhere, in Italy, & above all, GIVE ME YOUR <u>GENERAL</u> ADDRESS!! I embrace you all.

Ever your
H. James jr

I return your Missouri letter; the coolest of all the cool ones![15]

59.

JAMES TO HOWELLS, 20 March 1883, Boston

ALS Houghton
bMS Am 1784 (253) 48

131 Mount Vernon St
Boston. March 20<u>th</u>

My dear Howells.

Your letter from Siena[1] came to me yesterday, & you see I am not lazy about answering you. It was a real satisfaction to me to hear from you, as in this land of unscrupulous rumours & fictions all sorts of queer accounts of your movements & intentions had been wafted to me. I was sure you entered into our recent sorrow.[2] There is nothing to say about such things save that they *are*. My

---

12. David Douglas (1828–1916) of Edinburgh, who brought out authorized English editions of WDH's work from 1882 to 1898. In order to protect the English copyright in his work, WDH began to send duplicate magazine proofs directly to Douglas, who set type, deposited proofsheets for British copyright purposes, and then sent proofs back to WDH for corrections. WDH's corrected proofs were then stereotyped by Douglas and used for the English editions of his work. WDH economized further by having a set of plates returned to him for the publication of his American editions. WDH maintained this practice until the passage of international copyright legislation in 1891 prohibited the importation of plates manufactured abroad. See Scott Bennett, "David Douglas and the British Publication of W. D. Howells' Works," *Studies in Bibliography* 25 (1972): 107–24; see also the "Textual Commentary" to *The Rise of Silas Lapham* (Indiana University Press Edition), 375–78.

13. *A Modern Instance.*

14. Clarence King (1842–1901), first director of the U.S. Geological Survey and a member of the lively Washington literary circle that included John Hay, Henry Adams, and their wives. After his retirement in 1881, King became a speculator in mining properties.

15. The "cool" Missouri letter, presumably in response to *A Modern Instance,* has not been located.

1. Not extant.

2. HJ lost both his parents the preceding year. His mother had died in January, his father in December 1882.

return was painful & wretched, & my winter has not been delightful. However, I am "taking out" now what might have been scattered over years, & it is probable that when I return to Europe (not before some months) it will be for a—to put it mildly—longish stay. But even that depends on my sister, who is alone now but for me, & whose health, as you know, is none of the best.[3] She is mending, or tending to mend, I think, but I shall not leave her till I see her well on her feet. We live here together in the little house which my Father took when he left Cambridge (a place that seems to me now "unspeakable",) & which my sister will probably occupy for the next couple of years. I have spent quiet weeks (including a journey to Wisconsin with the mercury at 30 below zero)[4] but I haven't done much work. I have indeed done none whatever in the way of fiction—except offer a novel to the *Century*, which (though I left the terms to them) they refused. I should add that this refusal has since been somewhat modified. But in the meantime I have virtually (though not yet formally) engaged to give my next thing to Osgood to dispose of as he lists, so that if they take it they will have to do so on his terms.[5] I insert this fragment of "shop" to divert you—as you probably don't have much shop in Central Italy. I envy you Central Italy, I envy you even the tramontana[6] of Siena. I envy you the most delicious occupation in life—going round among the minor Italian towns to invent phrases about them. I shall devour every word you write about them.[7] I wish you had told me more about Florence & what you had seen & done there—& about the society through which you "crazily ran." Remember that I am surrounded by the social desolation of Boston—where the one feature is Mrs. Jack Gardner's flirtation with Frank Crawford, the American novelist of the future.[8] We, like T. & D.[9] are already of the past. Have you read *Mr. Isaacs?*—&

3. Bereft of her invalid father, AJ soon became a patient herself. After spending several weeks with her friend Katharine Loring (1849–1943) at Beverly, Massachusetts, Alice hospitalized herself at the Adams Nervine Asylum in Jamaica Plain from May to August 1883, where doctors monitored her diet and administered a version of the popular "rest cure." See Jean Strouse, *Alice James: A Biography* (Boston: Houghton Mifflin, 1980), 214–26.

4. Named as executor in his father's will, HJ had visited his brothers Wilkie and Bob at Milwaukee to begin the process of settling the estate.

5. On 13 April 1883 HJ signed an agreement with James R. Osgood, pledging himself to produce a novel and a series of tales and giving Osgood all rights in the material for a period of five years. *The Bostonians*, which ran in the *Century* (February 1885–February 1886), was covered by this contract, together with the stories that made up *Tales of Three Cities* (1884).

6. North wind.

7. As part of his long-term contract with James R. Osgood, WDH first serialized the chapters of *Tuscan Cities* (1885) in the *Century* (February–October 1885), where Joseph Pennell's accompanying illustrations also appeared.

8. Isabella Stewart ("Mrs. Jack") Gardner (1840–1924), art collector and flamboyant matriarch of Boston society, had recently befriended Francis Marion Crawford (1854–1909), author of *Mr. Isaacs: A Tale of Modern India* (1882). On 26 March 1882 Crawford told a close friend, "If you hear rumors of my attachment to a certain married lady, do not be distressed. She has been a good friend to me in trouble and is one of the purest and best women living—in spite of the slandering tongues of petty Boston." See Francis Marion Crawford to Louisa Terry, 26 March 1882, in John Pilkington Jr., *Francis Marion Crawford* (New York: Twayne, 1964), 47.

9. Thackeray and Dickens.

do you see a future in it? The brawny Crawford appears to act his novels as well as write them, though he has produced a serial for the much-desiring Aldrich?[10] Have you seen the amiable article about you in the *2 Mondes*, where the good M$^{\underline{me}}$ Fentryn describes you & me as the *disciples* (the *Émules* is the word she uses) of the good T. B.?[11] For the rest, articles about you & me are as thick as blackberries—we are daily immolated on the altar of Thackeray & Dickens. I enclose you the last (the *Tribune*,) which is not an immolation, however; on the contrary.[12] Thank you for your very kind remarks on the *Siege of London*,[13] which please me the more as it appears, publicly, to have fallen rather flat. I reward you by reading you in the *Century* with a poignant curiosity & perpetual relish.[14] When do you go to London? Whenever it is, I shall, I much fear, not be there. But we must arrange not to cross each other. I hope, indeed, you are

10. Thomas Bailey Aldrich, who succeeded WDH as editor of the *Atlantic*, serialized Crawford's *Roman Singer* (July 1883–June 1884).

11. "Les Nouveaux Romanciers Américains," *La Revue des Deux Mondes*, 3d. ser. 55 (1 Feb. 1883) by "Th. Bentzon," Mme. Marie Thérèse de Solms Blanc (1840–1907), French novelist and critic, at the time Mme. Fentryn. Surveying recent American novels, Mme. Fentryn concludes, "enfin les études profondément intéressantes de la vie contemporaine en Amérique, signées Howells, Henry James . . . ces émules d'Aldrich, qui, avant tous les autres, fit connaître ici, avec *Marjorie Daw, Prudence Palfrey*, et *la Reine de Saba*, la nouvelle école américaine d'un si délicat réalisme." (Finally, profoundly interesting studies of contemporary American life, exemplified in the work of Howells and Henry James . . . disciples of Aldrich, who, even more than they, has become known in France with his novels *Marjorie Daw, Prudence Palfrey*, and *The Queen of Sheba*, suggest that the new American school is one of very refined realism [636]).

12. On 18 March 1883 the New York *Tribune* ran an editorial (probably by John Hay) in support of Howells and James. Surprised by the disparaging tone of many recent newspaper notices about the two novelists, the *Tribune* wondered what could account for the apparent shift in attitude.

> With regard to Mr. James perhaps the case is not quite so queer. There has always been a party hostile to him in the American press, an American literary clique angrily refusing to accept him as an American novelist, owing to an uncomfortable doubt whether he had any desire for patriotic fellowship. The present outbreak against Mr. James is the extension of an old grievance rather than the discovery of a new one. . . . The clamor against Mr. Howells is so sudden, so violently in contrast with the praises lately lavished upon him, so grotesquely improper when we consider the amiability of his character and the cheerful, genial, unaffected tone of his writing, that the dispassionate observer is both puzzled by it and amused. What has he done all at once? Is Mr. James to be cast forth because Mr. Howells praises him, and Mr. Howells at the same time to be laid under the ban because he praises Mr. James?

The editorialist went on to speculate that the true source of the new hostility toward WDH was his incisive portrait of Bartley Hubbard in *A Modern Instance*:

> There are some hundreds of men whom a tolerant public maintains in American newspapers—men of coarse fibre, selfish instincts, weak morals, untruthful, undisciplined, not respecting other people because they do not respect themselves, and wanting only temptation to develop into rascals. Mr. Howells has read them. He has gone to the bottom of their vulgar little souls and turned them inside out.

See "The Case of Mr. Howells," New York *Tribune*, 18 March 1883, 6:2–3.

13. HJ, "The Siege of London," *Cornhill* (January–February 1883).

14. *A Woman's Reason* was serialized in the *Century* (February-October 1883).

deciding to stay another year. I am sorry to hear that Winnie droops[15] & give her my better hopes. The best to your wife.

Ever yours
H James

60.

JAMES TO HOWELLS, 21 February 1884, Paris   ALS Houghton
bMS Am 1784 (253) 50

Paris. Feb. 21$\underline{\text{st}}$ *1884.*

My dear Howells.

Your letter of the 2$\underline{\text{d}}$ last[1] gives me great pleasure. A frozen Atlantic seemed to stretch between us, & I had had no news of you to speak of save an allusion, in a late letter of T. B. A., to your having infant-disease in your house.[2] You give me a good account of this, & I hope your tax is paid for the year at least. These are not things to make a hardened bachelor mend his ways.—Hardened as I am, however, I am not proof against being delighted to hear that my Barberina tale[3] entertained you. I am not prepared even to resent the malignity of your remark that the last 3$\underline{\text{d}}$ is not the best. It isn't; the American part is squeezed together & écourté.[4] It is always the fault of my things that the head and trunk are too big & the legs too short. I spread myself always, at first, from a nervous fear that I shall not have enough of my peculiar tap to "go round." But I always (or generally) have and therefore, at the end, have to fill one of the cups to overflowing. My tendency to this disproportion remains incorrigible. I begin short tales as if they were to be long novels. Àpropos of which, ask Osgood to show you also the sheets of another thing I lately sent him—"A New England Winter."[5] It is not very good—on the contrary; but it will perhaps seem to you to put into form a certain impression of Boston.

—What you tell me of the success of Crawford's last novel[6] sickens & almost paralyses me. It seems to me (the book) so contemptibly bad & ignoble that the idea of people reading it in such numbers makes one return upon one's self &

15. Winifred Howells's health had been unstable for the past several years; at various times her symptoms included severe neuralgia, fatigue, vertigo, and, finally, acute anorexia nervosa.

1. Not extant.

2. Thomas Bailey Aldrich, then editor of the *Atlantic*; John Mead Howells was sick with scarlet fever.

3. "Lady Barberina," *Century* (May–July 1884). WDH must have seen advance sheets sent by HJ to James R. Osgood.

4. Cut short.

5. "A New England Winter," *Century* (August–September 1884).

6. Francis Marion Crawford, *To Leeward* (1883). Publisher's records indicate that 9,787 copies of the American edition were sold within a year of publication. See Houghton, Mifflin Copyright Accounts Ledger: 1881–1891, p. 76 (Houghton Mifflin Archive, Harvard).

A LITERARY COMBINATION.

Mr. H—w-lls: ARE YOU THE TALLEST NOW, MR. J—MES?
Mr. J—mes (ignoring the question): BE SO UNCOMMONLY KIND, H—W-LLS, AS TO LET ME DOWN EASY;
IT MAY BE WE HAVE BOTH GOT TO GROW.

The New School of Fiction, as satirized by *Life* (1883), inspired by Howells's flattering remarks about James in the *Century* (November 1882).

ask what is the use of trying to write anything decent or serious for a public so absolutely idiotic. It must be totally wasted. I would rather have produced the basest experiment in the "naturalistic" that is being practised here than such a piece of sixpenny humbug. Work so shamelessly bad seems to me to dishonour the novelist's art to a degree that is absolutely not to be forgiven; just as its success dishonours the people for whom one supposes one's self to write. Excuse my ferocity, which (more discreetly & philosophically) I think you must share; & don't mention it, please, to any one, as it will be set down to green-eyed jealousy.—I came to this place three weeks since—on the principle that anything is quieter than London; but I return to the British scramble in a few days. Paris speaks to me, always, for about such a time as this, with many voices; but at the end of a month I have heard all it has to say. I have been seeing something of Daudet,[7] Goncourt, & Zola; & there is nothing more interesting to me now than the effort & experiment of this little group, with its truly infernal intelligence of art, form, manner—its intense artistic life. They do the only kind of work, to-day, that I respect; & in spite of their ferocious pessimism & their handling of unclean things, they are at least serious and honest. The floods of tepid soap and water which under the name of novels are being vomited forth in England, seem to me, by contrast, to do little honour to our race. I say this to you, because I regard you as the great American naturalist. I don't think you go far enough, & you are haunted with romantic phantoms & a tendency to factitious glosses; but you are in the right path, & I wish you repeated triumphs there—beginning with your Americo-Venetian—though I slightly fear, from what you tell me, that he will have a certain "gloss."[8] It isn't for me to reproach you with that, however, the said gloss being a constant defect of *my* characters; they have too much of it—too damnably much. But I am a failure!—comparatively. Read Zola's last thing: *La Joie de Vivre.*[9] This title of course has a desperate irony; but the work is admirably solid & serious.—I haven't much London news for you. I see the genial Gosse occasionally, & the square-headed Tadema,[10] whose *d*'s & *t*'s are so mixed; & they frequently ask about you. Miss Fenimore Woolson[11] is spending the winter here; I see her at discreet intervals, & we talk of you and Mrs. *you*. She is a very intelligent woman, & understands when she is spoken to; a peculiarity I prize, as I find it more & more rare.—I am very happy as to what you tell me of Perry's having a large piece of work to do;[12] & I pray it may yield him some profit & comfort.

7. Alphonse Daudet (1840–97), French novelist and friend of HJ, was, like Edmond de Goncourt and Emile Zola, a champion of documentary realism in fiction.

8. WDH had contemplated writing a story in which, as he told his publisher Osgood, he could contrast the nascent nationality of America and the dying nationality of Venice in the adventures of a young Puritan shipscaptain . . . who sails from Salem or Duxbury for Venice about the year 1790, and gets fallen in love with by a beautiful and noble Venetian. I mean that the affair shall "end up" well; and the story as it lies in my mind is a pretty and merry one, as well as romantic.

HJ harbored a lifelong suspicion of the historical novel, an attitude that WDH eventually came to share: this projected work was never written. For the letter quoted above, see WDH to James R. Osgood, 12 July 1882, *SL* 3: 20; another letter to Osgood (16 October 1882, *SL* 3: 36–37) amplifies WDH's intentions.

9. *The Joy of Life.*

10. Lawrence Alma-Tadema (1836–1912), a Dutch artist elected to the Royal Academy in 1879. His wife was Edmund Gosse's sister-in-law. WDH had met him in London in 1882.

11. Constance Fenimore Woolson (1840–94), American writer who became much attached to HJ.

12. From 1884 to 1887 Thomas Sergeant Perry lectured in the Harvard Annex (the forerunner of Radcliffe College) on Shakespeare and Augustan literature. He had recently published *English*

Sad indeed has been hitherto the history of his career, & the cynical indifference of the public to so good a production (in spite of weaknesses of form) as his *18th Century* makes me blush for it. As you see, I am blushing a good deal for the public now. Give Perry my love, please, when you see him next, & tell him I am acutely conscious of owing him, & indeed his wife, a letter; they shall really have it soon. Addio—stia bene.[13] I wish you could send me anything *you* have in the way of advance-sheets. It is rather hard that as you are the only English novelist I read (except Miss Woolson,) I shouldn't have more comfort with you. Give my love to Winny: I am sure she will dance herself well.[14] Why doesn't Mrs. Howells try it too?

Tout à vous[15]
Henry James

61.

JAMES TO HOWELLS, 31 July 1884, London   ALS Houghton
bMS Am 1784 (253) 51

3 Bolton St. W.
July 31st

My dear Howells.

Being in the highest degree pressed with work, having just come to a renewed sense of terrible arrears, & having fifty other things to do, the moment seems remarkably good for writing you a few leisurely, friendly lines. A visit from Osgood this a.m. has put the pen in my hands. He tells me of your having bought a house in Beacon St.,[1] overlooking the lagoon (if I understand it right) & I hasten to express all my satisfaction at your being so happily & healthily domiciled. I see you in a lovely study that commands the shining estuary, visited by a muse whom the most pressing engagements elsewhere cannot induce to leave so sweet a spot. What charming things she will say to you, & how you will always find her with her cheek on her hand at your back-window! You will find yourself writing too well, & will sigh for the prosier prospects of Florence Venice & London. I wish you, seriously, every domestic & social felicity, & to Mrs. Howells the amplest consciousness of modern improvements. This is mainly what I wished to say; but with our rareness of opportunities I must put more in. I am at the present moment what I imagine you most naturally suppose me to be—a battered relic of the London Season. It is fortunately over, & I possess my

---

Literature in the Eighteenth Century (1883) and was at work on a critical study of neoclassicism entitled *From Opitz to Lessing* (1884), which he dedicated to WDH.

13. Farewell—be well.

14. Winifred Howells was preparing to make her social debut in Boston, an event later canceled owing to her declining health.

15. Ever yours.

1. Earlier that summer WDH had purchased a house on the water side of Beacon Street (No. 302) in Boston's Back Bay.

soul once more. I have tried hard to lead a quiet life, but have succeeded only in being infinitely interrupted & distracted. Moral—I shall next year seek safety in absence. Meanwhile, however, I remain uninterruptedly in London, on which with the last week, a holy calm has descended. I shall have no absence & no "country" (thank heaven,) but peg away at two fictions which I have undertaken & the minor (shorter) of which is to keep company to one of yours (I believe) in the *Century* for a while.[2] The other decorates the *Atlantic* a year hence. The Atlantic lately brought me Aldrich, that gilded youth, who edits periodicals from Brown's Hotel.[3] As he appears to have everything the world can give, he is afraid he may have the cholera, so returns presently to his homes. I hope he won't take the microbe with him, to decimate the twins. I see Gosse every now & then & we generally talk of you; of course you know (as indeed you are the author) of his American plans.[4] His Cambridge lectureship here is a good thing for him, but arduous at the start.[5] Where are you?—in what country? The rustle of the 'bus-wheels in Piccadilly & the fragrance of the opposite chimney-pots are all *my* touch of nature. Do you see T. S. P.?[6] Embrace him for me. Be embraced yourself & believe me ever of your Bostonianship the very faithful devotee—

Henry James

62.

HOWELLS TO JAMES, 22 August 1884, Kennebunkport

ALS Houghton
bMS Am 1094 (239)

Kennebunkport, Maine,
Aug. 22, 1884.

My dear James:

It is very good of you to write me when I've so long owed you a letter, and to make my buying a house "on the water side of Beacon" the occasion of

---

2. Originally envisioned as a six-part serial, *The Bostonians* (1886) eventually ran to thirteen installments in the *Century* (February 1885–February 1886), where WDH's *Rise of Silas Lapham* also appeared (November 1884–August 1885). HJ's next novel, *The Princess Casamassima*, appeared first in the *Atlantic* (September 1885–October 1886).

3. Throughout the 1880s, *Atlantic* editor Thomas Bailey Aldrich summered in Europe. In addition to his sprawling country place at Ponkapog, Massachusetts, in 1883 Aldrich had purchased a large house at 59 Mount Vernon Street on Beacon Hill in Boston.

4. WDH had helped to arrange American lecture engagements for Edmund Gosse, who traveled to America during the winter of 1884–85; his lectures, *From Shakespeare to Pope*, were published in 1886.

5. In May 1884 Gosse was appointed to the Clark Lectureship in English Literature at Trinity College, Cambridge, a post just vacated by Leslie Stephen's resignation. "The offer from Cambridge is all the more flattering," Gosse told WDH, "because I made no sort of appeal for it, not indeed having the vaguest notion that it was open." See Gosse to WDH, 7 May 1884, in *Transatlantic Dialogue*, 141.

6. Thomas Sergeant Perry.

forgiving my neglect. The greatest pleasure the house has yet brought me is this; but it is a pretty house and an extremely fine situation, and I hope it is not the only joy I shall have from it. I have spent some desolate weeks in it already, putting my books on their shelves, while the family were away at mountain-side and seaside, and I can speak confidently and authoritatively of the sunsets from the library-windows. The sun goes down over Cambridge with as much apparent interest as if he were a Harvard graduate: possibly he is; and he spreads a glory over the Back Bay that is not to be equaled by the blush of a Boston Independent for such of us Republicans as are going to vote for Blaine.[1]—Sometimes I feel it an extraordinary thing that I should have been able to buy a house on Beacon str., but I built one on Concord Avenue of nearly the same cost when I had far less money to begin with.[2] In those doubting days I used to go and look at the cellar they were digging, and ask myself, knowing that I had had barely money to pay for the lot, "*Can* blood be got out of a turnip?" Now I know that some divine power loves turnips, and that somehow the blood will be got out of the particular turnip which I represent. Drolly enough, I am writing a story in which the chief personage builds a house "on the water side of Beacon," and I shall be able to use all my experience, down to the quick.[3] Perhaps the novel may pay for the house.

I am just back from a visit of a few days at Campobello,[4] which is so far off that I feel as if I had been to Europe. It is a fashionable resort, in spite of its remoteness, and I saw many well-dressed and well-read girls there who were all disposed more or less to talk of you, and of your latest story, A New England Winter.[5] Generally speaking I should say that its prime effect had been to imbue the female Boston mind with a firm resolve to walk on the domestic roof at the first opportunity. The maiden aunt gives universal satisfaction, especially in her rage with her nephew when he blows her a five-fingered kiss. I myself having the vice of always liking you, ought perhaps to be excluded from the stand, but I must bear my witness to the excellence particularly of some of the bits of painting. In just such a glare of savage sunshine I made my way through Washington street in such a horsecar as you portray, the day I read your advance sheets. Besides that, I keenly enjoyed those fine touches by which you suggest a more celestially difficult and evasive Boston than I ever get at. The fashionableness which is so unlike the fashionableness of other towns—no one touches that

---

1. James G. Blaine (1830–93), Republican candidate for president in the bitterly contested election of 1884. Blaine, who had been accused in 1876 of taking kickbacks from railway companies and never completely exonerated, was narrowly defeated by Grover Cleveland (1837–1908), the reform governor of New York state. During the campaign, Cleveland, who had fathered an illegitimate child, was also tarred by journalists and cartoonists.

2. The Cambridge house at 37 Concord Avenue was built in 1872–73.

3. *The Rise of Silas Lapham* (1885).

4. WDH's family was vacationing in Canada. His impressions of Campobello figure in *April Hopes* (1887).

5. "A New England Winter," *Century* (August–September 1884). In the story one of HJ's characters, Miss Lucretia Daintry, accompanies a repairman to inspect the roof of her house.

but you; and you contrive also to indicate its contiguity, in its most etherial intangibility, to something that is very plain and dully practical. It is a great triumph which Pauline Mesh embodies. The study pleases me throughout: the mother with her struggles—herculean struggles—with such shadowy problems; the son with the sincere Europeanism of an inalienable, wholly uninspired American. As for the vehicle, it is delicious.

I don't know whether I've bragged to you of all the work I've done the past winter. One piece of it was an opera which Henschel set to music,[6] and we had a contract with the Bijou Theatre for its production in November. The other night the manager with whom we contracted, in trying to get aboard his yacht in the fog, fell and fractured his skull, poor man. He died, and with him our legal hold upon a potential fortune. I dare say the Theatre will still want it; but I wait the return of the puissant Osgood, who put our contract through before knowing.—The Madison Square people have bought the London dramatization of A Foregone Conclusion, and have sent it to me for revision.[7] As yet we have not got beyond the point of my having refused to do it for next to nothing. Sometime, when we meet, I will tell you how those gifted brothers led me on protesting over the same path you trod to the same flowery pitfall with another play.[8]—I really begin to admire them; they are masters of no common skill.

We are expecting the Gosses at our house early in December, and have plans for making them like the country, which ought to succeed at least so long as they are in it.

Before Perry went away for the summer I saw him very often. Since that time we have developed into political enemies: men to whom the private vices of Cleveland and the civic crimes of Blaine are reciprocally virtues of the most pleasing complexion.

There is no literary news to give you in this dull season, at this little seaport, where loverless maidens superabound in the hotels and the rowboats on the river in such numbers as would furnish all the novelists with heroines indefinitely. The family joins me in love.

Yours ever
W. D. Howells

6. WDH's libretto for A Sea-Change; Or, Love's Stowaway was set to music by George Henschel (1850–1934), who from 1881 to 1884 was the first conductor of the Boston Symphony Orchestra. Completed in 1885, the opera was never performed, because of the accident described in the letter and the extravagant staging the work entailed. WDH eventually published the libretto in Harper's Weekly (14 July 1888); as a volume it appeared (with substantial emendations) under Benjamin Ticknor's imprint later that year. See Meserve, Complete Plays, 269–99.

7. George S. Mallory (1838–97), joint proprietor with his brother, Marshall, of New York's Madison Square Theatre, was in the audience and proposed an American production of the play. A series of matinee performances were staged in 1886. See Meserve, Complete Plays, 314–37.

8. In 1882–83 the Mallory brothers had urged HJ to complete a dramatic version of "Daisy Miller" but then refused to produce it. In his notebook HJ referred to the theater managers as "asses and sharpers combined" (CN 232).

63.

JAMES TO HOWELLS, 23 May 1885, Bournemouth   ALS Houghton
                                                          bMS Am 1784 (253) 52

St. Alban's Cliff
Bournemouth
May 23$\underline{d}$

My dear Howells—

William enclosed me a note of yours (to him)[1] a few days since—in relation to some inquiry he had made of you about the consequences of the wretched Osgood's failure[2]—which gave a point to the sharp desire I already had of writing to express a friendly hope that that catastrophe has not fallen heavily upon *you*. As to this your note (to W$\underline{m}$) gives no information & I wait with some anxiety to learn—praying for you hard in the interval. I take for granted that Osgood's collapse terminates your particular connection with him—as I don't suppose that even your benevolent spirit will regard him as entitled to another—& a third—chance. But I trust he hasn't failed owing you any large sum of money. If he hasn't don't be—or rather don't feel—incommoded. You can make new arrangements which will be as fruitful as the old & of less ricketty a character. I am sorry to say that my own connection with the defunct has not been one on which I could congratulate myself. He has six books of mine in his hands—3 new ones—& I made before I last left America an agreement with him for the *Bostonians*—he to have the book (in 2 countries)—serial right &c—for a sum. He sold it to the Century—but I shall never have a penny of the money from him. Fortunately I shall recover the book—but the *Century*, I fear, will have enjoyed my calumnious prose for nothing (as far as I am concerned.) However, I didn't mean to go into these sordid details—but mainly—after asking whether *you* were hurt—to express my surprise & regret at the reve-

---

1. Not extant.

2. On 2 May 1885 James R. Osgood & Company went into receivership. For the next several months Osgood attempted to negotiate with his creditors; ultimately he was forced to transfer the business to a new group of managers, headed by Benjamin H. Ticknor, who reorganized the firm as Ticknor & Company. HJ had asked his brother William to consult with WDH and the family's attorney about the best means for him to protect his interests in the wake of Osgood's collapse: the four thousand dollars pledged for *The Bostonians* had not yet been paid. In two letters to WDH, William pressed for information. Already anticipating his brother's concern, William wrote on 5 May: "Harry will no doubt be rather impatient to learn whether he is likely to lose much by Osgood's failure. If you know in your own case how matters are to stand, can't you tip him a line of information? Or can you tell me how to find out?" A week later, William was still not satisfied: "I suppose you know how Osgood's affairs are going. I know absolutely nothing, nor of the thing to be done under such circumstances. Do you suppose it would lessen Harry's risks in any way if I were to put his interests into a lawyer's hands to look after?" After weeks of protracted negotiations, HJ sold the book rights for *The Bostonians* to Macmillan for an advance of five hundred pounds (slightly less than twenty-five hundred dollars) against a 15 percent royalty. The sum paid by the *Century* for the novel's serial rights, however, was unrecoverable. See WJ to WDH, 5 and 12 May 1885 (Howells Papers, Harvard); and Anesko, *"Friction with the Market"*, 102–7.

lation I find in your note to my brother that I owe you two letters. Here is one, without delay—if you will honour it by such a name. I am down here—& have been for weeks—looking after my sister who, I grieve to say, is in a wretched condition.[3] The place disagrees with her, yet she is too ill to be moved, & I am waiting for some better possibility: which seems slow to come. Bournemouth is a very good place, however, to make up literary arrears (& mine are fearful,) & the climate favours me as much as it incommodes poor Alice. My only social resource—except that it is a social resource to be out of London in May & June—is Robert Louis Stevenson,[4] who is more or less dying here & who (in case that event should take place) gave me the other day a message of a friendly—very friendly—character to give to you when I should next see you.[5] I shall wait till then—it is too long for a short letter. He is an interesting, charming creature, but I fear at the end of his tether: though indeed less apparently near death than he has been at other times. I congratulate you heartily on "Silas Lapham"—it has an immense reality & ranks among your highest flights. It is most remarkable. You do catch hold of life & give its impression.

—I am sickened by the idiotic, impudent outcry against my tale in the Century—a thing made up of the thinnest, airiest, rustiest *guesswork*, & fancifullest induction from glimpses of New England females in horse-cars 10 & 15 years ago—attacked on the ground of "personality" & invasion of privacy![6] The fault of my tale is its beastly ignorance & vagueness, as you will easily have perceived. Basta. I hope things are domestically well with you & am ever with love to your wife

very faithfully yours
Henry James

*Henry James, "William Dean Howells," Harper's Weekly 30 (19 June 1886):
394-95.*

As the existence of a man of letters (so far as the public is concerned with it) may be said to begin with his first appearance in literature, that of Mr. Howells,

3. After spending several months at the Adams Nervine Asylum in Jamaica Plain and then going on to New York for galvanic treatments, Alice James and her companion, Katharine Loring, traveled to England in search of a more permanent cure for her neurasthenic disorder.

4. Robert Louis Stevenson (1850–94), English novelist and poet, was ill with tuberculosis.

5. HJ emphasizes the conciliatory tone of Stevenson's overtures because, married to a divorced woman, he had reacted violently to *A Modern Instance*, mistaking that novel for an ad hominem attack. In 1882 Stevenson broke off relations with WDH, who had planned to visit him in France during the family's European sojourn. See *LiL* 1: 332–33.

6. Affronted by HJ's satiric treatment of Miss Birdseye, the frumpy ineffectual reformer (presumably inspired by Elizabeth Palmer Peabody [1804–94], Hawthorne's sister-in-law and venerable transcendental bluestocking), American newspaper reviewers had accused HJ of modeling *The Bostonians'* characters upon living persons. HJ first denied and then grudgingly admitted that he might have had Peabody in mind when creating Miss Birdseye, but he insisted that the novel's treatment of her was altogether affectionate. See HJ to WJ, 14 and 15 February 1885, *CWJ* 2: 7–9.

who was born at Martinsville, Ohio, in 1837, and spent his entire youth in his native State, dates properly from the publication of his delightful volume on *Venetian Life*—than which he has produced nothing since of a literary quality more pure—which he put forth in 1865, after his return from the consular post in the city of St. Mark which he had filled for four years. He had, indeed, before going to live in Venice, and during the autumn of 1860, published, in conjunction with his friend Mr. Piatt, a so-called "campaign" biography of Abraham Lincoln;[1] but as this composition, which I have never seen, emanated probably more from a good Republican than from a suitor of the Muse, I mention it simply for the sake of exactitude, adding, however, that I have never heard of the Muse having taken it ill. When a man is a born artist, everything that happens to him confirms his perverse tendency; and it may be considered that the happiest thing that could have been invented on Mr. Howells's behalf was his residence in Venice at the most sensitive and responsive period of life; for Venice, bewritten and bepainted as she has ever been, does nothing to you unless to persuade you that you also can paint, that you also can write. Her only fault is that she sometimes too flatteringly— for she is shameless in the exercise of such arts—addresses the remark to those who cannot. Mr. Howells could, fortunately, for his writing was painting as well in those days. The papers on Venice prove it, equally with the artistic whimsical chapters of the *Italian Journeys*, made up in 1867 from his notes and memories (the latter as tender as most glances shot eastward in working hours across the Atlantic) of the holidays and excursions which carried him occasionally away from his consulate.

The mingled freshness and irony of these things gave them an originality which has not been superseded, to my knowledge, by any impressions of European life from an American stand-point. At Venice Mr. Howells married a lady of artistic accomplishment and association, passed through the sharp alternations of anxiety and hope to which those who spent the long years of the civil war in foreign lands were inevitably condemned, and of which the effect was not rendered less wearing by the perusal of the London *Times* and the conversation of the British tourist. The irritation, so far as it proceeded from the latter source, may even yet be perceived in Mr. Howells's pages. He wrote poetry at Venice, as he had done of old in Ohio, and his poems were subsequently collected into two thin volumes, the fruit, evidently, of a rigorous selection. They have left more traces in the mind of many persons who read and enjoyed them than they appear to have done in the author's own. It is not nowadays as a cultivator of rhythmic periods that Mr. Howells most willingly presents himself. Everything in the evolution, as we must all learn to call it to-day, of a talent of this order is interesting, but one of the things that are most so is the separation that has taken place, in Mr. Howells's case, between its early and its later manner. There is nothing in *Silas Lapham*, or in *Doctor Breen's Practice*, or in *A*

1. WDH's 1860 campaign biography of Lincoln, *Lives and Speeches of Abraham Lincoln and Hannibal Hamlin*, was coauthored by John L. Hayes (1812–87), not John J. Piatt (1835–1917). Piatt collaborated with WDH in publishing *Poems of Two Friends*, which appeared in December 1859.

Modern Instance, or in *The Undiscovered Country,* to suggest that its author had at one time either wooed the lyric Muse or surrendered himself to those Italian initiations without which we of other countries remain always, after all, more or less barbarians. It is often a good, as it is sometimes an evil, that one cannot disestablish one's past, and Mr. Howells cannot help having rhymed and romanced in deluded hours, nor would he, no doubt, if he could. The repudiation of the weakness which leads to such aberrations is more apparent than real, and the spirit which made him care a little for the poor factitious Old World and the superstition of "form" is only latent in pages which express a marked preference for the novelties of civilization and a perceptible mistrust of the purist. I hasten to add that Mr. Howells has had moments of reappreciation of Italy in later years, and has even taken the trouble to write a book (the magnificent volume on *Tuscan Cities*) to show it. Moreover, the exquisite tale *A Foregone Conclusion,* and many touches in the recent novel of *Indian Summer* (both this and the *Cities* the fruit of a second visit to Italy), sound the note of a charming inconsistency.

On his return from Venice he settled in the vicinity of Boston, and began to edit the *Atlantic Monthly,* accommodating himself to this grave complication with infinite tact and industry. He conferred further distinction upon the magazine; he wrote the fine series of "Suburban Sketches," one of the least known of his productions, but one of the most perfect, and on Sunday afternoons he took a suburban walk—perfect also, no doubt, in its way. I know not exactly how long this phase of his career lasted, but I imagine that if he were asked, he would reply, "Oh, a hundred years." He was meant for better things than this—things better, I mean, than superintending the private life of even the most eminent periodical—but I am not sure that I would speak of this experience as a series of wasted years. They were years rather of economized talent, of observation and accumulation. They laid the foundation of what is most remarkable, or most, at least, the peculiar sign, in his effort as a novelist—his unerring sentiment of the American character. Mr. Howells knows more about it than any one, and it was during this period of what we may suppose to have been rather perfunctory administration that he must have gathered many of his impressions of it. An editor is in the nature of the case much exposed, so exposed as not to be protected even by the seclusion (the security to a superficial eye so complete) of a Boston suburb. His manner of contact with the world is almost violent, and whatever bruises he may confer, those he receives are the most telling, inasmuch as the former are distributed among many, and the latter all to be endured by one. Mr. Howells's accessibilities and sufferings were destined to fructify. Other persons have considered and discoursed upon American life, but no one, surely, has felt it so completely as he. I will not say that Mr. Howells feels it all equally, for are we not perpetually conscious how vast and deep it is?—but he is an authority upon many of those parts of it which are most representative. He was still under the shadow of his editorship when, in the intervals of his letter-writing and reviewing, he made his first cautious attempts in the walk of fiction. I say cautious, for in looking back nothing is more clear than that he had determined to advance only step by step. In his first story, *Their Wedding Journey,* there are only two persons, and in his next, *A Chance Acquaintance*, which contains one of his very happiest studies of a girl's character, the number is not lavishly increased.

In *A Foregone Conclusion*, where the girl again is admirable, as well as the young Italian priest, also a kind of maidenly figure, the actors are but four. To-day Mr. Howells doesn't count, and confers life with a generous and unerring hand. If the profusion of forms in which it presents itself to him is remarkable, this is perhaps partly because he had the good fortune of not approaching the novel until he had lived considerably, until his inclination for it had ripened. His attitude was as little as possible that of the gifted young person who, at twenty, puts forth a work of imagination of which the merit is mainly in its establishing the presumption that the next one will be better. It is my impression that long after he was twenty he still cultivated the belief that the faculty of the novelist was not in him, and was even capable of producing certain unfinished chapters (in the candor of his good faith he would sometimes communicate them to a listener) in triumphant support of this contention. He believed, in particular that he could not make people talk, and such have been the revenges of time that a cynical critic might almost say of him to-day that he cannot make them keep silent. It was life itself that finally dissipated his doubts, life that reasoned with him and persuaded him. The feeling of life is strong in all his tales, and any one of them has this rare (always rarer) and indispensable sign of a happy origin, that it is an impression at first hand. Mr. Howells is literary, on certain sides exquisitely so, though with a singular and not unamiable perversity he sometimes endeavors not to be; but his vision of the human scene is never a literary reminiscence, a reflection of books and pictures, of tradition and fashion and hearsay. I know of no English novelist of our hour whose work is so exclusively a matter of painting what he sees, and who is so sure of what he sees. People are always wanting a writer of Mr. Howells's temperament to see certain things that he doesn't (that he doesn't sometimes even want to), but I must content myself with congratulating the author of *A Modern Instance* and *Silas Lapham* on the admirable quality of his vision. The American life which he for the most part depicts is certainly neither very rich nor very fair, but it is tremendously positive, and as his manner of presenting it is as little as possible conventional, the reader can have no doubt about it. This is an immense luxury; the ingenuous character of the witness (I can give it no higher praise) deepens the value of the report.

Mr. Howells has gone from one success to another, has taken possession of the field, and has become copious without detriment to his freshness. I need not enumerate his works in their order, for, both in America and in England (where it is a marked feature of the growing curiosity felt about American life that they are constantly referred to for information and verification), they have long been in everybody's hands. Quietly and steadily they have become better and better; one may like some of them more than others, but it is noticeable that from effort to effort the author has constantly enlarged his scope. His work is of a kind of which it is good that there should be much to-day—work of observation, of patient and definite notation. Neither in theory nor in practice is Mr. Howells a romancer; but the romancers can spare him; there will always be plenty of people to do their work. He has definite and downright convictions on the subject of the work that calls out to be done in opposition to theirs, and this fact is a source of much of the interest that he excites.

It is a singular circumstance that to know what one wishes to do should be, in the field of art, a rare distinction; but it is incontestable that, as one looks about in our English and American fiction, one does not perceive any very striking examples of a vivifying faith. There is no discussion of the great question of how best to write, no exchange of ideas, no vivacity nor variety of experiment. A vivifying faith Mr. Howells may distinctly be said to possess, and he conceals it so little as to afford every facility to those people who are anxious to prove that it is the wrong one. He is animated by a love of the common, the immediate, the familiar and vulgar elements of life, and holds that in proportion as we move into the rare and strange we become vague and arbitrary; that truth of representation, in a word, can be achieved only so long as it is in our power to test and measure it. He thinks scarcely anything too paltry to be interesting, that the small and the vulgar have been terribly neglected, and would rather see an exact account of a sentiment or a character he stumbles against every day than a brilliant evocation of a passion or a type he has never seen and does not even particularly believe in. He adores the real, the natural, the colloquial, the moderate, the optimistic, the domestic, and the democratic; looking askance at exceptions and perversities and superiorities, at surprising and incongruous phenomena in general. One must have seen a great deal before one concludes; the world is very large, and life is a mixture of many things; she by no means eschews the strange, and often risks combinations and effects that make one rub one's eyes. Nevertheless, Mr. Howells's stand-point is an excellent one for seeing a large part of the truth, and even if it were less advantageous, there would be a great deal to admire in the firmness with which he has planted himself. He hates a "story," and (this private feat is not impossible) has probably made up his mind very definitely as to what the pestilent thing consists of. In this respect he is more logical than M. Émile Zola, who partakes of the same aversion, but has greater lapses as well as greater audacities. Mr. Howells hates an artificial fable and a denouement that is pressed into the service; he likes things to occur as they occur in life, where the manner of a great many of them is not to occur at all. He has observed that heroic emotion and brilliant opportunity are not particularly interwoven with our days, and indeed, in the way of omission, he has often practised in his pages a very considerable boldness. It has not, however, made what we find there any less interesting and less human.

The picture of American life on Mr. Howells's canvas is not of a dazzling brightness, and many readers have probably wondered why it is that (among a sensitive people) he has so successfully escaped the imputation of a want of patriotism. The manners he describes—the desolation of the whole social prospect in *A Modern Instance* is perhaps the strongest expression of those influences—are eminently of a nature to discourage the intending visitor, and yet the westward pilgrim continues to arrive, in spite of the Bartley Hubbards and the Laphams, and the terrible practices at the country hotel in *Doctor Breen*, and at the Boston boarding-house in *A Woman's Reason*. This tolerance of depressing revelations is explained partly, no doubt, by the fact that Mr. Howells's truthfulness imposes itself—the representation is so vivid that the reader accepts it as he accepts, in his own affairs, the mystery of fate—and partly by a very different consideration, which is simply that if many of his characters are disagreeable, almost all of them are extraordinarily good, and with a goodness which is a ground for national complacency. If American life is on the whole, as I make no doubt whatever, more innocent than that of any other country, nowhere is the fact more patent than in Mr. Howells's novels, which exhibit so constant a study of the actual and so small a perception of evil. His women, in particular, are of the best—except, indeed, in the sense of being the best to live with. Purity of life, fineness of conscience, benevolence of motive, decency of speech, good-nature, kindness, charity, tolerance (though, indeed, there is little but each other's manners for the people to tolerate), govern all the scene; the only immoralities are aberrations of thought, like that of Silas Lapham, or excesses of beer, like that of Bartley Hubbard. In the gallery of Mr. Howells's portraits there are none more living than the admirable, humorous images of those two ineffectual sinners. Lapham, in particular, is magnificent, understood down to the ground, inside and out—a creation which does Mr. Howells the highest honor. I do not say that the figure of his wife is as good as his own, only because I wish to say that it is as good as that of the minister's wife in the history of *Lemuel Barker*, which is unfolding itself from month to month at the moment I write. These two ladies are exhaustive renderings of the type of virtue that worries. But everything in *Silas Lapham* is superior—nothing more so than the whole picture of casual female youth and contemporaneous "engaging" one's self, in the daughters of the proprietor of the mineral paint.

This production had struck me as the author's high-water mark, until I opened the monthly sheets of *Lemuel Barker*, in which the art of imparting a palpitating interest to common things and unheroic lives is pursued (or is destined, apparently, to be pursued) to an even higher point. The four (or is it eight?) repeated "good-mornings" between the liberated Lemuel and the shop-girl who has crudely been the cause of his being locked up by the police all night are a poem, an idyl, a trait of genius, and a compendium of American good-nature. The whole episode is inimitable, and I know fellow-novelists of Mr. Howells's who would have given their eyes to produce that interchange of salutations, which only an American reader, I think, can understand. Indeed, the only limitation, in general, to his extreme truthfulness is, I will not say his constant sense of the comedy of life, for that is irresistible, but the verbal drollery of many of his people. It is extreme and perpetual, but I fear the reader will find it a venal sin. Theodore Colville, in *Indian Summer*, is so irrepressibly and happily facetious as to make one wonder whether the author is not prompting him a little, and whether he could be quite so amusing without help from outside. This criticism, however, is the only one I find it urgent to make, and Mr.

Howells doubtless will not suffer from my saying that, being a humorist himself, he is strong in the representation of humorists. There are other reflections that I might indulge in if I had more space. I should like, for instance, to allude in passing, for purposes of respectful remonstrance, to a phrase that he suffered the other day to fall from his pen (in a periodical, but not in a novel), to the effect that the style of a work of fiction is a thing that matters less and less all the while.[2] Why less and less? It seems to me as great a mistake to say so as it would be to say that it matters more and more. It is difficult to see how it can matter either less or more. The style of a novel is a part of the execution of a work of art; the execution of a work of art is a part of its very essence, and that, it seems to me, must have mattered in all ages in exactly the same degree, and be destined always to do so. I can conceive of no state of civilization in which it shall not be deemed important, though of course there are states in which executants are clumsy. I should also venture to express a certain regret that Mr. Howells (whose style, in practice, after all, as I have intimated, treats itself to felicities which his theory perhaps would condemn) should appear increasingly to hold composition too cheap—by which I mean, should neglect the effect that comes from alternation, distribution, relief. He has an increasing tendency to tell his story altogether in conversations, so that a critical reader sometimes wishes, not that the dialogue might be suppressed (it is too good for that), but that it might be distributed, interspaced with narrative and pictorial matter. The author forgets sometimes to paint, to evoke the conditions and appearances, to build in the subject. He is doubtless afraid of doing these things in excess, having seen in other hands what disastrous effects that error may have; but all the same I cannot help thinking that the divinest thing in a valid novel is the compendious, descriptive, pictorial touch, *à la Daudet*.

It would be absurd to speak of Mr. Howells to-day in the encouraging tone that one would apply to a young writer who had given fine pledges, and one feels half guilty of that mistake if one makes a cheerful remark about his future. And yet we cannot pretend not to take a still more lively interest in his future than we have done in his past. It is hard to see how it can help being more and more fruitful, for his face is turned in the right direction, and his work is fed from sources which play us no tricks.

2. In reviewing *The Story of a Country Town* (1883), an unsparing look at western life by Edgar Watson Howe (1853–1937), WDH observed, "It is needless to note that, having something to say, the author has said it well; that follows. I do not care to praise his style, though, as far as that increasingly unimportant matter goes, it is well enough; but what I like in him is the sort of mere open humanness of his book." See "Two Notable Novels," *Century* 28 (Aug. 1884): 633.

64.

JAMES TO HOWELLS, 19 October 1886, London

ALS Houghton
bMS Am 1784 (253) 53

October 19$\underline{th}$

34, DE VERE GARDENS, W.

My dear Howells.

It is more weeks than I venture to count since I have been owing you a letter—though it took some big preventive, at the time I received your last,[1] to suppress certain words I then wished to speak to you—words of explanation as to the, I fear, rather dry tone of the poor little tribute to your genius in the *Harper* newspaper.[2] That tone, & the general poverty of the article were the result of a desire not to injure you by appearing too much to "return the compliment" of your so generous article about me, in the *Century,* in the past time.[3] I had a horror of appearing too mutual & reciprocal, & cultivated (in your own interest) a coldness which I didn't feel. If I had been more free, I should have twined much fairer garlands round your brow. But all this you of course (& your letter showed it) read between the lines, & I need scarcely insist. But I should have liked to have more space—to have spoken of certain things more in detail.—It is very good news to me that you come abroad next year, & I envy you immensely having a boy to make an architect of.[4] That is a luxury—having your own artist of that sort in the family, that my thin individualism appears never destined to produce—& I haven't that pretext, which I should value, for going to spend a year in Paris. But if you come there, pretexts will not be wanting to me for at least shorter periods. Six weeks hence I hope to go down to Florence & Rome for a month or two—which makes me wish that time might roll backward in its flight & enable me to find you—as I might once have found you—there. This will be the 1$\underline{st}$ absence I have made from England—& almost from London, in a long time. It is easy to stay here—which is very surprising, considering how easy it is to get away. I did however spend a week at Broadway[5] in September, & foregathered with poor Gosse, Excuse this inadvertent *jamb!*[6] who had a house there for a month. I say "poor" Gosse because he has just been made the object of a singularly inhuman attack in the last Quarterly, denouncing him on the strength (or rather the weakness) of his little book *From Shakspeare to Pope,* as unfit for the post of instructor in English Literature at Cambridge.[7] The article, which is by one Churton Collins, an old friend of his, from

---

1. Not extant.
2. See "William Dean Howells," immediately preceding this letter.
3. See "Henry James, Jr.," pp. 229-35.
4. John Mead Howells was studying architecture at the Massachusetts Institute of Technology and would enroll at the École des Beaux-Arts in Paris the following year.
5. A fashionable country retreat in Worcestershire, visited by the Gosses in September 1885.
6. HJ uncustomarily skipped the facing half-sheet of stationery at this point.
7. "English Literature at the Universities," *Quarterly Review* 163 (October 1886): 289–329. The author of this article, John Churton Collins (1848–1908), severely criticized Gosse's latest book. In

whom he has been separated by a quarrel, & which bears the marks of the most premeditated ill-nature, has attracted much attention (to the way the University has filled the chair &c,) been reproduced in the newspapers, elicited letters, mainly non-complimentary to Gosse, &c, & in short I fear will do him a sensible injury. It points out some awkward slips & inaccuracies—but all the same Gosse remains a clever man & the author of the article a malignant mediocrity. G. is a good deal knocked up by it, will have to answer it, &c, & I think would value a word of comfort if you were to send him one.[8] It is a case in which a man counts his friends. In his place I shld. neither have sought nor accepted the Cambridge chair; but he will live to do very good work yet. His lately published little life of Raleigh I think a singularly admirable & artistic piece of narration, of the old fashioned personal kind; a book very capable of living.[9] I stopped reading your Lemuel Barker[10] after the 1st couple of months on account of the exasperation of the interruption, which made me hate him & you; but I shall fall upon him with accumulated curiosity the instant he is fully attached & be certain to love you both. I suspect him of being very triumphant: I won't speak of my own work, as it appears to interest no man or woman to-day. I have lately published 2 long-winded serials[11]—lasting between them far more than 2 years—of which in all that time no audible echo or reverberation of any kind, either in America or here, has come back to me. If I had not my bread & butter to earn I should lay down my pen tomorrow—hard as it is, at my age, to confess one's self a rather offensive fiasco. Notify me when you sail, & I will again take rooms for you. At least I am good still for that sort of thing. Commend me kindly to your wife & believe me ever, my dear Howells,

very faithfully yours
H. James

1884 Gosse had been elected to succeed Leslie Stephen as Clark Lecturer at Trinity College, Cambridge, even though he himself had never attended a university. Gosse's reputation never fully recovered from the charges of inaccuracy hurled at him by Collins.

8. See WDH to Edmund Gosse, 7 November 1886, *SL* 3: 167–68.

9. Edmund Gosse, *Raleigh* (London: Longmans, Green, 1886). WDH favorably reviewed the book in *Harper's Monthly* (74 [December 1886]: 158–59).

10. *The Minister's Charge; Or, The Apprenticeship of Lemuel Barker* first appeared in the *Century* (February–December 1886); it was published in book form by Ticknor & Company in 1887.

11. *The Bostonians* and *The Princess Casamassima.*

65.

JAMES TO HOWELLS, 7 December 1886, Milan   ALS Houghton
bMS Am 1784 (253) 130

Milan, Hotel de la Ville
December 7<u>th</u>.

My dear Howells.

Though you *did* write to me some time ago,[1] I can't despoil myself of a certain sense that in writing to you I drop my letter into an abyss too deep for echoes—nevertheless the impulse that drives my pen to-day is irresistible, & I write not for an answer—but just to write. The last thing I did before leaving London three days & ½ ago was to purchase "Lemuel Barker"[2] (you never think of sending me your books—that is, I hope you don't, because you don't do it,) & though I laid him down 24 hours ago I am still full of the sense of how he beguiled & delighted & illumined my way. The beauties of nature passed unheeded & the St. Gothard tunnel, where I had a reading lamp, was over in a shriek. The book is so awfully good that my perusal of it was one uninterrupted Bravo. It is wholly perfect—better than anything yet—even than Bartley & Silas,[3] I think—in short quite your capo d'opera.[4] And the best of it is that one sees you abundantly capable of doing better still, because you are so absolutely in the right track & the right sense. Where this comes from you will find no end more. Pause not, therefore, nor falter—but keep doing it every time! This whole thing is without fault or flaw—there isn't a false note, or a weak place. The girls are sublime, their speech & tone a revelation, & wonderful the way you have kept every one & everything in exactly the very pitch & *nuance* of reality—without straying for an instant into the unobserved. You must be very happy to have done anything so good—& I am almost as happy for it as you can be. In short, I congratulate you from my heart—& I congratulate your wife & your children, & even the servants, & the furnace-man, & your butcher & baker. 'Manda Grier is so fine that I felt, as I went, as if I were writing her. Not every one (great as the success of the book must be) will know how good she is—but that is but part of the general density & doesn't matter—it won't prevent you from doing "the likes" of her again.

—This is all I started to say—& I am waiting to be called for my train to Pisa. I am on my way to Florence to spend the rest of this month—after which I hope for 2 or 3 weeks of Rome & Naples, & a week of Venice. It is my summer vacation which I didn't take, by the almanac. When I left London the other day I had been there for 13 months without an absence. It's joyous to be in Italy

1. Not extant.
2. *The Minister's Charge.*
3. HJ refers to Bartley Hubbard in *A Modern Instance* (1882) and to *The Rise of Silas Lapham* (1885).
4. Masterpiece.

again—the sunshine is as yellow as of old & the colour of the shadows as pretty. I suppose you have heard from poor Gosse & know he has emerged—some-what—from his *année terrible*.[5] He has paid, fearfully, the penalty of a false posi-tion—for (between ourselves) I think he is in one in being at Trinity. But he stays there for the present—& he is right. Go on to glory, my dear Howells, & believe me

ever your faithfully plausive
Henry James

66.

HOWELLS TO JAMES, 25 December 1886, Boston · · · · · · · · · · · · TLS Houghton
bMS Am 1094 (240)

302 Beacon St., Boston, Dec 25, 1886.

My dear James—

I'm ashamed to send you a type-written letter; but I'm almost obliged to do so, for my wrist has weakened again and my handwriting has gone all to pieces. This sort has at least the merit of clearness; and you can forgive something to mere modernity in me.—Your most kind letter from Milan caused great excite-ment and rejoicing in this family. What could I ask more, even if I had the cheek to ask half so much? One doesn't thank you for such a thing I suppose, but I may tell you at least of my pride and pleasure in it. I'm disposed to make the most of the abundance of your kindness, for in many quarters here the book meets with little but misconception. If we regard it as nothing but an example of work in the new way—the performance of a man who wont and can't keep on doing what's been done already—it's reception here by most of the reviewers is extremely discouraging. Of all grounds in the world they take the genteel ground, and every

"Half-bred rogue that groomed his mother's cow,"[1]

reproaches me for introducing him to low company. This has been the tone of "society" about it; in the newspapers it hardly stops short of personal defama-tion.[2] Of course they entirely miss the very simple purpose of the book. Never-theless it sells, and sells bravely, and to my surprise I find myself not really caring a great deal for the printed animosity, except as it means ignorance. I suspect it's an effect of the frankness about our civilization which you have sometimes

---

5. Year of catastrophe. See letter #64, note 7, for the source of Gosse's troubles.

1. Oliver Wendell Holmes, "Astrea: The Balance of Illusions," l. 334.

2. Already annoyed by the glimpses of low life afforded by *The Rise of Silas Lapham*, many reviewers derided *The Minister's Charge* and its author for his "mania for the commonplace." WDH's treatment of "scenes of common and sordid life" required "no particle of imagination," according to the New York *Tribune*; indeed, his choice of material "would have made the fortune of a newspaper reporter." For this and other reviews, see the Indiana University Press edition of *The Minister's Charge*, xvii–xix.

wondered I could practice with impunity.[3] The impunity's gone, now, I assure you.—But all this is too much about myself. The other day the Harpers told me they had a new story from you[4] which they seemed immensely pleased with. I understood that it was on international ground, and I was glad they seemed disposed to rejoice with me that it was so. I took occasion to say to them that I hoped you would never allow yourself to be disturbed there by any outside influence. It is pre-eminently and indefeasibly your ground; you made it, as if it were a bit of the Back Bay; and the character that must pass under your eye is increasingly vast in quantity. I feel myself a recreant in not yet having read your two last books; I now read a good deal for reviewing, or whatever my work in Harper may be called; and I leave the books till I have the occasion to talk of them. I know certain passages and characters in The Bostonians quite well, and I think Olive Chancellor miraculously good; but the Princess Casamassima I don't know at all yet. Lowell goes about proclaiming it your best, and I've heard only good of it on all hands.—The furore caused by the Hawthorne outrage has pretty well died away.[5] It was a cruel atrocity, and all the more detestable because of that incurable single-heartedness of Lowell's, to which Hawthorne's treachery was inconceivable. A curious phase of the affair was that Hawthorne actually found credence for his version of it with some decent people; all the blackguards—and we've a lot of them—instinctively took sides with him.—I see Perry every other day, and we talk literature perpetually. Pellew[6] has come back to town, & I find him very interesting. He's a very able fellow, and distinctly a literary promise. Another man whom you will hear of is a Mr. John Heard,[7] a

3. Stung by the harsh reception that greeted *The Bostonians*, HJ was bewildered by the fact that WDH apparently escaped censure for his depictions of American civilization. "Everyone here admires extremely the truth and power of 'Silas Lapham,' including myself," HJ wrote to Grace Norton. "But what hideousness of life! They don't revile Howells when he does America, and such an America as that, and why do they revile me? The 'Bostonians' is sugar-cake, compared with it." See HJ to Grace Norton, 9 December 1885, *HJL* 3: 106.

4. "Louisa Pallant," *Harper's Monthly* (February 1888).

5. As literary editor of the New York *World*, Julian Hawthorne had interviewed James Russell Lowell, who had recently returned to the United States after serving as American ambassador to Great Britain. Without Lowell's consent, on 24 October Hawthorne published the interview, in which the former ambassador spoke freely about English politics and personalities. Lowell immediately responded in a letter to the Boston *Advertiser* of 25 October (to which WDH refers), refuting the opinions expressed in the interview and challenging Hawthorne's decision to publish them. After another more heated exchange of letters, Lowell retreated into silence; on 11 November the *World* printed a long personal letter from Hawthorne to Lowell and an editorial insisting that the paper had obtained the former minister's consent to publish his views. See George Knox, "The Hawthorne–Lowell Affair," *New England Quarterly* 29 (1956): 493–502.

6. George Pellew (1859–92), Harvard poet and literary critic, who would later defend WDH's editorial recommendation of Zola's novel *La Terre*. See "A Word for Mr. Howells," Boston *Post*, 27 February 1888.

7. John Heard Jr. was soon publishing stories in *Scribner's*, *The Century*, *Harper's Weekly*, and *Cosmopolitan*. In 1892 the Harpers brought out his collection entitled *A Charge for France, and Other Stories*.

Paris-born Bostonian, whose later life has been passed in Mexico; he writes equally well in French and English, and has contributed to the Revue Internationale of Florence. These, with a young Russian, are the people I see most. Into Boston society I'm asked very little and go less. I would like to go oftener to Cambridge; but it's very far off; and I'm looking forward to our escape next summer to Paris, where John is to go on with his architectural studies in the Ecole des Beaux Arts if he can get in. He's a youth of parts, and has hitherto done what he's attempted. Just now, he's very much absorbed in his first dress-suit which he gets into every night after dinner for some social occasion.—We expect to be two years in Paris, and when we return, I hope that we can contrive to spend the year pretty equally between Washington and Cambridge. Certainly I think we shall always winter hereafter in Washington; if it hadn't been for John's going into the Tech., here, we should have been there this winter.—I see Aldrich more rarely than I should like, these days, for the comfort of mere old friendship is very great. —I'm sick of this confounded machine, and you shall have the rest through the pen.—Last summer, which I spent in my house, here, I went several times to see Grace Norton, always gay company, and full of the literary interest which I care for almost alone. She gave me news of you, and sometimes read passages of your letters, which always amazed me by their excellent abundance. How can you get time to write them? By the way I find your Little Tour in France[8] delightful reading: it's a more absolute transference to literature of the mood of observation than anything else that I know.

We have been having a decently merry Christmas, and the children have enjoyed it; but I notice a decadence from the more robust and resolute Christmas of the old Dickens days, when holly was such a panacea. If one came back to Boston fifty years from now I fancy he would find it even soberer than now on Christmas. That reminds me I shall be fifty my next birthday, the 1st of March. I've heard people say that they are not conscious of growing older; but *I* am. I'm perfectly aware of the shrinking bounds. I don't plan so largely as I used, and without having lost hope I don't have so much use for it as once. I feel my half century fully. Lord, how it's slipped away!—Our Winny, who's been ailing so long, seems at last to have got her feet on the rising ground again. I wish you would give all our loves to your sister, and give us some good news of her when you write. The family join me in affectionate regards to yourself, whom we count upon seeing next year. If this letter follows you to Italy, salute the Arno and the Grand Canal for me; the Tiber I don't feel quite up to. Salute also the Bootts and their Devoneck,[9] and believe me

Ever yours
W. D. Howells.

---

8. *A Little Tour in France* (1885).

9. Francis Boott and his daughter, Elizabeth, who studied under and then married the American painter Frank Duveneck (1848–1919); all three were living in Florence.

67.

JAMES TO HOWELLS, 25 February 1887, Venice   ALS Houghton
                                                              bMS Am 1784 (253) 128

Venice
Palazzino Alvisi
February 25$\underline{th}$

My dear Howells.

It was in Florence, where I have been spending not much less than three months, that your delightful letter of Xmas day came to me; & it was from Florence that I intended to send you a rejoinder before the end of my stay—which occurred three days ago. However, you have a still better right to a Venetian letter—& I feel that in writing to you from here I am giving you a sort of account of your property. I can't do that in much detail as yet, as I have had but a couple of days to look about. It is the 1$\underline{st}$ time I have seen Venice in winter—for it is winter by the measure of the fact that a big plastered stove at the present moment rumbles in my ear. But it looks like summer, with yellow sunshine & gondoliers beckoning you upon the deep—or rather upon the shallow. At any rate it looks like Venice—which is my main requirement, as it had finally become most important for me to find something that didn't look like Florence. There are too many people there—for what they are, & I was chased away by the amiable effort that was manifested to retain me. By the time this occurred I had seen most of the people & could leave with a good conscience. I left a memento behind me in the shape of a pure profile begotten of several sittings to your ingenuous brother-in-law.[1] He insisted on altering the shape of my head—but with this exception I think the work better than any of the medallions that he has lately executed—better e.g. than yours. The world will owe it to the munificence of John Hay, to whom it goes, I believe, in bronze eterne. In Larkin, it seemed to me, the child of Vermont is more "immanent" as they say now, than in any incarnation the genius of that state has achieved. He ought to be the recipient of a national prize, as the American on whom Europe *can't* act! He took great pains with my medallion & I greatly hope, for him, that it will prove "generally acceptable." I am lodging here—rather provisionally—with Mrs. Bronson,[2] whom I think you know, & who has a kind of outhouse, or detached wing, which she very kindly puts at the disposition of her friends. But I only see her in the evening, as I "keep" myself, with the aid of a sympathetic "cooking-gondolier," during the day. It turns out that I am making a much longer absence from London than I expected; having lent my sister my apart-

---

1. At John Hay's request, Larkin Mead Jr. (1835–1910), Elinor's brother, executed a medallion of HJ in 1887. Mead had sculpted a medallion of WDH in 1883.

2. Katherine De Kay (Mrs. Arthur) Bronson (d. 1901), of New York and Newport, frequently entertained HJ at her Venetian home, Casa Alvisi, on the Grand Canal. HJ memorialized her in "The Late Mrs. Arthur Bronson," *The Critic* 40 (February 1902): 162–64; this article was reprinted in *Italian Hours* (1909).

ment there, I hope to stay in these latitudes till she is ready to vacate it by leaving town for the summer. A *long* absence from London is for me, every now & then, a great luxury: there is rest & relief in the smaller & lighter life of *any* other place one may go to. One finds that one has more time & possesses more one's soul. I had—just now—Florence ½ on top of me—but I felt the ½ of Florence infinitely less than the millionth part of London. And I hope to feel the whole of Venice, if it does me the honour to perch upon me, less than the moiety of the Tuscan capital.—The manner in which you tell me it pleased you that I wrote to you about Lemuel Barker gives me, my dear Howells, real delight. If anything I happen to say consoles you in any degree for the stupidity of the age, you are a thousand times welcome to it. The vulgar-mindedness of the public to which one offers the fruits of one's brain would chill the artist's heart if those fruits were not so sweet to his own palate! One mustn't think of the public *at all*, I find—or one would be nowhere & do nothing. It is everywhere the same—the form & profession of dulness and density are different; but the hatred (it is not too much to say) of any independent evolution is equal. You have the great advantage of knowing what you want to do, magnificently well & of having an equally superior capacity to do it; therefore don't let yourself be perturbed by people who, in the nature of the case, are foredoomed to the pettiest jealousies & bemuddlements & don't know anything about anything. I have left to the last to tell you what pleasure I take in the idea that you are going to be my neighbour (for it amounts to that,) for 2 years. I don't know when or whither you sail—but I confide in you to command me, in advance, if I can help you, on your arrival. I take it that I shall be in the north at that time. Tanti saluti[3] to your wife & tante cose[4] of every kind to the rest. Ever, my dear Howells,

very faithfully yrs.
Henry James

William Dean Howells, "Editor's Study" [The Princess Casamassima], *Harper's Monthly 74 (April 1887): 824–29.*

. . . That fiction has made a good beginning in the right direction, as we have always said in the Study's darkest moods, we see fresh evidence in the group of novels which have accumulated during the last two or three months on our table. They are not the only novels, of course, which have been published within this period, but they fairly represent the American activity in that industry, and we think, upon the whole, the showing that they make for us is one that we need not be ashamed of in any general competition. When Mr. Henry James contributes a work to this *concours*,[1] only Zola, or Daudet, or Tolstoï, or Thomas Hardy, can dispute the first prize with him. . . .

3. Regards.
4. Good wishes.
1. Gathering.

We find no fault with Mr. Henry James's *Princess Casamassima:* it is a great novel; it is his greatest and it is incomparably the greatest novel of the year in our language. It has to do with socialism and the question of richer and poorer, which grows ever more burning in our day, and the scene is contemporary London. Its people are the types which the vast range of London life affords, and they are drawn not only from the highest and the lowest, but from the intermediate classes, who are so much more difficult to take alive. The Princess Casamassima is our old acquaintance Miss Light, of *Roderick Hudson* fame, come with her beauty and splendor to forget her hated husband in semi-sincere sympathy with the London socialists, and semi-personal lovemaking with two of the handsomest. The hero is the little, morbid, manly, aesthetic bookbinder Hyacinth Robinson, son of an English lord and a French girl, who kills her betrayer. For the climax, Robinson, remembering his mother, kills himself—inevitably, not exemplarily—rather than shoot the political enemy whom the socialists have devoted to death at his hand. A striking figure is the plain, good, simple, romantic Lady Aurora, who goes about among the poor, and loves the tough-hearted chemist's assistant, Paul Muniment, and devotes herself to his sister, the unconsciously selfish little cripple. Another is Pynsent, the old dress-maker, who has brought Robinson up, and who lives and dies in awe of him as an offshoot of the aristocracy; another is Captain Sholto, the big, handsome, aimless swell, *dilettante* socialist, and hopeless lover of the Princess; another the Prince, with his passion for his wife and his coarse primitive jealousy of her; others yet are the real Socialists—English, French, and German; and the ferment of the ideals and interests of all these is the story. From first to last we find no weakness in the book; the drama works simply and naturally; the causes and effects are logically related; the theme is made literature without ceasing to be life. There is an easy breadth of view and a generous scope which recall the best Russian work; and there is a sympathy for the suffering and aspiration in the book which should be apparent even to the critical groundlings, though Mr. James forbears, as ever, to pat his people on the back, to weep upon their necks, or to caress them with endearing and compassionate epithets and pet names. A mighty good figure, which we had almost failed to speak of, is the great handsome shop-girl Millicent Henning, in whose vulgar good sense and vulgar good heart the troubled soul of Hyacinth Robinson finds what little repose it knows.

Mr. James's knowledge of London is one of the things that strike the reader most vividly, but the management of his knowledge is vastly more important. If any one would see plainly the difference between the novelist's work and the partisan's work, let him compare *The Princess Casamassima* and Mr. W. H. Mallock's last tract, which he calls *The Old Order Changes*, and which also deals with socialism.[2] No one can read it and deny Mr. Mallock's extraordinary cleverness, or its futility. His people are apparently real people till he gets them into

---

2. William Hurrell Mallock (1849–1923), a High Anglican Tory, attacked the economic theories of Henry George in a book-length essay entitled *Social Equality* (1882) as well as in works of fiction, of which *The Old Order Changes* (1886) was the most popular.

his book, and then they turn into stalking-horses for his opinions, those who would naturally disagree with him coming helplessly forward to be overthrown by those wonderful Roman Catholics of his—so very, very fine; so very, very wise; so very, very rich; so very, very good; so very, very proud and wellborn. We have some glimpses of an American girl, who seems at first a reality; but she ends by turning into an impossibility to oblige the author.

68.

JAMES TO HOWELLS, 2 January 1888, London   ALS Houghton
                                                             bMS Am 1784 (253) 54

34 De Vere Gardens W.
January 2$\underline{^d}$ 1888

My dear Howells.

Your pretty read book (that is a misprint for *red*—but it looks well, better than it deserves; & so I let it stand:) the neat & attractive volume, with its coquettish inscription and its mystifying date, came in to me exactly as a new-year's gift.[1] I was delighted to get it, for I had not perused it in the pages of Harper, for reasons that you will understand—knowing as you must how little the habit of writing in the serial form encourages one to read in that odious way, which so many simple folk, thank heaven, think the best. I was on the point of getting *April Hopes* to add to the brave array of its predecessors, (mine by purchase, almost all of them,) when your graceful act saved me the almost equally graceful sacrifice. I can make out why you are at Buffalo[2] almost as little as I believe that you believe that I have "long forgotten" you. The intimation is worthy of the most tortuous feminine mind that you have represented—say this wondrous lady, with the daughter, in the very 1$\underline{^{st}}$ pages of April Hopes, with whom I shall make immediate & marvelling acquaintance. Your literary prowess takes my breath away—you write so much & so well. I seem to myself a small brown snail crawling after a glossy antelope. Let me hope that you *enjoy* your work as much as you ought to—that the grind isn't greater than the inevitable (from the moment one really tries to *do* anything.) Certainly one would never guess it, from your abounding page. How much I wish I could keep this lonely new year by a long personal talk with you. I am troubled about many things, about many of which you could give me, I think (or rather I am sure,) advice &

1. With many other books by WDH, HJ's inscription copy of *April Hopes* was dispersed from his library after World War II. Its date would have been "mystifying" because, though sent by WDH in December 1887, the year printed on the book's title page is 1888. As with most of WDH's *Harper* serials, this novel completed its magazine run in November, thus timed to be available in hardcover for Christmas purchase.

2. WDH and his family were staying at Buffalo at the request of Winifred Howells's doctors, who were treating her at a sanatorium in Dansville, New York. On 13 November 1887 WDH wrote to his father that Winifred's "care must be moral quite as much as physical, and the doctors, after carefully studying her case, prefer us to be away from her" (*SL* 3: 206).

direction. I have entered upon evil days—but this is for your most private ear. It sounds portentous, but it only means that I am still staggering a good deal under the mysterious & (to me) inexplicable injury wrought—apparently—upon my situation by my 2 last novels, the *Bostonians* & the *Princess*, from which I expected so much & derived so little. They have reduced the desire, & the demand, for my productions to zero—as I judge from the fact that though I have for a good while past been writing a number of good short things, I remain irremediably unpublished. Editors keep them back, for months & years, as if they were ashamed of them, & I am condemned apparently to eternal silence. You must be so widely versed in all the reasons of things (of this sort, to-day,) in the U. S. that if I could discourse with you a while by the fireside I should endeavour to draw from you some secret to break the spell. However, I don't despair, for I think I am now really in better form for work than I have ever been in my life, & I propose yet to do many things. Very likely too, some day, all my buried prose will kick off its various tombstones at once. Therefore don't betray me till I myself have given up. That won't be for a long time yet. If we could have that rich conversation I should speak to you too of your monthly polemics in *Harper*[3] & tell you (I think I should go so far as that) of certain parts of the business in which I am less with you than in others. It seems to me that on occasions you mix things up that don't go together, sometimes make mistakes of proportion, & in general incline to insist more upon the restrictions & limitations, the *a priori* formulas & interdictions, of our common art, than upon that priceless freedom which is to me *the* thing that makes it worth practising. But at this distance, my dear Howells, such things are too delicate & complicated—they won't stand so long a journey. Therefore I won't attempt them—but only say how much I am struck with your energy, ingenuity & courage, & your delightful interest in the charming questions. I don't care how much you dispute about them if you will only remember that a grain of example is worth a ton of precept & that with the imbecillity of babyish critics the serious writer need absolutely not concern himself. I am surprised sometimes, at the things you notice & seem to care about. One should move in a diviner air.— Two or three nights ago Edmund Gosse came to share my solitude & my beef-steak, & we talked, al volito,[4] of you. He has I think quite recovered from the immediate effects of his horrid imbroglio of a year & a half ago—out of which he came very well; but not from some of its remoter ones. Nor will he do this, I fear, so long as he continues to hold his Cambridge professorship. I shall be glad when that is over, as I think he will then be in a much freer, sounder, position. He is the only man of letters I ever see here—to speak of, or to speak to. I have many good friends here, but they are not in that class, which strikes me as mostly quite dense & puerile. I even confess that since the *Bostonians*, I

3. WDH's regular "Editor's Study" column in *Harper's Monthly*, the forum in which he promulgated his views on literary realism. In 1891 WDH collected and revised many of these pieces as *Criticism and Fiction*.

4. In passing.

find myself holding the "critical world" at large in a singular contempt. I go so far as to think that the literary sense is a distinctly waning quality. I can speak of your wife & children only interrogatively—which will tell you little—& me, I fear, less. But let me at least be affirmative to the extent of wishing them all very affectionately, & to Mrs. H. in particular the happiest New Year. Go on, my dear Howells, & send me your books always as I *think* I send you mine. Continue to write only as your admirable ability moves you & believe me

ever faithfully yours
Henry James

William Dean Howells, "Editor's Study" [stories reprinted in The Aspern Papers *and* A London Life *and* The Reverberator], *Harper's Monthly* 77 (*October 1888*): *799–804.*

It is hardly worth while to attempt a full record of what has been done in fiction since the Study last gave its attention to that branch of literature. To note even the important events in it with the hope of doing justice to specific achievements is something beyond us. At best one can expect merely to appreciate with loose generality the work of new hands, and gratefully to welcome the increasing skill and power of some old ones.

Among these it seems to us that the touch of Mr. Henry James is of such excellent maturity in the short stories which he has lately printed that it would be futile to dispute his primacy in most literary respects. We mean his primacy not only among fabling Americans, but among all who are presently writing fiction. It is with an art richly and normally perfected from intentions evident in his earliest work that he now imparts to the reader his own fine sense of character and motive, and gives his conceptions a distinctness and definition really unapproached. There never was much 'prentice faltering in him; the danger was rather that in one so secure of his literary method from the first, a mere literary method might content to the end; but with a widening if not a deepening hold on life (all must admit that his hold has widened, whoever denies that it has deepened) this has clearly not contented him. No one has had more to say to his generation of certain typical phases than he, and he has had incomparably the best manner of saying it. Of course it can always be urged by certain mislikers of his—and he has them in force enough to witness the vast impression he has made—that these typical phases are not the important phases; but if they do this they must choose wholly to ignore such a novel as *The Princess Casamassima.* It is in a way discreditable to our time that a writer of such quality should ever have grudging welcome; the fact impeaches not only our intelligence, but our sense of the artistic. It will certainly amaze a future day that such things as his could be done in ours and meet only a feeble and conditional acceptance from the "best" criticism, with something little short of ribald insult from the common cry of literary paragraphers. But happily the critics do not form an author's only readers; they are not even his judges. These are the editors of the magazines, which are now the real avenues to the public; and their recent unanimity in presenting simultaneously some of the best work of Mr. James's life in the way of short stories indicates the existence of an interest in all he does, which is doubtless the true measure of his popularity. With "The Aspern Papers" in *The Atlantic*, "The Liar" in *The Century*, "A London Life" in *Scribner's* and "Louisa Pallant" and "Two Countries" in *Harper's*, pretty much all at once, the effect was like an artist's exhibition. One turned from one masterpiece to another, making his comparisons, and delighted to find that the stories helped rather than hurt one another, and that their accidental massing enhanced his pleasure in them.

Masterpieces, we say, since the language does not hold their betters for a high perfection of literary execution at all points. "Louisa Pallant," for instance, is an unmixed pleasure if you delight in a well-taken point of view, and then a story that runs easily from the lips of the imagined narrator, characterizing him no less subtly than the persons of the tale, in English to the last degree informal and to the last degree refined. Just for attitude, just for light, firm touch, the piece is simply unsurpassed outside the same author's work. We speak now only of the literature, and leave the doubter to his struggle with the question whether a mother would have done all that about a daughter; and we will not attempt to decide whether the American wife in the "Two Countries" would have killed herself if her English husband had written a book against her native land. These were to us very minor points compared with the truthfulness of the supposed case and the supposed people, just as in "A London Life" it doesn't so much matter whether poor Laura marries or not as whether the portrait of Mr. Wendover is not almost too good to be felt by the public which reads in running, and whether some touch of Selina's precious badness may not be lost. There are depths under depths in the subtle penetrations of this story, the surprise of which should not be suffered to cheapen the more superficial but not less brilliant performance in "The Liar"; for there too is astonishing divination, and a clutch upon the unconscious motives which are scarcely more than impulses, instincts.

[T]o Mr. Cable in his inter-related sketches called *Bonaventure*[1] we owe the pleasure of some fresh characters in a romantic atmosphere where we could not have hoped for anything better than types. The book is no such book as *The Grandissimes*; let that be fairly understood before we praise it for qualities proper to its slighter texture. *The Grandissimes* is one of the novels of our time, whereas *Bonaventure* is simply one of the gracefulest romances, in which high motive, generous purpose, and picturesque material answer for the powerful realities of the other. The facts of the case—the aspiration and the heroic self-sacrifice of the young creole school-master among the Acadians of Louisiana—are given by a species of indirection, a kind of tacking, which recalls Judd's method in his *Margaret*,[2] a book which Mr. Cable could not have had in mind, but to which

---

1. *Bonaventure: A Prose Pastoral of Acadian Louisiana* (New York: Scribner's, 1888) was authored by George Washington Cable, a Southern liberal and local colorist.

2. Sylvester Judd (1813–53), Unitarian minister and reformer. His best-known work, *Margaret* (1845), addressed a multitude of American social ills (false theology, intemperance, mistreatment of Native Americans, capital punishment) as they impinge upon the developing consciousness of a

his work assimilates itself in the romantic atmosphere common to them both. It has its charm, but it also has a misty intangibility which baffles, which vexes. Nevertheless this too is the work of a master who gives us for the time what he thinks best, and who has not yet begun to deliver his whole message to a world where few of the prophets have both head and heart. We see in him a curious process of evolution, in which the citizen, the Christian, seems to threaten the artist; but out of which we trust to see them issue in indissoluble alliance for the performance of services to humanity higher than any yet attempted. It is the conscience of Mr. Cable that gives final value to all he does; it will avail him with readers similarly endowed against any provincial censure, and will not suffer him to slight any side of his most important work, or to forget that art is the dearest medium of truth.

It is a very delicate medium, however, and it breaks unless the ethical intention it is meant to carry is very carefully adjusted. . . .

It was not because the censure of Mr. Cable was sectional or local that we were tempted just now to call it provincial, but because it was narrow-minded, the censure of people who would rather be flattered than appreciated; and in this sort the sum of our national censure of Mr. James is provincial. It is extraordinary that any one could read *The Reverberator* and not cry out in grateful recognition of its thorough Americanism; it makes one afraid that the author's patriotism has mistaken us, and that we are really a nation of snobs, who would rather be supposed to have fine manners than good qualities; or that we are stupid, and cannot perceive the delicate justice that rights us in spite of ourselves. But there is no mistake in his art, which, beginning with such a group of Americans as the Dossons and their friend the reporter of the society newspaper on the plane of their superficial vulgarity, ends with them having touched into notice every generous and valuable point in them, and espoused their cause against that of the grander world. In the case of the obtuse Flack this effect is almost miraculous, in that of Mr. Dosson and his daughter Delia it is charming, and in that of Francie Dosson adorable. We leave the Probert group of Gallicized Americans to those who know them better, though Francie's lover Gaston goes to one's heart; but the Dossons are all true and verifiable in their inexpugnable innocence at any turn in the international world which Mr. James has discovered for us. Francie Dosson, with her beauty, her fineness, her goodness, and her helpless truth, is a marvelous expression of the best in American girlhood. She unwittingly does her lover's people an awful mischief, and to the end she remains half persuaded of Mr. Flack's theory that people really like to have their private affairs written up in the papers; but all the same she remains lovable, and Gaston loves her. "*Sie war liebenswürdig und er liebte sie.*"[3] Mr. James makes you feel once again that this settles it.

---

young woman. To critics who complained of the book's haphazard structure, Judd responded, "May there not be a moral as well as a material plot—a plot of ideas as well as incidents? 'Margaret' is a tale not of outward movement but of internal development." See "Author's Note," *Margaret*, rev. ed. (Boston: Phillips, Samson, 1851), v.

3. She was lovable and he loved her.

As for Flack, he is perfect, the very genius of society journalism. But apparently, however indigenous with us, his species is not confined to our own country in its origin, if we may believe Señor Valdés in his latest novel, *El Cuarto Poder*, or *The Fourth Estate*,[4] or the newspaper press mainly as it exists in the little seaport city of Sarrió, somewhere in northwestern Spain of today. Sinforoso Suarez is the resonant Spanish of the nature if not of the name of Flack, though with a mellifluousness and a malignity added which are foreign to Flack; for as a rule the American interviewer wishes his victim no harm, and does not ordinarily aim at fine writing even when he achieves it. But, as in James's story, journalism is a subordinate interest of Señor Valdés's novel, which is mainly a picture of contemporary life in a Spanish town.

69.

JAMES TO HOWELLS, 29 September 1888, London   ALS Houghton
                                                                                        bMS Am 1784 (253) 55

34 De Vere Gardens W.
Sept. 29th 1888

My dear Howells—

You are really very delightful in the October *Harper*[1]—generous & sympathetic beyond my expectations or my deserts. Let me thank you promptly, heartily, joyfully. It's really a strange, startling, reviving sensation to be *understood*—I had so completely got used to doing without it. You console me for all kinds of stupidities & ineptitudes. *They* have been for a long time the only things I look for. Or rather, I don't look for them—I take them for granted. I don't even look *at* them, but go my way now perfectly without annoyance, & only with a certain amount of despair, which is easier to put up with. You have washed me down deliciously with the tepid sponge of your intelligence. I have talked of you lately with the good Mrs. Fairchild of Boston—her of the pretty daughters (& pretty self,) who has been spending the summer in England & whom I encountered at Broadway.[2] I liked almost everything she told me of you save that you haven't any home—which made me feel that you have even less excuse then than I supposed for not returning to Europe. I figured you one of the fathers of Beacon St. I have one now, essentially, & find it *everything* for my work.[3] I shld. go to pieces without it. The proof of this is that I haven't been out of it for 15 months—not even during the last two, save for casual clusters of days. On Octo-

---

4. Armando Palacio Valdés (1853–1938), whose book *The Fourth Estate* (1888) also treats the world of journalism with irony.

1. See WDH, "Editor's Study," in the preceding selection.

2. Lily Nelson Fairchild, wife of Charles Fairchild, the Boston financier who leased Red Top in Belmont to WDH. The couple had five children, at least one of whom, Lucia (1872–1924), accompanied her mother to England in the summer of 1888.

3. In December 1885 HJ had signed a twenty-one-year lease for an apartment in Kensington at 34 De Vere Gardens; he moved in the following spring.

ber 10th however, I go abroad for a few weeks. I have seen no one to speak of, or even to, for a long time, & the tendency of my life is ever to see rather fewer persons than more. I have seen too many in the past; & have crossed my meridian. Gosse I sometimes have speech with. He is very intelligent, but *manque de fonds*,[4] & has lately lost his unspeakable father, inherited a little money & discovered the pedigree of his mother—an American, to his extreme surprise, by parentage, & of old Massachusetts: *Hancock* &c. stock: whereat he is made excited.[5] The circumstance is indeed rather curious, in view of his many American propensities & associations—seeming to supply a mystic reason for them which he unconsciously obeyed.—What you said about the *Reverberator* gave me singular pleasure—so happily have you read in it *all* my pure little intentions. You make me think for a moment that the public might be really a little less idiotic than it is—though tomorrow, no doubt, I shall again perceive that it mightn't. It doesn't matter—the idea is the only thing; on the whole it takes care of itself. One must write for that—to write for the public is to follow the scent of a red herring. I wait, as always, for the book, to read your current fiction in *Harper*.[6] I am doing a longish thing for next year's *Atlantic*[7]—which now keeps me busy, belated & nervous. Aldrich was here the other day, encompassed with his queer impenetrable atmosphere of travel, luxury & purchase.[8] I wish every good to Mrs. Howells & to your children. I shake hands with you both on general & particular grounds & am ever, my dear Howells,

affectionately yours
Henry James

70.

HOWELLS TO JAMES, 10 October 1888, Little Nahant

ALS Houghton
bMS Am 1094 (241)

Little Nahant,
Oct. 10, 1888.

My dear James—

I found your letter here when I came home this morning from a house-hunt in New York. I write at once, or I shall never write, to say that it gave me great joy to know from you that I had given you pleasure. These things needed to be said, and I was glad to say them; I wish I could have said them more at length;

4. Lacks steadfastness of purpose; shallow-minded.

5. Emily Bowes (1802–56), Gosse's mother, was born in Wales of American parents; her father was the grandson of Nicholas Bowes, an early graduate of Harvard. After her death, Gosse's father, the British naturalist Philip Henry Gosse (1810–88), married Eliza Brightwen (1813–1900).

6. *Annie Kilburn*, serialized in *Harper's Monthly* (June–November 1888).

7. *The Tragic Muse* first appeared in the *Atlantic* (January 1889–May 1890); in terms of installments, it was HJ's longest-running serial.

8. Thomas Bailey Aldrich, then editor of the *Atlantic*; see letter #61, note 3.

and I want to tell you now that I think your Partial Portraits[1] wonderfully good work. It makes all my critical work seem clumsy and uncouth. Surely you were born with the right word in your mouth; you never say the wrong one, any way.—Of course the bestialità[2] will keep being said; but I think there is distinctly a tendency to a better sense of you here, if you really care for the fact. I'm not in a very good humor with "America" myself. It seems to me the most grotesquely illogical thing under the sun; and I suppose I love it less because it wont let me love it more. I should hardly like to trust pen and ink with all the audacity of my social ideas; but after fifty years of optimistic content with "civilization" and its ability to come out all right in the end, I now abhor it, and feel that it is coming out all wrong in the end, unless it bases itself anew on a real equality. Meantime, I wear a fur-lined overcoat, and live in all the luxury my money can buy. This now-ended summer it bought us the use of a wide-verandahed villa on forty acres of seclusion where poor Winny might get a little better possibly. The experiment isn't wholly a failure; but helplessness and anguish still remain for her; and this winter she will go to New York with us, for such doctoring as we can get there. I've found an apartment in two floors, in a huge old house overlooking Livingstone Place, where we shall dwell in some rooms of rather a European effect. (I have mainly in mind a metal-framed mirror.) I fancy the place would please Gosse, whom kindly tell with my love of our whereabouts. I'm glad he's half one of us, and rather sorry he denies us a great poet; he's a great American poet himself on his mother's side, it seems.[3]

Pillà draws in a life class in New York, and that is one of the larger reasons why we go there. But at the bottom of our wicked hearts we all like New York, and I hope to use some of its vast, gay, shapeless life in my fiction.[4] I suppose our home—such as it is—will be there hereafter in the winter, though we expect always to drift back to this good Boston region for the summer.

Mrs. Howells charges me to say that her heart was in all those words of mine that pleased you; and that she reads no one else with half so much pleasure. Pilla follows you with as much ardor as her mother.—John is a sophomore, weighty and learned, but not literary, and poor Winny hasn't read a book in years.

We all join in love to you.

Yours cordially
W. D. Howells.

1. *Partial Portraits* (London and New York: Macmillan, 1888), a collection of critical essays.
2. Stupidities.
3. In "Has America Produced a Poet?" *Forum* (October 1888), Gosse claimed that no American poet could rank with the "twelve worthies" of English poetry. Since Gosse himself had listed thirteen names, WDH could not resist an ironic rejoinder: see "Editor's Study," *Harper's Monthly* 78 (February 1889): 489.
4. WDH's New York experiences figure most directly in *A Hazard of New Fortunes* (1889–90), but he also exploited his daughter's art training in *The Coast of Bohemia* (1893).

71.

JAMES TO HOWELLS, 20 March 1889, London   ALS Houghton
                                    bMS Am 1784 (253) 129

34 D. V. G. W.*
Mch. 20$\underline{\text{th}}$
* De Vere *Gardens* W.

My dear Howells.

I this morning hear from young Balestier[1] of the great sorrow & shock that has fallen on you & on your wife.[2] I don't attempt to talk to you about it; I only wish not to let the day pass without sending you a sign of affectionate sympathy. I *can't* talk of death without seeming to say too much—I think so kindly of it as compared with life—the only thing we *can* compare it to. I remember your grave & tender little Winnie in years further away, probably, than any of your friends today—far years of Sacramento St. & small childhood undreaming of later woes. The later woes I have never ventured to speak to you of—they were *un*talkable—& I knew they were for you a perpetual fountain of pain. When a man loses a loved child everything that is most tender in him must be infinitely lacerated: yet I hope there is a sort of joy for both of you in the complete extinction of so much suffering. To be young & gentle & do no harm, & only to pay for it as if it were a crime—I *do* thank heaven, my dear Howells, both for your wife & yourself, that *that is* over. What an endlessly touching memory!

Ever faithfully yours
Henry James

72.

HOWELLS TO JAMES, 7 June 1889, Cambridge   ALS Houghton
                                    bMS Am 1094 (242)

Mt. Auburn Station, Cambridge,
June 7, 1889.

My dear James:

I shall never be able to thank you rightly for that letter you wrote me about Winny. My wife and I both felt that you had given words to the mute despair and wonder we were in, and had lightened our burden by speaking out its very form and essence for us. My phrase offends me now by its coldness, but indeed

---

1. Charles Wolcott Balestier (1861–91), author and publisher, who at this time was helping HJ manage his business affairs. Balestier had sent stories and essays to the *Atlantic* during WDH's editorial tenure.

2. Winifred Howells died of cardiac arrest on 3 March 1889, two days after WDH's fifty-second birthday.

none could impart the tender, fond gratitude we felt toward you. I thought I would write you at once, but I could not, for I wished to make you the intimate of our sorrow, and I found that in the letters which I did write I was breaking my heavy heart into mere rhetoric. In every way the expression of our bereavement escapes me; and I suppose we do not yet realize what has happened. For twenty-five years she was ours, and for three months we have lost her, after such long defeated hopes of having her back strong & well. You know perhaps the poor child was not with us when she died; she died homesick and wondering at her separation, in the care of the doctors who fancied they were curing her. "All happiness is alike, but every sorrow has its own physiognomy,"[1] and every trait of anguish is in this experience. I wonder we live; it seems monstrous. But the fact is real only in the little stabs it gives us through every beautiful or joyous thing that she does not share with us. When I came out to see this lovely old place, which we've taken for the summer I thought, "How Winny will like it!" No bird sings, no flower blows but to the effect of some such pang.—It's no use; I might as well stop. For a time I felt like a wretched worm that had been trodden on; I could only writhe.—About the future we profess to know nothing. If I could believe I was to meet her again I should be the lightest hearted man alive.—I hope some time to write you a letter worthier your friendship, but I want to tell you now how much you are present with us all in the story you are writing. Each number of the Tragic Muse we say we will read aloud; then we find each has read it. I am glad that as *I* read it I can own its superiority without a pang. No work equals it, for its subtle penetrations; it's incomparable in language and in clear sense of things. I wish it would never end; it satisfies me inexpressibly. I wish you could see how fully not only Mrs. Howells, but our young Pillà appreciates your work in it.

—We are in the Brooks Place,[2] next the Cushing Place, which you must remember of old. We look across meadows and market gardens to Fresh Pond, on whose shores I have wandered with you—on whose waters, I rowing, you told me the plot of Roderick Hudson.[3]

All join me in love.

Yours affectionately
W. D. Howells.

1. In a letter to Edwin L. Godkin dated 29 March 1889 (Godkin Papers, Harvard), WDH uses this phrase and attributes it to Leo Tolstoy (1828–1910), the Russian novelist whom he had embraced as a fellow critic of acquisitive culture. WDH may have been thinking of a famous line from the first chapter of *Anna Karenina*, "All happy families resemble one another; every unhappy family is unhappy in its own fashion."

2. A twenty-acre estate in Belmont; WDH used the Mt. Auburn Street station address in Cambridge for his mail.

3. See "The American James" (1920), pp. 471–73, for WDH's further reflections on his early years of friendship with HJ.

73.

JAMES TO HOWELLS, 17 May 1890, Milan   ALS Houghton
bMS Am 1784 (253) 56

Hotel de la Ville
Milan. May 17<u>th</u>

My dear Howells.

I have been not writing to you at a tremendous, an infamous rate, for a long
time past; but I should indeed be sunk in baseness if I were to keep this pace
after what has just happened. For what has just happened is that I have been
reading the *Hazard of N. F.*[1] (I confess I shld. have liked to change the name
for you,) & that it has filled me with communicable rapture. I remember that
the last time I came to Italy (or almost,) I brought your Lemuel Barker,[2] which
had just come out, to read in the train & let it divert an intensely professional
eye from the most clamorous beauties of the way—writing to you afterwards
from this very place I think, all the good & all the wonder I thought of it. So I
have a decent precedent for insisting, to you, now, under circumstances exactly
similar (save that the present book is a much bigger feat,) that, to my
charmed & gratified sense, the *Hazard* is simply prodigious. I read the 1<u>st</u> vol.
just before I left London—& the second, which I began the instant I got into
the train at Victoria, made me wish immensely that both it & the journey to
Bâle & thence were formed to last longer. I congratulate you, my dear Howells
unrestrictedly, & give you my assurance—whatever the vain thing is worth—
that, for me, you have never yet done anything so roundly & totally good. For,
(after the flat-hunting business is disposed of) the whole thing is almost equally
good—or would be, that is, if the Dryfooses were not so much better than even
the best of the rest, & than even the best of S. Lapham, & the best of what has
been your best heretofore. I don't know whether you can bear to see the off-
spring of your former (literary) marriages sacrificed so to the last batch—but it
is the sort of thing you must expect if you *will* practise so prolific a polygamy.[3]
The life, the truth, the light, the heat, the breadth & depth & thickness of the
Hazard, are absolutely admirable. It seems to me altogether, in abundance,
ease & variety, a fresh start for you at what I would call "your age" didn't I fear
to resemble a Dryfoos—so that I'll say instead that to *read* the thing is a fresh
start for me at mine. I should think it would make you as happy as poor happiness will let us be, to turn off from one year to the other, & from a reservoir in
daily domestic use, such a free, full rich flood. In fact your reservoir deluges me,

1. *A Hazard of New Fortunes*, 2 vols. (1890).
2. *The Minister's Charge* (1887); see letter #65.
3. HJ refers to WDH's practice of carrying over sets of characters from one novel to the next.
In *A Hazard of New Fortunes* WDH deals again with the Marches (Basil, his wife, Isabel, and their
children, Tom and Bella), characters largely modeled after WDH and his family. Basil and Isabel
were the protagonists of WDH's first novel, *Their Wedding Journey* (1870). The Dryfooses (old Jacob
and Elizabeth, and their children, Christine, Conrad, and Mela) were new inventions.

altogether, with surprise as well as other sorts of effusion: by which I mean that though you do much to empty it you keep it remarkably full. I seem to myself, in comparison, to fill mine with a teaspoon & obtain but a trickle. However, I don't mean to compare myself with you or to compare you, in the particular case, with anything but life. When I do that—with the life you see & represent—your faculty for rendering it seems to me extraordinary & to shave the truth—the general truth you aim at—several degrees closer than anyone else begins to do. You are less *big* than Zola, but you are ever so much less clumsy & more really various, and moreover you & he don't see the same things—you have a wholly different consciousness—*you* see a totally different side of a different race. Man isn't at all *one* after all—it takes so much of him to be American, to be French, &c. I won't even compare you with something I have a sort of dim, stupid sense you might be and are not—for I don't in the least know that you might be it, after all, or whether, if you were, you wouldn't cease to be that something you are which makes me write to you thus. We don't know what people might give us that they don't—the only thing is to take them on what they do & to allow them absolutely & utterly their conditions. This alone, for the taster, secures freedom of enjoyment. I apply the rule to you, & it represents a perfect triumph of appreciation; because it makes me accept, largely, all your material from you—an absolute gain when I consider that I should never take it from myself. I note certain things which make me wonder at your form & your fortune (e.g.—as I have told you before—the fatal colours in which they let *you*, because you live at home—is it?—paint American life; & the fact that there's a whole quarter of the heaven upon which, in the matter of composition, you seem to be consciously—*is* it consciously?—to have turned your back;) but these things have no relevancy whatever as grounds of dislike—simply because you communicate so completely *what* you undertake to communicate. The novelist is a particular *window*, absolutely—& of worth in so far as he is one; & it's because you open so well & are hung so close over the street that *I* could hang out of it all day long. Your very value is that you choose your own street—heaven forbid I should have to choose it for you. If I should say I mortally dislike the people who pass in it, I should seem to be taking on myself that intolerable responsibility of selection which it is exactly such a luxury to be relieved of. Indeed I'm convinced that no reader above the rank of an idiot—this number is moderate I admit—can really fail to take any view that's really *shown* them—any gift (of subject) that's really given. The usual imbecillity of the novel is that the showing & giving simply don't come off—the reader never touches the subject & the subject never touches the reader: the window is no window at all—but only childishly *finta*,[4] like the ornaments of our beloved Italy. This is why, as a triumph of *communication*, I hold the Hazard so rare & strong. You communicate in touches so close, so fine, so true, so droll, so frequent. I am writing too much (you will think me demented with chatter;) so

---

4. Sham, artificial.

that I can't go into specifications of success. It is *all* absolutely successful, & if a part or two are better than the others it isn't that the others are not so good as they ought to be. These last have the deuce of an effort in making it appear that nothing ought *ever* to be less good than they. That is, you set a measure & example of the prehensile perception—& so many things, in future, will seem less good than they ever *could* be, for not coming up to such a standard. The Dryfooses are portraiture of the very first magnitude, the old man magnificent, without flaw or faintness anywhere, & the whole thing, in short, so observed, so caught, so felt, so conceived & created—so damningly & inexplicably American. How can they stand each other? (so many of them!) I asked as I read, reflecting that they, poor things, hadn't *you*, as I had, to make me stand them all. Or rather they *had* you, really—& that's the ward of the enigma. You pervade & permeate them all, my dear Howells, just enough to save them from each other & from the unlimited extension of the movement of irresistible relief by which Christine D. scratches Beaton's face & even old Dryfoos smites his blank son (an admirable, *admirable* business, the whole of that). Go on, go on, even if *I* can't—& since New York has brought you such *bonheur*[5] give it back to her with still larger liberality. Don't tell me you can't do anything now, or that life isn't luxurious to you, with such a power of creation. You live in a luxury (of that kind) which Lindau wd. reprehend, or at any rate have nothing to meet, & that I am not sure even poor March wd. be altogether easy about. Poor March, my dear Howells—what tricks you play him—even worse than those you play Mrs. March! Just let me add that Conrad D. is a 1ST CLASS idea, as the son of his father & a figure in the Dryfoos picture. But *all* the picture, I repeat, is of the highest worth. How the devil did you do it? You'll found a school—that of your "3$\underline{d}$ manner" & I shall come to it.—I left London four days ago, with the cunning purpose of staying away from it for June & July & returning to it for August & September. I hope to spend June in Venice—July perhaps in some blue Giorgionesque background.[6] I continue to scribble, though with relaxed continuity while abroad; but I can't talk to you about it. One thing only is clear that henceforth I must do, or ½ do, England in fiction—as the place I see most & to day, in a sort of way, know best. I have at last more acquired notions of it, on the whole, than of any other world, & it will serve as well as any other. It has been growing distincter that America fades from me, & as she never trusted me at best, I can trust *her*, for effect, no longer. Besides I can't be doing *de chic*,[7] from here, when you, on the spot, are doing so brilliantly the *vécu*.[8]—The *vécu* indeed reached me in a very terrible form, in London, just before I came away, in the shape of the news of the rejection at Washington of

---

5. Happiness.

6. Giorgione (1477–1510), Italian artist whose canvases and frescoes had a liberating effect on Venetian painting.

7. A stylized version of life.

8. The real thing.

the International Copyright Bill.[9] That was the great news there, & it has made a very bad state of things—so that I was glad to come away, for a time at least, from the shame & discomfort of it. It seems as if this time we had said, loudly, that whereas we had freely admitted before that we in fact steal, we now seize the opportunity to declare that we *like* to steal. This surely isn't what we really *mean*, as a whole people—& yet apparently we do mean it enough not to care to make it clear that we mean anything else. It is a new sort of national profession, under the sun, & I am sorry the originality of it should belong to us.[10] Of course however there will be another big fight before the civilization of the country accepts such a last word. I have lately seen much the admirably acute & intelligent young Balestier,[11] who has been of much business use to me, & a great comfort thereby—besides my liking him so. I think that practically he will soon "do everything" for me. Also your (also acute) young friend H. Harland,[12] whom I had to fish out of a heaped-up social basket *as* your friend. I shall be glad to make him mine if he'll be so—he seems a very clever fellow. But why won't you ever project these young stars into my milky way? If it's to "spare" me you don't, because I always—at last—discover them & then have to try to lavish myself on them the more to make up to them for the unnatural rigour with which you've treated them. Please give my love to Mrs. March & tell her I could "stand" *her* if she'd only give me a chance. Do come out again, with Tom & Bella, whom I press to my heart, & I will take you to a better hatter, in London, than Dryfoos did. Ever, my dear Basil,

enthusiastically yours
Henry James

William Dean Howells, "Editor's Study" [The Tragic Muse], *Harper's Monthly 81 (September 1890): 638–43.*

It is difficult to say what manner of poet a certain poet is; to be quite modest, it is impossible; and yet, like the question of the first cause and the last end, it is

9. For the twelfth time since 1843, the U.S. Congress defeated a bill that would have established copyright protection for foreign authors. In 1887 HJ had written a public appeal for such legislation, which was finally enacted in 1891. See HJ to the American Copyright League, 15 November 1887 (*Selected Letters of Henry James*, 87); and Anesko, "Friction with the Market", 163–66.

10. WDH also spoke out against congressional lassitude on this issue. In his "Editor's Study" column in *Harper's Monthly* (82 [December 1890]: 152–56) WDH sketched an Altrurian fantasy in which he describes "Mount Restitution" as "a mighty heap of books of all sizes and shapes, but mostly those cheap paper editions of foreign authors"—a perpetual reminder to a newly regenerate book-buying public of its former piratical ways.

11. In addition to serving as a publisher's representative, Balestier was helping HJ launch his career as a playwright by assisting in his negotiations with theatrical managers and actors.

12. Henry Harland (1861–1905), an author who—under the pseudonym of Sidney Luska—had published a series of novels about immigrant Jews in America. He had recently arrived in London and would soon become the founding editor of the *Yellow Book*. WDH favorably greeted Harland's second novel, *Mrs. Peixada*, in his July 1886 "Editor's Study" column; in May 1889 he called Harland "a born story-teller [who] attracts you from the first word, and goes on to the end with a cumulative interest" (*Harper's Monthly* 78 [May 1889]: 987).

always tempting endeavor. As for Mr. Hay's work[1] one feels as if he were saying in this or that instance of it, "Here is what I could do in a given direction if I chose. We wish he had chosen to do more in one kind or another, but perhaps this is only an impulse of the baffled critical faculty which prefers something distinctively ranged, finally classified. But again perhaps a wiser criticism than ours (we imagine it with considerable effort and reluctance) will be more and more content with each artist for just what it finds him, if it finds him good; and if it must still place and label him will say of such a poet as Mr. Hay: "Ah, yes! An unclassifiable. This is nice. Put him with the class of the unclassifiables."

We fancy him in company there with another American who is chiefly recognizable as American because he is not recognizable as anything else, and who must be called a novelist because there is yet no name for the literary kind he has invented, and so none for the inventor. The fatuity of the story as a story is something that must early impress the story-teller who does not live in the stone age of fiction and criticism. To spin a yarn for the yarn's sake, that is an ideal worthy of a nineteenth-century Englishman, doting in forgetfulness of the English masters and grovelling in ignorance of the Continental masters; but wholly impossible to an American of Mr. Henry James's modernity. To him it must seem like the lies swapped between men after the ladies have left the table and they are sinking deeper and deeper into their cups and growing dimmer and dimmer behind their cigars. To such a mind as his the story could never have value except as a means; it could not exist for him as an end; it could be used only illustratively; it could be the frame, not possibly the picture. But in the mean time the kind of thing he wished to do, and began to do, and has always done, amidst a stupid clamor, which still lasts, that it was not a story (of *course*, it was not a story!), had to be called a novel; and the wretched victim of the novel-habit (only a little less intellectually degraded than the still more miserable slave of the theatre-habit), who wished neither to perceive nor to reflect, but only to be acted upon by plot and incident, was lost in a endless trouble about it. Here was a thing called a novel, written with extraordinary charm; interesting by the vigor and vivacity with which phases and situations and persons were handled in it; inviting him to the intimacy of characters divined with creative insight; making him witness of motives and emotions and experiences of the finest import; and then suddenly requiring him to be man enough to cope with the question itself; not solving it for him by a marriage or a murder, and not spoon-victualling him with a moral minced small and then thinned with milk and water, and familiarly flavored with sentimentality or religiosity. We can imagine the sort of shame with which such a writer, so original and so clear-sighted, may sometimes have been tempted by the outcry of the nurslings of fable, to give them of the diet on which they had been pampered to imbecility; or to call together his characters for a sort of round-up in the last chapter.

1. John Hay, *Poems* (Boston: Houghton, Mifflin, 1890).

The round-up was once the necessary close of every novel, as it is of every season on a Western cattle ranch; and each personage was summoned to be distinctly branded with his appropriate destiny, so that the reader need be in no doubt about him evermore. The formality received its most typical observance in *The Vicar of Wakefield*,[2] perhaps, where the modern lover of that loveliest prospect of eighteenth-century life is amused by the conscientiousness with which fate is distributed, and vice punished and virtue rewarded. It is most distinctly honored in the breach in that charming prospect of nineteenth-century life, *The Tragic Muse*, a novel which marks the farthest departure from the old ideal of the novel. No one is obviously led to the altar; no one is relaxed to the secular arm and burnt at the stake. Vice is disposed of with a gay shrug; virtue is rewarded by innuendo. All this leaves us pleasantly thinking of all that has happened before, and asking, Was Gabriel Nash vice? Was Mrs. Dallow virtue? Or was neither either? In the nineteenth century, especially now toward the close of it, one is never quite sure about vice and virtue: they fade wonderfully into and out of each other; they mix, and seem to stay mixed, at least around the edges.

Mr. James owns that he is himself puzzled by the extreme actuality of his facts; fate is still in solution, destiny is not precipitated; the people are still going uncertainly on as we find people going on in the world about us all the time. But that does not prevent our being satisfied with the study of each as we find it in the atelier of a master. Why in the world should it? What can it possibly matter that Nick Dormer and Mrs. Dormer[3] are not certainly married, or that Biddy Dormer and Sherringham certainly are? The marriage or the non-marriage cannot throw any new light on their characters; and the question never was what they were going to do, but what they were. This is the question that is most sufficiently if not distinctly answered. They never wholly emerge from the background which is a condition of their form and color; and it is childish, it is Central African, to demand that they shall do so. It is still more Central African to demand such a thing in the case of such a wonderful creature as Gabriel Nash, whose very essence is elusiveness; the lightest, slightest, airiest film of personality whose insubstantiality was ever caught by art; and yet so strictly of his time, his country, his kind. He is one sort of modern Englishman; you are as sure of that as you are of the histrionic type, the histrionic character, realized in the magnificent full-length of Miriam Rooth. *There* is mastery for you! There is the woman of the theatre, destined to the stage from her cradle: touched by family, by society, by love, by friendship, but never swayed for a moment from her destiny, such as it is, the tinsel glory of triumphing for a hundred nights in the same part. An honest creature, most thoroughly honest in heart and act, and most herself when her whole nature is straining toward the realization of some one else; vulgar, sublime; ready to make any sacrifice for her art, to "toil

---

2. Oliver Goldsmith (1730?–74), Anglo-Irish poet, novelist, and man of letters, published *The Vicar of Wakefield* in 1766. The story concludes with a mirthful double marriage ceremony.
3. Julia Dallow.

terribly," to suffer everything for it, but perfectly aware of its limitations at its best, while she provisionally contents herself with its second-best, she is by all odds so much more perfectly presented in *The Tragic Muse* than any other like woman in fiction, that she seems the only woman of the kind ever presented in fiction.

As we think back over our year's pleasure in the story (for we will own we read it serially as it was first printed), we have rather a dismaying sense of its manifold excellence; dismaying, that is, for a reviewer still haunted by the ghost of the duty of cataloguing a book's merits. While this ghost walks the Study, we call to mind that admirable old French actress of whom Miriam gets her first lessons; we call to mind Mrs. Rooth, with her tawdry scruples; Lady Dormer, with her honest English selfishness; Mrs. Dallow, with her awful good sense and narrow high life and relentless will; Nick's lovely sister Biddy and unlovely sister Grace; Nick himself, with his self-devotion to his indefinite future; Sherringham, so good and brave and sensible and martyred; Dashwood, the born man of the theatre, as Miriam is the born woman; and we find nothing caricatured or overcharged, nothing feebly touched or falsely stated. As for the literature, what grace, what strength! The style is a sweetness on the tongue, a music in the ear. The whole picture of life is a vision of London aspects such as no Englishman has yet been able to give: so fine, so broad, so absolute, so freed from all necessities of reserve or falsity.

Its modernity, its recognition of the very latest facts of society and art, and of that queer flirtation between them that can never be a marriage, is one of the very most valuable, most delightful things about the book. Modernity, indeed, is always somehow a charming thing when you get it skilfully expressed in a picture or a story. . . .

74·

HOWELLS TO JAMES, 25 September 1890, Lynn   ALS Houghton
                                                            bMS Am 1094 (243)

                                                        Prescott House, Lynn,
                                                            Sept. 25, 1890.

My dear James:

The vain wish to write you something worthy in answer to that magnificent letter of yours about my book[1] has kept me from writing to you at all. Now I come meekly, guiltily, and own that I never could have fitly acknowledged it, and that I ought to have known I couldn't. I don't even know how to thank you. Your praise is princely; when I read your letter I felt as if I had been created a peer, or something. Then, Balestier comes along six months later, and full of the memory of your kindness for me, uses me as if I were really a titled person. That youth made a gay time for us while he stayed with us in Saratoga, and we

1. See letter #73.

have ever so much talk of you. He will have told you of our plan of getting you to come and live there, in a house with a bronze boot-black for a fountain on its lawn, and amusing you with a toboggan-slide, to the perpetual music of McGinty and Annie Rooney.[2] We said, "Saratoga is the place for James. It's the *only* place that would reconcile him to America." I suppose we thought no other place could be so bad, even in America, and the whole country would profit by the contrast. We spent three weeks there, Mrs Howells and I with great amusement, and Pilla with rebellion and abhorrence.—But I wont speak of our goings and comings, or of our stayings, for Balestier will tell you all. Now we're back near Boston, waiting to get into our flat, if we can't exchange it for a furnished house.—I've just finished another novelette (An Imperative Duty)[3] which completes my work for the year, and I have three months of distracting leisure before me. I'm in despair how to employ it unless I give it to writing letters to you, and trying to retrieve myself.—I'm glad to say that The Tragic Muse is almost the tutelary deity of our reading public, as I hope the publishers' returns will persuade you to believe. It's a pity they don't publish fifty cent editions of your books, as I now have the Harper's do simultaneously with the bound editions of mine. You ought to be got into the hands of the people.—My wife wants me to thank you for your good will towards her sister; I hope Mrs. Shepard[4] may yet see you.—I gave Osgood's young partner[5] a note to you; McIlvaine is an admirable fellow.—Scudder, the new *Atlantic* editor told me with great pleasure of the letter you had written him.[6] He will make a good editor, and I think your relations with him will be very agreeable—he's so intelligent and jolly.—I wish you could see a bit of this American weather today—so bright and thin and keen, you can almost hear it rattle. But I wish more I could meet you in London,

2. Two popular songs: "Down Went McGinty to the Bottom of the Sea" by Joseph Flynn and "Little Annie Roonie" by Michael Nolan.

3. *An Imperative Duty* appeared serially in *Harper's Monthly* (July-October 1891).

4. WDH's sister-in-law, Joanna Mead Shepard (1842–1914), was also visiting Italy that summer.

5. Clarence W. McIlvaine (1865–1912), formerly employed by Harper & Brothers, joined James R. Osgood to form Osgood, McIlvaine & Company, the London representative of Harper's. When Osgood died in 1892, the concern was absorbed by Harper's, and McIlvaine took charge of the London office. In this capacity he had frequent dealings with HJ.

6. Horace E. Scudder (1838–1902) edited the *Atlantic* from 1890 to 1898. HJ's letter (not extant) was in response to Scudder's invitation to him to contribute four short stories to the magazine before 1892. HJ's first submission ("The Pupil"), however, was rejected by Scudder:

my reluctant judgment insists upon regarding the story as lacking in interest, in precision and in effectiveness, and however you may temporarily regard it, I should not be surprised if you came to take the same view of it. The situation seems to me too delicate to permit quick handling, and with such a family to exploit I should suppose a volume would be necessary. At any rate I find the structure of the story so weak for carrying the sentiment that I am afraid other readers will be equally dissatisfied, and say hastily—"vague"—"unformed." I hate to write all this but I should hate myself still more if I didn't!

See Horace E. Scudder to HJ, 30 October 1890, Houghton Mifflin Letter Books 3: 57 (Houghton Mifflin Archive, Harvard). In spite of this initial setback, Scudder quickly published HJ's next three submissions: "The Marriages" (August 1891), "The Chaperon," (November–December 1891), and "The Private Life" (April 1892).

which I don't know now that I shall ever do. I look forward to the winter in Boston with a feeling of satiety towards the place. I can only console myself by reflecting that it is much too good for me. I have that consolation in regard to everything, but I don't find it makes me less exacting.

Since we got back we've seen no one. I heard from Perry (whom I *did* see, however) that Lowell is still poorly, and is low spirited. Your brother Wm. I had a glimpse of the other day at Lynn station, when he waggled his hand to me from the car window—I suppose he was going home from the mountains.

Balestier told me of the play you've been writing,[7] and of the processes of selfsacrifice you've been through for it. I hope with all my heart they'll avail. From time to time I yearn towards the stage, but I don't suppose I shall ever do anything for it. The novel is such a *free* fight, you don't want ever afterwards to be tied up to any Queensbury rules.[8] We've just been visited by a young poet, from Louisville, Kentucky,[9] a young man of great promise and some beautiful performance, whom we had the pleasure of seeing look upon the ocean for the first time. He's a most gentle, refined creature, whose hard fate it is to be an accountant in a betting-house, the head of which has killed his man, and never goes out at night without an armed guard. He's killed *two* men, but one was black, and he doesn't count *him*. Just now a judge is holding court in one of the vendetta districts of Ky., with a regiment of soldiers. I mentioned this to Cawein, and he said, "Oh, they *always* have to have troops where there are feuds."—My wife and daughter join me in love.

Yours ever
W. D. Howells
(c/o Harpers.)

75.

JAMES TO HOWELLS, 10 January 1891, London   ALS Houghton
bMS Am 1784 (253) 58

January 10th
1891
34, DE VERE GARDENS, W.

My dear Howells.

It's a terrible time now that I've been owing you a letter—to thank you for your own charming one of something very like last summer (sure enough—from

---

7. HJ's dramatization of *The American* opened on 3 January 1891 at the Winter Gardens Theatre in Southport, a few miles north of Liverpool.

8. The rules of boxing, drafted in 1865 by John Sholto Douglas (1844–1900), Marquis of Queensberry, and standardized in 1889.

9. Madison J. Cawein (1865–1914), whose first volume of poetry, *Blooms of the Berry* (1887), had been lauded by WDH in the "Editor's Study" (*Harper's Monthly* 76 [May 1888]: 964–69).

Lynn beach;) & then for the lovely little memorial to Winnie[1]—which, touching & charming, produced for me feelings that made me enter into those—delicate & sacred as they were—that had led you to put it forth. I had gracefully plotted to send you a literal new year's greeting, but life is a mush of compromise even when it is not of concession—& 1891 is already beginning to swagger & feel its chin before I get my salutation off. It is only a salutation, my dear Howells—only a friendly twiddle of the fingers, across the wintry sea; & an expression of heartiest hopes & wishes for you. I posit or postulate you in Boston—though I don't presume to put my finger on your particular perch. Your nomadic ways give me an overwhelming impression of large free power—and make me feel like a corpulent fireside cat, tied by a pink ribbon to the everlastingly same fender. For weeks indeed, here, this has been the place for us to crouch—for we have had a dark and dreadful winter—the ugliest I have encountered since I came to live in London. Fog and frost pervade our very tissues, & month after month we live & move & have our being by lamplight. England in *extreme* cold is a comfortless land—& the chance to "skate" in impenetrable brown gloom a questionable solace. It is spoken of here by every age, sex and condition, as a bliss to make up for everything; such is the preference of the British people for bodily movement over mental. I am hoping from one week to another to go to Paris for a month, & if I could I would pierce the Alps—which I am told an icy blast, making itself at home in Florence & Venice (both buried in snow,) has already pierced. I'm rather afraid there is to be no Italy for me this year till next autumn—perhaps you'll all meet me there then. I am bent on clearing out of London the 1ˢᵗ May; and I have fanciful dispositions to have a period in Ireland—squalidly muddled as that country is. Indeed it is precisely on that account.—Meanwhile let me say in answer to your friendly words on the matter of my embracing the sordid profession of the playwright—let me say above all in *extenuation* of a course so unlovely—that I have simply *had* to. It isn't the love of art and the pursuit of truth that have goaded me into such miry ways; it is the definite necessity of making, for my palsied old age, more money than literature has ever consented, or evidently *will* ever consent, to yield me. My books simply don't sell—ecco.[2] So I hate to *talk* about what I am trying to do, & what I mean to try hard, repeatedly & scientifically, for the next 2 or 3 years, to do for the theatre—inasmuch as that represents one as attaching an intellectual importance to the business, of which the mean conditions that one has to meet and adjust one's self to on its behalf are a direct negation. It's only within certain rigid limits that I pretend to take my experiment seriously. These limits make a deplorably small field, artistically & psychologically; therefore if you see me taking microscopic paces & getting down on all fours, you will know the reason why—& know that *I* know it. The only thing that dignifies such diminutions is

---

1. As a memorial to his daughter, WDH collected Winifred's poetry and wrote a chronicle of her short life. One hundred copies of *Winifred Howells* were privately published on 1 February 1891 and circulated among family and close friends.

2. So there you are.

that they are really very difficult. I have lately written 3 plays—one of which[3] was performed (au fond de la province)[4] a week ago—with complete & gratifying success, I am happy to say; and I have found the affair a mighty challenge to ingenuity, patience, calculation & even—to speak frankly—talent. It is (but you know—you have done it,) an altogether special effort—& if one could get 4 hours for representation, as Dumas and Sardou[5] do, one might do something large—make a picture with something of the scale of life. But a paltry 2 h. & ½ is the most the Anglo-Saxon public will stand, & that means—for the representation of anything the least complex—the skimpiest & paltriest treatment. Fortunately, however, in a sense the same fine old Anglo-Saxon public won't stand, either, anything in the least complex. So one must deal with the primitive—all the more that the interpretation is booked to be primitive, at the very outset—that is the main, underlying condition. The most one can dream of is that one may, one's self, *raise* the conditions a little; & that, I confess in your private ear, is what I do dream of. Meanwhile, too, I hope to rescue myself from the spectre, as it were, of haggard want.—Balestier kindly joined me at Southport—a big kind of residential winter watering-place near Liverpool—& upheld me through the nervous *gère*[6] of a dramatization, in 4 acts, of my poor dear stale old novel of the "American." He was even a greater blessing than the success of the piece which (I am almost ashamed to say) was marked, & which we fondly hope, will, (through an arrangement which sounds perverse, but is really sensible & requires explanations that I won't bore you with,) be extended and continued through the country before the play is produced in London.[7] It will be only *after* it is produced in London that it will affront the American—& eke the Australian!—glare.[8] Fortunately I have a very agreeable & clever actor (Edward

3. *The American*.

4. In the depths of the provinces.

5. Alexandre Dumas, the younger (1824–95) and Victorien Sardou (1831–1908), French dramatists much admired by HJ.

6. Handling; management.

7. On 17 January 1891 Balestier wrote WDH from London and reported that *The American* was a consuming and delightful success at Southport two weeks ago tonight. I went down to see it; and thought of you—wondering whether you wouldn't think it worth a voyage across the Atlantic to see James dragged before the curtain by the star in response to cries of "Author." It is quite apparent that James has really had locked up in him all these years the most extraordinary capacity for the stage. He seems to embrace all the technique intuitively: he divines the dramatic laws of which managers make so much. I suppose it is his "inbred histrionism"—like Mrs. Farrell. "The American" *is* literary, as you would imagine; but it is primarily actable, workable, practicable. The most delightful part of the success of the piece is its effect on James. He is like a runner ready to run a race. He has the air of one just setting out—a youngster with an oldster's grip and mastery: surely the most enviable of situations. (Howells Papers, Harvard)

8. After some twenty-five performances at various provincial theaters, *The American* opened in London on 26 September at the Opéra Comique Theater and ran through 3 December 1891. See *The Complete Plays of Henry James*, ed. Leon Edel (New York: Oxford University Press, 1990), 47–55, 179–91.

Compton[9]—son of the old Shakspearean Compton, one of the best & most artistic of contemporary English comedians,) for my principal interpreter. He is also a very good sympathetic fellow—which makes me the more sorry that I shall probably not be rash enough to let him embody the typical Christopher Newman to indigenous eyes—to say nothing of ears. The peerless artist worthy of that opportunity is yet to be found. But basta—basta. Don't think me sunk into the garrulity of fatuity.—I remember that when Balestier (who by the way, I grieve to relate, doesn't content one with his state of health—he has been rather seriously ill, & isn't right yet—though he flies about the country on masterly errands)—when he returned from the U. S. last summer he dazzled & charmed me with categorical accounts of your productivity—your more & more thick coming fancies. You're as architectural as one of the great Roman fountains—the Acqua Paolina—& the plash of your multitudinous waters makes me want to strip & plunge. Extend then soon the depths of your marble basin. I seem to believe that you have masterpieces flowing into Harperian receptacles that I see not. But I speedily see & drain the books. I hope you are having a happy, yet not besotted winter. Your little monument to Winnie is exquisite & wrought of elements too fine for criticism to touch. Commend me to your wife & make me an *obscure* warning to your children. Hurry up the preliminaries & come out. Or rather, as I feel it to be, come *in*. I am keeping the door open for you. Ever my dear Howells,

affectionately yours
Henry James

76.

JAMES TO HOWELLS, 12 December 1891, Dresden   ALS Houghton
bMS Am 1784 (253) 59

Hotel de l'Europe.
Dresden
Dec. 12 th '91.

My dear Howells.

Your cable about the *Cosmopolitan*[1] came to me yesterday—forwarded from Devere Gardens to this place, for which, when it reached London, I had already started in obedience to pious but dismal obligations created by poor Wolcott Balestier's death. Of this miserable event you will probably have heard a day or

9. Edward Compton (1854–1918), one of the leading actors of his day, the son of Henry Compton (1805–77) and father of Compton Mackenzie (1883–1972), whose early works—*Carnival* (1912) and *Sinister Street* (1913–14)—HJ favorably mentioned in "The New Novel" (1914). See *Literary Criticism* 1: 124–59.

1. Not extant. On 8 December 1891 WDH had signed a contract with John Brisben Walker (1847–1931), owner and publisher of the *Cosmopolitan*, agreeing to co-edit the magazine for at least one year. The cable to HJ clearly conveyed this information and solicited his contributions.

two after it occurred here—last Sunday afternoon. His mother & sisters[2] were near him—but I knew that they were very helpless and lonely—& I supposed they would be very desolate, & as W$^{\underline{m}}$ Heinemann, his "English Library" partner &c. was coming, I came with him.[3] We travelled hard & reached Dresden in time for the poor boy's funeral which took place on Thursday last, with but 6 persons at the grave. He died of a most terribly poisonous typhoid—caught from the drinking of bad water somewhere—& which carried him off in little more than a fortnight. He was in a private hospital—& had all the help possible. It is miserably ugly & sad, for he was full of possibilities & capacities—of ideas and energies & life. I had seen much of him ever since his $1^{\underline{st}}$ coming to London & he had—with his wonderful understanding of ways & means—rendered me admirable service. He had become in a measure part of my life, part of my future—had entered into all *that* so that I feel helpless & lonely without him. His intelligence was beautiful & his spirit really great. What he would have done in literature I am not sure of—& what he has left (unpublished) gives an imperfect measure. He was too much in the marketplace & the bustle. But—later—he probably would have done much. At any rate he had made himself a large place in London & touched the lives of innumerable workers. Therefore—& for other reasons—I offered you, yesterday, by cable, a little reminiscential notice of him. There is no reason, nor fitness, in writing *much* on him—it will be a grievous mistake to overdo it. But something—outside of the interested *Century*—may fitly be said for youth & high brightness so massacred in their flower. I return to London almost immediately, & shall have to wait till then to write these few pages—very few—but I will get them off as soon as I can.[4]—But what, my dear Howells, is the *Cosmopolitan*—why—oh, why (let me not be odious!) are you hanging again round your neck the chain & emblem of bondage? I will be bold enough, at this distance, to tell you that I hate the idea most bitterly, that I hold you too high for such base uses & want you to write only other & yet other American chronicles. *That* is your genius, and not the handling of other people's ineptitudes. I want absolutely to know that there are millions in it; nothing less would satisfy me. Only then, however, the satisfaction would be to know simply that you had refused them. I wish I were nearer & could interfere. At my distance I can only contribute. I will, my dear Howells, & am ever at the end as at the beginning,

> your palpitating protégé
> *Henry James.*

P. S. How I should have talked to Wolcott about this, & how he would have been interested & illuminating! He was about everything.

---

2. Anna (Smith) Balestier (d. 1919) and her two daughters, Caroline and Josephine. Caroline Starr Balestier (1865–1939) married the English poet Rudyard Kipling (1865–1936) in 1892.

3. William Heinemann (1863–1920), in partnership with Balestier, had begun a new publishing venture to compete with the Tauchnitz continental editions of English-language books. Heinemann became the principal British publisher of HJ's books in the 1890s.

4. HJ, "Wolcott Balestier," *Cosmopolitan Magazine* (May 1892).

77.

HOWELLS TO JAMES, 23 February 1892, New York   ALS Houghton
bMS Am 1094 (244)

241 East 17th st.,
Feb'y 23, 1892.

My dear James:

Your paper on our dear Balestier[1] is absolutely fit. Nothing could be better, and I am exceedingly glad to have it. I shall put it into the May no., which is now the next and my first, and it will appear about April 20th. 50,000 copies of that edition will go to England, and Heinemann must wait his book for it.[2] I referred H.'s letter to Mr. Walker,[3] and if arrangements already made should lapse, H. will hear from W. The Cosmoptn will at once lead all the N. Y. magazines in literary quality; that is not much, but it is a beginning, and I shall count on your help as often as you can give it.

I was at Cambridge yesterday (the break-up of the Glacial Epoch underfoot and Italy overhead; you know) for the musical commemoration of Lowell's birthday,[4] and saw your wholesome brother a moment. His hopes are gadding Europeward already.—I had a long talk with Norton, and bathed my soul in sorrow for the past. I meet my ghost at every turn in that town. In the evening to Perry's, where we always talk of you, and so home. If this indeed be home! How droll I should be here! But why not?

All join me in love to you.

Yours ever
W. D. Howells.

78.

HOWELLS TO JAMES, 25 March 1892, New York   ALS Houghton
bMS Am 1094 (245)

241 East 17th st.,
March 25, 1892.

My dear James:

I have been trying, on other sheets, to say something to you about your sister's death.[1] But there seems nothing to say except that my wife and I feel it

---

1. HJ, "Wolcott Balestier," *Cosmopolitan Magazine* (May 1892).

2. In June 1892 William Heinemann published a collection of Balestier's short stories, *The Average Woman*, with HJ's eulogistic essay as a preface.

3. See letter #76, note 1.

4. A posthumous tribute to James Russell Lowell (b. 22 February 1819) was held in the Appleton Chapel at Harvard, where WDH saw some of his closest Cambridge friends: William James, Charles Eliot Norton, and Thomas Sergeant Perry.

1. Alice James died of breast cancer on 6 March 1892.

in itself and for you as I think you wish us to feel it. Otherwise, it is inexpressible. I knew, from your brother, of her willingness, her eagerness to be gone,[2] but I know that this is no measure of your bereavement.—I remember her as she used to be in Cambridge, sitting in the library, where your father used to write in the midst of his family, and how she looked and laughed; a clear, strong intelligence, housed in pain. Her memory is eternally dear to me for what she wrote us of Winny.[3]

Perhaps you may sometime write me of her last days; that would be precious.

—I have had them send you the Balestier paper,[4] which I hope will come duly to hand.

My wife and daughter join me in love to you.

Yours ever
W. D. Howells.

79.

JAMES TO HOWELLS, 19 October 1892, London

ALS Houghton
bMS Am 1784 (253) 60

October 19th
34, DE VERE GARDENS. W.

My dear Howells.

I am feeling rather nervous about a story that I sent you at the *Cosmopolitan* some time (I think) during the last fortnight of August—a thing called *The Wheel of Time*[1] & of the arrival of which I haven't heard—no more than of its

---

2. On 30 July 1891 Alice wrote to William about her terminal diagnosis:
It is the most supremely interesting moment in life, the only one in fact, when living seems life, and I count it as the greatest good fortune to have these few months so full of interest & instruction in the knowledge of my approaching death. It is as simple in one's own person as any fact of nature, the fall of a leaf or the blooming of a rose, & I have a delicious consciousness, ever present, of wide spaces close at hand, & whisperings of release in the air.
See *The Death and Letters of Alice James*, 186.

3. AJ's letter to WDH after the death of his daughter Winifred has not been located. But in response to it, WDH wrote,
your message, with its memory of another world, completely past, is an intimation that we may somewhere else survive that of today, too, and of all earthly morrows. . . . Our dear girl is gone—we begin to realize it, to yield, almost to consent. But whether we consent or not, we are helpless. I conjure her back in gleams and glimpses of her old childish self, presently obscured by the sad phantom of the long suffering before the close. It is useless; we shall go to her, but she shall not return to us. This fact has changed the whole import of death and life; they seem at times almost convertible.—I wish I could say something fit about her. I cannot. Only this I say, that she now seems not only the best and gentlest, but one of the wisest souls that ever lived. It is hard to explain; but she was *wise*, and of such a truth that I wonder she could have been my child. (*SL* 3: 251)

4. Proofs of HJ's "Wolcott Balestier," *Cosmopolitan Magazine* (May 1892).

1. "The Wheel of Time," *Cosmopolitan Magazine* (December 1892–January 1893).

prospects. I suppose it is all right—but my uneasiness arises partly from the rumour that reaches me in regard to your abdication of the editorship & which, within a few days, has been confirmed by your dear young John.[2] I rejoice in your resignation—you were meant for better things—but I can't help asking you if your successor[3] will tolerate *me*—to the extent, at least, of the said *Wheel of Time*, & if you will even kindly mention to him that it will be a relief to me that he shall let me know that he has cognizance of it—& whether or no he proposes to use it. In the latter case I should like very much to have, if possible, the type-copy (as it is a much-revised one,) back from him. Who is he? and what does he, in literary parlance, amount to?—Very much do I congratulate you on getting your head out of a noose which I fear was being drawn to strangulation. I haven't read your current things[4]—I never read you till I have you *all* palpably in my lap—but it is to them—I mean the likes of them—surely that you exclusively owe yourself.—I should have written you at any rate—even had I not had this small matter on my mind—to tell you what pleasure I have had in renewing acquaintance with the young John—a pleasure very great and very unreserved. He delighted me with his intelligence, *bonne grace*[5] & personal charm (he has lunched with me a couple of times,) & his face called up all sorts of old time resemblances & reverberations. I enter heartily into the joy you must feel in him and in the excellent place (a real achievement, I think,) that he has taken in Paris. I know it's too much to expect you to write to me—but I launch this into the abyss—& I am yours, my dear Howells, & your wife's & the young Mildred's

very faithful, always,
Henry James

2. Complaining of "hopeless incompatibility" between himself and John Brisben Walker, WDH severed his editorial connection with the *Cosmopolitan Magazine* in June (WDH to William Cooper Howells, 30 June 1892, SL 4: 21). John Mead Howells had passed the entrance examinations for the École des Beaux-Arts and had come to Europe to study architecture.

3. Immediately after WDH's resignation, John Brisben Walker resumed full editorial control of the magazine. In 1893 Arthur Sherburne Hardy (1847–1930) took over WDH's job as associate editor.

4. HJ probably refers to WDH's recently serialized novels *An Imperative Duty* (*Harper's Monthly* [July–October 1891]); *The Quality of Mercy* (syndicated in various American and Canadian newspapers from October 1891 through January 1892); and *The World of Chance* (*Harper's Monthly* [March–November 1892]).

5. Fine manners.

80.

JAMES TO HOWELLS, 29 January 1893, London   ALS Houghton
bMS Am 1784 (253) 61

34 DE VERE GARDENS. W.

My dear Howells.

Two beneficent notes have I had from you[1] since last I wrote you a word: one in regard to looking, effectively, after some *Cosmopolitan* business in the Autumn;[2] the other, a heavenly remark or two (still further sublimated by Mildred's lovely photograph) in lately forwarding me—with a courtesey worthy of a better cause—a particularly shameless autograph-seeker's letter. For each & all of these good gifts I am more thankful than the hurrying days have left me much of a chance to tell you. Most especially am I grateful for the portrait of the beautiful, beautiful maiden. Please thank her from me if not for sending it, at least for so felicitously sitting for it. It makes me jump the torrent of the years & reconstruct from her fine features the mythological past—a still tenderer youth than her present youth. (I ought to be able to mean my *own*; but I can't manage it—her profile won't help me to *that*.) I envy you & your wife her company & I rejoice for you in her presence. I rejoice for myself, my dear Howells, about your so delicate words to me in regard to a bit of recent work.[3] They go to my heart—they go perhaps still straighter to my head! I am so utterly lonely here—on the "literary plane"—that it is the strangest as well as the sweetest sensation to be conscious in the boundless void—the dim desert sands—of any human approach at all or any kindly speech. Therefore please be very affectionately thanked.

—All this while I never see anything that you yourself have lately flowered with—I mean the volumes that you freehandedly scatter. I console myself with believing that one or two of your last serial fictions are not volumes yet. Please hold them not back from soon becoming so. I see you are drawing a longish bow in the *Cosmopolitan*[4]—but I only read you when I can sit down to a continuous feast and all the courses. You asked me in your penultimate—I am talking now of your early-in-the-winter letter, if I should object to being made a feature of your composed reminiscences.[5] To which I reply that I only wish I could enrich them better. I won't pretend that I like being written about—the sight of my own name on a printed page makes me as ill (& the sensibility increases

1. Neither is extant.
2. See letter #79.
3. Probably *The Lesson of the Master* (1892), a collection of tales.
4. WDH's *A Traveller from Altruria* ran in the *Cosmopolitan Magazine* from November 1892 to October 1893.
5. WDH was negotiating with the Harpers for the series of "personal reminiscences" of American literary life that eventually became *Literary Friends and Acquaintance* (1900). In that volume HJ is mentioned only in passing. WDH did include a discreet paragraph about HJ in *My Literary Passions* (New York: Harper & Brothers, 1895), 224–25.

strangely with time,) as that of one of my creations makes me well. I have a morbid passion for personal privacy & a standing quarrel with the blundering publicities of the age. I wince even at eulogy, & I wither (for exactly 2 minutes & ½) at any qualification of adulation. But on the other hand I like, I love, to be remembered by you & I surrender myself to your discretion. I hope your winter, & Mrs. Howells's, & the fairest of daughters's, is rich and full & sane. How you must miss the Boy. I go abroad soon & hope to see him in Paris. When do you do the same?

> Yours always, my dear Howells,
> *Henry James*

Jan. 29<u>th:</u>

81.

JAMES TO HOWELLS, 1 July 1894, Venice   ALS Leeds

> Casa Biondetti
> S. Vio, 715. *Venice.*
> July 1<u>st</u>.

My dear Howells.

I don't know at all how to get at you directly; so I send this to you through kind mediation of Edmund Gosse; to whom, as soon as I rec'd. your too nude, crude card, & Mildred's (forwarded to me by my servant,) I addressed immediate & frantic inquiries about you.[1] He gives me, this morning, the shocking news that you are in Paris & that it is questionable if you come back to London at all. This will be dark work, & I beg you to give me, in all charity, some word that may lighten it. I expect to be here till the 10<u>th</u>, & then to start for home, reaching London about the 20<u>th</u> or 25<u>th</u>. But if there were any means of catching you in Paris, I would come there straight—come sooner. Will you give me an *address?*—will you send me 3 lines on receipt of this? This I earnestly beg. It will be quite sickening if you go off without my seeing you. I am very sorry indeed to hear your father is ill—Gosse mentions that as a possible provocation of your earlier return. If you are *not* coming to London I will seek you elsewhere. But *where?*—& when? I will *hurry* even—only do communicate with me. I am sorry for the delay of the roundabout journey, by London, of this. I am delighted there is so much as a chance of seeing you. Tanti saluti affetuosè[2] to the daugh-

---

1. WDH and his daughter arrived in London on 9 June and left for Paris three days later. The day after their arrival, WDH learned that his father, back in Ohio, had suffered a stroke. WDH sailed for the United States on 1 July and therefore did not receive this letter, which was never forwarded by Gosse. HJ had been on the Continent since April; in Venice he occupied the rooms formerly kept by Constance Fenimore Woolson, who died there at the end of January. Her death— quite possibly a suicide—prompted HJ to assist her family and also to retrieve his letters to her, which he destroyed.

2. Many affectionate greetings.

ter—& not less to the son. What a joy they must both be to you. But be a joy to *me,* you, my dear Howells, by surrendering yourself somewhere & somehow to

> your devotissimo
> *Henry James*

82.

JAMES TO HOWELLS, 9 August 1894, London

ALS Houghton
bMS Am 1784 (253) 62

34 De Vere Gardens W.
August 9$\underline{th}$. '94

My dear Howells.

I have delayed too long (after my return from the continent—3 weeks ago,) to tell you what a heartbreak it was to me to learn that you had returned to America without my seeing you & how much sympathy I feel for your sadly disastrous adventure. All I know of the matter is the little that Gosse has been able to tell me—& this does not include any light upon the issue of your father's illness or the situation that met you on your return. Whatever these things may have been be assured of my participation. Your card & Mildred's, left at my door & void of any address (you are the most addressless man I know!) were forwarded me in Venice—whereupon, in my eagerness & hope & fear, I immediately wrote you a letter which I enclosed to Gosse, entreating him to convey it to you somehow in Paris. In this letter I begged you to let me know where you were & how we might delightfully meet—I was eager to hurry away even from Italy to be with you. But this effort aroused no echo & when I at last reached London I heard from Gosse that he hadn't been able (through your precipitate flight,) to communicate with you. I am afraid you have been in much anxiety & trouble—& the 2 Atlantic voyages in the compass of so few weeks represent to me an almost tragic experience. I hope the daughter was not too sore tried by them. Not less do I hope that the sight of the son was a comfort for many woes—it must surely have been.—For myself, I am heavily-stricken. I wanted to see you more particularly than I can tell you—& had accumulations of precious things to say. There was so much I wanted to ask you & commune with you about, my dear Howells—& now I want it more than ever, but with prospects infinitely blighted. I don't venture to speak to you—after such discomfiture—of any "next" times or other times. So I simply utter my wretched disappointment. I can't begin to hint to you all I wanted to say to you—there are things I've been keeping for years to ask you. I have owed you a letter from months & months—ever since your goodness in sending me the *World of Chance*[1]—admirable fiction, which I never have had the grace to thank you for. And still this

---

1. *The World of Chance* (1893).

letter is not the letter I owe you. Faint glints & whispers of you reach me from time to time—but more often they do not. Individuals whom I am eager to see as bearing a note from you to me leave the note mockingly at my door with "Off to Germany" scrawled, with it, on a card without a clue. Others write to tell me that they *have* notes but have lost them, and when I write to ask them to come to see me, all the same, reply that they won't. So I am reduced to vain imaginings of your wonderful busy & beneficent life. Your activity & fecundity astound, & what is more to the point, constantly occupy me. It was of all these things that I wanted to discourse with you—to get at some of your secrets, to master some of your mysteries. I spent 4 months on the continent—almost all of the time in Venice. All Boston was there—& I think the Adriatic, of old, would have refused the Doge if he had brought her so much of Marlborough St. There is nothing left but to refuse the Adriatic! Another thoroughfare stopped. I cast this small loaf upon the waters—I would write to you constantly if I only knew how to direct to you. I try the Harpers this time. I send my love to Mildred whom I am simply furious at not having seen. I have a portrait of her which is at the root of that fury. I have lost sight of John—he comes no more to London. But my interest in him abides. Also, tell your wife, in *her*. That it does in you, my dear Howells, I should have proved had I seen you. Abime![2]

> Yours none the less faithfully
> *Henry James*

83.

HOWELLS TO JAMES, 21 August 1894, Magnolia, Mass.   ALS Houghton
bMS Am 1094 (246)

Magnolia,
Aug. 21, 1894.

My dear James:

Your letter came yesterday, and my wife and I read it with that pleasure-pain which must come from the assurance of your affectionate disappointment in our failure to meet. Imagine from your own my vaster grief! I can't begin to say it. But the whole affair was baffling, almost stupefying. I didn't want to start, and I sailed with a heart heavy enough to sink the ship; but once on the other side I found myself suddenly in the humor of it. I fell in love with Paris on sight. Then, the first morning, I found at the bankers' a telegram saying my father had a stroke of paralysis. After that I lived a double life, thinking of him, and yet trying not to spoil Pilla's pleasure, till the dispatch came two weeks later, calling me home. I found him better, and he is now on foot, and getting well, at 87.[1]— I left Pilla in Paris, at a pension, under John's care, and she has been the last

2. Rather!
1. Contrary to WDH's expectations, William Cooper Howells died one week later on 28 August.

month at Étretat. By the time this reaches you, I suppose they will both be in London, and if they have not reported themselves to you, it will not be because they have not been almost violently urged to it. But John has fits of insuperable shyness. He is a fine fellow, though, and I will own that I admire my daughter. I don't believe you have a more intelligent reader in all your elect following. I hope the child has seen you; for it would be next to my seeing you myself.— There are a thousand things that I suppose must now go unsaid between us, but I don't despair of a meeting; for though the sea is a bore, it is not so wide as it used to be. I would like to know your mind about many things. Nothing so much dismays me in myself as finding myself always so far from the mind I was of last year. The mere jolting about from place to place may partly account for it; but I shed my convictions and ideals at a frightful rate. I don't know what I shall write next, for my love of American life seems to be failing me. For the first time, I got the notion of something denser on the other side. Here, everything seemed so thin, so thin, when I got back; and after Paris what a horror that loathsome New York was!—Sometimes, I think I should like to give up the author's trade, altogether, and go back to journalism; but that is a squalid fight. Your things seem to me always and evermore finer and better. I cannot tell you what delight I read you with. There was something in the Yellow Book, not your best, but any one else's best, that I read in Paris with joy.[2] I go back to earlier things of yours, for lack of later, and I wish you wrote a story every week.—What of your plays? Do you still intend them, or do them?[3]—I have found the theatre always a snare, and yet, how I should like to do a successful play! The form is so perfect.—I shall leave you out of my Cambridge reminiscences, as you will be relieved to know; for I find that I cannot speak of the minority rightly.[4] My wife joins me in love.

Yours ever
W. D. Howells

John's address is Drexel, Harjes & Co. Paris.

My address is always 40 West 59th st., N. Y. The faithless Gosse knew my Paris address.

2. "The Coxon Fund," *Yellow Book* (July 1894).

3. Frustrated by the reluctance of theater companies to take on his recent work, HJ published two volumes of his unproduced plays in 1894: *Theatricals* in June and *Theatricals: Second Series* in December. Also in December the actor-manager George Alexander (1858–1918) would begin rehearsals of *Guy Domville*. The mixed reaction to that play—the author was both applauded and hooted from the stage at its premiere on 5 January 1895—effectively terminated HJ's pursuit of a playwriting career.

4. See letter #80, note 5. WDH's "My First Visit to New England," the first installment of *Literary Friends and Acquaintance*, had appeared in *Harper's Monthly* (May–August 1894).

84.

HOWELLS TO JAMES, 13 December 1894, New York   ALS Houghton
                                                             bMS Am 1094 (247)

40 West 59th street,
Dec. 13, 1894.

My dear James:

There was a note of unjustified discouragement in your letter of some weeks ago,[1] which my heart protested against with a promptness that puts my pen to shame. I wished to say to you that so far as literary standing is concerned there is no one who has your rank among us. That is, you, and not I, or another, are he on whom the aspiring eyes are bent of those that hope to do something themselves; and I believe that if now you were to write a novel of the same quality as your Lesson of the Master, or the Death of the Lion, you would address a larger public than you ever have reached before.[2] We are suffering at present from an invasion of little British romanticists,[3] but this is something that cannot last, and I am sure that if you proposed a story to a magazine here it would be welcomed by any editor. There are to be two new magazines, by the way: one in New York, and one of not less ambitions in Chicago; and the field is widening.[4] You have but to come in and occupy it. I wish you would come *over* and occupy it; but not while I am in England, as I may possibly be next year. The tie that held me here so long is loosed; my father is dead; and I may go without that anxiety for him which always tugged at my heart; and John is to be another year in Paris. I long to see you and talk of all the things we have common. I am glad your evil dream of the stage is past, and I wish now you might give yourself altogether to the novel; and don't abandon the international field, which you created, or at least cleared. You do English people past all Englishmen, but nobody has approached you in a certain sort of your own countrymen and countrywomen. You must know, you are very modern; my daughter, who is *commencement de siecle*[5] in her tastes, finds your Boston types as true as

---

1. Not extant.

2. "The Lesson of the Master," *Universal Review* (16 July and 15 August 1888), collected in 1892 in a volume of the same title, and "The Death of the Lion," *Yellow Book* (April 1894).

3. WDH probably had in mind the work of "Anthony Hope" (Sir Anthony Hope Hawkins) (1863–1933) and "Ian Maclaren" (John Watson) (1850–1907). Hope's *Prisoner of Zenda* and Maclaren's *Beside the Bonnie Brier Bush* were runaway best-sellers in 1894.

4. WDH was probably thinking of *The Bookman*, begun in 1895 by Frank Howard Dodd (1859–1916), president of Dodd, Mead & Company of New York, and *The Chap-Book*, which first appeared in 1894, published by the new Chicago firm of Stone & Kimball. HJ serialized "The Way It Came" (1 May 1896) and *What Maisie Knew* (15 January–1 May 1897) in *The Chap-Book*. The American editions of *What Maisie Knew* (1897) and *In the Cage* (1898) also appeared under the Chicago imprint of Herbert S. Stone & Company, which became independent in 1896 when the partnership of Herbert S. Stone (1871–1915) and Hannibal Ingalls Kimball Jr. (1874–1933) was dissolved.

5. Fashionably up-to-date.

if you had just done them. I suppose she didn't even try to express to you the great joy—and it's a fine and wise joy, a joy that knows—she has in everything you do. But that is heredity; the boy has it, too; and it is more largely national than you can realize at your distance.—I am trying to reply to your half-question as to "American chances and opportunities." It seems to me that you have only to suggest yourself, and they will rise at you.—From time to time I have a scheme of my own for serial publication: three, or four, or five known and "selected" novelists to publish together in a monthly number. If I can persuade some publisher, I will appeal to you to join me. The thing might run a year; and if it succeeded be taken up when we were ready again with a novel.—For the present I am doing short things; odds and ends of fiction; but I hope soon to get at a novel.[6] It is strange how the love of doing it survives. Of course, there is the need, too, but the love seems as great as ever. With the family love,

> Yours ever
> W. D. Howells.

I was dining last night with Hay and King,[7] and they were of the same mind with me about you.

85.

JAMES TO HOWELLS, 22 January 1895, London

ALS Houghton
bMS Am 1784 (253) 64

January 22$^{\underline{d}}$ 1895
34, DE VERE GARDENS. W.

My dear Howells.

I have 2 good things—& have had them for some time—to thank you for. One is John's charming paper about the Beaux Arts[1] which I was delighted you should have sent me—so lovely it is & young & fresh & vivid & in every way calculated to minister to the "fondness of a father" & the frenzy of a mother— to say nothing of the pride of an affectionate old friend. The dear boy seems to have been born to invent new ways of being filially gratifying & generally delectable. Happy you—happy, even if you had *only* him! Surely, surely you *must* all come out this summer to visit him with your condign tenderness. Any other course will be utterly shabby of you. I regard this as quite settled.—Secondly (or firstly it shld. have been,) I am indebted to you for your most benignant letter

---

6. Over the next two years, WDH completed three novelettes: *The Day of Their Wedding* (1896), *A Parting and a Meeting* (1896), and *An Open-Eyed Conspiracy* (1897). His next full-length novel was *The Landlord at Lion's Head* (1897). After parting company with John Brisben Walker and the *Cosmopolitan*, WDH tried to interest the Appleton publishing company and Harper's in a new literary periodical, but neither firm considered the plan commercially feasible.

7. John Hay and Clarence King.

1. John M. Howells, "Architect at the Gates of the Beaux-Arts," *Harper's Weekly* 38 (22 December 1894): 1221–22.

of December last. It lies open before me & I read it again & am soothed & cheered & comforted again. You put your finger sympathetically on the place & spoke of what I wanted you to speak of. I *have* felt, for a long time past, that I have fallen upon evil days—every sign or symbol of one's being in the least *wanted*, anywhere or by anyone, having so utterly failed. A new generation, that I knew not, & mainly prize not, had taken universal possession. The sense of being utterly out of it weighed me down, & I asked myself what the future wd. be. All these melancholies were qualified indeed by one redeeming reflection— the sense of how little, for a good while past (for reasons very logical, but acci-dental & temporary,) I had been producing. I *did* say to myself "Produce again— produce; produce better than ever, & all will yet be well"; and there was suste-nance in that so far as it went. But it has meant much more to me since *you* have said it—for it *is*, practically, what you admirably say. It is exactly, moreover, what I mean to admirably do—& have meant, all along, about this time to get into the motion of. The whole thing, however, represents a great change in my life, inasmuch as what is clear is that periodical publication is practically closed to me—I'm the last hand that the magazines, in this country or in the U. S., seem to want. I won't afflict you with the now accumulated (during all these past years,) evidence on which this induction rests—& I have spoken of it to no creature till, at this late day, I speak of it to you. But, until, the other month (2 mos ago,) Henry Harper,[2] here, made a friendly overture to me on the part of his magazine, no sign, no symbol of any sort, has come to me from any periodical whatever—& many visible demonstrations of their having, on the contrary, no use for me. I can't go into details—& they wd. make you turn pale! I'm utterly out of it *here*—& Scribner, the Century, the Cosmopolitan, will have nothing to say to me—above all for fiction. The *Atlantic*, & H. & M.,[3] treat me like the dust beneath their feet; & the Macmillans, here, have cold-shouldered me out of all relation with them. All this, I needn't say, is for your segretissimo[4] ear. What it means is that "production" for me, as aforesaid, means production of the little *book* pure & simple—independent of any antecedent appearance; &, truth to tell, now that I wholly *see* that, & have at last accepted it, I am, incongruously, not at all sorry. I am indeed very serene. I have always hated the magazine form, magazine conditions & manners, & much of the magazine com-pany. I hate the horrid little subordinate part that one plays in the catchpenny picture book—& the negation of all literature that the insolence of the picture book imposes. The money-difference will be great—but not so great after a bit as at first; & the other differences will be so all to the good that even from the economic point of view they will tend to make up for that & perhaps finally even completely do so. It is about the distinctness of one's *book-position* that you have so substantially reassured me; & I mean to do far better work than ever I

2. Joseph Henry Harper (1851–1938), partner in the Harper & Brothers publishing firm, proba-bly invited HJ to become a regular correspondent for *Harper's Weekly*, to which HJ contributed numerous articles in 1897.

3. Houghton, Mifflin & Company.

4. Most private.

have done before. I have, potentially, improved immensely—& am bursting with ideas & subjects: though the act of composition is, with me, more & more slow, painful & difficult. I shall never again write a *long* novel; but I hope to write 6 immortal short ones—& some tales of the same quality. Forgive, my dear Howells, the cynical egotism of these remarks—the fault of which is in your own sympathy. Don't fail me this summer. I shall probably not, as usual, absent myself from these islands—not be beyond the Alps as I was when you were here last. That way Boston lies, which is the deadliest form of madness. I sent you only last night messages of affection by dear little "Ned" Abbey, who presently sails for N. Y. laden with the beautiful work he has been doing for the new B. public library.[5] I hope you will see him—he will speak of me competently & kindly. I wish all power to your elbow. Let me hear as soon as there is a sound of packing. Tell Mildred I rejoice in the memory of her. Give my love to your wife, & believe me my dear Howells

yours in all constancy
Henry James

86.

JAMES TO HOWELLS, 30 March and 6 April 1896,   ALS Houghton
London   bMS Am 1784 (253) 65

March 30th 1896.
34, DE VERE GARDENS. W.

My dear Howells—

It was a great joy to me to receive from you a few days ago a sign of your remembrance in the shape of a beautiful little book of your own making. It was a still greater joy to find in it, on the fly-leaf, an expression of that affection which went to my heart.[1] And it was the greatest joy of all to discover in *The Day of Their Wedding*, as soon as I sat down to it, a perfect little masterpiece. It is, my dear Howells, a magnificent small—or rather a magnificent big—thing: so true, so touching, so droll, so vivid, so *juste*.[2] How you *know* those people & express them, how you feel them & inhabit them! The idea is admirable—a little treasure; & the way you have rendered it, the total effect, makes the little book, in its rounded adequacy & happy proportion, perhaps in a manner the greatest success you have ever perpetrated. It moved me & delighted me to the quick—& again & again I gloated over the blissfulness of the idea. What a

---

5. Edwin Austin Abbey (1852–1911), American artist and illustrator, was composing a series of Arthurian paintings, "The Quest for the Holy Grail," for the Boston Public Library. HJ assisted the artist's wife in writing the catalogue for a London exhibition in January of the first five panels. See *A Bibliography of Henry James*, 218–22.

1. After HJ's death, many of his books—including this inscription copy—were dispersed from his library.

2. Accurate.

lesson to the nonsense-mongers! If I myself had been appointed of heaven to do it, I shld. probably have felt impelled to sacrifice more to the painting of the picture, as it were, the evocation of the *ambiente*, the surrounding fantasmagoria. But I should have been wrong—for you. . . .[3]

April 6ᵗʰ. I was interrupted a week ago in the middle of that sentence; I have only at this hour found myself able to go on; & I don't know now quite what I was going to impute to you. But the beauty of your book abides with me. I gave it a day or two ago (by which of course I mean lent it,) to poor little Jonathan Sturges,[4] who, after a couple of years of Paris, has been ill here all winter—but is now as convalescent as his frail & frustrated little mortality will ever, I fear, permit him to be. I periodically ask him if he *thinks* you won't come out again this summer, but he takes refuge in dark prevarications, & I am reduced to thinking you won't all by myself. The fear, the dismal fear, is father to the thought. I am still prostrate with the bitterness of that horrid failure to catch you summer before last. Now I feel the chances ebbing if, as I suppose, your boy, in Paris, is gathering up his multitudinous laurels for departure. When he goes you won't come—if you don't come (to speak of—or rather to speak *to!*) even while he stays. Apropos of him, what an extension of your life it will be to see him piling up towers into the American sky! I've not been to Paris for 2 years & when he came, with his sweet sister, to see me here last summer, I was at a distance, in the depths of Devonshire, making a long retreat.[5] I leave London again May 1ˢᵗ for 6 months, & have taken a humble cottage in Sussex[6] (close to little sleepy red-roofed Rye,) which contains exactly a room for your visitation. Isn't there a pale ghost of a hope of it? The years bring no nearer, I'm sorry to say, the vision of any westward movement of my own. It would be a high luxury, several months in which I should do no work (*that* would inevitably go to the dogs;) & the stern moral of this would be that I couldn't afford it. I can only go in a paying way—forgive the sordid glance—& that way doesn't present itself. The events of this winter have brought home to me the length of my absence—& how the huge world over there is one that I've ceased to know or to understand. The Anglophobe delirium reached me as if it came from China or another planet.[7] Thank heaven it seems to have abated. Those were weeks

---

3. HJ's ellipses.

4. Jonathan Sturges (1864–1909), an invalid expatriate whose friendships included HJ and the painter James Abbott McNeill Whistler (1834–1903). It was in Whistler's Paris garden—just prior to WDH's abrupt return to the United States in July 1894—that the novelist advised Sturges, "Live all you can: it's a mistake not to. It doesn't so much matter what you do—but live." This remark, repeated to HJ on 30 October 1895, became the germ for *The Ambassadors* (1903). See CN 140–42.

5. From July to November 1895 HJ spent most of his time at Torquay.

6. Point Hill, at Playden. After three months HJ moved into the Old Vicarage in Rye.

7. HJ refers to the Venezuela Boundary Dispute, a crisis in Anglo-American relations touched off by Venezuela's request that the United States arbitrate a settlement with Great Britain to establish the border between Venezuela and the colony of British Guiana. Part of the territory in dispute was believed to contain gold reserves. In June 1895 Secretary of State Richard Olney (1835–1917) demanded that Great Britain resolve the claim in favor of Venezuela. Because Olney had invoked

of black darkness for me. I thanked you from my heart for your admirable pronouncement on Cleveland's war-cry.[8] I shall have had, I hope, however, in spite of war cries, I *believe* even—a really productive year. I feel myself (absit omen!)[9] in a better & longer current than for a long time back—or rather, to utter the real & monstrous truth, than *ever!* It may interest you to know that. Absit omen! Will you add to the charming obligation that rests on me by sending one of your books that I don't possess, that I long to read & that I have asked for here without being able to get it? I mean the "Coast of Bohemia".[10] And will you put my name, & yours, in it? Tante grazie[11]—in advance. I see Edmund Gosse with a certain frequency, & we try & pretend—to each other—that we are in relation with you. But it's hollow work. However, I shall exult over him with the *D. of T. W.,* & allow him to read it as soon as J. S. returns it. He is restlessly & exhaustingly, but not so very solidly busy. He has no margin—lives too cleverly, & I care enough for him to be anxious about him. Somehow I'm not about *you*—though I care for you too. And for Mildred & Mrs. Howells (what a reversed order: which the American mother will forgive.) And above all, my dear Howells, for the fond idea that you will perhaps write to

your devotissimo, fedelissimo
Henry James

---

the Monroe Doctrine in an unusually aggressive way—he claimed that the United States was "practically sovereign on this continent"—the British government refused to accept the American stipulations, and for a brief time war clouds gathered. President Grover Cleveland then asked Congress to appoint an independent commission to establish the boundary. After protracted diplomatic negotiations, the commission's findings were adopted in 1897. Venezuela's claims were only partially upheld, but the country retained control of the Orinoco River delta.

8. In his "Life and Letters" column (*Harper's Weekly* 40 [4 January 1896]: 6–7) WDH hoped that reason would soon displace misguided passion in the conduct of American foreign policy:

The patriotic emotion does not appear so fine a thing as it did at first sight. One cannot even be sure that it was really a patriotic emotion. It may have been merely a vindictive impulse, the explosion of a shabby desire to humiliate and abase an ancient enemy. There is in the American heart a hatred of England which, if not undying, is certainly not dead yet, and I suspect it was this that glutted itself in her imagined disaster and disgrace, when we all read the President's swaggering proclamation, in which he would not yield to the enemy so far as even to write good English. (7)

9. Knock on wood!

10. *The Coast of Bohemia* (New York: Harper & Brothers, 1893). No separate English edition was issued when the novel was first published, but it was reprinted in London and New York in 1899. This "Biographical Edition" included an introductory sketch by WDH.

11. Many thanks.

87.

JAMES TO HOWELLS, 11 October 1897, London   ALS Houghton
                                                         bMS Am 1784 (253) 66

Oct: 11th 1897.
34, DE VERE GARDENS, W.

My dear Howells.

Your news & your nearness are most exciting,[1] though charged with the lurid possibility of my losing you; which, however, I am determined not to do if I can help it. I am, alas, as you see, *not* in Paris: would to heaven I were! I *must* be there later in the autumn—early in the winter—but rather than really miss you—I mean if your hideous plan of going home *is* enacted—I will dash over, for a few days, to catch you. Only, 1st, let me appeal to you *thus*. Shall you know by the end of this week if you do *not* stay in Europe; & can you let *me* know by Saturday or Sunday? If you sail at the end of the "fortnight" you speak of, I suppose that means Sat: 23d: doesn't it? I beseech you not to; but if you *are* so cold & criminal I will come over on *Tuesday* 19th & get of you all I can. I am very sorry to say that I can't, thanks to causes too manifold to afflict you with, come this week or on an earlier day. But I do hope to hear from you that you elect to winter. Then—in that case—shan't you be in Paris somewhat longer? If you go to Italy; oh, I will come to you there. This is a sacrosanct vow. But do write me as soon as you are clear. If you *are* to sail & I receive your letter on Monday a.m. I can still manage Tuesday. Tanti saluti[2] to your wife & Mildred & to the Boy if he be still with you—in Paris, I mean. I am impatient.

Yours always
Henry James

88.

JAMES TO HOWELLS, 16 or 23 October 1897, London   ALS Houghton
                                                         bMS Am 1784 (253) 68

34, DE VERE GARDENS, W.

My dear Howells.

I deeply regret that you *don't* remain, & rashly & indelicately wonder at your madness; yet at the same time snatch voraciously the crumb of comfort of the prospect of seeing you here. Only I wish to God the crumb were more of a slice. I gathered somehow, from your original non-mention of London that if you should sail it would be by a French steamer: thence my idea of catching you in Paris as my only chance. But if you are to be here by the 29th—that is, if you

1. In July the Howellses sailed for Germany, WDH's doctor having prescribed the waters at Carlsbad as a cure for the author's persistent colic. After an extended visit to Germany and Holland, the family returned to New York in October, stopping in Paris and London on the way.
2. Many greetings.

get, in London, even but one day, or rather *take* it, miserable man, the 28$\underline{^{th}}$—I wont try to put in but 2 scraps of days, myself, on your actual side of the channel. I am under great obligation to be there later, & this wouldn't serve me as well as, or instead of, that. Therefore I await you here; but *can't* you, by a stretch of benevolence, make your "one day"—ghastly words—*two?* However, give me what you can, & I shall be grateful enough. Only I quite press upon you that— if you arrive on the evening, as I suppose, of the 28$\underline{^{th}}$ (but *do* make it the 27th!!) I shall put in a claim to you on the spot & from the very 1$\underline{^{st}}$ hour: what I shall like, above all, awfully to do being to meet you at the Station. Then, on the morrow, I shall be with you at the peep of dawn—under your window, & Mildred's, with a guitar. Isn't there, in relation to this, anything I can do for you in advance—as to taking rooms at an hotel &c.? I shall be delighted, I assure you. If you are here but for 2 or 3 nights I shld. think you wd. find one of the *Station* hotels (the Charing X, or The Grosvenor, at Victoria) the easiest & simplest thing. Or perhaps even the Northwestern at Euston, whence, for Liverpool, you wd. re-start. Command me in *any* way. And won't you all—force this on your wife—dine or lunch or, at the very least, tea with me on the 29$\underline{^{th}}$? (There is a special a.m. train to the Campania,[1] as you know, *on* the 30$\underline{^{th}}$.) If dining may conflict with an early start on the morrow, you must at least do much else. But I shan't, the whole of that day, quit you for a minute. So you are warned, & it will serve you right.—Don't think I try to boss you too much if I say: *Don't* fail to write a line to Gosse! His interest in you is always intense & his affection unabated—& there wd. be a tragedy. DO let me know your preferred Station, & do let me get rooms for you. Heaven speed you. All greetings.

Yours always
Henry James

Saturday.

89.

JAMES TO HOWELLS, 27 October 1897, London   ALS Houghton
bMS Am 1784 (253) 69

Wednesday
34, DE VERE GARDENS, W.

My dear Howells

This is but a word of renewed welcome & applause. May it greet you this p.m. as you alight. *Poveri voi*[1]—but, if it has been a dull day here I reflect that liveliness, on the channel, is just exactly what is to be deprecated. Therefore I

---

1. H.M.S. *Campania*, one of the swiftest transatlantic passenger ships of the Cunard line, launched in 1893.

1. Poor you; in this context, "Unfortunate travelers."

hope you will all be blooming. But give your companions, please, unlimited contingent sympathy. And do come EARLY tomorrow—as early in the a.m. as you can. Arrive—arrive! Since I last wrote your Saratoga book[2] has arrived— all dappled & sun-spotted & shade-flecked with your humour & truth even as the Saratoga street itself, under the trees & by the verandahs. Tarry not!

Yours always
Henry James

90.

JAMES TO HOWELLS, 27 November 1897, London   ALS Houghton
                                                      bMS Am 1784 (253) 67

Nov: 27$\underline{\text{th}}$ 1897.
34, DE VERE GARDENS, W.

My dear Howells.

I have been more touched than I can say by the swift evidence I have received (from H. L. Nelson,)[1] of the beneficent activity of the spirit in which you quitted me the other day in that deadly, dreary medium. I am sure you will be glad to know what your magic voice has wrought—a proposal, on Nelson's part, to which I have already lucidly responded. It seems therefore as if *The Awkward Age* were indeed to see the light, next year, in the amiable *Weekly*. You were wholly right as to the fee or guerdon—£600 ($3000) is exactly what would have been the form of *my* golden dream, and is what I have directly named. I am supposing that this applies to the *American* serial rights only, & that the English wd. be still *disponibles*;[2] but as to that I shld. doubtless be still humbly subject to correction. I could probably get £250, or £300 for the English affair.—But enough of that element. What is more to the point is that you will never know at how psychological a moment you appeared to me the other day— but I almost *can* tell you, nevertheless, how beautiful a kind of poetic justice I find, & thank fortune, & yourself, for, in your so clearing up things for me (for you *have*, really, to a wondrous degree) in the fulness of these years that crown our long friendship. I wanted to say so to you *then*, much better than I did—but one is tongue-tied at all great moments. But one feels it not the less. Never forget, at all events, for *I* never shall, that it *was* a psychological moment. I felt myself, somehow perishing in my pride or rotting ungathered, like an old maid against the wall & on her lonely bench. Well, I'm *not* an old maid (for the blessed trade) quite yet. And you *were* Don Quixote!

The proof of it is, my dear Howells, that you were so Quixotic as to return! And I'm sure Mrs. Howells plays Sancho to *that!* Yes, I desire to rub it in; you

---

2. *An Open-Eyed Conspiracy: An Idyl of Saratoga* (1897).

1. Henry Loomis Nelson (1846–1908), then editor of *Harper's Weekly*, which serialized *The Awkward Age* (1 October 1898–7 January 1899).

2. Available.

might perfectly be in Rome; & I might (more imperfectly,) come down to see you there. Do *not*, at any rate, I beseech you, be afraid to come & see me next time. You have done it once for all, & I shall do nothing worse than embrace you. It was a joy to me to be reminded by your wife (please tell her so,) of a thousand tender things of the old sweet time. And I love your daughter—I break it to you thus. *Try my amanuensis!*—especially to tick it out to me loud & clear that you are coming again.[3] Yours, my dear Howells,

> most affectionately
> Henry James

91.

JAMES TO HOWELLS, 28 January 1898, London ALS Houghton
bMS Am 1784 (253) 70

34, DE VERE GARDENS, W.
January 28ᵗʰ 1898.

My dear Howells.

Too long, too long have I delayed to thank you for your last good letter;[1] yet if I've been thus guilty the fault—as it were! the deep responsibility—is largely your own. It all comes from that wonderful (& still-in-my-ears-reverberating) little talk we had that morning here in the soft lap, & under the motherly apron, of the dear old muffling fog—which will have kept every one else from hearing *ever*—& only let me hear—& have been heard! I mean that the effect of your admirable counsel & comfort was from that moment to give the sense of being, somehow, suddenly, preposterously, renewingly & refreshingly, at a kind of practical high pressure which has—well, which has simply, my dear Howells, made all the difference! There it is. It is the absurd, dizzy consciousness of this difference that has constituted (failing other things!) an exciting, absorbing feeling of occupation & preoccupation—& thereby paralysed the mere personal activity of my pen. H. L. Nelson's letter,[2] following your first, completed & rounded off the petrifying new birth! You did, in that matter, naught but pure golden good—so far as we've got! I sent H. L. N. a detailed statement of subject, to which he replied genially that he & Alden[3] were already, as it were, disputing over it—as to whether the latter hadn't better take the thing outright for the Magazine. And to this end—of helping to settle that—he invited me to let them know what price I would attach to the thing for the English serial rights

---

3. HJ had recently employed a secretary typist, William MacAlpine, to whom he began dictating many of his letters and virtually all manuscript drafts.

1. Not extant.

2. Henry Loomis Nelson had made a definite proposal to serialize *The Awkward Age* in *Harper's Weekly*.

3. Henry Mills Alden (1836–1919), editor of *Harper's Monthly*, which (unlike *Harper's Weekly*) also had a sizable circulation in Great Britain.

(as represented by the Magazine here.) Then it was that, truly, I yearned &
hungered for your presence again, for I felt in myself no certainty of wisdom.
But I gouged out of my beating heart a tremulous "£300" more for the English
serial rights. I didn't say *more* than that for obvious reasons—& I didn't say less
because I didn't wish to "give away" my English opportunity too much in comparison with my American—& make the American guerdon seem perhaps
thereby excessive. Therefore I called the English addendum *half*. I haven't yet
heard in rejoinder to this—but I am waiting & hoping—hoping I haven't put
my foot in it.[4]—I am after all, also, doing some other things. But let me, àpropos
of other things, beseech you *not*, by any accident, to glance at a small serial
from my pen that has just begun to run in *Collier's Weekly*[5] & that they have
too portentously announced. It is an unblushing pot-boiler of a "ghost-story" (in
40 000 words!) & can give out but little air of ingenuity save as a total. Read it
then—if you *can!* I hope you have by this time roared—& not *wholly* with
rage & despair!—through the tunnel of your dark consciousness of return. I dare
say you are now quite out on the flowery meads of almost doubting of having
been away. This makes me fear your promise to come back—right soon—next
summer—may even now have developed an element of base alloy. I rushed off
to see Mrs. Harland[6] the instant I heard *she* was back, & got hold of you—& of
Mildred—for 5 minutes (& of all the handsomest parts of both of you,) in her
talk. She had left a dying mother, however, & her general situation has, I fear,
its pressure & pinch. What an interest indeed your boy's outlook must be to
you! But, as you say—seeing them *commence* . . . ![7] Well, they never com-
menced before; & the pain is all in *us*—not out of us. The thing is to keep it
in. But this scrawl—or sprawl—is about all my poor hand can now sustainedly
perpetrate—if I continue I shall have to clamour for a mount—a lift—from my
brave boy of the alphabetic hoofs.[8] But I spare you those caracoles. I greet you
each again, affectionately, & am yours, my dear Howells,

> intensely
> *Henry James*

---

4. The Harpers agreed to accept HJ's proposal, but only if they retained the option of publishing
The Awkward Age as a volume in England. HJ's prior commitment of the book to William Heinemann made this impossible; therefore, the serial was reserved for *Harper's Weekly*, which did not
circulate outside the United States.
   5. "The Turn of the Screw," *Collier's Weekly* (27 January–16 April 1898).
   6. Aline Merriam Harland (1860–1939), wife of Henry Harland, the editor and author.
   7. HJ's ellipses. John Mead Howells had returned to New York with his family and begun his
professional career as an architect.
   8. HJ's baroque reference to his typewriting amanuensis, whose "alphabetic hoofs" would enable
the author to write more, to turn new phrases: hence the mention of "caracoles"—half-turns in
horsemanship.

92.

HOWELLS TO JAMES, 17 April 1898, New York

ALS Houghton
bMS Am 1094 (248)

40 West 59th st.,
April 17, 1898.

My dear James:

In spite of your instructions Pilla and I have been reading your Turn of the Screw, week by week, and simply jumping up and down between times in our impatience. Mrs Howells has been warned by the sight of our sufferings, and has held off till the story should be finished, and now she will have her reward in one gulp, while we are still waiting for the last sip. I can't imagine how you end it, and of course I don't care. You've done it in any event, and the thing has interested me beyond any ghost story I ever read. Perhaps you think that is not saying much; but the kind is one that I am fond of, and I mean a lot of praise.— We all greatly liked your first letter (second unseen) in *Literature*; Mrs. Howells copied, for the joy of having it in holograph, apparently, the passage about the "immitigable womankind," which she thinks supreme, and has already used effectively in putting me to shame for an attempted letter of my own for the same place.[1] You may see that, and then I hope you will read my reluctance between the lines. My first decision against writing was wise; and in my poor endeavor I was hampered by the wish, not my own, that the thing should address itself both to the English and the American public. If I do anything more I shall aim straight at the British heart.—I am launched in the sort of travel-novel I am doing for Harper's Monthly for '99, and I seem, after long struggle with adverse winds and currents, to be going somewhere in it.[2] Of course I am distracted by

---

1. HJ had begun writing the "American Letter" for *Literature*, a weekly supplement to the London *Times*. His first piece, "The Question of Opportunities" (26 March 1898), surveyed the field of current American fiction and lamented its impoverished treatment of a vigorous and increasingly complex business civilization. WDH's *Rise of Silas Lapham* may have been the exception that proved the rule; it thus may have led Elinor Howells to copy the following passage of HJ's text:

"Business" plays a part in the United States that other interests dispute much less showily than they sometimes dispute it in the life of European countries; in consequence of which the typical American figure is above all that "business" man whom the novelist and the dramatist have scarce yet seriously touched, whose song has still to be sung and his picture still to be painted. He is often an obscure, but not less often an epic, hero, seamed all over with the wounds of the market and the dangers of the field, launched into action and passion by the immensity and complexity of the general struggle, a boundless ferocity of battle— driven above all by the extraordinary, the unique relation in which he for the most part stands to the life of his lawful, his immitigable womankind, the wives and daughters who float, who splash on the surface and ride the waves, his terrific link with civilization, his social substitutes and representatives, while, like a diver for shipwrecked treasure, he gasps in the depths and breathes through an air-tube. (*Literary Criticism* 1: 655)

WDH's first contribution, "Puritanism in Fiction," appeared on 14 May 1898. Fifty-seven others would follow (despite his misgivings here). HJ's tenure as American correspondent was much briefer: eleven of his columns ran from 26 March to 9 July 1898.

2. *Their Silver Wedding Journey* appeared in *Harper's Monthly* (January–December 1899).

the noises of the most stupid and causeless war that was ever imagined by a kindly and sensible nation.[3] If there could be anything worse than the Zola trial[4] it would be our behavior to Spain. But very likely it will end in talk; the Senate and House are at a deadlock, and there is a chance for reason again. The strange thing is that nobody, except the newspapers and the politicians, want war. It will set every good cause back, and heaven knows when people will want to read novels again; one jingo journal has amusingly promised the public relief from mine if the war comes.—I dined last night to meet Mrs. Matthew Arnold at her daughter's,[5] and the Godkins and Sedgwicks were there; it might all have been twenty years ago; but still I remained sixty-one. We are all, in constant regard for you, pretty well.

Yours ever
W. D. Howells.

93.

JAMES TO HOWELLS, 4 May 1898, London   ALS Houghton
                                                    bMS Am 1784 (253) 71

34, DE VERE GARDENS, W.
May 4$\underline{^{th}}$ 1898.

My dear Howells.

Very much in relation with you your good letter of the mid-April seems to put and keep me—all the more that I see as most unanimously affected by the dire events that have culminated since you wrote & that, here, in spite of Manila—or still more by reason of it—make one's life a haunting nightmare.[1] I don't say it here freely, of course—but I hate & loathe the war & have an

---

3. Sparked by a revolt in Cuba, where American business interests were threatened, the sinking of the battleship *Maine* in Havana harbor, and the sensationalized reporting of rival newspaper chains, the United States declared war against Spain in April 1898. Despite Spain's offer to accede to virtually all American demands, President William McKinley (1843–1901) authorized the full deployment of U. S. military forces, resulting in the swift American annexation of the Philippine Islands, Puerto Rico, and Guam, and protectorate status for Cuba.

4. After publishing "J'accuse" in January 1898—a denunciation of the trial of Captain Alfred Dreyfus—Émile Zola was himself prosecuted and found guilty of libel. This conviction was overturned in April 1898 and a new trial scheduled, but Zola chose not to appear and went into exile in England for almost a year. However, Zola's exposé forced the French government to reopen the Dreyfus case and resulted in a pardon for Dreyfus in 1899 and full exoneration in 1906. Dreyfus, a Jew, had been accused of selling military secrets to Germany; his trial, based on false charges of high treason, was marred by vicious anti-Semitism.

5. In 1884 the elder daughter of Matthew Arnold, Lucy Charlotte Arnold (1859–1934) married Frederick Wallingford Whitredge (1852–1916), an attorney in New York.

1. On 1 May 1898, less than a week after Congress declared war against Spain, Commodore George Dewey led an American naval squadron into Manila Bay and destroyed the entire Spanish Pacific fleet, which lay at anchor. While the Spanish/Philippine forces suffered many casualties, only seven American seamen were wounded. The city of Manila was not occupied by troops until August.

ineradicable pity & tenderness for poor old proud, plucky, ruined Spain—so harmless & decorous, so convenient & romantic in Europe, with all her ruin & her interest, & her charming little boy king & lovely, gallant, admirable Queen-Regent,[2] so continentally appealing & irresistible. I wish we had waited to pitch in to some one of our size. The victory in the Philippines has mainly, for me, of meaning, that it *may* mean brevity—as I hope everything eventual *will* mean, for us, magnanimity & moderation. Sickening to me is the vulgarity of all triumph that doesn't almost blush!—Meanwhile, here, at home, I blush a good deal—though I wear a brazen front in public. In general here there is more approval for us than I (save on some grounds,) quite understand: at the same time that there is (socially,) enough silly utterance of an adverse kind to throw me back on patriotism, at moments, more than I *want* to be thrown. But governmentally—as to the purely political class—one feels the country *with* us—& I think there is in all that rather a new situation altogether. But it all equally makes work & concentration (at a moment when I intensely require it,) an immense effort at 10 a.m. At the same time, when the effort succeeds, the work's a refuge. All thanks for your appreciation, & your wife's, of my *Literature* drivel. I have succumbed, in that matter, *purely* to the pecuniary argument, backing H. Harper's earnest approach. It means £40 a month, which I simply couldn't afford not to accept. But I am too out of it all, & too ignorant. Perhaps, indeed, that helps & is a merit. You're delightful about the *T. of the Screw*—the most abject, down-on-all-fours pot-boiler, pure & simple, that a proud man brought low ever perpetrated. He will do it again & again, too, even for the same scant fee: it's only a question of a chance! I'm but speculatively busy, save for the delightful *Awkward-Age*-business—the English serial rights whereof, however, I can do nothing for here. But mention not this.—I don't leave town till next month; & am meanwhile, thank heaven, quiet enough. May some other handful of the great black cloud, by the time this reaches you, have been torn away! I congratulate you from my boots on your immersion in 1899. I re-embrace you all—& hope Doña Pilar is fairly flaunting her mantilla. Tell Mrs. Howells she always likes the things I want her to—& have, really, written *for* her. I press you to my bosom, my dear Howells, & am

yours at every point
Henry James

2. Alfonso XIII (1886–1941) did not assume control of the Spanish government until 1902, when he reached his sixteenth year; until then the Queen Regent, Maria Cristina of Austria (1858–1929), was the nominal monarch.

94.

HOWELLS TO JAMES, 31 July 1898, York Harbor   ALS Houghton
                                                              bMS Am 1094 (249)

York Harbor, Maine,
July 31, 1898.

My dear James:

It was good of you to speak those friendly words about my Story of a Play, which I found very just.[1] You know my experience of the theatre was comic, rather than tragical, and I treated of it lightly because it was light. Of course the husband-and-wife business was the chief thing; and I was glad you recognized that. It is strange how the stage can keep on fooling us; what the burnt child does *not* dread is the fire, or at least the blue fire of the theatre. I have lately been fool enough to dramatize Silas Lapham for an actor who wanted it, and now does *not* want it. What a race! Their obligations are chains of flowers.[2]—Just before I left New York, my wife got back a North American Review, which she lent her sister twenty-five years ago; and in it was your notice of A Foregone Conclusion[3]—something so beautiful and wise that I am sure your maturity wouldn't want to disown it. My heart warmed itself over in the glow

---

1. In his "American Letter" (*Literature* [9 July 1898]: 18), HJ wrote:
Mr. Howells' short and charming novel, which perhaps might more fitly have been named "The Story of a Wife," moves . . . in a world of wit, perception, intellectual curiosity which have at their service an expression highly developed. The book—admirably light, and dealing, for the most part, only with the comedy of the particular relation depicted—is an interesting contribution to the history of one of the liveliest and most diffused necessities of the contemporary man—and perhaps even more of the contemporary woman-of letters, the necessity of passing a longer or a shorter time in the valley of the shadow of the theatre. The recital of this spasmodic connexion on the part of almost any one who has known it and is capable of treating it can never fail to be rich alike in movement and in lessons, and the only restriction Mr. Howells' volume has suggested to me is that he has not cut into the subject quite so deep as the intensity of the experience—for I assume his experience—might have made possible. It is a chapter of bewilderments, but they are for the most part cleared up, and the writer's fundamental optimism appears to have, on the whole matter, the last word. There can surely be no stronger proof of it. . . . It is sure to be, at the worst, a world all lubricated with good nature and the tone of pleasantry. Life, in his pages, is never too hard, too ugly, passions and perversities never too sharp, not to allow, on the part of his people, of such an exercise of friendly wit about each other as may well, when one considers it, minimize shocks and strains. So it muffles and softens, all round, the edges of "The Story of a Play." The mutual indulgences of the whole thing fairly bathe the prospect in something like a suffusion of that "romantic" to which the author's theory of the novel offers so little hospitality. And that, for the moment, is an odd consummation. (*Literary Criticism* 1: 700–1)
2. In 1897 WDH collaborated with the playwright Paul Kester (1870–1933) on a stage version of *The Rise of Silas Lapham*. The play was considered by the actor/playwright James A. Herne (1839–1901), who took the trouble to recommend numerous changes in the script but then abandoned all efforts to produce it.
3. HJ's review of the novel appeared in the *North American Review* (January 1875); the text is printed on pages 100–5.

of your praise, and I felt myself thirty-five again, with my years and my novels all before me.—I am working here at one of the latest which I hope is not the last, and am hazardously returning in it to my early method of mixing travel and story.[4] But it is insisting on a firmness of texture which I didn't intend, and is taking itself seriously.

I fancy you don't know this place, which has some tough and stubbed charms very much to my taste. I have a notion to write pretty closely of it in a paper for Literature[5] (where I like your work excessively and find it excellent in matter and simply bewitching in manner) for Mrs Smalley tells me that in England they do not know any summer-colony life like it. She is here with her sick daughter (getting well) and her younger son, a youth of portentous and most censorious solemnity. The poor things cling pathetically to their English past, which I fancy was not all that they remember it.[6]

We are in sight of peace. Our war for humanity has unmasked itself as a war for coaling stations, and we are going to keep our booty to punish Spain for putting us to the trouble of using violence in robbing her.

My wife and daughter join me in love.

Yours ever
W. D. Howells.

They are revamping Frank Leslie's magazine, and I have advised the editor to ask you for something.[7] If you send, fix a good price, and demand cash.

95.

JAMES TO HOWELLS, 19 August 1898, Rye

TLS Houghton
bMS Am 1784 (253) 72

LAMB HOUSE, RYE.
19th August, 1898.

My dear Howells,

I throw myself without hesitation into this familiar convenience,[1] for the simple reason that I can thus thank you to-day for your blessed letter from York

---

4. *Their Silver Wedding Journey* (1899).

5. WDH's "Confessions of a Summer Colonist" appeared in the *Atlantic* (December 1898) rather than *Literature*.

6. Phoebe Garnaut Smalley (1837–1923) and her husband were close friends of HJ when George W. Smalley was London correspondent for the New York *Tribune*. Their children were Evelyn Garnaut Smalley (d. 1938) and Emerson Smalley (1874–1945).

7. Miriam Florence Folline Leslie (1836–1914) assumed her husband's name after his death in 1882, and took on the editorship of *Frank Leslie's Popular Magazine* in 1898. By trimming its format and lowering its price, she greatly increased the magazine's circulation. HJ's short story "Paste" appeared there in December 1899.

1. HJ had first employed a secretary typist in 1897; this is the earliest surviving dictated typescript letter addressed to WDH.

Harbour, whereas if I were to wait to be merely romantic and illegible, I should perhaps have, thanks to many things, to put off *la douce affaire*[2] till week after next. If I strike, moreover, while the iron is hot, I strike also while the weather is—so unprecedentedly hot for this lukewarm land that even the very moderate cerebral performance to which I am treating you requires no manual extension. It has been delicious to hear from you, and, even though I be here domiciled in some gentility, in a little old quasi-historic wainscotted house, with a real lawn and a real mulberry tree of my own to kick my heels on and under, I draw from the folds of your page a faint, far sense of the old and remembered breath of New England woods and New England waters—such as there is still somewhere on my jaded palate the power to taste and even a little, over-built and over-planted as I at the best am, to languish for.

I am much touched by everything you say to me; and oh, had it come home to me more that you would have "really cared" at all, how much thicker I would have laid it on, not only the other day in Literature, but thirty years ago in the N.A.R., which, somehow, as I look back, seems to have been "literature" with rather more intensity than what I have for the most part been finding in my recent organ. Apropos of which recent organ, I have had to intermit for the time—to say nothing of having had to stop altogether my special "American" lucubrations. The people wrote to me practically, that they found they were, largely through my voluminosity, intensity, &c., &c., overdoing that department, and that unrest was visible among their clientèle, in consequence—so, would I, in short, mind writing on other things? It hadn't taken me long to arrive at the same perception, and the scant selection I was able to make of books that seemed to me at all worth talking about had an effect the opposite of inspiring: so I fell in—but only soon to fall out again; for, just now, I am obliged to concentrate, being frightfully nervous on the getting forward—and endward—with some other work, of which you wot something,[3]—from which I don't dare to steal, with my slow and roundabout processes, an ounce of cerebration. My very affectionate thanks, all the same, for your allusion to the manner of my Literature stuff. May all be well with you to the summer's end. By which I don't mean to leave any door open for anything ceasing to be so even then. I suppose your next door will open straight on New York again, as mine will on London, but as late in the autumn as I can make it. My little old house here is delightful, and I think my pomp of proprietorship will presently go the length of my sending you a photograph or two that I have just had taken of different aspects of it.[4] But oh what a poor way of showing it to you. I still closely count on a better one—extreme though, for all such countings, your habitual perfidity be. I really believe it to be a little focus of existence that will do much for me— by which I mean of course for possible productivity in both the near and the far

2. The pleasant task.
3. *The Awkward Age*, which began its run in *Harper's Weekly* on 1 October 1898.
4. In September 1897 HJ signed a twenty-one-year lease on Lamb House, in Rye, and began preparations to make it his permanent residence. He purchased the house in 1899, after the sudden death of his landlord.

(octogenarian though I be,) future. I am glad you are seeing something of my dear old friends the Smalleys, to whom my attachment, going back far and mingled with all sorts of old London associations and connections, is great enough for me to rejoice for them in any kind of accretion of advantage and kindness. I am very fond of Mrs. S. and very fond of Evelyn—excuse the apparent majesty with which I make the announcement. What I mean is that I like them the best—and what I should further mean if I further ventured to mean anything at all would be that there are all sorts of things in their history that make one tender of them the more one knows them. Basta! Be as gentle and genial to them as you can. If Emerson is sustained by inward upliftedness—or even by outward—in the not particularly discernible outlook of his young existence, I am afraid I rather rejoice than blush for him: so scattered and casual seem to me his other supports.

I can't speak to you of the war very much further than to admire the wit of your closing epigram about it, which, however, at the rate you throw out these things, you must long since have forgotten. But my silence isn't in the least indifference; it is deep embarrassment of thought—of imagination. I have hated, I have almost loathed it; and yet I can't help plucking some food for fancy out of its results—some vision of how the much bigger complexity we are landed in, the bigger world-contacts, may help to educate us and force us to produce people of capacity greater than a less pressure demands. Capacity for *what?* you will naturally ask—whereupon I scramble out of our colloquy by saying that I should perhaps tell you beautifully if you were here and sitting with me on the darkening lawn of my quaint old garden at the end of this barely endurable August day. I will make more things than that clear to you if you will only turn up there. Each of you, Mrs. Howells, Mildred, and John all included—for I have four spare rooms, tell it not anywhere—has been individually considered, as to what you would most like, in my domestic arrangements. Good-bye, good-bye. It is getting so dark that I can't see to dictate—which represents to you sufficiently the skill of my secretary. I am deeply impatient for your novel.[5] But I fear a painful wait. All thanks for the Frank Leslie tip. They have in fact sent me a circular, but of a coldly impersonal order.[6] Yours, my dear Howells,

evermore,
Henry James.

5. *Their Silver Wedding Journey*, which did not begin its run in *Harper's Monthly* until January 1899.

6. Nevertheless, HJ serialized "Paste" in *Frank Leslie's Popular Magazine* (December 1899). The story was placed through an author's syndicate.

part three

Legends of
Mastery

Biographical Overview

As they reach their years of full maturity, Howells and James must readjust to a rapidly changing literary marketplace. After decades of reluctance, in 1891 the United States finally signs a copyright agreement with the United Kingdom, ending the wholesale piracy of British fiction in America that had kept many firms (including Harper & Brothers) in the black. The nineties also witness a proliferation of truly mass-market magazines, greatly expanding the number of outlets available for manuscripts but also imposing new restraints upon them. The "popular" format, cheaply designed for easy reading and quick consumption, requires brevity and concision—qualities that James, especially, can seldom achieve. The "five thousand word tale" becomes his editorial nemesis. To help place stories and negotiate with white-collar professionals whom he now seldom knows firsthand, James engages a literary agent. By virtue of his long connection with Harper's (renewed after the firm's reorganization in 1900 following bankruptcy), Howells has more privileged access to their magazines; but even he is not immune from the new competitive pressures. With the exception of *The Son of Royal Langbrith* (1904), none of his later novels appears as a serial in Harper periodicals. Travel articles and briefer columns of literary and social commentary form the bulk of his magazine contributions for the rest of his life.

With his friend's generous advice and assistance, in 1904 James arranges to return to the United States for the first time in twenty-one years. Benefiting from Howells's experience on the lecture platform (1899), he tours the country—and pays his way—by addressing women's clubs on "The Lesson of Balzac." Before he returns to England, James spends several memorable days with Howells at Kittery Point, where a seaside home provides respite from the New York City summer.

While James is in the United States, his agent (James B. Pinker) arrives to help negotiate terms for a collected edition of the writer's work. Again, Howells supplies an important precedent, for he too has been trying to consolidate his work—and reputation. As publishing becomes increasingly ephemeral (and books a seasonal commodity), the imposing achievement of producing a collected edition seems to affirm a writer's peculiarly literary distinction and to offer a hedge against an obscure posterity. Since both men have distributed their titles among competing publishers, securing the cooperation of these rivals is the primary obstacle the authors face. With Pinker's aid (and also because his work is generally unremunerative), James succeeds; after the author revises much of his early fiction and composes significant prefaces for each major title, Scribners' twenty-four-volume New York Edition becomes a reality (1907–9). Ironically, because Howells remains a valuable literary commodity, he fails. Harper's issues six volumes of his handsome Library Edition in 1911, anticipating that thirty-five will be needed to complete the set; but when it cannot secure permission from Houghton Mifflin to reprint any of the writer's still popular early work, the project abruptly ceases.

Howells has seen this reversal of fortune coming for some time. Always a promoter of James, he continues his series of appreciative essays and endorsements, marveling at his friend's continued evolution of form and refinement of style. Knowing that the younger generation of writers looks not to him but to James for inspiration, Howells acknowledges that his own career may not effectively outlast the nineteenth century. In the dark night of the soul, he confesses to James, his many commemorative honors seem false and unmerited. James valiantly answers these objections, most touchingly in his last tribute to Howells in the form of a public letter written in 1912 on the occasion of the dean's seventy-fifth birthday.

Literary history has not been as kind or, perhaps, as perceptive. "What I wished mainly to put on record," James urged, "is my sense of that unfailing, testifying truth in you which will keep you from ever being neglected." Modern students of American culture neglect Howells only at their peril, for if they are attentive, they can still appreciate his work as James did, finding there the "exquisite notation of our whole democratic light and shade and give and take" which makes his fiction "in the highest degree *documentary*." James's work displays different virtues—quite possibly finer ones—but his friendship with Howells, the "give and take" of their letters, should not be neglected.

Parallel Chronology

	HOWELLS	JAMES	
1899	*Ragged Lady. Their Silver Wedding Journey.* Delivers "Novel Reading and Novel Writing" on lecture circuit. Bankruptcy of Harper and Brothers.	*The Awkward Age.* Purchases Lamb House, Rye, Sussex.	1899
1900	Harper firm in receivership. WDH begins "Editor's Easy	*The Sacred Fount. The Soft Side.*	1900

	HOWELLS	JAMES	
	Chair" column for flagship *Monthly*. *Literary Friends and Acquaintance*.		
1901	*Heroines of Fiction*. *A Pair of Patient Lovers*.		
1902	Purchases summer house at Kittery Point, Maine. *The Kentons*. *Literature and Life*.	*The Wings of the Dove*.	1902
1903	*Letters Home*. *Questionable Shapes*.	*The Ambassadors*. *The Better Sort*. *William Wetmore Story and His Friends*. Meets Edith Wharton.	1903
1904	Awarded Litt. D. from Oxford. Visits HJ at Lamb House; lays plans for HJ's American lecture tour. *The Son of Royal Langbrith*.	Returns to America for first visit in over twenty years. *The Golden Bowl*. Financing his travels with a lecture on "The Lesson of Balzac," HJ tours the South, the Midwest, and the Pacific coast.	1904–5
1905	*Miss Bellard's Inspiration*. *London Films*.	Arranges with Scribner's for the selective New York Edition of his novels and tales. *The Question of Our Speech*. *English Hours*.	1905
1906	*Certain Delightful English Towns*.	Extensively revises early work and composes prefaces for New York Edition.	1906
1907	*Through the Eye of the Needle*. *Between the Dark and the Daylight*.	*The American Scene*. First volumes of New York Edition appear in December.	1907
1908	Elected first president of the American Academy of Arts and Letters; continues in this office until his death. Trip to Italy. *Fennel and Rue*. *Roman Holidays and Others*.	Briefly renews interest in theater; poor sales of collected edition are profoundly disappointing.	1908

	HOWELLS	JAMES	
1909	Extended trip to England, Wales, and the Continent. *Seven English Cities.*	*Julia Bride. Italian Hours.*	1909
1910	Deaths of Mark Twain (April 21) and Elinor Howells (May 6). *My Mark Twain. Imaginary Interviews.*	Severe depression occasions psychosomatic illness. William James and his wife, Alice, come to Rye to lend support. All three travel to Bad Nauheim, Germany, where William seeks relief from heart ailment. When his condition worsens, brothers and Alice return to United States. William dies at Chocorua, New Hampshire (August 26). *The Finer Grain.*	1910
1911	Trips to Bermuda and Spain. Harper's begins Library Edition, but only six volumes (of projected thirty-five) published.	Receives honorary degree from Harvard before sailing for England.	1911
1912	Seventy-fifth birthday dinner.	Receives Litt. D. from Oxford.	
1913	*New Leaf Mills. Familiar Spanish Travels.*	*A Small Boy and Others.*	1913
		Notes of a Son and Brother. Work on *The Ivory Tower* interrupted by outbreak of war. *Notes on Novelists.*	1914
		Throws energies into war relief, especially Edith Wharton's efforts on behalf of Belgian refugees. Becomes naturalized British subject (July 28). Suffers series of strokes in December.	1915
1916	*The Leatherwood God. Years of My Youth.*	On New Year's Day King George V awards him the Order of Merit. Dies February 28. Ashes returned for burial at family plot in Cambridge, Mass.	1916

	HOWELLS	JAMES	
		The Sense of the Past. The Ivory Tower. The Middle Years.	1917
1920	Dies in New York (May 11). Buried in Cambridge Cemetery, near James's grave site. *The Vacation of the Kelwyns.*	*The Letters of Henry James,* edited by Percy Lubbock.	1920
1921	*Mrs. Farrell* (first appeared as "Private Theatricals" in the *Atlantic,* 1875–76).	*The Novels and Stories of Henry James,* in thirty-five volumes, edited by Percy Lubbock.	1921–23
1928	*Life in Letters of William Dean Howells,* edited by Mildred Howells.		

The Great Goethe,
the Good Schiller

Having accumulated a quantity of material during his 1897 European sojourn, Howells planned to rework his recent travels into literary form, which would take the shape of Basil and Isabel March's twenty-fifth-anniversary sequel to *Their Wedding Journey*. Provisionally entitled "The Discovery of Europe," this work signaled Howells's return to a field—the "international"—he had long since surrendered to James. With a salesman's bravado, he told the editor of *Harper's Magazine* (while asking for more "elbow room"—and substantially more money), "I hope to make it so light, new, and gay, so unique in conception and execution, that it will be successful, and that you will wish to continue it as long as I shall."[1] The waters at Carlsbad may not have cured him of anything else, but Howells was soon disabused of this optimism. Returning to his "early method of mixing travel and story" proved hazardous, as he told James. Getting the right start was especially troublesome; once under way, however, the book became diffuse and unmanageable. Critics have justifiably ignored this novel (when they have not dismissed it), but an author's failures still can speak to us if we ask the right questions of them. Why, contrary to all his expectations, should this book have been so difficult for Howells to write? Perhaps because, unlike any other, it betrays acute symptoms of the anxiety of influence.

After a very slow beginning, Howells finally found a vehicle for *Their Silver Wedding Journey* in the same narrative premise that James would employ in *The Ambassadors* (a middle-aged editor's return to Europe). Comparing Howells's book with James's preliminary notations for his novel (CN 141–42), one discovers parallels that can only seem uncanny, given their reverse chronology. Howells's autobiographical investment of himself (and Elinor) in the characters of Basil and Isabel vividly takes shape in James's imaginative construction of Strether and the background of his situation. "I can't make him a novelist—too like W.D.H., and too generally *invraisemblable*," James had noted. "But I want him 'intellectual,' I want him *fine*, clever, literary almost: it deepens the irony, the tragedy." Running through a series of rejected possibilities, James unwittingly supplies the list of fellow passengers that Howells would include on the Marches' sojourn: a lawyer (Triscoe), a journalist (Burnamy), a "mere man of business" (Stoller). At last James hits upon the proper type: "The Editor of a Magazine—that would come nearest."

In the opening pages of *Their Silver Wedding Journey*, the editor of *Every Other Week* hears from the Business End (that is, Fulkerson) that it's time for him to take an overdue sabbatical. A year in Europe would be just the ticket, but March seems reluctant. "It was your right to go, two years ago, and now it's your duty," Fulkerson urges. "Couldn't you look at it in that light?" " 'I dare say Mrs. March could,' the editor assented. 'I don't believe she could be brought to regard it as a pleasure on any other terms.' " James's imagined hero will be a widower, but his moral prospect is identical: "He has never really enjoyed—he has lived only for Duty and conscience—his conception of them; for pure appearances and daily tasks—lived for effort, for surrender, abstention, sacrifice." Abstractly, at least, a European holiday is something the Marches have already considered. "They had a tacit agreement that their youth, if they were ever to find it again, was to be looked for in Europe, where they met when they were young, and they had never been quite without the hope of going back there, some day, for a long sojourn." In this, too, Howells anticipates James's bittersweet theme. "He has married very young, and austerely," James's notebook entry reads. "Happily enough, but charmlessly, and oh, so conscientiously: a wife replete with the New England conscience." After twenty-five years of marriage, that conscience is still very much active in Isabel March. When her husband "tenderly" takes her hand, as he laments the passing of their youth, she discreetly withdraws it, "because though she could bear his sympathy, her New England nature could not bear its expression."[2]

In terms of structure (rather than character), Isabel finds her narrative equivalent in Maria Gostrey, without whom Strether could not hope to ascertain the possible meaning(s) of the events he observes. For Basil and Isabel, however, observation and evaluation are inseparable, self-contained, and usually definitive. As a couple, their joint witness becomes subordinate to the actions of others; they are (as James might say) permanent ficelles, which is why Howells's working title for the book is potentially misleading: no one "discovers" Europe in the way that Strether does, because the author makes little attempt to represent the Marches' interior process of consciousness. This is not a blind omission, however; almost from the first page, *Their Silver Wedding Journey* deliberately shunts its most Jamesian possibilities. Through the Marches' sprightly dialogue, Howells specifically invites such comparison and then humorously turns it aside. Thinking back on their first visit to Europe, Isabel remarks (à la *The American*),

> "I don't feel as if I really saw Europe, then; I was too inexperienced, too ignorant, too simple. I should like to go, just to make sure that I had been." He was smiling again in the way he had when anything occurred to him that amused him, and she demanded, "What is it?"
>
> "Nothing. I was wishing we could go in the consciousness of people who actually hadn't been before—carry them all through Europe and let them see it in the old, simple-hearted American way."
>
> She shook her head. "You couldn't! They've all been!"

"All but about sixty or seventy millions," said March.

"Well, those are just the millions you don't know, and couldn't imagine."

"I'm not so sure of that."

"And even if you could imagine them, you couldn't make them interesting. All the interesting ones have been, anyway."

"Some of the uninteresting ones too." (*SWJ* 1: 11–12)

At best, Basil's voice of Howellsian realism can only qualify Isabel's implied preference for more privileged Jamesian opportunities. Throughout the book March's occasional ironies register a muted form of social criticism, but they also betray his own complicity in the contentments of inequality. As the first edition's lavish illustrations make abundantly clear, he books their passage in a stateroom, not in steerage. Uncharacteristically out of touch with his market, Howells professed surprise when he learned that *Their Silver Wedding Journey* sold better in its gorgeous two-volume holiday format than in its plainer (and much less expensive) one-volume incarnation. One suspects that Basil March (and certainly Fulkerson!) would have known better.[3]

While a few of the other characters (notably the incorrigibly philistine Stoller)[4] serve as vehicles for Howells to disparage American materialism, the author's appraisal of the European scene is more genuinely critical. When the couple is not distracted by the novel's necessary (but comparatively insipid) romantic subplots, March sensitively directs his attention to "the great difference between Europe and America," which, observing the regal display of a sovereign before his subjects, he perceives as one of relative sincerity. March wonders

> whether the innate conviction of equality, the deep, underlying sense of a common humanity transcending all social and civic pretences, was what gave their theatrical effect to the shows of deference from low to high, and of condescension from high to low. If in such encounters . . . the prince did not play his part so well as the people, it might be that he had a harder part to play, and that to support his dignity at all, to keep from being found out the sham that he essentially was, he had to hurry across the stage amidst the distracting thunders of the orchestra. If the star stayed to be scrutinized by the soldiers, citizens, and so forth, even the poor supernumeraries and scene-shifters might see that he was a tallow candle like themselves. (*SWJ* 2: 226)

Grimly prophetic, March takes note of the imperial swagger of Prussian militarism, which parades itself in an endless array of hideously gargantuan statues in Berlin. In Düsseldorf he is pained by the anti-Semitism implicit in the "open neglect, throughout Germany, of the greatest German lyrist." There "would always be the question," he reflects, "whether the Jew-born Heine had even a step-fatherland in the Germany he loved so tenderly and mocked so pitilessly" (*SWJ* 2: 401). Howells's protagonist is no match for the "restless analyst" of James's *American Scene*, but without him *Their Silver Wedding Journey* would indeed be the empty confection that most critics negligently have assumed it is.

Naturally, the Marches' bookish itinerary also directs them toward Weimar and Würzburg, where they can pay homage to Goethe and Schiller. The pairing of these two greats is forever unequal, however, which inspires in March a peculiar feeling of pathos. He finds Schiller's birthplace rather commonplace, small and simply furnished. "It is all rather tasteless and all rather touching," March observes,

> and the place with its meagre appointments, as compared with the rich Goethe house, suggests that personal competition with Goethe in which Schiller is always falling into the second place. Whether it will be finally so with him in literature it is too early to ask of time, and upon other points eternity will not be interrogated. "The great Goethe and the good Schiller," they remain; and yet, March reasoned, there was something good in Goethe and something great in Schiller. (*SWJ* 2: 281)

The comparison affects March profoundly because his maker could not mistake a particularly poignant autobiographical parallel. No wonder the good Howells told the greater James that *Their Silver Wedding Journey* was "insisting on a firmness of texture" he did not really intend and was "taking itself seriously."

For his part, James expressed greater interest in *Ragged Lady* (1899), a feminized version of Horatio Alger's myth-making *Ragged Dick* (1868), in which Howells chronicles the worldly opportunities that happily avail themselves to a young person of character and stubborn determination. Through the intervention of some well-meaning city folk, Clementina Claxon, a simple country girl, comes to enjoy the same social advantages that James had once bestowed upon Isabel Archer: a first chance to see Europe and flirt with dashing English noblemen. But without *The Portrait of a Lady*'s justifying richness of psychological complication, Howells's novel quickly becomes a tedious piece of hackwork, patronizingly good enough, one might gather, for serialization in *Harper's Bazar* but consequently destined for intellectual oblivion. As he revised the first half of the novel, the author confessed to his sister that the job discouraged him. "I find it not nearly so good as I supposed," he lamented.[5] No subsequent critic has ever contradicted him.

Howells's disappointment is not altogether surprising when one considers that, at the time he was working on the book, he had decided (somewhat reluctantly) to try his luck on the literary lecture circuit and thus was finding himself preoccupied with wholly new anxieties. Howells's first stage appearances (at Bridgeport and Yonkers in the early months of 1897) proved more successful than he had anticipated, but these occasions also convinced him that he would find paying audiences more reliably in the towns and cities of the West, where competing cultural distractions were fewer. Two years later, Major James B. Pond, the country's foremost lecture agent, eagerly signed on Howells for a fifty-engagement tour through middle America, which promised to net the author ten thousand dollars—enough, that is, to liberate him from the incessant labor of literary journalism. Unaccustomed to the strains of constant travel and inescapable socializing, Howells scaled back the number of his appearances to twenty-five once he was on the road. ("It is the *kindness* . . . that kills," he told Pond. "I *cannot* refuse people's hospitality, and it is simply disastrous.") Even on this reduced schedule, however, Howells's "six weeks of rubbing elbows with American readers and lecture-goers" confirms the assertion that he "was the preeminent American man of letters at the turn of the century." Everywhere his audiences were ample: in the larger towns and on university campuses, sometimes more than one-thousand men and women gathered to hear him speak on "Novel-Writing and Novel-Reading."[6]

This amiable discourse owes much to James's celebrated essay on "The Art of Fiction" (1884) and thus signals a significant maturation of Howells's critical temperament. In his columns for the "Editor's Study," he had already begun to demonstrate a new catholicity of taste, an ability (almost a conscious desire) to work beyond the restrictive gentility of his *Atlantic* years. Now he could affirm that "truth may be indecent, but it cannot be vicious, it can never corrupt or deprave," and he was willing to say this "in defense of the grossest material honestly treated in modern novels as against the painted and perfumed meretriciousness of the novels that went before them." "Sometimes," Howells admitted,

> I have been vexed at its vicious pandering to passion, but I cannot think, after all, of any great modern novel which has not been distinctly moral in effect. I am not sorry to have had it go into the dark places of the soul, the filthy and squalid places of society, high and low, and shed there its great light. Let us know with its help what we are, and where we are.

In a humorous aside in his lecture, Howells confessed his debt to James by recounting an occasion (at the White House, no less) when a charming woman in the receiving line greeted him with effusive gratitude for the pleasure with which she was reading *The Bostonians*. "I could only thank her," Howells said, "and add that *I* liked The Bostonians too, as I did everything that Henry James wrote."[7]

By the late nineties, few readers would have repeated that mistake, for the texture of the writers' work was increasingly dissimilar. *The Spoils of Poynton*— with its central theme of renunciation, its acute analysis of the warped relation between aesthetic and social values, its triangular romantic plot, even its climactic scene of a great house going up in flames—effectively conceals its debts to *The Rise of Silas Lapham* by repudiating that novel's liberal desire for an "economy of pain" and insisting instead upon an inexorably punitive calculus of sacrifice. Whereas Howells (or Reverend Sewell) piously meditates on the ethics of self-sacrifice, James's characters (possibly excepting Fleda Vetch) flatly determine to sacrifice others; and similarly aggressive types come to the fore in all the Master's later fiction. As Charles Eliot Norton tartly remarked to Howells, "If these people are his 'Better Sort,' " (referring to one of James's titles), "what can the Worst Sort be?"[8]

Howells could appreciate the joke even though he did not share Norton's revulsion from the latter emanations of James's art, possibly because he could, on occasion, trace their genealogy back to himself. When, for example, Basil March reappears as the first-person narrator of *An Open-Eyed Conspiracy* (1897), his pronounced curiosity about the private lives of others he meets at Saratoga playfully anticipates the stranger intentions of James's anonymous voyeur in *The Sacred Fount* (1901). Delighting in the surreptitious observation of his subjects ("I sat eavesdropping with all my might, resolved not to lose a syllable"), March still cannot suppress a nervous delicacy about his appetite for information. "I resolved to keep as near to these people as I could," he muses, "and not to leave the place as long as they stayed; but I did not think it well to let them feel that I was aesthetically shadowing them, and I got up and strolled away toward the pavilion, keeping an eye in the back of my head upon them." With Isabel's customary assistance, Howells inevitably foreshadows James's sacralized title in the Marches' profane diction. Taunting her husband for his prying habits, Isabel observes, "I suppose you're feeling very proud that they're just what you divined." "Not at all," March answers;

> "I'm so used to divining people. How did you know I knew it?"
> "I saw you talking to him, and I knew you were pumping him."
> "Pumping? He asked nothing better than to flow. He would put to shame the provoked spontaneity of any spring in Saratoga."[9]

Compared to the almost frightening ambiguities of *The Sacred Fount*, however, the Marches' pastoral is indeed innocently open-eyed. Isabel's ironic banter, which mocks her husband's behavior by reminding him of analogous situations from their earlier fictional adventures, prevents his curiosity from becoming morbidly grotesque. The Marches comfortably take shelter in their past and invite the reader to relax in that shared foreknowledge. More radically isolated, James's nameless, faceless protagonist—a queer specter of modernity—inadvertently destabilizes epistemology itself.

Because (on the last page) *The Sacred Fount* imperils the sanity of its protagonist, readers who have interpreted the work autobiographically—beginning with Henry Adams—have considered this fiction an unintentional self-parody, a judgment made sufficiently plausible by the book's obsessive technique.[10] Significantly, when the novel was done, the author told Howells that finishing it had left him "rather depleted"—the same corporeal fate suffered by his own victimized subjects. To another correspondent, though, James dismissed *The Sacred Fount* as a "*jeu d'esprit*," "an accident, pure & simple, & not even an intellectual one." "It was a mere *trade*-accident," he added, "an incident of technics." Such books, James knew, were a hopeless professional liability. "I can't, the least little bit, afford to write them," he humbly admitted; "they lead to bankruptcy straight—and serve me right thereby."[11] James's potential exposure, then, was twofold, both aesthetic and commercial; and he correctly anticipated that with *The Sacred Fount* he would have to forgo his most lucrative means of support from literary labor—periodical publication.

More to his surprise, perhaps, Howells was also facing a similar dilemma. When the House of Harper went into receivership in December 1899, bankruptcy was not just a convenient metaphor to describe his literary situation; it was an imminent financial threat. Returning from his foreshortened western lecture tour, Howells read the news after suffering through a sleepless night in a Pullman car; the reality seemed grimly fantastic. ("I no more dreamt of their failing than of the U. S. government failing," he later told his sister.)[12] Although the reorganized firm eventually honored its outstanding debts to him and contracted to retain his editorial service and affiliation, Howells faced uncertain prospects at the beginning of the new century. In quick succession the *Atlantic* and *Scribner's* both rejected his new novel *The Kentons*, which (like James's recent experiment) was later published without the benefit of serialization—a sorry first for both writers. Reciprocally, their letters lick these recent wounds, assess diminished opportunities, and reflect nostalgically upon prior glories. As James immediately prophesied, the Harpers' "saddening & crushing" surrender to a finance capitalist like J. P. Morgan represented a move "farther & farther away from 'literature'—if indeed any move in any such direction have been, for a long time, left to be made."

Once Howells's continued relation with Harper's was legally secure and his role as literary adviser to the reorganized firm established, he worked diligently to prevent the company from drifting in the direction James rightly had feared. Indeed, one of his first tasks was to break a logjam in the editorial department and commit the *North American Review* to serializing *The Ambassadors*, which had lain idle in Harper's offices for almost two years.[13] To celebrate the novel's belated emergence, Howells also contributed his most perceptive critical essay on James to the same January number in which Lambert Strether disembarks at Chester. With its mature insights and delightfully familiar tone, "Mr. Henry James's Later Work" caps a lifelong career of distinguished appreciation. Howells rightly insists upon the fundamental continuity of James's work, as he traces the genealogy of Milly Theale, the fabulous heroine of *The Wings of the Dove*, back to Daisy Miller; but he also apprises us of the complex social history latent in that pattern of descent. "The sense of what money can do for an American girl without her knowing it, is a 'blind sense' in the character of Daisy," Howells shrewdly remarks, "but in the character of Milly it has its eyes wide open."

The most remarkable aspect of this essay, however, is one that few modern readers might suspect. Put on the defensive by his conjectural interlocutress, Howells promptly affirms the significance of James's experimental narrative forms, even putting in a good word for *The Sacred Fount*. "That troubled source," Howells admits,

> "is of a profundity," and in its depths darkles the solution which the author makes it no part of his business to pull to the top; if the reader wants it, let him dive. But why should not a novel be written so like to life, in which most of the events remain the meaningless, that we shall never quite know what the author meant? . . . In the scribbles which we suppose to be imitations of life, we hold the unhappy author to a logical consistency which we find so rarely in the original; but ought not we rather to praise him where his work confesses itself, as life confesses itself, without a plan? Why should we demand more of the imitator than we get from the creator?

The Melvillean cadences audible here are surpassed only by the Melvillean content; uncannily, this part of Howells's essay could be cribbed from chapter 14 of *The Confidence-Man* (which, as the author wryly suggested, might be "Worth the consideration of those to whom it may prove worth considering").[14] Howells's attitude toward the imaginary reader is less acerbic than Melville's, but their appeals for writerly latitude are surely of a piece.

Luckily for James, Howells offered the kind of public support that Melville never received (and desperately needed) from his literary confreres. Together with the long-awaited serialization of *The Ambassadors*, Howells's essay helped to break what James referred to as "the queer gruesome . . . spell" that previously had condemned him (in perpetuity, as it seemed) to loiter on "the mere shady side of the street." Surprisingly braced by renewed publicity, James was even considering a return to the United States, but the necessity of making the trip "somehow *pay*" baffled him. "*Encourage* me," James commanded his friend, "& you will add strength to my wings."

That strength came in the form of two valuable suggestions. Since Colonel George B. McClellan Harvey—whose deep pockets had helped salvage Harper's—had agreed to underwrite an English tour for Howells (which would yield material for two books of travel and a reliable supply of copy for the firm's magazines), perhaps the generous man at the top would do the same for another venerable contributor? (Already the McClure publishing syndicate had floated a similar proposal, inspiring James to rise to the possibility.) In short order the author's agent contracted with Harvey for a "Book of Impressions," at least eight chapters of which were to appear in *Harper's Monthly* or the *North American Review*, on terms that promised James a minimum return of fifty-two hundred dollars.[15] With some reluctance, Howells also intimated that a series of lecture engagements might help subsidize the cost of travel; but, remembering his own Midwestern experience in 1899, he was also aware of the physical and psychological liabilities inherent in such a plan. As Howells later told the editor of *Harper's Bazar* (who was charged with setting up the Master's itinerary), "he ought to lecture very, very few times, and *not* on any terms of public vastness." The most hospitable environment, Howells urged, would be "in drawing-rooms, country-club-rooms, and the like," where "the audience should be more or less invited, and made to feel itself privileged."[16]

Howells wrote these lines from Lamb House, to which he (and Mildred) had come for a brief visit before going on to Oxford, where the international distinction of an honorary degree (doctor of letters) awaited him. Such testaments of fame and the implied luxury of travel unintentionally provided James with renewed incentives to embark upon his western tour—and to make it a success.[17] If Howells could conquer England, James would tackle America. As they had done more than twenty years before, the two writers soon transposed residences. By the time James landed in Howells's adopted New York, the latter had spent six months crisscrossing the United Kingdom and was preparing to spend the winter in James's beloved Italy, where he efficiently gathered his recent impressions into the chapters of *London Films* and *Certain Delightful English Towns* (published, respectively, in 1905 and 1906). By contrast, James quickly despaired of working while he toured America. "I can't knock off pages like a war-correspondent, writing on his knee or his hat," he explained. "I want to do a really artistic & valuable book."[18] For that he needed time (and, emphatically, his amanuensis). Without a steady income from serial publication, however, the restless analyst was obliged to mount the lecture platform, compounding his gratitude for Howells's prescient intervention on that score.

Happily, Howells returned to the United States before his old friend left; wanting to reciprocate the Master's hospitality, he arranged for James to join the family first in New York and then at their seaside summer home at Kittery Point. Like most of James's older friends in America, Howells had worried about the impact that the country would make upon its alienated visitor. "He seems to have grown more and more inward, and to retire to his own interior to ruminate the morsels of his fellow men which he captures in his consciousness of things outside," Howells had noted when he first saw James again in 1904. How would such a nervously wrought creature tolerate the brusque, extroverted jostle of his former homeland? It came as no surprise that James symbolically declared independence by booking his return passage to England for the Fourth of July. On the fifth Howells told T. S. Perry, "Yesterday, H. J. sailed for the land of his adopted nativity. I dreaded for him his coming to these States, and I suspect it has been worse than I feared."[19]

From one of James's later letters, however, Howells inferred that their author bore "a tenderer heart than I should have supposed towards his native exile."[20] A similar tenderness informs much of "New England: An Autumn Impression," the first chapter of *The American Scene* (and the only one composed while James was in the United States). Fittingly enough, the final paragraph of this piece ends with the familiar initials of William Dean Howells, the eclipsed memory of whom reminds James that the "literary" Cambridge he once knew is now gone forever. When James revisited Fresh Pond, formerly a sylvan haunt of the aspiring Muse, he found the place transformed into a gregarious suburban park, "pervaded moreover by the rustle of petticoats too distinguishable from any garment-hem of the sacred nine." Remembering an earlier time "dedicated to shared literary secrets . . . I almost angrily missed, among the ruins, what I had mainly gone back to recover—some echo of the dreams of youth, the titles of tales, the communities of friendship, the sympathies and patiences, in fine, of dear W. D. H." With this deliberate inscription of literary fraternity, James supplied the terminal punctuation for the first installment of his remarkable testament to the "passion of nostalgia."[21]

Testamentary Acts

Not least among his motives in returning to America was James's desire to arrange for a new collected edition of his works. Scribner's had first proposed such a project five years earlier, but the germ they planted (like so many of James's) needed considerable time to mature in the writer's imaginative consciousness before it could flower. In that long interval James devoted his time and labor to the formidable novels of the "major phase"—*The Ambassadors, The Wings of the Dove*, and *The Golden Bowl*—and to the anxious preparations that preceded his American sojourn. Snared during that visit by a tangle of family obligations, social invitations, and speaking engagements (not to mention ferocious dental work), James watched his time in the States dwindle, provoking him at last to request his agent's help. "I shall feel some regret," he wrote back to London in May 1905, "if I shall have left the country without the question of my Collective Edition having in any degree been started, or the ground sounded for it."[1] The loyal Pinker responded by embarking for New York, where treacherous complications lay in store. Negotiating for reprint rights with all of James's competing publishers was neither simple nor inexpensive; indeed, a tedious array of legal and financial impediments came perilously close to aborting the embryonic venture.[2]

On that score, surely, Howells could recite chapter and verse, for similar crossfire between rival publishers was destined to consign his own "Edition Définitive" to pathetic oblivion. "What has become of it?" James asked in November 1906—"is it majestically proceeding?—though I don't see it advertised or proclaimed?—from which I infer *not*—but hope the 'not' doesn't breathe obstruction." Lamentably for Howells, his friend's negative inference was altogether correct and, in fact, prophetic. The majestic array of volumes that Harper's had planned to issue that autumn (a half dozen at first, running, eventually, to thirty-five in all) did not begin to appear for another five years, and even then (in 1911) the breath of obstruction blew hard against it. Howells's moment had passed. Almost overnight, Harper's Library Edition of "The Writings of William Dean Howells" became a bibliographical curiosity; Scribner's twenty-four-

331

volume set of "The Novels and Tales of Henry James" (the New York Edition, 1907–9) would become, in time, a bibliographical treasure. This reversal of fortune was hardly accidental, for James was uniquely situated to benefit (if not pecuniarily to profit) from the other writer's professional liabilities.

The production of handsome subscription sets of "standard authors" was a relatively new development in American publishing. Until the 1890s, almost no work recognized as literature was marketed this way; indeed, the frank commercialism of most subscription publishing houses and the vulgar products they turned out were viewed with considerable disdain by the established leaders of the book trade. The Dean himself once remarked that no books of literary quality were ever sold by subscription except those of Mark Twain; and Howells suspected that his succeeded "because the subscription public never knew what good literature they were."[3] Until the established publishers discovered the untapped market potential of the subscription audience, that avenue of the trade contented itself with gargantuan illustrated books, cheap encyclopedias and reference works, most with the "literary" content of a Sears, Roebuck catalogue (and often of similar dimensions).

Toward the end of the nineteenth century, however, different kinds of culturally legitimate writing found middle-class readers (or, at least, buyers) through canvassers and agents, or through direct-mail advertising. Mark Twain himself was a creative leader in developing this new market, not just with his own books but also with another enterprise freighted with extraordinary significance. In 1885 his deathbed subscription edition of *The Personal Memoirs of Ulysses S. Grant* immediately made publishing history, selling in numbers that only *Uncle Tom's Cabin* could rival. Through the summer of that year, the great general, afflicted with inoperable throat cancer, heroically fought on with his pen. With journalists bivouacked around the dying man's house and stationed near his side, the newspapers kept readers spellbound with pitiful accounts of Grant's final battle. Just days before his death, the closing words of his life history were committed to paper. Already Twain's newly organized publishing house (Charles L. Webster & Company, New York) had hired an army of Union veterans as canvassing agents, some of whom were privileged to carry hallowed sheets of their former commander's manuscript into the nation's parlors and living rooms for potential customers to touch and read. The effect was catalytic, and prepublication orders poured in at the rate of five thousand a day. After Grant's resplendent state funeral, the pace only accelerated; the former president's universal fame, moreover, ensured that foreign rights to the book would command a spectacular price. With great fanfare, Twain presented the general's widow with a cheque for two hundred thousand dollars two months after publication, the largest sum ever delivered to an author at one time.[4] Largely through Twain's promotional effort, subscription publishing (until then widely lamented as the scourge of the book trade) attained a new cultural legitimacy. "The result," as Grant's most recent biographer has observed, "was an astonishing number of two-volume sets sitting proudly on parlor tables in America in the 1880's."[5]

Those same parlor tables soon became the target of other aggressive marketing campaigns. Through the phenomenal success of Grant's *Memoirs*, the democratic marketplace had redefined the meaning of a classic. With understandable exuberance, Twain compared the book to Caesar's *Commentaries* but even his more temperate friend Howells was impressed. "I think [Grant] is one of the most natural—that is, *best*—writers I ever read," he told Clemens. "The book merits its enormous success, simply as literature. It's very handsome, too."[6] The success, as Howells noted, was both extrinsic and intrinsic: a matter of presentation as well as representation. In the columns of *Harper's Monthly* Howells went public with his praise, vindicating not only Grant's authorship but also the publication arrangement that had rescued the general's estate from the humiliation of poverty.[7]

"Quality" publishers (as they liked to distinguish themselves) quickly realized that multivolume sets of their own "standard" authors (as they liked to refer to their merchandise) could also be sold by subscription; and this method was now seen to possess a number of unusual marketing advantages. First of all, profit margins were kept high, because selling directly to the buyer eliminated the need to offer bookstores their customary discounts. Moreover, many of the authors sold by subscription were no longer protected by copyright; others, including James and Howells, were persuaded to accept reduced royalties on their collected editions. Most important, perhaps, was the discovery that through this mechanism, "culture" itself became a commodity newly available for conspicuous consumption. As one trade organ later observed, "in subscription form, if in no other, the 'reading public' does buy 'classics.' " Handsome libraries (such as President Eliot's famous five-foot Harvard shelf) could now be purchased on the installment plan, and hundreds were every day.[8]

One of the first firms to recognize the potential of this new market was Houghton, Mifflin and Company of Boston, which took great pride in publishing the works of Emerson, Longfellow, Dr. Holmes, and the other pillars of genteel New England culture. Howells, of course, had rubbed shoulders with these men in his early Boston years, when (as Holmes had quipped) he followed a line of almost apostolic succession in assuming the editorship of the *Atlantic Monthly*. But Howells also rubbed some of these men the wrong way—especially when he abandoned the *Atlantic* (and its new publisher, Henry Oscar Houghton) and became a free agent, letting the marketplace rather than personal loyalty dictate his literary allegiances. Nevertheless, it was to Houghton's successors that Howells appealed in the mid-nineties to publish a collected edition of his work. As usual, the Dean's take on the market was keen; more and more of these imposing sets were appearing every year: the time was certainly right to secure his place in an American canon that was just beginning to cohere. Howells correctly sensed that, with so much of American literature under its corporate control, Houghton, Mifflin was in a powerful position to establish (and preserve) that canon and was, indeed, accomplishing this through the mechanism of edition publishing.

The firm's ambivalent response to Howells starkly reveals an important, though still misunderstood, aspect of this cultural process. In spite of what some literary critics might like to believe, their recent declamations about the social and political determinants of canon formation are hardly new. Houghton,

Mifflin executives were very much aware of these factors in 1896, when Howells's proposal arrived at their Boston office. An exchange of letters and memoranda debating the merits of a new edition rapidly ensued between the company's headquarters and its field offices in New York and Chicago, where salesmen, editors, and production staff all were consulted. The company's president in Boston, George H. Mifflin, obviously relished the idea of once again publishing Howells, for he wrote to New York with great enthusiasm and conviction. "My own idea," he confided, "is that if we can make the proper kind of an arrangement with Harpers" (who had been publishing Howells for the last ten years) "it will be a good venture for the House, and quite a card. It means a complete and uniform Howells with introductory notes, etc. etc., and whatever may be said, Howells's position as one of our foremost men of letters is secure."[9] Mifflin's conviction would seem to have had a solid—almost an irrefutable—basis. By virtue of his abundant productivity and influential monthly columns in *Harper's Monthly,* Howells had indeed come to occupy a decanal position in the cultural hierarchy of American writers. (Even the man's middle name seemed providentially chosen, as interviewers liked to remark.) In fact, by the mid-nineties Howells arguably had reached the apex of his public career, with the triumph of *A Hazard of New Fortunes* (1889–90) recently behind him, and the popular success of *The Landlord at Lion's Head* just at hand (1896–97).

Much to his surprise, however, Mifflin learned that the company's field offices were rather cool to this proposal. Unfortunately, the internal memoranda sent from New York and Chicago have not survived, but Mifflin's responses to them have, in which the terms of a stubborn (and rather prophetic) debate become manifest. It is evident, at any rate, that the New York office in particular was dubious about the Howells project, for Mifflin repeatedly tried to answer their objections. How comprehensive was this edition likely to be? How many volumes? How would terms be negotiated for those titles to which Houghton, Mifflin did not control the copyright? Were the regular trade editions of Howells's work still selling in sufficient numbers to warrant a new edition? The Boston editorial group (informally known as "the Pow Wow") took up these questions right away. "You ask me for some information about Howells' books," Mifflin propmptly reported back. "We discussed the matter pretty fully at our Pow Wow yesterday," he continued,

and the conviction was unanimous that if proper arrangements could be made, and the matter could be compressed within a reasonable number of volumes that the Howells venture as a subscription work would be a good one. You see it would be the only uniform edition of Howells. His books are now in a most unsatisfactory shape, so far as get-up is concerned, no uniformity and no attractiveness about them in any way. The actual sales of Howells' books in the trade edition I do not think would form any safe guide, because the actual sales of Bret Harte you know through the trade are very meagre . . . and yet see what a tremendous success the subscription edition of Bret Harte so far has been. Howells' position in American literature we all think is far more permanently assured than Bret Harte's.[10]

To supplement this cultural rationale for publishing a collected edition of Howells, Mifflin also remarked that the firm might seize this opportunity to try something new in subscription marketing, for he was fearful that the house was losing its edge to New York competitors, whose increasingly lavish editions were less stuffy and sober than the deliberately drab "Household" series with which Houghton, Mifflin had made its reputation. "It might be desirable in the get-up of the edition to make a departure from any of our books," Mifflin suggested, "although that would be a matter for subsequent experimenting. You know the Scribners have made some rather handsome books of Stevenson's and Barrie's, and we might make a study of the matter so as to have a different get-up from our other standard editions." To clinch his argument in favor of Howells, Mifflin also returned to an obviously sore point: Howells's defection, years ago, when the old partnership between Houghton and James Ripley Osgood had broken up. "[Y]ou will remember," Mifflin added, "that Howells was about the only author who left us in 1880, and now he comes knocking at the door." To get him back now—after all the years of publishing with Harper's— would be "quite a card for the House." [11] Aesthetic, commercial, and even political factors were very much at work here. From a literary point of view, Howells's position seemed secure (at least to Mifflin); but from a business standpoint, his prodigal career raised concerns that might well supersede aesthetic considerations.

Knowing that the market for subscription editions was just then expanding, Howells was eager to come to terms. But Houghton, Mifflin refused to make a commitment until the firm could study all the relevant factors; and a principal anxiety was the question of the edition's size. To publish Howells complete would take a greater number of volumes than any of their other "standard" authors, and fixing a price ceiling on culture was very difficult to gauge. Would the public that bought Emerson in eleven volumes (at $2 a piece), or Hawthorne in twelve, be willing to sign on for Howells in twenty-four—or possibly more? "Our estimate of the enterprise from a commercial point of view," Mifflin told Howells, "would depend largely upon the practicability of confining the edition to a reasonable number of volumes and yet of making it entirely satisfactory to you." [12] Howells promptly recognized the dilemma and offered to limit the edition to contain only his novels, or perhaps those together with his popular travel writings. But to this Mifflin had to report that issuing these books alone would deprive the edition of its "strongest feature from the selling point of view," namely, its completeness. "I think the buying public in the subscription department attach great importance to this feature," he added. [13] To his business partners Mifflin was somewhat more explicit. To bring out the novels alone would "endanger the enterprise," he wrote to New York, and yet to extend the edition "into anything like 20 or 24 volumes would practically condemn the venture." A possible solution might be to double up the volumes, printing two or more titles between one set of covers by using a thin grade of paper in order to prevent the books from becoming cumbersome. "We have never had a word of complaint from scores of authors published in this way," he urged, "and once admit that Howells is a standard author, and I cannot believe that the doubling up would be such a fatal thing as it has seemed to you [in the New York office] all along."[14]

The interesting qualification here is Mifflin's stipulation of whether to admit that Howells was indeed a "standard author." In merely three weeks, the Dean had somehow slipped from his "position as one of our foremost men of letters" to that of a writer whose permanent rank remained in doubt. Three weeks may be somewhat longer than Andy Warhol's fifteen minutes of fame, but in cultural terms they are pretty much coterminous. Without the support of the firm's field offices, which never materialized, Mifflin was content, as he said, "to hang the Howells up."[15] He has remained on that peg ever since.

Although he apologized to Howells for the firm's decision and suggested that perhaps at some future time the enterprise might be taken up, Mifflin's private view changed remarkably and irreversibly. Within six months he would confide to another author (who had threatened to follow Howells's example of switching publishers and demanding higher than usual royalty rates) that the Dean's career was finished. "You speak of Howells getting for example 20 per-cent and being a 'rolling stone,'" Mifflin noted, from which he drew these sober conclusions:

> The first suggestion is I am sure a mistake, and I think Howells never made a more fatal false step than when he entered upon that fatal rolling stone policy. His books now simply don't sell, and he finds doors once so hospitably open now closed to him. I may say to you in strictest confidence that we recently had the offer of bringing together all his books for a final "definitive" Edition, which had it been made and sold by the methods we had in mind should have brought him in a permanent and steady income; but we declined the offer (though the copyright would not have been over half the sum you name) and this because owing to his methods, he has written himself out, has so scattered his works that he has killed the goose so to speak that "laid the golden egg!" He is almost the only one of "our authors" who thought he saw his interest in the "highest bid" policy, and the results in his case have been quite disastrous to his permanent place in literature and I believe also to his personal happiness.[16]

The perverse logic of Mifflin's argument can be disputed; indeed, the writer to whom it was addressed soon abandoned her connection with the firm and sought higher royalties elsewhere. But the publisher's conclusion about the negative impact of his firm's decision on Howells's "permanent place in literature" is probably correct.[17]

Houghton, Mifflin temporized about a collected edition, but Howells did not give up. In the first years of the new century, he renewed his quest, this time turning to Harper's, but clearly he was chastened and made somewhat skeptical by his earlier disappointment. Howells told Charles Eliot Norton in 1902 that prospects for a new Library Edition were looking good; but he also acknowledged, somewhat grimly, "it would take a Vatican library to hold me, almost."[18] The problem of dimensions had only gotten worse, because, with annual regularity, Howells kept producing novel after novel, and book after book of essays, travel, and literary criticism.

Harper's was genuinely interested in doing a complete edition of Howells, but now Houghton, Mifflin was in a position to make demands. It firmly insisted that, for the many titles to which it held copyright, all presswork and binding be subcontracted to the Riverside Press in Cambridge, and that Harper's pay it a royalty of 5 percent on each copy sold. Such an arrangement would necessarily drive up the cost of any edition; and it seems likely that Harper executives greatly overestimated Howells's personal advantage in bargaining with his old Boston employer. Harper's believed that, in deference to Howells's supposedly eminent position in American letters, Houghton, Mifflin would relent and liberally grant permission to reprint the early books. A curious triangular correspondence soon began, with both publishers writing delicately phrased letters to Howells (urging patience and hope), while they despatched increasingly blunt memos to each other (refusing to compromise on any terms). Keeping Howells in the dark apparently was crucial to both firms, and they largely succeeded in convincing him that the details of the contract were being ironed out. In May 1905 (significantly, just a week before James's visit to Kittery Point) Howells wrote to Mifflin, "I am glad you are arranging so amicably with Harpers about the library edition."[19] But the true relations of his competing publishers could more accurately be described as politely acrimonious. In July Howells sent a rather cryptic letter to his editor at Harper's, remarking that he had just received a letter from Mifflin. "It seems," he wrote, "to be the beginning of some sort of end." But an end to what—the negotiations, or the edition itself? Howells himself may not have been sure, for he continued, "If your purpose holds to begin the library edition of my books, I hope you will not let me fail to have the opening volumes for revision before you put them in type."[20]

Later that same year James and his agent confronted an identical dilemma, as Scribner's and Houghton, Mifflin sparred over terms for the New York Edition. In fact, the Boston firm's stern claims against Harper's provided a boilerplate for the proposal first sent to Scribner's. "The principle for which we have contended," as Houghton, Mifflin wrote,

> is that the publisher who has contracted for the sale of an author's works for the full term of copyright should have also the sole right of manufacturing the books, whether for himself or for issue under another imprint, and if he is prepared to make the book in the style and on the lines proposed by the publisher of the uniform edition, it seems to us that he has done all that can reasonably be expected.

Without mentioning Howells by name, the company nevertheless justified its demands by remarking that authors who "seek to collect their works after they have been issued by four or five different houses are surprised that there can be any difficulties or obstacles in the way, and have given no thought to the plates and stock in which the publisher has invested."[21] Having been apprised of Howells's prolonged difficulties, however, James was in a much better position to circumvent these obstacles, which he (and Pinker) promptly did. Only a month later an abashed George H. Mifflin stammered, "we should be the very last people to stand in the way of Mr. James's efforts to make a uniform edition of his works," adding that the firm's relations "with Mr. James extending now back for so many years would forbid any such attitude on our part."[22] Somewhat conspicuously, that argument never helped poor Howells, to whom it equally might have applied. In his case, Houghton, Mifflin was the first to stand in the way, and it never budged an inch.

Still unaware of the opposition's magnitude, Howells mapped out his Library Edition along lines that initially were quite similar to James's. He, too, wanted to revise and regroup his works, supply them with autobiographical prefaces, and suggest appropriate subjects for illustration. As the years passed, however, the material precedent of the New York Edition (and Harper's continued silence) adversely affected Howells's ambitions. With his publishers vacillating between enthusiasm and despair over the project, the author yielded to an impulse for sober self-reflection. "In going over my books," he told his brother Joe,

> I find that 18 or 20 volumes have been written since I came to Harper in 1886, and 10 or 12 before that. Of course, my meat went into the earlier ones, and yet there are three or four of the later novels which are as good as any. I hope I shall get my "wind" again, but just now I am fagged, there's no denying it. I can look back, and see that the like has happened before, but I wasn't then 72 years old.[23]

Howells was, in fact, seventy-four before the first volumes of his Library Edition were published in 1911. On the sixth of August (just as he and Mildred were embarking upon another European holiday), the New York *Times* reported that, before sailing, Howells had "settled with his publishers upon all the details" of a forthcoming complete edition of his works. Harper's announcement of the Library Edition of William Dean Howells seemed to confirm his status as "a writer of the first class" and to guarantee his rightful place in the nation's literary canon. "For half a century," the paper continued,

> William Dean Howells has been producing books which stand among the best in American literature. Looking back, he himself seems to stand in the group with Emerson, Longfellow, Lowell, Holmes, and the other great ones, and in truth he has preserved the tradition of these men, both the high devotion to letters and the characteristic spirit.

What the paper failed to mention, however, was that all "the other great ones" were published by Harper's major competitor in Boston.[24]

When the first volumes of Howells's Library Edition appeared, Houghton Mifflin dealt the series a finishing stroke by reminding Harper's of the complicated production agreement to which it was bound. Having learned of the edition's appearance only through the newspapers, the firm professed a willingness "to coöperate . . . in this worthy project of a complete edition," but it nevertheless refused to compromise on the terms hammered out nine years earlier. "As Mr. Howells is now abroad," their deceptively polite ultimatum continued, "we are taking this up with you direct, though the previous correspondence was, as you will recall, a three-cornered one." Even this reminder was an implicit rebuke

to Harper's strategy of seeking the author's personal intervention to win concessions from its Boston competitors. A feeble response from Franklin Square, the
last surviving document in the files, merely noted that arrangements were "not
altogether . . . completed" with respect to the manufacture of the other Howells
books. Unfortunately for the author, those volumes were simply not manufactured at all—by Harper's or by any one.[25]

Terminations

In this frustrating close to his career, Howells was victimized by conflicting estimates of his surplus value. Beginning in the mid-1880s, Harper's had appropriated that value in terms of the writer's unusual cultural authority. Through a series of monopolizing contracts with Howells (by which it had the right of first refusal to everything he wrote), the New York firm tightly controlled access to the aura of gentility and respectability with which Howells had become synonymous through the pages of its magazines. Harper's interest in Howells was thus directed more toward the future than to the past. What is more, Howells's value was not confined to his own literary production; it extended to any other work to which he might give critical endorsement through his serialized reviews and social commentary. Houghton, Mifflin, on the other hand, had appropriated Howells's surplus value more narrowly in terms of copyright (in the legal sense, that is, of intellectual property). The men in Boston controlled access to much of the author's most popular past work—the polite, domestic fiction with which he had begun his long career—and, as it turned out, were rather jealous guardians of that privilege.

"Publishers have their little theories," Howells once wrote, "their little superstitions, and their blind faith in the great god Chance which we all worship."[1] Perhaps it could be said that one of Harper's superstitions was a blind faith in the great god Howells' whom it assumed everyone else worshipped as devoutly as it did. In his centennial history of the house, the firm's literary patriarch, J. Henry Harper, proudly announced that the company was "just on the eve of publishing a complete Library Edition of the works of W. D. Howells." Echoing his publicity blurb, Harper testified, "For half a century Mr. Howells has been producing books which stand among the best in American Literature."[2] (Ironically, this little puff could have been lifted from one of the enthusiastic internal memoranda that George H. Mifflin had written sixteen years earlier.) In 1912, Harper's idolatry of Howells reached its zenith in the famous seventy-fifth-birthday extravaganza orchestrated by the firm's publicity-minded president, Colonel Harvey. In the wake of all the hoopla, however, the author felt horribly exposed and unworthy. With his edition frustrated and failing, what was there to celebrate? (In the first year, barely one hundred sets were sold.)[3] The dispro- portion was grotesque. It "was all, all wrong and unfit," he confessed to James, "but nobody apparently knew it, not even I till that ghastly waking hour of the night when hell opens to us." Utterly impatient with his friend's self-reproaches, James publicly reminded him "how the great and admirable Taine, in one of the fine excursions of his French curiosity, greeted you as a precious painter and a sovereign witness. But his appreciation," James insisted, would "be carried much further, and then . . . your really beautiful time will come."

Two years later Howells was still waiting for his "beautiful time," when he inquired again about preparing future volumes of his forlorn edition. "We are going ahead with the collected set," his editor falsely assured him, "but heaven knows 1913 was the worst year the American publishers have had in more than [a] decade. We have got to see a little daylight before we can begin to run again."[4] The other volumes of the Library Edition, however, would never see the light of day; Howells had gone into eclipse, a victim of the same market forces that he saw at work and analyzed so perceptively in *A Hazard of New Fortunes* and *The World of Chance* (not to mention *A Traveller from Altruria*). The great democracy, he once notoriously quipped, invited her novelists to look at the more smiling aspects of life as, indeed, the more American. Perhaps it would have been more accurate for Howells to single out the susceptibilities of publishers instead of novelists in this regard. In their different ways, both Houghton Mifflin and Harper's smiled on Howells and invited him to recipro- cate; nevertheless, they took the measure of his surplus value and, in the end, found him wanting. Without the material basis for lasting appeal, Howells's sta- tus within the canon (as George H. Mifflin prophetically knew) has at best been cyclical rather than assured. In stark contrast to James's promise of deferred recognition, Howells soon became "comparatively a dead cult" (as he himself confessed), "with my statues cast down and the grass growing over them in the pale moonlight." The monument he so desperately needed—a complete Library Edition—was never raised in time.

To say this is not to suggest that we can attribute the comparative decline of Howells's literary standing solely to material factors. The fact remains, however, that through the New York Edition James has exercised remarkable control over his posthumous reputation. Once they were rediscovered, the prefaces that James wrote for his edition provided a kind of formalist gospel for the New Critics, who attended to the Master's resurrection; only recently have exegetes begun to think of these texts heretically as apocrypha.[5] The brilliant success of James's "testamentary act" (as Michael Millgate has called it)[6] can almost be measured in the corresponding neglect of Howells's fiction, because the modern- ist values that later critics derived from *The Art of the Novel* were largely incom- patible with the registering or analysis of historical meaning.

Howells himself anticipated this outcome with neither malice nor regret. Charles Eliot Norton, on the other hand, chafed at the same prospect. Much annoyed by James's mature style, Norton was dismayed to learn that Howells could respond so indulgently toward a book like *The Wings of the Dove*. After reading the adulatory essay on "Mr. Henry James's Later Work" in the *North American Review*, Norton ransacked his files to recover those early letters (from the 1870s) in which James had so condescendingly dismissed Howells's first literary efforts. Almost as if to embarrass Howells into repudiating James, Norton coolly sent these documents down to New York, expecting them to have a decisive effect. In this he was disappointed. "It was kind of you to include James's early letters to yourself," Howells promptly responded,

> and I wont pretend I have read them with less interest because of certain allusions to me in them. In a way I think their criticism very just; I have often thought my intellectual raiment was more than my intellectual body, and that I might finally be convicted, not of having nothing *on*, but that worse nakedness of having nothing *in*. He speaks of me with my style, and such mean application as I was making of it, as seeming to him like a poor man with a diamond which he does not know what to do with; and mostly I suppose I *have* cut rather inferior window glass with it. But I am not sorry for having wrought in common, crude material so much; that is the right American stuff; and perhaps hereafter, when my din is done, if any one is curious to know what that noise was it will be found to have proceeded from a small insect which was scraping about on the surface of our life and trying to get into its meaning for the sake of the other insects larger or smaller. That is, such has been my unconscious work; consciously, I was always, as I still am, trying to fashion a piece of literature out of the life next at hand.[7]

In spite of Norton's tactics, Howells's equanimity really comes as no surprise, for he had long been accustomed to receiving James's criticism directly from the Master's hand. His modest response, as John Updike has suggested, is beautifully unanswerable.

James would have recognized (and appreciated) the characteristic serenity in his friend's attitude. In the last years of their lives, the two men preferred to cross paths, not each other. Howells's European travels (often subsidized by Harper's) could still excite envious wonder in James, who now felt too encumbered to travel; but James also perceived that his friend's "capacity to knock about" assuaged "a restlessness in him that makes it a sharp need." ("If it were all mere elderly fire & flame," he quickly added, "it would be *too* humiliating—to one's self.")[8] The sharpness, as James knew, was aggravated by the death in 1910 of Howells's beloved wife, Elinor. The two men soon were companions in suffering: William and Robertson James also died that year. The Cambridge Cemetery was making neighbors of the families again.

One by one their mutual literary friends and acquaintances fell away: Lowell, Norton, Jewett, Twain. When James himself was stricken, in a winter already darkened by the European war, Howells felt utterly bereft. "He is the last that is left of my earthly world," the elder man tenderly confided.[9] James's cherished memory helped Howells endure the solitary years that remained.

Notes

The Great Goethe, the Good Schiller

1. WDH to Henry Mills Alden, 1 July 1897, SL 4: 151.

2. WDH, *Their Silver Wedding Journey*, 2 vols. (New York: Harper & Brothers, 1899), 1: 2, 3, 242; hereafter cited parenthetically as *SWJ*.

3. "I have got my semi-annual statement from Harpers, and the money with it—nearly three thousand. They did much better with the gorgeous Silver Wedding Journey than I expected, having sold 2700 sets, besides 1600 of the ordinary edition. I expect they will get rid of the whole fine edition, this coming Christmas and the next . . ." (WDH to John M. Howells, 22 July 1900, SL 4: 244).

4. As Burnamy cynically observes of his employer, "He has a notion of trying to come forward in politics. He owns shares in everything but the United States Senate—gas, electricity, railroads, aldermen, newspapers—and now he would like some Senate" (*SWJ* 1: 163). The young man's business associates tellingly refer to Stoller as the "Bird of Prey," anticipating HJ's fearful description of Abel Gaw in *The Ivory Tower* as a man "incapable of thought save in sublimities of arithmetic," who perches "like a ruffled hawk . . . with his beak, which had pecked so many hearts out, visibly sharper than ever. . . ." See *The American Novels and Stories of Henry James*, ed. F. O. Matthiessen (New York: Knopf, 1947), 869.

5. WDH to Aurelia H. Howells, 17 January 1897, SL 4: 141.

6. WDH to James B. Pond, 10 November 1899, SL 4: 225; Harrison T. Meserole, "The Dean in Person: Howells' Lecture Tour," *Western Humanities Review* 10 (1956): 338. An epistolary chronicle of WDH's lecturing experience can be traced in SL 4: 131–33, 141–49, 215–26. WDH had also prepared another lecture on "Heroes and Heroines," which he read several times but found less successful. This work became the starting point for *Heroines of Fiction*, 2 vols. (New York: Harper & Brothers, 1901), first serialized in *Harper's Bazar*.

7. WDH, "Novel-Writing and Novel-Reading, An Impersonal Explanation," in *Howells and James: A Double Billing*, ed. Leon Edel and William M. Gibson (New York: New York Public Library, 1958), 8, 20, 12.

8. Charles Eliot Norton to WDH, 29 August 1903, SL 5: 62n4.

9. WDH, *An Open-Eyed Conspiracy: An Idyl of Saratoga* (New York: Harper & Brothers, 1897), 11, 14, 35.

10. "It is insanity," Adams wrote to Lizzie Cameron on 6 May 1901, "and I think Harry must soon take a vacation, with most of the rest of us, in a cheery asylum" (*The Letters of Henry Adams* 5: 248). In his reader's report for Scribner's, W. C. Brownell (speaking exponentially) affirmed, "It is surely the n + 1st power of Jamesiness. . . . It gets decidedly on one's nerves. It is like trying to make out page after page of illegible writing." Brownell (who was reading the book in manuscript for Scribner's) nevertheless concluded that *The Sacred Fount* was a literary tour de force: publishable but probably not salable. See Roger Burlingame, *Of Making Many Books: A Hundred Years of Reading, Writing and Publishing* (New York: Charles Scribner's Sons, 1946), 36–37.

11. HJ to William Morton Fullerton, 9 August 1901, *HJL* 4: 197–98.

12. WDH to Aurelia H. Howells, 29 April 1900, *SL* 5: 235.

13. In September 1900 Harper's London agent, Miliam D. Fitts, enthusiastically recommended HJ's story on the basis of the elaborate scenario he had read.

> I don't know when I have been so pleased and satisfied with a synopsis as with this one of James's. It is exactly what I wanted him to do. The American life in it, transplanted to Paris, where James is absolutely at home, will I am sure appeal to a large audience in the United States. . . . I feel sure from his letters and talks with me, that you will have one of the best novels written by him, and it looks to me as if it ought to become one of the books of the year.

When HJ's scenario reached New York, however, Henry Mills Alden, editor of *Harper's Monthly*, spurned it with a snub worthy of Woollett, Massachusetts. "We ought to do better," he flatly wrote. Embarrassed by these conflicting opinions, the new president of Harper's, Colonel George B. McClellan Harvey, rather astonishingly proposed that HJ could make the novel more suitable for publication by throwing half of it away—a suggestion that the bewildered novelist adamantly rejected. ("I am staggered," HJ told his agent, "by the unexpected barbarity of his asking me at this time of day to take 70 000 words out of a thing of 150 000, contracted with no dream of any such mutilation.") Compounding the insult, the firm then announced that its London branch would not publish the novel in England, requiring HJ's agent to renegotiate the sale of foreign rights. The stalemate persisted until WDH intervened on HJ's behalf. See Miliam D. Fitts to Harvey, 15 September 1900, and Alden's undated reader's report, interleaved with the original typescript of HJ's "Project of Novel" (Harper Archive, Morgan Library); and HJ to James B. Pinker, 19 April 1901 (Collection of American Literature, Yale).

14. Herman Melville, *The Confidence-Man: His Masquerade* (1857), ed. Harrison Hayford et al., Northwestern-Newberry Edition of The Writings of Herman Melville, vol. 10 (Chicago: Northwestern University Press, 1984), 69. In this and two other brief chapters (numbers 33 and 44), Melville digresses on various sites of contradiction between writer and reader. In a letter (now famous) about Emerson, Melville quipped, "for the sake of the argument, let us call him a fool;—then had I rather be a fool than a wise man.—I love all men who *dive*. Any fish can swim near the surface, but it takes a great whale to go down stairs five miles or more; & if he dont attain the bottom, why, all the lead in Galena can't fashion the plummet that will." See Melville to Evert A. Duyckinck, 3 March 1849, in Herman Melville, *Correspondence*, ed. Lynn Horth, Northwestern-Newberry Edition, vol. 14 (Chicago: Northwestern University Press and the Newberry Library, 1993), 121.

15. At this time Pinker also negotiated terms for a new novel about American life, but James never completed it. See James B. Pinker to Col. Harvey, 18 April 1904, Harper Contract Books, 11: 340 (*The Archives of Harper and Brothers*, reel 4).

16. WDH to Elizabeth Jordan, 1 June 1904, *SL* 5: 103. Hearing rumors of HJ's possi-

ble return to the States, the irrepressible Major James B. Pond immediately sent a "flaming appeal" for the Master to hit the popular lecture circuit—"to be as vividly declined as you may believe!" HJ said. HJ to Alice H. G. James, 16 May 1904 (James Papers, Harvard).

17. Indeed, when WJ tried to discourage his brother from purchasing Lamb House (a needless extravagance, he thought, for a bachelor), the novelist responded by comparing his own meager conditions with the amplitude of other writers. "My whole being cries out aloud for something that I can call my own," HJ answered,

> and when I look round me at the splendour of so many of the "literary" fry my confrères (M. Crawfords, P. Bourgets, Humphry Wards, Hodgson Burnetts, W. D. Howellses etc.) and I feel that I may strike the world as still, at fifty-six, with my long labour and my genius, reckless, presumptious and unwarranted in curling up (for more assured peaceful production), in a poor little $10,000 shelter—once for all and for all time—*then* I do feel the bitterness of humiliation, the iron enters into my soul, and (I blush to confess it), I *weep!* (*HJL* 4: 115)

18. HJ to James B. Pinker, 22 October 1904 (Collection of American Literature, Yale).

19. WDH to Elinor M. Howells, [April 1904], *SL* 5: 92n3; WDH to Thomas Sergeant Perry, 5 July 1905, *SL* 5: 126.

20. WDH to Charles Eliot Norton, 10 September 1905, *SL* 5: 133. On 14 August 1905 HJ had written to Elinor Mead Howells about his "2 wondrous days at Kittery Point and at Sara Jewett's place—so wondrous has everything become to me since my return here—in such iridescence does it all shine as seen from the re-entered, contracted tent of the Pilgrim at rest" (*If Not Literature*, 299).

21. HJ, *The American Scene*, in *Collected Travel Writings: Great Britain and America* (New York: Library of America, 1993), 414–15. To document HJ's motive of consecration, Rosalie Hewitt has shown that the final paragraph of the article was appended after it had been set up in galley proof for the *North American Review*; see "Henry James's 'Autumn Impression': The History, the Manuscript, the Howells Relation," *Yale University Library Gazette* 57 (October 1982): 39–51.

Testamentary Acts

1. HJ to James B. Pinker, 11 May 1905 (Collection of American Literature, Yale).

2. See Anesko, *"Friction With the Market"*, 141–62; and "Ambiguous Allegiances: Conflicts of Culture and Ideology in the Making of the New York Edition," in *Henry James's New York Edition: The Construction of Authorship*, ed. David McWhirter (Stanford: Stanford University Press, 1995), 77–89. Also useful are Philip Horne's overview and chronology of the New York Edition's history in *Henry James and Revision: The New York Edition* (Oxford: Clarendon Press, 1990), 1–19, 325–57.

3. William Dean Howells, "The Man of Letters as a Man of Business" [1893], *Literature and Life* (New York: Harper & Brothers, 1902), 15.

4. John Tebbel, *A History of Book Publishing in the United States*, 4 vols. (New York: Bowker, 1972–81), 2: 525–26. Grant's estate eventually received a total of $420,000 from Charles L. Webster & Company.

5. William S. McFeely, *Grant: A Biography* (New York: W. W. Norton, 1981), p. 501.

6. WDH to Clemens, 11 December 1885, *Mark Twain–Howells Letters*, 2: 545.

7. WDH, "Editor's Study," *Harper's Monthly* 72 (March 1886): 649–50.

8. "Subscription Books and 'The Library of Modern Authors,'" *The Book Buyer* 36 (September 1911): 134.

9. George H. Mifflin to Albert F. Houghton, 28 December 1896, Mifflin Letterbooks, 9: 792 (Houghton Mifflin Archive, Harvard). Subsequent references to unpublished letters from this series of letterbooks will be abbreviated GML, followed by the volume and page numbers.

10. George H. Mifflin to Albert F. Houghton, 30 December 1896, GML 9: 798.

11. George H. Mifflin to Albert F. Houghton, 30 December 1896, GML 9: 799–800. Mifflin's concern about the long-term viability of the firm's subscription department did not abate. In 1902 he suggested that "if in order to stop the dwindling sale of Standard Authors it is necessary to reduce prices, and change styles, we must face that problem. It may prove to be necessary to do this, or to make at least some radical change. Otherwise our business in Standard Authors may disappear" (Mifflin to Houghton, 8 August 1902, GML 11: 771). A collection of "prospectuses and other printed ephemera" for fine printing by firms other than Houghton, Mifflin & Company, assembled from 1901–3, also speaks to Mifflin's worries. These documents are preserved in the Houghton Mifflin Archive at Harvard (MS Am 2030.4 [11]).

12. George H. Mifflin to WDH, 5 January 1897, GML 9: 804.

13. WDH to George H. Mifflin, 8 January 1897, SL 4: 140; Mifflin to WDH, 22 January 1897, GML 9: 813.

14. George H. Mifflin to Albert F. Houghton, 22 January 1897, GML 9: 816.

15. George H. Mifflin to Albert F. Houghton, 1 Feb. 1897, GML 9: 829.

16. George H. Mifflin to Elizabeth Stuart Phelps Ward, 2 July 1897, quoted in Ellen B. Ballou, *The Building of the House: Houghton Mifflin's Formative Years* (Boston: Houghton Mifflin, 1970), 424.

17. Other internal documents from the company's files suggest that Houghton, Mifflin was also anxious about the future sales of Howells's work; this was, indeed, one of the criticisms that Mifflin first tried to deflect. Someone had his eye on the ledgers, for surviving records document that the sales of many Howells titles on the firm's list dropped off quite radically in 1895 and 1896, compared to prior years. For some books the decline is as much as 30 or 40 percent. Had Howells oversaturated his own market by virtue of his incessant productivity? Had his increasingly radical social and economic views (recently articulated in the utopian romance *A Traveller from Altruria* [1894]) alienated his public? Or was the decline in interest in Howells—especially in the very early books that Houghton controlled—simply a natural process, concomitant with age? Howells was also a very careful reader of royalty reports, and he, too, must have noticed the unusual shrinkage. Indeed, it is quite possible that declining sales prompted him to push for a new collected edition, which might serve precisely to rejuvenate his sagging market status. That had clearly been the effect of Houghton, Mifflin's 1891 "Holiday" edition of *Venetian Life*, for example, which sold five thousand copies the first year, in spite of a steep retail price of five dollars. See Houghton Mifflin Copyright Accounts, vol. 7 (Houghton Mifflin Archive, Harvard).

18. WDH to Charles Eliot Norton, 12 October 1902, SL 5: 137.

19. WDH to George H. Mifflin, 24 May 1905 (Houghton Mifflin Archive, Harvard).

20. WDH to Frederick A. Duneka, 7 July 1905, Harper Contract Books 11: 423 (*The Archives of Harper and Brothers*, reel 4). No record survives of a Houghton, Mifflin letter to Howells dated in early July, but it is possible that Howells is referring back to a letter of 25 May in which Mifflin assured him that the "Harper arrangement will undoubtedly work itself out to a satisfactory issue. We shall certainly do our part" (GML 9: 538).

21. Houghton, Mifflin & Co. to Charles Scribner's Sons, 25 October 1905 (Scribner Archive, Princeton).

22. George H. Mifflin to James B. Pinker, 25 November 1905 (Scribner Archive, Princeton).

23. WDH to Joseph A. Howells, 4 July 1909, *SL* 5: 279.

24. "Howells' Complete Works," *New York Times Book Review*, 6 August 1911, 480. Two weeks earlier, the paper had noted that "one of the chief tasks involved in bringing out this uniform edition of his works consists in negotiating with his various publishers for permission to include such titles as they control in this set." Since both these announcements probably were supplied by Harper editors, they represent a strategy to stimulate popular demand for the series, which might then embarrass and reverse Houghton, Mifflin's anticipated intransigence. See "New York Literary Notes," *New York Times Book Review*, 23 July 1911, 464.

25. Houghton Mifflin Co. to Harper & Brothers, 11 August 1911; Harper & Brothers to Houghton Mifflin Co., 13 August 1911, "Miscellaneous Correspondence Re: Contracts" (*The Archives of Harper and Brothers*, reel 57).

Terminations

1. WDH, "The Man of Letters as a Man of Business," 19.

2. J. Henry Harper, *The House of Harper: A Century of Publishing in Franklin Square* (New York: Harper & Brothers, 1912), 330.

3. Harper Royalty Ledgers, 8: 890; 10: 877 (*The Archives of Harper and Brothers*, reels 43, 45).

4. Frederick A. Duneka to WDH, 5 February 1914 (Howells Papers, American Antiquarian Society).

5. See, for example, Hershel Parker, "Deconstructing *The Art of the Novel* and Liberating the Prefaces," *Henry James Review* 14 (1993): 284–307.

6. Michael Millgate, *Testamentary Acts: Browning, Tennyson, James, Hardy* (Oxford: Clarendon Press, 1992).

7. WDH to Charles Eliot Norton, 26 April 1903, *SL* 5: 54.

8. HJ to Edmund Gosse, 19 September 1911, *Selected Letters of Henry James to Edmund Gosse*, p. 255.

9. WDH to Henry James III, 15 December 1915, *SL* 6: 89.

William Dean Howells in 1904. By permission of the Houghton Library, Harvard University.

Henry James at the time of his American tour (1904–5). By permission of the Houghton Library, Harvard University.

Letters and
Documents

96.

HOWELLS TO JAMES, 10 September 1899, Kittery Point   ALS Houghton
                                                            bMS Am 1094 (250)

Kittery Point, Maine,
Sept. 10, 1899.

My dear James:

I feel very guilty towards you, though you have had time enough to forget my sin of omission. The trouble was that I had not read The Awkward Age, and I was waiting to do so before I wrote. I have not read it even yet, though at last I am writing. I began with the brilliant beginning in the Weekly, and found that way of doing it too harassing; when the book came out, I promised myself to read it in the summer, and now it is September.[1] But I am always there, and so is the book. In the meantime I have come upon some old Atlantics in this house (the house of a sea-faring painter whose father was D. A. Wasson, a much-writing Unitarian parson of the '60s,)[2] and found in one a brave early story of yours, which I had never forgotten, called A Most Extraordinary Case.[3] I don't believe you've any idea how good it is; it is masterly, with an amazing grip on "cultivated American" character, which made me feel you ought never to have relaxed that hold. It made me feel proud of having admired you always, and eager to print your incomparable work.

Well, we have been here since Mid-June, beside a reefy and shippy shore, with sails by day and lamps by night, all over the water, and a sunrise and sunset gun from an obsolete fort across the harbor. The air is such as you breathe

---

1. Harper's published The Awkward Age as a volume in April 1899.
2. David A. Wasson (1823–87), Unitarian clergyman and author; his son, George S. Wasson (1855–1931), WDH's landlord, was a painter and magazine writer.
3. "A Most Extraordinary Case," Atlantic (April 1868).

nowhere else in the world, and the fisher-folk life quaint and old as the 17th century.—I have been writing some lectures, which I have been fool enough to agree giving this winter in the West,[4] and doing some other odd jobs: mainly the *Literature* letters which have fallen wholly to me since your time. They will stop with the year, me nothing sorry, and then I have a whacking scheme in view which I will tell you of later.[5] There have been cataclysmal changes at Franklin Square.[6] The earth there has opened and taken in McClure and his company, where never was anything but Harpers before. Really I lost half a night's sleep in surprise and grief, and well-nigh forgot the shame of the Phillipine war. The magazine goes down to $3 a year, but the quality will keep up, and the opportunities will remain the same; certainly they will be no worse. The new house will publish six periodicals.

Mrs. Howells, who joins me in these greetings, and I are just now alone, waiting for the children, as we still call them. Pilla has been away visiting a girl-friend in the Catskills,[7] and John all summer in New York. The first prize in the great California University Buildings competition,[8] goes to a Frenchman, but John's house comes in for the second, and ahead of all other competitors. He feels it a great triumph, and I dare say wont hear a word against the prime victor when he comes to-morrow: that is his high nature.

4. WDH's lecture tour began on 19 October 1899 in Ypsilanti, Michigan. Speaking on "Novel Writing and Novel Reading," WDH had twenty-five engagements in various midwestern cities. For details of the tour, see Harrison T. Meserole, "The Dean in Person: Howells' Lecture Tour," *Western Humanities Review* 10 (1956): 337–47; for the text of the lecture, see *Howells and James: A Double Billing*, ed. Leon Edel and Lyall H. Powers (New York: New York Public Library, 1958), 7–24.

5. WDH had begun negotiations with Clarke & Company of New York to edit a series of novels for newspaper syndication. His efforts to enlist HJ in this "scheme" are detailed in subsequent letters.

6. A victim of the economic turbulence of the 1890s, Harper & Brothers foundered in the spring of 1899. Unable to pay its debts, the company was reorganized by a new management team from the financial house of J. P. Morgan. Samuel Sidney McClure (1857–1949), who had pioneered the syndication of newspaper journalism in the 1880s, agreed to invest heavily in the company's stock and take over its direction, but was forced to withdraw in October 1899 when he failed to raise the needed capital. Morgan then asked Colonel George B. McClellan Harvey (1864–1928), a newspaperman who had also accumulated a fortune in public utilities transactions, to take charge. Harvey discovered that the firm was in even worse shape than anyone suspected, and he recommended that it go into receivership, which it did on 4 December 1899. Harvey then became president of the firm, acting as receiver for Morgan's State Trust Company. WDH first learned of the firm's collapse as he was returning from his western lecture tour; the morning paper brought him the news. "It was as if I had read that the government of the United States had failed," he recalled. "It appeared not only incredible, but impossible; it was, as Mr. J. Pierpont Morgan said, a misfortune of the measure of a national disaster." See J. Henry Harper, *The House of Harper*, 324.

7. Mildred Howells was vacationing with Julia S. Dwight (1870–1958), an artist friend, at her summer place in Haines Falls, New York.

8. In October 1896 Phoebe Apperson Hearst (1842–1919), a California mining heiress, organized an architectural competition for the design of the University of California campus at Berkeley. Nearly one hundred firms from around the world submitted plans; eleven, including the partnership of Howells, Stokes, and Hornbostel, were awarded prizes.

I hope you are well. Smalley-wise[9] I have had some news of you at your country-seat; but nothing satisfying, and I hardly dare ask anything direct.—I should think myself in pretty good shape, if it were not for the phantom of a small eliptical caterpillar which shows itself in my right eye. It is from a strain, I believe, and the oculists say it means nothing, but it annoys.—It is a divine day, of white sunshine and a southern wind. I hate to think of going back to New York in three weeks more.

Yours affectionately
W. D. Howells.

97.

JAMES TO HOWELLS, 25 September 1899, Rye   ALS Houghton
bMS Am 1784 (253) 73

Sept. 25th. 1899.
LAMB HOUSE, RYE.

My dear old Friend.

I take your genial letter from Kittery's Point as a great kindness & a great charity. Let us not, at this late day, have any question of "turns," in such communication, & communion, as may still contrive to enhance the comparatively contracted remnant of our years. I am quite capable, I warn you, (& even not improbable,) of following up this with other utterance even should temporary silence be your own necessity. *Giusto*.[1] I was (one says those things, but to this I'll swear,) on the point of writing to you to ask you to post to me the benefit of the *Ragged Lady*,[2] your novel that you mentioned to me so long as nearly 2 years ago as then finished, that has since then, I gather, been put forth as a book, & that I yearn to read in a copy not bought with vulgar gold but having my name in it as from your hand. Will you do this?—definitely? My articulate thanks will then be, *as* definitely, your portion. Àpropos of which matters I confess I'm sorry to hear from you that you've not read that much-battered (I'm told) *Awkward Age* that you so kindly (&, you may feel, so blindly,) godfathered: all the more that you won't ever, now—for it's one of those things that, if not done at the time, as it were, get fatally out of hand. On the other hand, I'm very glad you didn't read the thing serially, for I feel that it's only as a book that it compactly exists—that it isn't read *at all* unless so read. This, of course, was not my intention, but just the opposite: what happened was that I found the subject had much more to *give*, was still more curious & rich than it had first struck me as having & being, & that in short it grew & rounded itself on my

---

9. Phoebe Garnaut Smalley was summering in New England.

1. That's as it should be.

2. WDH completed *Ragged Lady* in the autumn of 1897; it was serialized in *Harper's Bazar* from July to November 1898 and appeared as a volume in February 1899.

hands.[3] This made it longer, much, than the 70,000 words intended—&, I'm afraid, awakened the disgust, thereby, of Editor & Publishers; at least I never heard from them, at all definitely that it *didn't:* so that I've sat in darkness ever since, under the dreadful sense of having failed (as if I were 25 again,) in the chance you had got for me. And yet, to my own perverse perception, nothing I've ever done is better—firmer, fuller, more unbrokenly sustained; in every way more expert & mature. *That* I only want to say to justify my regret at your not having been able to tackle it. But now wait for the next! I'm only sorry there is at present no track laid *for* a next—& I labour under the drawback that the *book* brings me still so little money that I can't afford to take the time to write one in the absence of *some* presumption of being able to serialize it. However, I shall fight this out better now that I'm really settled in the country—& meantime I didn't mean to afflict you afresh with my ignoble secrets. I'm doing a good deal in brevities—trying to learn to write "short stories" again as in the old days of the "Galaxy." The devil is that no periodical will *take* now anything of anything *like* the length of "The Extraordinary Case," your kind words about which, after long years, so greatly touch me. To be mature in 5000 words is rather, *for* the mature, (25 years can do it, doubtless,) a sickening effort.—Very strange, but less "intimate" to me, naturally, than to you, the transformation of the Harper business, periodicals &c.—very obscure also, so long as unexplained & unvivified. Also, further, somehow, rather saddening & crushing, as representing moves farther & farther away from "literature"—if indeed any move in any such direction have been, for a long time, left to be made. I hadn't realized the proportions of the particular abyss, which your letter seems to send a red spark fluttering down into. I had, just before it arrived, dropped (through my "literary agent,")[4] a small packet of MS. into the black gulf; addressed, that is, in spite of the A. A., a short fiction (about 8000 words,) to "Harper"—or addressed, rather, I believe, an inquiry as to whether they would care for it. Should you, by any remote chance, hear any of the now, (isn't it?) so strangely-commingled company, wondering if they *do* care for a small masterpiece called "The Beldonald Holbein," throw out a hint to them that they are quite probably enchanted with it.[5] Can you in any way reveal to me who is the new (or actual) editor of *The Atlantic?*[6] It's queer to be coming to you at this time of day with

---

3. Compare HJ's original journal entry, dated 4 March 1895: "The idea of the little London girl who grows up to 'sit with' the free-talking modern young mother—reaches 17, 18 etc.—comes out—and, not marrying, has to 'be there'—and, though the conversation is supposed to be expurgated for her, inevitably hears, overhears, guesses, follows, takes in, becomes acquainted with, horrors. A real little subject in this, I think—a real little situation for a short tale—if circumstance and setting is really given it" (CN 117–8).

4. After much deliberation, in 1898 HJ had engaged the services of James B. Pinker (1863–1922), one of the first and most successful literary agents, to help him place manuscripts and negotiate terms.

5. Henry Mills Alden eventually published HJ's story in *Harper's Monthly* (October 1901).

6. Horace E. Scudder's immediate successor at the *Atlantic* was Walter Hines Page (1855–1918), who edited the magazine during 1898–99; Page, in turn, was replaced by Bliss Perry (1860–1954), who stayed on as editor from 1899–1909.

such questions—but I'm in the grossest darkness, & have been for a long time, at the hands of that periodical, & yet it *may* come to pass that my "literary agent," though not of much use for anywhere but this country, shall find himself approaching the cold theatre of my early triumphs as a supplicant. But a truce to these sordid images.

—I'm infinitely interested in your personal & paternal news. How you make me yearn for a walk with you on the Maine rocks, or through the Maine woods, or by the Maine sea. Your summer history sounds delightful—& to have *all* that "& Heaven too" (by which I mean California too, & its golden crowns, in the form of the victorious John,) must indeed have warmed your innards. I rejoice immensely over what you tell me of John's career & the rate at which it moves. Please transmit to him my blessing & tell him that I pat him on the back till he chokes. Oh, I remember, too, "Wassons" & things. But they seem very ghostly. I have had a very quiet, solitary & extremely rural summer (since July 10$^{\underline{th}}$, when I came back from 4 months in Italy,) & I cultivate this prospect for the months to come—save that I am now looking, from week to week, for the advent of my brother W$^{\underline{m}}$ & his wife & daughter—he fresh (if fresh that can be called,) from a long cure at Nauheim where an evil *heart* has most woefully forced him to seek amelioration. He has in some degree found it, I believe, but he spends the winter on this side of the sea. I remain here till January or February—I find the country more & more a source of profit & even of rejuvenescence—a simplifica-tion to good ends. I send *Tanti saluti*[7] to Mrs. Howells & I keep tight hold of the memory of Mildred. *Don't* forget the Ragged Lady—& believe, my dear Howells, in the perfect fidelity of your very old friend,

the Ragged Gentleman
Henry James

98.

JAMES TO HOWELLS, 29 June 1900, Rye   TLS Houghton
bMS Am 1784 (253) 74

Lamb House, Rye.
29th June, 1900

My dear Howells,

I can't emulate your wonderful little cursive type on your delicate little sheets—the combination of which seems to suggest that you dictate, at so much an hour, to an Annisquam fairy; but I will do what I can and make out to be intelligible to you even over the joy it is, ever and always, to hear from you.[1] You say that had you not been writing me the particular thing you were, you fear you wouldn't have been writing at all; but it is a compliment I can better. I really believe that if I weren't writing you this, on my side, I *should* be writing

7. Many greetings.
1. WDH's letter, posted from Annisquam, on Cape Ann in Massachusetts, is not extant.

you something else. For I've been, of late, reading you again as continuously as possible—the worst I mean by which is as continuously as the booksellers consent; and the result of "Ragged Lady," the "Silver Journey," the "Pursuit of the Piano"[2] and two or three other things (none wrested from your inexorable hand, but paid for from scant earnings) has been, ever so many times over, an impulse of reaction, of an intensely cordial sort, directly *at* you—all, alas, spending itself, for sad and sore want of you, in the heavy air of this alien clime and the solitude, here, of my unlettered life. I wrote to you to Kittery Point—I think it was—something like a year ago, and my chief occupation since then has been listening for the postman's knock. But let me quickly add that I understand overwhelmingly well what you say of the impossibility for you, at this time of day, of letters. God knows they *are* impossible—the great fatal, incurable, unpumpable leak of one's poor sinking bark. Non ragionam'di lor[3]—I understand all about it; and it only adds to the pleasure with which, even on its personal side, I greet your present communication.

This communication, let me, without a shred of coyness, instantly declare, much interests and engages me—to the degree even that I think I find myself prepared to post you on the spot a round, or a square, Rather! I won't go through any simpering as to the goodness of your "having thought of me"—nor even through any frank gaping (though there might be, for my admiration and awe, plenty of that!) over the wonder of your multiform activity and dauntlessly universal life. Basta that I will write anything in life that anyone asks me in decency—and a fortiori[4] that *you* so gracefully ask. I can only feel it to be enough for me that you have a hand in the affair, that you are giving a book yourself and engaging yourself otherwise, and that I am in short in your company.[5] What I understand is that my little novel shall be of fifty thousand (50,000) words, neither more, I take it, nor less; that I should deliver it to you before December next; and that I shall receive the sum mentioned in the prospectus "down," in advance of royalties, on such delivery. (I shall probably in point of fact, in my financial humility, prefer, when the time comes, to avail

2. *Ragged Lady* and *Their Silver Wedding Journey*, both published by Harper's in 1899; "The Pursuit of the Piano," a short story, appeared in *Harper's Monthly* (April 1900) and was collected with several other tales in *A Pair of Patient Lovers* (Harper's, 1901).

3. Let us not speak of it. These were Virgil's words to Dante as they were crossing the gateway into hell (*Inferno* III).

4. All the more.

5. Earlier in 1900 WDH had agreed to edit a series of novels by prominent English and American authors for newspaper syndication, which was to be handled by James Clarke, president of Clarke & Company of New York. In pursuit of this enterprise, WDH solicited work from George Ade, Thomas Bailey Aldrich, James Lane Allen, George Washington Cable, Henry Blake Fuller, Hamlin Garland, Anstry Guthrie, Joel Chandler Harris, Henry James, Mary Noailles Murfree, Howard Pyle, James Whitcomb Riley, Francis Hopkinson Smith, Frank R. Stockton, Mark Twain, Mrs. Humphry Ward, Charles Dudley Warner, Mary E. Wilkins, and possibly others. HJ was one of the few who responded favorably, however; and when WDH discovered that Clarke was formerly a partner in the Canadian firm of Belford & Clarke, which had pirated his work years earlier, he abandoned the project altogether.

myself of the alternative right mentioned in the prospectus—that of taking, instead of a royalty, for the two years "lease", the larger sum formed by the so-much-a-word aggregation. But that I shall be clear about when the work is done; I only glance at this now as probable.) It so happens that I can get at the book, I think, almost immediately and do it within the next three or four months. You will therefore, unless you hear from me a short time hence to the contrary, probably receive it well before December. As for the absoluteness of the "order," I am willing to take it as, practically, sufficiently absolute. If you shouldn't like it, there is something else, definite enough, that I can do with it. What, however, concerns me more than anything else is to take care that you *shall* like it. I tell myself that I am not afraid!

I brood with mingled elation and depression on your ingenious, your really inspired, suggestion that I shall give you a ghost, and that my ghost shall be "international." I say inspired because, singularly enough, I set to work some months ago at an international ghost, and on just this scale, 50,000 words; entertaining for a little the highest hopes of him. He was to have been wonderful and beautiful; he was to have been called (perhaps too metaphysically) "The Sense of the Past";[6] and he was to have been supplied to a certain Mr. Doubleday[7] who was then approaching me—had then approached me—as the most outstretched arm of the reconstructed Harpers. The outstretched arm, however, alas, was drawn in again, or lopped off, or otherwise paralysed and negatived, and I was left with my little project—intrinsically, I hasten to add, and most damnably difficult—on my hands. Doubleday simply vanished into space, without explanation or apology; the proposal having been wholly his own and made, as pleaded, in consequence of a charmed perusal of the "Turn of the Screw." It is very possible, however, it is indeed most probable, that I should have broken down in the attempt to do him this particular thing, and this particular thing (divine, sublime, if I *could* do it) is not, I think, what I shall now attempt to nurse myself into a fallacious faith that I shall be able to pull off for Howells and Clarke. The damnable *difficulty* is the reason; I have rarely been beaten by a subject, but I felt myself, after upwards of a month's work, destined to be beaten by that one. This will sufficiently hint to you how awfully good it is. But it would take too long for me to tell you here, more vividly, just how and why; it would, as well, to tell you, still more subtly and irresistibly, why it's difficult. There it lies, and probably will always lie.

I'm not even sure that the international ghost is what will most bear being worried out—though, again, in another particular, the circumstances, combining with your coincident thought, seemed pointed by the finger of providence. What Doubleday wanted was two Tales—each tales of "terror" and making another duplex book like the "Two Magics". Accordingly I had had (dreadful deed!) to

6. After completing the first two and a half sections of this novel, HJ set it aside. He returned to it in 1914, when he dictated an elaborate plan for revising his original conception. The unfinished novel and HJ's surviving notes concerning it were published posthumously.

7. Frank Nelson Doubleday (1862–1934) had dissolved a publishing partnership with S. S. McClure and in 1900 joined with Walter Hines Page to form Doubleday, Page & Company.

puzzle out more or less a second, a different, piece of impudence of the same general type. But I had only, when the project collapsed, caught hold of the tip of the tail of this other monster—whom I now mention because his tail seemed to show him as necessarily still more international than No. 1. If I can at all recapture *him*, or anything like him, I will do my best to sit down to him and "mount" him with due neatness. In short, I will do what I can. If I can't be terrible, I shall nevertheless still try to be international. The difficulties are that it's difficult to be terrible save in the short piece and international save in the long. But trust me. I add little more. This by itself will begin by alarming you as a precipitate installment of my responsive fury. I rejoice to think of you as basking on your Indian shore. *This* shore is as little Indian as possible, and we have hitherto—for the season—had to combat every form of inclemency. To-day, however, is so charming that, frankly, I wish you were all planted in a row in the little old garden into which I look as I write to you. Old as it is (a couple of hundred years) it wouldn't be too old even for Mildred. But these thoughts undermine. The "country scenes" in your books make me homesick for New England smells and even sounds. Annisquam, for instance, is a smell as well as a sound. May it continue sweet to you! Charles Norton and Sally[8] were with me lately for a day or two, and you were one of the first persons mentioned between us. You were *the* person mentioned most tenderly. It was strange and pleasant and sad, and all sorts of other things, to see Charles again after so many years. I found him utterly unchanged and remarkably young. But I found myself, *with* him, Methusalesque and alien! I shall write you again when my subject condenses. I embrace you all and am yours, my dear Howells,

always,
Henry James.

I return Mr. Clarke's letter to you.

99.

HOWELLS TO JAMES, 15 July 1900, Annisquam, Mass.

TLS Houghton
bMS Am 1094 (251)

Annisquam,
July 15th, 1900.

My dear James:

Something in your cordial acceptance of my invitation for the great Authors and Newspapers enterprise alarms me with the fear that I did not make it plain how conditional the enterprise is. To most people I wrote that if a certain number could not be got to contribute, the thing would stop, and I now write to present this fact boldly to you if I failed to do it before. As yet I have got only six or seven authors to promise books, so many are highly contracted for, and so

8. Charles Eliot Norton and his daughter Sara.

many are governed by the reluctance of their regular publishers. The obstacles are many and the displeasures are such that my own courage has not held out as to my relation to the enterprise, but whether I keep on with it or not, I believe you will be safe in chancing a book with it, if it comes to trial. I think you will do well to take the proffered $2500, rather than the percentage on sales, and if you like, I will myself do your bargaining with the enterpriser; perhaps I can get better terms still, and at any rate I believe I can get better terms than you could. But what I am anxious about now is that you should not create your spectre without this warning that possibly the enterprise may fail him at the very hour when he needs its support. If as you say, you can place him elsewhere in such an event, go gaily on; I at least believe the chances are so good that they are worth your trying for, and whether I continue editor of the affair or not, I am myself going to contribute a book. I should like for once to see a book of mine thoroughly put before the public, instead of being left to grope its way. Of course one is more or less corrupted by the spectacle of the immense successes around one, and it galls me that I should sell only as many thousands as the gilded youth of both sexes are selling hundred thousands, and largely as I believe for want of publicity—that is the new word for advertising. You speak of one of the books which I have been guilty of not sending you (with shame I own it) and I cannot see the name of it even type-writing without rage, for Their Silver Wedding Journey was got out as a holiday book about a week before Christmas and then left to meet its fate after all the holiday books had been bought. After that they published the regular edition, and it was only by following the publishers up with unsparing vigor that I could make them let the public into the secret of its existence. Even yet I have not got them to announce it in the Harper periodicals!—But enough of this so sordid theme.[1]

I can understand your hunger for New England, in these later years. I feel it myself in New York, even, though it is not my country. It has a sort of strange, feminine fascination. It is like a girl, sometimes a young girl, and sometimes an old girl, but wild and shy and womanly sweet, always, with a sort of unitarian optimism in its air. Here on Cape Ann the charm is ruggeder than anywhere else, with a bleakness, which is irresistible, and a beauty that is indescribable. The house we have was the home of a granite quarry magnate, who made it everything that the family of such a man could desire, with hot and cold water, its own gasoline plant and all the modern improvements, not to mention a hill of red pines behind it and all Ipswich Bay before; and then died out of it, leaving it a dire possession to his widow.[2] It is walled and terraced up like Switzerland, and I have made my cornfield and melon patch in the old wilding flower gardens. There is an avenue of roses and syringas and smoke-trees to the trolley cars, and we look across a little hollow to the old Universalist church, on its green under its elms, across the roofs of white houses inhabited by old single

1. Harper's published a deluxe holiday edition of *Their Silver Wedding Journey* in two volumes on 8 December 1899 and, from new plates, in one volume in 1900.
2. Mrs. Elizabeth F. Bennett, wife of Henry H. Bennett.

women of all sorts, sometimes living alone in their great harking mansions, with burning heaps and masses of flowers in their dooryards. There is also the gray hut of a clam-man and the square, central chimneyed house of a short-lobster man—so called because he sells lobsters of less than the legal length—and the neat dwellings of many other villagers, half-farmers, half-fishers, mild-voiced, gentle-mannered, and every one ready for a joke. Half a mile off, down at the point where old piers are, from which the venturers of fifty years ago used to sail from their own doors for India and Cathay, is a settlement of summer folks, living in the primitive shells of thirty years ago, such as were built before people began to plaster their summer houses. They are rather an arid lot, and they leave us quite to ourselves, with either a savage indifference, or a savage diffidence, I don't know which, but at any rate acceptable. We are the freer to join in love to you, and the wish somehow to see you soon again. We read you with a touching constancy, and adore your art, with violent exceptions.

Yours ever,
W. D. Howells.

100.

JAMES TO HOWELLS, 9 and 14 August 1900, Rye

TLS Houghton
bMS Am 1784 (253) 75

Read P. S., (Aug. 14th first!)

Lamb House, Rye.
August 9, 1900.

My dear Howells,

I duly received and much pondered your second letter, charming and vivid, from Annisquam; the one, I mean, in reply to mine dispatched immediately on the receipt of your first. If I haven't since its arrival written to you, this is because, precisely, I needed to work out my question somewhat further first. My impulse was immediately to say that I wanted to do my little stuff at any rate, and was willing therefore to take any attendant risk, however measured, as the little stuff would be, at the worst, a thing I should see my way to dispose of in another manner. But the problem of the little stuff itself intrinsically worried me—to the extent, I mean, of my not feeling thoroughly sure I might make of it what I wanted and above all what your conditions of space required. The thing was therefore to try and satisfy myself practically—by threshing out my subject to as near an approach to certainty as possible. This I have been doing with much intensity—but with the result, I am sorry to say, of being still in the air. Let the present accordingly pass for a provisional communication—not to leave your last encompassed with too much silence. Lending myself as much as possible to your suggestion of a little "tale of terror" that should be also International, I took straight up again the idea I spoke to you of having already, some months ago, tackled and, for various reasons, laid aside. I have been attacking it again with intensity and on the basis of a simplification that would make it easier, and have done for it, thus, 110 pages of type. The upshot of this, alas, however, is that though this second start is, if I—or if *you*—like, magnificent, it seriously confronts me with the element of *length*; showing me, I fear, but too vividly, that, do what I will for compression, I shall not be able to squeeze my subject into 50,000 words. It will make, even if it doesn't, for difficulty, still beat me, 70,000 or 80,000—dreadful to say; and that faces me as an excessive addition to the ingredient of "risk" we speak of. On the other hand I am not sure that I can hope to substitute for this particular affair *another* affair of "terror" which *will* be expressible in the 50,000; and that for an especial reason. This reason is that, above all when one has done the thing, already, as I have, rather repeatedly, it is not easy to concoct a "ghost" of any freshness. The want of ease is extremely marked, moreover, if the thing is to be done on a certain scale of length. One might still toss off a spook or two more if it were a question only of the "short-story" dimension; but prolongation and extension constitute a strain which the merely *apparitional*—discounted, also, as by my past dealings with it, doesn't do enough to mitigate. The beauty of this notion of "The Sense of the Past" of which I have again, as I tell you, been astride, is precisely that it involves without the stale effect of the mere bloated bugaboo, the presentation, for folk both in and out of the book, of such a sense of gruesome *malaise* as can only—success being assumed—make the fortune, in the "literary world," of everyone concerned. I haven't, in it, really (that is save in one very partial preliminary and expository connection,) to make anything, or anybody, "appear" to anyone: what the case involves is, awfully interestingly and thrillingly, that the "central figure", the subject of the experience, has the terror of a particular ground for feeling and fearing that *he himself* is, or may be, may at any moment become, a producer, an object, of this (for you and me) state of panic on the part of others. He lives in an air of *malaise* as to the *malaise* he may, woefully, more or less fatally, find himself creating—and that, roughly speaking, is the essence of what I have seen. It is less gross, much less *banal* and exploded, than the dear old familiar bugaboo; produces, I think, for the reader, an almost equal funk—or at any rate an equal suspense and unrest; and carries with it, as I have "fixed" it, a more truly curious and interesting drama—especially a more human one. *But,* as I say, there are the necessities of space, as to which I have a dread of deluding myself only to find that by trying to blink them I shall be grossly "sold," or by giving way to them shall positively spoil my form for your purpose. The hitch is that the thing involves a devil of a sort of prologue or preliminary action—interesting itself and indispensable for lucidity—which impinges too considerably (for brevity) on the core of the subject. My one chance is yet, I admit, to try to attack the same (the subject) from still another quarter, at still another angle, that I make out as a possible one and which may keep it squeezable and short. If *this* experiment fails, I fear I shall have to "chuck" the supernatural and the high fantastic. I have just finished, as it happens, a fine flight (of eighty thousand words) *into* the high fantastic, which has rather depleted me, or at any rate affected me as discharging my obligations in that quarter. (But I believe I mentioned to you in my last "The Sacred Fount." This has been "sold" to Methuen here, & by this time, probably, to somebody else in the U. S.[1]— but, alas, not be serialized (as to which it is inapt.)—as to the title of which kindly preserve silence.) The *vraie verité*,[2] the fundamental truth lurking behind all the rest, is furthermore, no doubt, that, preoccupied with half a dozen things of the altogether human order now fermenting in my brain, I don't care for "terror" (terror, that is, without "pity") so much as I otherwise might. This would seem to make it simple for me to say to you: "Hang it, if I can't pull off my Monster on *any* terms, I'll just do for you a neat little *human*—and not the less International—fifty-thousander consummately addressed to your more cheerful department; do for you, in other words, an admirable short novel of manners, thrilling too in its degree, but definitely ignoring the bugaboo." Well, this I *don't* positively despair of still sufficiently overtaking myself to be able to think of. *That* card one has always, thank God, up one's sleeve, and the production of it is only a question of a little shake of the arm. At the same time, here, to be frank—and above all, you will say, in this communication, to be interminable— that alternative is just a trifle compromised by the fact that I've two or three things begun ever so beautifully in such a key (and only awaiting the rush of the avid bidder!)—each affecting me with its particular obsession, and one, the *most* started, affecting me with the greatest obsession, for the time (till I can do it, work it off, get it out of the way and fall with still-accumulated intensity upon the *others*) of all.[3] But alas, if I don't say, bang off, that *this* is then the thing I will risk for you, it is because "this", like its companions, isn't, any way I can fix it, workable as a fifty-thousander. The scheme to which I am *now* alluding is lovely—human, dramatic, International, exquisitely "pure," exquisitely everything; only absolutely condemned, from the germ up, to be workable in not less than 100,000 words. If 100,000 were what you had asked me for, I would fall back upon it, ("Terror" failing,) like a flash; and even send you, without delay, a detailed Scenario of it that I drew up a year ago; beginning then— a year ago—to *do* the thing—immediately afterwards; and then again pausing for reasons extraneous and economic. (Because—now that I haven't to consider my typist[4]—there was nobody to "take" it! The *Atlantic* declined—saying it

---

1. *The Sacred Fount* (London: Methuen, 1901; New York: Scribner's, 1901).

2. Real truth.

3. HJ refers to a preliminary exposition of *The Wings of the Dove*, which he had first outlined in his journal in November 1894 (CN 102–7). In 1899 a fuller synopsis (no longer extant) was sent in succession to several magazine editors, none of whom would commit themselves for serialization. HJ's work on this novel was interrupted by an invitation from Harper & Brothers for another serial, "a different and special thing," as he told James B. Pinker on 11 May 1900 (Collection of American Literature, Yale). HJ completed another scenario—for *The Ambassadors*—in September 1900 and sent it on to New York. A thorough account of HJ's complicated compositional schedule is provided by Sister Stephanie Vincec, " 'Poor Flopping *Wings*': The Making of Henry James's *The Wings of the Dove*," *Harvard Library Bulletin* 24 (1976): 60–93.

4. HJ's parenthetical remark is a holograph insertion in the typescript.

really only wanted "Miss Johnson"!)[5] It really constitutes, at any rate, the work I intimately want actually to be getting on with; and—if you are not overdone with the profusion of my confidence—I dare say I best put my case by declaring that, if you don't in another month or two hear from me either as a Terrorist or as a Cheerful Internationalist, it will be that intrinsic difficulties will in each case have mastered me: the difficulty in the one having been to keep my Terror down by *any* ingenuity to the 50,000; and the difficulty in the other having been to get, for the moment, in close quarters with any *other* form of Cheer than the above-mentioned obsessive hundred-thousander. I only wish you wanted *him*. Yet I have now in all probability a decent outlet for him.

Forgive my pouring into your lap this torrent of mingled uncertainties and superfluities. The latter indeed they are properly not, if only as showing you how our question does occupy me. I shall write you again—however vividly I see you wince at the prospect of it. I have it at heart not to fail to let you know how my alternatives settle themselves. Please believe meanwhile in my very hearty thanks for your intimation of what you might perhaps, your own quandary straightening out, see your way to do for me. It is a kind of intimation that I find, I confess, even at the worst, dazzling. All this, however, trips up my response to your charming picture of your whereabouts and present conditions— still discernible, in spite of the chill of years and absence, to my eye, and eke to my ear, of memory. We have had here a torrid, but not wholly a horrid, July; but are making it up with a brave August, so far as we have got, of fires and floods and storms and overcoats. Through everything, none the less, my purpose holds—my genius, I may even say, absolutely thrives—and I am

unbrokenly yours,
Henry James

14th August.

P. S. The hand of Providence guided me, after finishing the preceding, to which the present is postscriptal, to keep it over a few days instead of posting it directly: so possible I thought it that I might have something more definite to add—and I was a little nervous about the way I had left our question. Behold then I *have* then to add that I have just received your letter of Aug. 4—which so simplifies our situation that this accompanying stuff becomes almost superfluous.[6] But I let it go for the sake of the interest, the almost top-heavy mass of response, that it embodies. Let us put it then that all is for the moment for the best in this worst of possible worlds: all the more that had I not just now been writing you exactly as I am, I should probably—and thanks, precisely, to the lapse of days—be stammering to you the ungraceful truth that, after I wrote you,

5. Mary Johnston (1870–1936), whose *To Have and To Hold* was serialized in the *Atlantic* (June 1899–March 1900). The *Century* and at least one other magazine also declined to serialize *The Wings of the Dove*.

6. WDH's letter of 4 August is not extant.

my tale of terror *did*, as I was so more than half fearing, give way beneath me. It *has*, in short, broken down for the present. I am laying it away on the shelf for the sake of something that *is* in it, but that I am now too embarrassed and preoccupied to devote more time to pulling out. I really shouldn't wonder if it be not still, in time and place, to make the world sit up; but the curtain is dropped for the present. All thanks for your full and prompt statement of how the scene has shifted for you. There is no harm done, and I don't regard the three weeks spent on my renewed wrestle as wasted—I have, within three or four days, rebounded from them with such relief, vaulting into another saddle and counting, D. V.[7] on a straighter run. I have *two* begun novels;[8] which will give me plenty to do for the present—they being of the type of the "serious" which I am too delighted to see you speak of as lifting again, "Miss Johnson" *permettendolo*,[9] its downtrodden head. I mean, at any rate, I assure you, to lift *mine!* Your extremely, touchingly kind offer to find moments of your precious time for "handling" something I might send you is altogether too momentous for me to let me fail of feeling almost ashamed that I haven't something—the ghost or t'other stuff—in form, already, to enable me to respond to your generosity "as meant". But heaven only knows what may happen yet! For the moment, I must peg away at what I have in hand—biggish stuff, I fear, in bulk and possible unserialisability, to saddle you withal. But thanks, thanks, thanks. Delighted to hear of one of your cold waves—the newspapers here invidiously mentioning none but your hot. We have them all, moreover, *réchauffeés*,[10] as soon as you have done with them; and we are just sitting down to one now. I dictate you this in my shirt-sleeves and in a draught which fails of strength—chilling none of the pulses of

> yours gratefully and affectionately,
> *Henry James.*

William Dean Howells, "Editor's Easy Chair" [The Soft Side], *Harper's Monthly* 102 *(January 1901):* 316–20.

It is a curious psychological fact, which has been noted before this, that any instrument or vehicle of opinion seems to become itself vocal from the mere custom of expression. A newspaper which has been the organ of some man of original power apparently prolongs his thinking as well as his way of thinking after he has ceased to speak through it, and is mystically so imbued with his absent personality that it can hardly be made to interpret any other.

The new incumbent of the Easy Chair, with the best will in the world to

7. Abbreviated Latin for *Deo Volente:* God willing.
8. *The Wings of the Dove* and *The Ambassadors.*
9. Permitting it.
10. Rekindled.

take his own view of things, is aware of seeing them largely in the perspectives which the Chair so long commanded.[1] The perspectives are not only the same, but the range of objects is so often, in the turn of human events, the same, that he has wondered at times whether it would not be better to let the Chair speak directly for itself, than force it to the use of an inadequate and reluctant medium, and when he suggested this the other day, the Chair showed itself even too ready to take the floor.

"A friend of mine," the editor began, "who has just arrived from Europe, has been saying that nothing struck him so much on getting home as our bad manners. He was tingling with the shame for them which I think I have felt in my time, and he was not tingling the less, but rather the more, because he was contrasting our manners with those of the English, and not of the Continental peoples, whom we have always freely supposed to be so much better mannered. Are we really getting worse? If he could feel the contrast with English manners so painfully—"

"I see what you mean," said the Easy Chair, with an instant relish for the topic, but it paused a moment, as if adjusting itself to a hopeful point of view before it went on. "Still, I am not sure that what pained your friend and what pains us all when we step down that canvas gallery from the steamer, with the light of Europe still about us, and meet a smuggler's welcome from the United States customs, is just what he thought. I believe I should say that we had not bad manners so much as no manners. You may urge that it comes to the same thing, and so it does, but from a different cause."

"I don't know that I quite follow you," said the editor.

"Why, I mean that all manners come from taking thought of behavior. That is the reason why certain sects, like the Quakers and Shakers, who have only taken thought of behavior how most to simplify it, have charming manners. Any sort of discipline, like military training or sacerdotal training, gives good manners. But our American life is mainly commercial and civilian, and does not include taking thought of behavior, and so we are without manners. If we ever take thought of behavior, we shall have the best manners in the world, probably."

"I don't see why," said the editor, more in deference than in difference.

"Because we have the best hearts," the Easy Chair returned. "You won't expect me to prove that? You know that Lowell,[2] when he came home from his long stay abroad, complained that the average public servant he met—the conductor, the cabman, the porter, the waiter—would be kind, but he wouldn't be respectful. Some day that sort of man will imagine being respectful without

---

1. As part of his new contract with the Harper publishing organization, in 1901 WDH assumed responsibility for the "Editor's Easy Chair" column, which had been abandoned after the death of its originator, George W. Curtis (1824–92).

2. James Russell Lowell had served as America's ambassador to Spain (1877–80) and Great Britain (1880–85).

ceasing to be self-respectful. Then we shall have national manners of the highest type."

The Easy Chair leaned comfortably back, lifting the casters of its fore legs slightly from the floor. In an attitude so favorable to thoughtful disquisition it continued: "We are apt to judge people by their manners, and love them or hate them accordingly; but the manners of a people are not a perfect reflection of their morals; otherwise, the morals of the Latin races would not leave so much to be desired as they are now supposed to do. Still, manners are the tokens of character which form the only ground of judgment for the hasty observer. Observers of American manners have always been in a great hurry, and so we have fallen under heavier condemnation than we might if our visitors could have taken time to look into our morals. If these had been studied as tokens of our manners, we might now be famed for being the politest of the civilized peoples, instead of the rudest." . . . "It isn't easy to be specific in such an inquiry as this . . . but it seems to me the great fault of our manners, when we have them," said the Easy Chair, "is that they are personal and occasional manners. These, when they are good, are very good, but when they are bad they make you wish that the person's behavior was governed by a convention or a tradition of breeding which prescribed a certain type of conduct, not to be varied at will. That was the old ideal; but no Americans now have any ideal of politeness except the colored Americans. They seem really to love good manners, though perhaps they sometimes value them beyond good morals."

"But they are always delightful!"

"Yes, and no doubt their morals are better than they would be if their manners were bad. But I believe, of course," said the Easy Chair, rising on the wings of optimism again, "the actual state is merely transitional. We have no manners because we are waiting to get the best; and there is a play of rudeness in our life which is no real reflection of our character. But we must not wait too long! Manners are one of the most precious heritages from the past. We may disuse forms, but we must not disuse forms a great while. Goodness of heart, purity of morals, show themselves in forms, and practically do not exist without them. Forms in conduct are like forms in art. They alone can express manners; and they are built slowly, painfully, from the thought, the experience, of the whole race. In literature, for instance, they alone can impart the sense of style; they alone represent authority—"

The words of the Easy Chair lost themselves in an inarticulate murmur, but with the last the editor was reminded of something that seemed quite in the line of its thinking. It was something that a woman had said of Mr. Henry James's latest collection of his stories, which for reasons of his own he calls *The Soft Side*. "When you read most books," she said, "you feel merely that you are reading a book. But when you read a book of Henry James's you feel that you are reading *an author*."

She had a right to speak, for she was one of those devoted adherents of his who have read him from the beginning, and who alone are perfectly in his secret: not that they can always tell it! Perhaps she was the more devoted because so many women, of the sort that would rather be flattered than interpreted, are impatient of this master's work, and she wished to distinguish herself from them. In the talk that followed she was not very intelligible, though she was voluble enough, as to what in a writer imparted the sense of authorship; and the editor was left wondering whether it might not be a writer's power of getting at himself. Of course he would have to be of a quality worth getting at, but writers of inferior quality are so much and so finally on the surface that the fact of an author ever getting below it would itself be proof of his quality; and it seemed to him that of all the authors now writing English Mr. James had supremely this gift. It might be said in his reproach, but not by any critic worth while, that he was sometimes so subliminal that he was scarcely on the surface at all. "One may very well penetrate the depths below," this sort of critic might urge, "but why pull the hole in after one?" This would be the worst he could say, however, and how much he would then leave unsaid! It is not merely that Mr. James has supremely the gift of getting at himself, but that when he has got there he has arrived at a view of life such as no one else has framed; and his method of representing life, of making the reader share his view, is of a nature as delicate as it is peculiar. If we could imagine the perfume of a flower without the flower, the bouquet of wine without the wine, we should have something suggestive of the effect of his fiction with the sympathetic intelligence. In this last book of his there are certain pieces—like "The Great Condition," "In Europe," "Paste," "The Abasement of the Northmores," and "John Delavoy," to name no others—which are so captivatingly final in their way that one could not imagine anything better, or if there were anything better, could not desire it. No author has more fully perfected his method; but his control of the sympathetic intelligence is so absolute that this does not concern itself with the method, and is only in too much danger of forgetting it, of ignoring the consummate art, in the joyous sense of the life portrayed. Not since English began to be written has it so clearly embodied a literary intention of such refinement, or so unerringly imparted a feeling of character. In a time when the miasms of a gross and palpable fable are thick about us, this exquisite air breathes like a memory and a prophecy of days when fiction was and shall be valued for beauty and distinction. Here, aesthetically, are the good manners, the best manners, the form of the great world, the fashion of the modernity which is of all times, and to this school young aspirants may come to learn the art of being one's self from a master who is never more himself than when he is making you forget him.

101.

JAMES TO HOWELLS, 10 August 1901, Rye   ALS Houghton
                                                      bMS Am 1784 (253) 76

                                                      LAMB HOUSE, RYE.
                                                      August 10th 1901.

My dear Howells.

Ever since receiving & reading your elegant volume of short tales[1]—the arrival of which from you was affecting & delightful to me—I've meant to write
to you, but the wish has struggled in vain with the daily distractions of a tolerably busy summer. I should blush, however, if the season were to melt away without my greeting & thanking you. I read your book with joy & found in it recalls
from far, far away—stray echoes and scents as from another, the American, the
prehistoric existence. The thing that most took me was that entitled A Difficult
Case, which I found beautiful & admirable, ever so true & ever so *done*. But I
fear I more, almost, than anything else, lost myself in mere envy of your freedom
to do &, speaking vulgarly, to place, things of that particular & so agreeable
dimension—I mean the dimension of most of the stories in the volume.[2] It is
sternly enjoined upon one here (where an agent-man does what he can for me,)
that everything—every hundred—above 6 or 7 thousand words is fatal to "placing"; so that I do them of that length, with great care, art & time (much re-
boiling,) & then, even then, can scarcely get them worked off—published even
when they've been accepted. *Harper* has had a thing for nearly two years which
it has not thought worth publishing[3]—& Scribner another[4] for some 15 months
or so; & my agent-man has others that he can't place anywhere.[5] So that
(though I don't know why I inflict on you these sordid groans—except that I
haven't any one else to inflict them on—& the mere affront—of being unused
so inordinately long—is almost intolerable,) I don't feel incited in that direction. Fortunately, however, I am otherwise immersed. I lately finished a tolerably
long novel,[6] & I've written a third of another[7]—with still another begun[8] &
two or three more subjects awaiting me thereafter like carriages drawn up at the
door & horses chomping their bits. And àpropos of the 1st named of these,
which is in the hands of the Harpers, I have it on my conscience to let you
know that the idea of the fiction in question had its earliest origin in a circumstance mentioned to me—years ago—in respect to no less a person than your-

---

1. A *Pair of Patient Lovers*, published by Harper's on 23 May 1901.
2. The *Atlantic* printed "A Difficult Case" in two numbers (July–August 1900).
3. "The Beldonald Holbein," *Harper's Monthly* (October 1901).
4. "Flickerbridge," *Scribner's Magazine* (February 1902).
5. HJ probably was thinking of "The Story in It," which had been rejected by *Scribner's* and was eventually offered gratis to the *Anglo-American Magazine* (January 1902).
6. *The Ambassadors* (1903).
7. *The Wings of the Dove* (1902).
8. Probably *The Sense of the Past*.

self. At Torquay, once, our young friend Jon. Sturges came down to spend some days near me, and, lately, from Paris, repeated to me five words you had said to him one day on his meeting you during a call at Whistler's. I thought the words charming—you have probably quite forgotten them, & the whole incident— suggestive—so far as it was an incident; &, more than this, they presently caused me to see in them the faint vague germ, the mere point of the *start*, of a Subject. I noted them, to that end, as I note everything; & years afterwards (that is 3 or 4,) the Subject sprang at me, one day, out of my notebook.[9] I don't know if it be good; at any rate it has been treated, now, for whatever it is; & my point is that it had long before—it had in the very act of striking me as a germ—got away from *you* or from anything like you! had become impersonal & independent. Nevertheless your initials figure in my little note; & if you hadn't said the 5 words to Jonathan he wouldn't have had them (most sympathetically & interestingly) to relate, & I shouldn't have had them to work in my imagination. The moral is that you are responsible for the whole business. But I've had it, since the book was finished, much at heart to tell you so. May you carry the burden bravely!—I hope you are on some thymy promontory & that the winds of heaven blow upon you all—perhaps in that simplified scene that you wrote to me from, with so gleaming a New England evocation, last year. The summer has been wondrous again in these islands—4 or 5 months, from April 1st, of almost merciless fine weather—a rainlessness absolute & without precedent. It has made my hermitage, as a retreat, a blessing, & I have been able, thank goodness, to work without breaks—other than those of prospective readers' hearts.—It almost broke mine, the other day, by the way, to go down into the New Forest (where he has taken a house,) to see Godkin, dear old stricken friend.[10] He gave me, in a manner, news of you—told me he had seen you lately. He was perhaps a little less in pieces than I feared, but the hand of fate is heavy

9. HJ's journal entry for 31 October 1895 reads, in part:
I was struck last evening with something that Jonathan Sturges . . . mentioned to me: it was only 10 words, but it seemed, as usual, to catch a glimpse of a *sujet de nouvelle* in it. We were talking of W.D.H. and of his having seen him during a short and interrupted stay H. had made 18 months ago in Paris—called away—back to America, when he had just come— at the end of 10 days by the news of the death—or illness—of his father. He had scarcely been in Paris, ever, in former days, and he had come there to see his domiciled and initiated son, who was at the Beaux Arts. Virtually in the evening, as it were, of life, it was all new to him: all, all, all. Sturges said he seemed sad—rather brooding; and I asked him what gave him (Sturges) that impression. "Oh—somewhere—I forget, when I was with him—he laid his hand on my shoulder and said *à propos* of some remark of mine: 'Oh, you are young, you're young—be glad of it: be glad of it and *live*. Live all you can: it's a mistake not to. It doesn't so much matter what you do—but live. This place makes it all come over me. I see it now. I haven't done so—and now I'm old. It's too late. It has gone past me—I've lost it. You have time. You are young. Live!' " I amplify and improve a little—but that was the tone. It touches me—I can see him—I can hear him. Immediately, of course—as everything, thank God, does—it suggests a little situation. (CN 140–41)
See also HJ's detailed scenario, "Project of Novel," prepared for Harper's and dated 1 September 1900 (CN 541–76).
10. Edwin L. Godkin, founder and former editor of the *Nation*.

upon him. He has mitigations—supremely in the admirable devotion of his wife. And he is quartered for the time in the Forest of Arden. I am alone here just now with my sweet niece Peggy,[11] but my brother & his wife are presently to be with me again for 15 days before sailing (31st) for the U. S. He is immensely better in health, but he must take in sail hand over hand at home to remain so. Stia bene, caro amico, anche Lei[12] (my Lei is my joke!) Tell Mrs. Howells & Mildred that I yearn toward them tenderly.

Yours always & ever
Henry James

102.

JAMES TO HOWELLS, 25 January 1902, Rye   ALS Houghton
                                                      bMS Am 1784 (253) 77

LAMB HOUSE, RYE, SUSSEX.
January 25th 1902

My dear Howells.

It's a wonderful state of things that I am in your debt for two letters[1] & that for the first in particular—the charming one of the summer's end, long months ago—my failure to make sign of payment—has been aggravated & odious. It's useless to attempt to excuse or palliate such baseness: there *are*, I dare say, attenuating circumstances—but my exquisite literary art, even, I fear, would fail to make them worthy of your consideration. There's only one of them that I'll mention. That I'm *going* to write to you is always a delicious thought to me, which I hug & cherish even as the prospect of some joy, some social joy, to come: only I know not *what* social joy, in my battered age, casts so graceful a shadow before. At all events there has been that amount of preliminary gloating to stay my hand. After all, however, I do gloat over *having* written you, as well, & this I am proposing to do an hour or two hence. Your most kind communication, meanwhile, in respect to the miraculously-named "uptown" apartment-house[2] has at once deeply agitated & wildly uplifted me. The agitation, as I call it, is verily but the tremor, the intensity of hope, of the delirious dream that such a stroke may "bring my books before the public," or do something toward it—coupled with the reassertion of my constant, too constant, conviction that no power on earth can ever do that. They are *behind*, irremovably behind, the public, & fixed there for my lifetime at least; & as the public hasn't eyes in

---

11. Margaret Mary (Peggy) James (1887–1952), daughter of William and Alice Howe Gibbens James.

12. You also take care of yourself, my dear friend.

1. Neither extant.

2. On 19 January 1902 WDH wrote to Thomas Bailey Aldrich, "An apartment house here has been named 'The Henry James.' I cut out the advertisement and sent it to him, and I am wondering whether he will abhor or like it" (*SL* 4: 11).

THE HENRY JAMES,
801 WEST 113TH ST., COR. AMSTERDAM AV.
All outside light; 8 spacious rooms; bath, toilets, servants' stairs; most careful individual management; beautiful unobstructed views and healthful section; specially appeals to refined persons; liveried service; opposite St. John's Cathedral, Columbia University and many parks. Apply SUPERINTENDENT.

The Henry James, "the miraculously-named 'uptown' apartment-house," which *specially appeals to refined persons*, as advertised in the New York *World*, 10 November 1901.

the back of its head, & scarcely even in the front, no consequences can ensue. The Henry James, I opine, will be a terrifically "private" hotel, & will languish, like the Lord of Burleigh's wife, under the burden of an honour "unto which it was not born."[3] Refined, liveried, "two-toileted," it will have been a short-lived, hectic paradox, & will presently have to close in order to reopen as the Mary Johnson or the K. W. Wiggin or the James Lane Allen. Best of all as the Edith Wharton![4] Still, your advertisement gave me an hour of whirling rapture, against which I almost began to draw cheques. Then, in a vision I saw the thing catching the eye of my multitudinous publishers & *in* the eye I distinguished benevolent pity. They never have any for *me*, but I feel they are now having it, amusedly, for their floundering fellow-speculator.

—Very interesting as well, & scarce less tormenting—I mean in the way of making my mouth vainly water—the rest of your present letter, with its record of "big-sellers" to come, for you, or, what is almost as good, a prevision of "big-sellers" among the seats of the mighty. May the prevision be resoundingly made

3. Compare Tennyson's poem "The Lord of Burleigh," in which a village maiden languishes when she discovers that her newlywed husband is not, as she presumed, a simple landscape painter but rather the master of a grand estate. With some success she assumes

. . . all duties of her rank.

. . . .

But a trouble weighed upon her,
And perplexed her, night and morn,
With the burthen of an honour
Unto which she was not born

(ll. 72, 77–80).

4. Mary Johnston's most popular romance, *To Have and To Hold*, had been preferred by the *Atlantic* over *The Wings of the Dove*. Kate Douglas Wiggin (1856–1923), another best-selling author, is best remembered for *Rebecca of Sunnybrook Farm* (1903). James Lane Allen (1849–1925) wrote idealized tales and novels of Kentucky, such as *Summer in Arcady* (1896) and *The Choir Invisible* (1897). Although Edith Wharton (1862–1937) eventually became a close friend of HJ, he was seldom uncritical of her work. In 1902 she published *The Valley of Decision*, a historical novel that quickly earned more than ten thousand dollars in royalties.

good. I am delighted, at any rate, that you are not, as your letter of the autumn rather sadly portended, letting fiction slip away from you. All success to your *risorgimento!*[5] I await with barely decent patience the advent both of the serialized & the *lump* production.[6] You remain the sole & single novelist of English speech, now producing, whom I read—read the more, therefore, with concentrated passion. Where then should I be without you? The *little* American tale-tellers (I mean the two or three women,) become impossible to me the moment they lengthen. Mary Wilkins I have found no better than any other Mary, in the fat volume; & dear Sara Jewett sent me not long since a Revolutionary Romance, with officers over their wine &c, & Paul Jones terrorizing the sea, that was a thing to make the angels weep.[7] You wrote me of some inky maiden in the West, I think, who was superseding these ladies, but I watch for her in vain, & beg you to direct her to me.[8]

—Apropos of which articles (of diminutive fiction) you responded in your autumn letter to some remarks of mine—some, I fear, unmanly groans, on the subject of my difficulty in bringing my own diminutives to light; citing certain things of yours that had waited, in periodicals, ever so long. Your instances *were* very edifying—& the thing has no importance, save that I feel I appeared, seemingly, to have groaned out of tune. I didn't in the least mean that I was surprised at the small hospitality offered to things of 12 000, 15 000 words &c; for of that I long since sounded the depths. My surprise (over my own case,) was wholly in respect to things of six, seven, eight thousand words (I do no others now.) Artfully—& oh, so difficultly—constructed of those dimensions, to conciliate the fastidious editor, they none the less languish in the dark backward for periods of 2 years at a time. I just observed advertized in the Feb. Scribner a tiny thing that was "accepted" at a date remote by nearly that amount of time;[9] & my moral is all that even its tininess didn't smooth the way—more than this— for it. You will say that they might perfectly have refused it altogether, & when I reflect that that is gruesomely true, I doubly wonder why I fall—*have* fallen— into this strain of vain interrogation (say) of the silent stars—as if you pretended

5. Rebirth; revival.

6. The "lump" production was *The Kentons*, published by Harper's in April 1902 without serialization. *Letters Home* appeared in the *Metropolitan* (April–September 1903) before its issue as a Harper volume.

7. Mary Eleanor Wilkins Freeman (1852–1930) is—justifiably—better known today for her collections of short fiction, such as *A New England Nun* (1891), than for extended prose fictions like *The Heart's Highway* (1900), a historical novel. HJ had written to Sarah Orne Jewett (1849–1909) about *The Tory Lover* (1901), deprecating her exploitation of historical romance, which, HJ felt, "is . . . condemned, even in cases of labour as delicate as yours, to a fatal *cheapness.* . . . Go back to the dear country of the *Pointed Firs, come* back to the palpable present-*intimate* that throbs responsive, and that wants, misses, needs you, God knows, and that suffers woefully in your absence" (HJ to Sarah Orne Jewett, 5 October 1901, HJL 4: 208). HJ's preference for *The Country of the Pointed Firs* (1896) also has been vindicated by later critics.

8. WDH may have recommended the work of Willa Cather (1873–1947), whose poems and short stories about the Nebraska prairie had begun appearing in eastern periodicals around 1900.

9. "Flickerbridge," *Scribner's Monthly* (February 1902).

to speak for them! It is only that in reading over your older letter just now, I found first your passage relating your own experience. And little must any individual experience abide with you, or weigh for you, amid such a wealth of production. I marvel at the quantity of your work, & at what I venture to suppose the facility by which it *has* in some degree to be explained. You are magnificent, at any rate, & make me feel stranded & afar—I mean, in especial, by your journalistic abundance. When *I* try journalism—but I never *do!* (There I was at it again—so I'll *pretend* I never do.) The rest of your summer's end letter, about your Maine ways & Maine woods, was very grateful to me, & I felt, almost resentfully, that it was *I* who ought to have been with you when you went astray with your young parson, over the haunted house, & *not* the young parson—if young he was—whose familiarity (with you) I tend to resent.[10] There are no woods to get lost in here—though there *are* young parsons; with whom, however, I don't associate—so that I try to find it your one symptom of a compromised fortune that you are reduced to them in Maine. I should view a long drive with one—of the hereabouts pattern—as a confession of despair. However, that takes explanations—which wouldn't be interesting.—I scribble to you thus interminably, late, very late, at night—my only letter-writing time. A wild southwest gale howls round my old house, & I hear the lash of the rain in the intervals of the wind. My lamp burns still, my servants are long since at roost, & my faithful hound (a wire-haired fox terrier of celestial breed,) looks up from his dozing in an armchair hard-by to present to me afresh his extraordinary facial resemblance to the late James T. Fields.[11] It's one of the funniest likenesses I ever saw, (& most startling;) & yet I can't write to Mrs. Fields of my daily joy in it. So I thus relieve myself to you, even though you too be, in a manner, a residuary relict. I've had a workful autumn & early winter, finishing a novel which *should* have by this time been published—that is has been ready to be— but on which, as it is long, I fear too long, I've still several weeks' work. It's to be lumped (by Constable here & Scribner in America,) & has, I think, a prettyish title "The Wings of the Dove." It's moreover, probably, of a prettyish inspiration—a "love-story" of a romantic tinge, & touching & conciliatory tone. I pray

10. The clergyman is unidentified, but another letter from WDH to his sister Aurelia gives more information about his summer activities:

This afternoon I went to call on some nice old Boston people, and they made me get into their carriage which came up, and drive with them. We went a long way on the coast, past many rocky headlands, to see a pretty stone church, which a rich widow has had built on a bluff overlooking miles of sea and shore. It is a wild, lonely spot and strangely poetic. The widow's summer place is near, and she keeps a clergyman for the season paying all expenses herself, in memory of her husband. (WDH to Aurelia H. Howells, 7 July 1901, *SL* 4: 269)

The editors note that the Church of St. Peter by the Sea, adjacent to Bald Head Cliff, about five miles north of York Harbor, was donated in 1897 by Mrs. George W. Conarro, in memory of her husband, a prominent Philadelphia portrait painter.

11. James T. Fields, Boston publisher and editor of the *Atlantic*. WDH was his assistant when HJ's early short stories were first accepted for publication in the magazine. Annie Adams Fields (1834–1915), his widow, became Sarah Orne Jewett's close companion. She remained HJ's friend and occasional correspondent.

night & day for its comparative prosperity, but no publishers, alas (& they've had a mass of it for some time in their hands,) have told me that it has "taken their fancy." So I'm preparing for the worst, & yet at the same time panting (as *always* before the material has caught up with the mental finish of a book,) to get immediately next at two or three other besetting subjects. Meanwhile, unfortunately, my way is temporarily, I hope but very briefly, stopped by my having suffered to be gouged out of me long ago by the Waldo Storys[12]—a history in itself—a promise first to "look at" the late W.W.S.s papers & then to write a memorial volume of some sort about him. I've delayed quite desperately, & at last, quite *must*, as I've also promised W$^{\underline{m}}$ Blackwood here. But there is no *subject*—there is nothing in the man himself to write about. There is nothing for me but to do a *tour de force*, or try to—leave poor dear W.W.S. *out*, practically, & make a little volume on the old Roman, Americo-Roman, Hawthornesque & other byegone days, that the intending, & *extending*, tourist will, in his millions, buy. But pray for me *you*, over this—to do all that & Please the Family too! Fortunately the Family is almost cynically indulgent—& I hope not to be kept Pleasing it more than 3 or 4 months. But my lamp burns low. You must be single & stricken (each of you—with all respect to the other,) without Mildred. But I congratulate her on her winter tropics[13] & send her the assurance of my affectionate interest—if she can accept a gift so stale as that will be when it reaches her. You offered me her calendar[14]—& I gave no sign, brute that I was—& now I suppose it's gone forever. It would still be a joy to me, little as I deserve it. I surround Mrs. Howells with the solicitude of an antediluvian friend, & I bless the Boy as much as ever one can bless *up*, for I seem to see him perched on vertiginous platforms, far out of the line of vision of the likes of yours, my dear Howells,

always
Henry James

---

12. In 1897 Thomas Waldo Story had persuaded HJ to write a biography of his father, the sculptor William Wetmore Story (1819–95). HJ signed a contract that year with the Edinburgh publisher William Blackwood (1836–1912) but did not promise a delivery date for the manuscript. Blackwood published *William Wetmore Story and His Friends* in 1903.

13. Mildred Howells was spending the winter in Bermuda.

14. For the 1901 Christmas trade, Mildred Howells had published a "Whist Calendar for 1902," featuring verses and illustrations by her, together with monthly reminders of the rules of the game.

103.

HOWELLS TO JAMES, 14 February 1902, New YorkHOWELLS TO JAMES, 14 February 1902, New York   ALS Houghton
bMS Am 1094 (252)

48 West 59th st.,
February 14, 1902.

My dear James:

It will be long before your exemplary letter of Jan'y 27[1] can be fitly answered; a volume of wit and wisdom worth at least $100 a thousand words would be required even to acknowledge it; but now I must write you as enthusiastically as decency will permit of my pleasure in seeing your old, never-before-given Daly comedy done by the pupils of the Dramatic Arts School, yesterday.[2] It had got round to their teacher through Frohman,[3] who has inherited Daly and, it appears, you; and it has ripened into something delightful. It is excellent, and *goes* from first to last; the third act I felt a little *too* densely packed with incident, but that is a good fault, and the only one of the piece. Every point took; the house—most intelligent, almost too intelligent—laughed all through, and gave the company curtain after curtain, staying till 6 o'clock to see the very end, after being delayed from you by the fatuities of two brother-dramatists.[4] It was largely made up of friends and fellow pupils of the players and of the teacher. He, Franklin Sargeant is the son of Mrs. Sargeant who once "opened a saloon" of high literary quality in Boston, and is a good, reluctant critic:[5] he liked your piece as much as anyone, and praised it to me. I will try to find out if he looks for a future to it, and will let you know. If there is anything knowledgeous in the press I will send it; but knowledge is not the forte of the dramatic critic. I have indicated the comparative proficiency of the players on the enclosed pro-

1. WDH's error for HJ's letter of 25 January 1902 (#102).1. WDH's error for HJ's letter of 25 January 1902 (#102).

2. HJ's comedy *Mrs. Jasper* was written in 1891–92 for theater manager John August Daly and his troupe's leading actress, Ada Rehan (1860–1916). Despite numerous revisions made at Daly's insistence, the play was never produced. HJ published his original script, now titled *Disengaged*, in *Theatricals* (1894). The production WDH saw was based on the revised text HJ had prepared for Daly, which did not reflect his final artistic intentions. The premiere of *Mrs. Jasper* was staged by students of the American Academy of Dramatic Arts and the Empire Theater Dramatic School.

3. Charles Frohman (1860–1915) was the founder and manager of the Empire Theater.

4. Two one-act plays—*The New Year*, by Louisa Meigs Green, and *A Gentleman of the Road*, by Arthur Ketchum—were also performed.

5. In 1884 Franklin Haven Sargent (1856–1923) founded the Lyceum School of Acting, which later became the American Academy of Dramatic Arts. His mother, Mary Elizabeth Sargent, was the wife of a prominent Unitarian minister and abolitionist, John Turner Sargent. She maintained her salon, the Radical Club, from 1867 to 1880, attracting such luminaries as Emerson, Longfellow and, occasionally, William James. "Last night I went of all places in the world to mrs. Sargent's esthetic tea in Chestnut Street," William wrote HJ on 22 January 1876. "Certain individuals read poetry, whilst others sat and longed for them to stop so that they might begin to talk. The room was full of a decidedly good looking set of people—especially women—but new england all over! Give me a human race with some *guts* to them, no matter if they do belch at you now and then" (*CWJ* 1: 251).

gramme. Mrs. Jasper was a most beautiful creature—out of Western New York, I should think from the way she broke through into her native *Rs* (from the English accent which the school cultivates) in moments of high excitement. Coverley was altogether and unerringly delightful. As for the piece, to come back to it, I felt as if I had been reading one of your books, and I can't say better than *that*. To be honest, which is also to be disagreeable, I didn't suppose you had it in you. There!

Yours ever
W. D. Howells.

Think of my giving the very marrow of my morning to this letter, and then say there is no longer true friendship in the world!

104.

JAMES TO HOWELLS, 7 March 1902, Rye

ALS Houghton
bMS Am 1784 (253) 78

March 7$\underline{th}$: 1902
LAMB HOUSE, RYE, SUSSEX.

My dear, dear Howells.

My silence since I received your adorable "Mrs. Jasper" letter will have seemed to you unbelievably unbecoming: but I beg you none the less to take it from me that, in not making but one leap from the perusal of your amazing revelation to the clutch of my crazy pen, I yielded only to the most dismal forza maggiore.[1] I have, in fine, till ten days ago, been quite helplessly ill ever since I heard from you—& that (wretchedly waiting) is the only witchcraft I *could* use. I went up to London on Jan. 27$\underline{th}$, thinking to stay 3 months, but on 29$\underline{th}$ was suddenly laid low by an inward blight, & after 10 days of uncured, though overdoctored, misery there, I managed on Feb 11$\underline{th}$, to scramble back here, in a lull in the storm, & here at least elaborately, domestically & conveniently abase, I tumbled into bed with a bad relapse; but the nightmare is past. I am solidly convalescent—save for the gruesome consciousness of a mountain of agglomerated postal matter; & I mention the dreary weariness only that you may have chapter & verse for my not really having failed to thrill—to ecstasy, to delirium—at your weirdest of anecdotes! It beats the up-town "Henry James";[2] it beats everything that ever befell the obscure namesake of that structure. Really, it's most charming, amusing, beguiling, & I hold myself with 10 pair of hands not to say—hum!—Encouraging. It's *better* than that—it's absolute, unsurpassable, ultimissimo. I won't say I wish to goodness I had been there—but I gloat over the possibilities of goodness as I see that *you* couldn't help being! The dear young ingenuous benighted things! I could kiss them all with tears.

---

1. Greater power.
2. See letter #102.

A mixed review: Howells's annotated program for an unauthorized New York performance of *Mrs. Jasper*, one of James's unremunerative theatricals (first published in 1894 as *Disengaged*). By permission of the Houghton Library, Harvard University.

But the present woe to me is that there is so much, so ridiculously much more I could tell you about the poor little old ugly tragic joke of the original Mrs. J., & her squalid Daly-Rehan history (of 10 years ago,) than your very sweetest impression of her, even, could prompt you to tell *me*. But don't be afraid—now. The incident is buried deep; beneath fifty layers of dead nightmares. I only feel a weak natural pang as it seems irresistibly to come over me that the misguided darlings must have used for their text & study some contraband old type-copy of the play disinterred among Daly's posthumous relics (every rag of whose property in it had ceased long before his death, I receiving back, as I supposed, every syllable of the 3 acts:) and *not* from the fountainhead & classic & authentic last form—the printed play in one of 2 vols. of "Theatricals" published long since (though after Daly, of course,) by the Harpers & containing five other small wasted experiments of mine as well as Mrs. J. IF they knew the book, which, however, no human creature knows, they wd. belike, have chosen rather one or another of 2 or 3 alternative things in preference: conceivably most, perhaps, a shameless little piece of sharper actability called "The Album."[3] That & an allusion of yours makes me fear—! But fear *what*, at this pass? Vague and muddled my regret, for I don't even dimly recall any *fact* of difference between the 2 texts; nothing but a bare sense that the published was the measurably neater & livelier thing. And yet you divinely tell me that the thing you *saw* was, or could pass for, lively; & that is enough, & I swoon away, on it, into sublimities of universal acceptance. It "went," it "went," and, as *you* went, my cup sufficiently overflows from it! It isn't that I couldn't drink down oceans more; but one can't be more than gloriously drunk; & such now is my everlasting doom. Shall you ever again see the so fabulous (yet dimly reconstituted) young "parlour"-bred, essay-fed Sargent? If so, tell him, kindly, that, demented "sport" of such a stem as he strikes me, I yet love & honour him: only that he must really obtain, on these lines, the 2 vols. of Theatricals. They will eagerly rid themselves of the pair, on him, at the shop. Then he will know better where he is—& where *I* am. But dear, dear Howells, my pen is yet feeble in my grasp & my brain dull in my skull—whereby I embrace you for good night & am ever

affectionately & gratefully yours
Henry James.

105.

JAMES TO HOWELLS, 12 September 1902, Rye   TLS Houghton
bMS Am 1784 (253) 79

Lamb House, Rye, Sussex.
Sept. 12th, 1902.

My dear Howells.

An inscrutable & untoward fate condemns me to strange delinquencies—though it is no doubt the weakness of my nature as well as the strength of the said treacherous principle that the "undone vast", in my existence, lords it chronically & shamelessly over the "petty done". It strikes me indeed both *as* vast, & yet in a monstrous way as petty too, that I should have joyed so in *"The Kentons"*, which you sent me, ever so kindly, more weeks ago than it would be decent in me to count[1]—should have eaten & drunk & dreamed & thought of

---

3. Published in *Theatricals: Second Series* (1895).
1. *The Kentons* was published by Harper's in April 1902.

them as I did, should have sunk into them, in short, so that they closed over my head like living waters & kept me down, down in subaqueous prostration, & all the while should have remained, so far as *you* are concerned, brutishly & ungratefully dumb. I haven't been otherwise dumb, I assure you—that is so far as they themselves are concerned: there was a time when I talked of nothing & nobody else, & I have scarcely even now come to the end of it. I think in fact it is *because* I have been so busy vaunting & proclaiming them, up & down the more or less populated avenues of my life, that I have had no time left for anything else. The avenue on which you live, worse luck, is perversely out of my beat.

Why, however, do I talk thus? I know too well how *you* know too well that letters, in the writing life, are the last things that get themselves written. You see the way that this one tries to manage it—which at least is better than no way. All the while, at any rate, the impression of the book remains, & I have infinitely pleased myself, even in my shame, with thinking of the pleasure that must have come to yourself from so acclaimed & attested a demonstration of the freshness, within you still, of the spirit of evocation. Delightful, in one's golden afternoon, & after many days & many parturitions, to put forth thus a young, strong, living flower. You have done nothing more true & complete, more thoroughly homogeneous & hanging-together, without the faintest ghost of a false note or a weak touch—all as sharply ciphered-up & *tapped*-out as the "proof" of a prize scholar's sum on a slate. It is in short miraculously felt & beautifully done, & the aged—by which I mean the richly-matured—sposi[2] *as done* as if sposi were a new & fresh idea to you. Of all your sposi they are, I think, the most penetrated & most penetrating. I took in short true comfort in the whole manifestation, the only bitterness in the cup being that it made me feel old. *I shall never again so renew myself.*[3] But I want to hear from you that

2. Married couple.

3. After he revisited the United States in 1904–5, HJ had occasion to comment on the absence of mannered forms in American life, citing WDH's novels (and *The Kentons* in particular) as documentary. "For it is Mr. Howells," HJ wrote,

above all who helps us to recognize what has hitherto made our association possible and enabled us to hold out against the daily effect of our surrender of forms. He marks this surrender, at every point, with an infallible hand, and yet, in the oddest way in the world, a perfect gospel of optimism is to be extracted from his general picture. For here we get the exquisite detail of the mutual, the universal patience—with the strangest impression, as a whole, I think, of every one's, men's and women's alike, trying, all round them, by universal readiness and response, to deprecate and forestall the great peril of fatal aggravation.

Every one takes for granted everywhere an unlimited alacrity of service, sympathy, mercy, or, still more, active encouragement, and no one seems disappointed or betrayed, in a world where almost the only salient vital convenience is the ability of every one to get criticism restricted and errands obligingly, not mercenarily, done. What need for manners, any more than for any other detail of comfort, we thus seem eventually taught to wonder, in communities where nobody misses anything—by reason precisely of this merciful *pitch* of criticism? The pitch can with perfect convenience be low when passion and irritation are on their side so successfully kept down. It is as if every one feels the equilibrium too precious to be endan-

it has really—the sense & the cheer of having done it—set you spinning again with a quickened hum. When you mentioned to me, in I think your last letter,[4] that you had done The Kentons, you mentioned at the same time the quasi-completion of something else. It is this thing I now want—won't it soon be coming due?[5]—& if you will magnanimously send it to me I promise you to have, for it, better manners. Meanwhile, let me add, I have directed the Scribners to send you a thing of my own, too long-winded & minute a thing, but well-meaning, just put forth under the name of The Wings of the Dove.

I hope the summer's end finds you still out of the streets, & that it has all been a comfortable chapter. I hear of it from my brother as the Great Cool Time, which makes for me a blessed image, since I generally seem to sear my eyeballs, from June to September, when I steal a glance, across the sea, at the bright American picture. Here, of course, we have been as grey & cold, as "braced" & rheumatic & uncomfortable as you please. But that has little charm of novelty—though (not to blaspheme) we have, since I've been living here, occasionally perspired. I live here, as you see, still, & am by this time, like the dyer's hand, subdued to what I work in, or at least try to economise in. It is pleasant enough, for five or six months of the year, for me to wish immensely that some crushing stroke of fortune may still take the form of driving you over to see me before I fall to pieces. Apropos of which I am forgetting what has been half my reason—no, not half—for writing to you. Many weeks ago there began to be blown about the world—from what fountain of lies proceeding I know not—a rumour that you were staying with me here, a rumour flaunting its

---

gered; where there is so little other convenience, so little of the margin supplied by manners, that sole security counts double, and it is with peculiar intensity in every one's interest to be good-or in other words to be easy.

This then, this necessity of good-humor, is the great ease, the great bond and the great lubricant; so that it is as if the author's subtle sense of what the whole situation hangs by were the key to his wit and his pathos, his rare note of reality, his mastery of American truth. Such an expert study of the whole element as is supplied for instance in The Kentons catches in the very act the system to the working of which he all so ironically yet so incorruptibly testifies. This unsurpassed attempt to sound the grayest abysses of the average state and the middle condition projects for us the measure of how little their occupants may neglect the conviction, at least as a saving instinct, of the equal importance of all; all, that is, as a charge on the common forbearance or, to speak more nobly, the common humanity. The forbearance of Mr. Kenton in respect to his wife is only equalled by hers in respect to her husband, and the parental philosophy again only by that of the daughters, filially and fraternally. Nobody makes "short work," in a word, of any one or of anything, no matter how "impossible," and if we at moments rather fail to see how or why anybody finally either spares or is spared, we yet do see that on this strained basis the society depicted does in a manner creak along.

See "The Manners of American Women," Harper's Bazar 41 (July 1907): 646–51; rpt. in French Writers and American Women: Essays by Henry James, ed. Peter Buitenhuis (Brandford, Conn.: Compass, 1960), 76–77.

4. Not extant.

5. Although WDH published The Flight of Pony Baker in Septeı..ber 1902 and Literature and Life in October 1902, the work to which HJ refers was probably Letters Home, which did not appear as a volume until September 1903.

little hour as large as life in some of the London papers. It brought me many notes of inquiry, invitations to you, & other tributes to your glory—damn it! (I don't mean damn your glory, but damn the wanton & worrying rumour). Among other things it brought me a fattish letter addressed to you & which I have been so beastly procrastinating as not to forward you till now, when I post it with this. Its aspect somehow denotes insignificance & impertinence, & I haven't wanted to do it, as a part of the so grossly newspaperistic impudence, too much honour; besides, verily, the intention day after day of writing you at the same time. Well, there it all is. You will think my letter as long as my book. So I add only my benediction, as ever, on your house, beginning with Mrs. Howells, going straight through, & ramifying as far as you permit me. Yours, my dear Howells,

always & ever
Henry James

106.

JAMES TO HOWELLS, 11 December 1902, Rye   ALS Houghton
bMS Am 1784 (253) 80

LAMB HOUSE, RYE, SUSSEX.
December 11th 1902

My dear Howells.

Nothing more delightful, or that has touched me more closely, even to the spring of tears, has befallen me for years, literally, than to receive your beautiful letter of Nov. *30th*,[1] so largely & liberally anent *The W. of the D.* Every word of it goes to my heart & to "thank" you for it seems a mere grimace. The same post brought me a letter from dear John Hay, so that my measure has been full.[2] I haven't known anything about the American "notices," heaven save the mark! any more than about those here (which I am told, however, have been remarkably genial;)[3] so that I have *not* had the sense of confrontation with a public more than usually childish—I mean had it in any special way. I confess, however, that that is my chronic sense—the more than usual childishness of pub-

---

1. Not extant.

2. Hay's letter praising *The Wings of the Dove* has not survived, but in response HJ wrote: "Right noble & generous is it of you to have put your so persecuted hand to the beautiful words I have just received from you & which give me extraordinary joy. They are even as a cup of strong & clear wine for lips none so often or so lusciously moistened, & they nerve me, as the phrase is, to fresh efforts!" See HJ to John Hay, 16 December 1902, in *Henry James and John Hay*, 127–28.

3. See, for example, the review in the *Times Literary Supplement* (5 September 1902), which begins:

> Mr. Henry James is to be congratulated. It is a long time since modern English fiction has presented us with a book which is so essentially a book; a thing, conceived, and carried on, and finished in one premeditated strain; with unbroken literary purpose and serious, unflagging literary skill. *The Wings of the Dove* is an extraordinarily interesting performance.

This notice is reprinted in *Henry James: The Critical Heritage*, 319–21.

lics; & it is (has been,) in my mind, long since discounted, & my work definitely insists upon being independent of such phantasms & on unfolding itself wholly from its own "innards". Of course, in our conditions, doing anything decent is pure disinterested, unsupported unrewarded heroism; but that's in the day's work. The *faculty of attention* has utterly vanished from the general anglosaxon mind, extinguished at its source by the big blatant *Bayadère*[4] of Journalism, of the newspaper & the *picture* (above all) magazine; who keeps screaming "Look at *me, I* am the thing, & I only, the thing that will keep you in relation with me *all the time* without your having to attend *one minute* of the time." If you are moved to write anything anywhere about the *W. of the D.* do say something of that—it so awfully wants saying.[5] But we live in a lonely age for literature or for any art but the mere visual. Illustrations, loud simplifications & *grossissements*,[6] the big Building (good for John;) the "mounted" play, the prose that is careful to be in the tone of, & with the distinction of, a newspaper or bill-poster advertisement—these, & these only, meseems "stand a chance." But why do I talk of such chances? I am *melted* at your reading *en famille*[7] *The Sacred Fount*, which you will, I fear, have found chaff in the mouth & which is one of several things of mine, in these last years, that have paid the penalty of having been conceived only as the "short story" that (alone, apparently,) I could hope to work off somewhere (which I mainly failed of,) & then *grew* by a rank force of its own into something of which the idea had, modestly, never been to be a book. That is essentially the case with the *S. F.*; planned, like The Spoils of Poynton, What Maisie Knew, The Turn of the Screw & various others, as a story of from "8 to 10 thousand words" (!!) & then having accepted its bookish necessity or destiny in consequence of becoming already, at the start, 20,000; accepted it ruefully & blushingly, moreover, since, *given the tenuity of the idea*, the larger quantity of treatment hadn't been aimed at. I remember how I would have "chucked" *The Sacred Fount* at the 15th thousand word, if in the 1st place I could have afforded to "waste" 15 000, & if in the second I were not always ridden by a superstitious terror of not finishing, for finishing's & for the precedent's sake, what I have begun. I am a fair coward about *dropping*, & the book in question, I fear, is, more than anything else, a monument to that superstition. When, if it meets my eye, I say to myself "You know you *might* not have finished it," I make the remark not in natural reproach, but, I confess, in craven relief.

---

4. HJ's idiom invokes the seductive connotation of the French term (meaning a Hindu dancing girl) and the more graphic denotation of the English word "bayadere", a fabric with contrasting horizontal stripes (hence resembling a sheet of headlines and copy).

5. The reviewer for the *Times Literary Supplement* (see note 3) anticipated HJ's judgment:

This is, we repeat, an extraordinarily interesting performance, but it is not an easy book to read. It will not do for short railway journeys or for drowsy hammocks, or even to amuse sporting men and the active Young Person. The dense, fine quality of its pages—and there are 576—will always presuppose a certain effort of attention on the part of the reader; who must, indeed, be prepared to forgo many of his customary titillations and bribes. (*Henry James: The Critical Heritage*, 319)

6. Vulgar amplifications.

7. Aloud among the family.

But why am I thus grossly expatiative on the very carpet of the bridal altar? I spread it beneath Pillar's feet with affectionate jubilation & gratulation & stretch it out further, in the same spirit, beneath yours & her mother's.[8] I wish her & you, & the florally-minded young man (he *must* be a good 'un,) all joy in the connection. If he stops short of gathering samphire it's a beautiful trade, & I trust he will soon come back to claim the redemption of the maiden's vows. Please say to her from me that I bless her—*hard*.

—Your visit to Cambridge makes me yearn a little, & your walking over it with C. N. & your sitting in it with Grace.[9] Did the ghost of other walks (I'm told Fresh Pond is no longer a Pond, or no longer Fresh, only Stale, or something,) ever brush you with the hem of its soft shroud?[10] Haven't you lately published some volume of Literary Essays or Portraits (*since* the Heroines of Fiction) & won't you, munificently send me either that *or* the Heroines—neither of which have sprung up in my here so rustic path?[11] I will send you in partial payment another book of mine to be published on Feb: 27th.[12] Good night, with renewed benedictions on your house & your spirit.

Yours always and ever
Henry James

107.

JAMES TO HOWELLS, 8 January 1903, Rye   TLS Houghton
bMS Am 1784 (253) 81

Lamb House, Rye, Sussex.
Jan. 8th, 1903.

My dear Howells.

Let me beg you first of all not to be disconcerted by this chill legibility. I want to write to you *to-day*, immediately, your delightful letter of Dec. 29th[1] having arrived this morning, and I can only manage it by dictation as I am, in consequence of some obscure indiscretion of diet yesterday, temporarily sick, sorry, and seedy; so that I can only loll, rather listless (but already better of my poison) in an armchair. My feelings don't permit me to wait to tell you that the communication I have just had from you surpasses for pure unadulterated Charm any communication I have *ever* received. I am really quite overcome and weak-

---

8. In October 1902, Mildred Howells became engaged to David G. Fairchild (1869–1954), already a renowned botanist and agricultural explorer. For reasons that are not clear, she broke off the engagement by January of the following year.

9. Charles Eliot Norton and his sister Grace, whom WDH saw in Cambridge on 22 November. On this trip WDH also walked to the Cambridge cemetery to visit Winifred's grave.

10. HJ refers to the excursions he frequently took with WDH in the 1860s.

11. *Literature and Life* (1902) and *Heroines of Fiction* (1901).

12. HJ's next collection of tales, *The Better Sort*, was actually published on 26 February 1903.

1. Not extant.

ened by your recital of the generous way in which you threw yourself into the scale of the arrangement, touching my so long unserialized serial, which is manifestly so excellent a thing for me.[2] I had begun to despair of anything, when abruptly, this brightens the view. For I *like*, extremely, the place the N.A.R. makes for my novel; it meets quite my ideal in respect to that isolation and relief one has always fondly conceived as the proper *due* of one's productions, and yet never, amid the promiscuous petticoats and other low company of the usual magazine table-of-contents, seen them in the remotest degree attended with. One had dreamed, in private fatuity, that one would really be the better for "standing out" a little; but one had, to one's own sense, never really "stood" at all, but simply lain very flat, for the petticoats and all the foolish feet aforesaid to trample over with the best conscience in the world. Charming to me also is the idea of your own beneficent paper in the same quarter[3]—the complete detachment of which, however, from the current fiction itself I equally apprehend and applaud; just as I see how the (not-to-be-qualified) editorial mind would indulge one of its most characteristic impulses by suggesting a connection. Never mind suggestions—and how you echo one of the most sacred laws of my own effort toward wisdom in not caring to know the source of *that* one! I care to know nothing but that your relation to my stuff, as it stands, gives me clear joy. Within a couple of days, moreover, your three glorious volumes of illustrated prose have arrived to enrich my existence, adorn my house and inflame my expectations.[4] With many things pressing upon me at this moment as preliminary to winding-up here and betaking myself, till early in the summer, to London, my more penetrative attention has not yet been free for them; but I am gathering for the swoop. Please meanwhile be tenderly thanked for the massive and magnificent character of the gift. What a glorious quantity of work it brings home to me that you do! I feel like a hurdy-gurdy man listening outside a cathedral to the volume of sound poured forth there by the enthroned organist.— Don't fear, by the way, that to be "sacrificed" with you in the no. of the Atlantic that you speak of,[5] and which I shall probably not at all see, will give me any-

2. WDH interceded with Harper & Brothers to achieve serialization of *The Ambassadors* in the *North American Review* (January–December 1903).

3. "Mr. Henry James's Later Work," *North American Review* (January 1903); the text of WDH's appreciative essay follows this letter.

4. *Heroines of Fiction*, 2 vols. (1901), and *Literature and Life* (1902). The former, a collection of pieces also serialized in *Harper's Bazar* (May 1900–January 1902), included a sensitive appreciation of "Daisy Miller" (2: 164–76).

5. HJ refers to an acerbic review by Harriet Waters Preston (1836–1911) which attacked both WDH's *Kentons* and HJ's *Wings of the Dove* ("The Latest Novels of Howells and James," *Atlantic* 91 [January 1903]: 77–82). "Time was," Preston begins, "when to receive a package containing new books both by William Dean Howells and Henry James would have been a delightful and even exciting event. Such time was in the last century and ominously near a generation ago." Bliss Perry, the editor of the *Atlantic*, had sent proofs of the review to WDH in October 1902 because he "thought it only decent, in view of your former relations to the magazine, to give you the opportunity to 'kill' the article." But WDH refused to involve himself with the magazine's editorial policy: "I appreciate the kind motive you had in sending me Miss Preston's paper," WDH wrote, "and I

thing but a sense of amusing myself in the company I would most fondly se-
lect. The Atlantic, all the same, ought, in respect to you and me, to have better manners. Its behaviour to myself is the oddest mixture of the "rude" and
the almost sycophantic. Into the details of the former feature I needn't enter,
but the editor has just been asking of me an article on Zola,[6] and the publishers
another biography of Lowell, poor dear (!!)—both with blandishments. I have
promised the Zola and refused the Lowell; but I would have refused both
had I known they were being publicly impertinent to you; to whom two thirds
of any prestige still retained by their pale periodical is indelibly owing. But good-
night, my dear Howells, with every feebly-breathed, but forcibly-felt good
wish of

yours always and ever.
Henry James.

William Dean Howells, "Mr. Henry James's Later Work," North American
Review *176 (January 1903): 125–37.*

It has been Mr. James's lot from the beginning to be matter of unusually lively
dispute among his readers. There are people who frankly say they cannot bear
him, and then either honestly let him alone, or secretly hanker for him, and
every now and then return to him, and try if they cannot like him, or cannot
bear him a little better. These are his enemies, or may be called so for convenience' sake; but they are hardly to be considered his readers. Many of his readers, however, are also his enemies: they read him in a condition of hot insurrec-
tion against all that he says and is; they fiercely question his point of view, they
object to the world that he sees from it; they declare that there is no such world,
or that, if there is, there ought not to be, and that he does not paint it truly.
They would like to have the question out with him personally: such is their
difference of opinion that, to hear them talk, you would think they would like
to have it out with him pugilistically. They would, to every appearance, like to
beat also those who accept his point of view, believe in his world, and hold that
he truly portrays it. Nothing but the prevailing sex of his enemies saves them,
probably, from offering the readers who are not his enemies the violence to

---

thank you for that. But I think you must see how impossible it is for me to do anything more. It is
your affair as editor and her affair as author. If you are satisfied to print and she to write such a
criticism, it is certainly not for me, on any account whatever, to interpose an objection." (See Bliss
Perry to WDH, 30 October 1902, Houghton Mifflin Letterbook #27, p. 393 [Houghton Mifflin
Archive, Harvard]; and WDH to Bliss Perry, 31 October 1902, SL 5: 39). On 3 January 1903 Perry
apologetically wrote to Preston's other victim. If HJ had been "accessible," Perry also would have
given him the option of censoring it; now that it was published, he hoped "that these things mortal
move you not at all, but I should be genuinely sorry to have you think that the *Atlantic* is 'attacking'—as some of today's newspapers assert—two writers who have rendered it such yeoman
service in the past" (Houghton Mifflin Letterbook #27, pp. 740–41).

6. "Émile Zola," *Atlantic* 92 (August 1903).

which their prevailing sex tempts them. You cannot, at least, palliate his demerits with them without becoming of the quality of his demerits, and identifying yourself with him in the whole measure of these. That is why, for one reason, I am going to make my consideration of his later work almost entirely a study of his merits, for I own that he has his faults, and I would rather they remained his faults than became mine.

I

The enmity to Mr. James's fiction among his readers is mostly feminine because the men who do not like him are not his readers. The men who like him and are his readers are of a more feminine fineness, probably, in their perceptions and intuitions, than those other men who do not read him, though of quite as unquestionable a manliness, I hope. I should like to distinguish a little farther, and say that they are the sort of men whose opinions women peculiarly respect, and in whom they are interested quite as much as they are vexed to find them differing so absolutely from themselves.

The feminine enmity to Mr. James is of as old a date as his discovery of the Daisy Miller type of American girl, which gave continental offence among her sisters. It would be hard to say why that type gave such continental offence, unless it was because it was held not honestly to have set down the traits which no one could but most potently and powerfully allow to be true. The strange thing was that these traits were the charming and honorable distinctions of American girlhood as it convinced Europe, in the early eighteen-seventies, of a civilization so spiritual that its innocent daughters could be not only without the knowledge but without the fear of evil. I am not going back, however, to that early feminine grievance, except to note that it seems to have been the first tangible grievance, though it was not the first grievance. I, with my gray hairs, can remember still earlier work of his whose repugnant fascination was such that women readers clung to it with the wild rejection which has in a measure followed all his work at their hands.

It has been the curious fortune of this novelist, so supremely gifted in divining women and portraying them, that beyond any other great novelist (or little, for that matter) he has imagined few heroines acceptable to women. Even those martyr-women who have stood by him in the long course of his transgressions, and maintained through thick and thin, that he is by all odds the novelist whom they could best trust with the cause of woman in fiction, have liked his anti-heroines more,—I mean, found them realer,—than his heroines. I am not sure but I have liked them more myself, but that is because I always find larger play for my sympathies in the character which needs the reader's help than in that which is so perfect as to get on without it. If it were urged that women do not care for his heroines because there are none of them to care for, I should not blame them, still less should I blame him for giving them that ground for abhorrence. I find myself diffident of heroines in fiction because I have never known one in life, of the real faultless kind; and heaven forbid I should ever yet know one. In Mr. James's novels I always feel safe from that sort, and it may be for this reason, among others, that I like to read his novels when they are new, and read them over and over again when they are old, or when they are no longer recent.

II

At this point I hear from far within a voice bringing me to book about Milly Theale in *The Wings of a Dove*,[1] asking me, if *there* is not a heroine of the ideal make, and demanding what fault there is in her that renders her lovable. Lovable, I allow she is, dearly, tenderly, reverently lovable, but she has enough to make her so, besides being too good, too pure, too generous, too magnificently unselfish. It is not imaginable that her author should have been conscious of offering in her anything like an atonement to the offended divinity of American womanhood for Daisy Miller. But if it were imaginable the offended divinity ought to be sumptuously appeased, appeased to tears of grateful pardon such as I have not yet seen in its eyes. Milly Theale is as entirely American in the qualities which you can and cannot touch as Daisy Miller herself; and (I find myself urged to the risk of noting it) she is largely American in the same things. There is the same self-regardlessness, the same beauteous insubordination, the same mortal solution of the problem. Of course, it is all in another region, and the social levels are immensely parted. Yet Milly Theale is the superior of Daisy Miller less in her nature than in her conditions.

There is, in both, the same sublime unconsciousness of the material environment, the same sovereign indifference to the fiscal means of their emancipation to a more than masculine independence. The sense of what money can do for an American girl without her knowing it, is a "blind sense" in the character of Daisy, but in the character of Milly it has its eyes wide open. In that wonderful way of Mr. James's by which he imparts a fact without stating it, approaching it again and again, without actually coming in contact with it, we are made aware of the vast background of wealth from which Milly is projected upon our acquaintance. She is shown in a kind of breathless impatience with it, except as it is the stuff of doing wilfully magnificent things, and committing colossal expenses without more anxiety than a prince might feel with the revenues of a kingdom behind him. The ideal American rich girl has never really been done before, and it is safe to say that she will never again be done with such exquisite appreciation. She is not of the new rich; an extinct New York ancestry darkles in the retrospect: something vaguely bourgeois, and yet with presences and with lineaments of aristocratic distinction. They have made her masses of money for her, those intangible fathers, uncles and grandfathers, and then, with her brothers and sisters, have all perished away from her, and left her alone in the world with nothing else. She is as convincingly imagined in her relation to them, as

1. WDH's text consistently refers to *The Wings of the Dove* by this title.

the daughter of an old New York family, as she is in her inherited riches. It is not the old New York family of the unfounded Knickerbocker tradition, but something as fully patrician, with a nimbus of social importance as unquestioned as its money. Milly is not so much the flower of this local root as something finer yet: the perfume of it, the distilled and wandering fragrance. It would be hard to say in what her New Yorkishness lies, and Mr. James himself by no means says; only if you know New York at all, you have the unmistakable sense of it. She is New Yorkish in the very essences that are least associable with the superficial notion of New York: the intellectual refinement that comes of being born and bred in conditions of illimitable ease, of having had everything that one could wish to have, and the cultivation that seems to come of the mere ability to command it. If one will have an illustration of the final effect in Milly Theale, it may be that it can he suggested as a sort of a Bostonian quality, with the element of *conscious* worth eliminated, and purified as essentially of pedantry as of commerciality. The wonder is that Mr. James in his prolonged expatriation has been able to seize this lovely impalpability, and to impart the sense of it; and perhaps the true reading of the riddle is that such a nature, such a character is most appreciable in that relief from the background which Europe gives all American character.

III

"But that is just what does not happen in the case of Mr. James's people. They are merged in the background so that you never can get behind them, and fairly feel and see them all round. Europe *doesn't* detach them; *nothing* does. 'There they are,' as he keeps making his people say in all his late books, when they are not calling one another dear lady, and dear man, and prodigious and magnificent, and of a vagueness or a richness, or a sympathy, or an opacity. No, he is of a tremendosity, but he worries me to death; he kills me; he really gives me a headache. He fascinates me, but I have no patience with him."

"But, dear lady," for it was a weary woman who had interrupted the flow of my censure in these unmeasured terms, and whom her interlocutor—another of Mr. James's insistent words—began trying to flatter to her disadvantage, "a person of your insight must see that this is the conditional vice of all painting, its vital fiction. You cannot get behind the figures in any picture. They are always merged in their background. And there you are!"

"Yes, I know I am. But that is just where I don't want to be. I want figures that I *can* get behind."

"Then you must go to some other shop—you must go to the shop of a sculptor."

"Well, why isn't *he* a sculptor?"

"Because he is a painter."

"Oh, that's no reason. He ought to be a sculptor."

"Then he couldn't give you the color, the light and shade, the delicate *nuances*, the joy of the intimated fact, all that you delight in him for. What was that you were saying the other day? That he was like Monticelli[2] in some of his pastorals or picnics: a turmoil of presences which you could make anything, everything, nothing of as you happened to feel; something going on that you had glimpses of, or were allowed to guess at, but which you were rapturously dissatisfied with, any way."

"Did I say that?" my interlocutress—terrible word!—demanded. "It was very good."

"It was wonderfully good. I should not have named Monticelli, exactly, because though he is of a vagueness that is painty, he is too much of a denseness. Mr. James does not trowel the colors on."

"I see what you mean. Whom should you have named?"

"I don't know. Monticelli will do in one way. He gives you a sense of people, of things undeniably, though not unmistakably, happening, and that is what Mr. James does."

"Yes, he certainly does," and she sighed richly, as if she had been one of his people herself. "He does give you a sense."

"He gives you a sense of a tremendous lot going on, for instance, in *The Wings of a Dove*, of things undeniable, though not unmistakably, happening. It is a great book."

"It is, it is," she sighed again. "It wore me to a thread."

"And the people were as unmistakable as they were undeniable: not Milly, alone, not Mrs. Stringham, as wonderfully of New England as Milly of New York; but all that terribly frank, terribly selfish, terribly shameless, terribly hard English gang."

"Ah, Densher wasn't really hard or really shameless, though he was willing—to please that unspeakable Kate Croy—to make love to Milly and marry her money so that when she died, they could live happy ever after—or at least comfortably. And you cannot say that Kate was frank. And Lord Mark really admired Milly. Or, anyway, he wanted to marry her. Do you think Kate took the money from Densher at last and married Lord Mark?"

"Why should you care?"

"Oh, one oughtn't to care, of course, in reading Mr. James. But with any one else, you would like to know who married who. It is all too wretched. Why should he want to picture such life?"

"Perhaps because it exists."

"Oh, do you think the English are really so bad? I'm glad he made such a beautiful character as Milly, American."

"My notion is that he didn't 'make' any of the characters."

"Of course not. And I suppose some people in England are actually like that. We have not got so far here, yet. To be sure, society is not so all-important here, yet. If it ever is, I suppose we shall pay the price. But *do* you think he ought to picture such life because it exists?"

2. Adolphe Monticelli (1824–86), French painter admired by van Gogh for his depiction of dreamlike settings and courtly revels.

"Do you find yourself much the worse for *The Wings of a Dove?*" I asked. "Or for *The Sacred Fount?* Or for *The Awkward Age?* Or even for *What Maisie Knew?* They all picture much the same sort of life."

"Why, of course not. But it isn't so much what he says—he never *says* anything—but what he insinuates. I don't believe that is good for young girls."

"But if they don't know what it means? I'll allow that it isn't quite *jeune fille* in its implications, all of them; but maturity has its modest claims. Even its immodest claims are not wholly ungrounded in the interest of a knowledge of our mother-civilization, which is what Mr. James's insinuations impart, as I understand them."

"Well, young people cannot read him aloud together. You can't deny that."

"No, but elderly people can, and they are not to be ignored by the novelist, always. I fancy the reader who brings some knowledge of good and evil, without being the worse for it, to his work is the sort of reader Mr. James writes for. I can imagine him addressing himself to a circle of such readers as this REVIEW'S with a satisfaction, and a sense of liberation, which he might not feel in the following of the family magazines, and still not incriminate himself. I have heard a good deal said in reproach of the sort of life he portrays, in his later books; but I have not found his people of darker deeds or murkier motives than the average in fiction. I don't say, life."

"No, certainly, so far as he tells you. It is what he *doesn't* tell that is so frightful. He leaves you to such awful conjectures. For instance when Kate Croy—"

"When Kate Croy—?"

"No. I *won't* discuss it. But you know what I mean; and I don't believe there ever was such a girl."

"And you believe there was ever such a girl as Milly Theale?"

"Hundreds! She is true to the life. So perfectly American. My husband and I read the story aloud together, and I wanted to weep. We had such a strange experience with that book. We read it half through together; then we got impatient, and tried to finish it alone. But we could not make anything of it apart; and we had to finish it together. We could not bear to lose a word; every word— and there were a good many!—seemed to tell. If you took one away you seemed to miss something important. It almost destroyed me, thinking it all out. I went round days, with my hand to my forehead; and I don't believe I understand it perfectly yet. Do you?"

IV

I pretended that I did, but I do not mind being honester with the reader than I was with my interlocutress. I have a theory that it is not well to penetrate every recess of an author's meaning. It robs him of the charm of mystery, and the somewhat labyrinthine construction of Mr. James's later sentences lends itself to the practice of the self-denial necessary to the preservation of this charm. What I feel sure of is that he has a meaning in it all, and that by and by, perhaps when I least expect it, I shall surprise his meaning. In the meanwhile I rest content with what I do know. In spite of all the Browning Clubs—even the club which has put up a monument to the poet's butler-ancestor—all of Browning is not clear, but enough of Browning is clear for any real lover of his poetry.

I was sorry I had not thought of this in time to say it to my interlocutress; and I was sorry I had not amplified what I did say of his giving you a sense of things, so as to make it apply to places as well as persons. Never, in my ignorance, have I had a vivider sense of London, in my knowledge a stronger sense of Venice, than in *The Wings of a Dove*. More miraculous still, as I have tried to express, was the sense he gave me of the anterior New York where the life flowered which breathed out the odor called Milly Theale—a heartbreaking fragrance as of funeral violets—and of the anterior New England sub-acidly fruiting in Mrs. Stringham. As for social conditions, predicaments, orders of things, where shall we find the like of the wonders wrought in *The Awkward Age*? I have been trying to get phrases which should convey the effect of that psychomancy from me to my reader, and I find none so apt as some phrase that should suggest the convincingly incredible. Here is something that the reason can as little refuse as it can accept. Into quite such particles as the various characters of this story would the disintegration of the old, rich, demoralized society of an ancient capital fall so probably that each of the kaleidoscopic fragments, dropping into irrelevant radiance around Mrs. Brookenham, would have its fatally appointed tone in the "scheme of color." Here is that inevitable, which Mr. Brander Matthews has noted as the right and infallible token of the real.[3] It does not matter, after that, how the people talk,—or in what labyrinthine parentheses they let their unarriving language wander. They strongly and vividly exist, and they construct not a drama, perhaps, but a world, floating indeed in an obscure where it seems to have its solitary orbit, but to be as solidly palpable as any of the planets of the more familiar systems, and wrapt in the aura of its peculiar corruption. How bad the bad people on it may be, one does not know, and is not intended to know, perhaps; that would be like being told the gross facts of some scandal which, so long as it was untouched, supported itself not unamusingly in air; but of the goodness of the good people one is not left in doubt; and it is a goodness which consoles and sustains the virtue apt to droop in the presence of neighborly remissness.

I might easily attribute to the goodness a higher office than this; but if I did I might be trenching upon that ethical delicacy of the author which seems to claim so little for itself. Mr. James is, above any other, the master of the difficult art of never doing more than to "hint a fault, or hesitate dislike,"[4] and I am not

---

3. In an 1895 essay entitled "On Pleasing the Taste of the Public," the American critic and novelist Brander Matthews (1852–1929) suggested that the art of fiction had progressed through four distinct phases of development, concerning itself first with the Impossible (myth and legend), then with the merely Improbable (romance), the Probable (Balzac and Thackeray), and had culminated in the Inevitable (Hawthorne, George Eliot, Turgenev and Tolstoy). See his *Aspects of Fiction and Other Ventures in Criticism* (New York: Harper & Brothers, 1896), 63–64.

4. WDH quotes l. 204 of the "Epistle to Dr. Arbuthnot," from the *Prologue* to *Imitations of Horace* (1734) by the Augustan poet Alexander Pope (1688–1744).

going to try committing him to conclusions he would shrink from. There is nothing of the clumsiness of the "satirist" in his design, and if he notes the absolute commerciality of the modern London world, it is with a reserve clothing itself in frankness which is infinitely, as he would say, "detached." But somehow, he lets you know how horribly *business* fashionable English life is; he lets Lord Mark let Milly Theale know, at their first meeting, when he tells her she is with people who never do anything for nothing, and when, with all her money, and perhaps because of it, she is still so trammelled in the ideal that she cannot take his meaning. Money, and money bluntly; gate-money of all kinds; money the means, is the tune to which that old world turns in a way which we scarcely imagine in this crude new world where it is still so largely less the means than the end.

But the general is lost in the personal, as it should be in Mr. James's books, earlier as well as later, and the allegory is so faint that it cannot always be traced. He does not say that the limitless liberty allowed Nanda Brookenham by her mother in *The Awkward Age* is better than the silken bondage in which the Duchess keeps her niece Aggie, though Nanda is admirably lovable, and little Aggie is a little cat; that is no more his affair than to insist upon the loyalty of old Mr. Longdon to an early love, or the generosity of Mitchett, as contrasted with the rapacity of Mrs. Brookenham, who, after all, wants nothing more than the means of being what she has always been. What he does is simply to show you those people mainly on the outside, as you mainly see people in the world, and to let you divine them and their ends from what they do and say. They are presented with infinite pains; as far as their appearance (though they are very little described) goes, you are not suffered to make a mistake. But he does not analyze them for you; rather he synthesizes them, and carefully hands them over to you in a sort of integrity very uncommon in the characters of fiction. One might infer from this that his method was dramatic, something like Tourguénieff's, say; but I do not know that his method is dramatic. I do not recall from the book more than one passage of dramatic intensity, but that was for me of very great intensity; I mean the passage where old Mr. Longdon lets Vanderbank understand that he will provide for him if he will offer himself to Nanda, whom he knows to be in love with Vanderbank, and where Vanderbank will not promise. That is a great moment, where everything is most openly said, most brutally said, to American thinking; and yet said with a restraint of feeling that somehow redeems it all.

Nothing could well be more perfected than the method of the three books which I have been supposing myself to be talking about, however far any one may think it from perfect. They express mastery, finality, doing what one means, in a measure not easily to be matched. I will leave out of the question the question of obscurity; I will let those debate that whom it interests more than it interests me. For my own part I take it that a master of Mr. James's quality does not set out with a design whose significance is not clear to himself, and if others do not make it clear to themselves, I suspect them rather than him of the fault. All the same I allow that it is sometimes not easy to make out; I allow that sometimes *I* do not make it out, I, who delight to read him almost more than any other living author, but then I leave myself in his hands. I do not believe he is going finally to play me the shabby trick of abandoning me in the dark; and meanwhile he perpetually interests me. If anything, he interests me too much, and I come away fatigued, because I cannot bear to lose the least pulse of the play of character; whereas from most fiction I lapse into long delicious absences of mind, now and then comfortably recovering myself to find out what is going on, and then sinking below the surface again.

The Awkward Age is mostly expressed in dialogue; *The Wings of a Dove* is mostly in the narration and the synthesis of emotions. Not the synthesis of the motives, please; these in both books are left to the reader, almost as much as they are in *The Sacred Fount*. That troubled source, I will own, "is of a profundity," and in its depths darkles the solution which the author makes it no part of his business to pull to the top; if the reader wants it, let him dive. But why should not a novel be written so like to life, in which most of the events remain the meaningless, that we shall never quite know what the author meant? Why, in fact, should not people come and go, and love and hate, and hurt and help one another as they do in reality, without rendering the reader a reason for their behavior, or offering an explanation at the end with which he can light himself back over the way he has come, and see what they meant? Who knows what any one means here below, or what he means himself, that is, precisely stands for? Most people mean nothing, except from moment to moment, if they indeed mean anything so long as that, and life which is full of propensities is almost without motives. In the scribbles which we suppose to be imitations of life, we hold the unhappy author to a logical consistency which we find so rarely in the original; but ought not we rather to praise him where his work confesses itself, as life confesses itself, without a plan? Why should we demand more of the imitator than we get from the creator?

Of course, it can be answered that we are *in* creation like characters in fiction, while we are outside of the imitation and spectators instead of characters; but that does not wholly cover the point. Perhaps, however, I am asking more for Mr. James than he would have me. In that case I am willing to offer him the reparation of a little detraction. I wish he would leave his people more, not less, to me when I read him. I have tried following their speeches without taking in his comment, delightfully pictorial as that always is, and it seems to me that I make rather more of their meaning, that way. I reserve the pleasure and privilege of going back and reading his comment in the light of my conclusions. This is the method I have largely pursued with the people of *The Sacred Fount*, of which I do not hesitate to say that I have mastered the secret, though, for the present I am not going to divulge it. Those who cannot wait may try the key which I have given.

But do not, I should urge them, expect too much of it; I do not promise it will unlock everything. If you find yourself, at the end, with nothing in your hand but the postulate with which the supposed narrator fantastically started, namely, that people may involuntarily and unconsciously prey upon one another, and mentally and psychically enrich themselves at one another's expense, still you may console yourself, if you do not think this enough, with the fact that you have passed the time in the company of men and women freshly and truly seen, amusingly shown, and abidingly left with your imagination. For me, I am so little exacting, that this is enough.

The Sacred Fount is a most interesting book, and you are teased through it to the end with delightful skill, but I am not going to say that it is a great book like *The Awkward Age,* or *The Wings of a Dove.* These are really incomparable books, not so much because there is nothing in contemporary fiction to equal them as because there is nothing the least like them. They are of a kind that none but their author can do, and since he is alone master of their art, I am very well content to leave him to do that kind of book quite as he chooses. I will not so abandon my function as to say that I could not tell him how to do them better, but it sufficiently interests me to see how he gets on without my help. After all, the critic has to leave authors somewhat to themselves; he cannot always be writing their books for them; and when I find an author, like Mr. James, who makes me acquainted with people who instantly pique my curiosity by "something rich and strange,"[5] in an environment which is admirably imaginable, I gratefully make myself at home with them, and stay as long as he will let me.

V

"But,"—here is that interlocutress whom I flattered myself I had silenced, at me again,—"do you like to keep puzzling things out, so? I don't. Of course, the books *are* intensely fascinating, but I do not like to keep guessing conundrums. Why shouldn't we have studies of life that are not a series of conundrums?"

"Dear lady," I make my answer, "what was I saying just now but that life itself is a series of conundrums, to which the answers are lost in the past, or are to be supplied us, after a long and purifying discipline of guessing, in the future? I do not admit your position, but if I did, still I should read the author who keeps you guessing, with a pleasure, an edification, in the suggestive, the instructive way he has of asking his conundrums beyond that I take in any of the authors who do not tax my curiosity, who shove their answers at me before I have had a chance to try whether I cannot guess them. Here you have the work of a great psychologist, who has the imagination of a poet, the wit of a keen humorist, the conscience of an impeccable moralist, the temperament of a philosopher, and the wisdom of a rarely experienced witness of the world; and yet you come back at me with the fact, or rather the pretence, that you do not like to keep puzzling his things out. It is my high opinion of you that you precisely do like to keep puzzling his things out; that you are pleased with the sort of personal appeal made to you by the difficulties you pretend to resent, and that you enjoy the just sense of superiority which your continual or final divinations give you. Mr. James is one of those authors who pay the finest tribute an author can pay the intelligence of his reader by trusting it, fully and frankly. There you are; and if

5. Shakespeare, *The Tempest* I.ii.401.

you were not puzzling out those recondite conundrums which you complain of, what better things in the perusal of the whole range of contemporary fiction, could you be doing? For my part I can think for you of none. There is no book like *The Awkward Age,* as I said, for it is sole of its kind, and no book that at all equals it, since Mr. Hardy's *Jude,*[6] for the intensity of its naturalness. I don't name them to compare them; again I renounce all comparisons for Mr. James's work; but I will say that in the deeply penetrating anguish of *Jude,* I felt nothing profounder than the pathos which aches and pierces through those closing scenes of *The Awkward Age,* in Nanda's last talk with Vanderbank, whom she must and does leave for her mother's amusement, and her yet later talk with old Mr. Longdon, to whom she must and does own her love for Vanderbank so heartbreaking. What beautiful and gentle souls the new-fashioned young girl and the old-fashioned old man are, and how beautifully and gently they are revealed to us by the perfected art of the book in which they continue to live after we part with them! How——"

"Ah, there," my interlocutress broke in, as if fearful of not having the last word, "I certainly agree with you. I wish you were as candid about everything else."

108.

JAMES TO HOWELLS, 12 June 1903, Rye   TLS Houghton
                                                  bMS Am 1784 (253) 82

Lamb House, Rye, Sussex.
June 12th, 1903.

My dear Howells.

How shall I tell you without giving up the whole of my letter to it how abject, how fairly *spurnable,* I feel at having let an ancient purpose of writing to you again after my last (now more than four months old) drag itself on to this disgraceful day? Excuses and reasons, in such abasements, are in general, I know, not worth the paper they cover; and yet one feels ashamed to have been base only to adopt the doctrine that no account of it need particularly matter. My poor account, just now, can only be, at the best, that almost immediately after last writing to you I went up to London for a long stay, and that I have but within a very short time come back to this greater peace. You manage to write me letters from New York, and charming ones; so that I have no ground for trying it on you that anything worse, anything more fatal to self-respect, is the matter with London. I only find that, in practice, something insurmountable *is* the matter—when one's so rotten a correspondent as I am to start with; and this especially if I manage to gouge out of the day the due chunk of time for the regular stint of work—a thing I luckily, have *not,* this winter, failed of. That

---

6. *Jude the Obscure* (1895) was the last completed novel of Thomas Hardy (1840–1928). After the failure of *Jude,* Hardy abandoned the genre of fiction in favor of poetry.

leaves me the smaller space for fighting the general battle of London in—or, rather, for fighting my own particular one. I fall into thinking, in the midst of it all, of how much better certain overdue communications will get themselves uttered in *this* (here) small stillness—and my arrears pile themselves up till I take a week or two, on my return, to deal with them apologetically. It is a clumsy process, but I hope you mercifully won't feel that everything has been sacrificed by it. It is a joy to me, at all events, to find myself talking with you now.

Meantime it is too monstrous, truly, when I think, all the response, all the grateful appreciation, that I owe you. I am not clear as to whether or no my last did not, in very truth, follow *your* last; but that, at the best, makes no difference—inasmuch as it was certainly, in the larger sense, your very last that came swimming in to me on the silver flood of N.A.R. What it amounts to, as I gaze at it in my pain, is that I have never decently "thanked" you at all for your beautiful concomitant *étude* [1] in January, keen as was the pleasure, sugared the cup, lucent the syrup, that you administered; irresistible as these were, I say, at the time of tasting. But I can express what I owe you even better perhaps at this late hour than then, for I have had more time to measure all the good you there did me. I seem to myself distinctly to feel it in the air, to note it even in definite ways. You contributed (and the publication of the Ambassadors in the Review has also contributed) to break the queer gruesome (as it seems to me) spell that had long weighed upon the small faculty of getting at all into the *light*—the light of a garish Publicity—that nature had endowed me withal. This has been excellent for me, and has made me fairly believe that even if I don't get so far, so late in the day, as still ever to *bask* a little, I may yet not have to pursue the rest of my mortal course all on the mere shady side of the street. You have met me positively in the middle of the same—say as I attempted agitatedly to cross— and have there publicly recognised and accosted me, held me in parley long enough for passers-by to notice and perhaps even be scandalised. Let them be if they like—it has made me a different man! And since then—too long ago— have come the three goodly volumes of the Literature and Life and the Heroines, a gorgeous present, making my house more furnished and my manners, alas, more stark. Never were any two opposed quantities so disproportionate, and I despair of making them perceptibly less uneven. It has been delightful to possess both by the clutching hand and the lingering eye so much good reading of you. There's nothing in the L and L that doesn't touch and charm me. In the other case, frankly, I commune with you, I feel, less directly—with too many foreign substances, too many petticoats and chignons in particular, baffling and disturbing the embrace. It's like trying to taste good wine when the mouth is full of food. You are the wine in that metaphor—and your authors and authoresses, with their large female families, figure for me the beef and potatoes and pudding. I hope therefore, all the more, that you are back again at your own fiction in preference to that of others. I want more of the Kentons' strain from

1. Study.

you—in *that* you are fully vinous and go both to my head and to my heart. I don't see Harper's regular, or I should probably know what you're up to. However it's in the bottleful, that is the bookful, that I principally and really require you.

I did lately come as near seeing Harper's (one night in town) as one does in seeing Harvey,[2] whom I pumped for news of you, and who gave it good enough—only too general. He recited his usual fable about your having been on the very edge of accompanying him—from which I extracted the inevitable stern moral: to the effect, I mean, of course, that you will nevermore come at all. The moral of *that,* in turn, is that I am thinking as hard as ever I dare to of going to see you as soon as ever I can—which I mentioned to Harvey, so that, as my indiscretion may by this time have repeated itself to you, I shan't startle you over much by thus departing from reserve. It's soon to talk of it, and I only do so because it's still more impossible to write to you as if nothing were the matter. To be thinking of it (that is of going for 6 or 8 months in as merely doubtful and dim a way as I am, as I must as yet restrict myself to doing,)—this by itself makes me feel as if something enormous were the matter; the matter, always, with *me.* I shall go on thinking (under the essential difficulties) until I either do start—sometime next year, which is far off, or give it up as impossible. I must make it somehow *pay*—that is to do it at all; which it must somehow, accordingly, depend on. But there will be plenty of time to talk—so I won't bore you now. I will only write as many books, and as good ones as I can, in the interval, as that will add to the pence in the stocking. I shall live, in short, for the months to come, only *for* the stocking. I hope you are all facing by this time to some haunt of summer half as helpful, even, to you as this is to me. When does Mildred definitely give you away?[3] You see I as shamelessly want your news as if you had had no wrong from

yours, and your wife's, always
Henry James

109.

JAMES TO HOWELLS, 11 December 1903, Rye   ALS Houghton
bMS Am 1784 (253) 83

December 11$^{\underline{th}}$ 1903.
LAMB HOUSE, RYE, SUSSEX.

My dear Howells.

The vow is taken—not another hour shall I be dumb in the presence of benefits received from you. Two neat red volumes, the work of your cunning hand, still ornament my table, where I had sworn to keep them at once charmingly, & distressingly in my eye—until I had written to give you my blessing on

---

2. Colonel George B. McClellan Harvey, president of the reorganized firm of Harper & Brothers.

3. HJ was unaware that Mildred Howells's engagement had been broken off; see letter #106, note 8.

them. This doesn't mean, I hasten to add, that they haven't also played their part in enriching my mind & delighting my imagination. I have read *Letters Home* & *Questionable Shapes*[1] with the same rich response with which I have read you, always, from the 1st immemorial day—reading into you and reading out of you, I make bold to declare, more than all your other readers put together are capable of doing, vast though their number & inflamed their spirit. The "Letters" are a vivid, & humorous, & charming thing, altogether, but I am not sure that I didn't find in The Apparitional Tales a gentle beauty of peace & quietness, let alone of soothing comedy, that I liked as well. You do the apparition, truly, from the happiest point of view—yielding perhaps more than the old unhappy far-off one. Both books, at any rate, quite hum with your own fine note.—I am afraid that I make a poor show, in respect to liberal dealing, over *The Ambassadors*, my "author's copies" of which were energetically tumbled out to me, from Franklin Square,[2] here, across the sea, before I had had time, or presence of mind, to ask that they should be distributed at home. I have sent 3 or 4 of them back to waiting recipients in the U.S., but I haven't gone through this form with *your* copy, in view of your so close and easy relations with the publishers. If they haven't given you one, will you kindly ask them to do so, "with my love", so far as they are capable of cognizance of that sort of commodity? As for the terribly perfunctory little vols. on W. W. Story,[3] (extorted from me by the inexorable pressure of the family,) I am sorry to say I have no material interest nor property in the American edition—having long ago, on a dark day, parted with *all* rights, for a beggarly dole, to Blackwoods here. But now I hear that the American edition is perversely *selling*—in a degree sufficient, at all events, for my confusion.[4] My point, however, is that I have had no single copy to give away (else you should have had one;) Houghton & Mifflin haven't even sent me one for a compliment. I'm afraid I have no great story of anything else for you: my migrations here, are but from the blue bed to the brown. We have had a horrible season of 6 months—the most so, for ferocity of spring, summer, autumn, of all my English years, & it goes, with tempests & floods, an eternal deluge, from bad to worse; but I stick on here, as always, till well after the New Year, when I go up to London for 3 or 4 months—& enjoy it, in a manner, as I had pretty well ceased to do while continuously living there. I am trying meanwhile to persuade myself, by mere naked force of thought, that it will be possible for me to come over & see you in the course of the coming year—there being nothing but that nudity, as yet, to make the idea practisable or invest the dream. There are, in other words, large roaring lions in the path, & the more I listen to them the louder their roar becomes. But I *want* to come, quite pathetically & tragically—it is a passion of nostalgia; & I shall nurse the tender project in my

1. Both *Letters Home* and *Questionable Shapes* were published by Harper's in 1903.

2. The New York address of Harper & Brothers.

3. *William Wetmore Story and His Friends*, 2 vols. (Edinburgh and London: William Blackwood & Son, 1903; Boston: Houghton, Mifflin, 1903).

4. By the end of 1903, Houghton, Mifflin & Company had imported 1,250 sets of sheets of *William Wetmore Story and His Friends* from Blackwood.

arms—till it is snatched from me to have its brains dashed out. The difficulty is in the time of stay (the time of going wouldn't be before the summer's end.) I see my way to it for 2 or 3 months—I don't for 6 or 8—which alone wd. make it worth while & enable me to look about. I should greatly like before I chuck up the game to write another (another!!) American novel or two—putting the thing *in* the country; which wd. take, God knows,—I mean wd. require—some impressions. So, in short, I am groping my way, & if light should break you will be the first person I shall advise of the same (after my brother.) *Encourage* me by some winsome word & you will add strength to my wings. It will in fact be almost enough for me if you simply tell me that all the Howells's want to see me. I want at any rate to see them, & am yours & theirs

very constantly
Henry James

110.

JAMES TO HOWELLS, 8 January 1904, Rye

TLS Houghton
bMS Am 1784 (253) 84

Lamb House, Rye, Sussex.
Jan. 8th, 1904.

My dear Howells.

I am infinitely beholden to you for two good letters,[1] the second of which has come in to-day, following close on the heels of the first and greeting me most benevolently as I rise from the couch of solitary pain. Which means nothing worse than that I have been in bed with odious and inconvenient gout, and have but just tumbled out to deal, by this helpful machinery, with dreadful arrears of Christmas and New Year's correspondence. Not yet at my ease for writing, I thus inflict on you without apology this unwonted grace of legibility.

It warms my heart, verily, to hear from you in so encouraging and sustaining a sense—in fact makes me cast to the winds all timorous doubt of the energy of my intention. I know now more than ever how much I want to "go"—and also a good deal of why. Surely it will be a blessing to commune with you face to face, since it is such a comfort and a cheer to do so even across the wild winter sea. Will you kindly say to Harvey for me that I shall have much pleasure in talking with him here of the question of something serialisable in the North American, and will broach the matter of an "American" novel in *no* other way until I see him.[2] It comes home to me much, in truth, that, after my immensely

---

1. Neither extant.

2. In anticipation of his return to the United States, HJ eventually agreed to write two books for Harper & Brothers: a "Book of Impressions," which became *The American Scene* (1907) and a novel of contemporary American life. HJ began to work on the novel in the fall of 1907, but the incessant labor of revising his productions for the twenty-four-volume New York Edition forced him to postpone it. His initial conception for the novel was eventually superseded by a new donnée— for *The Ivory Tower*—but neither project was ever completed.

long absence, I am not quite in a position to answer in advance for the quantity and quality, the exact form and colour, of my "reaction" in presence of the native phenomena. I only feel tolerably confident that a reaction of some sort there will be. What affects me as indispensable—or rather what I am conscious of as a great personal desire—is some such energy of direct *action* as will enable me to cross the country and see California, and also have a look at the South. I am hungry for Material, whatever I may be moved to do with it; and, honestly, I think, there will not be an inch or an ounce of it unlikely to prove grist to my intellectual and "artistic" mill. You speak of one's possible "hates" and loves— that is aversions and tendernesses—in the dire confrontation; but I seem to feel, about myself, that I proceed but scantly, in these chill years, by those particular categories and rebounds; in short that, somehow, such fine primitive passions *lose* themselves for me in the act of contemplation, or at any rate in the act of reproduction. However, you are much more passionate than I, and I will wait upon *your* words, and try and learn from you a little to be shocked and charmed in the right places. What mainly appals me is the idea of going a good many months without a quiet corner to do my daily stint; so much so in fact that this is quite unthinkable, and that I shall only have courage to advance by nursing the dream of a sky-parlour of some sort, in some cranny or crevice of the conti- nent, in which my mornings shall remain my own, my little trickle of prose eventuate, and my distracted reason thereby maintain its seat. If some gifted creature only wanted to exchange with me for six or eight months and "swap" its customary bower, over there, for dear little Lamb House here, a really deli- cious residence, the trick would be easily played. However, I see I must wait for all tricks. This is all, or almost all, to-day—all except to reassure you of the pleasure you give me by your remarks about the A's[3] and cognate topics. The "International" is very presumably indeed, and in fact quite inevitably, what I am *chronically* booked for, so that truly, even, I feel it rather a pity, in view of your so-benevolent colloquy with Harvey, that a longish thing I am just finishing should not be *disponible*[4] for the N.A.R. niche; the niche that I like very much the best, for serialisation, of all possible niches. But "The Golden Bowl" isn't, alas, so employable—being contracted for, with Methuen here and the Scribners in New York, as a volume only, and on no brilliant terms.[5] Fortunately, however, I still cling to the belief that there are as good fish in the sea—that is in *my* sea—! I am sorry you failed of the sight of Harland,[6] if only that he might have pleased you (for he has greatly matured and solidified with Success!) more than his recent inspirations can have done. They truly are "rum" phenomena—

3. *The Ambassadors* (1903).

4. Available.

5. Later that year HJ did leap at the possibility that the *Century* might take *The Golden Bowl* as a serial; but his agent's negotiations with the magazine eventually fell through.

6. Henry Harland, formerly editor of the *Yellow Book,* had recently published two romantic fictions—*The Cardinal's Snuff-Box* (1900) and *The Lady Paramount* (1902)—which reaped huge fi- nancial returns.

scarcely less rum than the Success in question. And I speak of his gain of ripe-
ness even in the face of a most unutterable Interview journalistically had with
him in N. Y. and transmitted me by some importunate hand—in which I seem
to have been sacrificed with the best good faith in the world on the most fantastic altar.[7]—But *non ragionam'* [8] of these luridities; the fruit, so absolutely and so
strangely, of conscientious devotion on dear H's part. Such are the slings and
arrows of the truest loyalty! You mention to me a domestic event—in Pilla's
life—which interests me scarce the less for my having taken it for granted.[9] But
I bless you all.

> Yours always
> Henry James

III.

JAMES TO HOWELLS, 9 March 1904, London   ALS Houghton
                                                        bMS Am 1784 (253) 85

REFORM CLUB, PALL MALL. S. W.
Mch. 9th 1904

My dear Howells.

   This is brave & beautiful news[1]—a perfect fairy-tale of an announcement, &
I feel it press within me the spring of a fairly vociferous welcome. These hasty
lines start this instant for Bath, charged, for both of you, with my affectionate
blessing & greeting. I am in London, most congruously, & shall be here till well
on into next month, or, if possible, as long as you & Mildred are, & then leave
it only to take you with me, or prepare your rooms in advance, at Lamb House.
May England, from this moment, be better & balmier to you than, during long
diluvian months, it has been to us amphibians. And may Bath be a saturation
both of memories & remedies. I am so impatient to get you *here* without too

   7. HJ probably did more than sneeze when he read "A Pinch from '*The Cardinal's Snuff-Box*,'"
an interview with Harland that appeared in the New York *Herald* (13 December 1903, 3rd sec., 4–
5). The article featured such ejaculations as "Henry James! His intellect is of the same order as
Aristotle," among other profundities. When asked if he had taken HJ as a stylistic model, Harland
modestly confessed: "I? Oh, what am I, what can I ever do that I should exist in the same sentence
with Henry James? A mere butterfly, perched above a bowlder—a mote, a speck dancing in a great,
full beam!" Harland's final advice to the newspaperman was:

> I like this, now really I do. . . . Interviews aren't so half bad, after all. Be sure to put in a
> lot of James, and let me out of it, because, you know, when we talk of him we speak, as you
> are doubtless aware, of the very greatest mind that has ever been devoted to the writing of
> fiction in any language since the beginning of created literature.

   8. I hardly take notice.
   9. The event was the fact that Mildred Howells's engagement had been broken off.
   1. WDH and his daughter, Mildred, had sailed for England on 3 March 1904; after landing at
Plymouth and touring Exeter, they traveled west to Bath.

much delay that I permit myself to wonder if even the shade of Jane A.[2] mayn't induce satiety *before* April 1$^{\underline{st}}$. In any case if you find Bath does hold you, or promise to, long enough for you to turn round, as it were, I should like most awfully to come down & see you for the *day*—for luncheon & tea, say—& for an early date. The excellent G. W. trains[3] make this very feasible. So give me but a sign of assent, & I take the 10.50 from Paddington. Make me, benevolently *some* sign that you are landed, housed & happy.

With all love yours always
Henry James

112.

JAMES TO HOWELLS, 3 April 1904, London

ALS Houghton
bMS Am 1784 (253) 97

Sunday a.m.
REFORM CLUB, PALL MALL. S. W.

My dear Howells.

I am indebted to you & to Pilla, almost alike, for beautiful little letters,[1] & yours, in particular, I wd. fain have thanked you for the hour it arrived, or, at latest, some time yesterday. But every hour has been, in one way & another, going straight down, even now, the great Dragon-maw of this insatiable city. I am infinitely grateful for your still maturer thought on the subject of Harvey's possible relation to the Vol. of Impressions[2]—but shall be able to thank you much more in detail when I see you. It's a "vast" comfort, as you say at Bath, that this is to be so soon, & I plead with you to wire me on receipt of this as to where you go on Tuesday night & what I can arrange for you.[3] Command me so, by wire, or otherwise, & nothing will be easier than to serve you. On the eve of Easter[4] London is empty, & you will be able to get in anywhere. I said to you something about Great Western Hotel Paddington, but perhaps (*if* you're

---

2. Jane Austen (1775–1817), a novelist much admired by WDH and his family. From 1801 to 1806 she resided in Bath, a setting which figures in *Northanger Abbey* and *Persuasion* (both published posthumously in 1818).

3. The Great Western Railway.

1. Not extant.

2. In the fall of 1903 HJ had received an offer from S. S. McClure to write a book of "Impressions, Notes, Experiences, or whatever" in the event of his return to the United States. HJ apparently discussed this possibility with WDH, who brought the matter to the attention of Col. George Harvey, president of Harper & Brothers. Harvey must have outbid his rival, for on 18 April 1904 James's agent concluded an agreement with Harper's for a "Book of Impressions." See HJ to Witter Bynner, 8 January 1904 (Bynner Papers, Harvard), and James B. Pinker to Col. Harvey, 18 April 1904, Harper Contract Books 11: 340 (*The Archives of Harper and Brothers*, reel 4).

3. Because of inclement weather, WDH and Mildred abandoned a plan to stay on the Isle of Wight, and instead came up to London on 4 April.

4. The date for this letter is established by the fact that in 1904 Easter Sunday fell on 3 April.

going to Folkestone,[5] where quarters must have been *promised* you,) you wd. find the Charing Cross (railway hotel for railway hotel!) *more* convenient. It is blessedly close to me here (& to all other things,) & you wd. slip straight out of it into your Folkestone train. Only let me know, that I may seek you immediately after luncheon; with my morn's work done. Love to Pilla, & heaven speed you! Don't trouble to write—*wire*.

Ever your
Henry James

113.

JAMES TO HOWELLS, 13 May 1904, Rye

ALS Houghton
bMS Am 1784 (253) 88

LAMB HOUSE, RYE, SUSSEX.
May 13th 1904.

My dear Howells.

I spent yesterday, under urgency, in town, & came back last night late—having rec'd. your letter[1] just as I was hurrying off in the a.m. I shall be delighted to see you at luncheon on Monday, & beseech you to cultivate this possibility in the meanwhile, & to train Pilla, to whom I send my love, up to the cultivation of it. You will catch the train that leaves Ashford about *one* o'clk.,—reaching here 1.30—& then will go up to town by the 4.9 from here—via Hastings to Victoria, much the best & quickest way—I going with you to Hastings. There you *are*—it is perfect! I delight to know that things continue well with you at F.,[2] & that the proper effects take place from all the proper causes. Go, if you have time, to *Lymne* (ruined castle on steep,) not very far beyond Shorncliffe.[3] Any fly-driver will know. I haven't been, but am told it's admirable. *Wells* will know—I hope you will have comfortably seen that fine-eyed little man of intelligence & genius.[4] But I hurry this off!

Yours & Pilla's always
Henry James

5. WDH and Mildred stayed in London—and saw HJ frequently—until 28 April, when they moved to the channel town of Folkestone.

1. Not extant.

2. WDH and Mildred were still at Folkestone.

3. The present castle at Lympne dates from 1360, but earlier fortifications there go back to the time of the Roman settlement.

4. Herbert George Wells (1866–1946), English novelist, whom WDH had recently visited at Sandgate. On 14 May Wells advised WDH that if he and Mildred were staying at Folkestone until Tuesday (17 May), they could do their "neglected duty to Lympne Castle on Monday" (Howells Papers, Harvard).

114.

JAMES TO HOWELLS, 16 May 1904, Rye   ALS Houghton
                                                      bMS Am 1784 (253) 89

LAMB HOUSE, RYE, SUSSEX.

My dear Howells.

It was a blow, this a.m.—the household had so projected itself into your advent, & I had lain awake the previous night so long, listening to the roar of the fatted calf during his elaborate killing.[1] This please relentlessly tell Pilla— as also that I had provided a very handsome & rising young man for her further consumption at luncheon—who made me a good deal of a scene when he arrived at Lamb House & found the Attraction wanting. However, we sat down together & consoled each other by railing at female faith. If you only *will* come down from town after the efforts of Oxford[2] have subsided, all will be forgiven. But do send me your new address on a post-card that I may regularly work on you to that end. Here I sit, indefinitely, & your arrival will *always* be welcome. You have only to announce it—the fatted calf will be warmed up. I hope Oxford will really be for you all that Oxford *can*. That is immensely much; especially at this May time. *Stiano bene.*[3] I rejoice you liked the Wellses, who have written to me (by his hand—I scarcely know *her*) effusively thanking me for the Howellses.[4] Summon me to town without scruple for any convulsion, climax or crisis, & believe me

Yours ever, & Pilla's even still,
Henry James
May 16$\underline{\text{th}}$ 1904.

115.

HOWELLS TO JAMES, 17 May 1904, London   ALS Hayes

. . . CHARING CROSS HOTEL.
May 17th 1904.

Dear James:

This is deplorably enough my address for tonight and tomorrow night; then Oxford c/o Louis Dyer, (an old young friend),[1] Sunbury Lodge, 68 Banbury Road, till Monday; then London c/o Harpers till we are settled again, locally.

---

1. WDH had to cancel his visit to Rye because of some indisposition on Mildred's part.
2. WDH was to be awarded an honorary Doctor of Letters degree from Oxford University on 22 June; his visit in May was preliminary to the formal commencement ceremony.
3. Be well.
4. Not extant.
1. Louis Dyer (1851–1908), an author and lecturer in classics, was a friend from WDH's Cambridge days. He was graduated from Harvard in 1874, went to Balliol College, Oxford, for advanced study, and later took up residence there.

Pilla's heart is wrung as much even as an indignant host could wish. She does not know what to say, or I for her; we both live in the wish to retrieve ourselves. Everything seems to go wrong with the poor child, except her amiable self, and she feels bitterly the disappointment she has inflicted on you at her own expense.

I have had a line from Harvey, but nothing about the Women's Clubs.[2] Would you like me to jog him?

Yours ever
W. D. Howells.

116.

JAMES TO HOWELLS, 28 May 1904, Rye   ALS Houghton
                                                      bMS Am 1784 (253) 90

LAMB HOUSE, RYE, SUSSEX.
May 28th 1904

Dearest W. D. H!

I feel a kind of horror of my having made you no sign for so long—since your touching note from the Charing X Hotel in fact; though the motives of my neglect have been of the purest. I have but just escaped from the considerable social burden laid on me by Whitsuntide—the Edith Whartons[1] having been with me in force & Jonathan Sturges in even greater—*he* having stayed till yesterday. Under the complexity created by these & other combinations (Richard Cobden's daughter,[2] with a note of introduction, for 2 days &c,) *with* the hauntingness of my backward Book[3] &c, I have but smiled sweetly, wanly, fixedly, at the sense of my correspondence, & many other things, going to pieces. And then I have had, all the while, hopes for a kind of sublime joy, on your & Pilla's part, at Oxford, as would best consort with being left alone on your summits & not reminded of meaner things. However, I am alone again (for

2. The possibility of delivering a lecture to women's organizations was a new development in HJ's plan for visiting the United States. A series of lecture engagements in various cities would allow HJ to see more of the country and would help underwrite his expenses. HJ earlier had rejected an offer from Harvard to give the Lowell Lectures for 1904–5 because this would have committed him to remaining in Cambridge for an undesirably extended time. See HJ to Alice H. G. James, 19 January 1904 (James Papers, Harvard).

1. Edith Newbold Jones had married Edward Robbins ("Teddy") Wharton in April 1885. She and HJ had exchanged books and notes for several years, but they first met in London the day before Christmas 1903. The Whartons' visit to HJ was the first of many such descents in their chauffeur-driven motorcar, a practice that earned her HJ's sobriquet as the Angel of Devastation.

2. Richard Cobden (1804–65), the member of Parliament chiefly responsible for the repeal of the Corn Laws, left five surviving daughters. HJ's guest was probably either Jane Unwin, wife of the publisher T. Fisher Unwin (1848–1935), or Anne Cobden-Sanderson, wife of the great bookbinder Thomas James Cobden-Sanderson (1840–1922).

3. *The Golden Bowl.*

3 hours,—Phil Burne-Jones[4] arrives at 6.30!) & I yearn toward you even through the rose-coloured mantle in which I wrap you. Put your hand through when you *can*—for 3 strokes of the pen—& tell how it has been & how it still is! I hope & pray that you have been having impressions sharp & sweet, with no other sharpnesses, nor even excess of sweets, to spoil them. You see, however, I have nothing but vague affectionate murmurs to waft you—no "news," thank heaven; & I hope you twain are keeping clear of news other than such as you exchange, each with the other, about your felicity. Tell Pilla to sit tight & take a few small current penalties for *granted,* & then she will get *used* to the mixture & like it, get used to *not* getting used! As soon as you have a domicile I shall cynically invent a pretext for deserting—that is for escaping from the lash of my awful muse for a day—& come up to prune & water you, to straighten you on your stems, even, if necessary, by training you on sticks—though I seem to hear Pilla's wit echo to this that so, already, you've been a good deal trained. I want at any rate to assure myself with my eyes of your being-well, as you won't be able to tell me otherwise. Courage, courage, *& hold on:* you will find you *can.* All thanks for your kind offer of stimulating Harvey on the great Ladies' Club subject.[5] He had perhaps at the time of his first writing you not had time & margin enough, but if nothing comes by the end of a week or two more, I should regard your service as a deed of real mercy. I must know whether to *do* something! And yet I shall probably do it on the chance. I hope you are "somewhere pleasant" this perfect day (here.) Your rooms languish for you here, by the same token, & I am

yours always & ever
Henry James

117.

JAMES TO HOWELLS, 30 May 1904, Rye   ALS Houghton
bMS Am 1784 (253) 95

Monday *p.m.*
LAMB HOUSE, RYE, SUSSEX.

My dear Howells.

I wired you this p.m., & this is a word to confirm, intensely, my welcome. I shall be but too delighted to see you tomorrow afternoon, & the 4.28 from Charing ✝ *is* the train of the day. Be put into an Ashford carriage, & change of course at A; also tell Pilla to attach a label (a penny a dozen, with strings affixed,)—a label *L. H., Rye*—to her best bandbox if her b.b. is put into the van. You arrive here 6.35, & it will be rare to have you. Likewise, *blasès*[1] &

---

4. Philip Burne-Jones (1861–1926), English painter.
5. See letter #115, note 2.
1. Weary.

battered as you must both now be, this humble nook wears at present a sweetness of face! But I don't dare to swagger. I shall be of course at the stazione;[2] &
am

> yours impatiently
> *Henry James*

118.

JAMES TO HOWELLS, 6 June 1904, Rye ALS Houghton
bMS Am 1784 (253) 96

LAMB HOUSE, RYE, SUSSEX.

My dear Howells.

I am delighted you can have me to dine on the 14th, tomorrow, Tuesday,
week, & shall be glad if you can give me till *eight* o'clk (as I shall take that 4.9
train via Hastings—which will enable me, however, to be punctual.) I hope
then to convince you that your broodings, together, on my overwrought domestic sensibility were strictly morbid: the ghost that you & Pilla saw here, to that
extent, was but a sheet flopping on a pole—not the charming real thing like the
Oxford young man's. (All thanks to Pilla for *her*—she *is* the real thing.)[1] I have
had a spacious "week end"—thanks to Edward Warren's (Herbert's—of Magdalen—brother,)[2] having put himself off from Saturday last to *this* week (when,
however, he comes from *Friday* to Monday, to make up for it!)[3] and my young
man who followed you was only a night & a day! I just hear from W. E. Norris:[4]
"I envy you the society of your friend Howells. I've always loved his books &
shld. love him too, if he is at all like them. But people so seldom *are!*" I am
writing him that you are the image of Silas Lapham & Ragged Lady, & even
that he may call on you if he *can*. But he lives at Torquay & is to be in town
but from the 11th.

> Yours, both, ever
> *Henry James*
> June 6th.

2. Station.

1. Mildred Howells must have picked up a ghostly anecdote during her earlier visit to Oxford.

2. Edward Warren (1856–1937) was the architect whom HJ had consulted about renovations to
Lamb House; his brother, Sir Thomas Herbert Warren (1853–1930), was president of Magdalen
College, Oxford.

3. HJ's familiar defensive attitude—the inevitable result of an artist besieged by intrusive visitors—obscures the fact that he had invited Warren to come down for the weekend of either 4 or 11
June. See HJ to Edward Warren, 26 May 1904 (Huntington).

4. William Edward Norris (1847–1925), minor English novelist with whom HJ first became
acquainted at Torquay in 1894.

119.

JAMES TO HOWELLS, 22 June 1904, Rye   TLS Houghton
bMS Am 1784 (253) 92

LAMB HOUSE, RYE, SUSSEX.
June 22nd, 1904.

My dear Howells.

I unblushingly resort to print to thank you—after all but with due distinctness—for your most kind note enclosing Miss Jordan's letter.[1] I came back
late last night from a week in town, produced by an original necessity of two
days there—which I couldn't afford to lose; so that I boldly made them seven, a
period for which I could engage a typist and go on, unretarded, under my fictive
Old Man of the Sea. I come back to unanswered letters—and hence these gri-
maces. Miss J's communication to myself has not yet turned up—it doubtless
will soon;[2] but meanwhile I see the prospect (in the particular matter) as quite
conceivably not brilliant, and I am doubting if it will be my best economy to
take the time necessary for the fabrication of an harangue. I fabricate so
slowly—in the directions in which I've had no practice. And the incitement of
the glittering fee rather dim, I am afraid I pusillanimously shrink. Certainly, if
the personal exposure is out of proportion to the tip—! But I await the kind
Miss J, and reaffirm with effusion my indebtedness to the still kinder W.D.H.
All greetings meanwhile to the disembarked Lady.[3] I send her my love and
entreat her to back you up in every disposition to pleasing adventure. The most
pleasing would be for you all to be in London about July 11th, when I am
obliged to be there again for twenty-four hours. I hope you're having thunders
of applause at Oxford, and am

yours, all, always
Henry James

1. Prompted by HJ's anxiety about his upcoming American visit, WDH had written to Elizabeth
Jordan (1867–1947), editor of *Harper's Bazar*, about plans for HJ to deliver "a lecture, on some
literary subject, to deserving Women's Clubs." WDH asked Jordan to advise HJ directly about this
possibility, so that he might know whether to prepare a lecture in advance of his departure. Later in
the summer HJ met with Jordan and Col. Harvey in London and discussed these plans further, but
no definite engagements were arranged until HJ arrived in America. See WDH to Elizabeth Jordan,
1 June 1904, *SL* 5: 102–3.
2. Elizabeth Jordan's letters to HJ are not extant.
3. Elinor Howells had arrived in Liverpool on 18 June to attend the Oxford festivities.

120.

JAMES TO HOWELLS, 5 July 1904, Rye

ALS Houghton
bMS Am 1784 (253) 93

July 5th p.m. *1904*
LAMB HOUSE, RYE, SUSSEX.

My dear Howells.

I thank you for Miss Jordan's fresh communication, & rejoice to be able to place you again, especially in London—as I hope to see you there next week. I *did* hear from Harvey, on Miss J.'s behalf, as it were, & reporting her report—all in a sense that I have taken as discouraging & deterrent. I wrote to H. of course, promptly, & I shall now write to her—to whom I haven't hitherto written, though meaning to in my gratitude—for illusions dispelled![1] And I owe you, on this latter valuable head, renewed declarations—you having brought about the tonic revelation. In what a correspondence, too, I have all but involved you! But this last has *nothing* for you to answer. I go up on Monday afternoon next, to keep an engagement in London fondly but rashly made some month ago; & also, a good deal, to keep off a visitor or two—or three—whom I should otherwise be receiving here. And I shall probably find it the best economy to remain there for several days—as well (in respect to your house,) as the best pleasure. I shall come to see you as soon as the immediate complications that await me permit. You've immense arrears of Wahrheit & Dichtung[2] to make up to me. Be thankful that you have, this time, Mrs. Howells to help you in it, & tell her from me, with my love, how thankful *I* am.

Yours & hers always
Henry James

1. In his letter to Jordan of 5 July, HJ acknowledged that he should postpone work on a lecture until definite commitments from appropriate audiences could be secured:

> The field, I gather, will not deny a very modest harvest to the artful, the *very* artful gleaner,— a formula of the matter with which I for the present content myself & on which I can practically rest. It is moreover exactly the account of the question that I thought most probable & most conformable—to general trust!—& I shall be able to take action on it or not, according to my needs, abilities (such as they are!) &, above all, opportunities as [are] on [the] spot made manifest.

See "Henry James and the *Bazar* Letters," in Edel and Powers, *Howells and James: A Double Billing*, 35.

2. Figuratively, personal news. *Dichtung und Wahrheit* was the title of Goethe's multivolume autobiography (1811–32).

121.

JAMES TO HOWELLS, 5 August 1904, London   ALS Houghton
                                                            bMS Am 1784 (253) 94

THE ATHENAEUM, PALL MALL. S. W.
Aug. 5$\underline{th}$ 1904

My dear Howells.

Your good letter[1] was a benediction to me 2 or 3 days ago (rather *correcting* those otherwise lurid visions I have been having of your possible hunted & heated state;) & I have waited even this much to say only because till last night I also have been a little hunted, since receiving it: to say nothing of my being quite overwhelmingly heated. In the act of writing you (before coming up here on urgent business, for a day or two,) I was suddenly called to Folkestone by 2 just disembarked foreign friends whom I wished to prevent thereby from invad-ing Lamb House[2]—& I spent 24 hours there in that machination. This has been my 1$\underline{st}$ free hour since. Let me say too that ever since we parted 3 (?) weeks ago in Sloane St. I have had a letter (of yearning exhortation,) on my tongue's end *à votre adresse*[3]—but which kept *not* coming out at my pen's be-cause I had promised then to give you next some certainty about myself—& certainty had remained till 3 or 4 days ago too obscured. Worriment & suspense were, rather acutely my portion for a fortnight—in respect to my being *able*, after all, to embark for the U. S.—the failure of which wd. have been, I confess, a great humiliation & disappointment to me. I feel my going not only as a lively desire but as a supreme necessity—& I rejoice to say that it appears to be now definitely settled that I *do* embark. The good Pinker, my "literary agent," came to my aid in intention, zealously, by thinking a month ago that he had a good opportunity—or possibility—of arranging to *serialise* the *Golden Bowl* for me in the U.S. (so as to realise very much more on it—& in spite of that not having at all previously been in view.) So I feverishly divided it into 12 instalments, (& it *cut* far better than might have been,) & it was despatched, or 11 Parts out of the 12 were, across the Atlantic for judgment. I waited in a great state of tension, & the people, whoever they were (I don't know, & don't want to,)[4] took a fortnight, or almost, to consider & decide. Then they cruelly cabled "Decline", & the Golden Dream was as broken, outside, as the Golden Bowl within. If I had only known, or tried, *before* (instead of forming the book inde-pendently,) I am pretty sure I could have captured them—but that is one of the

1. Not extant.
2. The French novelist Paul Bourget (1852–1935) and his wife, Minnie.
3. Addressed to you.
4. Richard Watson Gilder (1844–1909), editor of the *Century*, rejected Pinker's offer. HJ con-fided that the possibility of serializing the novel had, in the suspenseful interlude, "been worrying me within an inch of my life, and during which, or the worst of it, I found myself behaving as if I had no other matter at all to think of." See HJ to Joseph Pennell, 29 July 1904 (Pennell Papers, Library of Congress).

vain "if's." It makes rather a chill, or snub, to "land" on—but it has luckily become possible for me to land all the same—& to make up for it a little, I at the same moment let my house—badly, too cheaply, for the mere amt. of the Servants' wages, but still let it, & for six months.[5] That is a facilitation—& yesterday, as soon as I got here, I bought a steamer trunk & ordered some clothes on the strength of it. All this gives me a rich & desperate sense of "going," & I am highly impatient & don't care what happens now. So be at ease about me— which this long story takes so extravagantly for granted your capacity for not being! What I have really all the while wanted *much* more to say to you is that my desire is, above all, to know you at ease about yourself—as I felt you insufficiently to be as we walked away together from Eaton Terrace[6] that last evening. You expressed some doubt, I remember, as to whether the N. Y. people wd. "like" something you had sent over (about Folkestone I think)[7]—as well as a general *malaise* about your footing of production (abroad,) which I longed at the moment to combat with high emphasis, & which it has since haunted me that I have been leaving unrefuted. What I mean is that your questioning in detail, at this time of day, that immense "liked" & likeable state which is the very air your work draws breath in & the very ground it has under its feet, was to "borrow trouble" as wantonly (as who shld. say,) as if you were borrowing Hall Caine or M. Corelli.[8] Sink luxuriously into your *position*, your immense record of admirable labour & the right of *leaning back*, on your own terms, that crown this as with the wreath of honour & of ease, & you will do what every one concerned wants quite exceedingly to understand you as doing—& as understanding that you *must* do. But it's all work scribbling in this stifling London air, & my hand has gone to pot, quite. But if we could talk again! I'm afraid we can't! I rejoice in your news of John, & your vision of Naples.[9] Yes, Malvern must be dull enough & how burnt the round hills. Life went from it with the decline of the water-cure—which had made it—for "movement." But there are lots of places, Welsh & others—though none, I do fear, with the Karnival of Kittery.[10] You & Mrs. Howells must do all your confetti-throwing at each other. I wish I could

5. HJ leased Lamb House to a couple of newlyweds, Louise Horstmann and John Boit, for five pounds a week.

6. When WDH and his family returned to London from Oxford, they resided at 86 Eaton Terrace, where they were neighbors of HJ's close friend Elizabeth Jessie Jane ("Goody") Allen (1845–1918), whose number was 74. Miss Allen had entertained WDH and Mildred at Eaton Terrace earlier in the spring.

7. "In Folkestone Out of Season," *Harper's Monthly* (November 1904).

8. "Hall Caine" (Sir Thomas Henry Hall Caine) (1853–1931) and "Marie Corelli" (Mary MacKay) (1855–1924), two popular English novelists.

9. John Mead Howells was touring Italy that summer.

10. After receiving the honorary degree from Oxford in June, WDH traveled extensively through England, Scotland, and Wales, gathering impressions for the serial pieces that would later be collected in *London Films* and *Certain Delightful English Towns*, both published by Harper's in 1906. WDH and his wife were especially interested in Wales because of his family's ancestry. From England WDH and his family went to Italy for the winter, hence HJ's anticipatory reference to the "Karnival," and his sly contrast with the native scenery of Kittery Point, Maine.

catch some of it in its passage. But I greet you both affectionately—attend & adjure you with much flourish of insistence & insistence of flourish. Believe me therewith

yours ever
Henry James

122.

JAMES TO HOWELLS, 1 March 1905, Cambridge   TLS Houghton
bMS Am 1784 (253) 98

95 Irving St., Cambridge, Mass.[1]
March 1, 1905.

Dear W. D. H.

The sense of my hideous long silence takes on from day to day such an accumulation of horror to me that I am now well nigh paralyzed with the fear of possibly hearing you are back before I have had the decency to break into sound.[2] Nothing would induce me to "meet" you (the terrific American word that I fear has, all winter, rung oftenest and sharpest in my ears!) before putting myself in the position to speak to you, with however red a face, about my having written. Let me postpone till then at least the miserable recital of all the reasons why I am doing so only now and thus. They are better, the wretched reasons, than you might really believe; and as an account of them, truly, would be very much of an account of my life since we last parted, this is a further inducement for my keeping the dish over to serve to you with my own hand, which will then endearingly point out to you the morsels least tough! Suffice it for the hour that I have been the victim of Fate and the creature of helplessness; simply clutching the sides of the car of the balloon for dear life, and feeling, with the vast movements of the monster, that this was all that could be asked of me. I will so subtly convince you of this when we do meet that I really believe your heart will be softened for me. I believe, clingingly, myself, in our ultimate encounter—before I leave these shores, (which I have arranged to do on July 4th) because it is somehow much in the air that you are to be sailing back rather early in the spring—as who should say between April and May.[3] By that time I shall have come back from California et cetera, to which dim distance I now begin in two or three days to commit myself; and shall be wanting to put in two or three weeks more in New York, where heaven send I shall find you! I have spent, all the winter, but some three weeks there, scarce more—bolting

---

1. The residence of William James.

2. HJ had promised to write "an early letter" from America, but WDH knew "how these things go" and did not want to reproach him. See WDH to Charles Eliot Norton, 4 November 1904, *SL* 5: 110.

3. The Howellses arrived in New York from Genoa on 17 April and moved on to Kittery Point at the end of May.

prematurely after that amount of taste of its worst mid-winter conditions. Since then I have put in such time as I could in Philadelphia, Washington, and the South, notably Florida, whence I returned but a few days since. My whole time here has been ravaged by the Dentist—through the circumstance of my having fallen, early in the winter, a victim to the fiendish ambition of a very perfect performer, in that line, in Boston, who conceived a vast and comprehensive plan of campaign at my expense, which he is still (whenever I can scramble back to him) ruthlessly carrying out. That whole business has made, truthfully speaking, such a deep dark hole in my time, my nerves, my strength, my ability to do anything else, that I literally came near going quite to pieces under it, and have had to sacrifice work, correspondence, opportunities and obligations of many kinds, just in order to survive. Ask *him*, when you return, why I couldn't write to you—just when I was beginning to mature toward doing so, and he will but too luridly answer your question. But it has been all a dreadful consciousness that I strive now to brush by!

I wrote a word to John, in N.Y., weeks ago, which contained a message for you, and which he may have sent on to you;[4] and I will forward him this, to be dealt with according to his knowledge of your whereabouts and movements. The real clog on my utterance now, is that I have too much to say to begin at all to tell you of it. I have had, in spite of everything, a very interesting time, and am glad to have come, and even to have engaged for the work you wot of: but I very soon found, on the spot, that working, producing, in the conditions of circulating, seeing, getting impressions and making myself acquainted, was a process practically quite defiant of production, concentration, any achievement *whatever*, almost, of the occasional privacy without which I can't arrive at any sort of expression. My getting *at* expression, in short, seems eternally postponed—and I fear it will only come (beyond a few dribblings already squeezed out)[5] when I get back to the privacy of my normal life and am able to feel myself really in *possession:* (I mean of impressions, memories, the whole subject.)

4. In his letter of 8 January 1905 HJ apologized for not arranging to see John Mead Howells: I am very sorry indeed to be leaving New York (for the *time*) after only missing (under the storm & stress of the complications of a very short & burdened stay here of 15 days) every chance & hope of seeing you or being able in some way to put my hand on you. My cousin Bay Emmet hoped to arrange it—but that escaped us, & now I am hurried off tomorrow to Washington with all my imperfections on my head. We must make it up later—for I am coming back for a better stay after I have done a few other things—coming back to a kinder season & more margin for old friends. *Then* I shall get hold of you as I exceedingly desire to do. I am the more afflicted now as news of your father fails me—be the authentic form in which you can give it me. And then my messages to them & these I have been keeping only with this horrid little sense of their being wasted. But give them my love & tell them I yearningly *await* them here (not sailing away till June or July;) you might even enclose them this as a sign of my baffled interest in you all & a whiff of my uncontagious fever. I add, for their benefit, that I am staying here with Mrs. Wharton & that I go [to] Washington for some 3 months. (Howells Papers, Library of Congress)

5. Only one chapter of *The American Scene* appeared serially while HJ was still in the United States: "New England: An Autumn Impression," *North American Review* (April–June 1905).

I have found so few *things*, objects, scenes, pictures, "monumental" phenomena of any sort to make copy of, that the whole business has reduced itself to impressions of the social (in the larger sense of the term) order, as to which I could do nothing till my saturation was complete. So I should have been really much of a lame duck if I hadn't more or less managed to follow your advice on the subject of preparing a lecture. That advice has been blest to me for it is helping to see me through. Without it, I really think I should have had to collapse. It isn't that I have read the stuff often (I call it "The Lesson of Balzac", and it seems to serve its purpose,) for I have exposed myself as yet only twice—both times at Philadelphia, that is the second at Bryn Mawr; but the consequences have been fruitful, and I go now to *re-spout* it in three or four cities of the West.[6] It makes traveling possible, and in short I find I can do it: though only to the tune of a few times and for a positively quite maximum fee. (I very soon became conscious, here on the spot, that I couldn't at all face the prospect of doing it in many smaller places, on minor terms.) But of all this, and of many other things, we will talk. I long to be *a quattrròcchi*[7] with you, for you too will be rich in revelation. I really hope with all my heart that your ordeal has been not too grim; by which I mean your wife's in particular. Pilla, I know, will have taken it all as opera and ballet, carnival and carouse. Give them both all my love, and judge me now more mercifully than you can possibly hitherto have thought of doing. I have mortally envied you the felicity of your charming distillations into the pictured Harper[8]—so light and so bright and so informed with the fine spirit of acquittal of your vow. They have been stabs at the heart of my own stagnancy and sterility—but I have none the less magnanimously surrendered to their charm. I surrender now to luncheon time, and oh! how I speed you hitherward! Come to me, come *for* me, and believe me,

Yours always, as ever,
Henry James

6. HJ's itinerary included speaking engagements at St. Louis, Chicago, Notre Dame, Indianapolis, and Los Angeles; he spoke to several different groups in some cities. See Marie P. Harris, "Henry James, Lecturer," *American Literature* 23 (November 1951): 302–14.

7. Face to face.

8. In addition to his piece on Folkestone (see letter #121, note 7), WDH had also published "London Films" (*Harper's Monthly* [December 1904]) and "In the Season, London Films—Part II" (*Harper's Monthly* [March 1905]).

123.

JAMES TO HOWELLS, 19 May 1905, New York

ALS Houghton
bMS Am 1784 (253) 99

May 19ᵗʰ 1905.
21, EAST ELEVENTH STREET

My dear Howells.

Only a word to say that I will, yearningly, come in at luncheon time tomorrow Saturday, if I hear nothing from you in an adverse way.[1] And I shall ask you very mercifully to let me make luncheon time about 1.45 or even 2—not at all waiting for me yourselves, but setting down—letting me drop into my chair without having delayed you. Much love.

Ever yr.
Henry James

124.

JAMES TO HOWELLS, 12 March 1906, London

ALS Houghton
bMS Am 1784 (253) 100

THE ATHENAEUM, PALL MALL. S. W.
12.3.1906.

My dear Howells.

I don't quite know where this will reach you, but I suppose, & hope, in N. Y.—though I suffer from the inability to enclose you, in the mental vision, between the walls & under the protecting roof, of a Home of Your Own. Mrs. Howells sent me a gentle postcard—I mean a vivid emblazoned one, a few weeks ago, which offered me an hotel at Atlantic City as your *then* solution of that question, but I somehow seem to like to think that you are not at Atlantic City still[1]—lovely as I pretended to many persons that I found it last June. Kindly thank Mrs. Howells for her gracious demonstration, & tell her I shall greatly value, always, any such help from her to realizing you, on your boards as you walk—anywhere. But you will meanwhile think, I fear, that I am realizing you but coldly & conveniently when I tell you that after making you no sign for so long I am now making you one on behalf (as it were,) of H. G. Wells, who goes to the U. S. on the 27ᵗʰ for some 2 or 3 months of lecturing or reading, or

1. HJ visited WDH at 340 West 57th Street on 20 May 1905. On this occasion WDH passed on an invitation for HJ to renew his lecture series for the fall and winter season, but he declined. The offer came from John Kendrick Bangs (1862–1922), a popular humorist and lecturer, who would later write a chapter ("The Son-in-Law") for *The Whole Family* (1908), the group novel to which WDH and HJ also contributed. See WDH to [John Kendrick] Bangs, 20 May 1905 (Howells Edition Center photostat, Indiana University).

1. WDH and his wife were in Atlantic City from 30 January to 18 March 1906, after which they returned to New York and took up residence in the Regent Hotel at Broadway and 70th Street.

other public performance & private inquiry. He will, I dare say, come to see you—& you must take him very easy (thoroughly good & even I think very remarkable little genius as he is;) for he will be grateful for little, will pass quickly & will be *inquiring* right & left—far from your door! (Any *public* aspect of N. Y.—the stranger the better—that you can show him will do.) But what I wanted particularly to say is that I have said to him that I would help him to a temporary *club-invitation* in N. Y. if I could—& it occurs to me that it will probably occur to *you*, if you see him, to ask that he be put down at the Century.[2] If you should kindly think of this I shall be grateful, & it will help me to redeem my vow to him (in respect to which also I have said a word to Lawrence Godkin,[3] to whom I have given him a note.) Have you read his *Kipps?*[4]—very admirable & indeed quite wonderful, I think—read it if you haven't! This is all about *him*—& he may perhaps have written you. If he does come & go—& especially when he goes—do, at your convenience, give me some word about him.[5] I mean by that really, you see, give me some about yourself. I hope you have had an easy & simplified winter & have written, more or less, another felicitous Fiction. I am in town for 8 or 10 weeks—after 7 or 8 steady months of Rye. I have written an American book (DON'T read it piecemeal,) & must write another to use up the rest of my material—in fact have already partly done so.[6] The trouble is it all fades from me so before I slowly *do* it. Tanti saluti[7] to all of you. Your English vol.[8] (which you never sent me!) is charmingly spoken of right & left here, & the pattern in your carpet is always affectionately recognised & exquisitely appreciated by

your constant old
Henry James

2. The ever-industrious Wells had already anticipated both HJ and WDH. On 17 February, more than a month before his departure, he told WDH, "Bushnell Hart has put me up at the Century Club (of West 43d St) and I shall be very glad *if* I can find a chance of talking to you a little more about things American." See H. G. Wells to WDH, 17 February 1906 (Howells Papers, Harvard). Albert Bushnell Hart (1854–1943) was a professor of history at Harvard.

3. Lawrence Godkin (1860–1929), the son of the late E. L. Godkin (founder of the *Nation*), was a New York attorney.

4. H. G. Wells, *Kipps: The Story of a Simple Soul* (1905).

5. On 8 April WDH hosted a literary luncheon for Wells, at which Mark Twain and several other writers and artists were present. WDH was happy to return the favor to Wells, who in 1904 had shown courtesies to WDH and Mildred at Sandgate. In a letter to his sister Aurelia, WDH described Wells as "a little cockney man, but of a brave spirit, who is socialistic in his expectations of the future, and boldly owns to having been a dry goods clerk in his own past." See WDH to Aurelia H. Howells, 8 April 1906, *SL* 5: 170.

6. *The American Scene* (1907); HJ never completed a second volume of "Impressions," although he expressed the desire to do so to many other correspondents.

7. Greetings.

8. *London Films* (1906) was issued by Harper's on 12 October 1905.

125.

JAMES TO HOWELLS, 13 September 1906, Rye   ALS Houghton
bMS Am 1784 (253) 101

LAMB HOUSE, RYE, SUSSEX.
September 13$\underline{\text{th}}$ 1906.

My dear Howells.

You see how I like the sense of a letter "between" us, that, being more sure that it *is* so held in suspense, perhaps, when my own hand holds it than when yours does, I have kept it dangling, week after week, till this hour. If I had written you long since (on receipt of your so obliging news of what you had done, so handsomely done, in N. Y., for the unattenuated Wells, &c)[1] I should not have enjoyed, these three months, the consciousness of what was intended for our communication. I shouldn't have been sure of *your* intentions, whereas I have been so fondly certain of my own. Please don't think that they at last too meagrely flower. I have finally also *seen* the said H. G. W. since his return from his adventure—I went over to Sandgate from a Saturday to a Monday (some 3 weeks ago,) when he reported of you rosily & gratefully. He exhaled fewer impressions than I had looked for (partly because, perhaps, he was laid up, in considerable pain, with a strained knee;) but he said he had spent the most interesting month of his life—& he has already written a book about the same, which has been journalistically appearing, but which I shan't see till it becomes, in a month or two, a volume.[2] He publishes, however, before that I believe (very soon,) a longish new Fiction,[3] & the fiction I shall the more interestedly attend to. His speculative "cheek" applied to other forms (to the U. S. for instance) vitiates a good deal, for me (by its excess of assurance & of simplification) an indubitable play of genius. But basta on that head. One's only personal news here just now is inevitably of one's sense of the prodigious summer we have been (& are still) having, radiant & rainless & beautiful (*four* wholly rainless months) beyond recorded memory. I have spent it largely in my garden; which has never had so many birds, bees, butterflies, roses and sweet-peas (these last in hedges 10 feet high)—& peace & steady labour have on the whole been with me—in spite of a little too many visitations & vomitations of the motor—which has become here a monstrous *new* assailant of the quiet life—stirring up a so much wider circle of complication. But I haven't the heart to advert to you on anything *done*. I have finished (some time since) an American volume, which awaits but the magazine-publication of its 2 or 3 last chapters;[4] but it doesn't

1. WDH's letter about H. G. Wells is not extant.

2. H. G. Wells first serialized *The Future in America: A Search After Realities* in *Harper's Weekly* (14 July–6 October 1906) before publishing it later that year.

3. *In the Days of the Comet* was published in October 1906.

4. Of HJ's three remaining chapters, only one—"Richmond"—appeared in a periodical, the *Fortnightly Review* (November 1906).

exhaust my "material", & yet the sense of a remainder on my hands even now—at this distance of time—& still to be worked off—invests the whole exhibition with an air of staleness which—which in short you will understand. Wooing *back* freshness is hard—but we live (or we write at least, I think,) from one vouchsafed miracle to another. Your English distillations unfailingly charm me, & I marvel at the economy of conquest which enabled you to gather such golden sheaves in so brief a reaping. I wonder if you want to come back—as I, distinctly & perversely, shld. like to return to—well, to Kittery Point. I think ever so tenderly of Kittery Point, & I live over, romantically, each hour of those 2 days striped so contrastedly with the effects of the oven & of the iceberg. My old wounds ache again—by which I mean my old mosquito-bites itch—with my renewed yearning. Wells told me of your having said that a Novel[5] had again been engaging you—whereat a rosy light seemed to shine for me. But what has become of that so true & so droll little beginning you read me (on the tropic day, & I don't speak of it as an aggravation)—about the people in the country lodgings (or with the farmer & his wife who did for them.)?[6] I revert to it with appetite. But good night—I am sitting up to a later hour than I dare to confess to you—it would sound like swagger, over this poor result! I greet Mrs. Howells faithfully, & bless you all, & am

yours always
Henry James

126.

JAMES TO HOWELLS, 1 November 1906, Rye   ALS Houghton
bMS Am 1784 (253) 102

LAMB HOUSE, RYE, SUSSEX.
November 1st 1906.

My dear Howells.

I lay you down but to take you up—which is much better, you will grant, than taking you up but to lay you down! It is but form against form—as I had your last English paper in *Harper*[1] in my hand last night when your good letter from Kittery[2] was brought in to me. This didn't prevent my eagerly breaking the seal—any more than my having done that & devoured you alive prevented my going back & hanging about you again at Southampton. Very interesting to me your account of all your actualities of deed & disposition, & above all very

5. *Through the Eye of the Needle* (1907).
6. WDH had begun a novel called "The Children of the Summer," which Harper's published posthumously in 1920 as *The Vacation of the Kelwyns*.
1. "By Way of Southampton to London," *Harper's Monthly* (November 1906).
2. Not extant.

wonderful & (to my habit of hugging the shore,) humiliating. When you tell me that you can't rest from change & travel & from the fierce life of hotels & all their monstrous brood—I grow green with envy of the very youth & strength of it. I can scarce bring myself to budge from the compass of my little garden, & my inability to move & wander is morbid & maniacal. There are still things I want to do, thank goodness, but vain motion & vague going forth affect me as menacing them to the very death! I wish it weren't so—it used not to be—but my habitational shell becomes more & more a *condition* for me, & represents more the fixed actual world out of which alone I can project the imaginary &c. That makes, I fear, much against my going back to the U. S. to Lecture—that & the fact that I ought to have tackled the job in question 12 years ago instead of 2. Nobody asked me *then*—when I was yearning for "employment" & greatly needing it, & now it's too late. Everything comes too late—to the belated. Still, I don't mean this for a wail—except, as I say, of envy! When you tell me that you plan Atlantic City for the winter, however, the twain of you (for I've been at Atlantic City & have—perhaps for use still—my notes of it,) I do feel a bit the perversity of things, in the sense that from the moment you do *that* sort of thing I feel it an injury that you don't do it nearer Rye—where you can do it, I really hold, better: even at Hastings & St. Leonard's, even at Brighton & Eastbourne, Bournemouth, Weymouth! Come & see, since you do confess to the rage for it. That is more logical than my going home to lecture at you! I am meanwhile ever so interested in your being "tired" of doing your English papers—ever so ingenious & artful & charming as I have found them! God knows I am tired of *my* (that is of the *pumping-up* of my now so tepid) supposititious impressions—& wish I could lay down the pen. But I have several more still to do, though a book, here, is all filled with a 1st batch & there will have to be another (shorter & Westerner) one. The book (the 1st) awaits the delay of the Harpers, who have consented to serialise me with no continuity, but subject me without pity, afar off & helpless as I am, to the most painful gaps & intervals.[3] Under these inconveniences I do sometimes yearn for the Platform! I am wonderstruck, under your (impressionistic) fecundity with the magnificent *Economic* art of your series—your having got such a majestic array out of so brief a transit—& there are some *few* of your articles I've missed. (One about the Kent country—but when did you ever miraculously get *at* it?—& with a tribute to

3. Harper's delayed serialization of HJ's travel pieces—and slipshod accounting for them—eventually frustrated his high hopes for *The American Scene*. HJ postponed the English edition of the book in order that its final chapters ("Richmond," "Charleston," and "Florida") appear serially in America; but neither *Harper's Monthly* nor the *North American Review* would print them. "I extremely resent their whole indifferent, cavalier, uncivil treatment of my stuff," HJ complained to his agent, "as if it were beneath their notice; & this not for the failure of the money—though that *is* inconvenient—but because common self-respect demands that one shouldn't in such a case be simply passive & grovelling" (HJ to James B. Pinker, 2 May 1907 [Collection of American Literature, Yale]).

this place,[4] that I have heard of & that has slipped me, but which I shall look up tomorrow at a club—as I make in the morn., a 3 days dash to London.) That's what I am *trying* to do—the economic swell—with my own American deposit—which I find alas, now that I'm so far away, so thin a pictorial & other soil to dig in. Therefore I feel with each punch of the spade, as if I were against bare boards. I am getting back also, with infinite relief, to the "imaginative"— for which my appetite has again opened itself—only, I confess, I find it so much harder every time! Apropos of which I delight to hear that you are *at* the so charming & amusing thing you read me that hot a.m. in your garden-house & the very perspiration of listening to which breaks out on me as I recall it.[5] It was one of your happiest & most *your* beginnings, I thought, & I wish strength to the renewed beat of your wings. Have you (as you mention him in that connection—of his having indeed reported to *me* on it) read Wells's Cometary novel[6]—with its bad title & too thinly-evoked final Utopia, but, as seems to me, admirable general force & fury, admirable realization of the passion & condition of his young man (the 1st 2 thirds of the book)? Wells, in these things, manifests, to my sense, a great talent & uses a great verity (though with dreadful roughnesses of hand that at times come near for me to breaking the spell,) which make him pretty well the only one of *les jeunes*[7] now performing in our language who is for me personally worth two cents. He too has been doing a "Future in America" (after 9 weeks at most, I think,)—which has as yet, however, appeared but piecemeal, where I haven't seen it.[8] So much Future (to so little Present,) has the air to me of rather giving it away. What else shall I tell you?—save that we are in the midst here of a colossal Book-Row (really a big air-darkening fight,) between the Times Book-Club & big cheap-selling Shops & the Publishers leagued with the other booksellers.[9] It is to me sordid & squalid

4. "Kentish Neighborhoods, Including Canterbury," *Harper's Monthly* 113 (September 1906): 550–63. At the end of the article, WDH gives a brief sketch of Rye,

> an endearing little town, one of hundreds (I had almost said thousands) in England, with every comfort in the compass of its cozy streets; with a church, old, old, but not too dotingly Norman, and a lane opening from it to the door of a certain house where one might almost live on the entrancing perspective of its tower and its graveyard trees. . . . What is precious about Rye is that with its great charm it does not insist upon being dramatically different from those hundreds or thousands of other lovely old towns. It keeps its history to itself, and I would no more invite the reader to intrude upon its past than I would ask him to join me in invading the private affairs of any English gentleman. (562–63)

The "certain house" down the lane is Lamb House.

5. The opening chapters of *The Vacation of the Kelwyns* (1920); see letter #125.

6. H. G. Wells, *In the Days of the Comet* (1906).

7. The younger generation.

8. Wells's collection of essays *The Future in America* was serialized in *Harper's Weekly*, 14 July–6 October 1906.

9. The so-called Book War of 1906–8 pitted the newly formed Times Book Club against the major publishing firms of Great Britain, which had agreed in 1899 upon a sales mechanism that enforced a uniform pricing policy for retailers and wholesalers of books. The Book Club attempted to circumvent these restrictions by circulating books at no charge to its members and then allowing subscribers to purchase the handled volumes at substantial discount. The popularity of this scheme

all, & I feel poor dear old Literature crouch within me & hold both her breath & her nose while it goes on—but it's rather a big Drama—*as* a Drama—& the end of it no man can say. My "sympathies" are on the whole with the publishers—but with such reservations, all round, that it isn't—*they* aren't—worth talking about. My sympathies are with Literature only—not one mention of which, not one care or thought for which—gets itself uttered in the mere rage of commercialism. The whole thing is of the last Documentariness as to our grand old Anglo-Saxon practical spirit. —And all the while you don't tell me a word of your Edition Définitive.[10] What has become of it?—is it majestically proceeding?—though I don't see it advertised or proclaimed?—from which I infer *not*—but hope the "not" doesn't breathe obstruction. *Mine* is becoming a reality—will, after the New Year, & the minute revising of my 1st 3 Novels has lain heavy upon me this summer. It was absolutely impossible to me to hand them over to new & high honours of type, paper, form, plates, prefaces (these latter very "important",) without retouching their original roughness—& from the moment one does retouch the only consistency, I hold, is in completeness. So I have retouched completely—but it has been a job! However, you will see—& I hope you won't deride. After the 1st three the need will be much less & will go *diminuendo*.[11] But what a letter! Yet I wish I could take another sprawl to tell you what an admirable long golden season you have missed here—arrested in its luscious length only a week ago. It has been for enclosed—though not uninvaded—garden-life the summer of one's life, & a monument to the possibilities of this unappreciated climate. It makes me say "why should I want to go to Atlantic City?" However, please tell Mrs. Howells, with my love, that I would do this in a moment for the sake of riding with *her* in a twin-perambulator there. What perambulations you will have! But if you'll only write 'em, I shall, my dear Howells, be more & more than ever & ever

your affectionate old
Henry James

P. S.
Do you, does Mildred, (to whom tender love,) ever see the (I fear) truly tragic *Smalleys???*[12]

---

threatened the viability of trade bookshops, which, by virtue of the 1899 "Net Book Agreement," could not lower prices. The publishers retaliated by suspending their advertising in the *Times* (and its influential literary supplement). The "war" finally subsided when the book club agreed to delay the distribution of remaindered volumes and to accept restrictions on its role as a bookseller. See Frederick Macmillan and Edward Bell, *The Net Book Agreement, 1899, and The Book War, 1906–1908* (Glasgow: University Press, 1924), and *The History of the Times. Vol. 3: The Twentieth-Century Test, 1884–1912* (London: Times Publishing Co., 1947), 448–59, 829–34.

10. Harper's flirted with the idea of publishing the first six volumes of WDH's Library Edition in the fall of 1906, but these were eventually postponed until 1911. The project for a collected edition of WDH's work was then abandoned.

11. Decreasingly.

12. Evidence from later letters suggests that Evelyn Smalley began to show signs of nervous breakdown, possibly aggravated by her continued proximity to her mother, Phoebe Garnaut Smalley.

127.

JAMES TO HOWELLS, 10 March 1908, Rye

ALS Houghton
bMS Am 1784 (253) 103

LAMB HOUSE, RYE, SUSSEX.

My dear Howells.

It has been deliciously delightful to hear from you[1]—& I can't begin to tell you above all what intense pleasure your so handsome pat on the back to the March *Harper* stuff[2] has given me. I value *no* pats as yours—or ever have: your supreme expertness & intimate intelligence & "technical" insight & general possession of the whole art & mystery make your judgements for me—well, the *only* ones (to be flatly frank,) that raise in my aged breast today the slightest braze. It is *murderous* to the little story to have divided it (it being really really all unity & close continuity) & it is good enough to have made an exception for. They have kept it unpublished since year before last, as if I were some obscure suppliant or neophyte—& I supposed that this was at least in order that they *might* run it together. Basta!

— Your being, all, kind of *near*[3] thrills me—but also *chills* me, the moment you begin to be so monstrously vague about coming to England. Why, we have been taking that for the "whole point" & never doubting but that you were quite in a flutter to reach us. That legend has filled the air here these many weeks & I personally have nursed it in my bosom. I have lucidly & so naturally believed, that you were to find here afresh a collection of the happiest little pegs for further, for furthest irresistible prose[4]—& have in fact been having in my eye a dozen or so to point out to you. In fine it's all *arranged:* so come (you, dear Mrs. Howells, & *you,* subtle Mildred, turn on the current) as the plainest & pleasantest matter of course in the world. After a very long winter here (since last July, when I came back from Rome & Venice) I shall be in London from about Easter on, & all through May, & yearning to render you any service that will pave your way & crown your confidence. I detest somehow your romping off to Gibraltar—it's so horridly on the way to New York. But let me vaticinate that if you weakly succumb to the vulgar—the so much *too* vulgar obviousness of that fact—you'll ever so quickly & bitterly rue it ("that's all I can say!")—rue

---

After Evelyn was placed in an asylum, HJ lamented that the "absolute impecuniosity, the wholly penniless state" of the Smalley family made any medical alternatives for her impossible. See HJ to Elizabeth Jordan, 17 April 1912 (Jordan Papers, New York Public Library); some of HJ's other letters to Jordan (e.g., those dated 7 July, 19 and 29 August 1909) also refer to the family's declining prospects.

1. Not extant.

2. "Julia Bride," *Harper's Monthly* (March–April 1908).

3. WDH and his family sailed to Rome in January for the winter. They would return to the United States in June, first traveling west through France to London, where they saw HJ.

4. WDH's basis for his journey was a series of travel pieces he serialized, by special arrangement with Harper's, in the New York Sunday *Sun.* These were later collected as *Roman Holidays and Others* (1908).

it even more than we the deluded & betrayed here. Therefore *book* somehow betimes for London. Tom Perry writes me every week from Paris as to whether Sister Anne sees nothing coming.[5] *He* will lay all carpets for you there. Yes, I can well believe how the Rome of today differs for you (& *so* for the worse *I* find,) from the unspeakable old Rome of the "Roman Pearls" in *Italian Journeys*—the last word on *that* golden age, as I remember I used to think them (the Pearls.)[6] I was there last May–June; but to go forth from this little old Sussex corner to invoke still more thrilling antiquities & to find the air darkened simply, as you say, with a colossal American teapot, & the American tongue wagging as fast as possible in the Locca Romana—no I couldn't face it again: never, never, I think, never—though, strange to say, I think I shld. be capable again of Venice.[7] Such questions, however, really die out for me, & I have now been kept sedentary for months as almost never before by the really immeasurable labour involved in my 24 volumes of the Edition:[8] the handling of which in the manner in which I have been doing it has absolutely driven everything else to the wall; that is everything but a still more desperate & more uncanny adventure (now breaking not a little into my time:) the production "experimentally" in Edinburgh on the 26th of this month of a little pig of a Play: a 3-act comedy which Forbes Robertson & his wife Gertrude Elliott (more intelligent sister of the bloated *Maxine*) have gouged out of me by the hint of the possibility of some sort of appreciable guerdon.[9] As they are on "tour" I go a few days hence to Manchester & the said Edinburgh for supreme rehearsals (I had a while back to give up precious days to preliminary ones in London;) & in fine beg you to pray for me, all, very hard on Thursday 26th. I am of course doing the abject

5. Compare the anxious cry of Fatima, one of the wives of Bluebeard: "Sister Anne, do you see any one coming?" HJ may be alluding sardonically to Perry's wife, whom he thought tyrannical; hence the masculine emphasis in the next sentence. Both WDH and HJ converged on Perry in May, while HJ was visiting Edith Wharton.

6. "Roman Pearls" was the heading for chapter twelve of *Italian Journeys* (1867). Even then, WDH wrote,

> Modern Rome appeared, first and last, hideous. It is the least interesting town in Italy, and the architecture is hopelessly ugly—especially the architecture of the churches. The Papal city contrives at the beginning to hide the Imperial city from your thought, as it hides it in such a great degree from your eye, and old Rome only occurs to you in a sort of stupid wonder over the depth at which it is buried. (152)

7. In *Roman Holidays and Others* (New York: Harper's, 1908), WDH actually wrote more favorably of modern conditions in Rome. After noting the beneficial effects of recent reforms in housing and sanitation, for example, WDH pointedly remarks, "I do not see why a Londoner, who himself lives in a well-kept town, should join with any of my fellow-barbarians in hypocritically deploring the modern spirit which has so happily invaded the Eternal City" (80).

8. Scribner's New York Edition of *The Novels and Tales of Henry James* was published by subscription in twelve two-volume installments between 14 December 1907 and 1 July 1909.

9. HJ's play *The High Bid* was a resuscitated version of "Covering End," written in the 1890s and then converted by HJ for publication as a short story to flesh out *The Two Magics* (1898), where it was paired with "The Turn of the Screw." When Johnston Forbes-Robertson (1853–1937) and Gertrude Elliott (1874–1950) took the play to London, it ran for only five matinee performances. Like her sister, Gertrude, Maxine Elliott (1868–1940) was a popular actress and theater manager.

thing with the sole thought of its making me a little money—by which I mean (if it goes,) a good deal: *something* that will do that having become of the last importance to me. (My books absolutely decline to do anything—though I am building a little on the Edition: which has long kept me from doing anything else.) If the play ("The High Bid") does anything worthwhile in a few provincial places in (during) April, it will be produced in London early in May—not otherwise; but let the idea of possibly assisting there at the first night throw a mystic weight into the scale that books you for a summer. That is a pompous speech, but represents a little the disorder of mind in which the possible loss of you plunges

your (*all* your) affectionate old friend
Henry James

P. S. A complete portentous set of the Edition will await your acceptance on your return to New York.

March 10th 1908.

128.

HOWELLS TO JAMES, 2 August 1908, Kittery Point   TLS Houghton
bMS Am 1094 (253)

Kittery Point,
August 2, 1908

My dear James:

   This is the third letter I have started to you, the others having been unsuccessfully attempted with the pen. My old age is tormented with scruples unknown to my brash middle life, and I fancied that something I had said about your prefaces in your most admirable library edition might not be so wholly pleasing as I meant it.[1] Those prefaces have given us all great satisfaction, as read aloud by me. We especially enjoyed you where you rounded upon yourself, and as it were took yourself to pieces, in your self-censure. The analysis of The American seemd happiest, but all the analyses were good, most subtle, and wise, and just, and the biographies of the three novels—Roderick Hudson and The

---

   1. In talking with HJ about the prefaces to the New York Edition, WDH may have been influenced by the unfavorable report of them he had received from Charles Eliot Norton. In his letter of 26 March 1908, Norton told WDH:

> Our chief literary concern has been of late with Henry James' new prefaces. I have not read them, but Sally has read them and finds them too self-occupied, and dislikes the disturbances of her old associations with the stories, and dislikes also the unreality which this criticism of the old characters gives to them. She does not like to have her puppets taken to pieces and the wires which moved them shown to her; nor does she think it a dignified proceeding to take for granted so largely the interest of the public in the conception and execution of the work of the living writer. (*SL* 5: 248n7)

Portrait of a Lady were the other two which I have yet received—were full of instruction for me, who as their godfather had fancied I knew all about them, but had really known them only from their birth, and not from their conception through their gestation.[2] I remember so well your telling me, on such a Sunday afternoon as this, when we were rowing on Fresh Pond, what R. H.[3] was to be. You have done a lot of good work, but nothing better than the last half of each of those prefaces; and I think the public will understand from them what I tried to note to you, that miserable hot afternoon when we sat glued to our chairs here: the fact, namely, that you have imagined your fiction, as a whole, and better fulfilled a conscious intention in it than any of your contemporaries. It took courage to do those introductions, and a toil as great, but how you must have liked doing them—or having done them!

I am, as usual, in the midst of a book which as usual, I did not distinctly mean to write, a book of "Roman Holidays and Others," the stuff of which has been appearing for the last six months in the Sunday edition of the New York Sun. The only thing that pleases me wholly is that the stuff seems to have been so much liked by the people who have read it there. The success has brought back my sense of success in the Venetian Life letters printed forty odd years ago in the Boston Advertiser.[4] But of course the Roman stuff is without any such authority as the Venetian, and is the reflex of my youthful fires, such as they were. Still it has amused me to find myself taking the old point of view, the old attitude, quite helplessly.

During the month we have been here my wife has suffered almost constantly from toothache, and at last she determined to have the wretched tooth out, so we all went up to Boston, and she took the gas, and Pilla and I sat quaking till she came to, all right. Then during her day's rest at the hotel, I went out and saw Norton one afternoon. His daughters happened to be away, and he was alone in the house, a chance which made him seem forlorn and very old and broken. It was a sadder time than I have ever had with him, though now and then he plucked up the courage to talk of old times. He read me with joyous affection from your brother a letter which Wm. had written him from Durham,[5]

2. WDH refers to his editorship of the *Atlantic*, during which five of HJ's novels were serialized: *Watch and Ward* (1871), *Roderick Hudson* (1875), *The American* (1876–77), *The Europeans* (1878), and *The Portrait of a Lady* (1880–81).

3. *Roderick Hudson*.

4. Portions of WDH's first important book, *Venetian Life* (1866), were initially serialized in the Boston *Advertiser* from 1863 to 1864. See William M. Gibson and George Arms, *A Bibliography of William Dean Howells* (New York: New York Public Library, 1948), 19–20.

5. WJ was traveling in England after having delivered the Hibbert Lectures ("The Present Situation in Philosophy") at Manchester College, Oxford. In his letter to Norton of 6 July 1908, WJ wrote, in part:

> The whole scene at Durham was tremendously impressive (though York Cathedral made the stronger impression on me). It was so unlike Oxford, so much more American in its personnel, in a way, yet nestling in the very bosom of those medieval stage-properties and ecclesiastical-principality suggestions. Oxford is all spread out in length and breadth, Durham

but there was nothing else to lift us. He told me frankly that poor D.'s affair[6] had aged him, and I tried, from you as well as myself, to make him see it a little from the general point of view. But it was very melancholy.

We had John and his wife[7] here for a fortnight after we came, but now they are in the Catskills, finishing out the month before they shall go to New York, and begin housekeeping in a little house they have taken in Washington Place, west of Sixth Avenue. John makes much of their being in a sort of nook, with a yard backing against that of a convent, but when I thought of the convents which one could back against in Rome, I had to feign my pleasure in his. His wife is an extremely pretty girl, wonderfully New Yorky, but very intelligent, and much disposed to overrate her fatherinlaw's literature.

Pilla is just home from a week's visit at the shrines in Art in Cornish, Vermont, where half a dozen painters, and our great novelist Winston Churchill are livelier in their social relation than they are friendly;[8] or perhaps uncritical is the word. I fancy Cornish is something like Broadway, as it used to be. The sweetest spirit of all, the great and good Saint Gaudens, is now disembodied;[9] but to meet a visitor they all meet amicably enough, and Pilla had a good time. It is a frightfully hot place, as every place in this hemisphere seems to be, but very pretty, on heights above the Connecticut River. I don't know but you may have been there.

It is only five or six Sundays since we went that pleasant walk through the Park to South Kensington, which I should like so much to go again. When you parted with me you forbade my doing anything for you in the lecturing way, and so I have attempted nothing, though I should have been so glad to try. The country is prosperous again, and when Taft is elected, as there seems no doubt he will be,[10] the people will be in the mood of cultivating their minds again.

---

concentrated in depth and thickness. There is a great deal of flummery about Oxford, but I think if I were an Oxonian, in spite of my radicalism generally, I might vote against all change there. It is an absolutely unique fruit of human endeavor, and like the cathedrals, can never to the end of time be reproduced, when the conditions that once made it are changed. Yet other places of learning go in for all the improvements! The world can afford to keep her one Oxford unreformed.

See *The Letters of William James* 2: 306–7.

6. WDH's reference is obscure; "poor D." may refer to his Oxford friend Louis Dyer, a loyal student of Norton's, who had died on 20 July 1908.

7. John Mead Howells had married Abby Macdougall White in New York on 21 December 1907.

8. Winston Churchill (1871–1947) rose to fame in the early years of the century as the author of popular historical romances and contemporary problem novels. In 1899 he built a mansion in Cornish, New Hampshire (on the Vermont border), a town that had already been colonized by writers and artists.

9. Augustus Saint-Gaudens (1848–1907), the eminent American sculptor, established his studio at Cornish in 1885.

10. With Theodore Roosevelt's support, William Howard Taft (1857–1930) defeated William Jennings Bryan (1860–1925) by more than a million popular votes in the election of 1908.

I have always wondered how you liked your tea on the terrace with our Scotch M. P.,[11] in whose company I saw you so strangely walking off that day. We all join in affectionate remembrances.

Yours ever,
W. D. Howells.

129.

JAMES TO HOWELLS, 17 August 1908, Rye

TLS Houghton
bMS Am 1784 (253) 105

LAMB HOUSE, RYE, SUSSEX.
17th: August 1908

My dear Howells.

A great pleasure to me is your good and generous letter just received—with its luxurious implied licence for me of seeking this aid to prompt response; at a time when a pressure of complications (this is the complicated time of the year even in my small green garden) defeats too much and too often the genial impulse. But so far as compunction started and guided your pen, I really rub my eyes for vision of where it may—save as most misguidedly—have come in. You were so far from having distilled any indigestible drop for me on that pleasant *ultimissimo* Sunday, that I parted from you with a taste, in my mouth, absolutely saccharine—sated with sweetness, or with sweet reasonableness, so to speak; and aching, or wincing, in no single fibre. Extravagant and licentious, almost, your delicacy of fear of the contrary; so much so, in fact, that I didn't remember we had even spoken of the heavy lucubrations in question,[1] or that you had had any time or opportunity, since their "inception", to look at one. However your fond mistake is all to the good, since it has brought me your charming letter, and so appreciative remarks you therein make. My actual attitude about the Lucubrations is almost only, and quite inevitably, that they make, to me, for weariness; by reason of their number and extent—I've now but a couple more to write. This staleness of sensibility, in connection with them blocks out for the hour every aspect but that of their being all done, and of their perhaps helping the Edition to sell two or three copies more! They will have represented much labour to this latter end—though in that they will have differed indeed

---

11. John Ebenezer Sutherland (1854–1918) represented the borough of Elgin and was chairman of the Scottish Temperance and Social Reform Association. On 3 May 1908 WDH reported to his sister Aurelia from Paris:

> Elinor and Pilla have shared the week between them in bed with bad colds, but are both getting over them, so that tonight we are going to have a Scotch M. P. *to,* for I am glad to say, not *for* dinner. He is a Roman hotel acquaintance, and a very good man. He represents the borough of Elgin, and is a Liberal verging hard upon Socialism. (Howells Papers, Harvard)

1. HJ's prefaces for the New York Edition.

from no other of their fellow-manifestations (in general) whatever; and the re-semblance will be even increased if the two or three copies *don't,* in the form of an extra figure or two, mingle with my withered laurels. They are, in general, a sort of plea for Criticism, for Discrimination, for Appreciation on other than infantine lines—as against the so almost universal Anglo-Saxon absence of these things; which tends so, in our general trade, it seems to me, to break the heart. However, I am afraid I'm too sick of the mere doing of them, and of the general strain of the effort to avoid the deadly danger of repetition, to say much to the purpose about them. They ought, collected together, none the less, to form a sort of comprehensive manual or *vade-mecum* for aspirants in our arduous profession. Still, it will be long before I shall want to collect them together for that purpose and furnish *them* with a final Preface. I've done with prefaces for ever. As for the Edition itself, it has racked me a little that I've had to leave out so many things that would have helped to make for rather a more vivid completeness. I don't at all regret the things, pretty numerous, that I've omitted from deep-seated preference and design; but I do a little those that are crowded out by want of space and by the rigour of the 23 vols., and 23 only, which were the condition of my being able to arrange the matter with the Scribners at all. Twenty three do seem a fairly blatant array—and yet I rather surmise that there may have to be a couple of supplementary volumes for certain too marked omis-sions; such being, on the whole, detrimental to an at all professedly comprehen-sive presentation of one's stuff. Only these, I pray God, without Prefaces! And I have even, in addition, a dim vague view of re-introducing, with a good deal of titivation and cancellation, the too-diffuse but, I somehow feel, tolerably full and good "Bostonians" of nearly a quarter of a century ago; that production never having, even to my much-disciplined patience, received any sort of jus-tice. But it will take, doubtless, a great deal of artful re-doing—and I haven't, now, had the courage or time for anything so formidable as touching and re-touching it. I feel at the same time how the Series suffers commercially from its having been dropped so completely out.[2] *Basta pure—basta!*

I am charmed to hear of your Roman book and beg you very kindly to send it me directly it bounds into the ring.[3] I rejoice moreover, with much envy, and also a certain yearning and impotent non-intelligence, at your being moved to-day to Roman utterance—I mean in presence of the so-bedrenched and vulgar-ised (I mean more particularly *commonised*) and transformed City (as well as, alas, more or less, Suburbs) of our current time. There was nothing, I felt, to myself, I could *less* do than write again, in the whole presence—when I was there some fifteen months agone.[4] The idea of doing so (even had any periodical wanted my stuff, much less bid for it) would have affected me as a sort of give-

2. Eventually, the edition ran to twenty-four volumes. For details of its complicated publishing history, see Anesko, *"Friction with the Market,"* 141–62.

3. Harper's published *Roman Holidays and Others* on 22 October 1908.

4. In the spring and early summer of 1907, HJ traveled to Paris, Rome, and Venice—his last extended visit to the Continent.

away of my ancient and other reactions in presence of all the unutterable old Rome I originally found and adored. It would have come over me that if those ancient emotions of my own meant anything, no others on the new basis could mean much; or if any on the new basis should pretend to sense, it would be at the cost of all imputable coherency and sincerity on the part of my prime infatuation. In spite, all the same, of which doubtless too pedantic view—it only means, I fear, that I am, to my great disadvantage, utterly bereft of any convenient *journalistic* ease—I am just beginning to re-do (on a meagre understanding with Houghton & Mifflin, re-attenuated by the involvement of Pennell) certain little old Italian papers,[5] with titivations and expansions, in form to match with a volume of "English Hours" re-fabricated three or four years ago on the same system. In this little job I shall meet again my not much more than scant, yet still appreciable, old Roman stuff in my path—and shall have to commit myself about it, or about its general subject, somehow or other. I shall trick it out again to my best ability, at any rate—and at the cost, I fear, of your thinking I have re-titivation on the brain. I haven't—I only have it on (to the end that I may then have it a little consequently *in*) the flat pocket-book. The system has succeeded a little with "English Hours;" which have sold quite vulgarly—for wares of mine; whereas the previous and original untitivated had long since dropped almost to nothing. In spite of which I could really shed salt tears of impatience and yearning to get back, after so prolonged a blocking of traffic, to too-dreadfully postponed and neglected "creative" work; an accumulated store of ideas and reachings-out for which even now clogs my brain.

We are having here so bland and beautiful a summer that when I receive the waft of your furnace-mouth, blown upon my breakfast-table every few days through the cornucopia, or improvised resounding trumpet, of The Times I groan across at my brother William (now happily domesticated with me:) "Ah why *did* they, poor infatuated dears? why *did* they?"—and he always knows I mean Why did you three hie you home from one of the most beautiful seasons of splendid cool summer, or splendid summery cool, that ever was, just to swoon in the arms of your Kittery *genius loci* (genius of perspiration!)—to whose terrific embrace you saw me four years ago, or whatever terrible time it was, almost utterly succumb. In my small green garden here the elements have been, ever since you left, quite enchantingly mixed; and I have been quite happy and proud to show my brother and his wife and two of his children,[6] who have been more or less collectively and individually with me, what a decent English season can be. I stayed on in town a little after that sad sweet Sunday with you—and there kept itself up still, for a few weeks, a certain overdone swing of the pendulum (I mean hither and yon; but always back hither again with renewed glee) and yet I had but that *one* pleasant séance with the good Scotch Member[7]—through

5. *Italian Hours* (1909) and *English Hours* (1905) were both published with illustrations by Joseph Pennell (1860–1926), husband of HJ's actress-friend Elizabeth Robins (1865–1952).

6. Margaret Mary ("Peggy") and Alexander Robertson James.

7. See letter #128, note 11.

the conjunction you and Mildred had so suddenly, and almost violently, precipitated. I greatly liked my tea on the Terrace with him (though with three or four others too whom he gathered in;) and thought him a very kindly and honest and sturdy, and above all *native*, Scotch Member indeed. That's as far as I went—and I thought I descried the limits of the ground I should ever be moved to cover (rapturously) at the best. However, I shall be sure to see him again— perhaps in the autumn (for there's to be an autumn Session, beginning Oct. 12th:, Mildred may be interested to know; if indeed she doesn't already know, and by profuse communication, a great deal more about it all than I can pretend to.) Perhaps even at an October Tea there will be a chance of my meeting her afresh in person: though, more seriously, I regard this as too much either to hope or to fear. Only tell her, please, with my love, that she really did, by the mere indirect whisk of her skirt, before she left, (she and the Scotch Member together—he by the mere imposition of his large parliamentary hand) improve my social position inordinately. I had never before, in the almost half-century, had tea on the Terrace at all; but immediately thereafter it so befel I had it twice, from different entertainers; though unfortunately without again encountering our friend. I like him, on the whole, indeed, more than I fear him—and shall not let him escape my further analysis. Tell Mildred, please, that, rather than this, I'm prepared to perish by Tea!

Let me thank you again for your allusion to the slightly glamour-tinged, but more completely and consistently forbidding and forbidden, lecture possibility. I refer to it in these terms because in the first place I shouldn't have waited till now for it, but should have waked up to it eleven years ago; and because in the second there are other, and really stouter, things, too definite ones, I want to do with which it would formidably interfere, and which are better worth my resolutely attempting. I never have had such a sense of almost bursting, late in the day though it be, with violent and lately too much repressed creative (again!) intention. I *may* burst before this intention fairly or completely flowers, of course; but in that case, even, I shall probably explode to a less distressing effect than I should do, under stress of a fatal puncture, on the too personally and physically arduous, and above all too gregariously-assaulted (which is what makes it *most* arduous) lecture-platform. There is one thing which may conceivably (if it comes within a couple of years) take me again to the *contorni*[8] of Kittery; and on the spot, once more, one doesn't know what might happen. *Then* I should take grateful counsel of you with all the appreciation in the world. And I *want* very much to go back for a certain thoroughly practical and special "artistic" reason; which would depend, however, on my being able to pass my time in an ideal combination of freedom and quiet, rather than in a luridly real one of involved and exasperated exposure and motion. But I may still have to talk to you of this more categorically; and won't worry you with it till then. You wring my heart with your report of your collective Dental pilgrimage to Boston in Mrs Howells's distressful interest. I read of it from your page, somehow, as I

8. Environs.

read of Siberian or Armenian or Macedonian monstrosities, through a merciful attenuating veil of Distance and Difference, in a column of the Times. The distance is half the globe—and the difference (for me, from the dear lady's active afflictedness) that of having when in America undergone, myself, so prolonged and elaborate a torture—in the Chair of Anguish, that I am now on t'other side of Jordan altogether, with every ghost, even, of a wincing nerve extinct and a horrible inhuman acheless void installed as a substitute. Void or not, however, I hope Mrs Howells, and you all, are now acheless at least, and am yours, my dear Howells,

ever so faithfully
Henry James

P. S. With all of which I catch myself up on not having told you, decently and gratefully, of the always sympathetic attention with which I have read the "Fennel and Rue"[9] you so gracefully dropped into my lap at that last hour, and which I had afterwards to toy with a little distractedly before getting the right peaceful moments and right retrospective mood (this in order to remount the stream of time to the very Fontaine de Jouvence[10] of your subject-matter) down here. For what comes out of it to me more than anything else is the charming freshness of feeling of it, and the general miracle of your being capable of this under the supposedly more or less heavy bloom of a rich maturity. There are places in it in which you recover, absolutely, your first fine rapture. You confound and dazzle me; so go on recovering—it will make each of your next things a new document on immortal freshness! I can't remount—but can only drift on with the thicker and darker tide: wherefore pray for me, as who knows what may be at the end?

130.

JAMES TO HOWELLS, 31 December 1908, Rye

ALS Houghton
bMS Am 1784 (253) 106

LAMB HOUSE, RYE, SUSSEX.
New Year's Eve *1908.*

My dear Howells.

I have a beautiful Xmas letter from you[1] & I respond to it on the spot. It tells me charming things of you—such as your moving majestically from one beautiful home to another, apparently still more beautiful;[2] such as the flow of

---

9. WDH's short novel *Fennel and Rue* (1908), almost self-consciously Jamesian, analyzes the problematic celebrity of authorship in an increasingly commercial culture.

10. Fountain of Youth.

1. Not extant.

2. While staying at 10 West 30th Street in New York, WDH and his family were readying a new twelve-room apartment at 130 West 57th Street for occupancy in the new year.

your inspiration never having been more various & more torrential—& all so deliciously remunerated an inspiration; such as your having been on to dear C. E. N.'s obsequies[3]—what a Cambridge *date* that, even for you & me—& having also found time to see & "appreciate" my dear collaterals, of the 2 generations (aren't they extraordinarily good & precious collaterals?;) such, finally, as your recognising, with so fine a charity, a "message" in the poor little old "Siege of London,"[4] which—in all candour, affects me as pretty dim & rococo, though I did lately find, in going over it, that it holds quite well together, & I touched it up where I could. I have but just come to the End of my really very insidious & ingenious labour on behalf of all that series—though it has just been rather a blow to me to find that I've come (as yet,) to no reward whatever. I've just had the pleasure of hearing from the Scribners that though the Edition began to appear some 13 or 14 months ago, there is, on the volumes already out, no penny of profit owing me—of that profit to which I had partly been looking to pay my New Year's bills! It will have landed me in Bankruptcy— unless it picks up, for it has prevented my doing any other work whatever; which indeed must now begin. I have fortunately broken ground on an American novel,[5] but when you draw my ear to the liquid current of your own promiscuous abundance & facility—a flood of many affluents—I seem to myself to wander by contrast in desert sands. And I find our art, all the while, more *difficult* of practice, & want, with that, to do it in a more & more difficult way; it being really, at bottom, only difficulty that interests me. Which is a most accursèd way to be constituted. I should be passing a very—or a *rather*—inhuman little Xmas if the youngest of my nephews[6] (William's *minore*[7]—aged 18—) hadn't come to me from the tutor's at Oxford with whom he is a little woefully coaching. But he is a dear young presence & worthy of the rest of the brood, & I've just packed him off to the little Rye annual subscription ball of New Year's Eve—at the old Monastery—with a part of the "county" doubtless coming in to keep up the tradition—under the sternest injunction as to his not coming back to me "engaged" to a quadragenarian hack or a military widow—the mature women being here the great dancers.—You tell me of your "Roman book,"[8] but you don't tell me you've sent it me, & I very earnestly wish you *would*—though not without suiting the action to the word. And *anything* you put forth anywhere or anyhow that looks my way in the least, I should be tenderly grateful for.—I just hear from Tom Perry,[9] restored to Paris after a good many weeks or months in Russia, Bohemia & suchlike places—& yet still having in his odd gaunt way managed

3. Charles Eliot Norton had died on 20 October. WDH attended a memorial service at Harvard's Appleton Chapel on 23 October, where he also met other members of the James family.

4. HJ's short story was first published serially in the *Cornhill* (January–February 1883); a revised text was included in volume 14 of the New York Edition.

5. This work, never completed, was pledged to Harper's as a companion to *The American Scene*.

6. Alexander Robertson James.

7. Youngest.

8. *Roman Holidays and Others* (1908).

9. Not extant.

to escape mostly any other existence than such bits as Lilla & her grim brood "leave over." He has also escaped—admirably—any loss of his honest, strong & clear, his humorous & really superior, vision of the things of the mind.—I should like immensely to come over to you again—really like it & for uses still (!!) to be possible. But it's materially, practically, physically impossible. Too late—too late! The long years have betrayed me—but I am none the less constantly

yours all
Henry James

P. S. Please tell Pilla that I have hoped all the autumn (for there has been a Session) for tea on the Terrace. But no sign has come. Has she failed me??

131.

JAMES TO HOWELLS, 3 May 1909, Rye

TLS Houghton
bMS Am 1784 (253) 107

LAMB HOUSE, RYE, SUSSEX.
3rd: May 1909

My dear Howells.

If I have disgracefully delayed to acknowledge, and with floods of gratitude, your beautiful kind letter of too many weeks ago,[1] please believe it the result of a particular situation—a situation that hasn't been very good, for me, but that, I'm happy to say, appears really to be mending. I have had a poor winter—not having been at all well or "fit"; though but from a special and perverse cause which has been, and is being, successfully dealt with.[2] It has been very blighting, however, to letter-writing and to still more urgent occupations, while it lasted; only I have had to struggle, in spite of demoralisation, for the so imperative sordid labour; while I could in strictness sacrifice my correspondents—in proportion as I loved them! As perhaps the most sacrificed of all you can accordingly judge of your place in my affection. Suffice it that I am better and easier, and that the divine primavera[3] is upon us (though for the moment here in rather cantankerous form;) whereby, in short, things in general are looking up. It was

---

1. Not extant.

2. Earlier that winter, HJ had suspected that he was suffering from heart disease, and in February had consulted an eminent specialist, Sir James Mackenzie (1853–1925), who tried to allay his fears. On 19 April 1909 HJ wrote to Edith Wharton:

> I *have* had—to be frank—a bad and worried and depressed and inconvenient winter—with the serpent-trail of what seemed at the time . . . a tolerably ominous cardiac crisis—as to which I have since, however, got considerable information and reassurance—from the man in London most completely master of the subject—that is of the whole mystery of heart-troubles. I am definitely better of that condition of December–January, and really believe I shall be better yet; only that particular brush of the dark wing leaves one never quite the same. (*HJL* 4: 518)

3. Springtime.

heavenly good of you to go and see the performance of my little Dramatic Exercise of so many years ago.[4] I took the greatest pleasure in your report of it—though, frankly, I can't but seem to see it as an uncanny and unholy thing. The charity was very welcome to it, but I rather disliked the air it gave me of appearing disposed to play the theatric game with little old primitive cards—so imperfect a pack. The theatre is really, as it happens, knocking at my door quite loudly in these days,[5] and my fate seeming to call me—after having waited till I totter on the edge of the grave to do so; but I must take up the challenge with as new cards as possible, or at any rate work toward that as hard and as promptly. I will explain this cryptic utterance to you better some little time hence—meantime, at any rate, give me all your prayers. I have delighted in what you have told me of your great new installation and your admirable verdurous vigour.[6] Long may it continue to rejoice me! I am in truth rather *spent*—and even at this present moment of writing—with many things; and want to *break*, in other words a salutary absence hence, which I am on the point of taking by getting up to town within a day or two, for as many, many days as I can afford. Meanwhile have patience with me—I am not absolutely fit at this hour to say more. Except indeed two or three things; the first of which is that I find John's little Tale in the Atlantic,[7] which I thank you for having sent me, most neat and right and charming. It is done with a *hand*, and I almost shudder to think of the promise it reveals. I have often wondered how it feels to have extraordinary children—or indeed any at all; and also even a little how it feels to have architectural children. But to have literary children, "promising" ahead at such a rate, and especially architectural-literary children, more or less extraordinary in both ways, how does *that* feel? It strikes me as most formidable and incalculable—but you are probably used to it by this time, and would even rather John did things as compactly and happily as the story in the Atlantic, than as so many of the children of others (and of so *many* others!) do them. There seem at any rate so many things now to congratulate him on that I scarce know where to begin. But I lump them, massively, and assure him I rejoice in him all round.

And then you haven't, as you promised, sent me your Roman book[8]—as to which I suggest to you that there is still time; though I should have been glad to have it at any moment these last weeks, during which it would have contrib-

---

4. HJ's *Disengaged* had its first professional performance on 11 March 1909 at a benefit matinee at the Hudson Theater in New York. This was the same play—then called *Mrs. Jasper*—WDH had seen performed in 1902 by students at the American Academy of Dramatic Arts. See letter #103.

5. In June 1909 Herbert Trench (1865–1923), manager of the Haymarket Theater, paid HJ a hundred pounds for an option on *The Other House*, but the play was not produced. Originally written in dramatic form in 1894, *The Other House* was published as a novel in 1896. HJ refurbished the story yet again for Trench in 1909. Charles Frohman, the American producer, also asked HJ to write a comedy for the winter repertory season at the Duke of York's Theater. *The Outcry* was completed in December 1910.

6. WDH's family moved into their new apartment in January 1909.

7. John Mead Howells, "At the Café d'Orsay," *Atlantic* (April 1909).

8. *Roman Holidays and Others* (1908).

uted to keep me a little in the key for a more or less Roman job of my own: the packing-together, for base book-making and pot-boiling purposes, under the name of "Italian Hours", various old scraps from the far-away Atlantic and Nation of our prime (but all previously re-printed) and re-touching and re-titivating them as much as possible, in fact not a little re-writing them, with expansions and additions to trick the book out further, and with illustrations by Penell—to match a couple of others, Houghton and Mifflin and Heinemann Volumes[9]—crowning the mercenary edifice. Such efforts are dire and difficult, in being so terribly perfunctory. One has to live backward by so desperate a contortion, and gouge out the inspiration for doing it at all. But thank goodness it is just finished; and this I will send *you*, if you'll still let me have not only the Roman book, but the delightful "old style" fiction you read me the beginning of at Kittery (that torrid day is dear to memory now!) and which, as I understand you, you have finished and are putting forth;[10] all from your insolent new library I suppose, with its heroic proportions—though who has a right to such, you will say, if not the creator of so many heroes and heroines.

All thanks for your news of the dear Smalleys,[11] whom I have also, all winter, hideously sacrificed; yet to whom, also, I am just writing—since I ought to add that I do now feel myself considerably out of the wood.

Interesting to me too—*and* as "pathetic", certainly, as you please, your mention of your failure of effort to do something newspaper-correspondentially for Tom Perry in New York.[12] His noble serenity under a lifetime of that sort of thing is verily a lesson!—in spite of the fact that one sees, not less verily, the reason and the logic; I don't mean of the serenity—which has *had* to come, practically—but of the lesson. But I must wind up. I greet your wife all faithfully, and thank her for a droll little reminder, in the form of an international advertisement of the sort we like to see, in some current sheet.[13] I hope for you that you're getting soon to the country—where I wish I were getting with you again into that trolley-car (since your country is a trolley-car country) to go and see Sara Jewett; of whom I'm sorry to say I had the other day a scrap of a baddish account.[14] To her too I must now write!—so I'm

all constantly yours
Henry James

9. Illustrated re-issues of *A Little Tour in France* (1900) and *English Hours* (1905).

10. On the contrary, WDH had decided to delay publication of "The Children of the Summer" (published in 1920 as *The Vacation of the Kelwyns*). After going over the 175 pages already set in type, WDH told Harper's that he was not satisfied with the novel and wanted to "give it a thorough overhauling." See WDH to Frederick A. Duneka, 8 April 1909, quoted in *SL* 5: 271n4.

11. See letter #126, note 12.

12. Perry and his wife were still in Europe, but they returned home to Boston late in 1909.

13. Elinor Howells's letter is not extant.

14. Sara Orne Jewett had suffered a stroke in March 1909 and was partially paralyzed. Her home at South Berwick, Maine, was not far from WDH's retreat at Kittery Point; WDH had visited her on 25 April.

132.

JAMES TO HOWELLS, 23 July 1909, Rye   ALS Houghton
                                                        bMS Am 1784 (253) 108

LAMB HOUSE, RYE, SUSSEX.

My dear Howells.

I have had lately no less than 3 very valuable & interesting communications
from you—as well as one, no less welcome, from Mrs Howells[1] (whom I beg to
have just a trifle more patience with me;) but I won't plunge into the reasons
why I have perhaps struck you as backward in making you the responsive sign.
I am afraid there are always reasons enough for my being the most laggard &
limping of letter-writers—the very infirmity of my constitution to begin with;
but I have been in particular delayed from acknowledging your news about poor
dear Evelyn S.[2] by the fact that her catastrophe seems to have engaged me in a
constant—or considerable—flow of correspondence—& with "lady-writers."
Ever so many of these have had at heart that I should know everything—& I
confess I have gallantly polished *them* off while treasuring up this ampler end of
the month, & of the flurry, for you. There just comes in a letter from Mrs.
Smalley herself—most pathetic of women; but I have already, some days since,
written to her also; & I now give you earnest preference & attention. I am
immensely struck with your kindness in the matter of the mysterious Calendar,
as ill-starred as its author; & feel I should indeed already have satisfied you on
the head of the Preface that the merciful young Boston publisher you tell me of
seeks at my hand. Kindly let him know that I will write such a Preface with
pleasure (though that seems a strange word to use in all the dismal connection,)
but that I can't do so without sight of the Book—or whatever the thing is—
itself! I have no basis for inspiration without that—for, very privately speaking,
I don't in the least know what the composition or publication *is*. I don't conceive it or see it—& aren't there, or won't there be, *proofs*, that will, or can, be
transmitted to me? It appears that some sheets or pages of the thing were some
time—a long time—ago sent me; but I have no recollection of them, or of their
form or place, whatever; therefore, in fine, if the Editore will supply this missing
link to my conscious connection with the matter, I will do what I can for
him, & above all for poor Evelyn. It occurs to me that her condition may represent an arrest or lapse of all this—for it has been communicated to me that her
infinitely tragic case is one for which no recovery can be hoped. But if she is
sane *on this side* the carrying out of the idea may be of good effect to her—
though at the same time I quite conceive that a publisher shouldn't cling to
relations with an authoress in an Asylum. On the chance, I hold myself entirely

1. None extant.
2. Evelyn Garnaut Smalley, daughter of George Washburn and Phoebe Garnaut Smalley, had
recently been committed to an asylum. A devoted reader of HJ, she had collected appropriate passages from his work to make up *The Henry James Year Book*, a calendar volume published by Richard
Badger of Boston in 1911. For this book HJ and WDH contributed prefatory letters.

ready to oblige. Only, to repeat, I *must,* for this purpose, take cognizance of the Calendar.

The heart-breaking misery of this new chapter in the harrowing history of that sport of the gods that our afflicted friends live so up to their vocation for being has already wrung from me all the responsive sympathy that my pen is capable now of recording, & I won't again go into the particulars of it. I save myself for another letter to poor Mrs. S.—having already written to Emerson[3] too—not counting the one to Evelyn herself—in addition to those to the lady-friends. Your earlier letter—the earliest of your three, including the note just sent by Mr. Allen White[4]—speaks of interesting things & not least of the prodigy of the 35 vols. of your Edition. I heartily rejoice for you that this plan approaches fulfilment; but delightful as your Prefaces would be sure to have been had you written them, I can't but congratulate you on your wisdom in keeping out of so desperately arduous a job, which would have crowned your life with an intolerable fatigue.[5] I found mine—of much scanter number—an almost insurmountable grind toward the end—& your attempted perpetration of 35 would have qualified you, I feel sure, for a cot beside poor Evelyn! What a monstrously & brutally stupid race is the avid & purblind one of Publishers, who seem never dimly to guess that authors can't to advantage be worked like icecream freezers or mowing-machines. Mr. Allen White has sent me your note, & a very quaint little address of his own, & I have written him that I shall be

3. Emerson Smalley, Evelyn's brother.

4. William Allen White (1868–1944), editor of the Emporia (Kansas) *Gazette;* his note is not extant.

5. Although WDH's first intentions for the Library Edition of his works seem to have followed closely the recent example of HJ's New York Edition—each volume to be embellished with a photographic frontispiece and a preface by the author—he abruptly abandoned the effort in the summer of 1909. Having composed at least eleven "Bibliographicals," as WDH termed them, he told Frederick Duneka of Harper's that no more would be attempted:

> I have made a careful experiment of the type in an introduction to A Hazard of New Fortunes, and have convinced my self that I cannot write prefaces for the library edition, much as I would like to meet your wish in the matter. I believe I was right in wishing the volumes to go [before] the public without any word of explanation or comment from me, because they are already most intimately full of me, and are their own explanation and comment. I know that the typical one I have done is well done, but I know also that it is superfluous and impertinent. I cannot pretend to better your judgment as to the advantage of the prefaces with the subscribers, and I only state my insuperable repugnance to them. I not only feel this in regard to them intrinsically, but I feel that I should have the effect of following in James's footsteps, and that with critics this would be a just ground for censure. I know that you do not agree with me on this point, but I count on your kindness to let me have my way, and to let the books go without a personal word from me. (SL 5: 277)

Only six volumes of the Library Edition—including WDH's prefaces—were published by Harper's in 1911: *My Literary Passions* and *Criticism and Fiction; The Landlord at Lion's Head; Literature and Life; London Films* and *Certain Delightful English Towns; Literary Friends and Acquaintance* and *My Mark Twain;* and *A Hazard of New Fortunes.* The texts of five other prefaces (for *Heroines of Fiction, The Son of Royal Langbrith, The Shadow of a Dream, The Coast of Bohemia* and *The Story of a Play,* and *The Altrurian Romances*) were published by George Arms in the *New England Quarterly* 17 (1944): 580–91.

delighted to see him, but also conscientiously warning him that "calling upon" me at this distance from town is a most fatiguing & thankless job. You will wearily remember how far from suburban I am—& coming to see me within the day involves at least 5 hours of train. On the other hand all my conditions reduce to an infinitely small "percentage" the friends I can ask to stay—manage to put up & (all by myself & with my pressure of occupation) entertain. But I dare say the Whites will somehow gallantly brave the journey to luncheon, & I will in that case make them very welcome.[6] I am firmly settled here for the summer—after a few (6 or 8) rather late & cold & wet weeks in London; which were nevertheless of good effect for me after many months on end (8 or 10) of this blessedly, but at last sometimes oppressively, sane & safe villeggiatura.[7] We are having a charmless & chill season—with everything incongruously rank from excess of rain. The excesses of my famous Kittery Sunday are far from us. I think very tenderly (under that association) of poor stricken & gentle & frustrate Sara Jewett—life seems to me to have so failed, to her, of final kindness. I like to remember that I was moved to write to her with great benevolence not long before her death.[8] How magnificently you seem to be working—I wish I had your organs—of every kind. May great benefits of every sort continue to flow to you from them! Your health of body & brain, your freshness of life, are the miracle of the age. I feel very ancient, & yet even my ancientry, too, doesn't yet despair. The Theatre is knocking loud at my door, in definite guise, & I am labouring to respond, both because of the intrinsic solicitation of the play & because of the absolute need that besets me to gain a few pence before I am further stricken. Something will, I think, come of it. But I must go to bed, & am

> Ever yours all
> *Henry James*
> July 23. 1909.

133.

HOWELLS TO JAMES, 25 December 1909, New York   ALS Houghton
                                                            bMS Am 1094 (257)

                                                            130 West 57th street,
                                                            Christmas, 1909.

My dear James:

We are reading aloud now every night your Tragic Muse—very small shreds of her; for my wife's nervous strength is so slight and her interest in the book so

---

6. HJ's pocket diary notes a luncheon engagement with William Allen White on 5 August 1909 (CN 306).

7. Country retreat.

8. Sarah Orne Jewett had died on 24 June 1909; HJ's last letter to her has not been located.

intense that she can seldom let me go beyond a dozen pages.[1] She hates to have the story finished for as she says in a justifiable panic, "Where shall we find anything like it?" I have supposed some other story of yours, but she has no hopes of anything else so good, even by you. The other night she sighed over a certain tremendous complication of emotions and characters, and said, "I don't believe *I* could do anything with it from this point." Pilla listens too, and enjoys the author and the simple transports of his elderly readers. My wife no longer cares for many things that used to occupy her: *hohheits*[2] of all nations, special characters in history, the genealogy of both our families. "Well what *do* you care for?" I asked, and I found her answer touching. "Well, James, and his way of doing things—and you." I must own to you a constantly mounting wonder in myself at your "way," and at the fullness, the closeness, the density of your work; my own seems so meager beside it.—The winter has whipped by past its shortest days, and has witnessed few things outside of this house for me. My wife wont go out, and so I keep in, talking with her, and we play with our dear little grandson, who dwells so lovingly in a world of love and is so full of surprises at it and for us. I could not have believed that life still held an experience so sweet for me.

—Last week I went to Washington, where our poor Academy held its first public sessions.[3] The papers read were really fine, but I think the public did not care in the least. The President[4] had us all to tea in the White House, and was very civil. He is a mighty paunch of a man, with a prodigious good head atop, and no end of good feeling and happy laughter. He did not want the right sort of presence, either, in a straight American way. At night we went to the Architects meeting in the Corcoran gallery where he presided at the presentation to poor McKim's daughter of a medal,[5] and made a good, kind, wisely humorous speech. The place is all white, and the girls in solid blues, pinks, and greens hanging over the gallery rails, were wonderfully Roman, Pompeian, Alma Tademaish.[6] They were better still when they came out under the clear Italian night,

---

1. *The Tragic Muse* was first published in 1890; WDH was probably reading from the revised text of the novel, the seventh and eighth volumes of the New York Edition. Elinor Howells, whose health was never robust, had undergone surgery for the removal of swollen glands.

2. German (*die Hoheit*): royalty.

3. In 1904 both WDH and HJ were elected (on the first and second ballots, respectively) to the newly organized American Academy of Arts and Letters. In November 1908, by which time successive balloting had swelled the membership to its full complement of fifty, WDH was elected president, a post he held until his death in 1920.

4. William Howard Taft, Republican of Ohio, defeated William Jennings Bryan in the election of 1908.

5. On 15 December the American Institute of Architects posthumously awarded a gold medal to Charles F. McKim, who had died 14 September 1909. William R. Mead, WDH's brother-in-law and McKim's partner, accepted the award and presented it to Margaret McKim, the architect's daughter.

6. During his 1882 visit to London, WDH had met the artist Lawrence Alma-Tadema, a friend of Edmund Gosse.

and *walked* home with their heels clicking and their neat ankles showing. We all send love.

Yours ever
W. D. Howells.

134.

HOWELLS TO JAMES, 1 February 1910, New York   ALS Houghton
bMS Am 1094 (259)

. . . 130 WEST 57TH STREET
February 1, 1910.

Dear James:

You owe me two letters,[1] but I make you my debtor for a third because I can't resist writing to you about The Bostonians, which I've been reading out to my family. I'm still reading it, for there are a hundred pages left, and I wish there were a thousand. I've the impression, the fear that you're not going to put it into your collection,[2] and I think that would be the greatest blunder and the greatest pity. Do be persuaded that it's not only one of the greatest books you've written, but one of the masterpieces of all fiction. Closely woven, deep, subtle, reaching out into worlds that I did not imagine you knew, and avouching you citizen of the American Cosmos, it is such a novel as the like of has n't been done in our time. Every character is managed with masterly clearness and power. Verena is something absolute in her tenderness and sweetness and loveliness, and Olive in her truth and precision; your New Yorkers are as good as your Bostonians; and I couldn't go beyond that. Both towns are wonderfully suggested; you go to the bottom of the half frozen Cambridge mud. A dear yet terrible time comes back to me in it all. I believe I have not been wanting in a sense of you from the first, but really I seem only now to be realizing you now.

My wife and daughter share my feeling about the book, which holds my poor old dear above her nervous suffering, and would have kept my dear girl from Bermuda if anything could. But she is gone with a sigh of wonder for what is to happen to Verena. (I am much concerned about your brute of a Mississippian.)[3] She sailed on Saturday away from one of the bitterest, *poisonest* winters I have known for many years. The cold tries me in my age as it used not to do; perhaps we may go another winter to pass it all in the tropics. Of course I should like to live the rest of my winters in some climate where history dwelt with the etherial

---

1. In addition to his Christmas greetings of 1909, WDH had sent another letter on 16 January 1910, in which he praised The Bostonians ("so like Boston that we all shuddered").

2. See letter #129.

3. Basil Ransom, like his Yankee cousin Olive Chancellor, vies for the affections of Verena Tarrant.

mildness; but it will probably be some such place as Bermuda. Or, it may be a
gelid submission to the New York conditions.—I have an idea you are not very
well. Or is it that I've heard it from some imaginable Smalleys?[4]

I wish you could find it in you to write me. But if you can't I can always
commerce with you in your books.

Yours affectionately
W. D. Howells

135.

JAMES TO HOWELLS, 27 May 1910, Rye   ALS Houghton
bMS Am 1784 (253) 113

LAMB HOUSE, RYE, SUSSEX.
May 27th 1910

My very dear old Friend.

A letter from Tom Perry just brings me news of the straight & heavy blow
that has descended on you,[1] & this is a poor sign of the intensely tender participation with which it makes me turn to you. A poor—the very poorest—sign, I
say, because I have been interminably & wearily & dismally ill these five months
(ever since Xmas) & although the light of amendment has at last begun to
break I am limited as yet but to feeble demonstrations. I think of this laceration
of your life with an infinite sense of all it will mean for you—a sense only
equalled by that of which your long long years of exquisite, of heroic devotion,
the most perfect thing of the kind one has ever known, will always have meant
for *her*. To think of her, moreover, is, for me, to recall the far backward stretch—
from our melted, our unbearable-to-revive youth—of her unbroken gentleness &
graciousness, the particular sweetness of touch, through all my close association
with your domestic fortunes, in every phase of them, & your public fame. But
one can't *speak* of these things—especially with a lame pen & a broken utterance; & you will know how little I feel you, or feel Mildred, to appeal to my
insistance. May all this coming time now wind you two closer & more helpingly
together. T. S. P. says you come out[2]—so I shall see you before too long: though
I am *trying* to go abroad (with my sister in law,) for a few weeks—to first join

4. If WDH did hear such news from the Smalleys, it was not imagined. In January 1910 HJ
slumped into a severe psychological depression. This was probably one reason why he had not
responded to WDH's earlier letters. HJ's condition seems to have been aggravated by several causes:
his declining physical health; his sense of isolation at Rye; and continued anxiety about his professional career. The poor sales of the New York Edition were particularly nettlesome. HJ did not fully
recover until midsummer 1910 (see CN 312–13).
1. Elinor Mead Howells died on 7 May; Thomas Sergeant Perry's letter to HJ is not extant.
2. WDH and Mildred sailed for England on 14 June.

William at Bad-Nauheim.[3] I have had a black & heavy time (with your beautiful letters of the winter unanswered,) but am at last gradually working through. As T. S. P. gives me the impression of your starting *soon* I think best to send this to Albemarle St.[4] Or no—rather—that doesn't seem explicit enough—so I infer *Kittery* for the moment & send it there. Yours & Mildred's, my dearest old Friend's,

> more & more than ever
> Henry James

P. S. No—on the whole—Harpers.

136.

JAMES TO HOWELLS, 27 June 1910, Constance   ALS Houghton
bMS Am 1784 (253) 114

> Insel Hotel
> Bodensee
> (Constance.)
> June 27ᵗʰ 1910.

My dear Howells.

This is a word of very earnest & affectionate welcome to you & to Mildred—with the hope that you may find, in these days, that you have left behind you some fraction of the soreness of your pain. I am waiting about in these parts—where rain & floods prevail, with William & Alice (he seeking a mild Nachkur[1] after Nauheim,) for the simple reason that I have been & still am, alas, too ill to fend for myself & be left alone. I am getting better, but with sad checks & relapses even now. I think I have written you that I return to America with them on Aug. 12ᵗʰ—I cling to them abjectly. We shall be in England toward, or by, the (July) 20ᵗʰ—at 1ˢᵗ at Rye; & perhaps even sooner. I thank you ever so kindly for your letter from Boston—of the 9ᵗʰ;[2] by which I am greatly moved. How I long to see you both—poor demoralized thing as I myself feel!

Ever, my dear Howells,

> your devoted old
> Henry James

P. S. We go hence to Berne, Lausanne Geneva &c.

---

3. WJ and his wife, Alice H. G. James, had joined HJ at Rye in April to help him convalesce. From there William traveled to Bad Nauheim in early June, seeking treatment for his worsening heart condition. HJ and Alice planned to join him later in Germany and then tour Switzerland; all three had booked return passage to the United States in August.

4. Forty-five Albemarle Street was the London address of Harper & Brothers.

1. Convalescence.

2. WDH's note acknowledged HJ's consolation: "It was good to see your handwriting again," he wrote, "and sweet to have your pity." In a postscript he added, "Boston is a beautiful town and Cambridge a wonder of leaves and grass—but with graves under them everywhere."

137.

HOWELLS TO JAMES, 1 July 1910, London

ALS Houghton
bMS Am 1094 (262)

. . . 18, HALF MOON STREET, MAYFAIR. W.
July 1st, 1910.

My dear James:

The best thing in your letter from Constance is the fact that you will be in America next winter, though the cause grieves me. When we were in Cambridge the other day for the saddest of all errands,[1] it seemed to me I must go back there to live, or at least to die, and later I visited my Concord Avenue house.[2] I had somehow the hope that you might be coming there to visit your brother, and I thought of seeing you often, and Perry. But the house forbade me. It was dreadful in its ghostliness and ghastliness, and it has two trolley lines in front of it that would banish sleep. So we gave it up, and the dream of six months of fall and spring in Cambridge every year hereafter. Probably we shall go back to New York, and about Christmas go down to Bermuda where we fancy taking a house, and welcoming you there if you have the nerve for the rough voyage.

London is not London without the possibility of you, and there is only that one reason for my being here which seems less and less a reason. In a chaos like mine one changes almost from hour to hour, and if it were to do again, the coming away, "lo farei domani piutosto che oggi."[3] That is, I think so, but I really know nothing. I try to be decent, to be humble, to be grateful, and to say that if I must lose my wife it is all that the world can still give in keeping such a daughter as mine. I am ashamed to have her devote herself so to me, but I cannot help it, and I hope she will get some joy and some distraction from our being here.

I am sorry indeed for your suffering and I do trust that the "tetto natio"[4] will be a healing shelter to you. I wish I were going home on the same ship, but we shall hardly sail before October. John and his wife, who are now in Rome for the architecture will come to us here about the 25th, and will go home a week before you.

It has rained almost ever day since we landed, but now and then throughout the day it doesn't, and that is something. Then we venture out, and with

---

1. Elinor Mead Howells was interred next to Winifred in the Howells family plot at the Cambridge cemetery. WDH and Mildred probably visited the grave site before sailing from Boston.

2. WDH had moved his family from Sacramento Street to 37 Concord Avenue, Cambridge, in 1873.

3. I would rather put it off until tomorrow instead of doing it today.

4. Native home, i.e., America.

this variety, and heaps of the proofs[5] always following me, the time passes. Pil joins me in love to you and your family.

Yours ever
W. D. Howells.

138.

JAMES TO HOWELLS, 9 July 1910, Geneva
ALS Houghton
bMS Am 1784 (253) 115

GRAND HÔTEL BEAU-RIVAGE GENÈVE
July 9th *1910.*

My dear Howells.

It was only yesterday that your good & most moving letter from Half Moon St. reached me at this place—which we leave Monday a.m. for London, sleeping but a night in Paris.[1] Therefore this hurried word shall be brief—for it means that I shall happily see you soon. We are pushing on to England as straight as our anxieties allow—I say anxieties because William is very unwell as to heart, the drastic Nauheim having apparently done him more harm than good, & to cease moving (he can be comparatively quiet in England till we sail) is imperative for him. Our sky moreover has been overdarkened still more since yesterday by the cable news of our poor dear Brother Bob's death,[2] at Concord, of heart-failure in his sleep—horribly alone, as I can't but painfully feel—with his wife & son in Europe & his married daughter far away.[3] Infinitely tragic & pathetic to me the whole image—*his* whole one, & that of all his troubled stormy joyless life—though of late years much pacified—for *him*. With this aggravation of William's I am, by the mercy of heaven (if any such thing or place there be) much better of my long malady, working more free of it—& *appearing*, I gather, especially this last week, quite well. I take up nothing that your letter expresses of your own stricken & disconnected sense & broken spring—I shall show you how I enter into it all when we meet. Life still has both hands on your shoulders & will insist on showing you how much she is still concerned with you.

---

5. In addition to his uninterrupted "Editor's Easy Chair" contributions to *Harper's Monthly*, and his memorial essay, "My Memories of Mark Twain," which ran in the same magazine from July to September 1910, WDH was editing a new set of short fictions for the "Harper's Novelettes" series, begun in 1906 with Henry Mills Alden as coeditor. *Imaginary Interviews* was also published later that year (October 1910).

1. The Jameses arrived in Paris on Monday, 11 July, and crossed to England the next day.

2. Robertson James, HJ's youngest brother, died on 3 July.

3. Estranged by her husband's persistent alcoholism, Mary Holton James had sailed to Europe with their son, Edward Holton (Ned), in December 1909. Mary James Vaux and her husband, George, arrived at Concord from Bryn Mawr, Pennsylvania, shortly after they were notified of her father's death.

How Mildred must be concerned, tell her, with my love, I vividly see. I shall make you an instant sign in London, & am

ever your faithfullest
Henry James

139.

HOWELLS TO JAMES, 7 January 1911, New York

ALS Houghton
bMS Am 1094 (263)

10 West 30th street,
Jan'y 7, 1911.

Dear James:

I feel very guilty in having taken our tickets for Bermuda on the 11th, but such is the lamentable fact. We have longed to be off during the last six weeks of grippe and nervous breakdown, and we cannot put off going now, even for you, poor dear, whom I should so gladly stay for.[1] I have had my own Pocket Illiad, which is nothing to your folio, but illiad enough.[2] My management of the Mark Twain commemoration, with my loathing for any publicity but that of print, was of almost killing effect, and hard upon it followed three days of the Accursed Academy of Arts and Letters, me President![3] I assure you the whole thing was a nightmare, but thank heaven I am awake from it, though in a tremble and cold perspiration still.

We hope to find a house in Bermuda, and stay three months, but we must go first to an hotel. I count much upon the outing because, for one thing, it is a land of large sleep, and here I wake every morning at 2 or 3 and drink my sorrow dry, and then drug myself, one way other, back into oblivion.

---

1. In the company of his brother and sister-in-law, HJ returned to the United States in August 1910. The family immediately retired to William James's summer home at Chocorua, New Hampshire, where the ailing elder brother died on 26 August. HJ spent most of the autumn with Alice at 95 Irving Street in Cambridge, although his improving health allowed him to make occasional visits to New York. He was planning to return to New York on 13 January 1911.

2. In comparing his own minor illnesses to HJ's more serious breakdown, WDH may be referring to HJ's idiosyncratic habit of inscribing strings of black and red x's in his pocket diary as a record of his oscillating physical condition. See *CN* 312–27.

3. On 30 November WDH presided at a ceremonial commemoration of Mark Twain at Carnegie Music Hall. Less than two weeks later, the American Academy of Arts and Letters held its second public meeting in New York (8–9 December). In a letter to his brother Joseph, WDH described his ordeal:

> I have been public-speaking-on-the-stage out of all experience within the past fortnight, beginning with the Mark Twain commemoration on the 30th, and going through the sessions of the Academy of Arts and Letters; I am president, you know. It is all a terrible trial to me, but they say I did decently well. The Mark Twain business crowded the Carnegie Hall from floor to roof with 3500 people, and a thousand left on the sidewalk, who couldn't get in.

See WDH to Joseph A. Howells, 11 December 1910, *SL* 5: 337.

This is not cheering you up, which I should like to do, but perhaps it will help you a little if you know you have the company that misery loves. I will own that I am somewhat comforted when I think of you, and realize that I am not the only wretched man, selfish beast that I am.

Your sister wrote me a heavenly letter which I shall try to answer worthily by and by.[4] What angelic courage, what divine sympathy.

You may care to know that the brute Badger is stilled. He sent me a proof, and it has gone back to him without bothering you, and it is all right.[5]

Pilla has shared my influenza and nervous breakdown, and she needs the exile from New York even more than I. We shall taxi down to the steamer, hand in hand, next Wednesday, mingling our tears of nervous weakness, and of regret that we are not to see you here. Billy[6] and his family are the only things besides that we regret.

With our love to all your people,

Yours affectionately
W. D. Howells.

140.

JAMES TO HOWELLS, 17 March 1911, New York   ALS Houghton
bMS Am 1784 (253) 132

New York.
March 17th
21, EAST ELEVENTH STREET

Dearest Howells,

Beautiful & comforting & most opportunely welcome your letter—as I absolutely *sans phrase*,[1] had only been waiting to get back to this place (I came on yesterday,) to reach out & try to draw you closer. This last alas your absence of

---

4. The letter from Alice H. G. James, HJ's sister-in-law, is not extant. But from WDH's response, dated 8 January [1911] (James Papers, Harvard), it is clear that they had exchanged condolences:

Your letter was a great, sad joy to me, and of unimaginable help in what you said of *his* last moments, and in those last words of his. Yes, he had earned the right to die because his work had been all unselfish. Mine has been just my pleasure, first if not always, and I cannot rejoice as you bid me. In the strange, incredible interval when my wife seemed getting well we had a long full talk, and I told her that once I had been taught that I ought to go first and I wished it. If that might have been she would have supported this pain better than I; women have more courage, more strength than men; she would have known what to do, and I do not yet.

But it is no use my writing this except that in a community of suffering there is somehow hope, and perhaps it will avail you a little if you know of my constant, my intelligent sympathy.

5. WDH had received the proof for Evelyn Garnaut Smalley's *Henry James Year Book* from Richard G. Badger, the Boston publisher. The American edition of the book was issued in September 1911.

6. WDH's grandson.

1. Without beating around the bush.

any allusion to a meditated return to New York doesn't at all help me to do—though I pray the powers that I may have some sight of you before my 4 or 5 (or 6) weeks here, in all, as I hope, thresh themselves out. Robert Grant,[2] the other day, at the Tavern Club in Boston, gave me news of you as cheerful as his expressed belief that you would remain away "till the middle of April" permitted it to be. It will be then that my stay here (in New York) will pretty well terminate[3] & I have been fondly hoping that the vexed Bermoothes might in turn become vexing to you—though if they don't who could benevolently (I recognise) wish you to hurry back from a coral strand to an icy mountain—by which I mean a Murray Hill? However, I have taken my passage home only for June 14th,[4] & will forgive your basking in tropic suns & plashing in azure seas if Mildred will promise to make you allow her to ask me down to Kittery for not less than 3 days with you if you go there between the time of your own return & that of my final departure. Meanwhile I bless & envy the happy status for you of which Grant, as aforesaid, gave me a Bostonian picture. This has to be *my* Bermuda—but I shall make it serve. I was here for 3 weeks the other month,[5] & have so taken the measure of the field. I have a vague plan of going for a little to Washington, but otherwise I shall be back at Cambridge when I am not here, & here when I am not back at Cambridge.[6] The strange & perverse doom by which I find myself again renewing an ineluctable connection with the latter (to me—in itself) so scantly sympathetic locality—well, is intimately part & parcel, isn't it? of our old friend the irony of fate. But I have, in spite of everything, more or less successfully struggled out of my deep black hole there; & I recognise that even while thoroughly conscious that (putting my dear brother's dear house & all its helpfulness aside,) I should probably have effected that slow labour better in some other places. I find this one, New York, for instance, in many ways auspicious, but that would be still more the case if you were here—& Mildred *anche*.[7] I thank you ever so kindly for your news of your friend the so munificent & intelligent Mr. Wayland (?)[8]—even though it bewilders & depresses me that I have been leaving it for him, all these years, to place the poor old Story-book[9] in your hands. I can account for the graceless fact with difficulty at this time of day—it only comes over me that H. M. & Co.[10] handled the volumes very meagrely & illiberally for me (no penny has ever come to me

2. Robert Grant (1852–1940), Boston lawyer and novelist.

3. HJ returned to Cambridge on 20 April.

4. HJ eventually put off his departure until 30 July.

5. HJ had been in New York from 13 January to 5 February 1911.

6. Instead of going to Washington that summer, HJ divided much of his time between Nahant, on the shore north of Boston, and the Berkshires, where he stayed with Edith Wharton at The Mount, her majestic Lenox home.

7. too.

8. The question mark is HJ's; Julius Augustus Wayland (1854–1912) was a socialist editor and communitarian reformer.

9. *William Wetmore Story and His Friends* (1903). See letter #109 for details of its publishing history.

10. Houghton, Mifflin & Company.

from America for it—though that is doubtless the fault of canny Edinburgh Blackwoods—from whom few pence have ever come;) & that I couldn't even come by a copy to give my Brother. Your friend is charming about the volumes & their author—& I beg you kindly to thank him for me—I mean for his vicarious generosity. The Story itself has at least the merit of performing to the very maximum the miracle of the loaves & fishes, or at least the feat of bricks without straw. The nearer one got (tried to get) to him—to W. W. S.—the more one found there was Nothing—& yet I had to *invent* Something—& it was the very devil; in spite of which his foolish, or rather reprobate, progeny didn't like the book—though they could help me with nothing but a few, the very fewest, stray grains of trash toward doing it. But we will indeed talk of these fond & faded old things—only, mind, the sooner the better. I can't but hope that you have found balm & peace & some measure of healing on your coral strand—though do give me some inkling of the moment at which the right one of your winds (of which I hear so much—as to their blowing—though you don't mention them) will waft you this way. The above address will always reach me. I have seen very few people here just yet (it's but my second day;) but I saw several 6 weeks ago, & even went to a business-meeting of the Am. Academy—where some of the elements frankly appalled me.[11] I don't know what to do about that connection, but you will advise

> your both all faithfully
> *Henry James*

141.

JAMES TO HOWELLS, 20 April 1911, New York   ALS Houghton
bMS Am 1784 (253) 116

21, EAST ELEVENTH STREET
April 20$\underline{^{th}}$ *1911.*

My dear Howells.

I depart under my nephew's care this afternoon,[1] & I scrawl you this thanks for your consignment while I very limply wait—returning you herein the 2 letters. Bennett's, I am bound to say, I find poor & void—& I can't imagine an author's writing to a critic on such an occasion & being moved to communicate so little—so little of his own light.[2] It makes me doubt if he—if A. B.—really

11. HJ's diary entry for Wednesday, 25 January 1911, reads: "Went to business meeting of Am. Academy at University Club. Small attendance, but impression simply sickening" (CN 329).

1. WJ's eldest son, Harry (1879–1947), escorted his uncle back to Cambridge later that day.

2. Arnold Bennett (1867–1931), prolific English novelist, author of *The Old Wives' Tale* (1908) and *Clayhanger* (1910), had written to WDH in response to his favorable "Editor's Easy Chair" column in *Harper's Monthly* (March 1911). In his review, WDH divided Bennett's novels into "realities" and "fantasticalities" and tried to account for his pendulumlike shifts from good work to bad:

> apparently he has found a comfort, or a relaxation, or an indemnification in writing a bad book after writing a good one. It is very curious; it cannot be from a wavering ideal; for no

has any! I would at any rate give it all (what he does—so commonly!—say) for ten words from him on the question of what, for himself, such things as The Old Wives & Clayhanger represent & *signify*—what idea, to his own, imagination, they express. I cant see any picture of life save in the *conditions* of a picture, of all pictures & any; that is as having a determined subject & with the subject's having a determined centre. I doubt if A. B. can name in either of his cases any such matter—though I have found him in both cases interesting & "curious" in spite of it. Yet, all the same, imperfectly, precariously, confusedly & above all *leakingly*—as with a hole in the unwrought bottom, & a big one! I call a book interesting (in exuberant moments) if I *can* read it; & if I could read those two it was because the author has something, of sorts, to *report of* & that he keeps it as thick as he knows how. The recognition of that carried me on as I read; or dragged rather than carried—carrying is to my sense another matter. Your paper is at all events very handsome & charming—with things in it admirably said. But it isn't *d'un jour d'hui*[3] that you know I always feel that.

I am better today than you saw me yesterday; but there are strong reasons for my going. All love to Pilla.

Yours & hers ever

H. J.

---

man could have seen the truth about life so clearly as Mr. Bennett, with any after doubt of its unique value; and yet we have him from time to time indulging himself in the pleasure of painting it falsely. . . . Of course there is always the chance that there may be two Mr. Arnold Bennetts, rather than two selves of one. Or it may be that there is a pseudo–Mr. Arnold Bennett who is abusing the name of a master to foist his prentice inventions upon the public. (633, 636)

It was Bennett's defense of this practice (in a letter to WDH dated 1 March 1911) that HJ found abject. "I feel it is my duty," Bennett told WDH,

to reassure an observer so friendly as you are, on the subject of the pseudo–Arnold Bennett, author of unserious books. The need of money was the sole & sufficient explanation of those books. Although I flatter myself that I live to write, I should be ashamed if I did not write to live. The last of those books was written some years ago, & has just been published. *Denry the Audacious*. I must tell you, however, that I consider *Buried Alive*, though as you say a farce, as a quite serious 'criticism of life', & that I mean to continue at intervals in this vein. And further I want to rebut the charge of excessive length brought against *Clayhanger*. Everybody believes & says it is longer than *The Old Wives' Tale*. Far from being longer, it is 40,000 words (20 per cent) shorter. The optical illusion of excessive length is due to the typographical ingenuity of the publishers, who apparently desired to convince the American public that this book is the first third of 'a million word novel'. (See preliminary puffs.) As a fact, it is 160,000 words long (exactly)—that is to say, less than a third of the length of *Anna Karenina*, *La Chartreuse de Parme*, *Vanity Fair*, etc. It may *seem* long. For that I accept the blame.

See *The Letters of Arnold Bennett*, ed. James Hepburn, 3 vols. (New York: Oxford University Press, 1966–70), 2: 274.

3. The first time you've heard me say.

142.

HOWELLS TO JAMES, 19 May 1911, Tompkinsville   ALS Houghton
bMS Am 1094 (264)

Tompkinsville, Staten Island,
May 19, 1911.

My dear James:

Let not the uncouth name of my sojourn repulse you: it is the suburb, wholly accessible by water which John has chosen for his family till he can come to Kittery Point in late August. Not far off, on the other side of the hill, lived the urbane Curtis many years, and yesterday sweltering by in a most ammoniacally scented landau, with Billie piling over us all, I saw the heels of his widow or orphan protruding from a hammock on his veranda.[1] The whole neighborhood is a wonderful arrest in the architecture of 1880 when it seems to have been overbuilt. The scene is such as we should have so differently made our prey when we had the heart for that kind of thing, and I wish I could read what you would have written about it.

Come when you will to Kittery Point; you will always be most welcome.[2] I am only as sorry for the cause of your present delay as I am glad of your own health and evident courage of your health. Of course without my asking you to, you would have told dear Mrs. James of my share in your common anxiety. It will be good to know that what must be done has been done successfully, and that you are all at peace again.[3]

Pilla has been at K. P. this week and is now at Boston resting in the dentist's chair from the labors of the garden. I am going on next Monday and then she will return to K. P. with me, and I shall try to take up what is left of life.—But when I say something like this I feel it a pose; I am really very cheerful, and happy as ever in my work. With my children I always talk gayly of their mother, not purposely, but because her life and mine was mostly a life of pleasure in the droll and amusing things. I recall our thousand and one experiences in strange character, and first of all our own characters; and the pang is no longer a sense

1. George William Curtis (1824–92) edited *Harper's Weekly* from 1863 until his death.

2. HJ probably visited WDH at Kittery Point sometime in early July 1911, when he was staying at Intervale, New Hampshire. The early days of the month were remarkably hot, as HJ's diary notes, and he often resorted to motoring as a source of relief. A letter from WDH to Thomas Sergeant Perry dated 9 July makes reference to the unpleasant "H. James weather" (*LiL* 2: 299).

3. While Harvard's decision to award HJ an honorary degree was a primary factor in delaying his return to England, there were also, as he told several correspondents, "urgent and intimate family reasons." Among these may have been Alice H. G. James's promise to William that the family would conduct séances during the year after his death and try to communicate with his spirit. As a psychologist, William had always been interested in the extrasensory operations of consciousness; HJ, too, had an impulse to "reach beyond the laboratory-brain" (see "Is There a Life After Death," in *The James Family*, ed. F. O. Matthiessen [New York: Knopf, 1947], 614). See also HJ to Sir T. H. Warren, 29 May 1911 (*LHJ* 2: 188).

of hopeless loss, but of wonder that I did not make more of her keenly humorous criticism of all that we knew in common.

During the past few months I finished the story which I told you of taking up after an interval of fifty years;[4] and I think I found out the truth about it. The thing is roughly pulled together, and needs endless going over, but I am sure the truth is in it, and that more and more is what I care for.

I write and find greater happiness in writing than I ever did; and this, my dear old friend, is clumsily leading up to the hope and belief that you will soon begin writing again. You have been miserably interrupted, but you have great things ahead of you to do and to enjoy doing; and you must set yourself to realize this. Why shouldn't you, pending something inventive, speak (self-respectfully, as you would) of the literary times and places you have lived in?[5] That is something which the editorial soul would exult to have from you.

Yours ever
W. D. Howells.

143.

JAMES TO HOWELLS, 19 February 1912, London TLS Houghton
bMS Am 1784 (253) 120

Dictated

105, PALL MALL, S. W.
February 19th., 1912.

My dear Howells.

Horribly long have I owed you a letter—ever since the splendid great parcel of your preliminary Editional volumes[1] reached me; to become the richest ornament of my domestic foreground—for into the background they shall *not* retreat!—and a glorious monument of your friendship. I have been silent, I am sorry to say, through much persistent unwellness; which broke upon me—after much persistent recuperation and gain of apparently solid ground—just at the time your missive arrived. This has made havoc with letters, with work, with confidence, with everything; though I am beginning to hope that I shall fairly scramble out of my hole. I have scrambled out of so many that a certain presumption has been created.

However, what I want most particularly to say to you to-day (and I am reduced to this machinery for saying it) is that, hearing from 45 Albemarle Street

---

4. *New Leaf Mills: A Chronicle* (New York: Harper & Brothers, 1913).

5. After the death of his brother William, HJ planned to use the family papers in writing a memorial volume about him. His intentions were transformed, however, after William's eldest son, Harry, objected to the liberal use of his father's letters. The resulting books, *A Small Boy and Others* (1913) and *Notes of a Son and Brother* (1914), were more autobiographical in nature.

1. The first (and only) six volumes of WDH's "Library Edition," issued by Harper's in 1911.

of the birthday banquet to be so gracefully offered you on March 1st.,[2] and that "letters" contributive to this grace are in order for the occasion, I have wanted greatly to toss my little nosegay into the pile. But I have only been able to do this by a letter addressed to yourself—not to the "Firm"; jamais de la vie![3] It goes to Albemarle Street to-day to be properly forwarded and accelerated, and I have provided in it for its being as publicly and resoundingly as possible launched at your patient head. May it not arrive the day after the fair. The time has been short for me, the margin small, in my actual sharp unfitness for writing even current notes. So please allow for everything—and if I *should* be belated, which I shall deeply regret, do still let my poor words go upon record somehow.[4] This is all I can add to them at this hour; save that I am

> yours and Mildred's all devotedly
> Henry James

Henry James, "*A Letter to Mr. Howells*," North American Review *195 (April 1912): 558–62.*

It is made known to me that they are soon to feast in New York the newest and freshest of the splendid birthdays to which you keep treating us, and that your many friends will meet round you to rejoice in it and reaffirm their allegiance. I shall not be there, to my sorrow; and, though this is inevitable, I yet want to be missed, peculiarly and monstrously missed, so that these words shall be a public apology for my absence: read by you, if you like and can stand it, but, better still, read *to* you and, in fact, straight *at* you by whoever will be so kind and so loud and so distinct. For I doubt, you see, whether any of your toasters and acclaimers have anything like my ground and title for being with you at such an hour. There can scarce be one, I think, to-day who has known you from so far back, who has kept so close to you for so long, and who has such fine old reasons—so old, yet so well preserved—to feel your virtue and sound your praise. My debt to you began well-nigh half a century ago in the most personal way possible, and then kept growing and growing with your own admirable growth— but always rooted in the early intimate benefit. This benefit was that you held out your open editorial hand to me at the time I began to write—and I allude especially to the summer of 1866—with a frankness and sweetness of hospitality that was really the making of me, the making of the confidence that required help and sympathy and that I should otherwise, I think, have strayed and stum-

---

2. With his indefatigable instinct for publicity, Colonel Harvey of Harper's had organized a seventy-fifth-birthday celebration for WDH on 2 March, to which four hundred prominent guests— including President William Howard Taft—were invited. One week later a special section of *Harper's Weekly* was devoted to "A Tribute to William Dean Howells," replete with photographs and public testimonials.

3. Not on your life!

4. HJ's letter, the text of which follows, was too long for publication in *Harper's Weekly* and was held over for the April 1912 number of the *North American Review*.

bled about a long time without acquiring. You showed me the way and opened me the door; you wrote to me and confessed yourself struck with me—I have never forgotten the beautiful thrill of *that*. You published me at once—and paid me, above all, with a dazzling promptitude; magnificently, I felt, and so that nothing since has ever quite come up to it. More than this even, you cheered me on with a sympathy that was in itself an inspiration. I mean that you talked to me and listened to me—ever so patiently and genially and suggestively conversed and consorted with me. This won me to you irresistibly and made you the most interesting person I knew—lost as I was in the charming sense that my best friend was an editor, and an almost insatiable editor, and that such a delicious being as that was a kind of property of my own. Yet how didn't that interest still quicken and spread when I became aware that—with such attention as you could spare from us, for I recognized my fellow-beneficiaries—you had started to cultivate *your* great garden as well; the tract of virgin soil that, beginning as a cluster of bright, fresh, sunny, and savory patches close about the house, as it were, was to become that vast goodly pleasaunce of art and observation, of appreciation and creation, in which you have labored, without a break or a lapse, to this day, and in which you have grown so grand a show of—well, really of everything. Your liberal visits to *my* plot and your free-handed purchases there were still greater events when I began to see you handle yourself with such ease the key to our rich and inexhaustible mystery. Then the question of what you would make of your own powers began to be even more interesting than the question of what you would make of mine—all the more, I confess, as you had ended by settling this one so happily. My confidence in myself, which you had so helped me to, gave way to a fascinated impression of your own spread and growth, for you broke out so insistently and variously that it was a charm to watch and an excitement to follow you. The only drawback that I remember suffering from was that *I*, your original debtor, couldn't print or publish or pay you—which would have been a sort of ideal of *re*payment and of enhanced credit; you could take care of yourself so beautifully, and I could (unless by some occasional happy chance or rare favor) scarce so much as glance at your proofs or have a glimpse of your "endings." I could only read you, full-blown and finished, always so beautifully finished—and see, with the rest of the world, how you were doing it again and again.

That, then, was what I had with time to settle down to—the common attitude of seeing you do it again and again; keep on doing it, with your heroic consistency and your noble, genial abundance, during all the years that have seen so many apparitions come and go, so many vain flourishes attempted and achieved, so many little fortunes made and unmade, so many weaker inspirations betrayed and spent. Having myself to practise meaner economies, I have admired from period to period your so ample and liberal flow; wondered at your secret for doing positively a little—what do I say, a little? I mean a magnificent deal!—of Everything. I seem to myself to have faltered and languished, to have missed more occasions than I have grasped, while you have piled up your monument just by remaining at your post. For you have had the advantage, after all, of breathing an air that has suited and nourished you; of sitting up to your neck, as I may say—or at least up to your waist—amid the sources of your inspiration. There and so you were at your post; there and so the spell could ever work for you, there and so your relation to all your material grow closer and stronger, your perception penetrate, your authority accumulate. They make a great array, a literature in themselves, your studies of American life so acute, so direct, so disinterested, so preoccupied but with the fine truth of the case; and the more attaching to me always for their referring themselves to a time and an order when we knew together what American life *was*—or thought we did, deluded though we may have been! I don't pretend to measure the effect or to sound the depths, if they be not the shallows, of the huge wholesale importations and so-called assimilations of this later time; I only feel and speak for those conditions in which, as "quiet observers," as careful painters, as sincere artists, we could still in our native, our human and social element, know more or less where we were and feel more or less what we had hold of. You knew and felt these things better than I; you had learned them earlier and more intimately, and it was impossible, I think, to be in more instinctive and more informed possession of the general truth of your subject than you happily found yourself. The *real* affair of the American case and character, as it met your view and brushed your sensibility, that was what inspired and attached you, and, heedless of foolish flurries from other quarters, of all wild or weak slashings of the air and wavings in the void, you gave yourself to it with an incorruptible faith. You saw your field with a rare lucidity: you saw all it had to give in the way of the romance of the real and the interest and the thrill and the charm of the common, as one may put it; the character and the comedy, the point, the pathos, the tragedy, the particular home-grown humanity under your eyes and your hand and with which the life all about you was closely interknitted. Your hand reached out to these things with a fondness that was in itself a literary gift and played with them as the artist only and always can play: freely, quaintly, incalculably, with all the assurance of his fancy and his irony, and yet with that fine taste for the truth and the pity and the meaning of the matter which keeps the temper of observation both sharp and sweet. To observe by such an instinct and by such reflection is to find work to one's hands and a challenge in every bush; and as the familiar American scene thus bristled about you, so year by year your vision more and more justly responded and swarmed. You put forth A *Modern Instance*, and *The Rise of Silas Lapham*, and *A Hazard of New Fortunes*, and *The Landlord at Lion's Head*, and *The Kentons* (that perfectly classic illustration of your spirit and your form) after having put forth in perhaps lighter-fingered prelude *A Foregone Conclusion*, and *The Undiscovered Country*, and *The Lady of the Aroostook*, and *The Minister's Charge*—to make of a long list too short a one; with the effect again and again of a feeling for the human relation, as the social climate of our country qualifies, intensifies, generally conditions and colors it, which, married in perfect felicity to the expression you found for its service, constituted the originality that we want to fasten upon you as with silver nails to-night. Stroke by stroke and book by book your work was to become for this exquisite notation of our whole democratic light and shade and give and take in the highest degree *documentary*, so that none other, through all your fine long season, could approach it in value and amplitude. None, let me say, too, was to approach it in essential distinction; for you had grown master, by insidious practices best known to yourself, of a method so easy and so natural, so marked with the personal element of your humor and the play, not less personal, of your sympathy, that the critic kept coming on its secret connection with the grace of letters much as Fenimore Cooper's Leatherstocking—so knowing to be able to do it!—comes in the forest on the subtle tracks of Indian braves. However, these things take us far, and what I wished mainly to put on record is my sense of that unfailing, testifying truth in you which will keep you from ever being neglected. The critical intelligence—if any such fitful and discredited light may still be conceived as within our sphere—has not at all begun to render you its tribute. The more inquiringly and perceivingly it shall still be projected upon the American life we used to know, the more it shall be moved by the analytic and historic spirit, the more indispensable, the more a vessel of light, will you be found. It's a great thing to have used one's genius and done one's work with such quiet and robust consistency that they fall by their own weight into that happy service. You may remember perhaps, and I like to recall, how the great and admirable Taine, in one of the fine excursions of his French curiosity, greeted you as a precious painter and a sovereign witness.[1] But his appreciation, I want you to believe with me, will yet be carried much further, and then—though you may have argued yourself happy, in your generous way and with your incurable optimism, even while noting yourself not understood—your really beautiful time will come. Nothing so much as feeling that he may himself perhaps help a little to bring it on can give pleasure to yours all faithfully,

HENRY JAMES.

144.

HOWELLS TO JAMES, 17 March 1912, New York

ALS Houghton
bMS Am 1094 (267)

12 East 58th street,
March 17, 1912.

My dear James:

I owe you an answer for two letters, or two answers. The first, the public one, I do not know how to acknowledge. It almost convinced me that I had really been some help or service to you; at any rate, I am going to believe it as a

1. In 1888 the redoubtable critic Hippolyte Taine (1828–93) had enthusiastically recommended WDH's *Rise of Silas Lapham* for publication in French. "I have read it in English," Taine wrote, "with the greatest pleasure and with much admiration; it is the best novel written by an American, the most like Balzac's, the most profound, and the most comprehensive. Silas, his wife and his two daughters are for us new types, very substantial and very complete." These remarks were conveyed to WDH in a letter from John Durand (10 April 1888 [Howells Papers, Harvard]) and first published (in the original French) in *LiL* 1: 412.

pleasure to which I can turn in the night when I wake to the sense of what a toad I am and always have been. Your letter, so fully, so beautifully kind, will help to take away some of those dreadful moments of self-blame, and I can think, "Well, there must have been something in it; James would not abuse my dotage with flattery; I was probably not always such a worm of the earth as I feel myself at present." Your letter, meant for the public eye, brought before mine the vision of those days and nights in Sacramento street, "when my bosom was young,"[1] and swelled with pride in your friendship and joy in sharing your literary ambition, as if it were the "communion of saints." I do thank you for it, and I am eager for all men to read it in *The North American* to which, as alone worthy of reporting it, it has been transferred from the *Weekly*. I was rather glad it was not in our host's scheme to read it at the dinner, where the best, the finest effect of it would have been lost. No letters were read, but all will be printed in the Review—quaintly enough, as I feel, since they were some of them personally addressed to me, who may be supposed to smuggle them into print for the gratification of my vanity. But I believe it is the convention to ignore that sort of ostensibility; at any rate, I found the matter past my control. It is at the worst, part of the divine madness of an affair in which I still struggle to identify my accustomed self. It was really something extraordinary. Four hundred notables swarmed about a hundred tables on the floor, and we elect sat at a long board on a dais. Mrs. Clifford[2] was among us, two elbows from the President of the United States, and she can tell you better about it than I, who remained for the whole time in a daze from which I wrenched myself for twenty minutes to read my farrago of *spropositi*;[3] it was all, all wrong and unfit; but nobody apparently knew it, not even I till that ghastly waking hour of the night when hell opens to us.

I leave myself little room to say I am sorry you are not feeling so well as you promised to be; I hope by now you are trying to keep your promise. Your nephew and name-sake writes me from Cambridge that you have been sitting on an anti-suffrage platform;[4] we shall all be marching in the suffrage procession in May: John's *two* boys, their two grandfathers, John and his wife, the two White

1. The quotation is from W. S. Gilbert's *Trial by Jury*:
> When first my old, old love I knew,
> My bosom welled with joy;
> My riches at her feet I threw—
> I was a love-sick boy!

2. Lucy Lane Clifford (d. 1929) was an English novelist and playwright whom HJ had introduced to WDH in the spring of 1904.

3. Nonsense.

4. Largely out of curiosity, HJ attended an Anti–Female Suffrage meeting in Albert Hall on 28 February 1912 as the guest of Mary Augusta (Mrs. Humphry) Ward (1851–1920), the popular English novelist. He did not sit on the platform. (See letter #145 for HJ's clarification of this point.) An exemplar of Victorian moral purpose, Ward supported the movement for women's higher education but opposed female suffrage on the grounds that a woman's influence was stronger in the home than in public life.

girls and Pilla, shouting the battle cry of female freedom.[5] Nothing but distance will save the windows of Rye House.—John's new boy[6] is a beauty, and Billy remains as divine as ever. He now has a feverish passion for Indians.

Pilla sends her love with mine. We are off to Atlantic City tomorrow for the week.

Yours ever
W. D. Howells.

145.

JAMES TO HOWELLS, 27 March 1912, London   ALS Houghton
bMS Am 1784 (253) 121

THE REFORM CLUB
March 27th 1912

My dear Howells.

I have this moment, almost literally, a very beautiful & touching letter from you—only one element of which, your deplorable talk about the figure you make to yourself in the watches of the night, excites my animadversion. How you can take any view of your long career of virtue & devotion & self-sacrifice, of labour & courage & admirable & distinguished production, *but* the friendly & understanding & acceptingly "philosophic" view, I decline even to lift an eye to comprehending—& can only most affectionately & authoritatively enjoin upon you, with Mildred's fond & spirited backing, to turn right over & go to sleep again. We all fall short of our dreams—but of what can you have fallen short unless of some prefiguring *delirium?* In that case it hasn't been you but the delirium that was wrong. That is bad grammar but sovereign truth.

—As for the terrible banquet (for I think it must indeed have been terrible,) your account of it confirms to me both the very indulgent one (*viva-voce* here,) of Lucy Clifford & the more sardonic remarks, by letter, of poor dear delightfully & consistently pessimistic Tom Perry.[1] Truly was it an ordeal for you of the

---

5. On 4 May 1912 a large parade of woman's suffrage advocates, including nearly a thousand men, took place in New York.

6. John Noyes Mead Howells was born 11 March 1912.

1. Perry's letter is not extant, but in response to it (18 March 1912) HJ wrote:

[Y]our scathing exposure of the Howells dinner does me good and renews my—well, I won't say my youth but my convictions or several of them. One of the most irresistible, if not most cherished of these is that the Great Country *que vous savez* [which you know] has developed the genius for vulgarity on a scale to which no other genius for anything anywhere can hold a candle. But what an awful state of things when a quiet decent honest man like W.D.H. *has* to think he can't under peril of life, do anything but become part of the horror. An old friend of mine here, Lucy Clifford (W.K.'s widow) who was there and at the "high table" has sent me a catalogue of the guests which I hang over in the appallment of fascination—or the fascination of appallment; and which, as she has just returned and I am to see her tonight, she will fill out with hideous detail—though indeed she appears, by a line she wrote me, to have enjoyed, rather, the weird desolation of it. (*HJL* 4: 605–6)

1$^{\underline{st}}$ water (or I suppose *wine;*) through which, not less clearly, you passed un-
scathed as to your grace & humour & taste (the only things that were *there* on
the table—& quite enough things.) I confess I am sorry that the letter I contributed was not read out—as it was particularly & altogether "built" to be; I wanted
to testify publicly to you, & to be thereby present & participant; & it never
occurred to me that there wouldn't be competent provision for such a rendering
on the part of the manager or for such an audition on the guests. With those
things failing one asks one's self what conception the managerial mind can have
had of the delicacies & proprieties & amenities congruous with the celebration
of a fine feast of letters. Alas for a world & a time in which the vision & the
determination in such a case are all for gross numbers & noise! But since you
personally appropriated my declaration—I mean took it in & felt it yourself—
that is all I really shall have cared for. I saw Lucy Clifford at once after her
return hither, & she told me how on the occasion—as on all her N. Y. occasions, with which, without exception, she was delighted—she was most kindly
treated especially by *W. D. H.* himself. She comes back quite adoring New York,
bless her simple British heart!—

I follow you & Pilla meanwhile to Atlantic City—& wonder if it will make
you think of Algeciras.[2] If you go there for a literary purpose—& where *don't*
you go for that?—you are capable of proving that it did; which is perfectly good
literature.

—We have no news here but the prodigious & portentous Coal Strike,[3]
which darkens with black anxieties & possibilities our whole social & economic
sky. At the expiration of a month now the end is not yet—rather only the
beginning is, & we are really making history on an extraordinary scale & assisting at a great Revolution, which will leave things far away from where it
found them. What has happened is that wage-earning Labour, by a long slow
process of education, has got solidly on its feet, conscious & reflective, & then,
by a sudden bound, leaped into the very centre of the arena, where he will
remain long undisplaced. It is very interesting—painfully, hideously so; & in
some of its actual consequences of suffering, want, starvation, financial damage
of the biggest kind, inflicted on the nation at large, very dreadful & cruel. But
there will be more to come, & we don't yet in the least know where we are.
What is striking and very fine is the order & preserved peace & excellent temper displayed by both parties—the Strikers & the Stricken, the Miners & the
mass of the people (including the Coal-Owners.) This won't perhaps last as the
situation is aggravated, & I have a haunting sense—people in general have—
that there may easily be fighting in the streets, in fact a lively approach to Civil
War. The Suffragists meantime have been of a sudden relegated to an utter back
seat—the country while *this* goes on simply won't hear of them. But you are

2. In the late autumn and winter of 1911–12, WDH and Mildred toured the Iberian peninsula,
gathering material for a series of travel articles on Spain. These he published in *Familiar Spanish
Travels* (1913).
3. In 1912 severe labor troubles affected many British industries—railways, textiles, steel—but
violence in the coal pits was the most sensational. In March a work stoppage was narrowly averted

misinformed as to my having sat on an anti-suffrage platform. Mrs. Humphry Ward wrote & asked me if I would do so with her, & I replied that I would go to her meeting with pleasure, out of cold-blooded curiosity, if she would understand that shld. Mrs. Pankhurst[4] ask me the next week I would hold myself free to do exactly as much. She freely assented, but when the time came I hated even to appear to put myself in a false position (for I am utterly detached & uncommitted on the subject, which leaves me of a cold—!) & therefore went sneakingly in a box, as I might have gone to the Opera or the Hippodrome. The question simply overwhelmingly bores me—& I resent being hustled into *concluding* about it at all. Somehow, strangely, rather, I don't find it, even in its acute phase here, *interesting*—it is various other things but isn't that. One would have thought *a priori* that it *would* be—everything *else* about women is; but this is, to me, mortally tedious, & I don't warm to it one way or the other. But I am writing you a monster of a letter. Aren't you coming out again this spring—if there is any old England left to come to? Certainly you won't want to leave the New for the Newer. But I am catching, in this room, a fireless cold & am

> yours & Mildred's all & always
> *Henry James*

146.

JAMES TO HOWELLS, 13 May 1914, London

ALS Houghton
bMS Am 1784 (253) 123

21 CARLYLE MANSIONS
CHEYNE WALK S. W.
May 13$^{\underline{th}}$ 1914.

My dear Howells.

Very delightful to me your letter just received[1]—save that it relegates to the indifferent—by which I mean *indefinite*—vague the prospect of next seeing you; speaking as it does of your expecting to spend the summer on one of your estates rather than on this side of the sea. You might challenge my right to assume all the "coming out" to be on your side & none on mine; but you won't—simply— for you *like* to frequent Europe, & I don't like to frequent the U. S.—which is quite irrelevant, however, as this would be utterly impossible no matter what my yearning. It's a pang to me when you tell me that you & Mildred would be much disposed to come & stay if it weren't for your small items of posterity.[2] It makes me want to say: Well, weigh *prosperity* against posterity & let the former press down the balance. For—I can only give you my own personal sense of it—

by the Miners' Federation (their target was the Cambrian Coal Trust), but by November the deteriorating situation resulted in mob action.

4. Mrs. Emmeline Pankhurst (1858–1928), the militant leader of the woman's suffrage movement in Great Britain.

1. Not extant.

2. A reference to WDH's grandchildren.

not being here, not "waiting" here, & by that implication being & waiting in the conditions that actually surround you, would image for my own life the extremity of failure. That autumn, winter & spring (1910–11) which I spent in Cambridge & New York—well I shall go down to my grave without having breathed to another ear what I went through with them. And observe how little I breathe it into yours now. I don't really despair of you on this rich old scene even yet, however, & meanwhile I have been deeply touched by your expression of intimate interest in my late book.[3] You are one of the very few individuals I dreamed at all of reaching as I wrote, & I had you so often in mind that I rejoice to know from you that my message didn't fall short. You express to me this in a way that much moves me; your image of your going over it all with T. S. P. is the most genial I could desire—so much of my meaning must have been at this time of day wasted & missed by the "general" reader that I take comfort in your gathering it up, you two, together.[4] This volume & its predecessor have nevertheless been very liberally acclaimed here—where I quite expected their reference to such ancient alien things to handicap them—in spite of which they have succeeded as nothing of mine has ever done, & excited, I gather, none but intelligent & most kindly remark. That last chapter about my ghostly young cousin[5] I feared would "say" very little in this age & clime—whereas it has apparently said more than anything else in the book & my doubts & hesitations, had I yielded to them, would have been a great mistake.

You will, I am sure, be glad to know that Sargent's extraordinarily fine portrait of me (as I didn't paint it myself I don't see why I shouldn't unreservedly admire it,) which was horribly gashed a while back by an idiotic suffragette, is under such successful treatment that it will probably be restored to effective life & bloom again.[6] But those ladies really outrage humanity, & the public patience has to me a very imbecile side. Another of them has hacked with a

3. *Notes of a Son and Brother* (1914), the second of HJ's autobiographical volumes. *A Small Boy and Others*, the first, appeared in 1913.

4. Frustrated by WDH's incessant changes of address, HJ sent him a copy of *Notes of a Son and Brother* in care of Thomas Sergeant Perry. In a letter to Perry (13 April 1914) HJ wrote:

I rejoice in your repeated mention of dear W.D.H. as a conversational resource to you, which I can well believe,—& am led on to think what a comfort in that line you must be to *him!* I had to send him the Notes [of a Son and Brother] in your care—for never was there a friend who so effectually & systematically defeats all imputability of a *real* address. (Harlow, *Thomas Sergeant Perry*, 347)

5. The last—and longest—chapter of *Notes of a Son and Brother* is built around numerous extracts from the letters of HJ's cousin Mary ("Minny") Temple, who had died of tuberculosis in 1870. Her death, HJ wrote, "made a mark that must stand here for a too waiting conclusion. We felt it together as the end of our youth" (*Autobiography*, 544). Recently discovered copies of Temple's letters reveal that HJ drastically emended them to suit his personal aesthetic preferences. See Alfred Habegger, "Henry James's Rewriting of Minny Temple's Letters," *American Literature* 58 (May 1986): 159–80.

6. In honor of HJ's seventieth birthday, a group of his friends commissioned a portrait by John Singer Sargent (1856–1925). While the finished work was displayed at the spring exhibition of the Royal Academy, a suffragette named Mary Wood hacked three holes in the canvas with a meat cleaver. HJ was unknown to her; she chose his portrait because it seemed to be attracting the most attention. With the help of restoration experts, Sargent was able to repair the damage.

chopper another picture today (a Herkomer portrait;) & the work goes bravely on.[7] But good night, my dear old friend. Forgive this smutchy letter—my ink has too freely flowed. I have told dear T. S. P. how glad I have been to think of you under his wing.

Yours all faithfully
Henry James

147.

HOWELLS TO JAMES, 29 June 1915, York Harbor   ALS Houghton
bMS Am 1094 (270)

York Harbor, Maine,[1]
June 29, 1915.

Dear James:

If I wait to write you a fit letter, I shall write none; so here goes a faint response to the kind mentions you make of me in your Mr. and Mrs. J. T. Fields.[2]

7. The next victim at the Royal Academy was a portrait of the Duke of Wellington by Sir Hubert von Herkomer (1849–1914), which was bludgeoned three times with an axe by Mary Ansell ("a well known militant," according to the London *Times*). The paper noted with some satisfaction that because the likeness was hung so high, its face was not disfigured. See "Another Academy Outrage," London *Times*, 13 May 1914, 8.

1. In the summer of 1912 WDH purchased a cottage in York Harbor, where he had stayed eleven years earlier. Although he retained the house at Kittery Point, which was now used more frequently by his son's family, it remained a painful reminder of Elinor.

2. In his memoir–essay "Mr. and Mrs. James T. Fields" (*Atlantic* 116 [July 1915]: 21–31), HJ had occasion to remark upon WDH's influence upon his early career:

> the new American novel—for that was preparing—had at the season I refer to scarce glimmered into view; but its first seeds were to be sown very exactly in *Atlantic* soil, where my super-excellent friend and confrère W. D. Howells soon began editorially to cultivate them. . . . I absolutely *like* to remember, pressing out elated irony in it, that the magazine seemed pleased to profit by Howells, whether as wise editor or delightful writer, only up to the verge of his broadening out into mastership. He broadened gradually, and far-away back numbers exhibit the tentative light footprints that were to become such firm and confident steps; but affectionate appreciation quite consciously assisted at a process in which it could mark and measure each stage—up to the time, that is, when the process quite outgrew, as who should say, the walls of the drill-ground itself. . . . The charm I thus rake out of the period, and the aspect of the Fieldses as bathed in that soft medium—so soft after the long internecine harshness—gloss over to my present view every troubled face of my young relation with the *Atlantic*; the poor pathetic faces, as they now pass before me, being troubled for more reasons than I can recall, but above all, I think, because from the first I found "writing for the magazines" an art still more difficult than delightful. Yet I doubt whether I wince at this hour any more than I winced on the spot at hearing it quoted from this proprietor of the first of those with which I effected an understanding that such a strain of pessimism in the would-be picture of life had an odd, had even a ridiculous, air on the part of an author with his mother's milk scarce yet dry on his lips. It was to my amused W. D. H. that I owed this communication, as I was to owe him ever such numberless invitations to partake of his amusement; and I trace back to that with interest the first note of the warning against not

I read it aloud to Pilla for our common pleasure; she knew *her* if not him and last summer we passed a night at her house in Manchester. Your paper relumed so many old faded fires, and cast, most precious of all, a tender light on your own youth, which used to abash me by its worldly maturity. I remember F.'s bringing me a story of yours with the question of whether he should take it, and my saying, "Yes, and as many more by the same hand as you can get." That is what young ass't ed.s should be saying now; but are they? A change has passed upon things, we can't deny it; I could not "serialize" a story of mine now in any American magazine, thousands of them as they are.

We are much at war for you over here; but we do not seem to help much; we are almost as bad as Russians who don't fight as well as they write. All York Harbor is for the Allies beginning with Mrs. Bell,[3] who lives two doors away from me. She still is the brightest of octogenarians.—Perry was down to see me before dooming himself to that dismal Hancock of his.[4] He is your most pathetically constant adorer, and on the whole I should say your worship was spreading among us. I am comparatively a dead cult with my statues cast down and the grass growing over them in the pale moonlight.

There is now a great wash of young poetry on these shores, and some of it not so bad.[5]—Pilla and I spend our days gardening by day and reading at night.

"ending happily" that was for the rest of my literary life to be sounded in my ear with a good faith of which the very terms failed to reach me intelligibly enough to correct my apparent perversity. I labored always under the conviction that to terminate a fond aesthetic effort in felicity had to be as much one's obeyed law as to begin it and carry it on in the same; whereby how could one be anything less than bewildered at the non-recognition of one's inveterately plotted climax of expression and intensity? One went so far as literally to claim that in a decent production—such as one at least hoped any particular specimen of one's art to show for—the terminal virtue, driven by the whole momentum gathered on the way, *had* to be most expressional of one's subject, and thereby more fortunately pointed than whatever should have gone before. I remember clinging to that measure of the point really made even in the tender dawn of the bewilderment I glance at and which I associate with the general precarious element in those first *Atlantic* efforts. It really won me to an anxious kindness for Mr. Fields that though finding me precociously dismal he yet indulgently suffered me—and this not the less for my always feeling that Howells, during a season his sub-editor, must more or less have intervened with a good result.

3. Helen Choate Bell (1830–1918), a distinguished patron of literature and art and friend of WDH and HJ. The neutrality of the United States during the early years of World War I was a source of profound embarrassment and shame to HJ.

4. Thomas Sergeant Perry had a summer house in Hancock, New Hampshire.

5. In his "Editor's Easy Chair" column for *Harper's Monthly* (September 1915), WDH assessed several volumes of poetry, including the early work of Robert Frost, Edgar Lee Masters, Conrad Aiken, Amy Lowell, and others. In reacting to the "new" poetry, WDH said—with respect to *North of Boston*:

When we say Mr. Frost's work is unaffectedly expressive of New England life, we do not mean that it is unconsciously expressive; we do not much believe in unconscious art, and we rather think that his fine intelligence tingles with a sense of that life and beautifully knows what it is at in dealing with it. . . . Dirge, or idyl, or tragedy, or comedy, or burlesque, it is

We have a deliciously large, cool house—no such oven as we baked you in at Kittery Point ten years ago.—I am doing my most miserable memoirs,[6] which really make me sick; but I promised to do them. I end them with going off to Venice. It is something awful and I wonder the more at the grace and ease with which you carry off your past in those two blithe books of yours.[7]

Yours affectionately
W. D. Howells.

148.

JAMES TO HOWELLS, 21 July 1915, London

TLS Houghton
bMS Am 1784 (253) 124

21 CARLYLE MANSIONS
CHEYNE WALK S. W.
July 21st. 1915.

My dear Howells.

I wrote you the other day,[1] but here I am again, and this time in the form of a beggar hobbling on this mechanical crutch;[2] to which under all our stress and strain I am much reduced now.

The enclosed pair of prospectuses will help me to explain them a little. Mrs. Wharton, who is labouring in Paris with the last magnificence of ability and energy, has written me thence a request that I will intercede with you on behalf of The Book of the Homeless.[3] She beseeches me to beseech of you a contribution, however brief, to this beneficent volume. I am promising her one myself, and thus for the first time in my life setting an example to the contemporary from whom I have taken so many! I shall write her something—come and do likewise. You do with ease, I feel, what I do with anguish—therefore I invoke your noblest facility. Read the longer circular, and hang in particular over the sentence in italics at the top of the second page. It is for the benefit of those children that we shall do our bit. So there we are—by which I especially mean

---

always the skill of the artist born and artist trained which is at play, or call it work, for our delight. Amidst the often striving and straining of the new poetry, here is the old poetry as young as ever; and new only in extending the bounds of sympathy through the recorded to the unrecorded knowledge of humanity. (635)

6. *Years of My Youth* (1916).

7. *A Small Boy and Others* (1913) and *Notes of a Son and Brother* (1914).

1. Not extant.

2. That is, dictating.

3. In April 1915 the Children of Flanders Rescue Committee was organized by Edith Wharton at the request of the Interior Ministry of Belgium. To aid this charity and a group of American Hostels for Refugees, Wharton persuaded Scribners and Macmillan to publish an illustrated anthology of war poetry and prose pieces, which she solicited from nearly seventy contributors. The proceeds from *The Book of the Homeless* totaled almost fifteen thousand dollars.

there we shall be, together, more than ever together, and to the effect of your making me

more than ever and ever yours
Henry James

149.

JAMES TO HOWELLS, 20 August 1915, London   ALS Houghton
bMS Am 1784 (253) 125

21 CARLYLE MANSIONS
CHEYNE WALK S. W.

"Tear it up" forsooth, my dear Howells!—

I would as soon tear up—in fact much sooner—every existing page of every member of my own past procession of masterpieces. How can I sufficiently thank you on Mrs. Wharton's behalf & that of the Book of the Homeless for the admirable force & feeling of your precious little poem?[1] Oh you poets, how you are the only ones that really hit it & *do* it! She will thank you more authentically, for herself, as soon as she gets back from the Alsatian Front, which she is now marvellously visiting—after having visited every other & having achieved & revealed all these months the most astoundingly beneficent administrative & organizational activity & ability. I am sending your blest rhyme straight to the Scribners in N. Y., who are publishing the Book there free of all costs, with Robert Grant & Barclay Updyke[2] doing all the editorial & supervising part. You will be in all sorts of eminent company & I am devoutly glad you are not absent from the happy show. I have reason to believe, alas, that my own copy (4000 words of deadly prose,) will have gone down in this new foulness of ferocity of the torpedoed *Arabic*[3]—but I think I have a kind of rough 1st draft.[4] Good night now—be deeply rejoiced in & believe me

yours more than ever
Henry James
Aug. 20th 1915

1. WDH had written a sonnet entitled "The Little Children" for *The Book of the Homeless*. On 21 August HJ wrote Edith Wharton, "W. D. Howells, dear man, has sent me from York Harbour, Maine, also a lyric de sa façon [after his fashion], a fine & forcible & most feeling one called "The Children," really grim & strong & sincere, which I am sending straight to Scribner & your Editors for you." See *Henry James and Edith Wharton Letters, 1900–1915*, ed. Lyall H. Powers (New York: Scribners, 1990), 351–52.

2. Daniel Berkeley Updike (1860–1941) was one of the country's leading authorities on printing and book design. In 1893 he founded the Merrymount Press in Boston, which soon became famous for its superior craftsmanship. For Robert Grant the author, see letter #140, note 2.

3. On the morning of 19 August a German submarine sank the White Star ocean liner *Arabic* off the southern coast of Ireland. Even though the ship was torpedoed without warning, only thirty-nine lives were lost.

4. HJ salvaged his contribution, "The Long Wards," one of the last compositions he lived to complete.

150.

JAMES TO HOWELLS, 18 September 1915, London   TLS Houghton
bMS Am 1094 (253) 125a

21, CARLYLE MANSIONS,
CHEYNE WALK. S. W.
September 18th. 1915.

My dear Howells.

I rejoice more than I can say at your note (of Sept. 4th.)[1] this morning received in evidence of your feeling how strongly we feel about the indispensability of your splendid stanza for The Book of the Homeless.[2] We re-thank and re-bless, and re-rejoice in, you; and I at once dispatch to New York this slightly amended Copy,[3] with the corresponding MS. of the same, for the autographic value of the latter there.[4]

Your very faithful and grateful old
Henry James

151.

HOWELLS TO JAMES, 26 January 1916, St. Augustine   ALS Houghton
bMS Am 1094 (271)

St. Augustine, Florida,
246 St. George Street,
Jan'y 26, 1916.

My dear James:

I hope this may find you mending from your break,[1] which has been such a sorrow to all of us who love you. To me the news of it was so disabling that I

---

1. Not extant.

2. On 27 August HJ informed Edith Wharton that he was not "disconcerted by Howells's having just written to me to 'withdraw' his fine & brave little piece (as being too crude & imperfect in form). I am going, in respect to that to *passer outre* [take another step]—to write to him tomorrow that he is utterly deluded, that we greatly admire it & in fine decline to give it up" (*Henry James and Edith Wharton Letters*, 353).

3. WDH changed the wording of his last line: see illustration on page 464.

4. In addition to proceeds from the sale of *The Book of the Homeless*, its manuscript contents were auctioned off to benefit Edith Wharton's designated charities.

1. HJ had suffered a stroke on 2 December 1915, from which he never fully recovered. On 15 December WDH learned of HJ's condition from his nephew Harry and responded at once:

I had not heard of the sorrowful news you tell me. I cannot say anything. But I wish he could have lived to know the Allies were winning, however they seemed to be losing. If he is still living when your next letter reaches your mother let her give him my dearest love. He is the last that is left of my earthly world. (WDH to HJ, Jr., 15 December 1915, SL 6: 89)

Lapsing in and out of consciousness, HJ lingered until 28 February 1916.

The Children.

"Suffer little children to come unto me,"
Christ bade, and answering with infernal glee,
"Take them!" the arch-fiend mocked; and from the walls
Of their wrecked homes, and from the cattle's stalls,
And the dogs' kennels, and the hold
Of their dead mother's arms, and from the cold
Of ravaged fields, famished, and sick, and bare,
And maimed by shot and shell,
The master-spirit of hell
Caught them all up, and through the shuddering air
Of his God-forsaken world
The little ones he hurled;
And in the unmatched might
Of the perverted right,
Roared his delight:
The Anti-Christ of ~~their~~ Schrecklichkeit.

W. D. Howells.

The original typescript of Howells's contribution to *The Book of the Homeless*, edited by Edith Wharton (1916). By permission of the Houghton Library, Harvard University.

did not know how to make you the offer of my sympathy, but I knew you would know you had it. Though I have written so seldom to you, you may be sure that no event or circumstance of your life has been unnoted by me, and especially none in this *dies irae*,[2] when you have been moved and stirred so deeply. I am much older than you, and I shall soon be in my eightieth year; but I have

2. Time of God's wrath.

somehow always looked to you as my senior in so many important things. You have greatly and nobly lived for brave as well as beautiful things, and your name and fame are dear to all who honor such things.

Pilla is with me here where I have fled from the cold and colds of the North, and she joins me in the love which I need not protest to you. If Mrs. William James is with you as I hope, share it with her.[3]

Yours ever
W. D. Howells.

3. At the time of William James's death, Alice H. G. James vowed to attend to HJ when his time should come. She sailed for England as soon as news arrived of HJ's illness and ultimately returned his ashes to America for burial in the Cambridge cemetery.

Epilogue

Within a week of James's death, Howells received an invitation from Harper's to write a commemorative essay about his friend for the flagship *Monthly*. Somewhat impulsively, he agreed. "No one knew James as I did," he eagerly affirmed, promising that a substantial essay ("biographical, personal, critical") soon would follow. Announce it for an early number of the magazine, he told his editor, and "I will write for you such a paper as I wrote about Longfellow, about Lowell, about Holmes, and better." Perhaps embarrassed by his own exuberance, Howells then added a cautionary postscript to request that a specific deadline be deferred. "I think I had better not promise the paper for any certain time," he suggested; "you had better say it 'will appear in a forthcoming number.'" Still, Howells wanted his audience to understand that he acknowledged a specific duty. "I should like to have it heralded because people will naturally expect something of the kind from me, and perhaps wonder why they do not get it."[1] Not surprisingly, however, Howells discovered that writing about *this* subject would prove considerably more problematic than eulogizing those earlier New England worthies whose cultural status then seemed beyond dispute. For at the end—almost the very end—James had renounced his American citizenship, sworn allegiance to King George V, become a British subject, wanting (as he petitioned the prime minister) "to testify at this crisis to the force of my attachment and devotion to England and to the cause for which she is fighting." Implicitly, James also wanted to protest America's continued neutrality in the face of the European debacle.[2]

In the United States, James's renunciatory gesture abraded many old wounds, some of which traced back to the heresies of *Hawthorne* (1879). When rumor of James's intentions first reached Howells, he, too, was stunned: the prospect of denationalization cut to a kind of democratic nerve. "Are you ready to join with James in renouncing Wilson," Howells bristled to Thomas Sergeant Perry, "and swearing fealty to King Jorge? Or don't you believe he's done it, or means to?" While admitting that James's case was different—virtually blameless—Howells

466

refused to qualify his own democratic allegiance. "Nothing could persuade me," he stoutly urged, "to bow the knee to e'er a crowned head of them all."[3] With time, Howells came better to understand and to sympathize with James's motives, but in the spring of 1916 he could not easily reconcile them with either official American policy or public opinion. Whatever one might have thought about the poetry of Longfellow, or Lowell, or Holmes, no one was going to question their patriotism. When Harper's refused to pay the steep price ($2,500) he had demanded for his James essay, Howells was greatly relieved. "I doubt now whether I shall ever write the paper," he confessed—"certainly if I do it will not be immediately."[4]

Indeed, four years would pass before Howells again attempted to fulfill his obligation. In April 1920 the occasion of Percy Lubbock's two-volume *Letters of Henry James* rekindled the commemorative flame. Still an unflagging occupant of the "Editor's Easy Chair" for *Harper's*, Howells chose to devote a column to James's epistolary testament; unfortunately, he did not have time to complete it. One short month after Lubbock's edition appeared, Howells was dead, his final thoughts on James unpublished. At the time of her father's death, however, Mildred Howells discovered drafts of two compositions that she fittingly used to conclude her own two-volume *Life in Letters of William Dean Howells* in 1928. These fragments (the start of the "Easy Chair" piece on James's letters and another, "The American James," harking back to the melancholy springtime of 1916), she claimed, were "the last things Howells wrote and form the final act in a long friendship" (*LiL* 2: 394).

While Mildred's sentiment is probably correct, Howells's "final act" was considerably more ambiguous than her published texts represent. Unwitting errors of transcription and the deliberate omission of some rather suggestive critical passages give the *Life in Letters* texts a kind of comforting assurance—almost fraternal—that the manuscripts much less consistently affirm. Throughout the "Easy Chair" essay, for example, Howells must suppress initial phrasings that accentuate—rather than qualify—James's essential foreignness to America. Thus, Howells first concedes James's unabashed "love of alien ideals," but then mutes this to express merely his friend's "adoration of foreign conditions and forms." If at first James "grew more English" ("in the course of his long life in England"), in the revision Howells insists—to the contrary—that in all James's time abroad "he did not grow less American." If America rejected James, Howells writes, "it must be owned that he paid us back in kind"—an unsparing allegation (with its retributive first-person plural pronoun) that the author then crossed out.

Even more revealing, perhaps, are the last two sentences of Howells's draft (suppressed by Mildred) which call attention to "the sense" (as he delicately puts it) of James's "oddity." Howells's stammering approach to that word—the preceding sentences are rife with cancellations—nevertheless conveys the unusually physical quality of James's epistolary manner of address and his own struggle to make proper sense of it. The cumulative rhetoric of intimacy—James seems always to be clasping his friends (all of them male) "closer and closer . . . more and more personally and publicly"—discomfits Howells, who finds in it all "a strange exhibition to say the least." Here, perhaps, is a James he never knew: shoutingly familiar, jovially burly, assertively homosocial.

Outwardly, at least, "The American James" seems less at odds with itself, perhaps because it was probably begun in the weeks following James's death.[5] But here the contest is only more subtle. Howells's generous impulse to commemorate James vies with a desire to legitimate his own aesthetic priorities. In spite of best intentions, Howells cannot wholly escape comparison and contrast with his subject. Though willing to subordinate himself to James with regard to fiction-writing, Howells simultaneously enumerates an early bibliography of published volumes—*Venetian Life, Italian Journeys, Suburban Sketches*—that it would take James years to catch up with. Howells first asserts (but then suppresses) his prerogative as a student of American life. He smothers the pride that discovers a "directness" of approach to his material in *Suburban Sketches*; Howells's revision silences this specific valediction with a more abstract generalization about his manner of treatment ("as I have ever since studied it"). By the same tributary logic, James's Coleridgean "fancy" becomes a more dignified "art." Likewise, Howells cannot forget the James family's "common Irish derivation" (whatever their social pretensions)—but he will not aver it in print.

Because of their unusual interest as Howells's last thoughts on James, the final two entries in this book are presented as modified genetic texts, based upon manuscripts recently deposited at the Houghton Library. I have employed conventional editorial symbols to help the reader trace the author's process of composition. Words or phrases canceled in the original are enclosed by angled brackets; interlineations are indicated by up- and down-arrows. When these types of emendations follow sequentially, the reader can watch the document evolving in Howells's mind. One turn of phrase is rejected, another preferred and substituted. Second thoughts occasionally overrule first impulses; sometimes they confirm them. Several cancellations also betray signs of internal revision: double angled brackets enclose words deleted by Howells within phrases that themselves were subsequently crossed out. Variants not represented in the text of the two entries are included in the Textual Apparatus.

Notes

1. WDH to Frederick A. Duneka, 7 March 1916, *SL* 6: 92–93.
2. HJ to Herbert H. Asquith, 28 June 1915, *HJL* 4: 764. Pragmatic considerations also figured in HJ's motives; because, legally, he was an "alien" during a time of war, his freedom of movement (between London and Rye) was restricted.
3. WDH to Thomas Sergeant Perry, 24 July 1915, *SL* 6: 94.
4. WDH to Frederick A. Duneka, 23 March 1916, *SL* 6: 94.
5. Most biographers have accepted Mildred Howells's assertion that her father began this essay in the weeks prior to his death in 1920. In the burst of enthusiasm with which he first broached the topic to Harper's, however (and in the process of naming his steep price for it), Howells parenthetically exclaimed, "I have already begun it, you see!" Thus, the surviving fragment might date from 1916. See WDH to Frederick A. Duneka, 18 March 1916, *SL* 6: 94.

"*Editor's Easy Chair*" [The Letters of Henry James]   bMS Am 1784.16 (6)

⟨Probably S[*w.o.* s]o strangely⟩ The Letters of Henry James which his biographer, Mr. Percy Lubbock, has ⟨put⟩ ↑lately↓ put together and ⟨so massively⟩ put forth in two massive volumes holding well a thousand pages form a literary document of ⟨unequalled ch⟩ ↑a↓ nature and character which we should ⟨look⟩ ↑seek↓ far ⟨and⟩ ↑to find and↓ fail to find the like of. The reason is that there ⟨never⟩ has been but one Henry James, and that he ⟨wrote in⟩ poured himself out in letters such as no other man knew how to write or could help writing. They are ad-dressed to ↑half↓ a hundred or a hundred[1] different men and women, mostly English but more largely American than most Americans might think, though Americans of European texture and color, but alike in the ⟨European⟩ civiliza-tion which we share ⟨with⟩ surpassingly[2] with the English and ⟨then very «sub»far⟩ ↑incomparably↓ less[3] with the French. ⟨It is⟩ ↑These letters form↓ the report of English life in an inalienably American soul, for American was what James remained through all the perversities of his expatriation, and his ⟨love of⟩ adoration of ⟨alien ideals.⟩ ↑foreign conditions and↓ forms; and he throws himself into them with a↑n ardor↓ ⟨passion⟩ of ⟨friendship, of⟩ sympathy ⟨of passion⟩ which ⟨are⟩ ↑is↓ of the same ⟨sincerity⟩ ↑quality↓ whomever ⟨they the *illeg.* letters address, whether old or young, akin or⟩ he wishes to win ⟨by his appeal⟩ to his embrace. The range of his correspondents is every age and he greets them all with the same effusion in which there is no question of his ⟨aff⟩ sincerity.

The letters begin with those addressed to ⟨his *w.o.* the⟩ written to his father[4] and mother and his brother⟨s⟩ from his repatriation in Paris after his exile in America, where he came to his literary consciousness, and mainly continue through the forty years of ⟨the⟩ his home in England, where he did not succeed in becoming English, even by the formal renunciation of his nationality. This may be said with no cast of censure, for James was American to his heart's core to the ⟨death⟩ day of his death. He may ⟨succeed⟩ have made the English think him English; he may have made himself think so; but he was never anything but American, ⟨th and⟩ though by early ⟨educat⟩ sojourn and schooling he was French. He renounced us because he was rightly ashamed of our official, never our national, neutrality in the world's self-defence against Germany, an attitude which we now all feel so grotesque and contemptible, and must remember with ⟨self-⟩loathing. Of course we must ⟨feel his⟩ regard his means of saying so, of doing so, as ineffectual, but it was not the less ⟨sincere⟩ ↑unselfish↓ and self-sacrificial.

It at least enlarged him to the fellow⟨ship⟩ citizenship of the largest ⟨«and» and⟩ civilization in the world and enabled him to clasp in the ⟨same⟩ same ardor

1. *LiL* omits "or a hundred."
2. *LiL* reads "surprisingly."
3. *LiL* omits "less."
4. *LiL* reads: "addressed by the writer to his father."

⟨of⟩ this [*w.o.* the] ↑civilization in the↓ same embrace with the Americanism which he could not really undo in his nature.

In his very interesting and interested study of James's nature and character, Mr. Lubbock who edits his letters, has not been able ⟨to «search» search⟩ ↑quite to make↓ him out, for some very simple reasons. ↑One of↓ ⟨He fails to⟩ ↑these is that he↓ ignores the ⟨simple reason⟩ ↑cause↓ of James's going to live abroad which was that he was a sick man who was less a sufferer in Europe than in America. He was better in Paris than in Boston where he was always suffering and when his brief French sojourn became his English life of forty years ⟨the⟩ it was not mainly because he was better in England, but it was more and more largely so. The climate was kinder to him than ours; and the ⟨country was⟩ life was kinder than his native ⟨air⟩ ↑life↓ and his native land. In fact America was never kind to James. It was rude and harsh, unworthily and stupidly ⟨s⟩ so, as we must more and more own, if we would be true to ourselves. We ⟨own to⟩ ought to be ashamed of our part in this; the nearest of his friends in Boston would say they [*w.o.* he] liked him, but they could not bear his ⟨literature⟩ ↑fiction↓; and ⟨they were not aware that that their personal liking on these terms was an insult from people⟩ ↑and the people, especially the ↑women ⟨of the⟩↓ ⟨smaller Boston scattere⟩ conscious↓ of culture, especially women, in ⟨places where opinion⟩ ↑throughout New England,↓ ⟨out in⟩ ↑⟨and the⟩↓ ⟨country places where opinion was formed, he had⟩ ↑he had sometimes↓ outright insult.[5] At the same time ⟨he⟩ ↑his work anomalously[6]↓ found ⟨the gr⟩ favor with editors who eagerly sought ⟨his work for all⟩ ↑it in all↓ the leading periodicals. ⟨The case was very anomalous, and⟩ His [*w.o.* It] ↑case↓ was not ⟨very⟩[7] different in England when he went to live there except that the ↑popular↓ ⟨dislike was not united nor the so outrage⟩ rejection and contumely which met it ⟨at home⟩ ↑and the editorial↓ ↑⟨were not⟩↓ ↑were neither so ⟨noisy⟩ vicious nor so generous.[8]↓ But a public grew up in England such as never grew up in America, ⟨if not more⟩ and made England more like home to him.

⟨It must be owned that he paid us back in kind, «and dealt as» though in terms⟩[9] It was fine in him⟨, and sweet that h⟩ that he was able to use him to the condition↑s↓, and it is fine that in the course of his long life in England that [*w.o.* he] ⟨grew more English⟩ he did not grow less American. There is a tenderness in his remembrance of ⟨E⟩ America which ⟨indeed⟩ does not appear in his ⟨cor ↑printed↓ frequent criti⟩ ↑public↓ printed criticism of us, but which abounds in the⟨se⟩ letters which address ↑themselves↓ to more American⟨s⟩ friends than to English friends, and when the ↑civic↓[10] change began to work itself out in him it was without a moment of rancour, but never ceased from a

---

5. *LiL* reads: "We ought to be ashamed of our part in this; the nearest of his friends in Boston would say they liked him, but they could not bear his fiction; and from the people, conscious of culture, throughout New England, especially the women, he had sometimes outright insult."

6. *LiL* reads "unanimously."

7. *LiL* retains "very."

8. *LiL* reads "general."

9. After cancelling the beginning of the new paragraph, WDH continues the preceding one.

10. *LiL* omits "civic."

fine reluctance, tacit or ⟨relu⟩ explicit. He was deeply wounded by our ⟨unworthy⟩ ridiculous endeavor for neutrality where there could not be neutrality and he did not live to witness the generous abandon that contemptible policy.[11] ⟨Almost⟩ W[w.o. w]ord by word he renounces his birthright, ⟨with self-question⟩ with ruth, with ⟨self-compulsion, and⟩ ↑grief↓, but never with doubt of the only course ↑he saw↓ open to him; and if our ⟨later⟩ ultimate but still tardy embrace of the heroic part seemed to leave him without justification that was an unfair appearance.

The↑se↓ ⟨letters of this⟩ unparalleled paper↑s↓ which address themselves to this friend and that ⟨with⟩ with ⟨unvarying⟩ ↑an↓ intimacy and affection ⟨and intimacy⟩ which alone does not alone does not vary in them. They may ⟨vary⟩ vary ⟨in⟩ from person to person to person; but they do not vary in the ⟨vary⟩ in the desire to ⟨clap⟩ clasp the friend ⟨the friend⟩ closer and closer, to greet him ⟨with greater and greater intima⟩ more and more closely, more and more personally and ⟨personally⟩ publicly. It is a strange exhibition to say the least, on the part of a being who will [w.o. i] strike most of his ⟨new⟩ acquaintance at the first ↑personal↓ encounter ⟨th⟩ as the most withdrawn. ⟨His work⟩ He writes to his father [w.o. br], his mother, with a sort of jovial ⟨burly⟩ burliness, which seems almost grotesque, and of a kind with the general shouting familiarity with the rest of the letters and must confirm them in the sense of his oddity[w.o. ies].[12]

"The American James"   bMS Am 1784.16 (1)

It is not strange that I cannot recall my first meeting with Henry James, or for that ↑matter↓ the second or third or specifically any after meeting. It is so with every acquaintance, I suppose. All I can say is that we seemed presently to be always meeting, ⟨to be always in those k⟩ at his ↑father's↓ house and at mine, but [w.o. and] in the kind Cambridge streets rather [w.o. as] than those kind Cambridge houses which it seems to me I frequented rather[1] more than he. We seem to have been presently always together, and always talking of methods of fiction, whether we walked the streets by day or night; or ↑we↓ sat together reading our stuff to each other; his stuff which we both hoped might make itself into matter for The Atlantic Monthly, then mostly left to my[w.o. e] ⟨by⟩ editing by my senior editor Mr. Fields.

I was seven years older than James, but ⟨he⟩ ↑I↓ was much his junior in the art we both adored. Perhaps I did not yet feel my fiction definitely in me. I supposed myself a poet, and I knew myself a journalist and a traveller in such books as Venetian Life, and Italian Journeys, and ↑the volume of↓ Suburban

11. *LiL* reads: "to witness the abandonment of that contemptible policy."
12. *LiL* omits the last two sentences.
 1. *LiL* omits "rather."

Sketches where I was beginning to study our American life ⟨«in the fashion» with the directness and⟩ as I have ever since studied it. But I am ↑distinctly↓ aware of a walk late in the night up and down North Avenue, and of his devoting to our joint scrutiny the ⟨life and⟩ character of ⟨the⟩ remoter branches[2] of his family in the interest of art. They were uncles and cousins of New York origin and of that ⟨common Irish⟩ derivation which gave us their [*w.o.* a] whole most interesting Celtic race. His family was settled at Albany where his grandfather was a[3] chief citizen and a ↑foremost↓ business ↑man.↓⟨m⟩ From him branched off ⟨and⟩ ↑and↓ down those [*w.o.* the] uncles and cousins of his artistic[*w.o.* f] enquiry. ⟨His father was the «l» most⟩

Our walks were by day and by night, but [*w.o.* and] our sessions in my little house were twice or thrice ↑by night↓ a week and on Sunday were always after our simple family supper where he [*w.o.* we] joined us only in spirit, for he ate nothing then or ever,[*w.o.* .] ⟨He⟩ except the biscuit which he crumbled in his pocket and fed himself ⟨by⟩ ↑after↓ the prescription of ⟨the⟩ ↑a↓ famous doctor then prevalent among people of indigestion.[4] He was a constant sufferer, ta[*w.o.* e]cit and explicit, and it was ⟨his⟩ a form of ⟨his⟩ escape from this misery for ↑him↓ to ⟨read and⟩ talk of what he was writing with the ⟨youth *illeg.* pair⟩ ↑young pair whom[*w.o.* se] he frequented,↓ and to ⟨let⟩ read of it as far as it was written. ⟨He included⟩ We were of like ⟨European⟩ Latin sympathies, but he was ⟨sole⟩ inveterately and intensely French, and ⟨we of⟩ ↑with↓ the Italian use of our three or four year's life in Italy we could make him feel that we met on common ground. ⟨But America, was what, we no matter what was the subject & theme of our literature was what we ↑most↓ wished «most» ↑America↓ to shape and color «as» [*w.o. illeg.*] ↑our↓ literature. we hoped of our future.⟩ James could not ⟨help the French⟩ ↑always↓ keep his French background back, and ⟨often he wr⟩ sometimes he wrote an [*w.o.* a][5] ⟨Gallic⟩ English that the editor ↑easily↓ convicted of Gallicism; but ⟨what we «hoped and meant at heart was Americanism pure» most desired was to be American⟩ this was the helplessness of early use and habit from ⟨his French education and edu⟩ from his ⟨early⟩ life ⟨in France [*w.o.* French] life⟩ and school⟨ing⟩ in France throughout ⟨↑&↓⟩ boyhood.

⟨Nothing could Though we joined⟩

From whatever strangeness of ⟨the⟩ ↑this French↓ past we now joined in an American present around the airtight stove which ⟨may perhaps⟩ ↑no doubt↓ overheated our little parlor. ⟨where «James» we talked and dreamed and saved⟩ for ⟨«the» ↑our↓ guest. who talked and read It was a I But it was a French story⟩ I had learned to ⟨know and⟩ like his fiction from such American subjects as Poor Richard, but now it was such a French theme as Gabrielle de Bergerac

---

2. *LiL* reads: "of the remote branches."

3. *LiL* omits "a."

4. Possibly a follower of Sylvester Graham (1794–1851), whose *Treatise on Bread and Bread-Making* (1837) recommended consumption of unadulterated whole-grain products as the key to life and health.

5. *LiL* omits "an."

which had employed his [*w.o.* m] ⟨fancy⟩ ↑art↓, and which he first talked over with me and read to [*w.o.* as] ⟨my young wife and me⟩ ↑us↓ by the light of our ⟨best⟩ kerosene ↑globe-↓⟨lig⟩lamp. We were sufficiently critical, no [*w.o.* as] doubt as an editorial family should be, but we richly felt the ⟨alien⟩ alien quality and circumstance of the tale, which became the first of the ⟨unbroken⟩ ↑long↓ succession of tales and ⟨novle⟩ novels[6] which I eagerly ⟨exc⟩ accepted from him ⟨b⟩ save[7] one of a supposed humorous cast which we both grieved ⟨over⟩ as both to find unacceptable.

I do not ↑know↓ how many were the nocturnal rambles which followed one another ⟨far⟩ into the mild autumnal weather of the Jameses' coming to Cambridge; six months after our own settlement there. One of these ⟨strange⟩ aimless strolls ⟨were⟩ took us ⟨«aimlessly» aimlessly⟩ to the wooded quadrangle, now long ↑since↓ doubtless⟨ly⟩ vanished into forgotten formlessness where James ↑resentfully↓ identified in a much-windowed ⟨«façade» mansion the⟩ ↑very plain old[8]↓ mansion the house where he lodged when an unwilling student of the Harvard Law school. It is not known by whose volition he was studying law, but it was distinctly by his own that he ceased to do so, ⟨and⟩ perhaps wholly unopposed by his family, but that is a part of his story very dimly known to me.

Our walks by day were only in one direction and in one region. We were always going to Fresh Pond, in those days a wandering space of woods and water where people skated in winter and boated ⟨and swam⟩ in summer.

6. *LiL* omits "became the first . . . novels."
7. *LiL* reads "even."
8. *LiL* omits "old."

Textual Apparatus

Letters are identified in the textual apparatus by their sequential number and by an abbreviated form of their editorial headings. Following this, there appears a record of significant internal revisions and cancellations in the manuscript and emendations I have made. Each entry begins with a notation of the page number and number (or numbers) of the lines in the text of the printed letter in which the cited material occurs. Such numbering begins with the first line of the inside address, not with the formal editorial heading that precedes each letter.

Insertions into the running text of the document are indicated by placement within vertical arrows, ellipses being used to abbreviate longer passages. Thus:

↑levity↓ present↑ing↓ ↑(Because . . . "Miss Johnson"!)↓

When a word has been written over some other word or part thereof, this is indicated by the use of the abbreviation "*w.o.*" (for "written over") following the final reading and preceding the original. Thus:

a.m. *w.o.* p.m. ease, *w.o.* care,

Words canceled in the original are enclosed by angled brackets; they always appear in the context of citation to confirm their location for the reader. Thus:

literally ⟨form⟩ afford

An italic question mark within the brackets indicates a degree of uncertainty about the reading provided. Illegible words are abbreviated in the record as *illeg.* Combinations of these various symbols and abbreviations should be self-explanatory.

A left-opening bracket (]) flags an editorial revision. Preceding it appears the reading of the text as printed, and following it the reading of the original. When it has been necessary to supply words, letters, or punctuation absent from the original not by oversight but because of the present physical condition of the document (e.g., torn paper or blotted ink), the reconstructed portions are enclosed by vertical lines. Thus:

three more] three m|ore|

All other editorial comments, such as those indicating autograph corrections (or additions) to typescript (or dictated) letters, appear in italics within square brackets.

#1 HJ/WDH   10 May 1867
   59.8   ⟨lightness⟩ ↑levity↓ of your lightness
#10 HJ/WDH   9 September 1873
   87.4   ⟨belongs to⟩ ↑suggests↓
   .8   ↑even↓ temporarily
   .9   a ↑great↓ part
#11 HJ/WDH   18 October 1873
   89.4   ⟨mellow⟩ ↑bright-colored↓
#13 HJ/WDH   9 January 1874
   92.22   Age *w.o.* ⟨time⟩
   94.4   ↑quite↓ from
   .9   ↑positively↓ can't
#15 HJ/WDH   3 May 1874
   95.17   ⟨avoid⟩ ↑write↓
#16 HJ/WDH   13 January 1875
   106.4   a.m. *w.o.* p.m.
#18 HJ/WDH   19 or 26 March 1875
   115.22   ⟨neglect⟩ ↑neglect↓
#19 HJ/WDH   4 April 1876
   117.19   ⟨know⟩ ↑remember↓
#20 HJ/WDH   28 May 1876
   119.4   ⟨no⟩ ↑but one or two↓
   .22   ⟨brand⟩ ↑circle↓
   .30   ⟨subscriber⟩ ↑contributor↓
   120.13   ⟨society,⟩ ↑families,↓
#22 HJ/WDH   24 October 1876
   122.13   ↑in the conception of the tale,↓
   .18–19   should⟨nt⟩ only
#23 HJ/WDH   18 December 1876
   123.7   most ↑or than any:↓
#24 HJ/WDH   2 February 1877
   125.13   psychologically *w.o.* physic
   .24   fatally ⟨ill⟩ ↑bad↓
#25 HJ/WDH   30 March 1877
   126.21   interest of the ⟨tale⟩ ↑subject↓
   127.6   the ⟨resemblance⟩ ↑merit of a↓
   .28–29   their dyspepsia & ⟨their⟩ dissipates their
   .41   ↑But I shall give you it, or its equivalent, by Nov. next.↓
   128.17   yesterday ↑in comp'y.↓ with Browning,
#26 HJ/WDH   6 May 1878
   129.22   hope that ⟨in your⟩ ↑you↓ yourself
#29 HJ/WDH   7 April 1879
   132.15   ⟨exceedingly⟩ ↑richly↓ successful
   133.17–18   You can live elsewhere ⟨if⟩ ↑*before*↓ you have lived here

#30 HJ/WDH   17 June 1879
   134.18   I can't literally ⟨form⟩ afford it.
       .22   equivalent ↑almost↓ grotesquely small
       .25   the ⟨sale⟩ ↑whole American career↓
   135.1–2   I shall have made this year ↑much↓ more
#31 HJ/WDH   14 or 15 July 1879
   136.22   pledge myself ⟨very⟩ ↑so↓ long in advance
#34 HJ/WDH   23 August 1879
   139.20   more than to say, ↑*probably*↓ not less than six
#37 HJ/WDH   31 January 1880
   146.10–11   ⟨sage⟩ graceful strictures
       .20   I think it ⟨would⟩ ↑is↓ extremely provincial
       .13–16   genius will get on ↑only↓ by agreeing with your ⟨*illeg.*⟩ ↑view↓ of the
                    case—to do something great he must feel as you ⟨would⟩ feel about it.
                    But then I doubt whether such a genius↑—a man of the faculty of Bal-
                    zac & Thackeray—↓*could* agree with you!
#39 HJ/WDH   6 June 1880
   150.12   The article will ↑have↓ helped to make you ↑more↓ known
#40 HJ/WDH   20 July 1880
   151.22   English copyright: ↑an indispensable boon.↓
       .28   out ↑the American↓ copyright
   152.15   to die ⟨or⟩ ↑and↓ to marry
#41 HJ/WDH   18 August 1880
   153.2   should be ⟨published⟩ ↑begun↓ in Dec.
#42 HJ/WDH   11 September 1880
   154.6–7   I envy ↑you↓ it.
#43 HJ/WDH   20 September 1880
   154.8   length of the ↑individual↓ instalments,
   155.2–3   reply will not ↑appreciably↓ disappoint you.
#45 HJ/WDH   5 December 1880
   156.8   journey abroad, ↑later in the winter↓.
   157.13   encounters ↑& acquaintances↓ made
#46 HJ/WDH   4 October 1881
   217.6   what ⟨pleasu⟩ ↑satisfaction↓ the history
#49 HJ/WDH   3 January 1882
   220.3   most charming ⟨thing⟩ ↑fellow↓ in the world.
#50 HJ/WDH   9 January 1882
   221.2   three more] three m|ore|
       .3   richer complexion] richer comp|lexion|
       .3   by the ↑presence of the↓ Philadephian fair
       .6   too hard on the upper classes, & too ⟨har⟩ ↑soft↓ on
       .13   your wife & children] your |wife| & children
#51 HJ/WDH   28 July 1882
   222.5–6   There are two ways of coming ↑from Liverpool: —to the↓ ⟨—by Euston⟩
                    Euston Station, or to St. Pancras.
#53 HJ/WDH   12 August 1882
   222.6   my brother ↑Bob,↓
   223.8   Only ↑give your name↓ ⟨say⟩ to the hall-porter
#54 HJ/WDH   19 August 1882
   223.14   Your novel is admirable to the end, ↑(which I haven't quite reached,)↓

#55 HJ/WDH   14 September 1882
224.13   4 days & then ⟨return⟩ go down
#57 HJ/WDH   15 October 1882
228.15   (in which you ⟨are⟩ ↑were↓ my sponsor)
  .28   ↑write, above all, as soon as you reach Italy.↓
#59 HJ/WDH   20 March 1883
239.3–4   (not before some ⟨weeks⟩ ↑months↓) it will be for a↑— to put it
              mildly—↓longish stay.
  .10   with the mercury at ⟨zero⟩ ↑30↓ below zero
  .25   ↑We, like T. & D. are already of the past.↓
240.3   Have you seen the ↑amiable↓ article
#60 HJ/WDH   21 February 2884
241.20   Crawford's ↑last↓ novel sickens
242.1–2   trying to write ⟨something⟩ ↑anything↓ decent or serious for a public so
              absolutely idiotic. ↑It must be totally wasted.↓
243.15   a tendency to ⟨arb⟩ ↑factitious↓ glosses;
  .21   but the ⟨thing⟩ ↑work↓ is admirably solid
#61 HJ/WDH   31 July 1884
244.14   You will find yourself writing too ⟨illeg.⟩ well, & will ⟨wish⟩ ↑sigh↓
  .17   I must ⟨write⟩ ↑put↓ more in.
#62 WDH/HJ   22 August 1884
246.3   spent ↑some↓ desolate weeks
#63 HJ/WDH   23 May 1885
248.20–21   I shall never have a penny of ⟨it⟩ ↑the money↓
#64 HJ/WDH   19 October 1886
257.23   I am still good for that ↑sort of thing.↓
#65 HJ/WDH   7 December 1886
258.16   one sees you ↑abundantly↓ capable
  .27–28   will know ↑how↓ ⟨real⟩ ↑good↓ she is
  .30   This ⟨isn't⟩ ↑is↓ all I started to say—
#67 HJ/WDH   25 February 1887
262.26   the American on whom ⟨the⟩ ↑Europe↓ *can't* act!
  .27   I greatly hope, ↑for him, that↓ it will prove
263.14   ⟨You have⟩ ↑It is everywhere↓
#68 HJ/WDH   2 January 1888
266.10   ⟨secrets⟩ ↑reasons↓
  .20   that ↑on occasions↓ you mix things up
#69 HJ/WDH   29 September 1888
271.2   or ↑even↓ to,
  .7–8   he is ↑made↓ excited
#73 HJ/WDH   17 May 1890
275.22   than ↑even↓ the best
  .33   full, rich ⟨thing⟩ ↑flood.↓
  .33   your reservoir ⟨surprises⟩ ↑deluges↓
276.7   ⟨closer⟩ ↑several↓ degrees closer
  .21   I ⟨wonder at⟩ ↑note↓
  .28   a ↑particular↓ *window*,
  .38   touches the ⟨reader⟩ ↑subject↓
#75 HJ/WDH   10 January 1891
284.9   your ↑particular↓ perch.

284.11   corpulent ↑fireside↓ cat,
  .18   ⟨passion⟩ ↑preference↓
  .27   say ↑above all↓
  .29   ⟨meagre⟩ ↑miry↓
  .31   literature ↑has↓ ever
  .35   to ↑the↓ business
286.5   ⟨trans-Atlantic⟩ ↑indigenous↓ eyes
  .5   ⟨*That* peerless⟩ The peerless
#76 HJ/WDH   12 December 1891
286.7   ⟨occupations⟩ ↑obligations↓
  .17   But↑—later—↓
  .25   ⟨Century⟩ *Cosmopolitan*
#80 HJ/WDH   29 January 1893
291.23   freehandedly ⟨drop⟩ ↑scatter.↓
#82 HJ/WDH   9 August 1894
293.19   so few weeks ⟨offer⟩ ↑represent to↓ me
#85 HJ/WDH   22 January 1895
298.8   qualified ↑indeed↓
  .11   all will ↑yet↓
  .17   ⟨person⟩ ↑hand↓
  .32   ↑I am indeed very serene.↓
#86 HJ/WDH   30 March and 6 April 1896
301.2–3   ↑however, in spite of war cries,↓
#87 HJ/WDH   11 October 1897
302.17   ↑This is a sacrosanct vow.↓
#88 HJ/WDH   16 or 23 October 1897
303.16–17   ↑—force this on your wife—↓
#91 HJ/WDH   28 January 1898
305.15   the ↑mere personal↓ activity
306.25   scrawl↑—or sprawl—↓
  .26   a lift—from] a lift—
#93 HJ/WDH   4 May 1898
309.4   so ↑continentally↓ appealing
  .8   here, ↑at home,↓
  .17   & ⟨my⟩ ↑your↓ wife's,
  .21   most ↑abject,↓
  .24   question of a ⟨fee⟩ ↑chance!↓
#97 HJ/WDH   25 September 1899
351.24   as ↑having &↓ being
  .16   ↑anything *like*↓
  .24   the ↑particular↓ abyss,
#98 HJ/WDH   29 June 1900
353.7   to you ↑even↓ *[autograph insertion]*
355.10   *shall [autograph underscore]*
  .30   *difficulty [autograph underscore]*
356.27   I return . . . you.] *[autograph insertion]*
#100 HJ/WDH   9 and 14 August 1900
358.1   *Read P.S. . . . . first!] [autograph insertion]*
359.16   *apparitional [autograph underscore]*
  .26   *he himself [autograph underscore]*

359.40–41	↑at still another angle,↓ *[autograph insertion]*
.44	*into [autograph underscore]*
360.1–3	↑This has been . . . inapt.)↓ *[autograph insertion]*
.22	*others [autograph underscore]*
.24	*now [autograph underscore]*
.31	↑(Because . . . "Miss Johnson"!)↓ *[autograph insertion]*
362.14	*mine! [autograph underscore]*
#101 HJ/WDH	10 August 1901
366.16	↑—every hundred—↓
.30	↑the fiction↓ ⟨tale⟩ in question
367.2	⟨mentioned⟩ ↑repeated to me↓
.4–5	incident ↑—suggestive↓—
#102 HJ/WDH	25 January 1902
369.8	⟨wild⟩ ↑delirious↓ dream
.18–19	↑Best of all as the Edith Wharton!↓
.23	↑—& oh, so difficultly—↓
.29	↑—*have fallen*—↓
371.2–3	any ↑individual↓ experience
.27	*should* have ↑by this time↓
372.24	bless ↑*up*,↓ ⟨upwardly⟩
#105 HJ/WDH	12 September 1902
377.27	*I shall [autograph underscore]*
#106 HJ/WDH	11 December 1902
379.5	has ⟨touched⟩ ↑befallen me↓
380.4	↑unrewarded↓ heroism;
#109 HJ/WDH	11 December 1903
396.24	↑perversely↓ *selling*
397.5	↑(another!!)↓
#110 HJ/WDH	8 January 1904
397.18	*no other way [autograph underscore]*
#114 HJ/WDH	16 May 1904
402.8	Lamb House] L
#116 HJ/WDH	28 May 1904
403.5–6	my ⟨silent⟩ ↑neglect↓
404.13	↑sticks↓ ⟨stakes⟩
.17	the great ⟨Women's⟩ ↑Ladies'↓ Club
#120 HJ/WDH	5 July 1904
407.10	latter ↑valuable↓ head
.13	↑fondly but↓ rashly
#121 HJ/WDH	5 August 1904
409.6	⟨force⟩ ↑strength↓ of it.
.22	ease, *w.o.* care,
.24	you ⟨will⟩ ↑*must*↓
#122 HJ/WDH	1 March 1905
412.1	*things [autograph underscore]*
.1	pictures,] ↑pictures↓ *[autograph insertion]*
#135 HJ/WDH	13 September 1906
415.25	radiant & ⟨rubiant⟩ ↑rainless↓
416.7	such ↑golden↓ sheaves

#126 HJ/WDH   1 November 1906
  417.4   from ↑the compass of↓
    .7   ↑—it used not to be—↓
    .27   book ↑(the 1st)↓
  418.3   ↑—the economic swell—↓
    .12   the ↑renewed↓ beat
    .17   with ⟨great⟩ ↑dreadful↓
  419.1–2   hold ↑both her breath &↓ her nose
    .4–5   ↑—*they* aren't—↓
    .12   the ↑minute↓ revising
    .13   ↑absolutely↓ impossible
#127 HJ/WDH   10 March 1908
  420.29   ↑ever so quickly &↓ bitterly
  421.13   sedentary ↑for months↓
#129 HJ/WDH   17 August 1908
  426.37   *less [autograph underscore]*
  427.8   *journalistic [autograph underscore]*
    .28   *did . . . did [autograph underscore]*
#130 HJ/WDH   31 December 1908
  430.6   your ⟨feeling⟩ ↑recognising,↓
#132 HJ/WDH   23 July 1909
  434.24   ↑composition or↓ publication
  435.3   this ↑new↓ chapter
    .16   your ↑attempted↓ perpetration
    .18   avid & ⟨worthless⟩ ↑purblind↓
#140 HJ/WDH   17 March 1911
  445.16   Ber⟨moot⟩↑muda↓
    .33   has ↑ever↓ come
#141 HJ/WDH   20 April 1911
  446.6–7   ↑an author's↓ writing
  447.3   ↑represent &↓ *signify*
    .11   something, ↑of sorts,↓
#145 HJ/WDH   27 March 1912
  455.10   only ⟨trust ?⟩ ↑most↓
    .14   sovereign ⟨sense⟩ ↑truth.↓
  456.24   At the ⟨end⟩ ↑expiration↓
    .27   Labour, *w.o.* l
    .34   ↑preserved↓ peace
    .38   there ⟨will⟩ ↑may↓
#146 HJ/WDH   13 May 1914
  457.6   ↑—by which I mean *indefinite*—↓
  458.12   ↑by the "general" reader↓
#149 HJ/WDH   20 August 1915
  462.16   ↑from the happy show.↓
"Editor's Easy Chair" *[The Letters of Henry James]*
  469.2   Lubbock,] Lubbock
    .23   America,] America
    .23   consciousness,] consciousness
    .32   contemptible,] contemptib⟨b⟩le,
    .33   must *w.o.* r

470.31   more like home] more home like [*WDH's transposition*]
.37   criticism *w.o.* &
.38   to more] more to [*WDH's transposition*]
471.1   ↑civic↓ change] ↑civic↓ change,
.11   unparalleled *w.o.* unparaletted
.16   closely,] closely

"The American James"

471.9   both *w.o.* n

Index

For ease of reference this index is subdivided into five parts: (1) names of persons; (2) general subject headings; (3) titles by WDH; (4) titles by HJ; and (5) titles by other authors.

Names

General Subject Headings

Works by William Dean Howells

Works by Henry James

Works by Other Authors